CONTENTS

KU-654-413

Vietnam

THE ROUGH GUIDE

There are more than one hundred Rough Guide titles
covering destinations from Amsterdam to Zimbabwe

Forthcoming titles include
Austria • Bangkok • Edinburgh
Japan • Jordan • Syria

Rough Guide Reference Series
Classical Music • The Internet • Jazz • Reggae
Rock Music • World Music

Rough Guide Phrasebooks
Czech • French • German • Greek • Hindi • Indonesian • Italian
Mandarin Chinese • Mexican Spanish • Polish • Portuguese • Russian
Spanish • Thai • Turkish • Vietnamese

Rough Guides on the Internet
http://www.roughguides.com/
http://www.hotwired.com/rough

Rough Guide Credits

Text editor:	Alison Cowan
Series editor:	Mark Ellingham
Editorial:	Martin Dunford, Jonathan Buckley, Jo Mead, Samantha Cook, Amanda Tomlin, Annie Shaw, Catherine McHale, Paul Gray, Vivienne Heller
Online editors:	Alan Spicer (UK), Andrew Rosenberg (US)
Production:	Susanne Hillen, Andy Hilliard, Judy Pang, Link Hall, Nicola Williamson, Helen Ostick
Cartography:	Melissa Flack, David Callier
Finance:	John Fisher, Celia Crowley, Catherine Gillespie
Marketing & Publicity:	Richard Trillo, Simon Carloss (UK), Jean-Marie Kelly, Jeff Kaye (US)
Administration:	Tania Hummel

Acknowledgements

The editor thanks Jan and Mark for making work a pleasure; Susanne Hillen and Nicola Williamson for keeping everything on track; Andy Hilliard and Link Hall for stress-free setting and fancy fonts; Andrew Tibber and Nikky Twyman for diligent proofreading; David Callier, Melissa Flack and Micromap for inspired cartography; and Karen Sherman for the postcards. The authors would like to thank Alison Cowan for sympathetic and cool-headed editing; Carol Pucci and Cameron Donald for extra *Basics* research; Philip Blackburn and Simon Broughton for musical gems; and *Lexus* for linguistic expertise. Individually, the authors would like to thank:

Jan: Steve for inspiration, unwavering support and doses of reality in the Pyrenees; the wa Dodd, Trish and Phil for their enthusiasm, encouragement and tenacious sleuthing; John, June and Alison for holding the fort and much else besides; and Rob, Ha and Giang for sowing the seeds. In Hanoi, thanks to David Hulse, Lisa Jones, Rebeca and Jason Ramos, Rocky Dang of *Phoenix Travel (HK)*, Pham Hong Anh, Rolf Salme, Muriel Kirton, Jeanette Evers, Annalisa Koeman, Nguyen Ngoc Hung, Dr Robert Snell, Adam Schwarz and to Margot Kokke for the final touches. In Hué, thanks to Le Dinh Gia and Le Thi Nhan of *Hue Tourist Co.*, Nguyen Van Me, Nguyen Huu Loan, Mr Ngo and Tran Van Phuong. In Da Nang, thanks to Ho Minh Phuong, Nguyen Thi Minh Thanh and colleagues at *Danatours*, and Mark Proctor. Thanks also to Le Huy Can in Paris, Dr Dana Healey (SOAS, London), Rob Bromage, Mark Beukema, Stine Lund, Carolyn Hill; to Dr John Hartley and *AEA International* for additional medical information, and to *Vietnam Investment Review*. Finally, special thanks to Tuyet, Khai and Hai, who became friends.

Mark: More love and thanks than they can imagine to all family and friends, but especially to Jo and dear Gran. Thanks, too, to Craig Anderson at *STA* for his long-suffering fact-checking; to Sinh of *Sinh Café*, Nguyen and Mr Hung in Pham Ngu Lao; to Rick Craik; to Mr Dung and Mr Lang in Nha Trang; and to Mr Khin and Mr Huynh, for friendship and assistance in Kon Tum. Most of all, though, my eternal gratitude to Mr Tran Dinh Nhung in Plei Ku for his many kindnesses.

This first edition published November 1996 by Rough Guides Ltd, 1 Mercer St, London WC2H 9QJ. Reprinted in September 1997.

Distributed by the Penguin Group:

Penguin Books Ltd, 27 Wrights Lane, London W8 5TZ
Penguin Books USA Inc., 375 Hudson Street, New York 10014, USA
Penguin Books Australia Ltd, 487 Maroondah Highway, PO Box 257, Ringwood, Victoria 3134, Australia
Penguin Books Canada Ltd, 10 Alcorn Avenue, Toronto, Ontario, Canada M4V 1E4
Penguin Books (NZ) Ltd, 182–190 Wairau Road, Auckland 10, New Zealand

Typeset in Linotron Univers and Century Old Style to an original design by Andrew Oliver.
Printed in the UK by Cox & Wyman, Reading, Berks.
Illustrations in Part One and Part Three by Ed Briant.
Illustrations on p.1 and p.407 by Henry Iles.

512pp includes index

A catalogue record for this book is available from the British Library

ISBN 1-85828-191-1

Vietnam

THE ROUGH GUIDE

Written and researched by
Jan Dodd and Mark Lewis

With special contributions from
Steve Eckett and Jo Peggie

THE ROUGH GUIDES

ROUGH GUIDES

Travel Guides • Phrasebooks • Music and Reference Guides

We set out to do something different when the first **Rough Guide** was published in 1982. Mark Ellingham, just out of university, was travelling in Greece. He brought along the popular guides of the day, but found they were all lacking in some way. They were either strong on ruins and museums but went on for pages without mentioning a beach or taverna. Or they were so conscious of the need to save money that they lost sight of Greece's cultural and historical significance. Also, none of the books told him anything about Greece's contemporary life – its politics, its culture, its people, and how they lived.

So with no job in prospect, Mark decided to write his own guidebook, one which aimed to provide practical information that was second to none, detailing the best beaches and the hottest clubs and restaurants, while also giving hard-hitting accounts of every sight, both famous and obscure, and providing up-to-the-minute information on contemporary culture. It was a guide that encouraged independent travellers to find the best of Greece, and was a great success, getting shortlisted for the Thomas Cook travel guide award, and encouraging Mark, along with three friends, to expand the series.

The Rough Guide list grew rapidly and the letters flooded in, indicating a much broader readership than had been anticipated, but one which uniformly appreciated the Rough Guide mix of practical detail and humour, irreverence and enthusiasm. Things haven't changed. The same four friends who began the series are still the caretakers of the Rough Guide mission today: to provide the most reliable, up-to-date and entertaining information to independent-minded travellers of all ages, on all budgets.

We now publish 100 titles and have offices in London and New York. The **travel guides** are written and researched by a dedicated team of more than 100 authors, based in Britain, Europe, the USA and Australia. We have also created a unique series of **phrasebooks** to accompany the travel series, along with an acclaimed series of **music guides**, and a best-selling **pocket guide to the Internet and World Wide Web**. We also publish comprehensive travel information on our two **web sites**: http://www.hotwired.com/rough and http://www.roughguides.com/

HELP US UPDATE

We've gone to a lot of effort to ensure that this first edition of *The Rough Guide to Vietnam* is as up-to-date and accurate as possible. Vietnam changes fast, however, and if you feel there are places we've under-rated or over-praised, or find we've missed something good or covered something which has now gone, then please write; suggestions, comments or corrections are much appreciated.

We'll credit all contributions, and send a copy of the next edition (or any other Rough Guide if you prefer) for the best letters. Please mark letters: "Rough Guide Vietnam Update" and send to:

Rough Guides, 1 Mercer St, London WC2H 9QJ,
or Rough Guides, 375 Hudson St, 9th floor, New York NY 10014.
Or send e-mail to: vietnam@roughtravl.co.uk

Online updates about this book can be found on Rough Guides' website at
http://www.roughguides.com/

• CHAPTER 7: HA LONG BAY AND THE NORTHERN SEABORD 355–377

• CHAPTER 8: THE FAR NORTH 378–405

PART THREE   CONTEXTS   407

LIST OF MAPS

MAP SYMBOLS

▬▬ Railway	▲ Hindu temple
══ Main road	◈ Cao Dai temple
── Minor road	♠ Pagoda
----- Path	▭ Church
── River	⌘ Mosque
── Ferry route	◉ Hotel/guesthouse
----- Chapter division boundary	▣ Restaurant
▄▄▄ International boundary	⊠ Post office
▄▄ Province boundary	ⓘ Tourist office
Beach	⊞ Hospital
⇓ Waterfall	▰ Building
⇉ Pass	✈ Airport
⇘ Viewpoint	★ Bus stop
◆ Historic site	⚲ Golf course
▪▪▪▪ City wall/battlement	⚑ Lighthouse
⌓ Mountain range	⁺⁺ Cemetery
▲ Mountain peak	Park
◠ Cave	Marsh

INTRODUCTION

H istory weighs heavily on **Vietnam**. For more than a decade, reportage of the war that racked this slender country portrayed it as a netherworld of savagery and slaughter; and even after the American War ended it was further pigeon-holed by Hollywood's seamless chain of combat movies. Yet, only twenty-odd years after the war's end, this incredibly resilient nation is beginning to emerge from the shadows: access is now easier than ever, and the country has re-invented its old-style communist system as a free market economy that encourages contact. As the number of tourists finding their way here soars, the word is out that this is a land not of bomb craters and army ordnance, but of shimmering paddy fields and sugar-white beaches, full-tilt cities and venerable pagodas – often overwhelming in its sheer beauty.

The speed with which Vietnam's population of some 73 million has been able to put the bitter events of its recent past behind it, and focus its gaze so steadfastly on the future, comes as a surprise to visitors expecting to encounter shell-shocked resentment of the West and war fatigue. It wasn't always like this, however. The reunification of North and South Vietnam that ended twenty years of bloody civil war, in 1975, was followed by a decade or so of hardline centralist economic rule from which only the shake-up of **doi moi**, Vietnam's equivalent of *perestroika*, could awaken the country. By lifting the lid off private enterprise, *doi moi* has, since its conception in 1986, signalled a renaissance for Vietnam, and today a high fever of commerce grips the nation, as citizens clamour to claim their slice of the pie while the good times roll. Of course, the shift to a market economy would have been only notional without accompanying shifts in international relations – in particular 1994's ending of the US trade embargo, which released the log-jam of foreign investment; and the diplomatic rehabilitation that ensued once Vietnamese forces were pulled out of Cambodia in 1989, culminating in the restoration of US-Vietnamese diplomatic relations in July 1995. From a tourist's point of view, it's a great time to come – thanks to an intoxicating sense of vitality and optimism, not to mention the chance to witness a country in profound flux. What's more, after a decade and a half of isolation, there's a huge warmth and curiosity shown towards visitors by the Vietnamese, who tend to pounce voraciously on any chance to interact with foreigners.

Of course, that's not the whole story. *Doi moi* is an economic policy, not a magic spell, and life, for most of the population, remains hard. Indeed, *doi moi* has introduced its own problems, with the adoption of a market economy predictably polarizing the gap between rich and poor. Despite the numerous Japanese, Taiwanese

---

PRICING POLICY

Both the local currency, **dong**, and **US dollars** are used in Vietnam and are generally interchangeable. Despite government efforts to promote the dong, prices are more frequently quoted in US$, especially by hotels, restaurants, tour agencies and so on. For this reason and because dong amounts tend to be unwieldy and more volatile, we've largely given prices in US$ throughout the *Guide*.

and Korean assembly plants springing up, monthly incomes in cities remain at around US$50 per month, while in the poorest provinces workers may scrape by on as little as US$15 a month – a difference that amply illustrates the growing gulf between urban and rural Vietnam.

As you might expect, the long-standing antipathy and deep psychological divide between the **north and south** endures. This was around long before the American War, and is engrained in the bedrock of Vietnamese culture. Northerners are typically considered reticent, dour, law-abiding, and lacking the dynamism and entrepreneurial know-how of their more worldly-wise southern compatriots. A cartoonist's caricature of a southerner would most likely depict a flashy wheeler-dealer, shades on, barking into a mobile phone as he weaves his Honda Dream through the busy streets; while his northern counterpart would appear in green army tunic and helmet, tootling along on his duck-laden bicycle.

Many visitors find more than enough to amuse them in Hanoi, Ho Chi Minh City and the other major centres; but despite the cities' allure, it's the country's striking **landscape** that most impresses. Vietnam occupies a narrow strip of land that hugs the eastern borders of Cambodia and Laos, hemmed in by rugged mountains to the west, and by the South China Sea to the east. To the north and south of its narrow waist, it dovetails out into the splendid deltas of the Red River and the Mekong, and it's in these regions that you'll encounter the paddy fields, dragonflies, buffaloes and conical-hatted farmers that constitute the classic image of Vietnam. In stark contrast to the pancake-flat ricelands of the deltas, Ha Long Bay's labyrinthine network of **limestone outcrops** loom dramatically out of the Gulf of Tonkin – a magical spectacle in the early morning mist. None of Vietnam's mountains reach particularly impressive heights, so any trip to the remote upland regions of central and northern Vietnam is far likelier to focus upon the **ethnic minorities** who reside there. Elaborate tribal costumes, age-old customs and communal longhouses await those visitors game enough to trek into the sticks – though if you're sufficiently fortunate to sample the legendary hilltribe hospitality, you may find that the knockout rice wine they brew leaves memories hazy. As for **wildlife**, the discovery, in the early Nineties, of a previously unknown species of ox, the soala, speaks volumes for the wealth of Vietnam's biodiversity – that, despite the decade-long pasting the country received from American bombers – and makes the improving access to the country's several **national parks** all the more gratifying.

Where to go

The "Hanoi or bust" attitude, whereby new arrivals doggedly labour between the country's two major cities, no matter how limited their time, blights many a trip to Vietnam. If you want to travel the length of the country at some leisure, see something of the highlands and the deltas and allow for a few rest days, you'll really need to be in-country for a month. With only two weeks at your disposal, the choice is either to hopscotch up the coast calling at only the most mainstream destinations; or, perhaps better, to concentrate on one region and enjoy it at your own pace. However, if you *do* want to see both north and south in a fortnight, internal flights can speed up an itinerary substantially, and aren't so expensive that they should be rejected out of hand.

For the majority of new arrivals, **Ho Chi Minh City** provides a head-spinning introduction to Vietnam. Set beside the broad swell of the Saigon River, the southern capital is rapidly being transformed into a southeast Asian mover and shaker to compete with the best of them. In Ho Chi Minh, the absurd becomes common-

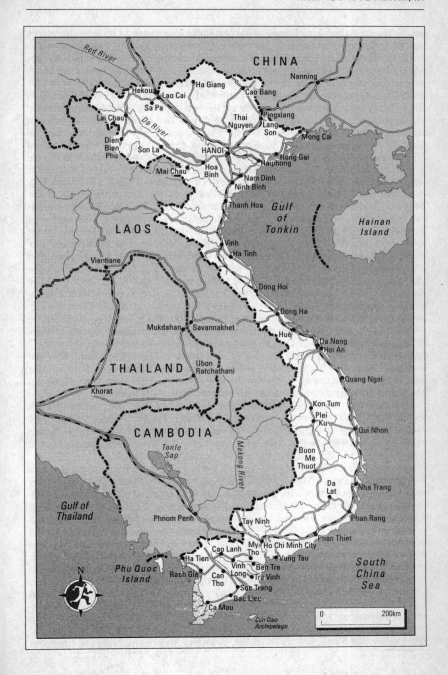

CHINA

Red River

Nanning

Ha Giang
Hekou
Lao Cai
Cao Bang
Sa Pa
Pingxiang
Lai Chau
Da River
Thai
Nguyen
Lang
Son
Mong Cai
Dien
Bien
Phu
Son La
HANOI
Hong Gai
Haiphong
Mai Chau
Hoa
Binh
Nam Dinh
Ninh Binh

LAOS
Thanh Hoa
Gulf
of
Tonkin
Hainan
Island

Vinh
Ha Tinh

Vientiane

Dong Hoi

Dong Ha

Mukdahan
Savannakhet
Hué

Da Nang
Hoi An

Ubon
Ratchathani
Quang Ngai

THAILAND
Kon Tum

Khorat
Plei
Ku
Qui Nhon

CAMBODIA
Tonle
Sap
Buon
Me
Thuot

Mekong River
Da
Lat
Nha Trang

Gulf of
Thailand
Phan Rang

Phnom Penh
Tay Ninh
Phan Thiet

My
Tho
Ho Chi Minh City

Cao Lanh
Vung Tau
South
China
Sea

Ha Tien
Vinh
Long
Ben Tre

Phu Quoc
Island
Rach Gia
Can
Tho
Tra Vinh

Soc Trang

Bac Lieu
Ca Mau
Con Dao
Archipelago

N

0   200km

place. The city's breakneck pace of life translates into a stew of bizarre characters and unlikely sights and sounds, and ensures that almost all who come here quickly fall for its singular charm. Furious commerce carries on cheek-by-jowl with age-old traditions; grandly indulgent colonial edifices peek out from under the shadows of looming office blocks and hotels; and cyclo drivers battle it out with late-model Japanese taxis in the chaotic boulevards. The city's unrelenting thrum of life is best soaked up over a roadside coffee and croissant. Few tourists pass up the opportunity to take a day-trip out of the city to **Tay Ninh**, the nerve centre of the indigenous Cao Dai religion. The jury is still out on whether the ostentatious Cao Dai Holy See constitutes high art or dog's dinner, but either way it's one of Vietnam's most arresting sights, and is normally twinned wih a stop-off at the Cu Chi Tunnels, where Vietnamese villagers dug themselves a warren stretching over two hundred kilometres, out of reach of US bombing. With Ho Chi Minh City seen off, most tourists next venture southwest to explore some or all of the **Mekong Delta**, where one of the world's truly mighty rivers finally offloads into the South China Sea; its skein of brim-full tributaries and waterways has endowed the delta with a lush quilt of rice-rich flats and abundant orchards. You won't want to depart the delta without having enjoyed a day's messing about on the water, typically arranged through the boat operators of **My Tho** or **Vinh Long** – though if you push on to **Can Tho**, the delta's largest settlement, you'll be able to incorporate a trip to a floating market into your waterborne idling. Far removed from the stereotype of the Asian city, **Da Lat**, the "capital" of the southern and central highlands, is chalk to Ho Chi Minh City's cheese. Life passes by at a rather more dignified pace at this altitude, and the raw breezes that fan this oddly quaint hillside settlement provide the best air-conditioning in Vietnam. **Minority peoples** inhabit the countryside around Da Lat, but to visit some really full-on *montagnard* villages you'll need to push north to the modest towns of **Buon Me Thuot**, **Plei Ku** and **Kon Tum**, which are surrounded by Ede, Jarai and Bahnar communities. Opt for Buon Me Thuot, and you'll also be well-poised to visit **Ban Don National Park** and hitch a ride on one of its sizeable population of elephants.

Less than two hours' bus ride southeast of Ho Chi Minh City, meanwhile, lies **Vung Tau**, erstwhile seaside retreat of Vietnam's French colonists. Today, its charm lies somewhat tarnished by the glut of unlovely hotels that have been thrown up to cater for the city's vast domestic tourist industry, though Bai Sau, its longest strip of sand, can still seem hugely appealing after the onslaught of Ho Chi Minh. East of Vung Tau, Highway 1, the country's jugular, girds its loins for the arduous journey up to Hanoi and the north. Unless you investigate the dramatically heaped sand dunes east of **Phan Thiet**, your first stop is likely to be **Phan Rang** – a sloppy little place, but blessed with some of the most splendid examples of the **Cham towers** that punctuate Vietnam's south-central coast. **Nha Trang** has grown into a crucial stepping stone on the Ho Chi Minh–Hanoi run, and the tirelessly touted boat trips around the city's outlying islands are a must. North of Nha Trang, **Son My** village attained global notoriety when a company of American soldiers massacred some 500 Vietnamese, including many women and children; unspeakable horrors continue to haunt the village's unnervingly idyllic rural setting.

Once a bustling seaport, the diminutive town of **Hoi An** perches beside an indolent backwater, its narrow streets of wooden-fronted shophouses and weathered roofs making it an enticing destination. Inland, the war-battered ruins of **My Son**, the greatest of the Cham temple sites, lie mouldering in a steamy jungle-filled valley. **Da Nang**, just up the coast, lacks Hoi An's charm but good transport links make it a convenient base for the area, while echoes of the American War still resound across the sands of China Beach. From Da Nang a corkscrew ride over cliff-top Hai Van Pass brings you to the aristocratic city of **Hué**, where the Nguyen emperors established their capital in the nineteenth century on the banks of the languid Perfume River. Despite the ravages of time and war, the temples and palaces of this highly cultured city still testify to past splendours, while its imperial mausoleums are masterpieces of architectural refinement, slumbering among pine-shrouded hills. Only a hundred kilometres north of Hué, the tone changes as war-sites litter the Demilitarized Zone (**DMZ**), which cleaved the country in two from 1954 to 1975. Two decades of peace have done much to heal the scars, but these windswept, wasted hills bear eloquent witness to a generation that lost their lives in the tragic struggle between South and North. The DMZ is most easily tackled as a day-trip from Hué, after which most people hop straight up to Hanoi. And there's little to detain you on the northward trek, save the glittering limestone caverns of **Phong Nha**, the entrance to a massive underground river system tunnelling under the Truong Son Mountains. Then, on the very fringes of the northern Red River Delta lie the ancient incense-steeped temples of **Hoa Lu** and, nearby, the mystical landscape of **Tam Coc–Bich Dong**, where paddy fields lap at the feet of sugar-loaf hummocks.

Anchored firmly in the Red River Delta, **Hanoi** has served as Vietnam's capital for close on a thousand years and is layered with history. It's a small, rather reserved city, a place of pagodas and dynastic temples, tamarisk-edged lakes and elegant boulevards of French-era villas, of national monuments and stately government edifices. But Hanoi is also being swept along on a tide of change as Vietnam forges its own shiny high-rise capital, and as the city's population dip their toes in the unfamiliar waters of the market economy. Though life proceeds at a gentler pace than in Ho Chi Minh, Hanoi is still an all-absorbing place, a city on the move, throwing up new hotels and restaurants by the week as it gears up for international investors and the swell of tourists. From Hanoi the majority of visitors strike out east to where northern Vietnam's premier natural attraction, **Ha Long Bay**, provides the perfect antidote to such urban exuberance, rewarding the traveller with a leisurely day or two drifting among the thousands of whimsically sculpted islands anchored in its aquamarine waters. Bai Chay, a resort town on the northern coast, is the usual embarkation point for Ha Long Bay, but a more appealing gateway is mountainous **Cat Ba Island**, which defines the bay's southwestern limits and is inhabited mostly by fisherfolk. The route to Cat Ba passes via the north's major port city, **Haiphong**, an unspectacular but genial place with an attractive core of faded colonial facades.

To the north and west of Hanoi mountain ranges rear up out of the Red River Delta. Vietnam's northern provinces aren't the easiest to get around, but these wild uplands are home to a patchwork of ethnic minorities and the country's most dramatic mountain landscapes. At weekends the little market town of **Sa Pa**, up near the Chinese border in the far northwest, is transformed into a showcase of minority style, while, far to the south the stilthouse-filled valley of **Mai Chau** makes for another manageable destination. Though few people venture further inland, rough backroads heading upcountry provide a tenuous link between isolated outposts and access to the northwest's only specific sight, where the French colonial dream expired in the dead-end valley of **Dien Bien Phu**. East of the Red River Valley lies an even less-frequented region, whose prime attraction is its varied scenery, from the limestone crags and multi-layered rainforest of **Ba Be**

National Park, over immense, empty hill country to the remote valleys of **Cao Bang**, farmed by communities still practising their traditional ways of life.

When to go

Vietnam has a tropical monsoon **climate**, dominated by the south or southwesterly monsoon from May to September and the northeast monsoon from October to April. The southern summer monsoon brings rain to the two deltas and west-facing slopes, while the cold winter monsoon picks up moisture over the Gulf of Tonkin and dumps it along the central coast and the eastern edge of the central highlands. Within this basic pattern there are marked differences according to altitude and latitude; temperatures in the south remain equable all year round, while the north experiences distinct seasonal variations.

In **southern Vietnam** the dry season lasts from December to late April or May, and the rains from May through to November. Since most rain falls in brief afternoon downpours, this need not be off-putting, though flooding at this time of year can cause problems in the Mekong Delta. Daytime temperatures in the region rarely drop below 20°C, occasionally hitting 40°C during the hottest months (March, April and May). The climate of the **central highlands** generally follows the same pattern, though temperatures are cooler, especially at night. Again, the monsoon rains of May to October can make transport more complicated, sometimes washing out roads and cutting off remoter villages.

Along the **central coast** the rainfall pattern reverses under the influence of the northeast monsoon. Here the wet season starts with a flourish in September and continues to February, though even the dry season (March to August) brings a fair quantity of intermittent rain. Hué and Da Nang in particular bear the brunt of the onslaught; if possible it pays to visit these two cities in the spring (February to May), just before the rains break in September or as they begin to fizzle out in November. Temperatures reach their maximum (often in the upper 30s) from June to August, when it's pleasant to escape into the hills. The northern stretches of this coastal region experiences a more extreme climate, with a shorter rainy season (peaking in September and October) and a hot dry summer. The coast of central Vietnam is the zone most likely to be hit by **typhoons**, bringing torrential rain and hurricane-force winds. Though notoriously difficult to predict, the coast around Hué seems most vulnerable in April and May, while further north the typhoon season lasts from July to November.

Northern Vietnam is generally warm and sunny from October to December, after which cold winter weather sets in, accompanied by fine persistent mists which can last for several days. Temperatures begin to rise again in March, building to summer maximums that occasionally reach 40°C between May and August, though average temperatures in Hanoi hover around a more reasonable 30°C. However, summer is also the rainy season, when heavy downpours render the low-lying delta area almost unbearably hot and sticky, and flooding is a regular hazard. The northern mountains share the same basic regime, though temperatures are considerably cooler and higher regions see ground frosts, or even a rare snowfall, during the winter (December to February).

With such a complicated weather picture, there's no one particular season to recommend as the **best time** for visiting Vietnam. Overall, autumn (September to December) and spring (March and April) are probably the most favourable seasons if you're covering the whole country.

VIETNAM'S CLIMATE

		J	F	M	A	M	J	J	A	S	O	N	D
Ho Chi Minh City													
Av daily temp	°F	80	81	84	86	84	82	82	82	81	81	80	79
	°C	27	28	29	30	29	29	28	28	27	27	27	27
Av monthly rainfall	inches	0.6	0.1	0.5	1.7	8.7	13	12.4	10.6	13.2	10.6	4.5	2.2
	mm	15	3	13	43	221	330	315	269	335	269	114	56
Relative humidity (pm)		61	56	58	60	71	78	80	78	80	80	75	68
Da Nang													
Av daily temp	°F	71	73	75	80	84	86	85	85	82	78	76	73
	°C	22	23	24	27	29	30	30	30	28	26	25	23
Av monthly rainfall	inches	4	1.2	0.5	0.7	1.9	1.7	3.9	4.6	17.6	20.1	8.7	8.2
	mm	102	31	12	18	47	42	99	117	447	530	221	209
Relative humidity (all hours)		86	86	86	85	81	77	78	77	84	85	86	86
Hanoi													
Av daily temp	°F	62	64	69	76	82	85	86	84	82	78	71	66
	°C	17	18	20	24	28	30	30	29	28	26	22	19
Av monthly rainfall	inches	0.7	1.1	1.5	3.2	7.7	9.4	12.7	13.5	10	3.9	1.7	0.8
	mm	18	28	38	81	196	239	323	343	254	99	43	20
Relative humidity (pm)		68	70	76	75	69	71	72	75	73	69	68	67

PART ONE

THE

BASICS

GETTING THERE FROM BRITAIN AND IRELAND

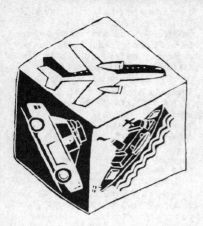

Although it's not yet possible to fly non-stop to Vietnam, many airlines offer indirect services (in other words, flights routed through one or more stops, usually including the carrier's domestic hub) to both Hanoi and Ho Chi Minh City. Taking these stops into account, flight times average 16–18 hours. Travelling from Glasgow, Manchester, Birmingham or other British airports, it's not necessarily cost-effective to build London into your schedule. Coming from Ireland, though, it may well work out more economically to take a cheap flight or ferry over to England, and start your long-haul flight from there.

With time in hand, you can work your transits to your advantage if you build a **stopover** into your schedule. By allowing you to experience a second

AIRLINES IN BRITAIN AND IRELAND

Aeroflot, 70 Piccadilly, London W1V (☎0171/355 2233). Five weekly no-frills flights to Bangkok via Moscow.

Air France, 177 Piccadilly, London W1Z (☎0181 /742 6600). Three flights a week to Ho Chi Minh, and two a week to Hanoi, via Paris and Bangkok.

Alitalia, 27–28 Piccadilly, London W1P (☎0171/602 7111). Extremely competitive flights to Bangkok via Rome, six days a week.

Cathay Pacific, 52 Berkeley St, London W1X (☎0171/747 8888). Pricey but comfortable daily flights to Hong Kong, with onward connections to Hanoi and Ho Chi Minh.

Emirates Airlines, 125 Pall Mall, London SW1Y (☎0171/930 5356). Two flights a week to Ho Chi Minh, via Dubai.

Finnair, 14 Clifford St, London W1 (☎0171/408 1222). Flights to Bangkok via Helsinki on Tuesday, Thursday and Sunday.

KLM, 8 Hanover St, London W1 (☎0181/750 9000). Twice-weekly services from Amsterdam to Ho Chi Minh, with connecting flights from UK regional airports.

Kuwait Airlines, 16 Baker St, London W1M (☎0171/412 0006). Four flights weekly to Bangkok via Kuwait City.

Lauda Air, 123 Buckingham Palace Rd, London SW1 (☎0171/630 5924). One flight weekly from Manchester and London via Vienna, stopping at Bangkok en route to Ho Chi Minh.

Lufthansa, 10 Old Bond St, London W1X (☎0345/737747). Three flights weekly to Frankfurt, and then non-stop to Ho Chi Minh.

Malaysia Airlines, 61 Piccadilly, London W1V (☎0181/740 2626). Four flights a week to Ho Chi Minh and two a week to Hanoi, all routed through Kuala Lumpur.

Singapore Airlines, 143–147 Regent St, London W1R (☎0181/747 0007). Daily flights to Ho Chi Minh, and three a week to Hanoi, changing in Singapore.

Tarom, 27 New Cavendish St, London W1M (☎0171/224 3693). Two flights weekly to Bangkok, routing through Bucharest.

Thai International, 41 Albemarle St, London W1M (☎0171/491 7953). Daily services to Ho Chi Minh, and five a week to Hanoi, all transiting in Bangkok.

Vietnam Airlines, c/o *Jetair UK*, 188 Hammersmith Rd, London W6 (☎0181/970 1533). *Jetair* issue composite tickets comprising *Air France* shuttle to Paris, and then picking up the *Vietnam Airlines* Paris–Hanoi and Paris–Ho Chi Minh services (both four flights weekly), all transiting in Dubai.

FLIGHT AGENTS IN BRITAIN AND IRELAND

Campus Travel, 52 Grosvenor Gardens, London SW1W 0AG (☎0171/730 8111); 541 Bristol Rd, Selly Oak, Birmingham B29 6AU (☎0121/414 1848); 61 Ditchling Rd, Brighton BN1 4SD (☎01273/570226); 39 Queens Rd, Clifton, Bristol BS8 1QE (☎0117/929 2494); 5 Emmanuel St, Cambridge CB1 1NE (☎01223/324283); 53 Forest Rd, Edinburgh EH1 2QP (☎0131/668 3303); 166 Deansgate, Manchester M3 3FE (☎0161/833 2046); 105–106 St Aldates, Oxford OX1 1DD (☎01865/242067). Student/youth travel specialists, with branches also in YHA shops and on university campuses all over Britain.

Council Travel, 28a Poland St, London W1V 3DB (☎0171/437 7767). Flights and student discounts.

Inflight Travel, 92–94 York Rd, Belfast 15 (☎01232/740187 or 743341). Long-haul flight specialist.

Joe Walsh Tours, 8–11 Baggot St, Dublin (☎01/676 3053). General budget fares agent.

North South Travel, Moulsham Mill Centre, Parkway, Chelmsford, Essex CM2 7PX (☎01245/492882). Friendly, competitive travel agency, offering discounted fares worldwide – profits are used to support projects in the developing world, especially the promotion of sustainable tourism.

Nouvelles Frontières, 11 Blenheim St, London W1Y 9LE (☎0171/629 7772).

STA Travel, 86 Old Brompton Rd, London SW7 3LH, 117 Euston Rd, London NW1 2SX, 38 Store St, London WC1 (☎0171/361 6262); 25 Queens Rd, Bristol BS8 1QE (☎0117/929 4399); 38 Sidney St, Cambridge CB2 3HX (☎01223/366966); 75 Deansgate, Manchester M3 2BW (☎0161/834

0668); 88 Vicar Lane, Leeds LS1 7JH (☎0113/244 9212); 36 George St, Oxford OX1 2OJ (☎01865/792800); and branches in Birmingham, Canterbury, Cardiff, Coventry, Durham, Glasgow, Loughborough, Nottingham, Warwick and Sheffield. Worldwide specialists in low-cost flights and tours for students and under-26s.

Stranmillis Travel, 84 Stranmillis Rd, Belfast BT9 5AD (☎01232/681457). Far Eastern specialist agent.

Trailfinders, 42–50 Earls Court Rd, London W8 6FT (☎0171/938 3366); 194 Kensington High St, London W8 7RG (☎0171/938 3939); 58 Deansgate, Manchester M3 2FF (☎0161/839 6969); 254–284 Sauchiehall St, Glasgow G2 3EH (☎0141/353 2224); 22–24 The Priory, Queensway, Birmingham B4 6BS (☎0121/236 1234); 48 Corn St, Bristol BS1 1HQ (☎0117/929 9000). One of the best-informed and most efficient agents.

Travel Bug, 597 Cheetham Hill Rd, Manchester M8 5EJ (☎0161/721 4000). Large range of discounted tickets.

Union Travel, 93 Piccadilly, London W1 (☎0171/493 4343). Competitive airfares.

World Travel Centre, 35 Pearse St, Dublin 2 (☎01/671 7155).

USIT, Fountain Centre, Belfast BT1 6ET (☎01232/324073); 10–11 Market Parade, Patrick St, Cork (☎021/270900); 33 Ferryquay St, Derry (☎01504/371888); Aston Quay, Dublin 2 (☎01/679 8833); Victoria Place, Eyre Square, Galway (☎091/565177); Central Buildings, O'Connell St, Limerick (☎061/415064); 36–37 Georges St, Waterford (☎051/72601). Student and youth specialists for flights and trains.

country, normally at no extra cost, stopovers can add extra spice to a holiday. If you fly with *Singapore Airlines*, for instance, you can enjoy a city-break in Singapore; with *Thai International*, you can stop off at Delhi or Bangkok (see box on p.3 for details of airlines and their routes).

Airlines that fly in and out of both Ho Chi Minh and Hanoi will normally be able to sell you an **open-jaw ticket**, which lets you fly into one city and out of the other, leaving you to travel up or down the country under your own steam. The cost for this more convenient means of seeing Vietnam equates to the most expensive return they sell – invariably the one to Hanoi.

Another option is a **round-the-world ticket** (RTW). Starting from around £750 for a one-year open ticket, these are a great means of designing your own, tailor-made trip around the globe. Many itineraries also offer the flexibility of substantial overland sections, for example London, Bangkok, HCM, overland to Hanoi, Bangkok, Sydney, overland to Melbourne, Auckland, LA, London (from £976). Although it's possible to include Ho Chi Minh or Hanoi in such a ticket, your choice of routes is usually wider if you route through Bangkok on your RTW ticket, and then pay the extra to bounce in and out of Vietnam from there.

FARES

For all flights you're best off booking through an established **flight agent,** although further discounts might be available to **students and under-26s** from certain agents, among them *Campus Travel* and *STA*. Tickets from discount agents are normally valid for a set period which could be anything from ninety days to a year. Always shop around before buying a ticket: airline ticketing is a notoriously complex and fickle business, governed largely by supply and demand. Scanning the small ads in Sunday papers, London's *Evening Standard* newspaper or *Time Out* magazine, or in regional newspapers and listings magazines, will give you some idea of the range of fares – though bear in mind that the ludicrously low fares cited are often simply a ploy to persuade you to call in the first place. Make sure any agent you deal with belongs to either *ABTA* or *IATA*, who will cover any debts if the agent goes bust.

High seasons differ from airline to airline. In general, though, July, August and December are the costliest months – and the most heavily booked, so plan ahead if this is when you want to travel. If you're not tied to particular dates, check the changeover dates between seasons: you might make a substantial saving by travelling a few days sooner or later. Discounted returns **to Ho Chi Minh** start from around £660 in the high season, and £540 at other times; to these prices, you can add £10–20 for flights **to Hanoi**. The most competitive prices are currently offered by *Lauda Air, Emirates, KLM* or *Thai International*.

The **cheapest** means of getting to Vietnam, though, can often work out to be a bargain-basement **flight to Bangkok**, followed by a **separate**

SPECIALIST TOUR OPERATORS

Bales, ☎01306/885991. Besides their whistlestop 8-day "Taste of Saigon" tour (3 days in Ho Chi Minh City, plus 5 days in Bangkok; from £1259), *Bales* offer a 17-day trip through Laos and Vietnam for £2690, and can also arrange tailor-made tours.

Earthwatch, ☎01865/311600, e-mail: ewoxford@vax.oxford.ac.uk. Runs several projects, mainly with an ecological or cultural slant, that accept volunteers; participants pay for their own travel and also help fund the research.

Exodus Expeditions, ☎0181/675 5550. The "Vietnam Adventure" trawls the length of Vietnam in 21 days, travelling by minibus and train, and staying in hotels, with prices starting at £1590. They also do a flexible 19-day cycling tour between Ho Chi Minh and Hanoi (£1700), with a back-up bus.

Explore Worldwide, ☎01252/319448. Itineraries include "Inside Vietnam" (14 days, from £1415), or the longer "Vietnam Explorer", which takes in Ha Long Bay and a trip to a minority village. A Cambodia extension, visiting Angkor Wat, can be added for an extra £500.

Frontier, ☎0171/613 1911, e-mail: enquiries @Frontier.mailbox.co.uk. Organize several 10-week field trips each year, combining biodiversity surveys in the forest and socio-economic work with local communities.

Kuoni Worldwide, ☎01306/40888. Holidays combining 2–3 nights in Ho Chi Minh City with

Hong Kong, Singapore, Thailand or Bali (from £899); their "Vietnamese Experience" (7 nights from £1595) takes in HCM City, Hué, Da Nang and Hanoi, bookended by stopovers in Thailand.

Regent Holidays, ☎0117/921 1711. Specialize in good-value, tailor-made travel arrangements throughout Indochina.

Silverbird Travel, ☎0181/875 9090. Far East specialists running an 11-night tour of northern hilltribes (£1070), and a tour of Ho Chi Minh, Hué, Hanoi and Vientiane by "lazy bicycle" (land-only £1105), among others; custom-made tours also arranged.

Simply Travel, ☎0181/995 8280. Offering a couple of very well-crafted, small-group tours: an upcountry yomp, and an extensive tour of the northern highlands that includes Mai Chau, Son La, Dien Bien Phu and Sa Pa. Prices range from £1490 to £1740 for 16 days.

Tennyson Travel, ☎0171/229 8612. Vietnam specialists, offering a range of tours, from stopovers in Ho Chi Minh and Hanoi up to a 21-day odyssey (£1695).

Thomas Cook Holidays, ☎01733/332255. The fully escorted, 13-night *Vistas of Vietnam* tour takes in Ho Chi Minh, Da Lat, Nha Trang, Da Nang, Hué and Hanoi, with all but the Nha Trang–Da Nang leg overland; sightseeing included, and optional tours available upon arrival. The trip weighs in at £2115 per person, excluding food, and includes 2 nights in Bangkok.

shuttle from there (operated by *Thai* and *Vietnam Airlines*, or, more expensively, *Air France*); *Aeroflot*, *Tarom*, *Kuwait Airlines*, *Finnair* and *Alitalia* offer some of the most affordable Bangkok returns, though creature comforts are noticeably by their absence on the first two of these airlines. Return fares from London to Bangkok can drop as low as £370, though such offers tend to get snapped up months in advance.

ORGANIZED TOURS

If you want to cover a lot of ground in a short time or have a specific interest you want to indulge, an organized tour might be worth considering. A raft of **specialist tour operators** offer packages that typically include flights, accommodation, day-time excursions and internal travel either by plane, train or road. These work out expensive compared to what you'd pay if you arranged everything inde-

pendently, but the more intrepid ones often feature activities it would be difficult to set up yourself. Before booking, make sure you know exactly what's included. Prices, which fluctuate throughout the year in line with airlines' high and low seasons, are based upon sharing a twin room; single supplements will add around £200–400 to the total cost. If you're concerned about costs, you can usually arrange much less expensive tours to all the sights, national parks and minority villages on the ground in Ho Chi Minh, Hanoi and other tourist centres through **local tour operators**: we've given details as appropriate throughout the *Guide*.

If you're keen to get a real **insight** into Vietnam, and are prepared to work to get it, there are also a couple of outfits undertaking research who allow paying volunteers to **participate** in their **projects** on a short-term basis; *Earthwatch* and *Frontier* both have offices in Britain (see box on previous page for details).

GETTING THERE FROM THE USA AND CANADA

Getting to Vietnam from North America is becoming cheaper and easier all the time. No American carriers offer direct services yet, but with diplomatic relations between the US and Vietnam restored, this state of affairs is sure to change in the very near future. *Northwest*, the only American carrier to fly non-stop from the US to Beijing, is

likely to be the first; in the meantime, there are many indirect flight options available on foreign airlines.

From the US, midweek, round-trip fares in the low season purchased through discount travel agents are as low as $1000 from **New York** (around a 21-hour journey, excluding stopovers) and $800 from major **West Coast cities** (around 17 hours); flying at the weekend adds about another $100. *China Airlines*, which flies via Taipei, and *Asiana* and *Korean Airlines*, which fly via Seoul, are the cheapest carriers. A round-trip ticket purchased directly from *China Airlines*, for instance, is $1100–1300 from the West Coast and $1400–1600 from the East. *EVA* can be slightly more expensive but worth considering for its added comforts. Some routings (see box opposite for details) require an overnight stay in another city such as Bangkok, Taipei, Hong Kong or Seoul, and often a hotel room will be included in your fare – ask the airline and shop around since travel agents' policies on this vary. Even when an overnight stay is not required, going to Vietnam can be a great excuse for a **stopover**. *Malaysia Air* and

AIRLINES AND AGENTS IN THE USA AND CANADA

AIRLINES

Air Canada, ☎1-800/776-3000; in Canada ☎1-800/555-1212. Daily service into Tokyo and Hong Kong from major Canadian cities with connections on other airlines to Ho Chi Minh City or Hanoi.

Asiana Airlines, ☎1-800/227-4262. Three flights weekly to Ho Chi Minh City from Los Angeles, San Francisco, New York and Vancouver via Seoul.

Canadian Airlines, ☎1-800/426-7000. Daily service to New York, Hong Kong or Bangkok from major Canadian cities with connections on other airlines to Ho Chi Minh City or Hanoi.

Cathay Pacific, ☎1-800/233-2742; in Canada ☎1-800/555-1212. Daily service to Ho Chi Minh City from Vancouver via Hong Kong; four times a week to Hanoi. Five flights a week from Toronto to Ho Chi Minh City via Hong Kong; four times a week to Hanoi.

China Airlines, ☎1-800/227-5118. Daily service to Ho Chi Minh City from Los Angeles and San Francisco via Taipei and service three times a week from New York via Anchorage and Taipei.

EVA Airlines, ☎1-800/695-1188. Daily service into Ho Chi Minh City from Los Angeles, San Francisco, New York and Seattle via Taipei.

Japan Airlines, ☎1-800/525-3663. Three flights weekly to Ho Chi Minh City via Osaka from Los Angeles and from New York via Tokyo and Osaka.

Korean Airlines, ☎1-800/438-5000. Twice-weekly service to Ho Chi Minh City from Los Angeles, San Francisco, Toronto-Montreal, Vancouver via Seoul.

Malaysia Air, ☎1-800/421-8641. Five flights a week into Ho Chi Minh City from Los Angeles via Taipei or Tokyo and Kuala Lumpur.

Northwest Airlines, ☎1-800/447-4747. Daily direct service from major US and Canadian cities to Hong Kong, Taipei or Singapore with connections on other airlines into Hanoi and Ho Chi Minh City. (*Northwest* has been given permission to start service into Ho Chi Minh City late in 1996.)

Philippines Airlines, ☎1-800/435-9725. Flies to Ho Chi Minh City three days a week from San Francisco or Los Angeles via Manila.

Singapore Airlines, ☎1-800/742-3333. Daily service from New York and Los Angeles to Ho Chi Minh City and Hanoi via Singapore. Twice-weekly flights from Vancouver via Singapore.

Thai International, ☎1-800/426-5204; in Canada, 1-800-668-8103. Four flights weekly to Ho Chi Minh City via Los Angeles and Seoul.

FLIGHT AGENTS AND CONSOLIDATORS

Air Brokers International, 323 Geary St, San Francisco, CA 94102 (☎1-800/883-3273; e-mail: airbroker@aimnet.com). Consolidator.

Air Courier Association, 191 University Blvd, Suite 300, Denver, CO 80206 (☎303/279-3600). Low-cost global courier fares.

Council Travel, 205 E 42nd St, New York, NY 10017 (☎1-800/743-1823). Discount travel agent offering student discounts, with branches in many US cities.

Educational Travel Center, 438 N Frances St, Madison, WI 53703 (☎1-800/747-5551). Student/youth discounts.

Flight Centre, S Granville St, Vancouver, BC (☎1-604/739-9539). Discount airfares to Asia from Canadian cities.

High Adventure Travel Inc, 253 Sacramento St, Suite 600, San Francisco, CA. 94111 (☎1-800/428-8735; e-mail: airtreks@highadv.com;

worldwide web site: http://www.highadv.com).

Last Minute Travel Club, 132 Brookline Ave, Boston, MA 02215 (☎1-800/LAST-MIN). Discount airfares, hotel packages.

Leisure Tyme Travel (☎1-800/322-TYME). Discounter that looks for lowest airfares.

New Frontiers/Nouvelles Frontières, 12 E 33rd St, New York, NY 10016 (☎1-800/366-6387); 1001 Sherbrook E, Suite 720, Montreal, H2L 1L3 (☎514/526-8444); other branches in San Francisco and Quebec City. French discount travel firm.

STA Travel, 48 E 11th St, New York, NY 10013 (☎1-800/777-0112). Discounts for students under 26.

Travel CUTS, 187 College St, Toronto M5T 1P7 (☎416/979-2406). Canadian student travel organization with branches all over the country.

Philippines Airlines allow one free stopover in each direction, while *Asiana* charges an extra $50.

From Canada, *Cathay Pacific* has the best service from either Vancouver (around 17hrs) or Toronto/Montreal (around 21hrs). A round-trip ticket for midweek travel purchased directly from the airline will run to CAN$1898–2150 for West Coast departures (overnight stay in Hong Kong required) and CAN$2123–2373 for East Coast departures, but discounted tickets are widely available. You can fly round-trip from Vancouver, Toronto or Montreal on *Korean Airlines* via Seoul, for instance, for as little as CAN$1328–1438 for East Coast departures and CAN$1460–1595 for West Coast departures. *Asiana Airlines*, with daily non-stop flights from Seattle to Seoul and connections three times a week into Ho Chi Minh City, is another inexpensive alternative for Vancouver-based travellers.

It's possible to include Vietnam on a **Circle-the-Pacific** deal, which allows four stopovers at no extra charge if tickets are bought fourteen to thirty days in advance, or on a **round-the-world** **ticket** (RTW). Some travel agents can sell you "off-the-shelf" RTW tickets that will have you touching down in about half a dozen cities; others will have to tailor-make one for you, which is apt to be more expensive. Sample low-season fares and routes are New York, Seoul, Hong Kong, Ho Chi Minh City (overland) Hanoi (overland) Laos, Bangkok, Taipei, New York for US$1752; and Los Angeles, Seoul, Hong Kong, Ho Chi Minh City (overland) Hanoi (overland) Laos, Bangkok, Jakarta, Denpasar, Los Angeles for US$1530. Add around US$140–180 for departures from Canadian cities.

Courier travel is also becoming an option because of increased interest in doing business in Vietnam, although the hit or miss nature of these makes them most suitable for the single traveller with a very flexible schedule.

SHOPPING FOR TICKETS

Airfares from North America to southeast Asia are highest from around early June to late August, and again from early December to early January.

SPECIALIST TOUR OPERATORS IN THE USA AND CANADA

Absolute Asia, ☎1-800/736-8187. A variety of tours in Vietnam, Laos and Cambodia starting at US$1485 for 4 nights in Hanoi and Ho Chi Minh City including transportation to and from Bangkok; tours can also be combined with other southeast Asian destinations.

Adventures Abroad, ☎604/732-9922. A Vancouver-based company with a good reputation for small-group tours, offering 2- to 3-week tours in Vietnam and Cambodia starting at US$1595 (land only) or US$3080 including airfare from New York and US$2755 with flights from the West Coast.

Asia Pacific Adventures, ☎213/935-3156. Small group (6–12 people) bicycle tours, tribal treks and tours for women only. A 9-day tribal trek starting in Bangkok is US$1474 not including airfare, and a 13-day rail tour from Hanoi to Ho Chi Minh City is US$1494. They'll also tailor-make trips.

Bolder Adventures, ☎1-800/642-2742. Small-group tours starting from US$2995 for a 16-day "Vietnam Discovery" tour including hiking and train travel in Ho Chi Minh City, Hanoi, Hué and Cuc Phuong National Park. The company also sells customized tours and trips combining Vietnam with other southeast Asian destinations: a 22-day Indochina tour, including transportation to and from Bangkok, starts at US$4100 (land only).

Cathay Pacific Holidays, ☎1-800/233-2742; in Canada ☎1-800/268-6868. Discounts on hotels and airport transfers through their "Stay a While" programme for those flying on *Cathay Pacific*. Hotels in Ho Chi Minh City and Hanoi can be booked directly through them before you leave.

The Center for Global Education, ☎612-330-1159. Educational tours focusing on the evolving relationship between Vietnam and the United States; 14-day tours cost US$2895 including airfare from the West Coast.

Global Volunteers, ☎1-800/487-1074. Offers 2- and 3-week volunteer service projects in Vietnam. Prices start at US$1790, not including airfare to Saigon. Participants pay programme and travel costs and donate their services.

Northwest World Wide Vacations, bookings via travel agents. A *Northwest Airlines* subsidiary, offering 2-night stays in Ho Chi Minh City starting at US$204 for hotel, airport transfers and a half-day sightseeing tour.

Orbitours, ☎1-800/235-5895. Australian company offering hotel and sightseeing packages only for independent travellers, and 10-day tours starting at US$1419 (land only).

All other times are considered low season. The price difference between the high and low seasons is only about US$200 on a typical round-trip fare, but you'll have to make your reservation further in advance during the high season or you could end up paying more than you'd counted on.

Whatever the airlines have on offer, there are any number of specialist travel agents which will set out to beat it. These are the outfits you'll see advertising in the Sunday newspaper travel sections, and they come in several varieties. **Consolidators** buy up large blocks of tickets to sell at a discount. They don't normally impose advance purchase requirements, but they do often charge very stiff fees for date changes; note also that airlines generally won't alter tickets after they've gone to a consolidator, so you can only make changes through the consolidator itself. Remember, as these companies' profit margins are pretty tiny, they make their money by dealing in bulk – don't expect them to entertain lots of questions. **Discount agents** also wheel and deal in blocks of tickets offloaded by the airlines, but typically offer a range of other travel-related services such as insurance, youth and student ID cards, car rentals, tours and the like. **Discount travel clubs**, offering money off air tickets, car rental and so on, may be worthwhile if you travel a lot; most charge annual membership fees. Don't automatically assume that tickets purchased through a travel specialist will be the cheapest available – once you get a quote, check with the individual airlines and you may be able to turn up an even better deal.

Finally, be advised that the pool of travel companies is swimming with sharks – *never* deal with a company that demands cash up front or refuses to accept payment by credit card.

PACKAGES AND ORGANIZED TOURS

There's a wide variety of airfare-hotel-sightseeing **packages** available, as well as **organized tours** that cover everything from hilltribe visits to trekking and biking. Tours range in length from a few days to several weeks. You can choose to explore Vietnam only, or combine a tour with Laos and Cambodia. Some tours also include transportation to and from Bangkok; see box on facing page for more details.

GETTING THERE FROM AUSTRALIA AND NEW ZEALAND

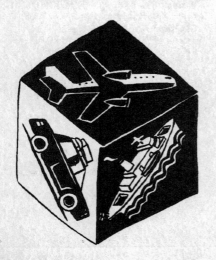

A reasonable range of flights ply the airspace between Australasia and Vietnam, flying either direct, or through one or other of southeast Asia's gateway airports. The main carriers with direct service from Australia to Vietnam are *Thai Airways, Singapore Airlines, Qantas* and *Vietnam Airlines*, or else there's the option of using services from Australia to Bangkok, Singapore or Hong Kong and then getting connecting flights to Hanoi or Ho Chi Minh City – leaving plenty of scope for stopovers.

Many people see Vietnam as part of a longer trip, either by flying over to Indonesia, travelling overland to, say, Bangkok, and hopping in and out from there; or on a **round-the-world ticket**, though routes including Vietnam are as yet uncommon, and it's more usual to take in Vietnam as a side-trip from either Bangkok or Singapore.

FARES

Return **fares** in the high season (mid-Nov until mid-Jan) purchased through agents cost around A$1500 from Sydney and A$1400 from Perth. Low-season fares (the rest of the year) from Sydney are about A$1300 and from Perth around $1100.

Thai Airways offers a service **from Sydney** through Bangkok that allows you to fly into Ho Chi Minh City, travel overland to Hanoi and fly out from there, or do the reverse for the same price –

A$1320 in the low season, A$1489 in the high. Slightly more expensive, *Qantas* offers a similar deal for overlanding between Ho Chi Minh City and Hanoi, with tickets for a low-season $1319 and a high-season A$1479. The same schedule but **from Perth** costs from A$1120 to A$1380. **From Darwin**, there are no direct flights to Vietnam, which leaves you the choice of either shuttling to another Australian city or flying to Bangkok and picking up a connecting flight there.

If you decide to take a look at Thailand or Indonesia on the way, cheapest fares to Bangkok

---

AIRLINES AND FLIGHT AGENTS

AIRLINES

Malaysian Airlines (low-call ☎13 2627; in NZ ☎09/373 2471). Auckland to Kuala Lumpur on Wed, Fri, Sun; from Kuala Lumpur on to Ho Chi Minh City on Tues, Thurs, Sat and Sun.

Qantas ☎02/9957 0111; in NZ ☎09/357 8900. Weekly service to Hanoi and Ho Chi Minh City from Sydney via Bangkok. Weekly Auckland-to-Ho Chi Minh City flight via Sydney and Bangkok.

Singapore Airlines ☎02/9350 0100 in Sydney; elsewhere, low-call ☎13 1011; in NZ ☎09/379 3209. Daily service from Sydney and Perth to Ho Chi Minh City via Singapore, plus 3 flights a

week to Hanoi. Flights from Auckland to Singapore Tues, Thurs, Sat and Sun, from where there are daily flights to Ho Chi Minh City.

Thai Airways ☎02/9844 0999; in NZ ☎09/377 3886. Hanoi from Sydney via Bangkok 5 times a week, and from Perth via Bangkok 3 times a week; Ho Chi Minh from Sydney via Bangkok daily, and from Perth via Bangkok 3 times a week.

Vietnam Airlines ☎02/9252 3303. Twice-weekly flights to Ho Chi Minh City from Sydney, and daily connecting flights from Bangkok, Hong Kong and Singapore; no service from Perth or Darwin.

FLIGHT AGENTS

Accent on Travel, 545 Queen St, Brisbane (☎07/3832 1777).

Anywhere Travel, 345 Anzac Parade, Kingsford, Sydney (☎02/9663 0411).

Budget Travel, 16 Fort St, Auckland; other branches around the city (☎09/366 0061; toll-free ☎0800/ 808 040).

Flight Centres Australia: Circular Quay, Sydney (☎02/9241 2422); Bourke St, Melbourne (☎03/9650 2899); plus other branches nation-wide. New Zealand: National Bank Towers, 205–225 Queen St, Auckland (☎09/209 6171); Shop 1M, National Mutual Arcade, 152 Hereford St, Christchurch (☎03/379 7145); 50–52 Willis St, Wellington (☎04/472 8101); other branches countrywide.

Harvey World Travel, 631 Princes Highway, Kogarah, Sydney (☎02/9567 6099); branches nationwide.

Northern Gateway, 22 Cavenagh St, Darwin (☎08/8941 1394).

Passport Travel, Kings Cross Plaza, Suite 11a, 4010 St Kilda Rd, Melbourne (☎03/9824 7183).

STA Travel, Australia: 855 George St, Ultimo, Sydney (☎02/9212 1255; toll-free ☎1800/637 444); 256 Flinders St, Melbourne (☎03/9654 7266); other offices in Townsville, state capitals and major universities. New Zealand: Travellers' Centre, 10 High St, Auckland (☎09/309 0458); 233 Cuba St, Wellington (☎04/385 0561); 90 Cashel St, Christchurch (☎03/379 9098); other offices in Dunedin, Palmerston North, Hamilton and major universities.

Thomas Cook, Australia: 321 Kent St, Sydney (☎02/9248 6100); 330 Collins St, Melbourne (☎03/9602 3811); branches in other state capitals. New Zealand: Shop 250a St Luke's Square, Auckland (☎09/849 2071).

Topdeck Travel, 65 Glenfell St, Adelaide (☎08/8232 7222).

SPECIALIST TOUR OPERATORS IN AUSTRALIA AND NEW ZEALAND

Explore, bookings through *Adventure World*, ☎1800/221931; in NZ ☎09/524 5118. A 12-day tour of Vietnam's major sights is A$1815/NZ$2085 per person; their 19-day "Vietnam Explorer" tour of the Ho Chi Minh trail includes hilltribe visits, bike rides and boat trips, and costs A$2335/NZ$2685. Accommodation is in hotels and guesthouses, and a 4-day extension into Cambodia (including Angkor Wat) can be taken for an extra A$1200/NZ$1368.

Intrepid Travel Pty Ltd, ☎1800/629186. The 2-week country-wide tour costs A$1390, the 3-week tour A$1890, and there are also 3-week adventure tours (A$1790) including hilltribe visits, trekking, cycling and island camping.
Orbitours, ☎02/9954 1399 in Sydney; elsewhere in Australia toll-free ☎1800/221176. Customized packages for independent travellers including trekking, diving and hilltribe visits, and 14-night group tours from Hanoi to Ho Chi Minh City by plane, bus and train for about A$1800.

---

with *Thai* are in the region of A$1200, while *Garuda* flies to Ho Chi Minh with a Bali stopover for A$1265–1375 from the eastern states, dropping to A$1060–1280 from Perth.

STA also sells return tickets on *Vietnam Airlines* from Bangkok to Ho Chi Minh for A$400 and Bangkok to Hanoi for A$460 (year-round prices).

From New Zealand, *Malaysian Airlines* flies to Hanoi for a year-round fare of NZ$1490, a service for which you'll pay NZ$1590 on *Qantas*. Otherwise, you could always fly from Auckland to either Bangkok, Hong Kong or Singapore, and con-

nect with a Vietnam flight – *Vietnam Airlines* tickets from Bangkok to Hanoi and back sell for approximately NZ$520 year-round.

PACKAGES AND ORGANIZED TOURS

An organized tour is worth considering if you have ambitious sightseeing plans and only a short time to accomplish them. Some of the "adventure"-orientated tours can also help you to get to more remote areas and organize activities that may be difficult to arrange yourself, such as trekking and cycling.

OVERLAND ROUTES TO VIETNAM

It's now possible to enter Vietnam overland from either Cambodia, Laos or China, and if you've got time to spare, taking this option means you can see that much more of Indochina than you would if you simply jet in.

From Laos, there's presently only one border crossing, at Lao Bao (see p.288), which is some 80km southwest of Dong Ha.

From Cambodia your only choice is to drop southeast from Phnom Penh to Moc Bai (see p.107), and from there to continue on to Ho Chi Minh City.

From China, however, there are more possibilities. The train that runs between Beijing and

Hanoi (see p.403 crosses into Vietnam at Dong Dang, north of Lang Son, but you can also cross further west at Lao Cai (see p.384).

For help with arrangements, you could always contact a reliable travel agent in Bangkok. *Diethelm Travel* in Bangkok can be contacted on the Internet, and reservations can be made by e-mail. Listings cover all of the company's southeast Asian itineraries, plus hotel information, transfers, transportation, with tariffs, maps and photographs. e-mail: dietravl@ksc.net.th, or access Diethelm's home page directory on the worldwide web: http://www.sino.net/diethelm /index.html.

VISAS AND RED TAPE

All foreign nationals need a visa to enter Vietnam. Tourist visas are generally valid for 30 days, and cost the local equivalent of US$40–60.

The majority of visitors apply for a visa in their country of residence, either from the embassy direct (see box on facing page), or through a specialist visa agent or tour agent. Processing normally takes between a week and ten days (longer for overseas Vietnamese); to be on the safe side, allow several weeks as mistakes are common and inexplicable delays often occur. For people travelling via neighbouring Asian countries, Bangkok is the most popular place to apply for a Vietnamese visa, since it's relatively quick (4–5 working days) and straightforward, though not necessarily any cheaper (around US$50 for a tourist visa).

To apply for a tourist visa, you have to submit two **application forms** with two passport-sized photographs and the fee. The 30 days is counted from the arrival date you specify on the form, so if you enter Vietnam later than anticipated, you lose time on your visa. On collecting the visa you will be given one copy of your application form with a photograph attached; keep this form with your passport as it's required by the immigration authorities on arrival in Vietnam. If you don't have it for some reason, blank forms are available at immigration or on the plane and all you'll need is a spare passport photo. People without a photo are charged for the services of a handy photographer (US$2–5).

Business visas are valid for three or six months and can be issued for multiple entry, though you'll need a sponsoring office in Vietnam to underwrite your application. Special circumstances affect **overseas Vietnamese**, who are generally only recognized as Vietnamese nationals by the government of Vietnam. Questions about dual nationality should be directed to the embassy in your country of residence.

On the application form you are also asked to specify your **exit and entry points**, which are then written in the visa. Unless you request otherwise, you will automatically be given "Noi Bai/Tan Son Nhat" (the airports of Hanoi and Ho Chi Minh City respectively). If you intend to enter by any of the land crossings (Dong Dang, Huu Nghi, Lao Cai, Lao Bao or Moc Bai) you need to state this when you apply for the visa, and check what eventually appears. Some embassies and consulates are reluctant to give entry points other than the two airports, in which case the only option is to try and get it changed in one of the neighbouring countries (Laos, Cambodia, China or Thailand); this seems to be slightly easier, though by no means guaranteed. (The exit point you originally specify is less vital as it can be changed in Vietnam, though you'll have to pay – see below.)

On **arrival** at the airport or border immigration desk you'll need the copy of your visa application form plus a completed Arrival and Departure Card. The Departure Card, which will be returned to you, is generally required to register at hotels and then has to be submitted when you eventually leave the country. As it's all too easy to leave it in a hotel, having a photocopy's not a bad idea – it won't be accepted in lieu of the original, but may help streamline things in case of loss.

If you decide to exit Vietnam **overland** and don't have the correct **exit point** in your Vietnam visa, you need to get this changed *after* obtaining the appropriate entry visa to Laos, China or Cambodia. This is relatively cheap and easy, but can only be handled by certain, officially approved tour agents in Hanoi, Ho Chi Minh City or Da Nang; ask at the city's Immigration Department (see "Listings" sections of main city accounts in the *Guide*) for details of these agents. Agents charge different amounts for changing the exit point (usually US$15–25) and take between two and four days, so it pays to shop around if you can. If you turn up at the border with the wrong exit point you'll be "fined" US$40–50, depending on the whim of the official you happen to deal with.

VIETNAMESE EMBASSIES AND CONSULATES

Australia 489 New South Head Road, Double Bay, Sydney. Visa enquiries ☎02/9327 1912; general enquiries ☎02/327 2539.

Cambodia Achar Mean St, Phnom Penh (☎23/362471)

Canada Contact: Mme Dinh T.M. Huyen, Ottawa (☎613/744 4963)

China 32 Quanghau Lu, Jianguomenwai, Beijing (☎10/532 1155)

Hong Kong 15th Floor, Great Smart Tower, 230 Wanchai Rd, Wanchai (☎259 4510)

Ireland Contact UK office (see below)

Laos 1 Thap Luong Road, Vientiane (☎5578)

Netherlands Contact Belgian office at Avenue de la Floride 130, 1180 Brussels (☎02/374 9133)

Singapore 10 Leeton Park, Singapore 1026 (☎468 3747)

Thailand 83/1 Wireless Rd, Bangkok 10500 (☎02/251 7201)

UK 12 Victoria Rd, London W8 5RD (☎0171/937 3174)

USA 1233 20th St NW, Washington DC 20036 (☎202-861-0737)

Note: visa information is also available on the Internet; address e-mail to Info@zvs.com.

It's important to be aware that if you are leaving Vietnam on the train through Lang Son to China, the exit point you need is Dong Dang (the train station) and *not* the Huu Nghi road crossing (see *The Far North* chapter, p.403, for more on travelling to China).

VISA EXTENSIONS

Until recently it was fairly easy to obtain a **visa extension** in Vietnam. However, in August 1995 the rules changed and now, in theory, no extensions are being given. Though the situation seems to have eased-up somewhat since then, it's unlikely to return to the days of cheap and trouble-free extensions. Check at the embassy or with specialist tour agents before you leave for the latest situation, or with the immigration police in Ho Chi Minh City or Hanoi.

Unless extensions become available again, the only option if you want to stay in Vietnam for longer than one month is to **leave the country and re-enter** on a new visa. The most popular cities to head for are Bangkok or Phnom Penh, as these are the cheapest to get to (Laos is a less attractive option, since an expensive – US$90–100 – tourist visa is required if you're returning to Vietnam). To save hanging around in Bangkok or Phnom Penh, you can apply for your new visa (costing around US$40–50) at a tour agent in Vietnam before you leave: the Immigration Department approval number will be faxed through to the embassy, then you simply turn up (with your approval letter citing the same number and 2 passport photos) to get your passport stamped, which usually takes just a day.

Incidentally, **overstaying** your visa will result in a hefty fine (up to US$2000), and is not recommended.

Holders of **business visas** can apply for an extension only through the same office that sponsored their original visa, backed up with reasons as to why an extension is necessary.

CUSTOMS

On arrival you have to fill out a Baggage Declaration Form declaring cameras, video and camcorders, tape recorders, portable computers and any other expensive electronic equipment or items of jewellery. It's a good idea to list any valuable items which you want to take out of the country again, even if it's not actually required. The **duty-free allowance** is 200 cigarettes, 1.5 litres of alcohol plus perfume and jewellery for personal use. The limit on currency is US$7000 (in either cash or travellers' cheques); anything in excess of this sum must be declared.

After your baggage has been checked, the yellow, duplicate copy of the Baggage Declaration Form will be given back to you – and will be required on departure (again, a photocopy might help matters should you lose it). Note that you have to show your baggage check when reclaiming luggage at any airport in Vietnam; the stub should be stuck to either your airline ticket or boarding pass.

Heading out again, note that **export restrictions** apply on items of "cutural or historical significance", so don't get too carried away buying Champa relics (see "Shopping and souvenirs", p.49, for more on this).

INSURANCE

Most people will find it essential to take out a good travel insurance policy. Bank and credit cards (particularly *American Express*) often have certain levels of medical or other insurance included if you use them to pay for your trip; this can be quite comprehensive, anticipating such mishaps as lost or stolen baggage and missed connections. Similarly, if you have a good "all risks" home insurance policy it may well cover your possessions against loss or theft even when overseas, and many private medical schemes also cover you when abroad – make sure you know the procedure and the helpline number.

If you plan to participate in water **sports**, or do some **trekking**, you may have to pay an extra premium; check carefully that any insurance policy you are considering will cover you in case of an accident. It's a good idea to make a note of the policy details and leave them with someone at home in case you lose the original. Note also that very few insurers will arrange on-the-spot payments in the event of a major expense or loss; you will usually be reimbursed only after going home. In all cases of loss or **theft** of goods, you will have to contact the local **police** to have a **report** made out so that your insurer can process the claim; for **medical claims**, you'll need to provide supporting bills. Keep photocopies of everything you send to the insurer and note any time period within which you must lodge any claims.

BRITISH AND IRISH COVER

In Britain and Ireland, travel insurance schemes (from around £35–50 a month for Vietnam) are sold by almost every **travel agent** or **bank**, and by specialist insurance companies. Policies issued by *Campus Travel*, *STA*, *Endsleigh*, *Frizzell* or *Columbus* (see box below for details) are all good value. *Columbus* and some banks also do **multi-trip policies** which offer twelve months' cover for around £125.

TRAVEL INSURANCE SUPPLIERS

BRITAIN AND IRELAND
Campus Travel, ☎0171/730 8111.
Columbus Travel Insurance, ☎0171/375 0011.
Endsleigh Insurance, ☎0171/436 4451.
Frizzell Insurance, ☎01202/292333.
STA, ☎0171/361 6262.
USIT, Belfast ☎01232/324073; Dublin ☎01/679 8833.

USA AND CANADA
Access America, ☎1-800/284-8300.
Carefree Travel Insurance, ☎1-800/645-2424.
Desjardins Travel Insurance (Canada only), ☎1-800/463-7830.

ISIS (International Student Insurance Service) – sold by STA Travel, ☎1-800/777-0112.
Travel Assistance International, ☎1-800/821-2828.
Travel Guard, ☎1-800/826-1300.
Travel Insurance Services, ☎1-800/937-1387.

AUSTRALIA AND NEW ZEALAND
AFTA, ☎02/9956 4800.
Cover More, in Sydney ☎02/9968 1333; elsewhere in Australia toll-free ☎1800/251881.
Ready Plan Australia toll-free ☎1800/337462; New Zealand ☎09/379 3399.
UTAG, in Sydney ☎02/9819 6855; elsewhere in Australia, toll-free ☎1800/809462.

US AND CANADIAN COVER

Before buying an insurance policy, check that you're not already covered. Private health plans typically provide some overseas medical coverage, although they are unlikely to pick up the full tab in the event of a mishap. Homeowners' or renters' insurance often covers theft or loss of documents, money and valuables while overseas. After exhausting these possibilities, you might want to contact a specialist travel insurance company; your travel agent can usually recommend one, or see the box on facing page.

Premiums for travel to Vietnam start at around US$65 for a two-week trip; $85 for three weeks to a month; $122 for two months and $180 for three months. Longer-term plans are also available. Note that most North American travel policies apply only to items lost, stolen or damaged while in the custody of an identifiable, responsible third party – hotel porter, airline, luggage consignment, etc. Even in these cases you will have to contact the local police within a certain time limit to have a complete report made out so that your insurer can process the claim.

AUSTRALIAN AND NEW ZEALAND COVER

Travel insurance is available from travel agents or direct from insurance companies (see box on facing page). Policies are broadly comparable in premium and coverage; a typical one will cost A$150 for one month, $220 for two months and $280 for three months.

HEALTH

Vietnam's health problems read like a dictionary of tropical medicine. Diseases that are under control elsewhere in southeast Asia have been sustained here by poverty, dietary deficiencies, poor health care and the disruption caused by half a century of war. However, by coming prepared (see also "Insurance", above) and taking a few simple precautions while in the country, you're unlikely to come down with anything worse than a cold or a dose of travellers' diarrhoea.

If you do get ill in Vietnam, international clinics in Hanoi and Ho Chi Minh City can provide diagnosis and treatment or sound advice. While you shouldn't run to a doctor at every headache or bout of diarrhoea, in general it's far better to seek medical advice at an early stage rather than attempting to treat yourself with potentially dangerous drugs or leaving it too late.

BEFORE YOU GO

When planning your trip it's wise to visit a **doctor** as early as possible, preferably at least two months before you leave, to allow time to complete any recommended courses of **vaccinations**. If you have any longstanding medical conditions, particular health concerns or are travelling with young children, consult your doctor and take any required medications with you. It's also advisable to have a trouble-shooting **dental check-up** – and remember that you generally need to start taking **anti-malarial tablets** one week before your departure.

For up-to-the-minute information, it may be worth visiting a specialized **travel clinic** (see box over); most clinics also sell travel-associated accessories, including mosquito nets and first-aid kits.

VACCINATIONS

No vaccinations are **required** for Vietnam (except yellow fever if you're coming directly from an area where the disease is endemic), but typhoid and hepatitis A jabs are **recommended**; it's also worth ensuring you're up to date with boosters such as tetanus and polio. Additional injections to consider, depending on the season and risk of exposure, are hepatitis B, Japanese encephalitis, meningitis and rabies. All these immunizations can be obtained at international clinics in Ho Chi Minh City and Hanoi, but it's less hassle and usually cheaper to get them done at home.

Typhoid vaccine is reasonably effective and can be administered either by injection or orally. Most medical authorities no longer recommend

MEDICAL RESOURCES FOR TRAVELLERS

BRITAIN AND IRELAND

British Airways Travel Clinic, 156 Regent St, London W1 (Mon–Fri 9am–4.15pm, Sat 10am–4pm; ☎0171/439 9584); branches at 101 Cheapside, London EC2 (☎0171/606 2977) and at the *BA* terminal in London's Victoria Station (☎0171/233 6661); plus regional clinics (call ☎0171/831 5333 for details of the one nearest to you).

Hospital for Tropical Diseases – at St Pancras Hospital, 4 St Pancras Way, London NW1 (☎0171/530 3454).

MASTA (Medical Advisory Service for Travellers Abroad), London School of Hygiene and Tropical Medicine. Operates a premium-rate Travellers' Health Line (☎0891/224100) 24 hours a day, 7 days a week, supplying written information tailored to your journey by return of post.

Travel Medicine Services, PO Box 254, 16 College St, Belfast 1 (☎01232/315220).

Tropical Medical Bureau, Grafton St Medical Centre, Dublin 2 (☎01/671 9200); Dun Laoghaire Medical Centre, 5 Northumberland Ave, Dun Laoghaire, Co Dublin (☎01/280 4996).

USA AND CANADA

Canadian Society for International Health, 170 Laurier Ave W, Suite 902, Ottawa, ON K1P 5V5 (☎613/230-2654). Distributes a free pamphlet, "Health Information for Canadian Travelers."

IAMAT (International Association for Medical Assistance to Travelers), 417 Center St, Lewiston, NY 14092 (☎716/754-4883) and 40 Regal Rd, Guelph, ON N1K 1B5 (☎519/836-0102). This non-profit organization provides lists of English-speaking doctors, climate charts and leaflets on various diseases and inoculations.

Travel Medicine, 351 Pleasant St, Suite 312, Northampton, MA 01060 (☎1-800/872-8633). Sells first-aid kits, mosquito netting, water filters and other health-related travel products.

Travelers Medical Center, 31 Washington Square, New York, NY 10011 (☎212/982-1600). Consultation service on immunizations and treatment of diseases for people travelling to developing countries.

AUSTRALIA AND NEW ZEALAND

Auckland Hospital, Park Rd, Grafton, Auckland (☎09/797 440).

Travellers' Medical and Vaccination Centre, Level 7, 428 George St, Sydney (☎02/9221 7133); Level 3, 393 Little Bourke St, Melbourne (☎03/9602 5788); Level 6, 29 Gilbert Place, Adelaide (☎08/8212 7522); Level 6, 247 Adelaide St, Brisbane (☎07/3221 9066); 1 Mill St, Perth (☎08/9321 1977).

Travellers Immunization Service, 303 Pacific Hwy, Sydney (☎02/9416 1348).

Travel Health and Vaccination Clinic, 114 Williams St, Melbourne (☎03/9670 2020).

Travel-Bug Medical and Vaccination Centre, 161 Ward St, North Adelaide (☎08/8267 3544).

---

the cholera vaccine for tourists since it has proved only fifty percent effective and can provoke a severe reaction.

Hepatitis is an inflammation of the liver in which the most distinctive characteristic is yellowing of the eyes and skin, usually preceded by tiredness, high fever, and pain in the upper right abdomen. There are many different strains but the most common are hepatitis A and B, both of which can be prevented by vaccination. For protection against **hepatitis A**, which is spread by contaminated food and water, the *Havrix* vaccine is expensive but extremely effective – a single injection provides immunity for up to ten years. If only gammaglobulin is available, leave the injection as late as possible before departure as it wears off after 3–6 months, depending on the dosage. **Hepatitis B**, like the HIV virus, can be passed on through unprotected sexual contact, blood transfusions and dirty needles. The very effective vaccine (3 injections over 6 months) is recommended for anyone in a high-risk category, including those travelling extensively in rural areas with access to only basic medical care.

The risks of contracting **Japanese encephalitis** are extremely small, but as the disease is untreatable, those travelling extensively in the countryside, especially in the north during and soon after the summer rainy season, should consider immunization. The course consists of two injections at two-week intervals plus a booster for longer protection, but is not recommended for those with liver, heart or kidney disorders, or for multiple-allergy sufferers. If your plans include long stays in remote areas your doctor may also recommend vaccination against **meningitis** (a single shot) and **rabies**. The pre-exposure vaccine for rabies consists of two injections over 1–3 months with a third a year later and then a booster every 2–5 years; if bitten, you still need to have shots but fewer than otherwise, and it gives you a little more time to reach medical help

Get all your shots recorded on an **International Certificate** of Vaccination: some travellers entering Vietnam from China have been asked to show certificates by immigration officers hoping to levy a "fine".

GENERAL PRECAUTIONS

There's no point in getting paranoid about your health while travelling in Vietnam but it's worth being aware of the dangers and taking several **commonsense precautions**. The most important measures are to keep your resistance high and allow adequate time to acclimatize to the heat, humidity and an unfamiliar diet. Ensure you eat sufficient quantities and maintain a balanced diet in order to keep up mineral and vitamin intakes; eating lots of peeled fresh fruit helps, though you may also want to bring some multi-vitamin and mineral tablets to make up for any shortfalls. If you tend to sweat a lot, add a little extra salt to your food and drink plenty of bottled water or hot tea. In tropical climates it's easy to get run down and become more susceptible to whatever's around, especially if you're doing a lot of travelling.

Personal hygiene is one area you can control and it pays to be vigilant in a climate where bacteria thrive. Wash your hands frequently, especially before eating, and avoid sharing drinks, cigarettes or toothbrushes. Infections take hold easily so treat even the smallest cuts, scratches and bites with care: clean thoroughly with boiled water, apply iodine or antiseptic (a spray is useful) and then keep them dry and covered; change dressings frequently and repeat the process after washing as the water is likely to be contaminated. It's advisable to wear shoes at all times, and flip-flops (thongs) in the shower – and don't slosh around in lakes and irrigation canals, since they often harbour snails which carry bilharzia (river blindness).

Bottled **water** is plentiful in Vietnam and there should be no difficulty finding it except on treks into the remoter regions (for more on water, see the box over the page). As regards **food**, the two most important precautions are to eat at places which are busy and look clean, and to stick to fresh, thoroughly cooked foods. Just because a restaurant is expensive doesn't mean it's necessarily safe, and you're generally better-off eating Vietnamese dishes wherever you are. Ingredients tend to be ultra-fresh, but if a dish seems tired or looks as if it might have been reheated give it a miss, and send back anything undercooked or luke-warm. Food that is boiled or fried in front of you – such as bowls of steaming-hot *pho* (soup) – is a good bet. Seafood is such a feature of Vietnamese cuisine that it's a shame to miss-out, but it pays to be extra wary of shellfish. Fresh fruit you've peeled yourself is safe; other uncooked foods such as salads and raw vegetables are risky, but as they're often an integral part of Vietnamese dishes it's difficult to avoid them entirely. Ice creams and yoghurts from reputable outlets in the main cities shouldn't cause problems.

Following these precautions will greatly increase your chances of staying healthy. However, if you do fall ill and are concerned by the symptoms, get yourself to Hanoi or Ho Chi Minh City for diagnosis. Nearly all the diseases mentioned here can be treated effectively with no long-term consequences as long as they're caught in the early stages.

INTESTINAL TROUBLES

As P J O'Rourke helpfully pointed out, travel in developing countries "entails an extraordinary amount of having to go to the bathroom". **Diarrhoea** is the most common ailment to afflict travellers, often in a mild form while your stomach adapts to an unfamiliar diet. If there are no other major symptoms then it will probably all be over in two or three days and shouldn't require any treatment. The sudden onset of diarrhoea accompanied by severe stomach cramps and vomiting could indicate food poisoning, which should also run its course within a couple of days. In either case, it is essential to drink lots of water and in severe cases replace lost salts by taking oral rehydration solution (commonly known as ORS); this is especially important with young children. Sachets are widely available, or you can

WHAT ABOUT THE WATER?

The simple rule is don't drink the **water** in Vietnam – and resist the temptation to have **ice** in your drinks. Contaminated water is a major cause of sickness due to the presence of pathogenic organisms: bacteria, viruses and cysts. These micro-organisms cause ailments and diseases such as diarrhoea, gastroenteritis, typhoid, cholera, dysentery, poliomyelitis, hepatitis A and giardiasis – and can be present even when water looks clean and safe to drink.

Fortunately there are plenty of alternative drinks around: most guesthouses and hotels provide thermos-flasks of boiled water, hot tea is always on offer while cheap, **bottled water** and carbonated drinks are widely available. When buying bottled water check the seal is unbroken as bottles are occasionally refilled from the tap. Water in Hanoi and Ho Chi Minh City is chlorinated and most travellers use it for brushing their teeth without problem, but this is not recommended in rural areas where water is often untreated. Particular care should be taken anywhere where there is flooding as raw sewage may be washed into the water system.

The only time you're likely to be out of reach of bottled water is trekking into remote areas when you'll be relying on **boiled water**. Boiling for ten minutes gets rid of most bacteria in water but at least twenty minutes is needed to kill amoebic cysts, a cause of dysentery. To be safe you may wish to use some kind of **chemical sterilization**. Iodine purification tablets or solutions are more effective than chlorine compounds, though still leave a nasty after-taste – and iodine products are unsuitable for pregnant women, babies and people with thyroid problems. The use of a **filter** helps improve the taste but will not take out smaller viruses and chemical pollutants.

Purification, a two-stage process involving both filtration and sterilization, gives the most complete treatment. A range of portable water purifiers, from pocket-size units weighing only 60 grams upwards, is now available. *Pre-Mac* make reliable purifiers, which are available in the UK from *British Airways Travel Clinics* (see box on p.16), *MASTA Ltd* (☎0171/631 4408), and specialist outdoor equipment retailers (call ☎01892/534361 for details of local stockists); in Ireland they are available through *All Water Systems Ltd*, Unit 12, Western Parkway Business Centre, Lr Ballymount Rd, Dublin 12 (☎01/456 4933); in the USA and Canada, contact Outbound Products (☎1-800/663-9262; in Canada ☎604/321-5464).

make your own ORS by adding half a teaspoon of salt and three of sugar to a litre of cool, bottled or previously boiled, water. At the same time avoid milk, greasy or spicy foods, coffee and most fruit, in favour of bland foodstuffs such as eggs, bread, rice, noodles, banana, papaya and soup. Anti-diarrhoea medication tends to undermine the body's own efforts to fight off the infection and masks the symptoms, though tablets such as Lomotil and Imodium can be a useful stop-gap measure if you need to travel. If diarrhoea persists beyond two or three days, is very painful or if you notice blood or mucus in your stools, then it could be something more serious and you should seek medical advice.

Dysentery is an intestinal inflammation, indicated by diarrhoea with blood and mucus plus abdominal pain. There are two main types to be wary of: bacillary and amoebic. **Bacillary dysentery** has an acute onset with fever, discomfort and vomiting, as well as serious abdominal pains with watery, bloody diarrhoea. In mild cases spontaneous recovery occurs within a week, but severe illness may require antibiotics.

Amoebic dysentery is the more serious as bouts last for several weeks and usually recur. Symptoms appear gradually and are marked by bloody faeces accompanied by cramps in the lower abdomen, but no fever or vomiting. If left untreated, amoebic cysts enter the bloodstream and may cause long-term problems, but a prompt course of antibiotics should be completely effective.

Two symptoms distinguish **giardia**: highly sulphuric belches and farts, plus discoloured stools but with no sign of blood or pus. Another strong indication is urgent but inconsistent diarrhoea which may lay you low one day and leave you feeling fine the next. Again the disease is treatable with antibiotics under medical supervision.

Typhoid and cholera are also spread via contaminated food and water, generally in localized epidemics. **Typhoid** symptoms are varied but usually include high fever, headaches, constipation and then diarrhoea in the later stages. The disease is highly infectious and needs immediate medical treatment but it's also difficult to diagnose. The first sign of **cholera** is the abrupt but painless onset of watery, copious and unpredictable diarrhoea, combined later with nausea, vomiting and muscle cramps. It's the rapid dehydration caused by diarrhoea that's the main danger rather than the intestinal infection itself. However bad the diarrhoea and vomiting, you can treat cholera well with plenty of oral rehydration solutions, but if you can't take enough fluids, seek medical help.

Finally, bear in mind that if you are suffering from diarrhoea, oral drugs, such as anti-malaria or contraceptive pills, pass through your system too quickly to be absorbed effectively.

MALARIA

Both Hanoi and Ho Chi Minh City have few incidences of **malaria** while the northern Red River Delta and coastal regions of the south and centre are also considered relatively safe. On the other hand malaria occurs frequently in the highlands and rural areas, where the majority of cases involve the most dangerous strain, *Plasmodium falciparum*, which can be fatal if not treated promptly. The key measure is to avoid getting bitten by mosquitoes (which carry the disease), but if you're travelling in high-risk areas it is advisable to take **preventative tablets**, of which the weekly drug mefloquine (*Lariam*) is the most effective since in Vietnam the parasite is now largely resistant to chloroquine. However, mefloquine has some nasty side-effects, including dizzy spells, nausea and neuropsychiatric disturbances, which can persist even after you've stopped taking the drug; ensure you discuss any concerns you might have with your prescribing physician. Women in the first trimester of pregnancy or during lactation should avoid mefloquine and it's also important not to get pregnant for three months after stopping the drug. The most commonly used alternative is daily proguanil (*Paludrine*) in combination with weekly chloroquine (*Avloclor*). Note that you need to start taking tablets a week before exposure, and then continue with them for four weeks after leaving a malarial region.

None of these is infallible and it is still possible, though rare if the regime is followed correctly, to contract malaria while taking preventative drugs. If you develop regularly recurring fevers with flu-like symptoms of shivering and headaches, you should seek medical advice. A blood test will confirm the diagnosis; when caught early, treatment can be quick and effective. If you can't get to a doctor immediately, take 600mg of quinine three times daily for seven days, then three *Fansidar* tablets in one dose (adult dosage) – and then still get medical help as soon as possible.

The most important means of combatting all mosquito-borne diseases is simply not to get bitten in the first place. Though mosquitoes lurk all day in dark, steamy forests, humid bathrooms and so on, they tend to be most rampant at dawn and dusk. At these times wear long sleeves, trousers and socks, avoid dark colours and perfumes, which attract mosquitoes, and put **repellent** on all exposed skin. Sprays and lotions containing around forty percent DEET (diethyltoluamide) are effective and can also be used to treat clothes, but the chemical is toxic: keep it away from eyes and open wounds – and follow the manufacturer's recommendations carefully, particularly with young children. DEET sometimes causes bad dreams, nausea and dizziness, in which case try *Mosi-Guard Natural*, *X-Gnat* or *Gurkha* repellents.

Most hotels and guesthouses provide **sleeping nets**, but you may want to bring your own if you intend to do much trekking in remote areas; a net which hangs from a single point is the most practical. Many nets are already impregnated with pyrethroids, but need re-treating every six months; all the gear is available from travel clinics (see box on p.16) and good travel shops. Tuck the edges in well at night, sleep away from the sides and make sure there are no tears in the mesh. Air-conditioning and fans help keep mosquitoes at bay, as do mosquito coils and knockdown, insecticide sprays (available locally), though none of these measures are as effective as a decent net.

OTHER MOSQUITO-BORNE AILMENTS

Mosquitoes are also responsible for transmitting dengue fever and Japanese encephalitis. The symptoms of **dengue fever** (also known as breakbone fever) are similar to malaria but with more pronounced and severe headaches, together with aching muscles and sometimes with a rash spreading from the trunk onto the limbs and face. It is carried by a variety of mosquito active in the daytime and occurs mostly in Ho Chi Minh City, although the chances of catching it are small. There's no specific cure but most people recover completely after a week of rest, paracetamol and plenty of fluids; aspirin should be avoided as it provokes internal bleeding. However, there is a more dangerous version called dengue haemorrhage fever, which primarily affects children but is extremely rare among foreign visitors to Vietnam. If you notice an unusual tendency to bleed or bruise, seek medical advice immediately. **Japanese encephalitis** produces symptoms ranging from mild, non-specific fevers to severe headaches, delirium, loss of consciousness and, in a tiny minority of cases, the disease can prove fatal.

BITES AND CREEPY CRAWLIES

Unfortunately, mosquitoes aren't the only things that **bite**. Bed bugs, fleas, lice or scabies can be picked up from dirty bedclothes, though this is relatively unusual in Vietnam. Try not to scratch bites which easily become septic. Ticks picked up walking through scrub may carry a strain of typhus; carry out regular body inspections and remove ticks promptly. **Rabies** is transmitted by a bite, or even a lick on broken skin or the eyes, from an infected animal. The best strategy is to give all animals, especially dogs, cats and monkeys, a wide berth. If bitten, wash the wound immediately but gently with soap or detergent and apply alcohol or iodine if possible. Find out as much as you can about the animal, and if there's any chance it might be infected get to a clinic for a course of injections.

Vietnam has several poisonous **snakes** but in general snakes steer clear of humans and it's very rare to get bitten. Avoid walking through long grass or undergrowth, and wear boots when walking off-road. If bitten, remain still to slow down absorption of the venom and stay calm until help arrives. If possible, get someone to clean and disinfect the bite thoroughly, and wrap a bandage around the wound, applying gentle pressure. It helps if you can take the (dead) snake to be identified, or at least remember what it looked like. **Leeches** are more common and, though harmless, can be unpleasant. Long trousers, shirtsleeves and socks help prevent them getting a grip. The best way to get rid of leeches is to burn them off with a lighted match or cigarette; alternatively rub alcohol or salt onto them.

Worms enter the body either via contaminated food, or through the skin, especially the soles of the feet. You may notice worms in your stools, or experience other indications such as mild abdominal pain leading, very rarely, to acute intestinal blockage (roundworm, the most common), an itchy anus (threadworm) or anaemia (hookworm). An infestation is easily treated with worming tablets from a pharmacy.

HEAT TROUBLE

If you're not used to travelling in tropical areas it can take a couple of weeks to acclimatize to the high temperatures and humidity, during which time you may feel listless and tire easily. And don't underestimate the strength of the tropical sun: **sunburn** can be avoided by restricting your exposure to the midday sun and liberal use of high-factor sunscreens. Dark glasses help to protect your eyes from damaging rays, while a wide-brimmed hat reduces the risk of sunstroke. Drinking plenty of water will prevent **dehydration** but if you do become dehydrated – signs are infrequent or irregular urination – drink a salt and sugar solution (see under "Intestinal Troubles", p.17). **Heat stroke** is more serious and may require hospital treatment. Indications are a high temperature, lack of sweating, a fast pulse and red skin. Reducing your body temperature with a lukewarm shower will provide initial relief. High humidity often causes **heat rashes, prickly heat** and **fungal infections**. Prevention and cure are the same: wear loose clothes made of natural fibres, wash frequently and dry-off thoroughly afterwards. Talcum powder helps, particularly zinc oxide-based products (prickly heat powder), as does the use of mild antiseptic soap.

AIDS

As yet Vietnam carries out very little screening for sex workers or other high-risk groups and **sexually transmitted diseases**, including AIDS (known locally as **SIDA**), are flourishing. It is, therefore, extremely unwise to contemplate casual, unprotected sex; Vietnamese condoms (*bao cao su*) are often poor quality, but more reliable imported varieties (*OK* and *Trust*) are also available.

If it becomes essential for you to have an injection or a transfusion in Vietnam, try to make sure that new, sterile equipment is used; blood for transfusions should come from a known donor rather than a blood bank. Don't undergo acupuncture or the like unless you're certain the equipment is absolutely sterile.

GETTING MEDICAL HELP

Pharmacies can generally help with minor injuries or ailments and in major towns you may well find a pharmacist who speaks French or even English. The selection of reliable Asian and Western products on the market is improving rapidly and both Ho Chi Minh City and Hanoi now have reasonably well-stocked pharmacies. That said, drugs past their shelf-life and even counterfeit medicines are rife, so inspect packaging carefully, check use-by dates – and bring anything you know you're likely to need from home. Local **hospitals** can also treat minor problems, but in a real emergency your best bet is to head for Hanoi or Ho Chi Minh. Hospitals in both these cities can handle most eventualities and you also have the option of one of the international medical centres. Addresses of clinics and hospitals can be found in our "Listings" sections for major towns in this book. Note that doctors and hospitals expect immediate cash payment for health services rendered; you will then have to seek reimbursement from your insurance company (hang onto receipts for any payments you make).

> Some of the illnesses you can pick up in Vietnam may not show themselves immediately. If you become ill within a year of returning home, tell whoever treats you where you have been.

INFORMATION AND MAPS

Tourist information on Vietnam is at a premium. The Vietnamese government maintains a handful of tourist promotion offices, and a smattering of accredited travel agencies, around the globe, but they can supply you with only the most generalized information, and you may find that a better source of information, much of it based on firsthand experiences, is the Internet and worldwide web (see box over).

Matters don't improve much on arrival. Tourist offices are profit-making concerns, and don't take kindly to being treated as information bureaux;

> **VIETNAM TOURISM OFFICES ABROAD**
> **Australia** No office.
> **Canada** No office.
> **France** 4 Rue Cherubini, 75002 Paris (☎42 86 86 37).
> **Ireland** Contact UK office.
> **New Zealand** No office.
> **UK** c/o *Westeast Travel*, 271–273 King St, Hammersmith, London W6 9LZ (☎0181/741 1158).
> **USA** No office.

and anyway, Western concepts of information don't necessarily apply here – bus timetables, for example, simply don't exist.

TOURIST OFFICES AND INFORMATION

There's a frustrating dearth of free and impartial advice available in Vietnam. State-owned **tourist offices** – under the auspices of either *Vietnam-tourism* or the local provincial organization – are in reality thinly disguised travel agencies, and their lacklustre and occasionally disdainful counter staff are reluctant to spend their time providing free information to independent travellers when there are tours to sell and cars to rent out.

Opening hours are usually Monday to Saturday 7–11am & 1–5pm, and sometimes Sunday.

Vietnamtourism has offices in Hanoi, Ho Chi Minh and other major tourist centres, while the biggest of the provincial organizations is Ho Chi Minh City's **Saigontourist**. Don't expect to be furnished with armfuls of glossy brochures and other hand-outs, though: the best they'll manage is a local map, a schedule of their tours and maybe lists of local **accommodation** – affiliated hotels only. In Hanoi or Ho Chi Minh City, you might have more luck, ironically, if you approach one of the many private **tour agencies** now appearing – those in Pham Ngu Lao in Ho Chi Minh and central Hanoi are growing quite accustomed to Westerners' demands for advice (see "Listings", p.105 and p.347). Your fellow travellers can also be good sources of up-to date, if sometimes idiosyncratic information. **Noticeboards** in cafés and guesthouses are worth casting an eye over – as are the **listings** publications you'll find in Hanoi and Ho Chi Minh.

VIETNAM ON LINE

There's an increasing amount of information about Vietnam to be found on the **Internet**. As yet, little is coming out of Vietnam itself, but instead is mostly generated by the overseas Vietnamese community (largely in Vietnamese), academics and returning travellers (see p.44 for information on getting connected in Vietnam). For interactive advice try one of the newsgroups listed below or, if you're looking for a specific topic (the more specific the better), the best place to start is one of the search engines, such as *AltaVista*, *Infoseek* or *Lycos*, which search both the World Wide Web and newsgroups. Below we've listed a few of the more useful and well-established sites available; inevitably this will change, but as all are well linked you'll discover the up-and-coming sites pretty quickly.

Discussion forums

rec.travel.asia and soc.culture.vietnamese. Unmoderated newsgroups where it's worth posting a message for answers to a specific question, or browsing for interesting message threads – but bear in mind that there's no guarantee the information is either accurate or up to date.

Environment

The *World Conservation Monitoring Centre* runs a huge site at http://www.wcmc.org.uk/infoserv/countryp/vietnam/ with everything you want to know about the environment and conservation in Vietnam, from an evaluation of the country's biodiversity resources to coverage of general development issues.

General sites

VietGATE at http://www.saigon.com/ posts a list of NGOs (non-governmental organizations) working in Vietnam and has archives of newsgroup messages. *Vietnamese Connection* at http://www.vietconnection.com/ runs a big site with a wealth of detailed information on Vietnamese culture, recommended book lists and so on, plus an extensive list of Vietnamese recipes.

Images

To whet your appetite, browse the *Vietnam Pictures Archive* photo gallery at http://sunsite.unc.edu/vietnam/ covering art, people, history, monuments and scenery.

Links

http://coombs.anu.edu.au/WWWVLPages/VietPages/WWWVL-Vietnam.html. A large, well-organized site with the definitive list of Vietnam links. Or, try http://vietinfo.com for a more selective, annotated listing.

Magazine articles

The digital version of *Destination: Vietnam* is mainly of interest for its articles focusing on travel, arts, cuisine and culture. The site, at http://www.well.com/user/gdisf/dvhome.html, also includes a fair number of images, plus book and film reviews.

War

For a list of links specifically related to the American War in Vietnam go to ftp://ftp.msstate.edu/docs/history/USA/Vietnam/vietnam.html, while veterans have their home page at http://www.vietvet.org/ – not about Vietnam as such, but interesting for vet-related issues.

Weather

Current weather information and five-day forecasts for Hanoi and Ho Chi Minh City are available at http://167.8.29.8/weather/basemaps/wast1.html provided by *USA Today*.

MAPS

Maps of Vietnam are widely available, although the regular name-changing that goes on means that country maps tend to give different names for the same settlement – especially for smaller villages. The best general maps are either the *International* 1:1,000,000 "Travel Map" of Vietnam or the *Nelles* 1:1,500,000 map of Vietnam, Laos and Cambodia. The 1:2,000,000 "Vietnam, Cambodia & Laos World Travel Map" from *Bartholomew* isn't too bad either, though it lacks any details of tourist attractions. All but the Nelles map feature plans of Ho Chi Minh City and Hanoi. If you need larger-scale **city maps** than the ones we provide in this book – which also show recommended hotels and restaurants – reasonable ones are available from street vendors in both Hanoi and Ho Chi Minh City – or try *Vietnamtourism* in either city.

MAP OUTLETS

BRITAIN AND IRELAND

Daunt Books, 83 Marylebone High St, W1 (☎0171/224 2295).

Easons Bookshop, 40 O'Connell St, Dublin 1 (☎01/873 3811).

John Smith and Sons, 57–61 St Vincent St, Glasgow G2 5TB (☎0141/221 7472).

National Map Centre, 22–24 Caxton St, SW1 (☎0171/222 4945).

Stanfords,* 12–14 Long Acre, WC2 (☎0171/836 1321); 52 Grosvenor Gardens, London SW1W 0AG; 156 Regent St, London W1R 5TA.

The Travel Bookshop, 13–15 Blenheim Crescent, London W11 2EE (☎0171/229 5260).

*Note: maps by mail or phone order are available from *Stanfords*, ☎0171/836 1321.

USA AND CANADA

Book Passage, 51 Tamal Vista Blvd, Corte Madera, CA 94925 (☎415/927 0960).

The Complete Traveler Bookstore, 199 Madison Ave, New York, NY 10016 (☎212/685 9007); 3207 Fillmore St, San Francisco, CA 92123 (☎415/923 1511).

Forsyth Travel Library, 9154 W 57th St, Shawnee Mission, KS 66201 (☎1-800/367 7984).

Map Link Inc, 25 E Mason St, Santa Barbara, CA 93101 (☎805/965 4402).

Open Air Books and Maps, 25 Toronto St, Toronto, ON M5R 2C1 (☎416/363 0719).

Phileas Fogg's Books & Maps, #87 Stanford Shopping Center, Palo Alto, CA 94304 (☎1800/233 FOGG in California; ☎1800/533 FOGG elsewhere in the USA).

Rand McNally,* 444 N Michigan Ave, Chicago, IL 60611 (☎312/321 1751); 150 E 52nd St, New York, NY 10022 (☎212/758 7488); 595 Market St, San Francisco, CA 94105 (☎415/777 3131); 1201 Connecticut Ave NW, Washington, DC 20036 (☎202/223 6751).

Sierra Club Bookstore, 730 Polk St, San Francisco, CA 94109 (☎415/923 5500).

Travel Books & Language Center, 4931 Cordell Ave, Bethesda, MD 20814 (☎1800/220 2665).

Traveler's Bookstore, 22 W 52nd St, New York, NY 10019 (☎212/664 0995).

Ulysses Travel Bookshop, 4176 St-Denis, Montreal (☎514/289 0993).

World Wide Books and Maps, 1247 Granville St, Vancouver, BC V6Z 1E4 (☎604/687 3320).

*Note: *Rand McNally* now has 24 stores across the USA; call ☎1-800/333 0136 (ext 2111) for the location of your nearest store.

AUSTRALIA AND NEW ZEALAND

Bowyangs, 372 Little Bourke St, Melbourne, VIC 3000 (☎03/9670 4383).

The Map Shop, 16a Peel St, Adelaide, SA 5000 (☎08/8231 2033).

Perth Map Centre, 891 Hay St, Perth, WA 6000 (☎09/322 5733).

Speciality Maps, 58 Albert St, Auckland (☎09/307 2217).

Travel Bookshop, 20 Bridge St, Sydney, NSW 2000 (☎02/9241 3554).

COSTS, MONEY AND BANKS

Despite what you might have heard, travelling in Vietnam needn't be much more expensive than in its southeast Asian neighbours. With the average annual income hovering around US$250, daily expenses are low by dint of economic necessity, and if you come prepared to do as the locals do, then food, drink and transport can all be incredibly cheap – and even accommodation needn't be too great an expense.

Bargaining is very much a part of everyday life: almost everything is negotiable, from fruit in the market to a room for the night – with the notable exception of meals. A few tricks of the trade are given on p.49, but don't get too carried away: a few thousand extra dong won't do irreparable damage to your budget, and will probably mean much more to the recipient than it does to you.

CURRENCY

Vietnam's unit of currency is the **dong**, which you'll usually see abbreviated as "d" after an amount – as in 1000d, 10,000d, and so on. **Notes** come in denominations of 200d, 500d, 1000d, 2000d, 5000d, 10,000d, 20,000d and 50,000d; there are no coins in circulation. In addition, the **American dollar** operates in parallel to the dong as unofficial tender. Until the practice was made illegal in late 1994, many businesses insisted on receiving payment in dollars; although in reality traders still welcome dollars, the legislation does at least mean your dong won't ever be refused. Indeed, the dong is now the most convenient currency to use, and if you have some left over at the end of your trip you can change them back into dollars at a bank or, failing that, at the airport. You'll require an exchange certificate showing that you changed the currency legally in the first place. Most travellers tend to retain some of their cash in dollars, which they find less bulky to carry, and which come in handy if a local bank won't change travellers' cheques.

At the time of writing, the **exchange rate** was around 18,000d to £1 and 11,000d to US$1; current rates are posted at all banks that change travellers' cheques or dollars. Though the country has seen massive inflation during the past decade – one dong notes were still being printed as recently as 1985 – Vietnam's currency is now relatively stable, with inflation down to around 10 percent per annum.

COSTS

By eating at simple *com* (rice) and *pho* (noodle soup) stalls, picking up local buses and opting for the simplest accommodation there's no reason why you shouldn't be able to adhere to a **daily budget** in the region of US$12–15. Upgrading to more salubrious lodgings with a few mod cons, eating good food followed by a couple of beers in a bar, and signing up for the odd minibus tour could bounce your expenditure up to a more realistic US$25; and from there, the sky's the limit, if you stay at the ritziest city hotels, dine at the swankiest restaurants and rent cars with drivers wherever you go.

> **PRICING POLICY**
>
> Because dong amounts tend to be unwieldy and more volatile, we've largely given **prices in US$** throughout the *Guide*. Incidentally, don't be alarmed if you notice that Vietnamese pay less than you in a train station, *Vietnam Airlines* office, hotel, or bus: Vietnam maintains a **three-tier pricing system**, with Westerners paying many times more than locals, and *Viet Kieu* (overseas Vietnamese) paying somewhere between the two.

TRAVELLERS' CHEQUES, CASH AND CARDS

Easily the safest and most convenient method of carrying money abroad is in the form of **travellers' cheques**. While sterling and other major currencies are accepted in Hanoi and Ho Chi Minh, American dollars are still far and away the best currency in which to buy them. Travellers' cheques are available for a small commission from most banks and building societies, and from branches of *American Express* and *Thomas Cook*; make sure you keep the purchase agreement and a record of cheque serial numbers safe and separate from the cheques themselves. Once in Vietnam, they can be cashed at major banks upon validation by means of a passport, for a commission of 1–2 percent depending upon whether you require dollars or dong. The bank might ask to see your proof of purchase for travellers' cheques, so it's as well to have your receipt with you.

Dong are not available outside the country at present, though if you take in some American **dollars** you'll have no problems getting by until you reach a bank. Major **credit cards** – *American Express*, *Visa*, *Mastercard* – are slowly becoming more acceptable in Vietnam: all top-level and many mid-level hotels will accept them, as well as a slowly growing number of restaurants; surcharges rise to a ceiling of 5 percent. Banks are increasingly **advancing cash** against cards, though only in Hanoi, Ho Chi Minh and one or two other major cities; see "Listings" in the relevant accounts for details. For their troubles they charge a 3–5 percent commission.

BANKS AND EXCHANGE

Banking hours are generally Monday to Friday 8–11.30am and 1–4pm and Saturday 8am–noon, though in Hanoi and Ho Chi Minh you'll be able to change money outside these hours, at exchange counters and hotels. The country's **major bank** is the *Vietcombank*, which has branches in most towns and cities; other banks that sometimes change travellers' cheques include *Incombank*, *Agribank* and *Sacombank*. It's worth noting that not all banks – especially in smaller towns – will change travellers' cheques; **always check** the position in your next port of call, and get into the habit of carrying a few dollars with you to allow for unforeseen circumstances such as public holidays. **Hotels** also change dollars sometimes, but at less favourable rates. A **black market** of sorts exists in Vietnam, and marketeers will sometimes approach you offering to change your cash, but the tiny profit you might make on such deals doesn't really justify the risks.

When you exchange money, ask for a **mix of denominations**. Changing US$100 will give you a huge wad of notes to carry if it comes in 5000d notes, while in some places, especially backwaters, bigger bills can be hard to split. Finally, refuse really motley banknotes, as you'll have difficulty getting anyone else to accept them.

EMERGENCY CASH

If you find yourself in dire straits and need to have money **wired**, you'll need to contact the *Vietcombank* in either Hanoi or Ho Chi Minh. *Vietcombank* has arrangements with only selected banks across the world: these include *Lloyd's Bank* in London, the *Commonwealth Bank* in Sydney; the *Royal Bank of Canada*; and the *Chase Manhattan Bank* and *Citibank* in New York (*Vietcombank* will furnish you with a full list). You'll need to contact one of the associated banks and supply them with details of the branch of *Vietcombank* to which you want the money sent, along with your own particulars. Payment can be made to you in dong or dollars, but note that hefty charges are levied at both ends, so treat this as a last resort.

GETTING AROUND

Bombed almost into oblivion during successive wars, Vietnam's transport network is only now returning to some semblance of efficiency. A relatively extensive network of roads skeins the country, while the rolling stock of the French-built train system is once again able to make the long haul from Ho Chi Minh to the Chinese border. Vietnam's main thoroughfare is Highway 1, which runs from Hanoi to Ho Chi Minh, passing through Hué, Da Nang and Nha Trang en route, and ghosted at almost every turn by the country's main rail line.

However, **public transport** remains shambolic: timetables are for the most part redundant, and an increasing number of tourists are now opting for internal flights or **private tours**, in order to escape the country's clapped-out buses and snail-slow trains. Doing as the locals do shouldn't be rejected out of hand, though: many visitors have their warmest encounters with the Vietnamese within the chaos of a public bus or train. **Security** is an important consideration on public transport: on buses, never fall asleep with your bag by your side, and never leave belongings unattended at a food-stop. On trains, be especially vigilant when the train stops at stations and takes on hawkers, ensure your money-belt is safely tucked under your clothes before going to sleep and that your luggage is safely stowed (preferably padlocked to an immovable object).

BUSES AND MINIBUSES

Though Vietnam's national **bus** network offers daily services between all major towns, the unlikely fleet of aged jalopies that kangaroos around the highways is a severe disincentive to travel. Cramped, stuffy and designed for the more diminutive southeast Asian frame, Vietnamese buses push patience and stamina to the limit. Seats are normally uncushioned, and once the roof is laden, luggage (which could be anything from live pigs in baskets to scores of sacks of rice) is piled into the vehicle itself. Breakdowns and punctures are frequent occurrences, and can sometimes necessitate a roadside wait of several hours while driver, fare collector and mechanic roll up their sleeves and improvise a repair. Even relatively healthy buses make agonizingly slow progress, as they stop frequently along the road to pick up passengers. You'll hear some buses referred to as "express" buses, but don't be taken in: the difference is negligible.

All towns have a **bus station**, and larger communities have both a local and a long-distance station. Though there are occasional early evening departures, most buses depart early, from 5am through to mid-morning, waiting only as long as it takes to muster a full-enough quota of passengers, so it pays to set your alarm if you want to be sure of a seat. That said, all is not lost if you oversleep or miss your connection: with so many buses plying the highways, it's often possible to **wave down** a bus that's headed your way, if you can get yourself to the nearest main road.

For longer journeys, **tickets** are best bought a day in advance: many routes are served by only one bus a day, and so can be heavily over-subscribed. **Prices** are becoming increasingly difficult to predict, since how much you pay depends very much upon where you are: certain tourist hotspots, especially in the south, are fast learning that they can charge what they like; elsewhere, you might pay the going price. Station staff will sometimes tell you to buy a ticket on the bus; if this happens, try to ascertain what the correct price is before boarding, as fare collectors will often take advantage of your captive position. Ominously, Da Lat's local tourist agency has taken to insisting that visitors pay many times over the odds for a seat on a **charter bus** (catering for the tourist market and wealthier Vietnamese, and advertised in tourist hotels and cafés); if this becomes more prevalent, your best bet will be to stand outside the bus station and wave down the public bus as it emerges: this way, you should pay something approaching the normal fare. Paying for **two seats** can be a good way of ensuring at least a modicum of comfort for yourself, if you aren't too embarrassed by such a display of extravagance, but be prepared for a struggle to maintain both seats throughout the journey. On long-distance journeys, buses make occasional **food stops** at roadside restaurants.

MINIBUSES

Privately owned **minibuses** are now becoming a regular fixture in Vietnam. If anything, they squeeze in more people per square foot than ordinary buses, and to pick up enough passengers to achieve this, they often drive interminably around town, touting for takers. On the other hand, they do at least run throughout the day, making them useful if you've missed the early-morning bus. Most common on well-trodden tourist routes such as Ho Chi Minh–Da Lat and Ho Chi Minh–Vung Tau, minibuses sometimes share the local bus station, or simply congregate on the roadside in the centre of a town; specific details are given in accounts throughout the *Guide*.

TRAINS

Vietnam's single-track **train** network comprises more than 2500km of track, all of it dating back to the colonial period. Though trains are slow, travelling on them can be a pleasant experience if you splash out on a soft-class berth or seat; scrimp on your ticket, on the other hand, and you'll probably regret it. This means that train travel is not a particularly cheap option, especially with **ticket prices** for tourists around four times higher than those for locals. The most **popular lines** with tourists are the shuttle from Da Nang to Hué (4hr), a bite-sized, picturesque sampler of Vietnamese rail travel; and the overnighters from Hué to Hanoi (14–17hr) and from Hanoi up to Lao Cai, for Sa Pa (10–11hr).

SERVICES

The country's **main line** shadows Highway 1 on its way from Ho Chi Minh City to Hanoi (1726km), passing through Nha Trang, Da Nang and Hué en route. From Hanoi, three branch lines strike out towards the northern coast and into its hinterlands. One line traces the Red River northwest to **Lao Cai**, site of a border crossing into **China**'s Yunnan Province. Another runs north to **Dong Dang**, and is the route taken by the two weekly

trains from Hanoi **to Beijing**. The third branch, a shorter spur, links the capital with **Haiphong**. All that remains of the **Phan Rang–Da Lat** branch line that once linked the central highlands with the southern coast is a truncated tourist excursion service that runs, upon request, from Da Lat to Trai Met, a few kilometres down the line.

When it comes to choosing which **class** to travel in, it's essential to aim high. At the bottom of the scale is a **hard seat**, which is just as it sounds, though bearable for shorter journeys; **soft seats** offer slightly more comfort, but are still fairly grim for long hauls. On overnight journeys, you'd be well advised to invest in a berth of some description. Cramped **hard-berth** compartments have six bunks, three either side – with the cramped top ones being the cheapest, and the bottom ones (under which there's handy storage space) the priciest. **Soft-berth** compartments, containing only four bunks, offer more sleeping space; while at the top of the range are two-bed **super-berth** compartments, though these are presently only available on the S1 and S2 services (see below).

At least one service each way travels between Hanoi and Ho Chi Minh daily, a journey that takes somewhere between 36 and 44 hours: these so-called "**Reunification Express**" trains are labelled S1 to S6; odd-numbered trains travel south, even ones north, hence the S4 (40hr) and S6 (44hr) depart daily from Ho Chi Minh City, and the S3 (40hr) and S5 (44hr) make the trip in the opposite direction. In addition to these, the S2 and S1 (both 36hr) operate on Mondays and Thursdays. On the **northern lines**, several trains per day make the run from Hanoi to Haiphong (2hr–2hr 30min), while there are two daily services, one of which travels overnight, to Dong Dang (8–10hr) and Lao Cai (10–11hr).

Beside these trains, **local** services shuttle along portions of the line. Of these, the most useful is the LH2, which runs from HCM to Hué every second day, stopping en route at Nha Trang and Da Nang. **Departure times** change regularly: current times are always displayed in stations, and trains generally leave pretty much on time.

Simple **food** is included in the price of the ticket on overnight journeys, but you might want to stock up with goodies of your own; you'll also have plenty of opportunities to buy snacks when the train pulls into stations – and from carts that ply the aisles.

TICKETS

Booking ahead is essential, and the further ahead the better, especially if you intend travelling at the weekend or over a holiday period; sleeping compartments should be booked at least three days before departure. You'll sometimes be asked to produce your **passport** when you buy a ticket.

Fares vary according to the class of travel and the train you take, and prices change regularly, but the following figures give some indication of what you can expect to pay on the slowest service from Ho Chi Minh to Hanoi (S6). A hard seat from Ho Chi Minh to Nha Trang costs US$10, and a soft berth $23; going as far as Da Nang, the same classes cost $21 and $50, respectively; while for the entire journey to Hanoi they cost $39 and $94. As a rule of thumb, the faster the service, the more expensive it is, though the difference between soft berth and super berth on the S1 and S2 is only a matter of a few dollars, so upgrading is worthwhile.

BOATS AND FERRIES

Ferries sail year-round to the three major islands off Vietnam's coastline, **Phu Quoc**, **Cat Ba** and **Con Dao**. In addition, a ferry runs from **Haiphong** to **Ha Long Bay**, and there's a hydrofoil service between Ho Chi Minh City and **Vung Tau**. Tickets can be bought on the boats, but it's better to get them in advance (details are given in the relevant chapters of the *Guide*). The other area you'll encounter passenger services is the **Mekong Delta**, where **river ferries** haul themselves from bank to bank of the various strands of the Mekong from morning until night. Numerous

---

MESSING ABOUT ON THE WATER

It's possible to **charter** a vessel in any seaside or riverside town simply by asking around at the water's edge, though some places are better geared up to tourists than others. In the **Mekong Delta**, the main centres for excursions are **My Tho** (p.120), **Vinh Long** (p.126), **Can Tho** (p.136) and **Ca Mau** (pp.139–140). **Ho Chi Minh City**'s waterways can be explored by motorboat, while up the coast, **Nha Trang**'s tour companies do a roaring trade in snorkelling trips (p.207). But perhaps the quintessential waterborne experience is to glide across island-strewn, magical **Ha Long Bay** (p.370).

---

aged (and often less than seaworthy) cargo vessels also dawdle between towns, and some ply the route to Ho Chi Minh City, but they tend to be slow and basic; we've outlined a handful of the more do-able ones in the text. If all you're really after is a pleasure trip on the water, check out the box above for ideas.

VEHICLE RENTAL

Renting a **private vehicle** is quite an economical means of transport if you are travelling in a group; moreover, it means you can plan a trip to your own tastes, rather than having to follow a tour company's itinerary. And although self-drive isn't yet possible in Vietnam, it's easy to hire a **car**, **jeep** or **minibus** complete with driver. The same companies, agencies and tourist offices that arrange tours (see over) will rent out swish air-conditioned vehicles, as well as more basic models for a few dollars less. Prices are in the region of US$35 per day for a car, and $50 per day for a minibus. In addition, a per-kilometre charge of approximately $0.40 is levied by some companies. When negotiating on the price, it's important to clarify exactly who is liable for what: things to check include who pays for the driver's accommodation and meals, fuel, road and ferry tolls, parking fees, repairs and what happens in the case of a major breakdown. There should then be some sort of contract to sign showing all the details, including an agreed itinerary, especially if you are renting for more than a day; make sure the driver is given a copy in Vietnamese. In some cases you'll have to settle-up in advance though, if possible, it's best if you can arrange to pay roughly half before and the balance at the end.

MOTORBIKES AND MOPEDS

Motorbike or **moped** rental is possible in most towns and cities regularly frequented by tourists, and pottering around on one or the other can be a most enjoyable and time-efficient method of sightseeing. Lured by the prospect of independent travel at relatively low cost, some tourists cruise the countryside on motorbikes, but you'd do well to think very hard – and check the small print on your insurance policy – before undertaking any **long-distance biking**, since Vietnam's roads can be distinctly dangerous (see 'Rules" of the Road" opposite). The appalling road discipline of most Vietnamese drivers means that the risk of an

"RULES" OF THE ROAD

There's no discernible method to the madness that passes as a **traffic** system in Vietnam so it's extremely important that you don't stray out onto the roads unless you feel 100 percent confident about doing so. The theory is that you **drive on the right**, though in practice motorists and cyclists swoop, swerve and dodge wherever they want, using no signals and their **horn** as a surrogate brake. **Right of way** invariably goes to the biggest vehicle on the road, which means that motorbikes and mopeds are regularly forced off the highway by thundering trucks or buses; note that overtaking vehicles assume you'll pull over onto the hard shoulder to avoid them. It's wise to use your horn to its maximum and also to avoid driving after dark, since many vehicles don't turn on their headlights.

On the whole the **police** seem to leave foreign riders well alone, and the best policy at roadside checkpoints is just to drive by slowly. However, if you are involved in an **accident** and it was deemed to be your fault, the penalties can be fairly major fines.

Parking your bike where it won't be tampered with can be a real pain: leaving it in a parking compound (*gui xe*) or paying someone to keep an eye on it may help, but there are no guarantees.

accident is very real – with potentially dire consequences should it happen in a remote area: well-equipped hospitals are few and far between outside the major centres, and there'll probably be no ambulance service to help you out. On the other hand, many people bike around with no problems and thoroughly recommend it, especially for day-trips or for touring the northern mountains and the Mekong Delta.

There are plenty of bikes **for rent** in Vietnam's major tourist centres, and we give details of outlets throughout the *Guide*. It costs around US$6 per day to hire a moped, and a few dollars more for a motorbike; in less well-touristed areas, ask at your hotel, or at the provincial tourist office. Often you'll have to pay in advance and leave some form of ID, while other places may ask you to sign a rental contract. If you're renting for a week or so, you may be asked to leave a substantial deposit, often the bike's value in dollars.

Although it's technically illegal for non-residents to own a vehicle, there is a small trade in **secondhand bikes** in the two main cities – try noticeboards in the travellers' cafés; so far the police seem to be ignoring the practice, but check the latest situation before committing yourself. Despite the heavy traffic, the most popular **route** is Highway 1, between Ho Chi Minh and Hanoi, a journey of around two weeks, averaging 150km per day. The majority of people travel from south to north, so it's generally easier to pick up a bike in Hanoi and sell in Ho Chi Minh. In peak season (Sept–Dec) you should be able to find a foreign buyer at either end, in which case you can expect to recover you costs. Otherwise, a Vietnamese will probably take your bike to sell on, though they know you're generally in a hurry to leave and won't offer much. The **bike of choice** is usually a Minsk 125cc; it's sturdy, not too expensive (US$350–400 secondhand), and is the easiest to get repaired outside the main cities. It's also fairly comfortable, though you might want to add some extra padding to the seat.

Whether you're renting or buying, remember to check everything over carefully, especially brakes, lights and horn. Though most Vietnamese don't bother, wearing a **helmet** is now a legal requirement as well as an essential safety precaution: it's best to bring your own, but you can buy less robust, locally made helmets in Hanoi and Ho Chi Minh for around US$40.

Road conditions are highly erratic, with pristine asphalt followed by stretches of spine-jarring pot-holes, and you'll probably need one or two simple repairs sooner or later. **Repair shops** are fairly ubiquitous – look for a Honda sign or ask for *sua chua xe may* (motorbike repairs) – but you should still carry at least a puncture-repair kit, pump and spare spark plug. Fuel (*xang*) is cheap (less than $0.40 per litre) and widely available, though it's best to fill up at town pumps as petrol sold in bottles beside the road is likely to be inferior quality. Vietnamese road-**maps** tend to be unreliable, so ask at junctions and check if the route ahead is driveable, especially in the mountains where summer rains regularly take out roads and bridges. Finally, try to travel in the company of one or more **other bikes** in case one of you gets into trouble, though you won't want to travel far with someone riding pillion on unmetalled roads.

BICYCLES

Cycling is perhaps the best way of sightseeing around towns, and you shouldn't have to pay more than US$1 per day for the privilege. Locally produced bikes are available to buy for as little as US$30, but with standards presently so low, you're far better off renting. If you decide upon a **long-distance cycling** holiday, you may well want to bring your own bike with you. Hardy **mountain bikes** cope best with the country's variable surfaces.

If you want to see Vietnam from the saddle, there are several companies that offer specialist cycling tours – see details of specialist tour operators on p.5 and p.11.

HITCHING

Although not really comparable to **hitching** in the Western sense, there is a tradition of drivers (especially truck drivers) picking up passengers from the roadside, in exchange for a small payment – and this system has been used to great effect by some travellers. However, in addition to the **risks** associated with hitching anywhere, you're also quite likely to be overcharged, due to the prevailing (and not unreasonable) assumption that all foreigners are wealthy. Set against the relatively low cost of other forms of tranpsort, hitching becomes an ill-advised and unattractive proposition.

PLANES

The Vietnamese national carrier, **Vietnam Airlines**, operates a reasonably comprehensive network of domestic flights across the country. Internal flights come into their own on longer hauls, and can shave precious hours or even days of journeys – the 2-hour journey between Hanoi and Ho Chi Minh City, for instance, compares favourably with the 40 hours you might spend on the train. Be aware, however, that many flights are not direct, and connections are often unwieldy and impractical. *Vietnam Airlines* has **booking offices** in all towns and cities with an airport; addresses and phone numbers are listed throughout the *Guide*. The only other airline operating internal flights is *Pacific Airlines*, a Taiwan-based airline currently flying a very limited range of routes.

Vietnam Airlines has a computerized reservations system, which has streamlined the booking process, but **ticketing** is still at a fairly basic stage, with options limited to standard single or return trips. Book as far ahead as you can: you'll need to have your **passport** with you, and tickets can be paid for in either dollars or dong. There's a US$1–1.50 **departure tax** on domestic flights.

The shuttle **between Hanoi and Ho Chi Minh** is the route most frequently used by tourists. *Vietnam Airlines* flies nine times daily each way, taking two hours, for a standard one-way fare of US$150; *Pacific Airlines* also flies once a day in each direction. Other useful services from Hanoi and Ho Chi Minh fly to **Hué**, **Da Nang** and **Nha Trang**; Ho Chi Minh City also has flights to **Phu Quoc Island**.

ORGANIZED TOURS

Ever-increasing numbers of tourists are seeing Vietnam through the window of a minibus, on **organized tours**. Ranging from 1-day jaunts to 2- or 3-week trawls upcountry, tours are ideal if you want to speedily acquaint yourself with the highlights of Vietnam; they can also work out much cheaper than car rental. On the other hand, by relying upon tours you'll have little chance to really get to grips with the country and its people, or to enjoy at your leisure places that appeal. If you're really pressed for time are still determined to cover a lot of ground, think about arranging a package tour to suit your interests before you leave home, though these tend to be expensive (see boxes on p.5, p.8 and p.11).

Hordes of tour companies have sprung up in Hanoi and Ho Chi Minh City, all offering similar ranges of tours, but at wildly differing prices. Tours sold by **state-owned companies**, *Vietnamtourism* and *Saigontourist*, are generally the most expensive, but their prices are undercut by scores of **private tour agencies**, which charge up to 50 percent less. **Prices** vary according to how many people there are in a group, so always try to join a tour that's already scheduled; some café-agencies stick tour programmes up on boards for you to add your name to. Generally speaking, a day-trip, say, from Ho Chi Minh to the Cu Chi tunnels and Tay Ninh, starts at around US$6 a head, a 2-day trip into the Mekong Delta from $20 a head, while an extended 10-day journey up the coast to Hué would be around $60 a head; all these prices are for a seat on a full minibus, but you'll pay more if there are fewer takers. While some tours include accommodation, meals and entry fees, others don't, so check exactly what you're getting before handing over any cash.

The other alternative is to set up your own **custom-made tour** by gathering together a group and renting a car or minibus plus driver (see "Vehicle rental" p. 28).

LOCAL TRANSPORT

In a country with a population so adept at making do with limited resources, it isn't surprising to see the diverse types of **local transport** dreamt up. **Taxis** are becoming an increasingly common sight on the streets of Hanoi, Ho Chi Minh City, Hué, Da Nang and Haiphong, while local **bus** services are also setting up in the two main cities. Elsewhere you'll have to rely upon a host of two- and three-wheeled vehicles for getting around.

Cheap, ubiquitous and fun, **cyclos** – three-wheeled rickshaws comprising a "bucket" seat attached to the front of a bicycle – are the quintessential mode of transport across much of the country. They can carry one person, or two people at a push, with a corresponding reduction in comfort. A **fair price** for a five- or ten-minute hop on a cyclo is 5–6000d, maybe fractionally less if you are out in the sticks, though if you hire one for a few hours' touring, you should budget on a figure of around 11,000d per hour. Secure a price before setting off, and make absolutely sure that the driver is in agreement with it. When haggling, ensure

you know which currency you are dealing in (5 fingers held up, for instance, could mean 5000d or US$5), and whether you're negotiating for a single or return trip, and for one passenger or two. Should a difference of opinion emerge at the end of a ride, having the exact fare ready to press into a stroppy driver's hand can sometimes resolve matters. The motorized version of the cyclo, found in the south, is known as the **cyclo mai**. A Mekong Delta speciality, the **xe dap loi** is also a variation on the cyclo theme, with passengers being pulled in a "wagon" tagged behind a bicycle; the motorized version is known as a **Honda loi**.

Xe lams (also known as **Lambros**) are three-wheeled, motorized buggies whose drivers squeeze in more passengers than you'd believe possible. These are as close as you get to a local bus service outside Hanoi and Ho Chi Minh, and rows of them are usually found either at the local bus station, or outside the local market, from where they make short hauls into the suburbs or surrounding countryside. A typical xe lam ride of a few kilometres costs 3–4000d.

Finally, there's the **Honda om** or motorbike taxi (*om* translates as "embrace"), known in the north as a **xe om**. Honda oms are invaluable in highland regions, where pedal power is useless; prices are approximately one and a half times as expensive as for cyclos.

ACCOMMODATION

You are unlikely to recall accommodation as one of the profoundest joys of your stay in Vietnam. Compared to other southeast Asian countries, it's no bargain either: expect to pay around £5.50/US$8 for the most basic double room with fan and attached bathroom, and at these prices, many of the lower-priced establishments are mangy and unhygienic. Injections of private investment are now a feature of the hotel scene, and standards are rapidly improving in Hanoi and Ho Chi Minh, though out in the sticks where competition is less intense, change is coming more slowly.

Vietnam's burgeoning tourist statistics are being mirrored by an exponential increase in the number of rooms available nationwide. If you require an international-class room, however, it always pays to **book ahead**: occupancy rates hover at around 90 percent in Hanoi, and are only marginally lower in Ho Chi Minh, and it'll be a while before the Hiltons, Hyatts and Sheratons are all up and running. Around **Tet** (see p.45 for the dates this falls from 1997–99), booking in advance is advisable whatever level of accommodation you require.

Finding a room is pretty much up to you. There's a booth at Ho Chi Minh airport that will phone through to reserve a room for you, and touts wielding hotel name-cards accost you outside both the country's international airports, but otherwise the only help you'll get is from cyclo drivers looking for a commission. Once you've found a hotel, look at a range of rooms before opting for one, as standards can vary hugely within the same establishment; you'll also need to check the bed arrangement, since there are many permutations in Vietnam. A "**single**" room could have a single or twin beds in it, while a "**double**" room could have two, three or four single beds, a single and a twin, and so on. Incidentally, not all places are permitted to take foreigners: if you walk into a place and the staff merely smile and shake their heads, chances are this is the case.

When you **check in** at a Vietnamese hotel or guesthouse, you are required to hand in your passport and to fill in a simple registration form, both of which are presented at the local police station later – though there's talk of this routine being phased out. Depending on the establishment, your **passport** plus departure card will either be kept as security until you move on, or returned to you later the same night. If you're going to lose sleep over being separated from yours, asking for it back sometimes works.

It's normally possible to **pay** your bill when you leave, although at some places you'll have to pay your first night in advance, and sometimes you'll even be required to shell out daily; payment can be made in dollars or dong. Foreigners pay far more than locals, and *Viet Kieu* (overseas Vietnamese) have to fork out somewhere between the two. Room rates fluctuate according to demand, so it's a good idea to try and bargain – making sure, of course, that it's clear whether both parties are talking per person or per room; your case will be

that much stronger if you are staying for several days. Establishments of a decent standard sometimes add **government tax** and **service charge**, usually totalling 15 percent, to your bill; some charge only 10 percent, and still others include it in their stated price. (Our price codes – see box opposite – include all applicable taxes.)

SECURITY AND OTHER HASSLES

Hotel **security** can be a big problem in Vietnam, though it's now sometimes possible to leave valuables in a safe or locked drawer at reception. Whatever you do, don't leave valuables in your room: reports of theft from rooms are not uncommon, and you are far better off keeping valuables with you at all times, in a money pouch. In many places, a padlock on the door of your room is the norm, and you can increase security by using your own lock.

In the basest digs, rooms are cleaned irregularly and badly, and **hygiene** can be a problem, with cockroaches and even rats roaming free; you can at least minimize health risks by not bringing foodstuffs or sugary drinks into your room. Finally, **prostitution** is rife in Vietnam, and in less reputable budget hotels it's not unknown for Western men to be called upon, or even phoned from other rooms, during the night.

TYPES OF ACCOMMODATION

Grading accommodation isn't a simple matter in Vietnam. The names used (guesthouse, rooms for rent, mini-hotel, hotel and so on) can rarely be relied upon to indicate what's on offer, and there are broad overlaps in standards. Some of Vietnam's largest hotels are austere, state-owned edifices styled upon unlovely Eastern European models and yielding only the most grim of rooms; while even the tiniest rooms-for-rent operations often make a real effort. What's more, some hotels cover all bases by having a range of rooms, from simple fan-cooled rooms with cold water, right up to cheerful air-conditioned accommodation with satellite TV, fridge and mini-bar. As a rule of thumb, the newer a place is, the better value it's likely to represent in terms of comfort, hygiene and all-round appeal.

Throughout the *Guide* we've given comprehensive listings of the options available and allocated price codes (see box on facing page).

BUDGET ACCOMMODATION

The very cheapest form of accommodation in Vietnam is a bed in a **dormitory**; there are no youth hostels as yet. Dormitories are not a new concept in Vietnam: many bus and train stations have on-site dorms known as *nha tro*, but these practically never take Westerners – which is just as well, since the risk of theft in them is considerable. However, backpackers' dorms are a new development on the accommodation scene in Hanoi and Ho Chi Minh, where you can expect to pay US$2–3 for either a bed or a mattress on the floor, sharing common facilities. The few dorms presently operating are located in the budget **guesthouses** (*nha khach*) and **rooms for rent** set-ups (private homes with a handful of rooms to let) that proliferate around Ho Chi Minh's Pham Ngu Lao enclave and, less so, in the Old Quarter of Hanoi.

Otherwise, you'll need to upgrade to a simple fan room sharing washing facilities, in either a room for rent or a state-run **hotel** (*khach san*) or guesthouse, which will set you back anywhere between US$4 and $8 (①). Don't expect much panache, though: rooms at this level are generally undecorated and decrepit, with fittings typically amounting only to a ceiling fan, mosquito net, Thermos of hot water and jar of tea. If you push your dollar expenditure into double figures (②), you should get the luxury of a private bathroom – although you're unlikely to get hot water for this price in the warmer south.

In major cities, the next rung is best served in Ho Chi Minh by a privately owned room for rent, and in Hanoi by a **mini-hotel** (a modest, privately owned hotel), where gauche but cheerful rooms with **air-con** and **hot water** go for around US$15–30 (③). Elsewhere, you'll probably have little choice but to upgrade in the local state-run hotel.

MID- AND UPPER-RANGE ACCOMMODATION

For upwards of US$30 per room a night, accommodation can begin to get quite rosy. At the ④ level, you can be sure of a comfortable and well-appointed room with air-con, hot water, fridge and maybe even satellite TV, in all but the most remote areas. Such a room could either be in a hotel or mini-hotel.

Paying US$40–75 will get you a room in a **middle-range hotel** of some repute, with in-house restaurant and bar, booking office, room service and so on; while at the **top of the range** (⑤–⑥) the sky's the limit – if you want the last word in splendour, you could easily spend up to US$200 a night. International-class hotels are for the moment confined to the two major cities, which also have some reasonably charismatic places to stay, such as the *Metropole* in Hanoi and Ho Chi Minh's *Continental*. With so many businesspeople flooding into the country, it's wise to book ahead: this level of accommodation is presently in short supply, and it's going to take a while to redress the shortfall.

STILTHOUSES AND CAMPING

As Vietnam's minority communities become more exposed to tourism in the future, visitors may have the choice of staying over in **stilthouses** or other village accommodation. At present, this option is restricted almost exclusively to the north of the country, notably around Sa Pa and in the Mai Chau Valley. You can either take one of the tours out of Hanoi which includes overnighting in a minority village (see p.349), or make your own arrangements when you get out there (see *The Far North* chapter for details). In the central highlands, the choice is limited to Yok Don National

Park, where rangers can arrange a stay at Ban Don (see p.177). Accommodation usually consists of a mattress on the floor in a communal room; those villages more used to tourists normally provide a blanket and mosquito net, but it's advisable to take your own net and sleeping bag to be on the safe side, particularly as nights get pretty cold in the mountains. Prices in the villages vary from US$2.50 to $10 per person per night, depending on the area, with a dollar or two extra for an evening meal according to how much you eat; unless you're arriving before midday, it's generally a good idea to take food for your first night. Villagers will welcome **gifts**: pens, pencils and writing pads all make useful offerings.

No provisions exist in Vietnam for **camping** at the present time. That said, there are so many yawning stretches of **beach** along the coast, that you may find yourself crashing out under the stars for the night, and this is unlikely to cause any problems.

EATING AND DRINKING

At its best, Vietnamese food is light, subtle in flavour and astonishing in its variety. Though closely related to Chinese cuisine, Vietnam has its own distinct culinary tradition, using herbs and seasoning rather than sauces, and favouring boiled or steamed dishes over stir-fries.

In the south, **Indian** and **Thai** influences add curries and spices to the menu, while other regions have evolved their own array of specialities, most notably the foods of Hué and Hoi An. Buddhism introduced a **vegetarian** tradition to Vietnam, while much later the **French** brought with them bread, dairy products, pastries and the whole café culture. Hanoi, Ho Chi Minh City and the major tourist centres are now relatively well provided for, with everything from hawker stalls to hotel and Western-style restaurants, and even ice-cream parlours. The quality and variety of food tends to be better in the **south** than the **north**, with Ho Chi Minh being considered Vietnam's culinary capital. You'll also generally eat better in the main towns than off the beaten track, where restaurants of any sort are few and far between. That said, you'll never go hungry; even in the back of beyond, there's always some stall selling a noodle soup or rice platter and plenty of fruit to fill up on.

WHERE TO EAT

Broadly speaking, there are three types of eating establishment to choose from. One step up from **hawkers** peddling their dish of the day from shoulder poles or hand-carts are **street kitchens**, inexpensive joints aimed at locals. More formal, Western-style **restaurants** come in many shapes and sizes, from simple places serving unpretentious Vietnamese meals to top-class establishments, offering high-quality Vietnamese specialities and international cuisine – the latter almost exclusively the preserve of foreign diners. Finally, there are the **travellers' cafés** which, among other things, lay on inexpensive if rather banal meals, along the lines of burgers and banana pancakes.

Throughout the *Guide* we've given phone numbers for those restaurants where it's advisable to make **reservations**. While most eating establishments stay **open** throughout the year, note that some close over Tet (see "Festivals and Religious Events", p.46, for more on the chaos surrounding Tet). Though places stay open later in the south, especially in Ho Chi Minh, the Vietnamese **eat early**: outside the major cities and tourist areas, food stalls and street kitchens rarely stay open beyond 8pm and may close even earlier. You'll need to brush up your **chopstick**-handling skills, too, although other utensils are always available in places used to tourists – and in French restaurants you won't be expected to tackle your *steak-frites* with chopsticks.

When it comes to **paying**, the normal sign language will be readily understood in most restaurants; in street kitchens you pay as you leave – either proffer a few thousand dong to signal your intentions, or ask *bao nhieu tien?* ("how much is it?").

STREET KITCHENS

Street kitchens range from makeshift food stalls, set up on the street round a cluster of pint-size stools, to eating houses where, as often as not, the cooking is still done on the street but you either sit in an open-fronted dining area, or join the overspill outside. Like the food stall, these streetside restaurants offer few concessions to comfort. But they are permanent, with an address if not a name, and serve basic rice- or noodle-based meals for next to nothing. Some places stay open all day (7am–8pm), while many close once they've run out of ingredients and others only open at lunchtime (10.30am–2pm). To be sure of the widest choice and freshest food, it pays to get there early (before 1 or 1.30pm at lunchtime, and by 7pm in the evening), and note that the best places will be packed around noon.

Often there's a sign announcing the type of food (frequently, "*com pho*" – rice dishes and noodle soups), but in general what's on offer is displayed in a glass cabinet or on a buffet-table. Recently *com binh dan*, or "people's meals", have become popular at lunchtime. Here you select from an array of prepared dishes, piling your plate with such things as stuffed tomatoes, fried fish, tofu, pickles or eggs, plus a helping of rice; expect to pay from around US$1 for a good plateful. Though it's not a major problem at these prices, some street kitchens overcharge, so double-check when ordering.

While regular restaurants in Vietnam are definitely improving, the food served at many street kitchens is often superior in quality and much cheaper; they're also a lot more fun. All you need is a bit of judicious selection – look for clean places where the ingredients are obviously fresh – plus a smattering of basic vocabulary (see "A Glossary of Food and Drink", p.40).

RESTAURANTS

If you're after more relaxed dining, where people aren't queuing for your seat, then head for a Western-style **Vietnamese restaurant** (*nha hang*) which will have chairs rather than stools, a name, a menu and be closed to the street. In general these places serve a more varied selection of Vietnamese dishes to foreigners, though they also attract wealthier locals in increasing numbers. The food on offer is often what's called speciality food (*dac san* or *dac biet*), consisting of a wide range of dishes categorized according to the principal ingredient, from pork, fish or duck, to venison, frog, eel or pigeon. Menus rarely show prices, and overcharging is a regular problem, making for tedious ordering as you check the cost of each dish or risk an astronomical bill at the end. Another thing to watch out for are the extras: peanuts, hot towels and packs of tissues on the table will be added to the bill even if untouched; ask for them to be taken away if you don't want them, and check the bill carefully. These local restaurants generally quote prices in dong and a modest meal for two will cost roughly US$8–10 (88,000–110,000d). Opening hours are usually during lunch, from 10.30am to 2pm, and in the evening from 5pm to no later than 9pm, or 8pm in the north.

The more **expensive restaurants** (including the smarter hotel dining rooms) tend to stay open later in the evening, perhaps until 9.30 or 10.30pm, have menus priced in dollars and, in some cases, accept credit cards. Usually their menus indicate if there's a service charge, but watch out for an additional 4–5 percent on credit-card payments. These restaurants can be relatively fancy places, with at least a nod towards decor and ambience, and correspondingly higher prices (a meal for two is likely to cost at least US$10 and often much more). The most popular **foreign cuisine** on offer is French, though both Hanoi and particularly Ho Chi Minh City boast some pretty good international restaurants, including Thai, Chinese, Tex Mex, Indian and Italian. As yet, high-class restaurants are scarce in the rest of Vietnam, though Hué, Da Nang and Haiphong are beginning to get in on the act.

TRAVELLERS' CAFÉS

Catering primarily to budget travellers, what have become known as **travellers' cafés** tend to serve fairly mediocre Western and Vietnamese dishes, from banana pancakes to steak and chips

BREAKFAST

Vietnamese traditionally breakfast on *pho* or some other **noodle soup**. Alternatively, you might find some early morning hawker peddling *xoi dau*, a wholesome mix of steamed **sticky rice** with soya bean, sweet corn and peanuts. Simple **Western breakfasts** (such as toast with jam, cheese or eggs, and coffee) are usually available in the travellers' cafés or hotels, though top-class hotels normally stretch to predictable options such as cereals and fresh milk and some lay-on the full works in their breakfast buffets. In towns, you could always buy jam and bread or croissants for a **do-it-yourself** breakfast; however, things get more difficult out in the sticks, where you may even develop a taste for starting the day on a *pho*.

or fried noodles – and have the advantage of **all-day opening**, usually from 7am to 11pm or midnight. If you crave a Western-style breakfast, fresh fruit salad or a mango-shake, these are the places to go. Such cafés naturally flourish in the popular tourist towns, notably Hanoi, Ho Chi Minh, Hoi An, Hué, Nha Trang and Da Lat.

VIETNAMESE FOOD

The staple of Vietnamese meals is **rice**, with noodles a popular alternative at breakfast or as a snack. Typically, rice will be accompanied by a fish or meat dish, a vegetable dish and soup, followed by a green tea digestive. **Seafood and fish** – from rivers, lakes, canals and paddy fields as well as the sea – are favoured throughout the country, either fresh or dried. The most commonly used **flavourings** are shallots, coriander and lemon grass, though ginger, saffron, mint, anise and a basil-type herb also feature strongly, and coconut milk gives some southern dishes a distinctive richness.

Even in the south, Vietnamese food tends not to be overly spicy; instead chilli sauces or fresh chillies are served separately. Vietnam's most famous seasoning is the ubiquitous **nuoc mam**, a nutrient-packed sauce which is either added during cooking or forms the base for various dipping sauces. *Nuoc mam* is made by fermenting huge quantities of fish in vats of salt for between six months and a year, after which the dark brown liquid is strained and graded according to its age and flavour. Phu Quoc Island is said to produce the finest quality, though both Phan Thiet and Phan

Rang also turn out a mean *nuoc mam*. Foreigners usually find the smell of the sauce pretty rank, but most soon acquire a taste for its distinctive salty-sweetness. The use of **monosodium glutamate** (MSG) can be excessive, especially in northern cooking, and some people are known to react badly to the seasoning. A few restaurants in the main cities have cottoned-on to the foibles of foreigners and advertise MSG-free food; elsewhere, try saying *Khong co My Chinh* (without MSG), and keep your fingers crossed. Note that what looks like salt on the table is sometimes MSG, so taste it first.

The most famous Vietnamese **dish** has to be **spring rolls**, variously known as *cha gio*, *cha nem* or just plain *nem*. Various combinations of minced pork, shrimp or crab, rice vermicelli, onions, beansprouts and an edible fungus are rolled in rice-paper wrappers, and then fried. In some places they're served with a bowl of lettuce or mint, in which case you're supposed to wrap some leaves around each roll – using deft chopstick manoeuvres – before dipping it in the accompanying sauce. In addition, a southern variation has barbecued strips of pork wrapped in semi-transparent rice wrappers, along with raw ingredients such as green banana and star fruit, and then dunked in a rich peanut sauce.

SOUPS AND NOODLES

Though it originated in the north, another dish you'll find throughout Vietnam is *pho* (pronounced "fur"), a noodle **soup** eaten at any time of day but primarily at breakfast. The basic bowl of *pho* consists of a light, beef broth, flavoured with ginger, coriander, and sometimes cinnamon, to which are added broad, flat rice-noodles, spring onions and slivers of chicken, pork or beef. At the table you add a squeeze of lime and a sprinkling of chilli flakes or a spoonful of chilli sauce. There are countless variations on the theme, such as adding a raw egg to make a more substantial meal. If you stray far off the beaten track, you're likely to become quite a connoisseur of *pho*.

Countless other types of soup are dished up at street restaurants. *Bun bo* is another substantial, beef and noodle soup eaten countrywide, though most famous in Hué, while in the south *hu tieu*, a soup of vermicelli, pork and seafood noodles, is best taken in My Tho. *Chao* (or *xhao*), on the other hand, is a thick rice gruel served piping hot, usually with shredded chicken or filleted fish, flavoured with dill and with perhaps a raw egg cooking at the bottom; it's often served with fried breadsticks (*quay*). Sour soups are a popular accompaniment for fish, while *lau*, a standard of most restaurant menus, is more of a main meal than a soup, where the vegetable broth arrives at the table in a steamboat (a ring-shaped metal dish on live coals or, nowadays, often electrically heated). You cook slivers of beef, prawns or similar in the simmering soup, and then afterwards drink the flavourful liquid that's left in the cooking pot.

FISH AND MEAT

Among the highlights of Vietnamese cuisine are its succulent seafoods and freshwater **fish**. *Cha ca* is a famous fish dish (fried at table in dill-flavoured butter and served with rice noodles) invented in Hanoi but now found in most upmarket restaurants, while *ca kho to*, fish stew cooked in a clay pot, is a southern speciality. Another dish found in more expensive restaurants is *chao tom* (or *tom bao mia*), consisting of savoury shrimp pâté wrapped round sweet sugar-cane and fried.

Every conceivable type of meat and part of the animal anatomy finds itself on the Vietnamese dining table, though you're unlikely to encounter anything more frightening than beef, chicken and pork in street food. **Ground meat**, especially pork, is a common constituent of stuffings, for example in spring rolls or the similar *banh cuon*, a steamed, rice-flour "ravioli" filled with minced pork, black mushrooms and bean sprouts; a popular variation uses prawns instead of meat. Pork is also used, with plenty of herbs, to make Hanoi's *bun cha*, small **hamburgers** barbecued on an open, charcoal brazier and served on a bed of cold rice-noodles with greens and a slightly sweetish sauce. One famous southern dish is *bo bay mon* (often written *bo 7 mon*), meaning literally **beef** seven ways, consisting of a platter of beef cooked in different styles.

Roving gourmets may want to try some of the more unusual meats on offer. **Dog** meat (*thit cay* or *thit cho*) is a particular delicacy in the north, where "yellow dog" (sandy-haired varieties) is considered the tastiest. Winter is the season to eat dog meat – it's said to give extra body heat, and is also supposed to remove bad luck if consumed at the end of the lunar month. **Snake**, like dog, is supposed to improve male virility. Dining on snake (*thit con ran*) is surrounded by a ritual, which, if you're guest of honour, requires you to swallow the still-beating heart. Another one

strictly for the strong of stomach is *trung vit lon*, embryo-containing **duck eggs** boiled and eaten only five days before hatching – bill, webbed feet, feathers and all. Pending a rumoured government ban on such trade, other exotica on the menu might include a whole list of endangered species, such as turtle (*rua*), pangolin (*truc*) and porcupine (*nhim*), which will probably be off-limits financially, even if you have no qualms on ecological grounds.

VEGETABLES – AND VEGETARIAN FOOD

If all this has put you off meat for ever, it is possible to eat **vegetarian** food in Vietnam, though not always easy. The widest selection of vegetables is to be found in Da Lat where a staggering variety of tropical and temperate crops thrive. Elsewhere, most restaurants offer a smattering of meat-free dishes, ranging from stewed spinach or similar greens, to a more appetizing mix of onion, tomato, beansprouts, various mushrooms, peppers and so on; places used to foreigners may be able to oblige with vegetarian spring rolls (*nem an chay*, or *nem khong co thit*). At street kitchens you're likely to find tofu and one or two dishes of pickled vegetables, such as cabbage or cucumber, while occasionally they may also have aubergine, bamboo shoots or avocado, depending on the season. However, unless you go to a **specialist** vegetarian outlet – of which there are some excellent examples in Ho Chi Minh City and Hué – it can be a problem finding genuine veggie food: soups are usually made with beef stock, morsels of pork fat sneak into otherwise innocuous-looking dishes and animal fat tends to be used for frying. The phrase to remember is *an chay* (vegetarian), or seek out a vegetarian rice shop (*tiem com chay*). Otherwise, make the most of the 1st and 14th/15th days of the lunar month when many Vietnamese spurn meat and you're more likely to find vegetarian dishes on offer.

SNACKS

Vietnam has a wide range of snacks and nibbles to fill any yawning gaps, from huge rice-flour **crackers** sprinkled with sesame seeds to all sorts of dried fish, nuts and seeds. The white, steamed **dumpling** called *banh bao* is a Chinese import, filled with tasty titbits, such as pork, onions and tangy mushrooms or strands of sweet coconut. *Banh xeo*, meaning sizzling **pancake**, combines shrimp, pork, beansprouts and egg, all fried and then wrapped in rice paper with a selection of greens before being dunked in a spicy sauce. A similar dish, originating from Hué – a city with a vast repertoire of snack foods – is *banh khoai*, in which the flat pancake is accompanied by a plate of star fruit, green banana and aromatic herbs, plus a rich peanut sauce.

Markets are often good snacking grounds, with stalls churning out soups and spring rolls or selling intriguing banana-leaf parcels of pâté (a favourite accompaniment for *bia hoi*), pickled pork sausage or perhaps a cake of sticky rice.

A relative newcomer on the culinary scene is **French bread**, made with wheat flour in the north and rice flour in the south. Baguettes – sometimes sold warm from streetside stoves – are sliced open and stuffed with pâté, soft cheese, or ham and pickled vegetables.

FRUIT AND SWEET THINGS

Vietnam is not strong on desserts, and restaurants usually stick to ice cream and fruit, although fancy, international places might venture into *crêpe suzette* territory. Those with a sweet tooth are better-off browsing around street stalls where there are usually candied fruits and other Vietnamese **sweetmeats** on offer, as well as sugary displays of French-inspired cakes and pastries in the main tourist centres.

Green-coloured *banh com* is an eye-catching local delicacy made by wrapping pounded glutinous rice around sugary, green bean paste. A similar confection, found only during the mid-autumn festival, is the "earth cake" *banh deo*, which melds the contrasting flavours of candied fruits, sesame and lotus seed with a dice of savoury pork fat. **Fritters** are popular among children and you'll find opportunistic hawkers outside schools, selling banana fritters, *banh chuoi*, or mixed slices of banana and sweet potato, *banh chuoi khoai*.

Most cities now have **ice-cream** parlours selling tubs or sticks of the local, hard ices in chocolate, vanilla or green tea flavours, though for health reasons it's safest to buy only from the larger, busier outlets – and not from street hawkers. More exotic tastes can be satisfied at the European- and American-style ice-cream parlours of Hanoi and Ho Chi Minh City, while frozen yoghurts are also increasingly available at ice-cream parlours and some cafés.

With its diverse climate, Vietnam is blessed with both tropical and temperate **fruits**, including dozens of banana species. The richest orchards are in the south, where pineapple, coconut,

papaya, mangoes, longan and mangosteen flourish. Da Lat is famous for its strawberries, while the region around Nha Trang produces the peculiar "dragon fruit" (*thanh long*), in season from May to September. The size and shape of a small pineapple, the dragon fruit has a mauvish-pink skin, studded with small protuberances, and smooth, white flesh speckled with tiny black seeds. The slightly sweet, watery flesh is thirst-quenching, and hence is often served as a drink, crushed with ice. A fruit you might want to give a miss is the durian, a spiky, yellow-green football-sized fruit with an unmistakably pungent odour reminiscent of mature cheese and caramel, but tasting like an onion-laced custard. Jackfruit looks worryingly similar to durian but has smaller spikes and its yellow segments of flesh are deliciously sweet.

DRINKS

Giai khat means "quench your thirst" and you'll see the signs everywhere, on stands selling fresh juices, bottled cold drinks or outside cafés and *bia hoi* (draft beer) outlets. Many drinks are served with **ice**: tempting though it may be, the only really safe policy is to avoid ice altogether – *dung bo da, cam on* (no ice, thanks) should do the trick. That said, ice in the top hotels, bars and restaurants is generally reliable, and some people take the risk in far dodgier establishments with apparent impunity.

WATER AND SOFT DRINKS

Bottled **water** is widely available at around US$1 or less per litre; avoid any other water, and even drinks that may have been diluted with suspect water (see p.18 for more on this). Locally made **soft drinks** are tooth-numbingly sweet, but are cheap and safe – as long as the bottle or carton appears well sealed – and on sale just about everywhere. The Coke, Sprite and Fanta hegemony also means you can find your favourite fizzy drink in surprisingly remote areas. Oddly, canned drinks are usually more expensive than the equivalent-sized bottle, whether it's a soft drink or beer – apparently it's less chic to drink from the old-fashioned bottle. A more effective thirst-quencher is fresh coconut milk, though this is more difficult to find in the north. Fresh juices such as orange and lime, are also delicious – just make sure they've been mixed with soda, bottled or treated water – or try sugar-cane juice (*mia da*) with a dash of lime. Pasteurized milk, produced by *Vinamilk*, is now sold in the main cities.

Somewhere between a drink and a snack, it's worth looking out for glasses of **chè**, usually on sale in the markets. *Chè* is made from green bean and served over ice with chunks of fruit, coloured jellies and even sweet corn or potato. In hot weather it provides a refreshing sugar-fix: in the cooler north, *chè* stalls tend to close in the winter, but are a year-round feature in the rest of the country.

TEA AND COFFEE

Tea drinking is part of the social ritual in Vietnam. Small cups of refreshing, strong, green tea are presented to all guests or visitors: the well-boiled water is safe to drink, as long as the cup itself is clean, and it's polite to drink at least a cupful. Although your cup will be continually replenished to show hospitality, you don't have to carry on drinking; the polite way to decline a refill is to place your hand over the cup when your host is about to replenish it. Tea is also served at the end of every meal, and is usually provided free in restaurants and at food stalls. If you can't live without tea bags, you can buy Lipton's in Hanoi and Ho Chi Minh, where cafés frequented by tourists may also offer regular tea, though it often comes laced with sweetened, condensed milk.

Vietnam's best tea is said to grow around Bao Loc, southwest of Da Lat in the central highlands, and the best **coffee** a few kilometres further north among the hills of Buon Me Thuot. The Vietnamese drink coffee very strong and in small quantities, with a large dollop of condensed milk at the bottom of the cup. Cafés accustomed to tourists often provide a Thermos of hot water so you can dilute the coffee, and some even offer fresh (pasteurised) milk. In general coffee is filtered at the table, by means of a small dripper balanced over the cup or glass, which sometimes sits in a bowl of hot water to keep it warm. If you're heading off into the more remote areas, where it's often difficult to find a cup of coffee, you may want to stock up with a supply of "3 in 1", sachets of powdered coffee, milk and sugar, available in the main cities.

THE HARD STUFF

Imported canned and **bottled beers** available in Vietnam include *Tiger*, *Heineken* and *San Miguel*, but there are plenty of good locally produced light beers around at more reasonable prices. The most

popular domestic beer is *333* (*Ba Ba Ba*), which is also the cheapest – and very drinkable. Some connoisseurs rate *Saigon Export* as the best, though *BGI* and *Bière la Rue* are also fine brews. There are many other locally produced beers and some towns boast their own brewery, such as *Huda* in Hué, *Da Nang* beer, *Thanh Hoa* and even *Son La* – all worth a try.

Roughly thirty years ago technology for making **bia hoi** ("draft beer"; also known in the south as *bia bock*) was introduced from Czechoslovakia and is now quaffed in vast quantities throughout Vietnam. *Bia hoi* tastes fairly weak, though it measures in at 4 percent alcohol. Quality varies from region to region, but it's cheap and unadulterated with chemicals – so, in theory at least, you're less likely to get a hangover. The beer is usually served warm from the keg and then poured over ice, though some outlets serve it ready chilled, especially in the south where it may also be bottled. *Bia hoi* has a 24-hour shelf-life, which means the better places sell out by early evening and you're unlikely to be drinking it into the wee hours.

There are dozens of *bia hoi* outlets in Hanoi and Ho Chi Minh, ranging from a few ankle-high stools gathered round a barrel on the pavement to beer gardens. A few serve proper meals, while most offer snacks of some sort, typically *nem chua* (pickled pork wrapped in banana leaf), *lac* (peanuts), *khoai tay ran* (potato chips). Nowadays you might also see signs for *bia tuoi*, a close relation of *bia hoi* that uses ingredients imported from Germany and is served from pressurized barrels. *Bia tuoi* comes in a light or dark brew and is stronger but also more expensive (at up to US$1 per half litre, more than double the regular stuff).

Almost anything edible in Vietnam is turned into **wine** or **spirit** (*ruou*), or steeped in it – including rice, strawberries, mulberries, snake and assorted herbs. As often as not, these drinks are medicinal tonics rather than alcoholic beverages, and there's a lively export trade in sending such efficacious brews up to China. The most common local wine is rice alcohol, which features heavily at festivals and for making toasts at official receptions. The ethnic minorities of the northwest (Thai and Muong) concoct their own version, called stem alcohol (*ruou can*) which is drunk from a communal jar using thin, bamboo straws. The recipe for *ruou can* is a closely guarded secret, but its basic constituents are sticky rice, herbs and

A GLOSSARY OF FOOD AND DRINK

The following list should give you an idea what to ask for where the menu's either Vietnamese-only or non-existent. For a comprehensive menu reader, check out the *Rough Guide Vietnamese Phrasebook*.

Note that the spelling of foods is not always consistent and that some names differ between north and south: (N) and (S) indicate the regional variants.

GENERAL TERMS AND REQUESTS

bat (N); *chen* (S)	bowl	*dua*	chopsticks
bao nhieu tien	how much is it?	*it duong*	a little sugar
can chen (N); *can ly* (S)	cheers!	*lanh*	cold
chuc suc khoe	to your good health	*nguoi an chay*	vegetarian
cop	cup	*toi khong an thit*	I don't eat meat or fish
da	ice	*nong*	hot
dung bo da cam on	no ice, thanks	*rat ngon*	delicious

RICE AND NOODLES

bun	round rice noodles	*com trang*	steamed or boiled rice
bun bo	beef with *bun* noodles	*chao*	rice porridge
bun bo gio heo	chicken, beef and pork with *bun* noodles	*mi xao*	fried noodles
		pho	flat rice noodles, usually in soup
bun ga	chicken with *bun* noodles	*pho bo tai*	noodle soup with rare beef
com	cooked rice	*pho bo chin*	with medium done beef
com rang (N); *com chien* (S)	fried rice	*pho co trung*	with eggs

FISH, MEAT AND VEGETABLES

ca	fish	*cai bap*	cabbage
ca ran (N); *ca chien* (S)	fried fish	*ca chua*	tomato
cua	crab	*ca tim*	aubergine
luon	eel	*dau*	beans
muc	squid	*gia*	bean sprouts
tom	shrimp or prawn	*khoai tay*	potato
tom hum	lobster	*khoai lang*	sweet potato
thit	meat	*mang*	bamboo shoots
bit tet	beefsteak	*ngo* (N); *bap* (S)	sweetcorn
bo	beef	*rau xao cac loai*	stir-fried vegetables
ga	chicken	*sa lat*	salad
lon (N); *heo* (S)	pork	*sa lat ca chua*	tomato salad
vit	duck	*sa lat rau xanh cac loai*	green salad
rau co or *rau cac loai*	vegetables		

MISCELLANEOUS

banh	cake (sweet or savoury)	*mut*	jam
		ot	chilli
banh mi	bread	*tao pho* (N); *dau hu* (S)	tofu
bo	butter	*tieu*	pepper
pho mat, fo mat or *fromage*	cheese	*trung*	egg
lac (N); *dau phong* (S)	peanuts (ground nuts)	*trung om let* or *op lep*	omelette
muoi	salt	*trung ran* or *trung op la*	fried eggs

DESSERTS AND FRUIT

banh ngot	cakes and pastries	*dua hau*	water melon
duong	sugar	*du du*	papaya
kem	ice cream or cream	*khe*	starfruit
mat ong	honey	*mang cau* (N); *qua na* (S)	custard apple
sua chua	yoghurt	*mang cut*	mangosteen
trai cay	fruit	*mit*	jackfruit
buoi	pomelo/grapefruit	*nhan*	longan
cam	orange	*qua bo*	avocado
chanh	lemon/lime	*sau rieng*	durian
chom chom	rambutan	*soai*	mango
chuoi	banana	*tao tay*	apple
dau tay	strawberry	*thang long*	dragon fruit
dua	coconut	*vai*	lychee
dua (N); *thom* (S)	pineapple		

DRINKS

bia	beer	*nuoc*	water
ca phé	coffee	*nuoc khoang*	mineral water
ca phé da	iced coffee	*nuoc so da*	soda water
ca phé den	black coffee	*nuoc cam*	orange juice
ca phé den khong duong	black coffee without sugar.	*nuoc chanh*	lime juice
		nuoc dua	coconut milk
ca phé nong	hot coffee	*ruou ran*	snake wine
ca phé sua	coffee with milk	*ruou trang* or *choum*	rice alchohol
ca phé sua nong	hot milk coffee	*so da cam*	orange soda
tra	tea	*so da chanh*	lime soda
tra voi chanh	tea with lemon	*sua*	milk
tra sua	tea with milk	*sua tuoi*	fresh milk
khong da	no ice	*sua ong tho*	long-life milk

spices which are heated together and then buried in the ground for a month or more to ferment. You can indulge in some of the best *ruou can* in Son La or Mai Chau.

Sometimes you'll come across a bottle of Chinese champagne or Russian vodka, but increasingly Western spirits, such as whisky, cognac and gin, are available in most big towns. Before being tempted by the cheap prices on the street, however, bear in mind that a lot of these products are fakes; check the cap is properly sealed and the bottle doesn't look used.

MAIL, TELECOMMUNICATIONS AND MEDIA

Vietnam has been investing heavily in its communications networks. International phone connections are among the most expensive in the world, but on the whole it's easy to phone or fax abroad, even from the smaller towns. International mail services also seem to work fairly efficiently and are reasonably reliable to or from any of the major cities.

Domestic telephone calls are less reliable, plagued by poor quality lines and dicky connections, while the most you can say about in-country post is that it gets there eventually. Satellite **TV** in English is available in more places than you might imagine but imported English-language **newspapers** are only sold in Hanoi and Ho Chi Minh City. Vietnam's English-language press has a wider distribution and normally makes it to wherever foreigners congregate in large enough numbers.

MAIL SERVICES

Mail can take anywhere from four days to four weeks in or out of Vietnam, depending largely where you are. Services are quickest and most reliable from the major towns, when eight to ten days is the norm. **Overseas postal rates** are reasonable: a postcard costs US$0.50 or less, while a standard letter is just under a dollar, depending on the weight; ideally you should have mail franked in front of you. **Express Mail**

Service (EMS) operates to most countries and certain destinations within Vietnam; the service cuts down delivery times substantially and the letter or parcel is automatically registered. The main post offices are **open** seven days a week, normally 7am–8pm; some may close for an hour at lunch while others stay open until 10pm. Rates for all post office services – phone, fax, telex, stamps or parcels – are posted up in the main halls.

Poste restante services are available in selected towns: Hanoi, Ho Chi Minh, Da Nang, Hué, Hoi An and Da Lat. Each city operates a different system: most charge a small amount per item, but in Hanoi it's free and you help yourself from the pigeonholes. At the moment, no one asks for ID when collecting mail, so you might want to get important letters sent by recorded delivery. How long they keep the mail varies but is usually somewhere between one and two months. To avoid misfiling, your name should be printed clearly, with the surname in capitals and underlined, and it's still worth checking under your first name, just in case. Have letters addressed to you c/o Poste Restante, GPO, town or city, province. Note that within Vietnam if you want to leave a message for someone in poste restante, you have to buy a local stamp.

Sending parcels out of Vietnam can be time consuming, especially if they decide to inspect each item, in which case novels or other material about Vietnam printed abroad can cause problems; you may also be charged customs duty on items such as CDs. Take everything to the post office unwrapped and keep it small: after inspection, and a good deal of form-filling (you may have to pay a nominal amount for the forms), the parcel will be wrapped for you. Surface mail is the cheapest option, with parcels taking between one and four months to reach their destination. Note that some parcel counters are only open in the morning.

Receiving parcels is not such a good idea: some parcels simply go astray; those that do make it are subject to long and thorough customs inspections, import duty and even confiscation of suspicious items – particularly printed matter, videos or cassettes.

PHONES

One benefit of Vietnam's late entry into modern telecommunications has been the opportunity to leap-frog straight in with the latest technology, and where the system does work, it works well. The massive amount of capital investment required is how the government justifies its notoriously high tariffs on **international calls**, which stand at around US$4–5 per minute, though they are gradually falling (see box below for details of dialling codes). The best place to call abroad is from the post office. There's no facility for reversed-charge calls but you can almost always get a "**call-back**": ask the operator for a minimum (one-minute) call abroad and get the phone number of the post office you're calling from; you can then be called back directly at the post office, at a total cost of a one-minute call plus a small charge for the service. A few post offices still insist on a three-minute minimum call but with enough persuasion you should be able to get just the one. In theory you can dial abroad direct from a public telephone (see below), but as phones seem to be located on the noisiest street corners, it's rarely worth the effort. Many **hotels** now offer international direct dialling (IDD) from your room, but you will usually be clobbered by rates at least 10 percent above the norm, and a minimum charge for 1–3 minutes even if the call goes answered.

Whether you telephone from your hotel or the post office, **cheap rates** (10 percent discount) for international calls apply between 11pm and 7am Monday to Saturday, all day Sunday and on public holidays; the telephone halls in both Ho Chi Minh and Hanoi GPOs are open 24 hours.

Long-distance domestic calls are far more reasonably priced, but again the cheapest option is to dial direct from the post office. Cheap rates apply between 10pm and 5am when there's a 20 percent discount. **Local calls** are free from private phones, hotels, restaurants (but not call boxes), and incur a small charge when made from the post office. Finding a phone number is not so easy: the better hotels should have up-to-date **directories** and their reception staff will usually help; otherwise, try asking in the post office, or calling the general enquiries number (☎108) and speaking to one of their English-speaking staff, for which you pay a small charge.

At the moment **public telephones** (all card phones) aren't much use since they have no protection from street noise, though this is due to change. Public phones are only found in the main cities and are either yellow or blue, which corresponds to the colour of phone card you need to use them; calls cost the same whichever colour system you opt for. Phone cards can be purchased at the post office: cards good for international calls cost around US$30 while those for domestic calls cost $3–4. Instructions are displayed on the phone in a variety of languages, including English.

International and domestic **fax** is now widely available at many hotels and nearly all post offices throughout the country. It is usually cheaper sending faxes from the post office, where charges are levied per page; some hotels charge by the minute. Both hotels and post offices charge for receiving faxes on your behalf (US$0.50–1 per page).

PHONING VIETNAM FROM ABROAD

To call Vietnam from abroad, dial your international access code (see below) + **84** + area code minus first 0 + number.

UK ☎00

USA ☎011

Canada ☎011

Australia ☎0011

New Zealand ☎00

PHONING ABROAD FROM VIETNAM

To call abroad from Vietnam, dial **00** + country code (see below) + area code minus first 0 + number.

UK ☎44

USA ☎1

Canada ☎1

Australia ☎61

New Zealand ☎64

PHONING WITHIN VIETNAM

Every province in Vietnam has an **area code** which must be used when phoning from outside that province. Area codes are included in telephone numbers throughout the *Guide* – omit them if dialling within the province.

TIME DIFFERENCES

Vietnam is 7 hours ahead of London, 15 hours ahead of Los Angeles, 12 hours ahead of New York, 1 hour behind Perth and 3 hours behind Sydney – give or take an hour or two when summer time is in operation.

E-MAIL AND THE INTERNET

Linking to the Internet from Vietnam as a short-term visitor requires a lot of patience, a healthy bank balance and a screwdriver. At the time of writing Vietnam has three commercial Internet access providers geared towards in-country **business users**, who pay a sign-up fee plus monthly subscriptions: *NetNam*, *VareNet* and *VietNet*. The first two operate like Bulletin Board Services and the only international facility available as yet is e-mail, with a limit on message length. *VietNet* offers restricted connection to the Internet but further development of international services is likely to be slow while the government puzzles over how to control this lucrative and potentially subversive means of communication.

At the moment, most **short-term visitors** who want to link-up access the CompuServe node in Hong Kong by means of an international phone call. If you intend to do this, it's wise to give your computer a trial run by connecting to the Hong Kong node before you leave home. Alternatively, you can dial into CompuServe in the US using call-back, but perhaps the best option for short-term visitors is to use *Sprintnet*, since the charges are added to your regular CompuServe bill; the *Sprintnet* number in both Hanoi and Ho Chi Minh is ☎1250.

Many **hotel phones** in Vietnam have the American RJ11 plugs but you'll also find plenty that are hard-wired – hence the screwdriver; a female-to-female RJ11 socket will come in handy where it's only the wall-socket that's hard-wired. Once you're plugged in the fun really starts if you're trying to connect to an overseas network: with each failed attempt potentially costing you a one- or three-minute minimum call, depending on the hotel's charging policy. The end result can be a phone bill that exceeds the cost of your room. Alternatively, one or two business centres in the big hotels of Hanoi and Ho Chi Minh now allow you to link your own computer and modem to their telephone lines; again check tariffs and charging policy first.

If you have specific questions about connecting up in Vietnam, try either of the newsgroups listed in the box on p.22. *Teleadapt* on http://www.teleadapt.com/ is the best place to go for advice on hardware and extra bits of kit required for different countries. (See "Directory", p.53, for information on power points and voltages.)

THE MEDIA

Vietnam has several English-language **newspapers** and magazines, most of which are geared to the foreign business community and potential investors. The most informative publications and those with the widest distribution are the weekly newspaper, *Vietnam Investment Review*, and the *Vietnam Economic Times*, a monthly magazine with a useful pull-out guide for visitors. Though short on general news, both these publications are worth looking at for an insight into what makes the Vietnamese economy tick. Both also print selective but up-to-date restaurant and nightlife listings, plus feature articles on culture and tourist destinations.

Vietnam Investment Review's "Time Out" section is the best available source for events in Hanoi; in Ho Chi Minh City, look out for the free monthly magazine, *What's On in Saigon*, which contains local listings and a few articles.

Foreign publications, such as the *International Herald Tribune*, *The Economist*, *Time*, *South China Morning Post* and the Bangkok papers are available in the newsstands of more upmarket hotels in Hanoi and Ho Chi Minh City. Older issues are sold on the streets, often "acquired" from airlines and hotel rooms, and at some of the larger bookstores (see Ho Chi Minh and Hanoi "Listings", p.105 and p.347).

The government **radio** station, *Voice of Vietnam*, began life in 1945 during the August Revolution. It became famous during the American War when "Hanoi Hannah" broadcast propaganda programmes to American GIs. Nowadays the station is on air for roughly eighteen hours a day, with local news bulletins in English repeated throughout the day. To keep in touch with international news, however, you'll need a short-wave radio to pick up *BBC World Service* (6195kHz), or *Voice of America* (8–10am 17740 or 21550kHz, 6pm–midnight 6110kHz); check *What's On in Saigon* for alternative frequencies.

Vietnamese **television** (VTV) is also government-run and airs a mix of films, music shows, news programmes, Russian broadcasts and a few aged American imports. VTV presents the news in English at the end of the day's viewing, usually sometime after 10pm. Hotels increasingly provide satellite TV in their mid- and top-category rooms.

OPENING HOURS AND PUBLIC HOLIDAYS

Basic hours of business are 7.30–11.30am and 1.30–4.30pm, though after lunch nothing really gets going again before 2pm. The standard closing day for offices is Sunday, and many also close on Saturday afternoon.

Banks tend to work Monday to Friday 7.30–11.30am and 1.30–3.30pm, Saturday 7.30 –11.30am, though some stay open a little later in the afternoon or may forego a lunch-break. **Post offices** keep much longer hours, in general staying open from 7am through to 8pm, or even 10pm at night, with no closing day. **Shops** and **markets** open seven days a week and in theory keep going all day, though in practice most stallholders and many private shopkeepers will take a siesta. Shops mostly stay open late into the evenings, perhaps until 8pm or beyond in the big cities.

The majority of **tourist offices** and tour agents keep fairly standard hours (7.30–11.30am & 1.30–5pm) and most are open at weekends, while the more switched-on keep going all day and into the evening. **Museums** usually close one day a week, generally on Mondays, and their core opening hours are 8–11am and 2–4pm. **Temples** and **pagodas** occasionally close for lunch but are otherwise open all week and don't close until late evening.

ADMISSION CHARGES

There's usually an admission charge levied at museums, historic sights, national parks and any place which attracts tourists – sometimes even

PUBLIC HOLIDAYS
January 1: New Year's Day
January/February: Tet, Vietnamese New Year (3 days – starting on Feb 7 in 1997, Jan 28 in 1998 and Jan 16 in 1999 – though increasingly offices tend to close down for a full week)
February 3: Founding of the Vietnamese Communist Party
April 30: Liberation of Saigon, 1975
May 1: International Labour Day
May 19: Birthday of Ho Chi Minh
June: Birthday of Buddha (eighth day of the fourth moon)
September 2: National Day
December 25: Christmas

beaches. Though the amount is often minimal (less than US$1), charges at some more **major sights** range from a dollar or two, such as Hanoi's Temple of Literature, the Cham ruins at My Son, up to Ho Chi Minh's Reunification Palace or Hué's citadel and royal mausoleums (US$5 each). Admission charges which exceed US$1 are given in the text; where no amount is shown, admission is either free, or a negligible amount (less than $1). Note that there is sometimes a hefty additional charge for **cameras** and **videos**.

Apart from those with some historical significance, **pagodas and temples** are usually free, though it's customary to leave a donation in the collecting box or on one of the altar plates.

FESTIVALS AND RELIGIOUS EVENTS

The Vietnamese year follows a rhythm of festivals and religious observances ranging from solemn family gatherings at the ancestral altar to national celebrations culminating in the exuberant festival of Tet, the Vietnamese New Year. In between are countless local festivals, most notably in the Red River Delta, honouring the tutelary spirit of the village or community temple.

The majority of festivals take place in spring, with a second flurry in the autumn months. Details are given below of the major festivals plus a number of local events. One festival that will definitely make an impact, whether you plan to participate or not, is **Tet**: not only does most of Vietnam close down for the week, but for several weeks either side of the holiday, hotels and local transport services are stretched to the limit and international flights are filled by returning overseas Vietnamese. (For dates of Tet and other public holidays, see "Opening Hours and Public Holidays", previous page.)

Many Vietnamese festivals are **Chinese** in origin, imbued with a distinctive flavour over the centuries, but minority groups also hold their own, specific celebrations. The ethnic **minorities** continue to punctuate the year with rituals that govern sowing, harvest or hunting, as well as elaborate rites of passage surrounding birth and death. The **Cao Dai** religion has its own array of festivals while **Christian** communities throughout Vietnam observe the major ceremonies. Christmas is marked as a religious event only by the faithful, but Christmas Day is now a public holiday in Vietnam and city-dwellers, particularly in Ho Chi Minh City, increasingly enter into the spirit of the occasion with parties and family gatherings.

Some festivities have seen a revival since *doi moi*, but on the whole the number of such celebrations is in decline, not least because of the expense involved. You may be lucky enough to happen on a local festival, but the ceremonies you're most likely to see are **weddings** and **funerals**. The tenth lunar month is the most auspicious time for weddings, though at other times you'll also encounter plenty of wedding cavalcades on the road, their hired buses decked out with red-paper stencils of the Chinese ideograph for "happiness". Funeral processions are recognizable from the white headbands worn by mourners, while close family members dress completely in white. Contrary to Western perceptions, it's considered lucky to meet a funeral procession: the deceased will soon ascend to heaven and might see fit to put in a favourable word with the gods on your behalf.

Most festivals take place according to the **lunar calendar**, which is also closely linked to the Chinese system with a zodiac of twelve animal signs. The most important times during the lunar month (which lasts 29 or 30 days) are the full moon (day 1) and the new moon (day 14 or 15). Festivals are often held at these times, which also hold a special significance for Buddhists who are supposed to pray at the pagoda and avoid eating meat during the two days. All Vietnamese calendars show both the lunar and solar (Gregorian) months and dates, but to be sure of a festival date it's best to check locally.

TET: THE VIETNAMESE NEW YEAR

"Tet", simply meaning festival, is the accepted name for Vietnam's most important annual event, properly known as **Tet Nguyen Dan**, or festival of the first day. Tet lasts for seven days and falls sometime between the last week of January and the third week of February, on the night of the new moon. This is a time when families get together to celebrate renewal and hope for the new year, when ancestral spirits are welcomed back to the household, and when everyone in Vietnam becomes a year older – age is reckoned by the new year and not by individual birthdays.

VIETNAM'S MAJOR FESTIVALS

SPRING FESTIVALS
(January–April)

Tet The most important date in the Vietnamese festival calendar is New Year (*Tet Nguyen Dan*). After an initial jamboree, Tet is largely a family occasion when offices are shut, and even shops and restaurants may close for the seven-day festival. Officially only the first three days are public holidays, though many people take the whole week (1st to 7th days of first lunar month; late Jan to mid-Feb – see p.45 for precise dates for 1997–1999).

Tay Son Festival Martial arts demonstrations in Tay Son District, plus garlanded elephants on parade (5th day of first lunar month; late Jan to mid-Feb).

Water Puppet Festival As part of the Tet celebrations a festival of puppetry is held at Thay Pagoda, west of Hanoi (5th to 7th days of first lunar month; Feb).

Lim Singing Festival Two weeks after Tet, Lim village near Bac Ninh, in the Red River Delta, resounds to the harmonies of "alternate singing" (*quan ho*) as men and women fling improvised lyrics back and forth. (13th to 15th days of the first lunar month; Feb–March)

Hai Ba Trung Festival The two Trung sisters are honoured with a parade and dancing at Hanoi's Hai Ba Trung temple (6th day of the second lunar month; March).

Perfume Pagoda Vietnam's most famous pilgrimage site is *Chua Huong*, west of Hanoi. Thousands of Buddhist pilgrims flock to the pagoda for the festival which climaxes on the full moon (14th or 15th day) of the second month, though the pilgrimage continues for two weeks either side (March–April).

Den Ba Chua Kho The full moon of the second month sees Hanoians congregating at this temple near Bac Ninh, to petition the goddess for success in business (March–April).

Thanh Minh Ancestral graves are cleaned and offerings of food, flowers and paper votive objects made at the beginning of the third lunar month (April).

SUMMER FESTIVALS
(May–August)

Phat Dan Lanterns are hung outside the pagodas and Buddhist homes to commemorate Buddha's birth, enlightenment and the attainment of Nirvana (8th day of the fourth moon; May).

Chua Xu Fesival The stone statue of Chua Xu at Sam Mountain, Chau Doc, is bathed, and thousands flock to honour her (23rd to 25th day of fourth lunar month; May).

Tet Doan Ngo The summer solstice (5th day of the fifth moon) is marked by festivities aimed to ward off epidemics brought on by the summer heat. This is also the time of dragon boat races. (late May to early June).

Trang Nguyen (or *Vu Lan*) The day of wandering souls is the second most important festival after Tet. Offerings of food and clothes are made to comfort and nourish the unfortunate souls without a home, and all graves are cleaned. This is also time for the forgiveness of faults, when the King of Hell judges everyone's spirits and metes out reward or punishment as appropriate. Until the fifteenth century prisoners were allowed to go home on this day (14th or 15th day of the seventh lunar month; Aug).

AUTUMN FESTIVALS
(September–December)

Do Son buffalo fighting festival Held in Do Son village, near Haiphong on the 9th and 10th days of the eigth lunar month (Sept).

Kate Festival The Cham New Year is celebrated in high style at Po Klong Garai and Po Re Me, both near Phan Rang (Sept–Oct).

Trung Thu The mid-autumn festival, also known as Children's Day, is when dragon dances take place and children are given lanterns in the shape of stars, carp or dragons. Special cakes, *banh trung thu*, are eaten at this time of year. These are sticky rice cakes filled with lotus seeds, nuts and candied fruits and are either square like the earth (*banh deo*), or round like the moon (*banh nuong*) and containing the yolk of an egg. (14th or 15th day of the eight lunar month; Sept–Oct).

Whale Festival Lang Ca Ong, Vung Tau. Crowds gather to make offerings to the whales (16th day of eighth lunar month; Sept–Oct).

Ghe Ngo Festival Boat-racing festival in Soc Trang (10th day of tenth lunar month; Nov–Dec).

Christmas Midnight service at Ho Chi Minh cathedral, and much revelry along Nguyen Hue and Le Loi as people throw glitter over each other (December 24).

There's an almost tangible sense of excitement leading up to midnight on the eve of Tet, which explodes into a cacophony of jubilant drums and percussion; though since firecrackers were banned in 1995, the ear-splitting noise has diminished – as has the number of injuries.

Tet kicks off seven days before the new moon with the **festival of Ong Tau**, the god of the hearth (23rd day of the twelfth month). Ong Tao keeps watch over the household throughout the year, wards off evil spirits and makes an annual report of family events, good or bad, to the Jade Emperor. In order to send Ong Tau off to heaven in a benevolent mood, the family cleans their house from top to bottom, and makes offerings to him, including pocket money and a new set of clothes. Ong Tau returns home at midnight on the first chime of the new year and it's this, together with welcoming the ancestral spirits back to share in the party, that warrants such a massive celebration.

Tet is all about **starting the year afresh**, with a clean slate and good intentions. Not only is the house scrubbed, but all debts are repaid and those that can afford it have a haircut and buy new clothes. To attract favourable spirits, good luck charms are put in the house, most commonly cockerels or the trinity of male figures representing prosperity, happiness and longevity. The crucial moments are the first minutes and hours of the new year as these set the pattern for the whole of the following year. People strive to avoid arguments, swearing or breaking anything – at least during the first three days when a single ill-word could tempt bad luck into the house for the whole year ahead. The first visitor on the morning of Tet is also vitally significant: the ideal is someone respected, wealthy and happily married who will bring good fortune to the family; the bereaved, unemployed, accident-prone and even pregnant women, on the other hand, are considered ill-favoured. This honour carries with it an onerous responsibility, however: if the family has a bad year, it will be the first-footer's fault.

The week-long festival is marked by **feasting** and special foods are eaten at Tet, such as pickled vegetables, strips of pork fat and sugared fruits, all of which are first offered at the family altar. The most famous delicacy is *banh chung* (*banh tet* in the south), a thick square or cylinder of sweet, sticky rice that is prepared only for Tet. The rice is wrapped round a mixture of green bean paste, pork fat and meat marinated in *nuoc mam*, and then boiled in banana leaves which impart a pale green colour. Good-quality cakes can go for as much as US$1 apiece. According to legend an impoverished prince of the Hung dynasty invented the cakes over two thousand years ago; his father was so impressed by the simplicity of his son's gift that he named the prince as his heir.

Tet is an expensive time for Vietnamese families, many of whom save for months to get the new year off to a good start. Apart from special foods and new clothes, it's traditional to give children red envelopes containing *li xi*, or lucky money, and to decorate homes with spring blossoms. In the week before Tet, flower markets grace the larger cities: peach is the most popular blossom, especially in the north, along with plum, kumquat (symbolizing gold coins) and, nowadays, the more showy blooms of rose, dahlia or gladioli.

SHOPPING AND SOUVENIRS

Souvenir-hunters will find rich pickings in Vietnam, whose eye-catching handicrafts and mementoes range from colonial currency and stamps to basketware crafted by the country's ethnic minorities, and from limpet-like conical hats to replica US Army-issue Zippo lighters.

Throughout the *Guide*, we've highlighted the best places to shop: the single best place is Ho Chi Minh, though Hanoi and Hué have their moments, too. Remember that **prices** in Vietnam are almost always open to negotiation (see box on facing page for some tips on successful bargaining).

CLOTHING, ARTS AND CRAFTS

Few Western tourists leave Vietnam without the obligatory **conical hat**, or *non la*, sewn from rain- and sun-proof palm fronds; at less than US$0.50, they're definitely an affordable keepsake. From the city of Hué comes a special version, the **poem hat** or *non bai tho*, in whose brim are inlays

THE ART OF BARGAINING

• The Vietnamese, not unreasonably, see tourists as wildly rich – how else could they afford to stop working and travel the world – and a **first quoted price** is usually pitched accordingly.

• The trick is to remain **friendly** and amused, but also to be realistic: traders will quickly lose interest in a sale if they think you aren't playing the game fairly. Any show of aggression, and you've lost it in more ways than one.

• If you feel you are on the verge of agreement, **moving away** often pays dividends – it's amazing how often you'll be called back.

• Keep a sense of **perspective**: if a session of bargaining is becoming very protracted, step back and remind yourself that you're often arguing the toss over mere pennies or cents – nothing to you, but a lot to the average Vietnamese.

which, when held up to the light, reveal lines of poetry or scenes from Vietnamese legend. Vietnamese women traditionally wear the **ao dai** – baggy silk trousers under a knee-length silk tunic slit up both sides. Extraordinarily elegant, *ao dai*s can be bought off the peg anywhere in the country for approximately US$25; or, if you can spare a few days for fitting, you can have one tailor-made for around US$40.

Silk from the highlands is sold by the metre in Vietnam's more sizeable markets, and embroidered **cotton**, in the form of pyjamas, sheets and pillowcases, are also sold along Dong Khoi in Ho Chi Minh City and in Hanoi's Hang Gai. Meanwhile, the sartorial needs of backpackers are well catered for in major tourist destinations, where **T-shirt** sellers do brisk business. Predictably popular designs include a portrait of Uncle Ho, the *Apocalypse Now Bar* logo, and the yellow communist star on a red background.

TRADITIONAL HANDICRAFTS

Of the many types of traditional handicrafts on offer in Vietnam, **lacquerware** (*son mai*) is among the most beautiful. Made by applying multiple layers of resin onto an article and then polishing vigorously to achieve a deep, lustrous sheen, lacquer is used to decorate furniture, boxes, chopsticks and bangles and is sometimes embellished with inlays of **mother of pearl** (which is also used in its own right, on screens and pictures). Common motifs are animals, fish

and elaborate scrolling. More recently, the lacquerware tradition has been hijacked by more contemporary icons, and it's now possible to buy colourful lacquerware paintings of Mickey Mouse, Tin Tin and Batman.

Bronze, **brass** and **jade** are also put to good use, appearing in various forms such as carvings, figurines and jewellery. In Hué, brass and copper **teapots** are popular. Ivory is worked too, though the savagery (not to mention illegality) involved in separating elephants from their tusks should be enough to dissuade most people from buying the stuff. Of the earthenware, porcelain and ceramics available across the country, thigh-high **ceramic elephants** and other animal figurines are the quirkiest buys – though decidedly tricky to carry home. Look out, too, for boxes and other knick-knacks made from wonderfully aromatic **cinnamon** and **camphor wood**. For something a little more culturally elevated, you could invest in a **water puppet** in Hanoi, or a traditional **musical instrument** (for more on both of these, see "Music and Theatre", p.447). Vietnam's **ethnic minorities**, or *montagnards* as the colonial French designated them, have yet to fully cash in on the possibilities of selling crafts to the tourist market. Fabrics – sometimes shot through with shimmering gold braid – are their main asset, sold in lengths and also made into **purses, shoulder bags** and other accoutrements. Some cloths woven in the central highlands feature intriguing designs that incorporate the helicopters and guns which strafed the region during wartime. The southern minorities are also adept at **basketwork**, fashioning backpacks, baskets and mats, and **bamboo pipes**. In the north, Sa Pa is a pop-

Bear in mind, especially when buying older artefacts, that **export restrictions** may apply on all items deemed to be of "cultural or historical significance". This includes objects made of bronze, porcelain, ivory or precious stones, works of art and anything over fifty years old. Export **licences** can be applied for in Ho Chi Minh and Hanoi (see p.104 and p.346) and take 2–3 days to process. The fee usually varies from 1 to 3 percent of the object's value, and may be more, depending on the view of the expert making the assessment. You might consider having purchases you're not sure about, even fake antiques, cleared by the ministry anyway as customs officials aren't always very discriminating and regularly confiscate items.

ular place to buy clothes, bags and **skull-caps** from the H'mong people, and you'll find lengths of woven fabrics or embroidery in markets throughout the northern mountains.

PAINTINGS

A healthy fine arts scene exists in Vietnam, and **painting**, in particular, is thriving. In the galleries of Hué, Hanoi and Ho Chi Minh you'll find exquisite works in oil, watercolour and charcoal by the country's leading artists, though you can expect to pay hundreds or even thousands of dollars. Artists, some of whom paint onto silk, inevitably look to the war with America for subject matter, though there's a wealth of non-martial painting, too. Many artists are also finding it lucrative to knock out hackneyed works featuring willowy women in *ao dais* walking or cycling through the streets of Hoi An, and conical-hatted workers tending paddy fields, and sell them through souvenir shops. This is a shame, as more original works are going unpainted as a consequence. Still, it's tempting to fork out for an original to take home with you. Watercolours that are anything but hackneyed are churned out nineteen to the dozen by **Vien Thuc**, the prolific "mad monk" of Da Lat (see p.170); his prices are negotiable, but US$2–3 apiece isn't untypical. If you can't even stretch to this, you could always snap up some of the charming hand-painted silk **greetings cards** sold in and around major post offices.

BOOKS, STAMPS AND COINS

In the bookshops of Hanoi and Ho Chi Minh, you can buy photocopied editions of almost all of the **books** ever published on the subject of Vietnam. You'll also occasionally come across genuine, secondhand books in Ho Chi Minh's bookstores looted from wartime US Army libraries, and with stamps on their inside front pages to prove it, as well as battered copies of guidebooks intended for GIs. Philatelists meanwhile will enjoy browsing through the old Indochinese **stamps** sold in and outside the GPOs of Hanoi and Ho Chi Minh, and also by street hawkers along Pham Ngu Lao in Ho Chi Minh. Similarly, old **notes** and **coins**, including French-issue piastres and US Army credits, are available.

MEMORABILIA AND TRINKETS

Army surplus is a big moneyspinner, though fatigues, belt, canteen and dog tags that may have been stolen from a dead or wounded GI aren't the most tasteful of souvenirs – if indeed they're genuine (most are fakes). The khaki **pith helmets** with a red star on the front, worn first by the NVA during the American War and now by the regular Vietnamese Army, also find many takers. Other items that sell like hotcakes are **Zippo lighters** bearing such pithy adages as "When I die bury me face down, so the whole damn army can kiss my ass" and "We are the unwilling, led by the unqualified, doin' the unnecessary for the ungrateful", though again they're unlikely to be authentic GI issue.

In the souvenir shops of Ho Chi Minh's Dong Khoi and Hanoi's Hang Khai or Hang Gai, French and Russian watches and other trinkets abound; while out in the street, nimble-fingered children hawk **model helicopters, planes and cars** recycled from discarded soft drinks cans; and beside the *Continental*, extravagant wooden model ships go for US$15–30. Nearby, the souvenir shop inside the *Rex Hotel* stocks an attractive range of chinaware – teapots, vases, ashtrays – embossed with its distinctive crown logo.

EDIBLE SOUVENIRS

Finally, **foodstuffs** that may tempt you include **coffee** from Buon Me Thuot, candied strawberries and **artichoke tea** from Da Lat, coconut **candies** from the Mekong Delta, preserved miniature **tangerines** from Hoi An and packets of **dried herbs and spices** from Sa Pa. As for **drinks**, most of the concoctions itemized on p.39 are securely bottled, with the exception of rice wine.

POLICE, CRIME AND HARASSMENT

Vietnam is a relatively safe country for travellers, including women travelling alone. In fact, given the country's recent history, many visitors are pleasantly surprised at the warm reception that foreign travellers, particularly Americans, receive. Given the crushing poverty that exists in Vietnam, it comes as no surprise that crime is on the rise – though it's still relatively small scale and shouldn't be a problem if you take commonsense precautions. Generally, the hassles you'll encounter will be the milder sort of coping with hawkers, touts and beggars.

PETTY CRIME

As a tourist, you are an obvious target for thieves (who may include your fellow travellers): carry your passport, travellers' cheques and other valuables in a concealed **money belt**. Don't leave anything important lying about in your room; if your hotel has a safe, use it. A cable lock, or **padlock** and chain, comes in handy for doors and windows in cheap hotels, and is useful for securing your pack on trains and buses. It's not a bad idea to keep US$100 or so separately from the rest of your cash, along with your travellers' cheques receipts, insurance policy details, and photocopies of important documents such as the relevant pages of your passport and visa, and baggage declaration form.

At street level it's best not to be ostentatious: forego eye-catching jewellery and flashy watches, try to be discreet when taking out your cash, and be wary in **crowds** and on **public**

transport. If your pack is on the top of the bus, make sure it is attached securely (usually everything is tied down with ropes) and keep an eye on it during the most vulnerable times – before departure and on arrival at your destination. On trains, either cable lock your pack or put it under the bottom bench-seat, out of public view. One or two cases have occurred where travellers have been drugged and then robbed, so it's best not to accept food or drink from anyone you don't know and trust. Bear in mind that when travelling on a cyclo you are vulnerable to moped-borne snatch-thieves.

On the whole, petty crime is more of a problem in the **south** than the north, and **Ho Chi Minh City** has a fairly bad reputation for thieves, pickpockets and con-artists; be wary of innocent-looking kids and grannies who may be acting as decoys for thieves – especially on or around Dong Khoi. Areas of the city where you'd be unwise to walk alone after dark – and, for that matter, in daylight – are District 4 (below the Ho Chi Minh Museum), and Thu Duc District, across the far side of the Saigon River. However, don't get paranoid: crime levels in Vietnam are a long way behind those of Western countries, and violent crime against tourists is extremely rare.

If you do have anything stolen, you'll need to get the **police** to write up a report in order to claim on your insurance: try to recruit an English speaker to come along with you – and be prepared to have to pay a "fee". Corruption among police and other officials can be a problem, fostered by low levels of pay: you might be stopped on the road or at border crossings and "fined", while trumped-up fines are often imposed on bus, cyclo or other drivers seen carrying a Westerner – fines you'll often be expected to pay. With a lot of patience, plus a few cigarettes to hand round, you should be able to resolve most "problems" and, so long as you keep your cool, "fines" can often be bargained down considerably. In general, however, the police steer clear of foreigners – partly under instructions from the government not to upset the lucrative tourist business.

"SOCIAL EVILS" AND SERIOUS CRIME

Since liberalization and *doi moi*, Vietnamese society has seen an increase not only in petty crime, but also in the more serious matters of drug-re-

EMERGENCY SERVICES

The following numbers apply throughout Vietnam; if possible, get a Vietnamese-speaker to phone on your behalf.

Police ☎13

Fire ☎14

Ambulance ☎15

lated crime, prostitution and so on. Most of what the Vietnamese have labelled "social evils" are viewed as a direct consequence of reduced controls on society and ensuing Westernization. These undesirable trends have prompted the government to instigate measures such as seizing pornographic videos and literature, censoring song lyrics and raiding gambling dens. Though this should have little effect on most foreign tourists, beyond perhaps earlier closing hours at clubs and pubs, it is as well to be aware of it and sensitive to the issues involved.

Finally, having anything to do with **drugs** in Vietnam is extremely unwise. City cyclo drivers will often offer to sell you drugs – outside Ho Chi Minh's *Apocalypse Now Bar* is a notorious hotspot – and many people take them up on it, but you could easily be turned in to the police. A substantial bribe might persuade them to drop the matter; otherwise, you're looking at fines and jail sentences for lesser offences, while the death penalty is common for smuggling large quantities.

Single Western males tend to get solicited by **prostitutes**, most commonly inside cheap provincial hotels: quite apart from any higher moral considerations, bear in mind that AIDS is on the increase in Vietnam.

MILITARY AND POLITICAL HAZARDS

Unsurprisingly, the Vietnamese authorities are sensitive about **military installations** and strategic areas – including border regions, military camps (of which there are many), bridges, airports and train stations. Anyone taking photographs in the vicinity of such sites risks having the film removed from their camera, or the ubiquitous "fine". **Unexploded ordnance** from past conflicts still pose a serious threat: the problem is most acute in the Demilitarized Zone, where each year a few local farmers or scrap-metal scavengers are killed or injured. Wherever you are, stick to well-trodden paths and never touch any shells or half-buried chunks of metal.

Needless to say, **political activists** aren't exactly welcome in Vietnam and anyone carrying political literature or in contact with known activists will be treated with suspicion, possibly tailed and even deported. Their Vietnamese contacts will be treated less leniently.

BEGGARS...AND CURIOSITY

Given the number of disabled, war wounded and unemployed in Vietnam, there are actually surprisingly few **beggars** around. Most people are actually trying hard to earn a living somehow, and in the circumstances it doesn't seem unreasonable to have your shoes cleaned more times than they might need, or buy a couple of extra postcards. At many tourist spots, you may well be swamped by a gaggle of **children** selling cold drinks, fruit and chewing gum. Although they can be a bit overwhelming, as often as not they're just out to practise their English and be entertained for a while; they may even turn out to be excellent guides, in which case it's only fair that you buy something from them in return.

Otherwise, the irritation you'll experience most often is **being stared at** from morning to night – a state of affairs that can become more than a little wearing; some onlookers, overcome by curiosity, may even reach out and stroke your soft, pink skin, uncalloused hands or light hair.

WOMEN TRAVELLERS

Vietnam is generally a safe country for women to travel around alone. Most Vietnamese will simply be curious as to why you are on your own and the chances of encountering any threatening behaviour are extremely rare. That said, it pays to take the normal precautions, especially **late at night** when there are few people around on the streets. Avoid taking a night-time cyclo by yourself in Ho Chi Minh City, Nha Trang or Hanoi; use a taxi instead. There are certain areas of Ho Chi Minh which are best avoided altogether (see above). Most Vietnamese women **dress** modestly and are covered from top to toe, and it helps to do the same, avoiding skimpy shorts and vests, which are considered offensive. Asian women travelling with a white man have reported cases of serious harassment, from verbal abuse to rock throwing – something attributed to the tendency of Vietnamese men to automatically label all such women as prostitutes.

DIRECTORY

ADDRESSES Locating an address is rarely a problem in Vietnam, but there a couple of conventions it helps to know about. Where two numbers are separated by a slash, such as 110/5, you simply make for no. 110, where an alley will lead off to a further batch of buildings – you want the fifth one. Where a number is followed by a letter, as in 117a, you're looking for a single block encompassing several addresses, of which one will be 117a. Vietnamese cite addresses without the words for street, avenue and so on; we've followed this practice throughout the *Guide* except where ambiguity would result.

CHILDREN The main concern for those travelling with children will probably be hygiene. Vietnam can be distinctly unsanitary, and children's stomachs tend to be more sensitive to bacteria. Sticking to a bland diet of bread, rice and soup, and avoiding spicy foods will help, but if children still become sick, it's crucial to keep up their fluid intake, so as to avoid dehydration. Disposable nappies are hard to come by, even in Hanoi and Ho Chi Minh City. Before planning your trip, give some thought to whether your child is resilient enough to cope with all the attention he or she will receive, and with long, hard journeys; don't make your itinerary too ambitious. Many budget hotels have rooms with three or even four single beds in them; while at more expensive hotels under-12s can normally stay free of charge in their parents' rooms, and baby cots are becoming more widely available.

CONTRACEPTIVES Medicines in Vietnamese pharmacies are limited and often way beyond their sell-by date, so if you are following a course of oral contraceptives, stock up before arrival. Condoms (*bao cao su*) are sold in Hanoi and Ho Chi Minh, but don't count on getting them easily elsewhere – reliable imported brands to look out for are *OK* and *Trust*.

DEPARTURE TAX Vietnam charges an US$8 departure tax on international flights (payable in dong or dollars) and a US$1–1.50 levy on domestic flights.

DISABLED TRAVELLERS Next to no provisions are made for the disabled in Vietnam, so you'll have to be pretty much self-sufficient. None of the country's **hotels** have rooms specifically adapted to the needs of the disabled; the best you can hope for is a ground-floor room, or a hotel with a lift. A little extra money can alleviate transport difficulties, by enabling you to take internal flights, or to hire a private minibus with a driver. Taxis are available in Hanoi, Ho Chi Minh and some other cities, and wheelchair users with collapsible chairs may be able to take cyclos, balancing their chair in front of them. Finally, expect to receive a lot of **attention**. All Westerners are subjected to staring and pointing, so a Westerner with apparent disabilities is liable to come under intense scrutiny. For more advice, contact one of the following organizations: *RADAR*, 12 City Forum, 250 City Rd, London EC1V 8AS (☎0171/250 3222, Minicom ☎0171/250 4119); *Mobility International USA*, PO Box 10767, Eugene, OR 97440 (Voice and TDD: ☎503/343-1284); *ACROD* (*Australian Council for Rehabilitation of the Disabled*), PO Box 60, Curtin ACT 2605 (☎06/682 4333).

ELECTRICITY Usually 220 volts, though you may come across 110 volts; plugs are two-pinned, with the pins rounded. Power supplies are erratic, though, so be prepared for cuts and surges.

ETIQUETTE When entering a Cao Dai temple, the main building of a pagoda or someone's home, it's the custom to remove your **shoes**; in a pagoda or temple you are also expected to leave a small **donation**. Women in particular should **dress** modestly, especially out in the countryside where shorts and vests can cause offense, and nudity on the beach is out. Most Vietnamese dress as smartly as they can afford to and if you're dealing with officialdom it pays to look neat and tidy. Passing round **cigarettes** (to men only) is always appreciated and is widely used as a social gambit aimed at progressing tricky negotiations, bargaining etc. As in most Asian countries, it's not done to get angry, and it certainly won't get things done any quicker. Other social conventions worth noting are that you shouldn't touch **children** on the head and, unlike in the West, it's best to ignore a young baby rather than praise it, since it's believed that praise will attract the attention of jealous spirits who will cause the baby to fall ill.

GAY AND LESBIAN VIETNAM There is no discernible gay or lesbian scene in either Hanoi or Ho Chi Minh.

LAUNDRY It's possible to get clothes washed at pretty much any guesthouse or hotel, for around US$3. Washing is almost invariably given a rigorous scrubbing by hand, so don't submit anything delicate; it's also common practice to write your room number on each item with a seemingly indelible pen. Top hotels in Hanoi and Ho Chi Minh offer a dry-cleaning service.

LEFT LUGGAGE Most hotels will have a room or cupboard earmarked for luggage. This system may not be 100 percent secure, but it's the best there is for now.

SPORTS AND OUTDOOR PURSUITS As long as you retain a healthy sense of respect for potentially dangerous undertows, any of the south-central coast's beaches are great for swimming. Snorkelling trips and scuba-diving courses are available in Nha Trang (see p.206), while Da Nang recently hosted Vietnam's first surfing competition. A trekking industry of sorts is starting to develop in the northern mountains, where the country's highest peak, Fan Si Pan, also offers a challenge to more adventurous hikers (see p.389).

TAMPONS are best brought from home, as in Vietnam they're prohibitively expensive – if you can find them.

TIME DIFFERENCES Vietnam is 7 hours ahead of London, 15 hours ahead of Los Angeles, 12 hours ahead of New York, 1 hour behind Perth and 3 hours behind Sydney – give or take an hour or two when summer time is in operation.

TIPPING, while not expected, is always appreciated.

WORKING Without a prearranged job and work permit, don't bank on finding work in Vietnam. With specific skills to offer, you could try approaching some of the Western companies now flooding into Hanoi and Ho Chi Minh. Otherwise, TEFL (Teaching English as a Foreign Language) is the best bet; having a TEFL qualification, while useful, isn't essential. Universities are worth approaching, though pay is better at private schools, where you could earn up to US$750–1000 a month. If a school requires your services, it should be able to arrange all the required paperwork. Private tutoring is an unwieldy way of earning a crust, as you'll have to pop out of the country every month to procure a new visa, unless extensions are reinstated. For long-term volunteer placements, apply to VSO (*Voluntary Service Overseas*; ☎0181/780 2266) in the UK; Australia's *Overseas Service Bureau* (☎03/9279 1788); or *CARE Australia* (☎1800/020046, fax 06/257 1938), which employs people on a contract basis for long-term development work in areas including agriculture and natural resources, healthcare and business development. (See p.5 and p.8 for details of short-term volunteer projects.)

CHINA

CHAPTER 8
THE FAR NORTH

CHAPTER 6
HANOI AND AROUND

BURMA

CHAPTER 7
HA LONG BAY AND
THE NORTHERN SEABORD

LAOS

CHAPTER 5
THE CENTRAL
PROVINCES

THAILAND

CHAPTER 4
THE SOUTH-CENTRAL
COAST

CAMBODIA

CHAPTER 3
THE SOUTHERN
AND CENTRAL
HIGHLANDS

CHAPTER 1
HO CHI
MINH CITY
AND
AROUND

N

CHAPTER 2
THE MEKONG
DELTA

0   400km

CHAPTER ONE

HO CHI MINH CITY AND AROUND

Twenty years after its humiliating defeat, [Ho Chi Minh] *looks and feels much as it did before. The southern metropolis has cast off the dour sackcloth the victor forced it to wear. That it has been able to do so with such aplomb is not really surprising. The hair shirt never fit.*

Henry Kamm, 1996

Washed ashore above the Mekong Delta, some 40km north of the South China Sea, **HO CHI MINH CITY** is a city on the march, a boomtown where the rule of the dollar is absolute. Fuelled by the sweeping economic changes wrought by *doi moi*, this effervescent city, perched on the west bank of the Saigon River, is in the throes of a breakneck programme of re-invention shaking it to its French-built foundations. Years of rubbing shoulders with the consumer-oriented Americans made the Saigonese wise to how to coin a profit. Now they are pressing old, near-forgotten skills back to work, as the market economy shifts into gear again, and Ho Chi Minh City is surging towards the new millennium, challenging Singapore, Kuala Lumpur and the other traditional southeast Asian powerhouses. While all the accoutrements of economic revival – fine restaurants, immaculate hotels, glitzy bars and clubs, and stores selling imported luxury goods – are here, so far they represent no more than occasional blips on the city's compellingly hotch-potch **landscape** of French stones of empire, venerable pagodas and austere, Soviet-style housing-blocks. And, sadly, Ho Chi Minh City is still full to bursting with people for whom progress hasn't yet translated into food, lodgings and employment. Street children range through tourist enclaves hawking T-shirts, postcards and cigarette lighters; limbless mendicants haul themselves about on crude trolleys; and watchful pickpockets prowl Dong Khoi on the look-out for unguarded wallets. Indeed, **begging** is now a problem of such epidemic proportions in Ho Chi Minh City that tourists must quickly come to accept it as a hassle that goes with the territory. Alarmingly, the arrival, en masse, of well-off Westerners seems to be nudging some women towards a resumption of the **prostitution** for which the go-go bars of Dong Khoi were so infamous during the American War.

If Hanoi is a city of romance and mellow charms, then Ho Chi Minh – locals prefer its pre-1975 name of Saigon – is its antithesis, a fury of **sights and sounds**, and the crucible in which Vietnam's rallying fortunes are boiling. No corner of the city affords respite from the ceaseless cacophony of construction work casting up swish new office-blocks and swanky hotels with logic-defying speed. French-era Renaults and Peugeots jostle with such an organic mass of state-of-the-

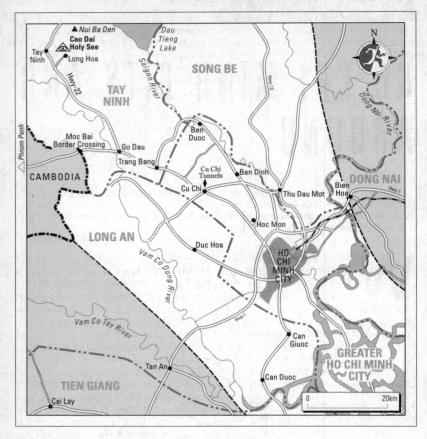

art jeeps, landcruisers, Hondas and cyclos, that tree-lined streets and boulevards will soon need to be re-sculpted to cope. And amid this melee of change, a population of six million goes about its daily life: schoolgirls clad in the traditional silk *ao dai* glide past streetside baguette-sellers; monied teenagers in designer jeans chirrup into mobile phones; and Buddhist monks walk with measured pace from shopfront to shopfront, in search of alms. Adding a **cosmopolitan** dash to the mix is the recent influx of Western tourists and expats, many of them French and American. Much of the fun of being in Ho Chi Minh City derives from the simple pleasure of **watching the day go by** and absorbing its flurry of activity – something best done from the safety of a roadside café. To blink is to miss some new and singular sight, be it a cyclo piled high with wicker baskets of fruit, or a boy rapping out a stacatto tattoo on pieces of bamboo to advertise a nearby soup-stall.

It's one of Ho Chi Minh City's many charms that once you've exhausted – or been exhausted by – all it has to offer, paddy fields, beaches and wide-open countryside are never far away. If you take only one trip **out of the city**, make it the one to **Cu**

Chi tunnels, where villagers dug themselves out of the range of American shelling. The tunnels are normally twinned with a tour around the fanciful Great Temple of the indigenous Cao Dai religion at **Tay Ninh**. A brief taster of the Mekong Delta at **My Tho** or a dip in the South China Sea at **Vung Tau** are also eminently possible in a long day's excursion, but we've covered these last two places together with the regions to which they belong, on p.117 and p.187 respectively.

The **best time to visit** tropical Ho Chi Minh City is in the dry season, which runs from December through to April. During the wet season, May to November, there's a short downpour every afternoon, though this won't disrupt your travels. Average temperatures, year-round, hover between 26 and 29°C; March, April and May are the warmest months.

HO CHI MINH CITY

Our knowledge of Ho Chi Minh City's early history is sketchy, at best. Between the first and sixth centuries, the territory on which it lies fell under the nominal rule of the **Funan Empire**, to the west. Funan was subsequently absorbed by the Kambuja peoples of the pre-Angkor **Chen La Empire**, but it is unlikely that these imperial machinations had much bearing upon the sleepy fishing backwater that would later develop into Ho Chi Minh City.

The Khmer fishermen who eked out a living here would recognize little today beyond the city's web of waterways; so besieged by forest and swampland were their homes, that they named their settlement **Prei Nokor**, "settlement in the forest". Set on stable ground just north of the delta wetlands, though, and surrounded on three sides by navigable waterways, the settlement was clearly destined for greater things. In time, Chen La segued into the Khmer empire of **Angkor**, which ruled the roost until the fifteenth century, and Prei Nokor flourished as an entrepôt for Cambodian boats pushing down the Mekong River. By the seventeenth century it boasted a Khmer garrison and a mercantile community that embraced Malay, Indian and Chinese traders.

Such a dynamic settlement was bound to draw attention from the north. By the seventeenth century's close, the **Viets** had trampled over the kingdom of Champa on their march south, and the following century saw this traditionally Khmer area swallowed up by Hué's **Nguyen Dynasty**. With new ownership came a new name, **Saigon**, thought to be derived from the Vietnamese word for the kapok tree. Upon the outbreak of the **Tay Son Rebellion**, in 1772, Nguyen Anh of the Nguyen dynasty hastened south to Saigon, which he named as his interim capital, and bricked the whole settlement into a walled fortress, the eight-sided **Gia Dinh Citadel**, built to resemble a lotus flower in bloom on the advice of his geomancers. Having quelled the rebellion, in 1802, Nguyen Anh returned to Hué as Emperor Gia Long; but Saigon remained his regional administrative centre in the south.

The army that put down the Tay Son brothers included an assisting **French** military force. From this early foothold the French grappled for seven decades to undermine Vietnamese control in the region and develop a trading post in Asia. Finally, in 1861, they seized Saigon, using Emperor Tu Duc's persecution of French missionaries as a pretext. The 1862 **Treaty of Saigon** declared the city the capital of French Cochinchina.

Ho Chi Minh City owes its form and character to the French colonists. As part of a broad **public works** programme, channels were filled in, marshlands drained, and steam tramways set to work along its regimental grid of tamarind-shaded boulevards, which by the 1930s sported such wildly incongruous names as Boulevard de la Somme and Rue Rousseau. Flashy examples of European architecture were erected, cafés and boutiques sprang up to cater for its new, Vermouth-sipping, baguette-munching citizens, and all in all the city was imbued with such a Gallic air that Somerset Maugham, visiting in the 1930s, found it reminiscent of "a little provincial town in the south of France...a blithe and smiling little place". The French *colons* (or "colonials") bankrolled improvements to Saigon with the vast profits they were able to cream from exporting Vietnam's **rubber** and **rice** out of the city's rapidly expanding seaport.

On a human level, however, French rule was at best harsh, and at worst cruel; dissent duly crystallized in Saigon – as in the rest of Vietnam – in the form of strikes through the 1920s and 1930s; but the nationalist movement hadn't gathered any real head of steam before **World War II**'s tendrils spread to southeast Asia. At its close, the **Potsdam Conference** of 1945 set the British Army the task of disarming Japanese troops in southern Vietnam. Arriving in Saigon two months later, they promptly returned power to the French, and so began thirty years of war (see p.417).

Designated the capital of the **Republic of South Vietnam** by President Diem in 1955, Saigon was soon both the nerve-centre of the American war effort, and its R&R capital, with a slough of sleazy bars along Dong Khoi (known then as Tu Do) catering to GIs on leave of duty. Despite the communist bomb attacks, and demonstrations by students and monks, that periodically disturbed the peace, these were good times for Saigon, whose entrepreneurs and wheeler-dealers prospered on the back of the tens of thousands of Americans posted here. The meal-ticket finally expired with the withdrawal of American troops in 1973, and two years later the **Ho Chi Minh Campaign** rolled into the city and through the gates of the presidential palace, and the communists were in control. Within a year, Saigon had been renamed **Ho Chi Minh City**.

The **war years** extracted a predictably heavy toll: American carpet-bombing of the Vietnamese countryside forced millions of refugees into the relative safety of the city, and ill-advised, post-reunification policies triggered a social and economic stagnation whose ramifications are plain for all to see today. To make matters worse, persecution of any southerners with links to the Americans saw many thousands sent to re-education camps, and millions more flee the country by boat.

Only in 1986, when the **economic liberalization** of *doi moi* was established, and a market economy re-introduced, did the fortunes of the city show signs of taking an upturn. Now this slumbering giant of a city has one eye on the future once more.

> The **telephone code** for Ho Chi Minh City is ☎08.

Arrival

With the lion's share of new **arrivals** to Vietnam flying into Ho Chi Minh City, Tan Son Nhat Airport is likely to provide you with your first glimpse of the country; it is also the terminus for all internal flights. Arriving overland from other regions of Vietnam, you'll end up either at the train station, a short distance north of the downtown area, or at one of a handful of bus terminals scattered across the city.

Options for **moving on** from Ho Chi Minh City are detailed on pp.106–107.

By plane

Tan Son Nhat Airport is a little under 7km northwest of the city centre, on Truong Son. Recent renovations have spruced up the arrival and departure lounges immeasurably, and facilities now run to duty-free, banks (daily 8am–midnight), a post office with telephone service (daily 9am–8pm), and a *Saigontourist* booth (daily 10am–6pm) that will sell you a city map ($1) and help out with booking accommodation of a certain standard. There's also a snack bar on site, and a reasonable restaurant across the car park. At the end of your trip, you can squander any remaining dollars on beer, burgers and hot dogs in the departure lounge's *Skyline Café*.

The only way to get into the city centre from the terminal doors is to take a **taxi**, and hordes of drivers will greet you as you emerge into the car park, along with touts brandishing hotel brochures. By far the cheapest option is to gather enough passengers (normally 6–8) to fill an estate car or minibus taxi ($1–2 per person). Otherwise, metered *Airport Taxi* (☎844 6666) or *Vinataxi* (☎844 2170) cabs make the run for $7–8, though these are undercut by a couple of dollars by the vintage – and perfectly legitimate – Peugeots that rove around the car park. If money is really tight, you could walk **outside the airport gates** (only a few hundred metres) where you can hail either a Honda om or cyclo (see "City transport", p.64); neither should cost more than $2, though the latter option will be a fairly leisurely ride.

By train

Trains from the north pull in at the **train station**, or *Ga Saigon*, 3km west of town, on Nguyen Thong. There's bound to be a cluster of cyclo drivers on the look-out for fares in the forecourt, but given the distance into the centre, you might opt for a taxi ($4) – even if it means ordering one (☎844 6666 or 844 2170).

By bus

Buses stop at a clutch of different terminals – the remotest of which are 17km away from each other. Arrivals **from Phnom Penh** in Cambodia terminate slap-bang in the centre of town at the **Phnom Penh Garage**, next to the *Rex Hotel* at 155 Nguyen Hue Boulevard, from where it's only a short cyclo ride to all the central hotels and guesthouses.

Most buses **from the north** arrive at sprawling **Mien Dong bus station**, 5km north of the city on Xo Viet Nghe Tinh; local buses shuttle between here and central **Ben Thanh bus station**, a five-minute walk from Pham Ngu Lao; or take a cyclo mai ($2–3) to save time. The only exceptions to the rule are certain minibus services from Da Lat, Phan Thiet and Vung Tau, which arrive at **Van Thanh bus station**, 3km north of the city centre on Dien Bien Phu – again, a cyclo mai is your best method of transport into town, though there are xe lams and cyclos if you aren't in a hurry.

Buses **from the south** terminate at **Mien Tay bus station**, 10km west of the city centre in An Lac District; local buses shuttle into town from here, passing along Pham Ngu Lao en route. Again, there are exceptions, with some buses out of My Tho stopping instead at **Cholon bus station**, from where air-conditioned *Saigon Star* buses provide an inexpensive and unusually comfortable means of

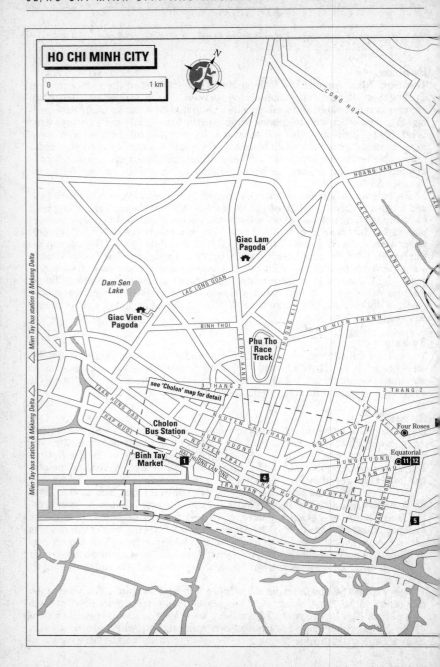

HO CHI MINH CITY

0   1 km

N

CONG HOA

HOANG VAN TU

LE VAN

CACH MANG THANG TAM

Giac Lam Pagoda

LAC LONG QUAN

LE DAI HANH

LY THUONG KIET

Dam Sen Lake

Giac Vien Pagoda

BINH THOI

TO HIEN THANH

Phu Tho Race Track

3 THANG 2

3 THANG 2

see 'Cholon' map for detail

LE HONG

LE HONG PHONG

NGUYEN CHI THANH

NGO GIA TU

HAI BA

Cholon Bus Station

Four Roses

TRAN HUNG DAO

HUNG VUONG

HUNG VUONG

Equatorial

Binh Tay Market

HAI THUONG LAN ONG

NGUYEN TRAI

TRAN PHU

11 12

DONG

1

NGUYEN TRAI

TRAN BINH TRONG

DAP MUOI

TRAN HUNG DAO

4

TRAN VAN KIEU

5

Mien Tay bus station & Mekong Delta

Mien Tay bus station & Mekong Delta

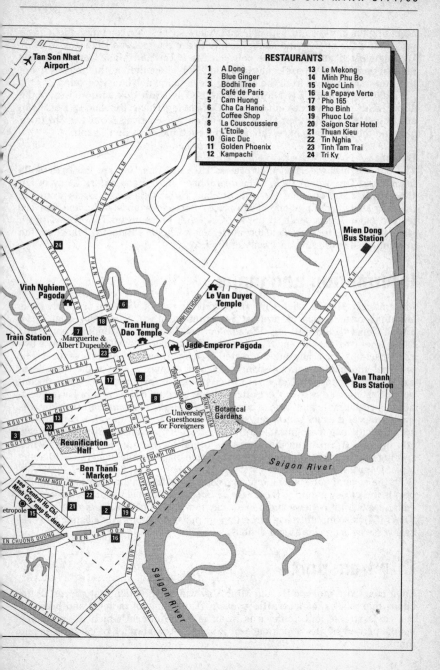

RESTAURANTS

1	A Dong	13	Le Mekong
2	Blue Ginger	14	Minh Phu Bo
3	Bodhi Tree	15	Ngoc Linh
4	Café de Paris	16	La Papaye Verte
5	Cam Huong	17	Pho 165
6	Cha Ca Hanoi	18	Pho Binh
7	Coffee Shop	19	Phuoc Loi
8	La Couscoussiere	20	Saigon Star Hotel
9	L'Etoile	21	Thuan Kieu
10	Giac Duc	22	Tin Nghia
11	Golden Phoenix	23	Tinh Tam Trai
12	Kampachi	24	Tri Ky

Tan Son Nhat Airport

Mien Dong Bus Station

Vinh Nghiem Pagoda

Le Van Duyet Temple

Tran Hung Dao Temple

Train Station

Marguerite & Albert Dupeuble

Jade Emperor Pagoda

Van Thanh Bus Station

Vo Thi Sau

Dien Bien Phu

University Guesthouse for Foreigners

Botanical Gardens

Nguyen Dinh Chieu

Reunification Hall

Ben Thanh Market

Saigon River

see 'Central Ho Chi Minh City' map for detail

etropole

EN CHUONG DUONG

BEN VAN DON

Saigon River

accessing the city – white, with blue and yellow stripes, you can't miss them if you walk out of the station and along Huynh Thoai Yen towards Binh Tay Market. Well-signposted **shuttle buses** between Mien Tay and Mien Dong terminals make it possible to bypass central Ho Chi Minh altogether, in the unlikely event that you want to travel from the Mekong Delta to the north or vice versa.

Finally, buses **from Tay Ninh** pull in at the **Tay Ninh bus station**, west of the airport and just above the confluence of Cach Mang Thang Tam and Le Dai Hanh, and linked by bus with Ben Thanh Bus Station; most arrivals **from Cu Chi town** also end their journeys here, though some continue on to Ben Thanh.

By boat

The only regular waterborne arrivals in Ho Chi Minh City are the **hydrofoils from Vung Tau**, which dock, when operational, at the **Passengers Quay of Ho Chi Minh City**, opposite the end of Ham Nghi. Otherwise, boats from the Mekong Delta float up to one of two places. Services from My Tho and Ben Tre tend to moor 1.5km south of the Ho Chi Minh Museum on Ton That Thuyet; while those from further afield terminate below Cholon's Binh Tay Market, at the junction of Chu Van An and Tran Van Kieu.

Information and maps

Frustratingly, Ho Chi Minh City, along with the rest of Vietnam, presently lacks any efficient and impartial **tourist information** office. *Saigontourist*, at 49 Le Thanh Ton (☎829 8914), and *Vietnamtourism*, Room 101, Mondial Center, 203 Dong Khoi (☎824 2000) and 234 Nam Ky Khoi Nghia (☎829 0776), the city's two largest set-ups, are really only interested in selling their own, expensive tours. For practical information with no strings attached, enquire at one of the **travellers' cafés** along Pham Ngu Lao, or at the **customer information** desk in a decent hotel. Casting an eye over the **noticeboards** in some of Pham Ngu Lao's guesthouses, restaurants and bars is also worthwhile. *Vietnamtourism* offers an adequate **map** of the city with a country map on the flipside, though a better, more accurate city map (recognizable by its blue border) is available from street hawkers; the pre-1975 plan on the reverse is useful for getting your bearings when reading wartime accounts of the city. The same map is available in the GPO at the top of Dong Khoi.

Of the several publications offering **what's on** information, far and away the best is the glossy monthly, *What's On in Saigon* ($2), which features a social calendar, restaurant reviews and a lively city news section. The *Vietnam Economic Times* ($4), also monthly, has a free 16-page pull-out visitor's guide listing subjects as diverse as art galleries and dentists.

City transport

Faint-hearted visitors to Ho Chi Minh City will blanch upon first glimpsing the chaos that passes for its **traffic system**. Thousands of mopeds and bikes fill the city's streets and boulevards in an insectile swarm which is now being supplemented by the appearance of a burgeoning number of cars, jeeps and minibuses.

SAMPLE FARES AROUND TOWN

Costs of local transport, excluding taxis, are extremely low and are usually paid in dong. For example, you can expect to pay a minimum of 5000d per kilometre for a **cyclo** or **Honda om** ride within central Ho Chi Minh, while the standard fare for **xe lams** and such **bus services** as exist is 1500–2000d. Below are some sample fares for one person travelling either by cyclo or Honda om; note that cyclo drivers charge a little extra for luggage, and that by "centre" we mean Dong Khoi.

Pham Ngu Lao to GPO: 5–6000d.	Centre to Jade Emperor Pagoda: 6–8000d.
Train station to centre: 6–8000d.	Mien Dong bus station to centre: 15,000d.
Pham Ngu Lao to Cholon: 10–12,000d.	Van Thanh bus station to centre: 12–14,000d.

Given the relatively high cost of taxis and the dearth of reliable bus services, the mode of transport you're likely to get most use out of in Ho Chi Minh is the **cyclo**. For the full city effect though, you'll want to do at least some of your exploring **on foot**. There's an art to jay-walking in Vietnam: besides nerves of steel, a steady pace is required – drivers are used to dodging pedestrians, but you'll confuse them if you stop in your tracks.

Cyclos

With over fifty thousand **cyclos** operating in Ho Chi Minh City, hailing one is never a problem, though it pays to be choosy – some of the cyclo drivers who congregate downtown were soldiers in the Southern Army, and their smattering of English makes life much easier. Unless you approach a driver outside a premier hotel, you'll find rates are pretty consistent throughout the city (see box of sample fares above); if you hire a cyclo and driver for a half- or whole day, about $1 an hour is the norm, though rates for a single hour will obviously be higher. Though it's quite possible to ride two to a cyclo, the corresponding rise in cost and lessening of comfort make this a false economy.

Finally, bear in mind that the roads around the central Dong Khoi area are off-limits to cyclos – if your driver follows a circuitous course, or drops you short of your destination, it's probably because he isn't able to get any closer.

Taxis and Honda oms

Taxis have become a much more common sight on the streets of Ho Chi Minh City of late, with two companies offering metered services in air-conditioned vehicles. You'll sometimes spot white *Airport Taxis* (☎844 6666) and yellow *Vinataxis* (☎844 2170) on the street, but if time is of the essence it's safer to book a car over the phone; expect a trip within the city centre to cost $2–3. No match for the modern fleets of *Airport Taxis* and *Vinataxis* in terms of comfort, but boasting bags of charm, are the colonial-era Peugeots that continue to operate around the city; you can track them down below Ben Thanh Market, along Pham Ngu Lao, and outside the *Rex Hotel* at the top of Nguyen Hue. Prices are a shade lower than their plusher competition.

The two-wheeled taxi or **Honda om** is a faster alternative to the cyclo. Translated, it means "Honda embrace": passengers ride pillion on a motorbike, hanging on for dear life. Honda oms are nowhere near as prevalent as cyclos, though if you ask around, there's sure to be someone who'll be glad to oblige and pocket some extra money; prices are similar to cyclo rates.

Buses and xe lams

So undeveloped is Ho Chi Minh City's public transport network that the only time you're even remotely likely to resort to a **bus** – apart from getting to one of the city's outlying long-distance bus terminals (see p. 106) – is if you visit Cholon. The air-conditioned *Saigon Star Co* service (daily 5am–10pm) loops between the south side of Mei Linh Square, and Huynh Thoai Yen, below Binh Tay Market. From Pham Ngu Lao, head down to the eastern end of Buu Vien to pick up the service en route to Cholon; on the return journey, you'll be dropped off at the far side of Tran Hung Dao.

Xe lams – three-wheeler buggies whose drivers pack in more passengers than you'd imagine possible – function as buses around the city. They're slightly less expensive than buses, but you'll often be in for an excruciating ride. If you're the sort who'll try anything once, xe lams gather at Ben Thanh Bus Station, and around the corner from Pham Ngu Lao and opposite *Easy Rider*, on Nguyen Thai Hoc.

Bike, motorbike, moped and car rental

Motorbike rental in Vietnam peaked in popularity a few years ago, when bi-king up- or downcountry was all the rage. With the tourist minibus network growing ever more comprehensive, this trend seems to be fading, though motorbiking is still an efficient and romantic means of viewing the city. You need to be wary, though, of the scams pulled by less reputable companies, as well as the dangers of Vietnamese roads (see *Basics*, p.29). Be vigilant at all times on the road. The same goes for **bike rental** – a charming way to see the city but fraught with danger if you aren't road-aware. Many hotels, guesthouses and cafés advertise bikes for rent, especially along Pham Ngu Lao (see p.104 for details of outlets).

Self-drive isn't an option yet in Ho Chi Minh City, but pretty much every one of the city's tour operators can arrange **car rental** plus driver for you; tour agencies are listed on p.105. Drivers rarely speak much English, so if you want a guided tour you'll have to pay extra for the guide. Given Ho Chi Minh City's one-way systems and traffic-flow, travelling by car doesn't represent the most efficient way of city sightseeing; but car rental *does* come into its own if you want to take a day-trip out of the city – to Tay Ninh or My Tho, for example – but don't relish being shoe-horned into a tour bus all day; prices average $35–40 per day.

Boat

Pass by the Passengers Quay of Ho Chi Minh City, opposite the end of Ham Nghi on Ton Duc Thang, and you're bound to be harangued by people offering **trips along the Saigon River** and its canals, at $4–5 an hour. These touts seem particularly keen to take you up Ben Nghe Channel to Cholon, though the trip – along a truly filthy and squalid stretch of water – is harder to recommend than the journey up the Thi Nghe Channel and past the back of the zoo. A far more wholesome option is to board one of the floating restaurants moored beside the *Floating Hotel*, and take a **dinner cruise** along the Saigon River (see p.92 and p.94).

Accommodation

Hotels have been spreading like wildfire across Ho Chi Minh City ever since *doi moi* paved the way for foreign investors and local entrepreneurs to chance their arm in the tourist sector, so finding **accommodation** should cause you no headaches: unfussy digs at the bottom end of the scale are easily affordable, while a room in an accredited hotel can be an absolute steal.

The recent influx of tourists and businesspeople to the city has kept occupancy rates consistently high. However, with existing hotels upgrading and expanding, tens of major new projects on the drawing board, and countless smaller concerns springing up overnight, there shouldn't be any need to **book in advance**. Exceptions to this are if you're hitting town around Tet (usually late Jan/early Feb), or if you want to be sure of staying at one of the city's finer addresses.

The **Saigontourist** booth at Tan Son Nhat Airport (daily 10am–6pm) purports to help new arrivals to find accommodation – though they won't be interested in grubbing around at the budget end of the market. Otherwise the only assistance you'll find will come from the **touts** handing out flyers and business cards outside the arrivals lounge. Once in the city centre, you can ask cyclo drivers to alert you to newly-opened places.

Generally the most pleasant and convenient area in which to stay is the region around **Dong Khoi**, which is home to several of Vietnam's most venerable hotels as well as a whole host of intermediate options; or consider the mid- and upper-range hotels up around **Dien Bien Phu**. Ho Chi Minh's budget enclave centres around **Pham Ngu Lao**, 1km west of the city centre. Pham Ngu Lao has been dubbed "Western Street" by locals, and it isn't hard to see why: besides its tens of budget accommodation choices, the road boasts travel agencies, restaurants, bars and shops catering for travellers – a bonus if you want to arrange inexpensive onward travel. **Hotels, mini-hotels, guesthouses** and **rooms for rent** are ten-a-penny in Pham Ngu Lao, with room-rates starting from $6–7 for a grim fan-cooled box with shared bathroom. However, if you're in town for a few days, you'd do well to shell out that much again and upgrade to a brighter air-con room with en suite bathroom. Only two **dormitories** operate at present, though this is bound to change quickly. **Security** is pretty good around Pham Ngu Lao, as all guesthouse lobbies are staffed round the clock. Even so, it pays to ensure that a room locks up adequately before you commit yourself to it. Finally, it's worth making the point that the north side of Pham Ngu Lao has been earmarked for a major shopping development scheme for several years now. Should this finally materialize, businesses on the southside will be unaffected, while **Bui Vien**, a block south, is destined to take on a far higher tourist profile.

ACCOMMODATION PRICE CODES

All accommodation listed in this guide has been categorized according to the following scale:

① under US$10 (under 110,000 dong)	② US$10–15 (110–165,000 dong)
③ US$15–30 (165–330,000 dong)	④ US$30–75 (330–825,000 dong)
⑤ US$75–150 (825–1,650,000 dong)	⑥ over US$150 (over 1,650,000 dong)

Rates are for the cheapest available double or twin room; breakfast is not usually included. During holiday periods, rates are liable to rise, and proprietors may be less amenable to bargaining. Although the law requires prices to be quoted in dong, most hotels also give their rates in US$; payment can be made in either currency.

For a more detailed discussion of accommodation, see pp.31–34.

Finally, staying in **Cholon** leaves you marooned in the bustle of Ho Chi Minh's Chinatown, a considerable distance from the city centre, but there are some bargain lodgings, far removed from the travellers' enclave.

Dong Khoi and around

All the following hotels and guesthouses are marked on the map opposite.

Asian, 146–150 Dong Khoi (☎829 6979, fax 829 7433). Stylish and central it may be, but this new, mid-range hotel needs time to mature before it can be classed truly comfortable. ⑤

Ben Nghe Guesthouse, 19 Ton That Thiep (☎822 2116). Colonial French visitors knew it as guesthouse *Lafayette*, American GIs visited the ground floor's raging *Mimi Bar*, and today it's a shabby yet endearing dive: bargain rooms share communal facilities and decor is nothing to write home about but sheets are spotless and you won't find a cheaper deal so near to the centre. ②

Bong Sen, 117–123 Dong Khoi (☎829 1516, fax 829 8076). An affordable hotel right at the heart of Dong Khoi; breakfast is included in the price of your room, and there's an in-house business centre. ④

Caravelle, 19–23 Lam Son Square (☎829 3704, fax 829 6767). It'll take some serious refurbishing for this famous address to keep up with the pack: all standard facilities are present, but rooms are lacklustre and overpriced, and furnishings slovenly. ⑤

Century Saigon, 68a Nguyen Hue (☎823 1818, fax 829 2732). Soulless but undeniably well-appointed rooms behind a grandly colonnaded facade slap-bang in the centre of the city – a good choice for businesspeople. ⑥

Continental, 132–134 Dong Khoi (☎829 9201, fax 829 0936). The grandly carpeted staircases, marbled floors and darkwood doors of this venerable address's halls and corridors convey a colonial splendour that sadly doesn't extend to its rooms – frankly, you're better off at a new hotel, though costlier rooms do boast commanding views down Dong Khoi. ⑤

Dong Khoi, 12 Ngo Duc Ke (☎829 4046). A lengthy overhaul should be complete by now, and the sea-blue tiling and Moorish dome of this charismatic building restored to its former glory. One thing's for sure: it'll no longer be a budget option. ⑤

Huong Sen, 70 Dong Khoi (☎829 1415, fax 829 0916). A heavily Oriental influence is at play in the lobby, beyond whose lacquerwork screens and chairs, and fan of pikes, rooms are perfectly adequate – likeable, even; back-up provided includes airline booking, money change and in-house movies. ④

Linh, 16 Mac Thi Buoi (☎824 3954, fax 824 3949). Well-appointed rooms and attractive bamboo furnishings make this cheery mini-hotel a fair proposition. ④

Majestic, 1 Dong Khoi (☎829 5517, fax 829 5510). A great, peach-coloured gem of a building, 1929-built and still oozing character, the *Majestic* was recently treated to sweeping renovations and is now a sight for sore eyes. All rooms are charming (some have a river view) and staff fall over themselves to be helpful. ⑥

Norfolk, 117 Le Thanh Ton (☎829 5368, fax 829 3415). Unfussy yet pleasantly co-ordinated rooms with access to all the usual facilities, and efficiently run by friendly staff. ⑤

Orchid, 29a Don Dat (☎823 1809, fax 829 2245). Rooms at this low-key, mid-range hotel are clean, if a little dated, and kitted out with TV, air-con and ensuite bathroom. Cheaper rooms don't have a lot of space so it's worth paying $5 extra to upgrade; rates include breakfast in the palatable ground-floor restaurant. ④

Rex, 141 Nguyen Hue (☎829 6043, fax 829 6536). The *Rex* shamelessly milks its fame – ashtrays, slippers and other fittings all bear a price – but its rooms are extremely comfortable; one of the stronger personalities on the Ho Chi Minh hotel scene. ⑤

Riverside, 18 Ton Duc Thang (☎822 4038). Grand colonial pile proudly eyeing the river from the base of Dong Khoi; rooms are unremarkable but perfectly decent. ⑤

Saigon Floating Hotel, 1a Me Linh Square (☎829 0783, fax 829 0784). Riverine wedge of hotel, long popular among businesspeople, that can count 3 restaurants, 3 bars, swimming

**ACCOMMODATION:
CENTRAL HO CHI MINH**

pool and health club among its facilities. The pastel shades in the rooms won't suit all tastes, but front rooms boast unrivalled views of the Saigon River. ⑤

Saigon Prince, 63 Nguyen Hue (☎822 2999, fax 824 1888). Within a lurid pink toytown exterior, a classy new boutique hotel – not to be confused with the *Prince* on Pham Ngu Lao – that has seen a sensitive designing hand at work; an extra $15 secures a river view. ⑥

Northwest of the cathedral
Both the following hotels are marked on the map on pp.62–63.

Marguerite & Albert Dupeuble, 146/15a Vo Thi Sau (☎824 3385). If both the spotless en suite rooms in the house French chef Albert shares with his Vietnamese wife are taken, they'll strive to find you quarters with one of the neighbours – a rare chance to experience home life, Vietnamese style. To reach the house, follow the northbound alley at no. 146 and take the first left turn. ③

University Guesthouse for Foreigners, 10 Dinh Tien Hoang (☎829 8686). Meant for visiting professors but also accepts tourists, of whom the more gregarious will enjoy the chance to converse with students in the leafy courtyard café; TV, air-con and bathroom in tremendous-value rooms, and two budget single rooms ($22); bicycle rental at $1 a day. ④

Around Ben Thanh Market

All the following hotels are marked on the map on p.69.

Que Huong, 129–133 Ham Nghi (☎822 4922). Spacious, airy rooms lent character by their crazily-tiled bathtubs – pay the extra $3 for a good view from a first-class room, or settle for gazing across the city from the tenth-floor restaurant. ④

Thai Binh Duong, 92 & 107 Ky Con (☎822 2674). Vast but reasonably charismatic rooms crammed with mid-century furniture; certain rooms have fridge and air-con, all have hot water; rooms in the annexe will sleep 4 for $5 extra. ②

Thanh Thao, 71 Le Thi Hong Gam (☎825 1836). Sparkling, minty-fresh rooms with air-con, fridge, telephone and hot water – a bargain, but it's a long haul to the upper floors. ③

Pham Ngu Lao and around

All the following hotels, guesthouses and rooms for rent are marked on the map below.

Bi Saigon, 185/26 Pham Ngu Lao (☎833 2947). Set off gloomy corridors, chintzy but comfortable rooms with shower, as well as 3 expansive suites leading onto balconies. ③

Coco Loco, 351 Pham Ngu Lao (☎832 2186). Above a restaurant, so you'll be ideally poised for hitting the breakfast special served below; 7 reasonable rooms, all with hot water, and with air-con available for a moderate surcharge. ②

Giang Tien, 38 Pham Ngu Lao (☎835 2979). Real effort has been made in this agreeable, if marginally overpriced mini-hotel: rooms feature hot water and air-con, and a couple even run to bathtubs. ③

Golden Road, 112 Bui Vien (☎835 3108). Opting to climb to a higher floor knocks a few dollars off the price, though all rooms have hot water and air-con. ③

Guest House 127, 127 Cong Quynh (☎833 0761). The genial family in charge pay more attention to detail than most, resulting in a range of wholesome rooms, some en suite, sleeping up to 4; a few economy rooms are planned, and there's free fruit and hot drinks. Recommended. ②

Hoan Vu, 265 Pham Ngu Lao (☎839 6522). A popular travellers' haunt now showing signs of its age, its spartan rooms and time-worn bathrooms comparing unfavourably with those of the nearby *Vien Dong* (see opposite); nonetheless, relatively inexpensive, and secure. ②

Le Le, 269 De Tham (☎832 2110). Typical of HCM's new breed of guesthouse: behind a smart frontage are 6 bright, clean rooms ranging from fan rooms sharing communal facilities, to a deluxe chamber that's ideal if you like a garden swing and fishpond on your balcony. ①–③

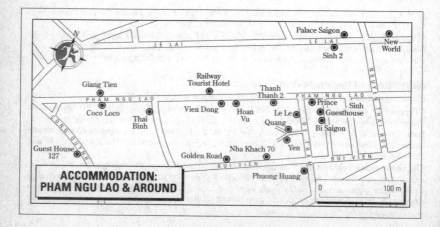

ACCOMMODATION:
PHAM NGU LAO & AROUND

New World, 76 Le Lai (☎822 8888). A benchmark on the Ho Chi Minh hotel scene upon its opening a few years back – luxurious rooms complemented by all the trimmings you could need. ⑥

Nha Khach 70, 70 Bui Vien (☎833 0569). A relative veteran of the scene, very friendly and offering free coffee and fruit. Of 9 rooms, 2 are hardly more than cupboards, the others airy and pleasant. ①–②

Palace Saigon, 82 Le Lai (☎833 1353). Drape a towel over the gaudy plastic flowers, and rooms are cheery, capacious, and a cut above most of the district's addresses; 4 sleep for the same price as 2 in the double rooms. ④

Phuong Huang, 25 Bui Vien (☎835 3231). The handful of rooms in this exceptionally friendly place have sofas and private bathrooms making them pleasing bolt-holes from street level – but push for one of the lighter front rooms, which have their own balconies. ③

Prince, 187 Pham Ngu Lao (☎832 2657). One of Pham Ngu Lao's handful of real hotels, the *Prince*'s down-at-heel, high-ceilinged rooms get cheaper, the more stairs you have to mount to reach them. ②

Quang, 217/12 De Tham (no phone). One of several private homes offering bargain rooms down the alleyway between 217 and 219 De Tham: 3 small but freshly painted rooms, with fan but shared WC; front rooms overlook the Dickensian alley-scene below. ①

Railway Tourist Hotel, 14 Pham Ngu Lao (☎835 5600). Ropey but competitively priced rooms off dingy corridors; a bicycle rental service is available. ①

Sinh Guesthouse, 185/4 Pham Ngu Lao (☎832 4877). The latest addition to the *Sinh Café* empire is a spruce operation set back slightly from Pham Ngu Lao; the cheapest rooms share common toilets. ①

Sinh 2, 1 Le Lai (☎835 5601). Up a spiral staircase over a café, 3 dorms as bare as they come, with mattresses tossed onto the floor and toilets out in the car park below. ①

Thai Binh, 325 Pham Ngu Lao (☎839 9544). Hugely unappealing, but cut-priced, and tolerable if needs must. The cheapest of the 28 substandard rooms fight it out over communal facilities, while a third occupancy costs $2 more. ①

Thanh Thanh 2, 205 Pham Ngu Lao (☎832 4027). Overwhelmingly friendly and efficient, though the forthcoming terrace bar up on the roof could disrupt the peace for its cluster of inviting, generously proportioned and good-value rooms – one of which can double as a dorm ($3 per person); air-con adds one-third again onto the bill. ①–②

Vien Dong, 275a Pham Ngu Lao (☎839 3001, fax 833 2812). With its broad span of facilities, ranging from fans and cold water to air-con, hot water, fridges and satellite TV, the *Vien Dong* is perennially popular, but there are usually rooms free, making it a dependable first-night destination. The elevator is a bonus for disabled travellers. ②

Yen, 217/29/6 De Tham (☎836 0200, ask for Yen). Like *Quang*, compact, simple rooms offering outstanding value in a private address off De Tham. ①

West of Pham Ngu Lao

All the following hotels and guesthouses are marked on the map on pp.62–63.

Equatorial, 242 Tran Binh Trong (☎839 0000, fax 839 0011). Brand spanking new, mustard-hued monolith – the latest in a respected Asian chain – offering the city's last word in comfort, and the full gamut of facilities. ⑥

Four Roses, 790/5 Nguyen Dinh Chieu (☎832 5895, fax 821 0088). Located in no-man's-land between Cholon and the city centre, a homestay in the literal sense: with its 4 rooms and tranquil bougainvillea garden, the family-run *Four Roses* offers the perfect antidote to hectic Ho Chi Minh; meals can be rustled up on request. ③

Metropole, 148 Tran Hung Dao (☎832 2021, fax 832 2019). Known as the *Binh Minh* in Vietnamese, a sedate and peaceful 94-room hotel, set slightly west of the city centre, but still worth considering for its business facilities and modest pool, and for its well turned out rooms enjoying 24-hour room service and free breakfast. ⑤

Cholon

All the following hotels are marked on the map on p.86.

Arc en Ciel, 52–56 Tan Da (☎855 4435, fax 855 0332). Standard mid-range hotel with a handful of facilities – though better value for money is available at the *Tan Da* (see below). ④

Hoa Binh, 1115 Tran Hung Dao (☎835 5113). Cheap rooms are the only possible attraction at this noisy hotel, patronized mainly by Chinese, Taiwanese and Vietnamese guests; pricier digs entitle you to air-con. ①–②

Phuong Huang, 411 Tran Hung Dao B (☎855 1888). An aesthetic nightmare, its cheapest rooms lacking windows, let alone bathrooms, but worth considering if you're hard up. In the credit column, you'll be well placed for soaking up Cholon's colour. ①

Tan Da, 22–24 Tan Da (☎855 5711). Friendly mini-hotel with extremely well-appointed rooms, bearing in mind the price. ③

The city

HO CHI MINH CITY – or Thanh Pho Ho Chi Minh, to give it its Vietnamese name – is divided into eighteen districts, though tourists rarely travel beyond districts One, Three and Five, unless it's to visit the rural district of Cu Chi (see p.107). The city proper hugs the west bank of the **Saigon River**, and its central area, District One, nestles in the hinge formed by the confluence of the river with the silty ooze of the **Ben Nghe Channel**; traditionally the French Quarter of the city, this area is still widely known as Saigon. **Dong Khoi** is its delicate backbone, and around the T-shape it forms along with **Le Duan Boulevard** are scattered most of the city's museums and colonial remnants.

Excepting the commercial fever of **Cholon**, its frenetic Chinatown, the city refuses to carve up into homogeneous, tourist-friendly districts, so visitors have to effect a dot-to-dot of the sights that appeal most. These almost invariably include one or more of the museums established to pander to the West's fixation with the American War, the pick of the bunch being the **War Crimes Museum** and **Revolutionary Museum**. For some visitors, the war is their primary frame of reference, and such historical hotspots as the **US Embassy** and the **Presidential Palace** rank highly on their itineraries; but of course the city predates American involvement by several centuries, and not all of its sights revolve around planes, tanks and rusting ordnance. Ostentatious reminders of French rule abound, among them such memorable buildings as dignified **Notre Dame Cathedral** and the grandiose **Hotel de Ville** – but even these look brand spanking new, compared to gloriously musty edifices like **Giac Lam Pagoda** and the **Jade Emperor Pagoda**, only a taster of the many captivating places of worship across the city. And if the chaos becomes too much, you can escape to the relative calm of the **Botanical Gardens** – home, incidentally, to the city's **History Museum**.

Dong Khoi

Slender **Dong Khoi**, running for just over 1 km from Le Duan to the Saigon River, has long mirrored Ho Chi Minh's changing fortunes. The French knew the road as Rue Catinat, a tamarind-shaded thoroughfare that constituted the heart of French colonial life. Here the *colons* would promenade, stopping at chic boutiques and perfumeries, and gathering at noon and dusk at cafés such as the *Rotonde* and the *Taverne Alsacienne* for a Vermouth or Dubonnet, before hailing a *pousse-*

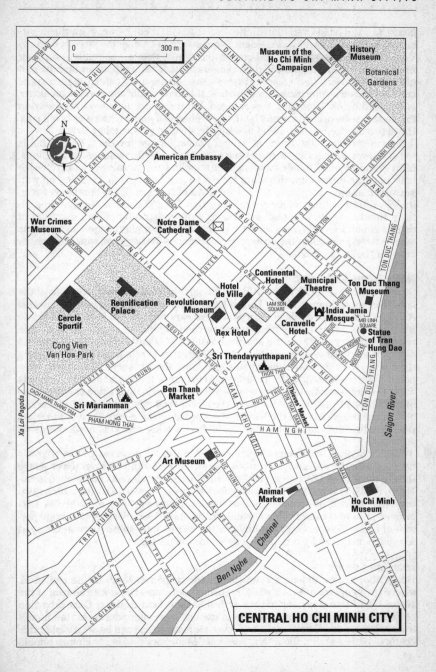

CENTRAL HO CHI MINH CITY

pousse (a hand-pulled variation on the cyclo) to run them home. With the departure of the French in 1954, President Diem saw fit to change the street's name to Tu Do, "Freedom"; and it was under this guise that a generation of young American GIs came to know it, their periods of R&R taking them around the glut of bars – *Wild West, Uncle Sam's, Playboy* – that sprang up to pander to their more lascivious needs. After Saigon fell in 1975, the more politically correct moniker of Dong Khoi, or "Uprising", was adopted, but the street quickly went to seed in the dark, pre-*doi moi* years, and by the Seventies had gone, in the words of Le Ly Hayslip, from "bejewelled, jaded dowager to shabby, grasping bag lady".

Ever receptive to the needs of Saigon's latest foreign invaders, Dong Khoi is today, however, enjoying a renaissance, and its eclectic melange of buildings, from grand colonial facades and slender shophouses, to unlovely concrete-slab halls of cards thrown up with scant regard for aesthetics, is fast topping up with **souvenir shops** catering to the recent wave of tourism. Each Sunday evening, the city's trendsetting teenagers converge on Dong Khoi and Nguyen Hue on their Hondas, to circle round and round, girlfriends riding pillion, in a kind of mating ritual. Inevitably, the street has also become a pilgrimage site for those who've fared less well in the economic resurgence – its **beggars**, with their weary litany of "hello, shoeshine".

Notre Dame Cathedral

Straddling the northern reach of Dong Khoi is the pleasing redbrick bulk of the late nineteenth-century **Notre Dame Cathedral**, whose twin spires the novelist Anthony Grey memorably compared to "the ears of a hidden jackrabbit". Aside from the few stained-glass windows above and behind its altar, and its marble relief *Stations of the Cross*, the interior boasts only scanty decoration, but there's plenty of scope for people-watching, as a steady trickle of women pass through in their best silk tunics and black pants, fingering their rosary beads, their whispered prayers merging with the insistent murmur of the traffic outside. Towards dusk, the neon-lit halo and blue neon words, *Ave Maria*, that shine above the figure of Christ at the head of the nave are disconcertingly reminiscent of a nightclub entrance. A statue of the Virgin Mary provides the centrepiece to the small **park** fronting the cathedral, where cyclo drivers loiter and kids hawk postcards and maps.

The cathedral's twin compass-point spires were, for decades, one of Saigon's handiest landmarks, but they've now been dwarfed by the telecom tower above the **General Post Office**, east of the park. Unchanged since its completion in the 1880s, the GPO is worth a peek inside for its nave-like foyer, lent character by two huge map-murals, one charting Saigon and its environs in 1892, the other the telegraphic lines of southern Vietnam and Cambodia in 1936. Further in, a huge portrait of Uncle Ho sporting a healthy tan and warm smile gazes down at the aged wooden benches and tables of the cavernous main hall.

Lam Son Square

Dong Khoi briefly widens a couple of hundred metres south of the cathedral, where the peppermint green walls, revolving globe and clay-coloured roof of the **Hotel Continental** announce your arrival in **Lam Son Square**. Once a bastion of French high society, and still one of the city's premier addresses, the hotel's front terrace – the *Continental Shelf* – was *the* place to see and be seen earlier this century. Little wonder, then, that Somerset Maugham's nose for a story should have led him here in the mid-Twenties: "Outside the hotels are terraces," he recounted, "and at the hour of the aperitif, they are crowded with bearded, gesticulating Frenchmen drinking the sweet and sickly beverages...which they drink in France and they talk nineteen to the dozen in the rolling accent of the Midi...It is very agreeable to sit under the awning on the terrace of the Hotel Continental, with an innocent drink before you, [and] read in the local newspaper heated controversies upon the affairs of the colony." Sadly the terrace no longer exists, so if you want to tap into the history of the place, the best you can do is to ensconce yourself in the hotel's gelateria, *La Dolce Vita* (see p.98).

Standing grandly on the eastern side of Lam Son Square, its cyclopean, domed entrance peering southwestwards down Le Loi, is the turn-of-the-century **Municipal Theatre**. The National Assembly was temporarily housed here in 1955, but today it once again offers a varied programme that embraces fashion shows, drama and dance. The ground in front of the broad sweep of its staircase once featured a statue of a group of South Vietnamese marines, but its days were numbered after Saigon fell in 1975. Just below the theatre, the runt of the litter of major buildings perched around the square, the 1958-built **Caravelle Hotel**, gazes enviously across the square at the more handsome *Continental*. Down at heel and unattractive, it nonetheless found favour with many of the Western journalists assigned to cover the war, and its terrace bar is said to have seen many a report drafted over a stiff drink. If you need a drink yourself, grab a table at the *Givral* (see p.98), facing the *Continental* and an ideal venue for watching the day go by.

From Lam Son, it's only a couple of minutes' walk down Le Loi to Nguyen Hue (see below) and the Hotel de Ville.

Down towards the riverbank

Though souvenir stores are in the ascendancy below the *Caravelle*, they haven't yet managed entirely to eradicate the past, and it's still possible to winkle out relics of old Saigon. Wander south of Lam Son and you'll soon meet Dong Du, where a left turn reveals the blue-washed walls of the 1930s **Indian Jamia Muslim Mosque**. There's really nothing to see here, and the empty, red-carpeted hall belies the drama of the four minarets sprouting from it, but there's a reassuring sense of peace that's enhanced by the slumbering worshippers lazing around the complex. (To avoid causing offence, heed the sign advising you not to enter in "tie shirt" or "short pants", or to "wear shoes enter the moss".) Heading on down Dong Khoi meanwhile, opposite the *Paloma Café* at no. 69f, you'll spot the flaking, mustard-coloured walls of the former Hotel Catinat, its name still emblazoned on the front but now missing an "h"; while at the corner of Dong Khoi and Mac Thi Buoi, a set of fire hydrants shipped from Alabama in 1963 adds another ingredient to the street's melting pot of influences.

Around Nguyen Hue

When Saigon's French administrators laid the 750-metre sweep of Charner Boulevard over a filled-in canal and down to the Saigon River, their brief was to replicate the elegance of a tree-lined Parisian boulevard. This they managed, for in its day their broad avenue was mooted as the *Champs Elysées* of the East. Since then, an insectile swarm of Hondas has laid siege to the thoroughfare – now known as **Nguyen Hue** – and any romance has been dispelled. Recent renovations have attempted to spruce it up, but though the paving may have been redone, and the slummy booths that spined it demolished, the facelift has failed to revive the street's glamour. Only at Tet does Nguyen Hue spring to life, when it hosts a vast, riotously colourful flower market which draws Vietnamese belles in their thousands to pose among its roses, sunflowers, chrysanthemums and conical orange trees in their best *ao dai*s.

The stately edifice that deigns to stand at Nguyen Hue's northern extent is the former **Hotel de Ville**, an ostentatious reminder of colonial Europe's stubborn resolve to stamp its imprint on the countries it subjugated, no matter how incongruous. Built in 1908 as the city's administrative hub, this yellow and white striped hat-box of a building today houses the People's Committee behind its showy jumble of corinthian columns, classical figures and shuttered windows; while not to everyone's taste, it at least adds a sense of age to Nguyen Hue. A statue of Uncle Ho cradling a small child in his lap mounts watch over the tiny **park** fronting the building, where roving photographers loll around touting polaroid snaps to passing pedestrians; while on the pavements around the park, hawkers brandish postcards, balloons, maps, toys crafted from beer cans and photocopied offprints of Graham Greene's *The Quiet American*.

Though the **Rex Hotel**, a few paces below the park at the junction of Nguyen Hue and Le Loi, may give the impression of being venerable, in fact it has only operated as a hotel since 1976. Having started out as a garage for the Renaults and Peugeots of the city's French expat community, during the Sixties it billeted American officers, and hosted regular press briefing sessions that came to be known by jaded members of the press as the "Five O'Clock Follies". From its fifth-floor *Rooftop Garden*, the hotel yields a superb view of the whirl of life on the street below, best enjoyed over a cool glass of *333* beer. At night, the hotel's emblem, a giant **crown**, lights up on the terrace, providing the city with one of its most memorable landmarks.

The southern face of the block south of the *Rex* hides peaceful **Sri Thendayyutthapani Temple**, whose crumbling *gopuram* (sculpted gate tower) stands at 66 Ton That Thiep. The place manages a certain rag-tag charisma, the lavish murals normally associated with Hindu temples replaced by faded paintings of Jawaharlal Nehru, Mahatma Gandhi, and various deities from the Hindu pantheon, plus a ceiling gaily studded with coloured baubles and lamps. Steps beyond the topiary to the right of the main sanctuary lead to a roof terrace that's dominated by a weather-beaten tower of deities, whose ranks have been infiltrated by two incongruous characters dressed like public schoolboys in braces, shorts and striped ties, and waving merrily. Across the road from the temple, you can duck down into Ton That Dam's so-called **Thieves' Market**. Goods stolen from US provisions stores magically used to turn up here in the war years and the stalls on its upper reaches, with their TVs, electronic equipment and pirate CDs, still have an intriguingly dodgy air.

The Revolutionary Museum

Of all the stones of empire thrown up in Vietnam by the French, few are more eye-catching than the former Gia Long Palace, a block west of the Hotel de Ville at 65 Ly Tu Trong, built in 1886 as a splendid residence for the governor of Cochinchina. Homeless after the air attack that smashed his own palace, Diem decamped here in 1962, and it was in the tunnels under the building that he spent his last hours of office, before fleeing to the church in Cholon where he met his death (see p.87). Ironically, nowadays it houses the **Revolutionary Museum**

(Tues–Sun 8.30–11.30am & 1.30–4.30pm), which makes use of photographs, documents and artefacts to trace the struggle of the Vietnamese people against France and America. Excepting the shock tactics of the War Crimes Museum (see p.82), it's the city's most engaging museum, and the promised English language signs will make it better still.

Things kick off in the chamber to the left of the entrance, where the years of French rule come under the microscope – *A bas le Fascisme Colonial* ("Down with colonial fascism") screams a faded press cutting, neatly summing up the gist of the gallery. There are some interesting photos casting light upon old Saigon on the walls here but if your history isn't up to scratch, the references to revolutionary players can be bewildering. The museum shifts into higher gear upstairs, where the focus turns to the war with America. The best exhibits are those showcasing the ingenuity of the Vietnamese – bicycle parts made into mortars, a Suzuki motorbike in whose inner tubes documents were smuggled into Saigon, a false-floored boat in which guns were secreted, and so on. Look out, too, for sweaters knitted by female prisoners on Con Dao Island, and bearing the Vietnamese words for "peace" and "freedom". Elsewhere, there's a cross-sectional model of the Cu Chi tunnels, and a rewarding gallery of photographs of the Ho Chi Minh Campaign and the fall of Saigon.

Before you leave, be sure to make an inspection of the **gardens**, where a tank, helicopter and artillery gun leer out from behind the frangipanis and well-groomed hedges.

Along the waterfront

For decades, the **quay** hugging the confluence of the Saigon River and Ben Nghe Channel provided new arrivals with their first real glimpse of Indochina – and a most exciting glimpse it would have been, as scores of coolie-hatted dock-workers lugged sacks of rice off ships, shrimp farmers dredged the oozy shallows, and junks and sampans bobbed on the tide under the vigilant gaze of *colons* imbibing at nearby cafés. The docking of a passenger ship must have caused a particular stir. Arriving by steamer in 1910, Gabrielle Vassal felt as if, "all Saigon had turned out…Some expected friends, others came in the hope of meeting acquaintances or as mere spectators. One was reminded of a fashionable garden party, for the dresses and equipages were worthy of Paris itself." These days there's no such activity and many of the boats docked here are floating restaurants (see p.92 and p.94), but a stroll along riverside Ton Duc Thang still unearths the odd heavily laden boat just in from the Mekong Delta. At night the river reflects the blue, green and red of the monumental *Canon*, *Carlsberg* and *DHL* signs on the far bank.

Take a left onto Ton Duc Thang at the base of Dong Khoi, and it's only a short skip to **Mei Linh Square**, long a popular haunt for early-morning practisers of *tai chi*, and radiating out from a statue of Tran Hung Dao, who points accusingly from his plinth at the *Floating Hotel* opposite. Ton Duc Thang draws its name from a former president of the Democratic Republic of Vietnam, whose life is celebrated at the nearby **Ton Duc Thang Museum** (Tues–Wed & Fri–Sun 7.30–11.30am & 1.30–4.30pm, Thurs 7.30–11.30am). Don't expect any fireworks here: beside some grim photographs highlighting the many years he spent de-husking rice on the prison-island of Poulo Condore (see p.197), a few evocative photos of old Saigon and some of the bric-a-brac of the man's life comprise the museum's principal highlights.

The Ben Nghe Channel

Back at the foot of Dong Khoi, a right turn whisks you to the mouth of the **Ben Nghe Channel**, where a signal mast marks the position of the **Pointe des Blagueurs** (Jokers' Point), once the epicentre of the colonial promenading circuit. With the bells of the evening Mass still ringing in their ears, French strollers would have hastened here to catch up on the latest gossip. The impressive Oriental roof of the mansion across the mouth of the channel broke onto the Saigon skyline in the 1860s. Known as the *Nha Rong*, or Dragon House, this former headquarters of a French shipping company is now home to the **Ho Chi Minh Museum** (Tues–Thurs & Sat–Sun 7.30–11.30am & 1.30–4.30pm; free) – an apposite venue, given that it was from the abutting wharf that Ho left for Europe in 1911. Sadly, the collection within fails to live up to the Dragon House's compelling fusion of Eastern and Western architectural styles, and if French translations of communist tracts aren't to your taste you'll need to wring all the interest you can out of personal effects such as Ho's walking stick, haircomb, chopsticks and watering-can, and of photographs charting his travels around the globe.

The days when Ben Nghe was choked with sampans are long gone, and now its pitch-black waters are eerily calm, but there's still a pocket of interest on its north bank, where a brace of austere buildings signals the city's **financial district**, home to the State Bank, right by the Dragon House bridge, and the mausoleum-like hulk of the Government Bank of Vietnam next door. Unless you relish seeing monkeys, snakes and lizards crammed into tiny cages you're best off spurning the **animal market** that cowers under the left-hand stairway of the disused metal bridge across the road. An alternative to wading back into the downtown area, is to push on southwest along the bank of the channel towards the base of Nguyen Thai Hoc, the focus of a full-on **street market**.

Ben Thanh Market and around

There's much more beneath the pillbox-style clock tower of **Ben Thanh Market** than just the cattle and seafood pictured on its front wall. The city's largest market for over eighty years now, and known to the French as the *Halles Centrales*, Ben Thanh's dense knot of trade has caused it to burst at the seams, disgorging stalls onto the surrounding pavements. Inside the main body of the market, a tight grid of aisles, demarcated according to produce, teems with shoppers, and if it's souvenirs you're after, a reconnaissance here will reveal conical hats, basketware bags and shoes, Da Lat coffee and Vietnam T-shirts. All this, though, is tame stuff compared with the wet market along the back of the complex, where you'll find buckets of eels, clutches of live frogs tied together at the legs, heaps of pigs' ears and snouts, and baskets wedged full of hens, among other gruesome sights. If you can countenance the thought of eating after seeing – and smelling – this patch of the market, *com*, *pho* and baguette stalls proliferate at the back left-hand side of the main hall.

The aroma of jasmine and incense replaces the stench of butchery a block northwest of Ben Thanh, at Truong Dinh's **Sri Mariamman Hindu Temple**. Less engaging than Sri Thendayyutthapani (see p.76), Sri Mariamman's imposing yellow walls are besieged by vendors selling oil, incense and jasmine petals, and topped by a colourful *gopuram*, or bank of sculpted gods. Inside, the gods Mariamman, Maduraiveeran and Pechiamman reside in stone sanctuaries reminiscent of the Cham towers upcountry, and there are more deities seated around the courtyard.

South of Ben Thanh

A short stroll from Ben Thanh Market, down Pho Duc Chinh, in a grand colonial mansion, Ho Chi Minh City's **Art Museum** (Tues–Sun 8–11.30am & 1.30–4.40pm) is disappointing, with a tedious montage of revolutionary posters – most depicting smiling, pith-helmeted soldiers aiding old women and children – and a collection of contemporary paintings and drawings that rely on hackneyed images of soldiers, war zones, and, inevitably, Uncle Ho. Of the few exceptions, U Van An's haunting *Halong* – a five-panel lacquerware painting of a shimmering nude – is a highlight. The second floor's array of antique urns, gilt Buddhas and Cham statues similarly warrants no more than fifteen minutes' inspection, though if it does manage to fire your imagination, you might afterwards cross the road to **Le Cong Kieu**, where antique shops sell Oriental and colonial bric-a-brac. Memorabilia reflecting Vietnam's more recent history sells at the army surplus stalls at the back of **Dan Sinh Market**, at 104 Nguyen Cong Tru, where you can pick up khaki gear, VC pith-helmets, old compasses and *Zippo* lighters embossed with saucy pearls of wisdom coined by GIs.

Along Le Duan Boulevard to the Botanical Gardens

Above Notre Dame, **Le Duan Boulevard** runs between the Botanical Gardens and the grounds of the Presidential Palace. Known as Norodom Boulevard to the French, who lined it with tamarind trees to effect a Gallic thoroughfare, it soon became a residential and diplomatic enclave with a crop of fine pastel-hued colonial villas to boot. Its present name doffs a cap to Le Duan, the secretary-general of the *Lao Dong*, or Workers Party, from 1959.

The former American Embassy

Turn northeast from the top of Dong Khoi and the sense of harmony created by Le Duan's graceful colonial piles is soon spoilt by the mildewed slab of white stone, entombed in a honeycomb casing of enforced concrete, that housed the **American Embassy** from 1967 until 1975. Its stained walls are still knotted with barbed wire and shadowed by pillboxes, and though it has recently been handed back to the United States, the embassy remains neglected while its future is decided. Two events have immortalized this imposing building. The first came in the pre-dawn hours of January 31, 1968, when a small band of VC commandoes breached the embassy compound during the nationwide **Tet Offensive**. That the North could mount such an effective attack on the hub of US power in Vietnam, was shocking to the American public; in the six hours of close-range fire that followed, five US guards died, and with them the popular misconception that the US Army had the Vietnam conflict under control.

Worse followed seven years later, during "Operation Frequent Wind", the chaotic **helicopter evacuation** that marked the United States' final undignified withdrawal from Vietnam. The embassy building was one of thirteen designated landing zones where all foreigners were to gather, upon hearing the words, "It is 112 degrees and rising" on the radio followed by Bing Crosby singing *White Christmas*. At noon, April 29, the signal was broadcast, and for the next eighteen hours scores of helicopters shuttled passengers out to the US Navy's Seventh Fleet off Vung Tau. Around two thousand evacuees were lifted from the roof of the embassy alone, before Ambassador Graham Martin finally left with the Stars and Stripes in the early hours of the following morning. In a tragic postscript to

US involvement, as the last helicopter lifted off, many of the Vietnamese civilians who for hours had been clamouring at the gates were left to suffer the communists' reprisals.

The Museum of the Ho Chi Minh Campaign

The lengthy revamp which transformed the city's Military Museum into the **Museum of the Ho Chi Minh Campaign**, nearby at 2 Le Duan (Tues–Sun 8–11.30am & 1.30–4pm), evidently lacked any imaginative force at its helm. By the time you're inside the building, you've already passed the museum's most interesting exhibits: the **tanks**, **planes** and **artillery guns** scattered around its grounds, which were instrumental in the North's final push on Saigon in 1975. Among them is one of the T54 tanks that burst through the palace gates (see box on facing page), and an F5E fighter plane that fired on Saigon in April 1975. Inside, below four stained-glass windows depicting comrades striving for the cause, the main hall features a huge bust of Ho Chi Minh eyeing a selection of shells, hardware and guns, and photos dating from the fall of the city. Exhibits are for the most part unidentifiable, though, since only a handful of signs are in English. At the hall's northeast extremity you'll find the usual muster of naive and idealized paintings depicting NVA soldiers embracing children and old women, and accepting bouquets of flowers from pretty maids in *ao dai*s.

The Botanical Gardens

The pace of life slows down considerably – and the odours of cut grass and frangipani blooms replace the smell of exhaust fumes – when you duck into the city's **Botanical Gardens** (daily 7am–9pm), accessed by a gate at the far eastern end of Le Duan, and bounded to the east by the Thi Nghe Channel. Established in 1864 by the Frenchmen, Germain and Pierre (respectively a vet and a botanist), the gardens' social function has remained unchanged in decades, and their tree-shaded paths still attract as many courting couples and promenaders as when Norman Lewis followed the "clusters of Vietnamese beauties on bicycles", headed there one Sunday morning in 1950, to find the gardens "full of these ethereal creatures, gliding in decorous groups... sometimes accompanied by gallants". In its day, the gardens harboured an impressive collection of tropical flora, including many species of orchid. Post-liberation, the place went to seed but nowadays a bevy of gardeners keep it reasonably well tended again, and portrait photographers are once again lurking to take snaps of you framed by flowers.

Stray right inside and you'll soon reach the **zoo**, home to camels, elephants, crocodiles and big cats, and komodo dragons – a gift from the government of Indonesia. It's not a happy sight, though: cages are ancient and dingy (worst off is the ill-starred Malayan bear) and the animal stench is sometimes overpowering. If you've got kids in tow, keep your fingers crossed that the motley rides of the **amusement park** are open – if not, you can always appease them with an ice cream or a coconut from one of the several **cafés** sprinkled around the grounds.

The History Museum

A pleasing, pagoda-style roof crowns the city's **History Museum** (Tues–Sun 8–11.30am & 1–4pm), whose main entrance is tucked just inside the gateway to the Botanical Gardens. It houses a train of galleries illuminating Vietnam's past from primitive times to the end of French rule, by means of a decent if unastonishing array of artefacts and pictures. Dioramas of defining moments in

Vietnamese military history lend the collection some cohesion – included are Ngo Quyen's 938 AD victory at Bach Dang (see p.365), and the sinking of the *Esperance*. Should you tire of Vietnamese history, you might explore halls focusing on such disparate subjects as Buddha images from around Asia; seventh- and eighth-century Champa art; and the customs and crafts of the ethnic minorities of Vietnam. There's also a room jam-packed with exquisite ceramics from Japan, Thailand and Vietnam; and you could round off your visit at the **water puppetry theatre** (shows half-hourly; $1).

The Reunification Hall and around

Five minutes' stroll through the leafy parkland northwest of the cathedral, a red flag billows proudly above the **Reunification Hall** (Mon–Sat 7.30–10.30am & 1–4pm, Sun 7.30am–4pm; $4 including guided tour; entrance on Nguyen Du), a whitewashed concrete edifice with all the charm of a municipal library, which occupies the site of the Norodom Palace, a colonial mansion erected in 1871 to house the governor-general of Indochina. With the French departure of 1954, Ngo Dinh Diem commandeered this extravagent monument as his presidential palace, but after sustaining extensive damage in a February 1962 assassination attempt by two disaffected Southern pilots, the place was condemned and pulled down. The present building was labelled the Independence Palace upon completion in 1966, only to be retitled the more politically correct Reunification Hall when the South fell in 1975 (see box below).

Spookily unchanged from its working days, much of the building's **interior** is a veritable time-capsule of Sixties and Seventies kitsch: pacing its airy banqueting rooms, conference halls and reception areas, it's hard not to think you've strayed into the arch-criminal's lair in a James Bond movie. Guides usher you through the hall's many chambers, proudly pointing out every piece of porcelain, lacquer-

---

THE BREACHING OF THE PRESIDENTIAL PALACE

If the frantic airlift from the roof of the US Embassy symbolized the American capitulation in Vietnam, then the **breaching of the presidential palace** grounds by a tank belonging to the Northern Army, on April 30, 1975, was the defining moment of the fall of Saigon and the South.

Of the many Western journalists on hand to witness the spectacle, none was better placed than English journalist and poet James Fenton, who conspired to hitch a ride on the tank that first crashed through the gates: "The tank speeded up, and rammed the left side of the palace gate. Wrought iron flew into the air, but the whole structure refused to give. I nearly fell off. The tank backed again, and I observed a man with a nervous smile opening the centre portion of the gate. We drove into the grounds of the palace, and fired a salute...An NLF soldier took the flag and, waving it above his head, ran into the palace. A few moments later, he emerged on the terrace, waving the flag round and round. Later still, there he was on the roof. The red and yellow stripes of the Saigon regime were lowered at last."

Inside the palace, Duong Van Minh ("Big Minh"), sworn in as president only two days before, readied to perform his last residential duty. "I have been waiting since early this morning to transfer power to you", he said to General Bui Tin, to which the general replied: "Your power has crumbled. You cannot give up what you do not have."

work, rosewood and silk on display. Most interesting is the **third floor**, where, as well as the presidential library (with works by Laurens Van Der Post and Graham Greene flush alongside heavyweight political tomes), there's a sassily curtained projection room, and an entertainment lounge complete with tacky circular sofa and barrel-shaped bar. Nearby, two stuffed tigers (a gift from a highland tribe) mark the way to the **movie room**, where a coherent potted account of the war is screened half-hourly. Once the credits roll, move on down to the atmospheric **basement**, where wood-panelled combat staff quarters yield archaic radio equipment and vast wall maps.

Adjoining the western edge of the Reunification Hall's grounds, is **Cong Vien Van Hoa Park**, a municipal park whose tree-shaded lawns heave with life each Sunday. During the colonial era, the park's northernmost corner was home to one of the linchpins of French expat society, the **Cercle Sportif**, a Westerners-only sports club where the *colons* gathered to swim and play tennis before sinking an aperitif and discussing the day's events, once the last set had been decided. Surveying the grandiose swimming pool, flanked by Grecian pillars, that has survived since those days, and the dilapidated old clubhouse, it's easy to conjure the tennis whites and parasols of Saigon's high society. In time, American names replaced French on the members' list; and today the place is called the *Workers' Sports Club* – though the many men who gather to play French *boules* provide a quaint link with their country's colonial past.

The War Crimes Museum

A block above the park at 28 Vo Van Tan, the **War Crimes Museum** (Tues–Sun 7.30–11.45am & 1.30–4.45pm) is probably the city's most popular attraction, a distressing compendium of the horrors of war that pulls no punches at all, though flawed by a one-sided, accusatory tone. The range of US military hardware parked out in the **courtyard** embraces an A37 plane, described, with ghoulish understatement, as having "rather strong fire effect"; and a menacing seven-ton "landshaking bomb", brooding under the skeletal frame of its parachute. There's also a guillotine that harvested heads at the Central Prison on Ly Tu Trong, first for the French and later for Diem. The centrepiece of the yard though is its *Huey* helicopter, which provides a photo-opportunity most visitors are unable to resist.

Inside, a series of halls present a grisly portfolio of **photographs** of mutilation, napalm burns and torture. Most shocking is the gallery detailing the effects of the 75 million litres of defoliant sprays dumped across the country: besides the expected images of bald terrain, hideously malformed foetuses are preserved in pickling jars. Give the distorted and inaudible videos of the **movie room** a miss, but peek at the mock-up of the **tiger cages**, the godless prison cells of Con Son Island (see p.197), which could have been borrowed from the movie set of *Papillon*. The **souvenir shop** outside vends US Army-issue fungicidal foot powder and dog tags, and models crafted from spent bullets, but if the museum has made any impression, you'll spurn such tastelessness, and spend your money instead at the **water puppetry theatre** (half-hourly; $2) opposite.

Xa Loi Pagoda

Vapid **Xa Loi Pagoda** (daily 7–11am & 2–5pm), a five-minute walk west of the museum at 89 Ba Huyen Thanh Quan, became a hotbed of Buddhist opposition to Diem in 1963. The austere, 1956-built complex is unspectacular, its most striking component a tall **tower** whose unlovely beige blocks lend it a drabness even

---

THE SELF-IMMOLATION OF THICH QUANG DUC

In the early morning of June 11, 1963, a column of Buddhist monks left the **Xa Loi Pagoda** and processed to the intersection of Cach Mang Thang Tam and Nguyen Dinh Chieu. There, **Thich Quang Duc**, a 66-year-old monk from Hué, sat down in the lotus position and meditated as fellow monks doused him in petrol, and then set light to him in protest at the repression of Buddhists by President Diem, who was a Catholic. As flames engulfed the impassive monk and passers-by prostrated themselves before him, the cameras of the Western press corps rolled, and by the next morning the grisly event had grabbed the world's headlines. More self-immolations followed, and Diem's heavy-handed responses at Xa Loi – some four hundred monks and nuns were arrested and others cast from the top of the tower – led to massed popular demonstrations against the government. Diem, it was clear, had become a liability; on November 2, he and his brother were assassinated in Cholon's Cha Tam Church (see p.87), the victims of a military coup.

---

six tiers of Oriental roofs can't quite dispel. The main **sanctuary**, accessed by a dual staircase (men scale the left-hand flight, women the right), is similarly dull: beyond a vast joss-stick urn inventively decorated with marbles and shards of broken china, it's a lofty, unatmospheric hall featuring a huge gilt Buddha and fourteen murals that narrate his life. Turn left and around the back of the Buddha, and you'll come across a shrine commemorating Thich Quang Duc and the other monks who set fire to themselves in Saigon in 1963 (see box above); Quang Duc's is the ghostly figure holding a set of beads, to the left of the shrine.

North of Dien Bien Phu

Take a stroll northwest from the zoo up Nguyen Binh Khiem, and ten minutes later you'll reach the broad boulevard of **Dien Bien Phu**. Once over Dien Bien Phu, Nguyen Binh Khiem peters out beside the banks of the Thi Nghe Channel; but Mai Thi Luu, one block to the west, yields up the spectacular **Jade Emperor Pagoda** (daily 6am–6pm), built by the city's Cantonese community around the turn of the century, and still its most captivating pagoda. If you visit just one temple in town, make it this one, with its exquisite panels of carved gilt woodwork, and its panoply of weird and wonderful deities, both Taoist and Buddhist, beneath a roof that groans under the weight of dragons, birds and animals.

Within the treelined **courtyard** out front is a grubby pond whose occupants have earnt the temple its alternative moniker of Tortoise Pagoda. Once over the threshold, look up and you'll see Chinese characters announcing: "the only Empire is in Heaven" – though only after your eyes have acclimatized to the all-pervading fug of joss-stick smoke. A statue of the **Jade Emperor** lords it over the main hall's central altar, sporting an impressive moustachio. It's the Jade Emperor who monitors entry into Heaven, and his two keepers of Heaven – one holding a lamp to light the way for the virtuous, the other wielding an ominous-looking axe – are on hand to aid him.

A rickety flight of steps in the chamber to the right of the main hall runs up to a **balcony** looking out over the pagoda's elaborate **roof**; set behind the balcony, a neon-haloed statue of Quan Am (see p.437) stands on an altar banked high with offerings of lotus flowers and fruit. Left out of the main hall, meanwhile, you're confronted by Kim Hua, to whom women pray for children; judging by the number of babies weighing down the female statues around her, her success rate is high. The Chief of Hell resides behind Kim Hua's niche. Given his job description, he doesn't look too demonic, though his attendants, in their sinister black garb, look suitably equipped to administer the sorts of punishments depicted in the ten dark-wood reliefs on the walls before them.

Less impressive, but still worthy of a flying visit if you're in the vicinity, **Tran Hung Dao Temple** (daily 7–11am & 2–4.30pm) is a few hundred metres west of the Jade Emperor Pagoda, at 36 Vo Thi Sau. Built in 1932, the temple is dedicated to legendary military tactician Tran Hung Dao, who in 1287 notched up a resounding victory against Kublai Khan's 300,000-strong invading Mongol hordes, by luring its fleet onto bamboo stakes driven into the banks of the Bach Dang River (see p.365). Tran Hung Dao confirmed his nationalistic credentials when he had the words *sat dat*, "death to the enemy", tattooed on the arms of his troops. A statue of the great man dominates the temple's modest courtyard, fittingly warlike except for its comical pair of curly-toed pixie boots. Beyond it, a couple of gaudy tigers stand guard in front of the unprepossessing exterior of the temple, their growling maws kept filled with raw meat by worshippers and janitors. There's a smaller statue of Tran Hung Dao inside, attired as for battle and framed by two whale ribs that curve like giant fangs; while murals around him depict his triumphs – though you'll be hard pressed to make out much detail in the gloomy half-light. Opposite the temple, **Le Van Tam Park** stands on the site of an early French colonial graveyard, the *Massiges Cemetery*, but nothing remains of the tombs of the pioneering soldiers, sailors, traders and settlers once laid to rest here.

Further north: Le Van Duyet Temple and Vinh Nghiem Pagoda

Another national hero is commemorated at the **Temple of Marshal Le Van Duyet** (daily 5.30am–4.30pm), at the top of Dinh Tien Hoang, in the region of the city where the **Gia Dinh Citadel** once stood. A military mandarin and eunuch who lived around the turn of the nineteenth century, Le Van Duyet succeeded in putting down the Tay Son Rebellion, and later became military governor of Gia Dinh. Sadly, his endorsements of French expansionism haven't endeared him to today's government, a fact which best explains the temple's down-at-heel appearance. Strolling the grounds reveals the two unmarked oval mounds under which the marshal and his wife are buried. The temple itself, which stretches through three halls behind a facade decorated with unicorns assembled from shards of chinaware, manages only to be shabby, rather than atmospheric. In the first hall, two portraits of the marshal stand on an altar teeming with dragons, unicorns and phoenixes, and beyond these lies a jumbled collection of artefacts – cut glass, chinaware, weaponry and gowns – that either belonged to the marshal or were left by devotees. Look out, too, for a tablet recording the names of donors to the renovations of 1937, on which the *colons* are predictably flattered with top billing. On the first day of the eighth lunar month, to coincide with the marshal's birthday, a **theatre** troupe dramatizes his life; and there's more activity around Tet, when crowds of pilgrims gather to ask for safe-keeping in the forthcoming year.

From here, you'll need to take a cyclo to reach swish but missable **Vinh Nghiem Pagoda** (daily 6.30am–noon & 1.30–9pm), whose spacious sanctuary and soaring tower face an austere-looking war memorial across Nam Ky Khoi

Nghia. There's a decidedly well-to-do air about this place, and its janitor obviously plans to keep it that way, with guests required to remove shoes, and joss-sticks confined to a lotus-shaped urn out front. Inside, a huge golden Buddha perched on a lotus gazes serenely over proceedings but it's the immensely intricate gilt woodwork through which your view of him is framed that'll strike you. A mass of wooden funerary tablets are crammed into the **memorial room** behind the altar. Each one bears the picture, name and death date of a deceased worshipper, and monks bustle around setting offerings of rice and tea before them.

A terrace runs from the hall round to the seven-storey **tower** – you can climb the tower, though there's nothing to see other than a statue of Quan Am on each level. Below the terrace, monks apply themselves diligently to their studies; while a copse of bamboo behind the main sanctuary reveals an ugly and angular **repository**, stacked to the rafters with thousands of decorous funerary urns.

Cholon

The dense cluster of streets comprising the Chinese ghetto of **CHOLON** was once quite distinct from Saigon, though linked to it by the five-kilometre-long umbilical cord of Tran Hung Dao. The distinction was already somewhat blurred by 1950, when Norman Lewis found the city's chinatown "swollen so enormously as to become its grotesque Siamese twin"; and the steady influx of refugees into the city during the subsequent war years saw to it that the two districts became joined by a seamless swathe of urban development. Even so, a short stroll around Cholon, whose name, meaning "**big market**", couldn't be more apposite, will suffice to tell you that it's lost little of its singularity. Even by Ho Chi Minh's standards, the full-tilt mercantile mania here is breathtaking, and from its beehive of stores, goods spill exuberantly out onto the pavements. You'll get most out of Cholon simply by losing yourself in its amorphous mass of life: amid the melee, streetside barbers clip away briskly, bird sellers squat outside tumbledown **pagodas and temples**, heaving markets ring to fishwives' chatter, and stores hawk mushrooms, dried shrimps and rice paper.

The **ethnic Chinese**, or **Hoa**, first began to settle here around the turn of the nineteenth century; many came from existing enclaves in My Tho and Bien Hoa. The area soon became the most sizeable Hoa community in the country, a mantle it still holds, with a population of over half a million. Residents tended to gravitate towards others from their region of China, with each congregation commissioning its own places of worship and clawing out its own commercial niche – thus the Cantonese handled retailing and groceries, the Teochew dealt in tea and fish, the Fukien were in charge of rice, and so on.

The great wealth that Cholon generated had to be spent somewhere. By the early twentieth century, sassy restaurants, casinos and brothels existed to facilitate this. Also prevalent were **fumeries**, where nuggets of opium were quietly smoked from the cool comfort of a wooden opium bed; among the expats and wealthy Asians that frequented them was Graham Greene, whose experiences are diarized in *Ways of Escape*. By the 1950s, Cholon had become a potentially dangerous place to be, with thriving vice industries controlled by the **Binh Xuyen** gang. First the French and then the Americans trod carefully here, while Viet Minh and Viet Cong **activists** hid out in its cramped backstreets – as Frank Palmos found to his cost, when the jeep he and four other correspondents were riding in was ambushed in 1968 (see p.460).

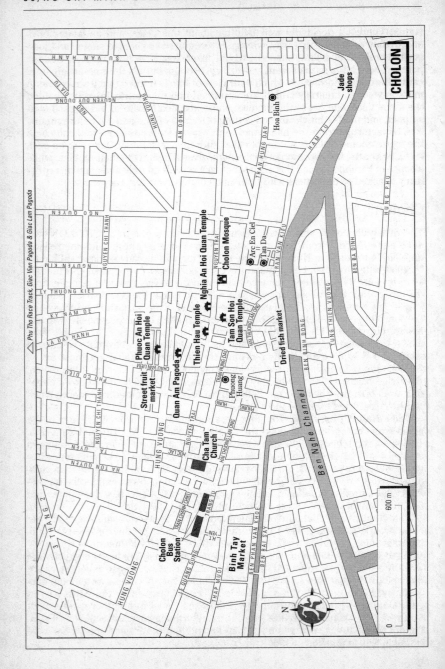

CHOLON

Jade shops

Hoa Binh

Arc En Ciel
Tan Da

Cholon Mosque

Nghia An Hoi Quan Temple

Thien Hau Temple

Tam Son Hoi Quan Temple

Phuoc An Hoi Quan Temple

Dried fish market

Street fruit market

Quan Am Pagoda

Phuong Huang

Cha Tam Church

Cholon Bus Station

Binh Tay Market

Ben Nghe Channel

Phu Tho Race Track, Giac Vien Pagoda & Giac Lam Pagoda

SU VAN HANH
GIA PHU
NGO QUYEN
NGUYEN DUY DUONG
HUNG VUONG
AN DONG
TRAN HUNG DAO
NAM TU
HUNG PHU
BEN BA DINH
NGO QUYEN
NGUYEN CHI THANH
NGUYEN KIM
LY THUONG KIET
KY NAM DE
LA DAI HANH
PHO CO DIEU
NGUYEN CHI THANH
TRA
UYEN
HA TON QUYEN
3 THANG 2
HUNG VUONG
CHAU VAN LIEM
NGUYEN TRAI
HUNG VUONG
HOC LAC
NGUYEN TRAI
HAI THUONG LAN ONG
HAI THUONG LAN ONG
HUNG DAO
PHUNG
TRAN CHANH CHIEU
THANG TU
HI YEN
PHO QUANG SUNG
THAP MUOI
BEN PHAN VAN KHOE
BEN BAI SAY
BINH DONG
VUNG THIEN VUONG
NGUYEN TRAI
TRAN HUNG DAO
NGUYEN TRAI

600 m

0

N

Post-reunification, Cholon saw hard times. As Hanoi aligned itself increasingly with the Soviet Union, Sino-Vietnamese tensions became strained. Economic **persecution** of the Hoa made matters worse, and when Vietnam invaded Chinese-backed Cambodia, Beijing launched a punitive **border war**. Hundreds of thousands of ethnic Chinese, many of them from Cholon, fled the country in unseaworthy vessels, fearing recriminations. Now, though, the authorities have come to value the business nous of the Chinese, and the distemper that gripped Cholon for over a decade has ended. Tran Hung Dao remains the jugular of the enclave; you'll reach Cholon's hub if you travel southwest along Tran Hung Dao from Ben Thanh Market, but the best and cheapest means of getting here is to take a bus to the west side of Cholon and then wander.

Binh Tay Market and around

Saigon Star Co buses disgorge their passengers in Huynh Thoai Yen, on Cholon's western border, from where seething **Binh Tay Market** is a stone's throw away, on Thap Muoi. First impressions of the market, with its multi-tiered, mustard-coloured roofs stalked by serpentine dragons, are of a huge temple complex. Once inside, however, it quickly becomes obvious that only mammon is deified here. If any one place epitomizes Cholon's vibrant commercialism, it's Binh Tay, its well-regimented corridors abuzz with stalls offering products of all kinds, from dried fish, pickled vegetables and chilli paste pounded before your eyes, to pottery piled up to the rafters, and the colourful bonnets crafted from knotted lengths of twine that Vietnamese women so favour. A pair of marvellously dilapidated blocks of shophouses, each capped by four Moorish domes, hems in the market; while a veritable army of cyclo-drivers lays siege to its front entrance. Beyond Binh Tay's south side, a shanty-town of makeshift stalls hawk cheap snacks to hungry shoppers and traders.

Walk north from Huynh Thoai Yen, and you'll soon reach **Tran Chanh Chieu**, a street clogged by a **poultry market** full of chickens, geese and ducks tied together in bundles, all clucking manically, and manhandled like so many bales of hay. **Cereals and pulses** are the speciality at the street's east end, with weighty sacks of rice, lentils and beans forming a sort of obstacle course for the cyclos that try to negotiate the narrow strip of roadway still visible.

The slender pink spire of **Cha Tam Church** peers down from above the eastern end of cramped Tran Chanh Chieu, but you'll have to walk either left or right, and round onto Hoc Lac, to find the entrance. It was in this unprepossessing little church, with its Oriental outer gate and cheery yellow walls, that President Ngo Dinh Diem and his brother Ngo Dinh Nhu holed up on November 1, 1963, during the coup that had chased them out of the Gia Long Palace (see p.76). Early the next morning, Diem phoned the leaders of the coup and surrendered. An M-113 armoured car duly picked them up, but they were both shot dead by ARVN soldiers before the vehicle reached central Saigon. With clearance from the janitor (who's always somewhere around hoping for a tip) you can clamber up into the **belfry** and under the bells, Quasimodo-style, to join the statue of Saint Francis Xavier for the fine views he enjoys of Cholon. He'll also point out the pew where Diem and his brother sat praying as they awaited their fate.

Shops specializing in Chinese and Vietnamese **traditional medicine** have long proliferated on **Hai Thuong Lan Ong**, a two-minute walk east of the church, and are identifiable by the sickly aroma that hangs over it. Named after a famous herbalist who practised and studied in Hanoi two centuries ago, the street is lined by dingy shophouses banked with cabinets whose old wooden drawers are crammed full of herbs. Step over the sliced roots laid out to dry along the pavement and peer inside any one of the shops, and you'll see rheumy men and women weighing out prescriptions on ancient balances. Steepled around them are boxes, jars and paper bags containing anything from dried bark and roots, to antler fur and tortoise glue. Predictably popular is **ginseng**, the Oriental cure-all said to combat maladies as varied as weakness of the heart and acne. Also available, though definitely under-the-counter material, are monkey-, tiger- and rhino-based medicines, despite a government ban on these products.

Down to the waterfront

Hai Lon Ong peels off southwards to meet waterfront Tran Van Kieu. Shops on the southside of Tran Van Kieu shield the **Ben Nghe Channel** from view, but if you turn right, past the pungent **dried fish market** and over the bridge, you'll be able to study the godowns, stilthouses and boat-houses on its oily waters. Old men crouch arthritically along the bridge trying to make a few dong from the motley arrays of bric-a-brac – odd shoes, spanners and spoons – laid out before them. Head east instead from the foot of Hai Lon Ong, and soon you'll delve into Ben Ham Tu, where dozens of stores pander to the Chinese predilection for **jade**.

Nguyen Trai and around

Cholon's greatest architectural treasures are its temples and pagodas, many of which stand on or around **Nguyen Trai**, whose four-kilometre sweep northeast to Pham Ngu Lao starts just beyond the row of streetside **barbers** above Cha Tam Church. Past the street's junction with Phung Hung (where a riotous street **fruit market** stands to your left, and a glut of shops selling scarlet Chinese roast pork, sausages and chickens to your right), is its intersection with Chau Van Liem; from here you can thread your way up to **Quan Am Pagoda**, set back from the bustle of Cholon on tiny Lao Tu, its existence betrayed by a cluster of stallholders selling incense and caged birds. An almost tangible air of antiquity broods over the place, enhanced by the film of dust left by the spiral incense sticks hanging from its rafters. Don't be too quick to dive inside, though: the pagoda's ridged roofs are impressive enough from the outside, their colourful crust of "glove-puppet" figurines, teetering houses and temples from a distance creating the illusion of a gingerbread house; while framing the two door gods and the pair of stone lions assigned to keeping out evil spirits, are gilt panels depicting petrified scenes from traditional Chinese court life – dancers, musicians, noblemen in sedan chairs, a game of chequers being played.

When Cholon's Fukien congregation established this pagoda well over a century ago, they dedicated it to the Goddess of Mercy, but it's **A Pho**, the Queen of Heaven, who stands in the centre of the main hall, beyond an altar tiled like a mortician's slab. A pantheon of deities throngs the open courtyard behind her, attracting a steady traffic of worshippers; most dominant are the two statues of **Quan Am** – one with its back to A Pho, the other a dignified burnt gold colour. Keep an eye out too for the calligrapher who sets up shop in the corridor to the right of the main chamber: for around $1 he'll daub your name on a prayer paper. The turtles in the pond beside him also come under his jurisdiction, and you'll sometimes catch him slipping them bananas between scribbling prayers.

Phuoc An Hoi Quan Temple three minutes' walk north, is a disarming place, seemingly erected bang in the middle of a turn-of-the-century Chinese merchant's residence. Beyond the menacing dragons and sea monsters patrolling its roof, and the superb wood carving depicting a king being entertained by jousters and minstrels hanging over the entrace, is the temple's **sanctuary**, in which stately Quan Cong sits, instantly recognizable by his blood-red face, and waited upon by two storks fashioned from countless plectrum-shaped ceramic shards. It's the **chambers** that lie either side of him, however, crammed with rosewood furniture, grand old clocks and framed mirrors, liver-spotted photographs, and mounted stags' heads, that really stoke the imagination.

Further along Nguyen Trai, extensive renovations have cheated grey-brick **Thien Hau Temple** of much of its charisma, but this doesn't stop local women coming in numbers to make offerings to Me Sanh, Goddess of Fertility and to Long Mau, Goddess of Mothers and newly born babies. When Cantonese immigrants established the temple towards the middle of last century, they named it after Thien Hau, Goddess of Seafarers. New arrivals from China would have hastened here to express their gratitude for a safe passage across the South China Sea. Three statues of her stand on the altar, one behind the other, while an eye-catching mural on the inside of the front wall depicts her guiding wildly pitching ships across a storm-tossed sea. Nowadays, the temple is somewhat marred by overt commercialization that even has the janitors sport matching T-shirts. The temple's salvation is its **roof**, bristling with so many figurines, you'll wonder how those at the edge can keep their balance.

Two more religious sites – both of them missable, if you're suffering from pagoda fatigue – face one another 100m further down Nguyen Trai. Beyond its impressively whiskered door gods, **Nghia An Hoi Quan Temple** has a quiet, shabby aura, disturbed only by the occasional rattle of fortune sticks at its altar; dominated by vast incense spirals, it's correspondingly dusty and drab. Ruddy Quan Cong again holds sway, sporting a lurid green robe and a rather comical red ribbon around his head; beside him are his *aides de camp*, General Chau Xuong and the mandarin Quan Binh. If you can bear to examine any more roof decorations, the peacocks, fish and frolicking lambs on the temple's eaves are pretty enough. Across the street, but accessed by an entrance on Trieu Quang Phuc, **Tam Son Hoi Quan Temple** is similarly sorry for itself these days. Quan Cong turns up yet again, as do Thien Hau and, to her left, Me Sanh, sitting with her daughters as if for a portrait photographer. Look out for the dragon dance costumes in the chamber to the left of the main hall. Across Nguyen Trai's intersection with Ly Thuong Kiet, **Cholon Mosque** strikes an oddly un-Chinese chord. White and duck-egg blue, with green railings, its unfussy architecture and slender minarets are in stark contrast to the pagodas nearby.

North of Cholon

Two of Ho Chi Minh City's more engaging places of worship, Giac Lam Pagoda and Giac Vien Pagoda, are kept under wraps out in the hinterlands to the north of Cholon – as is the thriving Phu Tho racecourse, if you fancy a bit of a flutter. Given their similarities, there's little to be gained by seeing both pagodas; whichever one you choose is sure to be known to downtown cyclo-drivers.

Giac Lam Pagoda

You'll see the gate leading up to **Giac Lam Pagoda** at 118 Lac Long Quan, a couple of hundred metres northeast of its intersection with Le Dai Hanh; from there, a short track passes a brand new tower (its 6 levels are scaleable and

---

PHU THO RACECOURSE

There's no more potent symbol of the regeneration of capitalism in Ho Chi Minh City than the resumption of horseracing at Cholon's **Phu Tho Racecourse** (☎855 1205). Upon the liberation of the South in 1975, gambling was declared an example of bourgeois decadence and outlawed, and it's only since 1989 that the country's political climate has become sufficiently liberal for the course to re-open. **Meetings**, which take place on Saturday and Sunday afternoons, and two Thursday afternoons a month throughout the year, attract punters in their thousands; collectively, they've been known to spend over $30,000 in a day. Ringing the course's dust track is a wire fence intended, it's said, to thwart spectators wanting to influence a race by throwing stones at the horses. Such tricks aren't confined to the grandstand, a dilapidated hangover from the colonial era: horse-drugging is not unheard of, and jockeys (many of whom are as young as 14) have been known to accept bribes to throw a race. Hundreds of racehorses are now bred in Ho Chi Minh; their numbers are boosted periodically by imports from Europe and Hong Kong, which are then put to stud in order to improve the bloodstock.

Foreigners are not barred from betting. **To win**, you have to select correctly both the first- *and* second-place horse; all gambling is on-course, and the maximum bet is around $2. Phu Tho Racecourse is just north of Cholon, at 2 Le Dai Hanh.

---

afford good city-views) and a cluster of monks' tombs on its way to the actual pagoda. Built in 1744 – and looking every bit its age – rambling Giac Lam is draped over 98 hardwood pillars, each inscribed with traditional *chu nom* characters (Vietnamese script, based on Chinese ideograms). From its terracotta floor tiles and extravagant chandeliers to the antique tables at which monks sit to take tea, Giac Lam is characterized by a quaint clutter that imbues it with an appealingly fusty feel, and a reassuring sense of age. Access is through an understated **entrance** at the rear of the right-hand wall, which leads into a cob-webbed **funerary chamber** flanked by row upon row of gilt tablets above photos of the deceased. The many-armed goddess that stands in the centre of the chamber, illuminated by shafts of light that slice through windows punched into the roof, is Chuan De, a manifestation of Quan Am. A right turn leads to a **courtyard-garden**, around which runs a roof studded with blue and white porcelain saucers. A quaint mini-mountain, complete with model bridges, pagodas and greenery, provides the garden with a centrepiece. Monks would once have sat studying Buddhism on the huge wooden benches in the peaceful old **classroom** at the back of the complex; today this is used by revising university students. The cloth panels in this chamber depict the ten Buddhist hells; study them carefully, and you'll see sinners variously being minced, fed to dogs, dismembered and disembowelled by toothsome demons.

To the left of the funerary chamber as you enter the pagoda is the **main sanctuary**, whose multi-tiered altar dias groans under the weight of the many Buddhist and Taoist statues it supports (remember to take off your shoes before entering). Elsewhere in this chamber you'll spot an ensemble of oil lamps balanced on a Christmas tree-shaped wooden frame. Worshippers pen prayers on pieces of paper which they affix to the tree and then feed the lamps with an offering of oil. A similar ritual is attached to the bell across the chamber, though in this case people believe that their prayers are hastened to the gods by the ringing of the bell.

Giac Vien Pagoda

From Giac Lam, you'll need to head southwest along Lac Long Quan to reach **Giac Vien Pagoda**; take the right-turn between nos. 247 and 249 – if you see Binh Thoi to your left you've gone too far – then turn left and then right. The track to the pagoda is lined by shanty houses that have encroached up to and over the monks' tombs outside. Founded in the eighteenth century, and said to have been frequented by Emperor Gia Long, the pagoda has much in common with Giac Lam. Here, too, there's a dark lived-in atmosphere – so dark, indeed, that bats hang in its smokey rafters, squeaking intermittently. Upon entering the pagoda's red doors daubed with yellow *chu nom* characters, visitors are confronted by banks of old photos and funerary tablets flanking long, refectory-style tables. The two rows of black pillars that spine it lend an arresting sense of depth to this first chamber, which is dominated by a panel depicting a ferocious-looking red lion, and a statue of a slouching Ameda, grinning and fiddling with a set of beads. Go on around the sky-blue-washed stone walls (crafted, incongruously, in classical Greek style) and into the **main sanctuary**, and you'll find a sizeable congregation of deities, as well as a tree of lamps similar to the one at Giac Lam. The monks residing in Giac Vien are hospitable to a fault, and you'll quite probably be sat down for a cup of tea poured from beneath a varnished coconut husk cosy.

Eating

If Hanoi is Vietnam's first city, then Ho Chi Minh is without doubt its culinary capital. Such is the size of the expat community here that the majority of new ventures opening up specialize in **non-Vietnamese foods**: whatever your craving – Tex Mex or tandoori, shish kebab or sushi – it's bound to be catered for, though **French** restaurants predictably comprise the most formidable foreign contingent in town. The French legacy is also evident in the city's abundance of **cafés**, which are currently enjoying a resurgence. Confronted by such a global restaurant scene, it's easy to ignore indigenous cuisine, but you do this at your peril: **Vietnamese food** comes no better than in Ho Chi Minh, whether taken in a sophisticated **restaurant** or at a **streetside stall**. Owing to the transitory nature of foodstalls, it's impossible to make specific recommendations, but there are plenty to choose from (see p.35 for more on how to spot a good one).

Most of Ho Chi Minh City's eating establishments stay **open** throughout the year, but remember that some will close down over Tet. Increasingly the demands of travellers are leading to more flexible hours; given this variability, we've specified exact times wherever possible.

Restaurants

One step up from street stalls are the **eating houses**, where good, filling *com* and *pho* meals are served from buffet-style tin trays and vast soup urns. **Travellers' cafés**, concentrated around Pham Ngu Lao, and catering exclusively for the banana-pancake brigade, are fine if you want an inexpensive steak and chips or some fried noodles, but hardly in the league of the city's heavyweights, its **specialist restaurants**. Of course, by Vietnamese standards, these restaurants are incredibly expensive – eat at one and you'll probably spend enough to feed a Vietnamese family for a month – but by Western standards they are low priced, and the quality of cooking is consistently high. What's more, ingredients are fresh, with vegetables transported from Da Lat, and meat often flown in from Australia. Certain swankier restaurants have taken to laying on live **traditional music** in order to lure diners – we've mentioned a few such places in our listings.

Upper Dong Khoi and around

All the following places are marked on the map opposite.

Annie's Pizza, 57 Nguyen Du. Passable pizzas ranging from medium to "jumbo" ($5–15) as well as Australian pies ($4); the branch at 59 Cach Mang Thang Tam (☎839 2577) does home deliveries. 11am–3pm & 5–11pm.

Chez Guido's, *Hotel Continental*, 132–134 Dong Khoi (☎829 9201). A cool Italian venue affording good views of Dong Khoi, its decor a successful amalgam of grand classical pillars and rustic furniture; chef Guido's specialities – paella Valenciana ($12) and couscous Algerienne ($11) – strike an oddly un-Italian chord, though there are also pizzas and other standards. 11am–10pm.

Cung Dinh Rex, *Rex Hotel*, 141 Nguyen Hue (☎829 2185). Some may find the lavish Oriental decor oppressive but there's no knocking the food: try the steamed chicken with lime leaves or braised catfish with caramel, or splash out on a set meal (from $15 per head). You'll need to book ahead. 10.30am–2.30pm & 5.30–10.30pm.

Madame Dai's Bibliotheque, 84a Nguyen Du (☎823 1438). Unmarked gates a stone's throw from Notre Dame yield an intriguing slice of old Saigon. The food (either French or Vietnamese set meals; $12 a head) isn't terrific, but it's the ambience you pay for: guests dine in the library, banked with legal tomes and antiques, of the home of Madame Dai, a Paris-trained lawyer and ex-member of Thieu's National Assembly, who floats around like royalty; performances of traditional music and dance follow weekend sittings. Book ahead.

Manhattan's, 1 Nguyen Van Chiem. American-style burger bar knocking out Ho Chi Minh's best burgers and fries, as well as flavoursome fried chicken. 10am–10pm.

Quan An 39, 39 Nguyen Trung Truc. Hectic streetside operation, a 10-min walk west of Dong Khoi, dishing up tasty set lunches – grilled pork on rice, veggies, soup and iced tea – all for less than $1. 10.30am–1.30pm.

Rex Garden, 86 Le Thanh Ton. A tank provides the incongruous backdrop to this pleasant Vietnamese establishment, backing onto the *Revolutionary Museum* gardens. 6am–10pm.

Spago, 158 Dong Khoi. American-style diner that rams home the US motif with wall-to-wall Hollywood posters; popular with well-off locals who enjoy the cajun chicken wings, steaks and sundaes (see "Cafés, ice cream and desserts", p.98) as much as the Americana; two eat for $16 upwards. 7am–11pm.

Lower Dong Khoi and the waterfront

All the following places are marked on the map opposite.

Augustin's, 10 Nguyen Thiep. Secreted down a narrow lane linking Dong Khoi and Nguyen Hue, an intimate bistro serving well-cooked French dishes. 11.30am–2pm & 6.30–10pm.

La Fourchette, 9 Ngo Duc Ke (☎823 1101). Varnished lightwood panelling and darkwood floor, Van Gogh prints and murals of rural France; the compact menu features melt-in-your-mouth imported steaks ($9) and a well-stocked cheeseboard. 11.30am–2pm & 6–10pm.

Lemongrass, 63 Dong Khoi (☎829 8006). Relatively expensive establishment whose highly rated food is eaten to the strains of serenading players. 11am–3pm & 5–11pm.

Maxim's Dinner Theatre, 15–17 Dong Khoi (☎822 5554). Choose from the extensive French and Chinese menus, sit back and enjoy the live music as you dine, and then move upstairs for dance if you aren't too full; book ahead for weekend dining. 4.30–10pm.

Restaurant 13, 13 Ngo Duc Ke. Touts outside this unpretentious joint are masters of the hard sell: yield to them and you can sample such delights as sweet leek and mussel soup, or the sublime stir-fried cubed beef. 7am–midnight.

Saigon Floating Restaurant, Ton Duc Thang. Cruises (Mon–Sat 8pm, Sun 5.30 & 8pm) cost $0.50 choose between set meals ($5 a head) and pricey seafood – or just order a drink and watch the river flow. 8am–10.30pm.

EATING AND DRINKING:
CENTRAL HO CHI MINH

0   100 m

American Embassy

Notre Dame Cathedral

Reunification
Palace

Ben Thanh
Market

Thieves' Market

Statue
of Tran
Hung Dao

MEI LINH
SQUARE

Saigon River

RESTAURANTS

1	Annie's Pizza
2	Ashoka
3	Augustin's
4	Chez Guido's
5	Cung Dinh Rex
6	Kruathai
7	La Dolce Vita
8	La Fourchette
9	Le P'tit Bistro
10	Lemongrass
11	Madame Dai's Bibliotheque
12	Manhattan's
13	Maxim's Dinner Theatre
14	Quan An 39
15	Quan Dua
16	Restaurant 13
17	Rex Garden
18	Saigon Floating Restaurant
19	Saigontourist Cruise
20	Sapa
21	Seoul House
22	Shunka
23	Spago
24	Tannam
25	Tex Mex
26	Vietnam House

CAFÉS

27	Brodard Restaurant
28	Chi Lang Café
29	La Dolce Vita
30	Givral Café
31	Kem Bach Dang
32	Kem Cong Truong
33	Napoli Café
34	Paloma Café
35	Le Pierrot Gourmand
36	Spago

BARS/PUBS

37	Apocalypse Now
38	Bar Catinat
39	Bia Hoi Thanh Nha
40	Buffalo Blues
41	La Dolce Vita
42	Hammock Saigon
43	Hard Rock Café
44	Hien & Bob's Place
45	Ice Blue
46	Mogambo
47	Q Bar
48	Red Rhino
49	River Bar
50	Rooftop Garden

Saigontourist Cruise, Ton Duc Thang (☎899 1831). Tickets ($20) for the dinner cruise include a cultural show upriver at *Binh Quoi Cultural Village* (see p.100); return journey is by car. Daily at 5pm.

Seoul House, 37 Ngo Duc Ke (☎829 4297). *Bulgogi* (marinated beef, barbecued at table), pork with *kimchi* (pickled cabbage), and other authentic Korean dishes, eaten between walls bearing *Korean Air* posters and ginseng ads; $12 feeds two. 11am–2pm & 5–10pm.

Tannam, 59–61 Dong Khoi (☎822 3407). Lacking the intimacy of nearby *Lemongrass*, but still a stylish place, with a beguiling garden terrace and a menu that includes several veggie options alongside its top-notch meat and fish dishes. 11am–2.30pm & 5–10.30pm.

Vietnam House, 93–95 Dong Khoi (☎829 1623). Occupying a splendid louvred colonial building, a cracking introduction to Vietnamese food, and manned by staff in traditional garb. There's traditional folk music at 7pm, and set meals from $9. 11am–2pm & 5–10pm.

Thi Sach and around

All the following places are marked on the map on p.93.

Ashoka, 17a/10 Le Thanh Ton (☎823 1372). A few silk paintings adorn the walls at this understated Indian address, but it's the food that does the talking: authentic moghul Indian dishes – some, such as *cho cho tikka* (chicken marinated in yoghurt), cooked in the tandoor – and a satisfying range of veggie dishes. 11.30am–2pm & 6–10pm.

Kruathai, 2 Thi Sach (☎829 8919). Outstanding Thai restaurant whose chefs do a mean *pad thai* ($2), and a *som tam* ($2) that'll bring tears to your eyes, as well as great curries ($3); choose from the short English menu, or scan the extensive photo-menu. 10.30am–10.30pm.

Le P'tit Bistro, 58 Le Thanh Ton (☎823 0219). With menus inside *Paris Match* covers, walls plastered with pages from French magazines, and soft French muzak, the Gallic connection is evident. Steaks (from $5 – choose from mushroom, mustard, roquefort or pepper sauce) are good, while crepes suzette or the French cheese platter rounds things off. Expensive but sleek: two pay around $25–30, all in. 11am–2pm & 6.30–10.30pm.

Quan Dua, 15b Thi Sach. Locals in the know make for Thi Sach when they want fine seafood; *Quan Dua* is an elder statesman of the Thi Sach scene, but still delivers cracking seafood dishes on its lively streetside terrace. 10am–11pm.

Sapa, 8a/8 Don Dat. Popular new restaurant-cum-bar, run by a Swiss expat, and working from a menu featuring fondue, schnitzel and, more surprisingly, snake. 7am–midnight.

Shunka, 17a/9 Le Thanh Ton (☎822 2182). Serene, two-floor Japanese restaurant with minimalist decor but enticing food. 11.30am–2pm & 6–11pm.

Tex Mex, 24 Le Thanh Ton (☎829 5950). Fair approximations of tacos, chilli and guacamole amid a predictable melange of cacti, bullfighting posters and sombreros. The set meal ($9) offers starter, grilled meat, dessert and coffee – though chucking down litres of San Miguel and margherita ($20 a litre) seems to be the priority for most regulars. 11.30am–1am.

Pham Ngu Lao and around

All the following places are marked on the map opposite.

Banana Café, 6/8 Pham Ngu Lao. Bamboo-walled joint whose pancakes and pizza pies have a loyal following; meals are tasty but ungenerous, so start with a plate of spring rolls. Videos are screened nightly at 7pm. 8am–midnight.

Cay Dua, 154 Le Lai. Also known as the *Coconut Tree* (two trees stand, sentry-style, out front), handily placed if you feel the need to duck out of Pham Ngu Lao. Braised rice with chicken in an earthenware pot is a speciality; two eat handsomely for $6. 10am–10pm.

Coco Loco, 351 Pham Ngu Lao. With dishes off the international menu at around $2, slightly pricier than the rest, though the English breakfast special (sausage, beans, eggs, bread, mushrooms and tomato; $2.50) will stoke you up through to dinner. 7am–midnight.

Dynasty, *New World Hotel*, 76 Le Lai (☎822 8888). The anodyne piano music wafting up to this dog-legged Cantonese restaurant from the lobby below may irritate, but there's no faulting the elegant decor (porcelain and bonsai), nor the splendid food, created by a Hong Kong

EATING & DRINKING: PHAM NGU LAO

0 _____ 100 m

RESTAURANTS & BARS

1	Banana Café	**8**	Kim Café	**15**	Sawaddee
2	Bar Rolling Stones	**9**	Le Le	**16**	Sinh Café
3	Bia Hoi Nguyen Chat	**10**	Long Phi	**17**	Terrace Bar
4	Cay Dua	**11**	Lotus Café	**18**	Thanh
5	Coco Loco	**12**	Mr Conehead's	**19**	Thanh Da
6	Dynasty & Hoa Mi	**13**	Quan Phong Anh	**20**	Thu Thuy
7	Easy Rider	**14**	Saigon Café	**21**	Zen

chef who knocks out more-ish *dim sum* every lunchtime; two can dine well for $20, but the sky's the limit if you plump for delicacies like bird's nest soup or shark's fin. Mon–Sat 11am–2pm & 6–10pm; Sun 7am–2pm & 6–10pm.

Hoa Mi, *New World Hotel*, 76 Le Lai (☎822 8888). A current pacesetter thanks to starters such as rice cake wrapped in banana leaves and served with shrimp mousse ($5), and main courses like wok-fried crab with tamarind ($15). There's traditional music (7–10pm) and even a water puppetry show on Sat evenings. Expensive, but worth it. 11am–2pm & 6–10pm.

Kim Café, 270 De Tham. Smaller, but brighter and better kept than *Sinh Café*, which may explain why its terrace is so heaving at night; besides breakfasts and veggie meals galore, there's guacamole, garlic bread, mashed potatoes, and a fantastic Malay-style chicken curry ($2). 7am–1am.

Lotus Café, 197 Pham Ngu Lao. The truly mountainous "big breakfast" is worth trying at least once, as is the banana dessert; dusty ledgers on a shelf are packed with comments – some useful – on Vietnam and the surrounding countries. 7am–11pm.

Quan Phong Anh, 134a Nguyen Thai Hoc. One of a rowdy gaggle of functional restaurants along Nguyen Thai Hoc; try barbecued beef wrapped in rice paper with mint leaves and noodles – fiddly but full of flavour – or the terrific *lau* (steamboat). 4pm–midnight.

Saigon Café, 195 Pham Ngu Lao. Always busy at breakfast due to its fine croissants, and eggs with pork chop for less than $1; the fruit salad receives plaudits, too. 7am–10pm.

Sawaddee, 252 De Tham. The Thai chef relies heavily upon coconut and chilli to create fiery sour and sweet dishes. Pork with peanut sauce comes recommended, while the bananas in coconut milk are a delicious way to clear the palate; a meal for two shouldn't exceed $9. 9am–11pm.

Sinh Café, 6 Pham Ngu Lao. The big daddy of the traveller scene, doling out average but affordable meals in its unsalubrious dining room, and rather dead after about 9pm; browsing the noticeboard on the wall might unearth something of use. Note that *Sinh Café* tours depart from *Sinh 2*, around the corner at 1 Le Lai. 7am–11pm.

Thanh, 207 Pham Ngu Lao. This simple joint at the hub of Pham Ngu Lao serves low-cost, mainstream Vietnamese food presented buffet-style at the entrance; don't miss the delicious stuffed tofu. 6am–7pm.

Thanh Da, 212 De Tham. Spit-and-sawdust *com* shop, unbeatable value and handy for Pham Ngu Lao; stuffed tomatoes and pork chops are sensational, though there's always *pho* on the go if they don't appeal. 8am–8pm.

Thu Thuy, 26 Cach Mang Thanh Tam. Banana-leaf parcels of cured pork hang along the frontage of this excellent *nem* specialist, a short walk north of Pham Ngu Lao. 11am–10pm.

Zen, 175/6 Pham Ngu Lao. One of the few really authentic eating options along Pham Ngu Lao. Decor couldn't be simpler, but what you're here for are bargain-priced, imaginative veggie dishes such as wild red rice and Chinese mushrooms braised in a claypot, and a coconut and pumpkin soup to die for; don't miss their divine fruit shakes either. 6.30am–11pm.

From Tran Hung Dao to the Ben Nghe Channel

All the following places are marked on the map on pp.62–63.

Blue Ginger, 37 Nam Ky Khoi Nghia (☎829 8676). Refined, low-ceilinged dining room with live traditional music as you tuck into quality Vietnamese food (main courses $4) – but kick off with an aperitif on one of the opium couches in the sleek bar out front; the express lunch ($5) offers good value. 11am–2.30pm & 4.30–10pm.

Cam Huong Restaurant, 228 Tran Hung Dao. Set in a charming sky-blue colonial villa, and run by an equally charming, French-speaking maitre d', this restaurant offers Vietnamese seven-ways grilled beef (*bo 7 mon*); $3 buys a sample platter for two. Noon–1pm & 4–11pm.

Ngoc Linh Restaurant, 58 Ho Hao Hon. Airy courtyard restaurant shaded by bamboo and frangipani trees and specializing in fresh seafood, prepared according to Vietnamese and Chinese recipes; two can eat for $8, though prices soar if you order imaginatively. 10.30am–9.30pm.

La Papaye Verte, 33a Ben Van Don. Set incongruously among warehouses on Ben Nghe Canal's south bank, a charming and good-value French bistro where carnivorous feasts like steaks and pork chops ($3) are best eaten with a rustic salad ($1). French expats come for the circular billiards table. 8am–midnight.

Phuoc Loi, 75 Ham Nghi. You won't find cheaper Chinese food anywhere in the city – though indelicate surroundings are the trade-off. 10.30am–2pm & 4.30–9pm.

Thuan Kieu, 114 Yersin. Canteen-style *com* operation where any one of an array of appetizing dishes served on rice and with iced tea to drink costs just over $1. 6am–9pm.

Tin Nghia, 9 Tran Hung Dao. Mushrooms and tofu provide the backbone to the inventive menu in this "pure vegetarian" restaurant, now into its seventh decade. You could do far worse than the tofu cooked with lemongrass and red pepper. 7am–8.30pm.

From Nguyen Thi Minh Khai to Dien Bien Phu

All the following places are marked on the map on pp.62–63.

Bodhi Tree, 265 Vo Van Tan. Set up by the nun who masterminded *Zen* (see above), so good veggie food is guaranteed; try *bi cuon* – rice cakes with a vegetable and potato filling, but not on the menu; or *lagu*, a hearty veggie stew eaten with French bread. 7.30am–11pm.

La Couscoussiere, 24 Nguyen Thi Minh Khai (☎829 9148). Carpets hanging on the walls bring a hint of Persia to *La Couscoussiere*, which is steadily building a reputation for premier-league Arabic and Indian food; the house speciality, predictably, is couscous, served with lamb, chicken or merguez (North African sausage) – the *Couscous Royal* ($15) is enough for two; phone for home delivery. 11am–2.30pm & 6–11pm.

L'Etoile, 180 Hai Ba Trung (☎829 7939). High-class French cuisine that's complemented by guitar music and expansive wine cellar, all housed in a charismatic villa; expect to pay $15 a head. 11.30am–2.30pm & 5–11pm.

Giac Duc, 492 Nguyen Dinh Chieu. Hole-in-the-wall eating house, specializing in Vietnamese and Taiwanese vegetarian foods, and favoured by local monks; soups, rice and a tempting spread of cakes, in addition to delicious spring rolls and *banh bao*. 6am–midnight.

Le Mekong, 32 Vo Van Tan (☎829 1277). Housed in a pastel-coloured villa along the road from the War Crimes Museum, polished *Le Mekong* draws the crowds with tempting French treats such as duck à l'orange and a baked apple tart that's second to none; serenading guitarists meander between the tables. 6–10pm.

Minh Pho Bo, 107/12 Truong Dinh. *Pho* is the staple product at this gaily painted noodle shop; if that doesn't sound substantial enough, the *lau bo*, or steamboat beef ($2 feeds two) will fill a gap. 6am–10pm.

Saigon Star Hotel, 204 Nguyen Thi Minh Khai (☎823 0260). Well-loved Singaporean classics such as *bak kut teh* (pork ribs in soy sauce), Hainanese chicken rice and fried noodles, all prepared to a dependable standard. 11am–11pm.

North of Dien Bien Phu

All the following places are marked on the map on pp.62–63.

Cha Ca Hanoi, 27e Nguyen Huu Canh. A Hanoi speciality, fried marinated fish served with noodles, that suffers none from the journey south. 10am–8pm.

Coffee Shop, *Saigon Lodge Hotel*, 215 Nam Ky Khoi Nghia. Malaysian cuisine a speciality: the halal Muslim section in the menu includes beef rendang, mutton and chicken korma and *nasi lemak*, all around $5, and all prepared by a Malaysian chef. 24hr.

Pho 165, 165 Dien Bien Phu. Cheap and cheerful soup kitchen, one of several along this stretch of Dien Bien Phu, dishing out flavoursome *pho* in workaday surroundings. 6am–11pm.

Pho Binh, 7 Ly Chinh Thang. A must-see for all war buffs: a wartime safe-house for communists, it was from here that the command was given to kick off 1968's Tet Offensive. Don't make the trip for the soup alone, though. 6am–11pm.

Tinh Tam Trai, 170a Vo Thi Sau. No-frills veggie restaurant where you choose your meal from the front window. A mural of Quan Am looks serenely down upon diners from the back wall. 6am–1pm & 3–9pm.

Tri Ky, 82 Tran Huy Lieu (☎824 0968). Located some way up towards the airport, this smart restaurant offers "jungle cuisine" – cobra, bat, wild boar, venison and turtle – to those who can stomach it. 11am–2pm & 6.30–10pm.

Cholon and the outskirts

All the following places are marked on the map on pp.62–63.

A Dong, 22–23 Hai Thuong Lan Ong. Sporting red lanterns and flame-red tablecloths, a vast ballroom of a place that draws Cholon diners in droves for classic Cantonese food. Noon–2pm & 5.30–10.30pm.

Golden Phoenix, *Hotel Equatorial*, 242 Tran Binh Trong (☎839 0000). A rising star in the Ho Chi Minh restaurant firmament, though its Szechuan and Cantonese treats don't come cheap – expect to pay upwards of $18 a head for a decent feed. 11.30am–2pm & 6.30–10pm.

Kampachi, *Hotel Equatorial*, 242 Tran Binh Trong (☎839 0000). Japanese chefs ensure that sushi, teppanyaki and other standards are up to scratch for the mostly Japanese diners that frequent this stylish and reputable joint; *sake* provides the perfect liquid accompaniment. Noon–2pm & 6–11pm.

BUYING YOUR OWN FOOD: MARKETS AND SUPERMARKETS

With baguettes, cheese and fruit in such abundant supply in Vietnam, making up a picnic is easy. All the basics can be found at any of the city's **markets**, though if you're homesick for peanut butter, Vegemite or other such exotica, you'll need to head for a specialist **supermarket** or **provision store**.

Markets

The handiest market for Pham Ngu Lao is **Thai Binh Market**, down at the street's southwestern end; hardly less close, and larger, **Ben Thanh Market** (see p.78), the central market in the city centre, is at the far eastern end of Tran Hung Dao. Cholon is served by **Binh Tay Market** (see p.87) on its southwestern border; and by **Andong Market**, northeast of it at the junction of Tran Phu and An Duong Vuong.

Supermarkets and provisions stores

Donamart, 63 Ly Tu Trong. Well stocked with baked beans and other uniquely Western comestibles.

Kim Thanh, 64 Ham Nghi. One of numerous stores between nos. 54 and 74 selling *Branston* pickle, *Hershey's* syrup, Russian caviar, imported biscuits, baked beans and other canned foods, as well as wines and spirits.

Minimart, *ITC*, 101 Nam Ky Khoi Nghia. Cheese, milk and Western tinned goods.

Nhu Lan Bakery, 66–68 Ham Nghi. Famed bakery selling bread, cakes, ham, cheeses and pâté.

Saigon Food Market, 162 Hai Ba Trung. Wines, canned and frozen foods, and the "most delicious sweeties and cakes".

Sama, 35 Dong Du. Classy *épicerie* specializing in French and Italian produce; also stocks champagne.

Seven Eleven, 16 Nguyen Hue. Not the genuine article, but a fair approximation: Slush Puppies, cold drinks, ice creams and food.

U-Save Mart, 57 Nguyen Du. Ravioli, Nescafé and other treats.

Cafés, ice cream and desserts

Café culture, introduced by the French, is once again very much alive in Ho Chi Minh, so once you've dined there are numerous places at which to round things off with an ice cream, crêpe or sundae. Earlier in the day, the same venues offer the chance to linger over a coffee and watch things tick along.

Brodard Restaurant, 131 Dong Khoi. Really more of a café, and a real throwback to the past, with doormen in peaked hats and dickie-bowed gents delivering coffees and sandwiches ($1.50) on trays. 6am–10pm.

Café de Paris, 274 Tran Hung Dao. Ideal for a cold drink and a creamy cake to break up your Cholon odyssey. 7am–11pm.

Chi Lang Café, Chi Lang Park, Dong Khoi. The *Chi Lang*'s commanding position, set back from and above Dong Khoi, makes it a prime site for people-watching; if you tire of that, you can browse around the art galleries flanking it. 8am–11pm.

La Dolce Vita, *Hotel Continental*, 132–134 Dong Khoi. *Gelateria* with an almost tangible sense of age (see "Bars and pubs", p.100), and superb ice creams. 11.30am–7pm.

Givral Café, 169 Dong Khoi. Munching a French pastry, sipping a coffee and listening to old crooners on the radio, it's as if the war never happened. A Ho Chi Minh institution, facing the *Continental* on Lam Son Square. 7am–10pm.

Kem Bach Dang, 26 & 28 Le Loi. Twin open-fronted ice-cream parlours revered for their extravagant creations, some of which feature fruits from Da Lat; unfortunately, it's a magnet for beggars who periodically stray inside. 8am–11pm.

Kem Cong Truong, 10 Pham Ngoc Thach. Locals swear by this roadside café, close to Dong Khoi's cathedral, and serving inexpensive ice creams, fresh coconuts and beers. 8am–10pm.

Mr Conehead's, 195 Pham Ngu Lao. Tiny frontage opposite *Kim Café* with a selection of papers and magazines to leaf through over one of a range of tasty ice creams. 8am–8pm.

Napoli Café, 5 Pham Ngoc Thach. Fresh-cut flowers, terracotta tiles and al fresco tables breathe a rustic sigh through the *Napoli*, a short stroll above the cathedral; choose from a modest selection of cakes, pastries and sundaes or indulge in the *mangia e bevi* – a sensational blend of ice cream, orange juice and fresh fruit. 8am–11pm.

Paloma Café, 26 Dong Khoi. Immensely popular café – candlelit and romantic at night – at the lower end of Dong Khoi; ice creams start at $2 on a menu that also runs to filling breakfasts. 7.30am–11.30pm.

Le Pierrot Gourmand, 19 Le Thanh Ton. Behind its lurid pink doors, actually a very cosy, French-run crêperie, where you can choose between sweet or savoury crêpes, or check out the splendid homemade ice creams. 8am–11.30pm.

Spago, 158 Dong Khoi. "Terminator", "Home Alone" and other movie-inspired ice cream sundaes, alongside American dishes (see "Restaurants", p.92). 7am–11pm.

Nightlife and entertainment

Ho Chi Minh boasts a range of **nightlife** that's expanding in direct proportion to the number of foreigners hitting town, so there's no need to head back to your hotel once dinner is through. **Bars** and **pubs** abound, and an increasing number of them now feature live music to pull the crowds – normally either Filippino or local covers bands, who play safe pop-rock sets that lean heavily on Creedence Clearwater and the Eagles. Home-grown talent is on display in **Cong Vien Van Hoa Park**, on Cach Mang Thang Tam, and **Son Tra Park**, on Nguyen Thai Hoc, where Vietnamese crooners in chintzy cocktail dresses and cockatoo hairstyles belt out Western and Vietnamese pop tunes to largely local audiences. It isn't unheard of for big showbiz names from the West to make appearances, either: Bryan Adams and Joan Jett have both performed in recent years, and if another eminent visitor is coming, the local press will ensure you know all about it. Later at night, a growing number of **clubs** and **discos** get going, enabling you to continue drinking and have a boogie.

The weekly magazine *What's On in Saigon* boasts the most up-to-the-minute **listings** of the city's latest bars, plus the hottest new clubs and any more highbrow entertainment on offer.

Traditional entertainment

Few places cater for Westerners wanting an insight into **Vietnamese culture**. For Western and Vietnamese **classical music**, the best thing you can do is drop by the *Conservatory of Music* (☎839 6646) at 112 Nguyen Du, and ask about the *HCM City Youth Chamber Music Club*'s forthcoming performances. There are regular performances of modern and traditional Vietnamese music, too, at 3 Thang 2's *Hoa Binh Theatre* (☎865 5199), as well as **traditional theatre** and **dance**, and dubbed **movies**. The *Youth Cultural House* at 4 Pham Ngoc Thach (☎829 4345) is another venue that mounts varied cultural events and movies;

while Lam Son Square's Municipal Theatre hosts fashion shows, traditional drama and dance. The only real tourist-oriented venue in the city is presently the **Binh Quoi Village**, whose nightly programmes ($5) of folk music, traditional dancing and **water puppetry**, organized by *Saigontourist*, can be coupled with a Saigon River dinner-cruise (see p.94). The village is at 1147 Xo Viet Nghe Tinh (☎899 1831) – or contact *Saigontourist* (☎829 8914). Water puppetry isn't as big in Ho Chi Minh City as it is in Hanoi, though if you aren't going to the north, you might attend one of the shows laid on at the *History Museum*, Le Duan (half-hourly; $1); and at the *War Crimes Museum*, 28 Vo Van Tan (half-hourly; $2).

Bars and pubs

Bars and **pubs** have taken the city by storm: Dong Khoi is predictably well endowed, while another boozy enclave has developed around Le Thanh Ton, Don Dat and Thi Sach, where a glut of bars ranging from slick yuppie haunts to earth-ier watering-holes harking back to the raunchy GI bars of the Sixties has devel-oped to cater for expats renting apartments nearby. At the other end of the scale, all Pham Ngu Lao's travellers' cafés turn their hand to drink at night – fine if you're willing to forego atmosphere in order to save a dollar or two on a beer, and great for meeting like-minded tourists.

Bars **open** either late in the morning, to catch the lunchtime trade, or early in the evening; most are shut by 1am (though many stay open an extra hour at the weekend), but one or two keep on through the night. **Prices** vary wildly: a couple of *BGI* beers at a streetside café won't be more than $1, but you can multiply that by four or five in a more upmarket bar; wines and spirits are only available at the upper end of the market, and prices are slightly steeper. One way to economize is to take advantage of early evening **happy hours**, when bars offer either half-price drinks or two drinks for the price of one.

With competition hotting up to such an extent landlords are having to explore varied means of attracting customers, among them live music, darts, pool and *karaoke* (or *KTV*), an unholy creation whereby drunken punters take to the microphone and sing along to hits by reading lyrics off a TV screen.

Apocalypse Now, 2c Thi Sach. The pioneer of the city's second coming of bar culture, recently relocated but still as rowdy and sweaty as ever. Sandbags, *Apocalypse Now* and *Platoon* posters, and a ceiling mural of a copter firefight that incorporates fans as rotary blades create a suitably Nam-ish atmosphere. Sadly, up-front prostitution inside and drug peddlers out front blight the place for many. 6.30pm–late.

Bar Catinat, 4 Nguyen Thiep. Slick joint beside *Augustin's* whose sophisticated clientele lean against an eye-catching bar crafted from a single tree trunk. 7pm–1am.

BIA HOI BARS

If you can't afford the price of a bottle of *BGI*, you might try a **bia hoi bar**, where locals glug cheap local beer over ice by the jug-full. These spit-and-sawdust bars crop up all over the city, but the two listed below are used to the foibles of Western tourists.

Bia Hoi Nguyen Chat, 159 Pham Ngu Lao. Streetside drinking, perched on rick-ety stools, at the eastern end of Pham Ngu Lao. If you get peckish they'll rustle up some simple snacks.

Bia Hoi Thanh Nha, 6 Hai Ba Trung. Right down at the junction of Hai Ba Trung and Mac Thi Buoi, modestly located in con-verted garage space below a grim concrete icehouse, but still well patronized by locals.

Bar Rolling Stones, 177 Pham Ngu Lao. Stones fans will get off on the music, but the atmosphere is unpredictable: mean and moody when full, dark and dull when empty; come late. 7pm–3am.

Buffalo Blues, 72a Nguyen Du. Decent live jazz and blues, *Bass* and *Tennant's* on tap, darts, bar billiards and light snacks. 11am–midnight, happy hour before 8pm.

Coco Loco, 351 Pham Ngu Lao. Pleasant bar-restaurant with a clientele that combines travellers and young expats; prices drop in the afternoon. 7am–midnight.

La Dolce Vita, *Continental Hotel*, 132–134 Dong Khoi. Slightly scruffy open courtyard, shaded by frangipanis; Fowler first met Pyle, the eponymous *Quiet American*, here or hereabouts in Grahame Greene's famous novel. 11.30am–7pm.

Easy Rider, 193 Nguyen Thai Hoc. Laid-back watering-hole with a mainly French clientele; unobtrusive music, except on Fri when a band plays. 11am–3am.

Hammock Saigon, Bach Dang Quay, Ton Duc Thang. Lovingly converted sampan offering fine views of the river; shoot a game of pool in *Café Boong* (8am–11pm) or head upstairs to the noisier *Hammock Bar*. 5pm–1am, happy hours 5–8pm & midnight–1am.

Hard Rock Café, 24 Mac Thi Buoi. Unofficial addition to the Hard Rock empire; just as noisy, just as keen to hawk T-shirts, but sleazier and more affordable. 4pm–2am.

Hien & Bob's Place, 43 Hai Ba Trung. Deliberately priced above the backpacker market, but favoured by expats who come to shoot the crap with Vietnam veteran Bob. Noon–2am, happy hour 5–8pm.

Ice Blue, 54 Dong Khoi. Supposedly modelled on a traditional English pub, though the wall-to-wall risqué beer ads aren't your standard pub decor; the 30 "world beers" on sale include *Boddington's* and *Bass* (both $4), happy hour is 3–8pm and there's a free burger with your second beer at the weekend. 11am–1am.

Le Le, 171 Pham Ngu Lao. Simply the best bar on Pham Ngu Lao: great music, inexpensive *BGI* and a busy pool table; recently closed for a season, but should have re-opened by now.

Long Phi Café, 163 Pham Ngu Lao. Sussed music, pool table, bar snacks and a cosy gallery upstairs; a small *BGI* is $1. 11am–2am.

Mogambo, 20 Thi Sach. One for a lads' night out – fish and chips, steaks, pies and Mexican food, a good stock of movies on video, and waitresses poured into decidedly un-PC leopard-skin dresses; pelts on the walls emphasize the faintly sassy feel. Noon–1am.

Q Bar, 7 Lam Son Square. Easily the most stylish address in town, with 3 sumptuous candlelit chambers carved from the bowels of the theatre and decorated with lavish murals; pricey. 6pm–2am.

Red Rhino, 8a Don Dat. Pale washed walls, wicker chairs, terracotta flooring and comic-strip murals make this a cool, breezy hangout, though the odd nook and cranny wouldn't go amiss. 5pm–3am.

River Bar, 5–7 Ho Huan Nghiep. Sleek bamboo-encrusted joint that evokes colonial days: order a cocktail, recline in a rattan chair and daydream; there's table football hidden upstairs, and happy hour from 5.30 to 7.30pm. 10am–2am.

Rooftop Garden, *Rex Hotel*, 141 Nguyen Hue. Sky-high prices, but a drink amidst the fairy-lit topiary and clumsy model animals of the *Rex* terrace is still *de rigueur* on a trip to the city; green tea ($1) is the cheapest tipple on the menu.

Terrace Bar, *Thanh Thanh 2*, 205 Pham Ngu Lao. As the name suggests, a top-floor open terrace that allows you to escape the shoeshine boys' clutches; barbecues are planned for the future. 10am–1am.

Discos and clubs

Although Ho Chi Minh's **disco and club scene** is in its infancy, things are picking up rapidly, and Vietnam's increased contact with the West is reflected in the improving standards of dance music on the city's turntables. That said, clubs are still extremely naive (refreshingly so, if you're used to the studied posturing of clubbers in London or New York), and the practice of employing hostesses in slit gowns to wait on table is still prevalent. In addition, some establishments continue to cater for the locals' love of **ballroom dancing** – a tradition which is sadly fading out, as MTV turns youngsters away from the foxtrot, and towards hip-hop. All clubs and discos levy a **cover charge** (normally $6–7) entitling you to your first drink free. Again, see *What's On in Saigon* for the hottest new clubs.

Cheers, *Vien Dong Hotel*, 275a Pham Ngu Lao. Bar-disco, popular with HCM's young, hip and trendy, who seem unperturbed by the sickly pastel and neon hues of its decor; covers bands play nightly, or make your own music in a private *karaoke* room ($40 a night). Mon–Fri & Sun 8pm–1.30am, Sat 8pm–2.30am.

Downunder, *Saigon Floating Hotel*, 1 Mei Linh Square. Deep in the underbelly of the hotel, a spangly venue whose dancefloor will suit aspiring John Travoltas; cover charge applies at the weekend. 8pm–2am.

Liberty, 80 Dong Khoi. A largely Vietnamese crowd waltzes along to the smoochy live music in this incredibly dark club; disco music takes over from 10pm. 8.30pm–1am.

Maxim's, 15–17 Dong Khoi. Sedate dancing upstairs after a meal in the restaurant (see p.92). 8.30–11.30pm.

Rosy Night Club, 119 Nguyen Hue. Best on Sat nights, when foreign DJs mount *Strictly Rhythm*, and expats dance the night away under an impressive lighting rig. 8pm–2am.

Starlight, *Century Saigon*, 68a Nguyen Hue. Dayglo stars and moons adorn the walls in this dark, atmospheric eleventh-floor club, whose superb downtown views lend it a truly cosmopolitan feel. Covers band plays from 9pm; pool table, too, and happy hour (6–8pm). 6pm–1am.

Truong Son Disco, 6d Dong Khoi. Youthful expats seem to have latched onto this pitchy black disco; entry is inexpensive. 7pm–1am.

Markets and shopping

Ho Chi Minh City may be no mecca for **shopping**, but there's no shortage either of souvenir shops allowing you to stock up with gifts before departure. Paintings, silk *ao dais* and lacquerware are all popular, as are **curios** such as opium pipes, antique watches, French colonial stamps and banknotes, and US army-issue cigarette lighters. Visitors interested in Vietnam's history will find a wealth of copied **books** on the subject; while tighter budgets will be grateful for the ubiquitous T-shirts and conical hats; predictably, the best selection of gift shops is along Dong Khoi. **Bargaining** is an essential skill to cultivate if you're going to be doing much shopping – see *Basics*, p.49, for some tips.

Shopping malls haven't reached Ho Chi Minh yet (though there are two big department stores), so **markets** remain the best place to head for, for varied stock. The big daddy of them all is **Ben Thanh Market** (p.78), at the junction of Tran Hung Dao, Le Loi and Ham Nghi; Cholon's equivalent is **Binh Tay Market** (p.87), below Thap Muoi on its southwestern edge. **Thai Binh Market**, at Pham Ngu Lao's western end, is modestly proportioned, but a mere stone's throw from the travellers' enclave up the street; while **Dan Sinh Market**, 104 Nguyen Cong Tru (p.79), has a section specializing in army surplus, both American and Vietnamese. For other manageable souvenirs, check out the booths inside the GPO on Dong Khoi (and on the street itself) for old **coins**, **stamps**, notes, and **greetings cards** featuring typical Vietnamese scenes hand-painted onto silk. **Antiques and curios** are available in several stores along Le Cong Kieu (see p.79), while intriguing **model ships** are sold on the street north of the Municipal Theatre, at the eastern flank of the *Continental*.

Generally speaking, shops will be **open** daily 10am to dusk, although some shopkeepers take an extended afternoon break, while larger stores often stay open beyond 8pm.

Department stores

Cua Hang Bach Hoa, 135 Nguyen Hue. Electronic goods, watches, pirate cassettes and videos, Vietnam T-shirts and lacquerware, all signposted with signs in Russian.

ITC, 101 Nam Ky Khoi Nghia. Ho Chi Minh's slickest shopping address to date, stocking electrical goods, clothes, toiletries and souvenirs; the *Minimart* supermarket is on the first floor.

Books, newspapers and magazines

Book Store, 20 Ho Huan Nghiep. Far and away the city's best bookshop, with photocopied reprints of almost every book extant on the American War.

Books & Music Store, 243 De Tham. Secondhand books bought and sold, plus a limited selection of pirate CDs.

Bookshop 33 Passage Eden, 104–106 Nguyen Hue. Modest selection of old novels in English and French.

Lao Dong, 104 Nguyen Hue. Opposite the entrance to the *Rex*, quite the best place in town for magazines and newspapers.

Mr Conehead, 195 Pham Ngu Lao (entrance opposite *Kim Café*, on De Tham). Several shelves of paperbacks, mostly in English, as well as recent editions of the *Bangkok Post*, and magazines to read if you buy one of their ice creams.

Fabrics, handicrafts and antiques

Albert, 22 Vo Van Tan. Recommended tailor.

Ant's, 91 Mac Thi Buoi. Ceramics, old watches, French *piastres* and assorted bric-a-brac.

Bach Tuyet, 141 Dong Khoi. Pure silk *ao dai*s a speciality, as well as "artistic embroidery and painting" on silk.

Bich Lien, 125 Dong Khoi. General souvenirs-cum-handicrafts, plus a good range of Tin Tin and Disney paintings on laquer.

Emily, 15 Le Loi. Toy planes, ships and cars made out of aluminium cans.

Minh Huong, 85 Mac Thi Buoi. Hand-embroidered cotton wares.

Nap, 63 Le Thanh Ton. Fair choice of tablecloths, napkins, hand-embroidered pictures, pyjamas, and *ao dai*s.

Ngoc Bich, 112 Nguyen Du. Specialist store with an arresting range of Vietnamese musical instruments.

Phuong Tam, 153 Dong Khoi. Tin Tin lacquerware, antique watches and handicrafts.

Rex Hotel Souvenir Shop, *Rex Hotel*, 141 Nguyen Hue. A vast range of *Rex* souvenirs, from ashtrays to flower vases.

Souvenir Shop, 159 Dong Khoi. Lacquer, ivory, silverware, semiprecious stones and wood carvings.

Xa Saigon, 259 De Tham. Stocks a smattering of traditional handicrafts such as montagnard bags and cloths, and Vietnamese musical instruments.

Paintings

Bichacultural Shop, 30 Dong Khoi. Sizeable shop selling ornaments as well as paintings.

Gallerie Lotus, 47 Dong Khoi. Paintings, some on lacquerware.

Hoang Hac, 73 Ly Tu Trong. One of the city's trendier galleries, stocking some classy stuff.

Nam Phuong, 156 Dong Khoi. One of several interesting galleries on Chi Lang Park.

Tu Do Art Gallery, 142 Dong Khoi. Paintings on silk, lacquer and canvas, as well as a number of wood carvings.

World Art Gallery, 12e Pham Ngu Lao. Painstaking copies of the world's classic works.

Listings

Airlines *Air France*, 130 Dong Khoi (☎829 0981); *Cambodia International Airline*, 16 Ho Huan Nghiep (☎829 9462); *Cathay Pacific*, 49 Le Thanh Ton (☎223203); *China Airlines*, 132–134 Dong Khoi (☎825 1388); *China Southern Airlines*, 52b Pham Hong Thai (☎829 1172); *Garuda*, 106 Nguyen Hue (☎829 3644); *KLM*, 244 Pasteur (☎823 1990); *Lao Aviation*, 39/3 Tran Nhat Duat (☎844 2807); *Lufthansa*, 132–134 Dong Khoi (☎829 8529); *MAS*, 116 Nguyen Hue (☎824 2885); *Pacific Airlines*, 27b Nguyen Dinh Chieu (☎823 0930); *Philippine Airlines*, 4a Le Loi (☎829 2113); *Qantas*, third floor, Administration Bldg, Tan Son Nhat Airport (☎842 4950); *Singapore Airlines*, 6 Le Loi (☎823 1583); *Thai Airways*, Han Nam Officetel, 65 Nguyen Du (☎829 2810); *Vietnam Airlines*, 116 Nguyen Hue (☎829 2118) and 229 Pham Ngu Lao (☎832 2261).

Banks and exchange At *Vietcombank*, 29 Chuong Duong (Mon–Fri 8–11.30am & 1.30–4pm, Sat 8–11.30am), you can receive money wired from abroad. For exchange outside normal banking hours, try the *Vietcombank* bureaux within *Fiditourist*, 195 Pham Nhu Lao (Mon–Sat 7.30–11.30am & 1.30–9.30pm, Sun 8–11am & 2–4pm), opposite the *Continental* at 175 Dong Khoi (normal hours), and at the airport (daily 8am–midnight). Slightly extended hours are also on offer at *Sacombank*, on the corner of Pham Ngu Lao at 211 Nguyen Thai Hoc (daily 8–11.30am & 1.30–4pm), and at the *Thai Military Bank*, 11 Chuong Duong (Mon–Fri 8.30am–3.30pm, Sat 8.30am–noon), which has marginally better rates. Finally, hotel reception desks can often change dollars, though at poor rates.

Bike, moped and motorbike rental Most rental operations are in Pham Ngu Lao; average daily costs are $1 for a bicycle and $6 for a moped. The *Prince*, 187 Pham Ngu Lao, has bicycles and mopeds, as do *Fiditourist* at no. 195, the nameless outfit at no. 267, and *Kim Café*, 270 De Tham. At *Hotel 211*, you can also rent 250cc motorbikes for $10 per day. In the city centre, try the *Ngoc Chau Handicraft Shop*, opposite the *Rex* at 108 Nguyen Hue, where bicycle rental costs $2 per day. If you want to buy a bike, check out the *Cua Hang Bach Hoa* department store, below the *Rex* at 135 Nguyen Hue, or the stores along the western end of Le Thanh Ton. There are scores of moped shops along the western end of Ly Tu Trong, and you'll occasionally see mopeds and motorbikes advertised in Pham Ngu Lao's cafés.

Car rental Hire-cars with drivers can be arranged through tour agencies (see opposite); self-drive is not an option, as yet.

Computing facilities You can rent the use of a computer by the hour at *PC*, 214 De Tham, and the *Saigon Business Centre*, 41–47 Dong Du. Otherwise, all decent hotels have business centres.

Consulates *Australia*, Landmark, 5b Ton Duc Thanh (☎826 0935); *Cambodia*, 180 Dien Bien Phu (☎829 6814); *China*, 39 Nguyen Thi Minh Khai (☎829 2457); *France*, 27 Xo Viet Nghe Tinh (☎829 7231); *Germany*, 126 Nguyen Dinh Chieu (☎829 1967); *India*, 49 Tran Quoc Thao (☎829 4498); *Indonesia*, 18 Phung Khac Khoan (☎822 3799); *Laos*, 181 Hai Ba Trung (☎829 7667); *Malaysia*, 53 Nguyen Dinh Chieu (☎829 9023); *New Zealand*, 455 Nguyen Dinh Chieu (☎839 6227); *Singapore*, 5 Phung Khac Khoan (☎822 5173); *Thailand*, Room 662, Rex Hotel (☎829 3115); *UK*, 261 Dien Bien Phu (☎829 8433).

Courier services *DHL* is based at 253 Hoang Van Thu (☎844 4268), and has a branch at the GPO; *Airborne Express* is just below the GPO at 80c Nguyen Du (☎829 4303).

Dentists Call *St Paul Hospital*, 280 Dien Bien Phu (☎822 5052), or the *Faculty of Dentistry*, Office 9, 652 Nguyen Trai (☎855 9225); or contact the *AEA International Clinic* (see below).

Emergencies Dial ☎14 in case of fire or ☎15 for an ambulance; better still, get a Vietnamese-speaker to call on your behalf.

Export licences Apply to the *Customs Service*, 21 Ton Duc Thang (☎829 0912).

Hospitals and clinics *AEA International Clinic*, Han Nam Officetel, 65 Nguyen Du (☎829 8520) has international doctors who will see you for a flat fee of around $40, and they can also arrange emergency evacuation if necessary. Otherwise, Cholon's *Cho Ray Hospital*, at 201 Nguyen Chi Thanh (☎855 4137), has an out-patients room for foreigners ($5 per consultation) and a foreigners' ward ($25 per night); or there's the *Emergency Centre*, 125 Le Loi (☎829 2071), whose English- and French-speaking doctors charge $8 or so per consultation.

Immigration Department 254 Nguyen Trai, at the junction with Nguyen Cu Trinh.

Laundry Most hotels and guesthouses will wash clothes for you; otherwise, try the Thanh Phong Laundry Service, near *Guest House 127*, at 123 Cong Quynh. For dry cleaning, head for one of the upper-bracket hotels.

Newspapers *Lao Dong*, 108 Nguyen Hue, sells the best crop of local and international newspapers and magazines; street vendors carry recent copies of the *Bangkok Post*, *Time* and *Newsweek*, as well as local papers.

Pharmacies Two of the best are at 199 Hai Ba Trung and 14a Nguyen Dinh Chieu, or make for the cluster of pharmacies in one block, at 60 Nguyen Du.

Post offices The GPO (daily 6.30am–10.30pm) is beside the cathedral at the head of Dong Khoi; *poste restante* is kept here, but incoming faxes (☎829 8540) are held nearby at 230 Hai Ba Trung, and there's a 50¢ pick-up fee. There's also a post office beside *Guest House 127*, at the western end of Bui Vien, and handy for those staying in Pham Ngu Lao.

Sports There are tennis courts at the *Saigon Floating* and *Rex* hotels, and (cheaper) *Workers' Club*, in the northern corner of the Cong Vien Van Hoa Park, on Nguyen Thi Minh Khai. The *World Gym* is at 26 Le Thanh Ton, and the *Hash House Harriers* meet at the *Floating Hotel* every Sun afternoon; check the local press for details.

Swimming There's an inexpensive but extremely busy pool at the *Workers' Club*, Cong Vien Van Hoa Park; for a little more peace and quiet, there are hotel pools at the *Rex*, *Floating Hotel*, *Metropole* and *New World* that you can use for a daily fee of around $10.

Tampons and sanitary towels are sold at *U-Save Mart*, 53 Nguyen Du, and *Minimart*, 101 Nam Ky Khoi Nghia.

Taxis These gather outside the *Rex* in the city centre; otherwise, phone *Airport Taxis* (☎844 6666) or *Vinataxis* (☎844 2170); a short trip across the city centre costs $3, while the trip out to the airport is around $7. In addition, old French Peugeots congregate alongside Ben Thanh Bus Station, and on Pham Ngu Lao.

Telephone services There are IDD, fax and telex facilities at the GPO, beside the cathedral at the top of Dong Khoi; otherwise, IDD calls can be made (more expensively) from most hotels.

Tour agencies *Ann's Tourist*, 58 Ton That Tung (☎833 2564), comes highly recommended; *Cam On Tours*, 32 Dong Du (☎829 8443), is a friendly oufit worth trying for genuine travel advice, visa services, car rental and tours; *Diethelm Travel*, International Business Centre, 1a Me Linh Square (☎829 4932), offers well-crafted tours, but at a price. *Fiditourist*, 195 Pham Ngu Lao (☎829 6264), is very reasonable, though not as slick as *Kim* and *Sinh*. *Gateway Tours*, 75 Le Thanh Ton (☎844 1187), specializes in treks to Cat Tien National Park, and mountain-biking tours are planned for the future. *Kim Café*, 270 De Tham (☎835 9859), is a veteran of the independent travel scene, with a popular and affordable Mekong Delta trip, plus longer trips and visa services. *Peace Tours*, 60 Vo Van Tan (☎829 0923), offers tours of up to one month, car hire ($36 per day), and *Vietnam Airlines* ticketing. *Sinh Café*, 179 Pham Ngu Lao (☎835 5601), is a pioneering travellers' café-cum-tour agency, offering cut-price, countrywide minibus tours, visa services, airport shuttles and car rental. Tours offered by the state-run agencies, *Saigontourist*, 49 Le Thanh Ton (☎829 8914), and *Vietnamtourism*, Room 101, Mondial Center, 203 Dong Khoi (☎824 2000), and 234 Nam Ky Khoi Nghia (☎829 0776), tend to be rather mediocre – and overpriced.

AROUND HO CHI MINH CITY

When Ho Chi Minh's chaotic streets become too much for you, you'll find you can get quite a long way **out of the city** in a day. With public transport slow and erratic, day-trips are best arranged through a tour agency (see above), though public buses also ply the routes. The single most popular trip out of the city takes in two of Vietnam's most memorable sights: the **Cu Chi tunnels**, for twenty years a bolthole, first for Viet Minh agents, and later for Viet Cong cadres; and the weird and wonderful **Cao Dai Holy See at Tay Ninh**, the fulcrum of the country's most charismatic indigenous religion. Southwest of the city Highway 1 runs

MOVING ON FROM HO CHI MINH CITY

For addresses and telephone numbers of airlines and foreign consulates in Ho Chi Minh City, see "Listings" p.104. Some sample fares to and from stations are given in the box on p.65.

PLANES

The easiest way to get to Tan Son Nhat is by taxi (see p.65), but if you're travelling solo it's more economical to sign up with *Sinh Café* or one of the other Pham Ngu Lao operations advertising airport shuttles ($2–5, depending on passenger numbers). If you save a few dollars by taking a cyclo or Honda om, be aware that you'll be dropped outside the gates, a few hundred metres from the departures terminal. Note, also, that there's a **departure tax** of $8 levied on all international flights, and of $1.50 on trips within Vietnam. **Flight enquiries** should be made at the office of the relevant carrier (see "Airlines", p.104).

TRAINS

Vietnamese trains are over-subscribed, so it's sensible to book as far ahead as possible – particularly if you want a sleeping berth (see p.27 for details). Travel agents and some hotels will help you out for a commission, but to be sure of getting what you want, go along in person: ignore the bank of counters on the right as you enter the station concourse and continue on to the **foreigners' enquiries counter** (daily 7–11am & 1–3pm; ☎844 3952), beside which a board details all arrivals and departures in English; a small charge is made for reservations. Beyond this counter, there's a **money changer** (Mon–Sat 8am–4pm) that changes dollars for dong at a competitive rate. The main station, *Ga Saigon*, is a fifteen-minute cyclo ride from the city centre.

BUSES AND TAXIS

To the Mekong Delta: the easiest way of kicking off a tour of the Mekong Delta, is to take a *Saigon Star Co* bus (p.66) to **Cholon Bus Station**, from where there are frequent departures throughout the day to My Tho (p.117). For all other destinations, you'll need to travel to distant **Mien Tay Bus Station**, just off Hung Vuong on the western edge of the city, where several buses a day leave for all the delta's major towns except Ha Tien (daily 5am & 3pm). Xe lams leave for Mien Tay from opposite the *Easy Rider Bar* on Nguyen Thai Hoc; or there are hourly buses from nearby Ben Thanh Bus Station. A cyclo costs $3 (but it's a very long haul) as does a Honda om.
To Vung Tau and the north: buses to **points north** depart from Xo Viet Nghe Tinh's **Mien Dong Bus Station**. More distant towns and cities are only served by one or two buses a day, and with these tending to leave well before dawn, it's wise to buy a ticket in advance – these are on sale at a blue one-storey building, marked "Phong Ve Toc Hanh" (daily 5am–4pm), to your left as you enter the terminal. Again, buses and xe lams run up to Mien Dong from Ben Thanh Bus Station.
   If you're heading for either **Da Lat** or **Phan Thiet**, however, your best bet is to take one of the regular minibus services from **Van Thanh Bus Station** on Dien

down to **My Tho** (see *The Mekong Delta*, p.117), where you can catch a glimpse of the Mekong River; while to the northeast, it breezes up to the dreary orbital city of **BIEN HOA**, from where Highway 51 drops down to the beaches of **Vung Tau** (see *The South-Central Coast*, p.187). Though both can be reached within a day, they really warrant an overnight stay.

Bien Phu. Van Thanh isn't presently accessible by local bus so you'll have to take a taxi, cyclo or similar. There are also frequent minibus departures to **Vung Tau** from Van Thanh, but it's far easier to pick up a Vung Tau shuttle in town – either along Ham Nghi, or opposite the mosque on downtown Dong Du.

Finally, buses bound for **Cu Chi and Tay Ninh** work out of the **Tay Ninh Station**, west of the airport. Buses to the station depart regularly from below Ben Thanh Market, from where there are also some direct services to Cu Chi Town.

To Cambodia: buses bound for Phnom Penh leave daily from the garage at 145 Nguyen Du, though you'll need to buy your ticket at 155 Nguyen Hue a day before departure – and you'll need a Cambodian visa (allow at least 7 days for processing); the consulate is at 180 Dien Bien Phu (☎829 6814). Another option is to sign up for a shared **taxi** in Pham Ngu Lao ($20–25 for a full car); this will take you as far as the **Moc Bai border crossing**, from where you can walk over the border and connect with a local bus ($5) to Phnom Penh. Note that the political situation in Cambodia is unpredictable, to put it mildly, and that tourists have been targeted by guerrilla groups; seek advice before travelling here.

BOATS

Hydrofoils to Vung Tau should once again be operational by the time you read this, after a lengthy lay-off – enquire at the Passengers Quay of Ho Chi Minh City for details.

In addition, cargo **boats to the delta** are sometimes prepared to take passengers on board, space allowing. Their docking sites are subject to change, but presently they leave from one of two places – Ton That Thuyet (cross the bridge at the end of Calmette, turn right onto Ton Dan and then right again at the waterfront), or in Cholon at the junction of Chu Van An and Tran Van Kieu. The image of a slow boat up the Mekong may sound romantic, but don't be deluded: the vessels are slow, old and potentially dangerous, and run to no discernible schedule. What's more, once upriver you are at the mercy of the crew, and could find that the quoted fare rises dramatically. All in all, you'll probably have a more relaxing time if you make your way to the delta by land, and then go about arranging a boat trip once there.

ORGANIZED TOURS

Tour agencies abound in Ho Chi Minh and offer a range of itineraries, from one-day whistle-stop tours around the region, to lengthy trips upcountry. Tours can be arranged either at a travellers' café, or through a private company or (more expensive) state-run agent; operators on Pham Ngu Lao generally offer the most competitive prices. Popular jaunts include a one-day trip to Tay Ninh and the Cu Chi tunnels, for around $5; two- or three-day tours of the Mekong Delta; the ten-day trawl up to Hué, taking in the central highlands and the south-central coast en route; and even all the way to Hanoi – though the overnight train from Hué to the capital is a better option. Tours travel by **bus** or **minibus**, depending upon passenger numbers, and operators can also lay on **private cars** and personal **guides** for you.

Recommended tour agencies are listed on p.105; see *Basics*, p.30 for provisos and tips on signing up for a tour in Vietnam.

The Cu Chi tunnels

During the American War, the villages around the district of **Cu Chi** supported a substantial VC presence; faced with American attempts to neutralize them, they quite literally dug themselves out of harm's way, and the legendary **Cu Chi tunnels** were the result. Today, tourists can visit a short stretch of the tunnels, drop to their hands and knees and squeeze underground for an insight into life as a tunnel-dwelling resistance fighter. The tunnels have been widened to allow passage for the fuller frame of Westerners but it's still a dark, sweaty, claustrophobic experience, and not one you should rush into unless you're confident you won't suffer a subterranean freak-out.

There are two sites where you can see tunnels: Ben Dinh and, 15km beyond, **Ben Duoc** ($4), which has the dubious additional attractions of a grounded helicopter and a firing range. By far the most popular and convenient site is **Ben Dinh** (daily 8am–5pm; $2), which is best reached by taking a **tour** out of Ho Chi Minh City (see p.107): most combine Cu Chi with the Cao Dai Cathedral, described on p110. If you don't want to squeeze into a minibus, four people will pay around $40 for a **taxi** following the same itinerary. **Buses** covering the 30km to **CU CHI** town depart from Ben Thanh and Tay Ninh stations in Ho Chi Minh (see p.107), but from the town you'll need to take a Honda om for the final 10km to the site; on a **motorbike**, turn right off the highway when you reach Cu Chi post office.

The **guided tour** of Ben Dinh kicks off in a **classroom**, where a wall chart, a cross-section of the tunnels and an inaudible movie fill you in on the background. From there, you head out into the bush, where **tripwires** connected to fire-crackers are rigged up to give a taste of the fear factor for American GIs who had to search for tunnels. Your guide will point out lethal booby traps, a tiny trap-door and an abandoned tank, but it's the **tunnels** themselves that are most thought-provoking; while negotiating them, bear in mind that people lived below ground here for weeks on end.

Digging the tunnels

When the first spades sank into the earth around Cu Chi, the region was covered by a rubber plantation tied to a French tyre company. Anti-colonial **Viet Minh** dug the first tunnels here, in the late 1940s; intended primarily for storing arms, they soon became valuable hiding places for the resistance fighters themselves. Over a decade later, **Viet Cong** (VC) activists controlling this staunchly anti-government area, many of them local villagers, followed suit and went to ground. By 1965, 250km of tunnels criss-crossed Cu Chi and surrounding areas – just across the Saigon River was the notorious guerrilla power base known as the **Iron Triangle** – making it possible for the VC guerrilla cells in the area to link up with each other, and to infiltrate Saigon at will; one section daringly ran underneath the Americans' Cu Chi Army Base.

Though the region's compacted red clay was perfectly suited to tunnelling, and lay above the water-level of the Saigon River, the **digging parties** faced a multitude of problems. Quite apart from the snakes and scorpions they encountered as they laboured with their hoes and crowbars, there was the problem of inconspicuously disposing of the soil by spreading it in bomb craters or scattering it in the river under cover of darkness. With a tunnel dug, ceilings had to be shored up securely: after American bombing made timber scarce, the tunnellers had to resort to stealing iron fence posts from enemy bases. Tunnels could be as small as 80cm wide and 80cm high, and were sometimes four levels deep; **vent shafts** (to disperse smoke and aromas from underground ovens) were camouflaged by thick grass and termites' nests. In order to throw the Americans' dogs off the scent, pepper was sprinkled around vents, and sometimes the VC even washed with the same scented soap used by GIs.

Tunnel life

Living conditions below ground were appalling for these tenacious "human moles". Tunnels were foul-smelling, and became so hot in the early afternoon, that inhabitants had to lie on the floor in order to get enough oxygen to breathe. The darkness was so profound that some long-term dwellers suffered temporary blindness upon reaching the surface. At times it was necessary to stay below ground for weeks on end, in living quarters shared with bats, rats, snakes, scorpions, centipedes and fire ants. Some of these unwelcome guests were co-opted to the cause: boxes full of scorpions and hollow bamboo sticks containing vipers were secreted in tunnels, where GIs might unwittingly knock them over.

Within the multi-level tunnel complexes, there were latrines, wells, meeting rooms and dorms. Rudimentary **hospitals** were also scratched out of the soil: operations were carried out by torchlight using instruments fashioned from shards of ordnance, and a patient's own blood was caught in bottles and then pumped straight back using a bicycle pump and a length of rubber hosing. Such medical supplies as existed were secured by bribing South Vietnamese Army (ARVN) soldiers in Saigon; doctors also administered herbs and acupuncture – even honey was prized for its antiseptic properties. **Kitchens** cooked whatever the tunnellers could get their hands on. Once American chemical weapons and artillery had destroyed rice and fruit crops, this meant a meagre diet of tapioca, leaves and roots, unless enough bomb fragments could be transported to Saigon and sold as scrap to buy food. Maintaining morale was a constant challenge, one met in part by **performing troupes** that toured the tunnels, though their politically correct songs – "He who comes to Cu Chi, the Bronze Fortress in the Land of Iron, will count the crimes accumulated by the Enemy" was one – were hardly in Bob Hope's league.

The end of the line

American attempts to **flush out** the tunnels proved ineffective. Operating out of huge bases erected around Saigon in the mid-Sixties, they evacuated villagers into strategic hamlets and then used defoliant sprays and bulldozers to rob the VC of cover, in "scorched earth" operations such as January 1967's **Cedar Falls**. Even then, tunnels were rarely effectively destroyed – one soldier at the time compared the task to "fill[ing] the Grand Canyon with a pitchfork". GIs would lob down gas or grenades or else go down themselves, armed only with a torch, a knife and a pistol; those die-hard soldiers who specialized in such underground activities came to be known as **tunnel rats**, their unofficial insignia *Insigni Non Gratum Anus Rodentum*, meaning "not worth a rat's arse". Booby traps made of sharpened bamboo stakes awaited them in the dark, as well as "bombs" made from Coke cans and dud bullets found on the surface. Tunnels were low and narrow, though, and entrances so small that GIs often couldn't get down them, even if they could locate them. Maverick war correspondent Wilfred Burchett, travelling with the NLF in 1964, found his Western girth a distinct impediment: "On another occasion I got stuck passing from one tunnel section to another. In what seemed a dead end, a rectangular plug was pulled out from the other side, and, with some ahead pulling my arms and some pushing my buttocks from behind, I managed to get through...I was transferred to another tunnel entrance built especially to accommodate a bulky unit cook".

Another of the Americans' diverse tactics aimed at **weakening the resolve** of the VC guerrillas involved dropping leaflets and broadcasting bulletins that played on the fighters' fears and loneliness. Although this prompted numerous desertions, the tunnellers were still able to mastermind the **Tet Offensive** of 1968. Ultimately, the Americans resorted to more strong-arm tactics to neutralize the tunnels, sending in the B52s freed by the cessation of bombing of the North in 1968 to level the district with **carpet bombing**. The VC's infrastructure was decimated by Tet, and further weakened by the **Phoenix Programme** (see p.423). By this time, though, the tunnels had played their part in proving to America that the war was unwinnable. At least 12,000 Vietnamese guerrillas and sympathizers are thought to have perished here during the American War, and the terrain was laid waste – pockmarked by bomb craters, devoid of vegetation, even the air poisoned by lingering fumes.

The Cao Dai Holy See at Tay Ninh

Above Cu Chi, Highway 22 pushes on northwestward through idyllic paddy flatlands. After several kilometres the highway runs through **TRANG BANG**, where the photographer Nick Ut captured one of the war's most horrific and incisive images – that of a naked girl with her back in flames running along the highway, fleeing a napalm attack. A sign marked "Tay Ninh 10km, Long Hoa 4km" signals the turning off the highway to **LONG HOA**, the site of the enigmatic **Cao Dai Cathedral**, or Great Temple, of the Holy See of Tay Ninh District. **Joss-stick factories** line the road into Long Hoa, their produce bundled into mini-haystacks by the roadside to dry; around 4km later you reach Long Hoa's **market**, from where the cathedral itself is another 2km. **Buses** to Tay Ninh depart from Ho Chi Minh City's Tay Ninh Bus Station, but a **tour** is preferable (see p.107).

The cathedral

A grand gateway marks the entrance to the grounds of the 1927-built Cao Dai Cathedral. Beyond it, a wide boulevard escorts you past a swathe of grassland used on ceremonial occasions, to the wildly exotic cathedral itself, over whose left shoulder rises distant **Nui Ba Den**, Black Lady Mountain.

On first sighting, the **Cathedral** seems to be subsiding, an optical illusion created by the rising steps inside it, but your first impressions are more likely to be dominated by what Graham Greene described as a "Walt Disney fantasia of the East, dragons and snakes in Technicolor". Despite its dayglo hues and rococo clutter, this surreally gaudy construction somehow manages to bypass tackiness. Two square, pagoda-style **towers** bookend the front facade, whose central portico is topped by a bowed, first-floor balcony and a **Divine Eye**. The most recurrent motif in the cathedral, the eye is surrounded by a triangle, as it is on an American dollar bill. A figure in semi-relief emerges from each tower: on the left is Cao Daism's first female cardinal, Lam Huong Thanh, and on the right, Le Van Trung, its first pope.

The eclectic ideology of Cao Daism is mirrored in the **interior**. Part-cathedral and part-pagoda, it draws together a pot-pourri of icons and elements under a vaulted ceiling, and daubs them all with the primary colours of a Hindu temple, to create Norman Lewis's vision of "fun-fair architecture in extreme form…one expected continually to hear bellowing laughter relayed from some nearby Tunnel of Love". Men enter the cathedral through an entrance in the right wall, women by a door to the left, and all must take off their shoes. Inside the lobby, a

mural shows the three "signatories of the 3rd Alliance between God and Mankind": French poet Victor Hugo and the fifteenth-century Vietnamese poet, Nguyen Binh Khiem, are writing the Cao Dai principles of "God and humanity, love and justice" in French and Chinese onto a shining celestial tablet. Beside

CAO DAISM

The basic tenets of **Cao Daism** were first revealed to **Ngo Van Chieu**, a civil servant working in the criminal investigation department of the French administration on Phu Quoc Island, at the beginning of the 1920s. A spiritualist, Ngo was contacted during a seance by a superior spirit calling itself Cao Dai, or "high place". This spirit communicated to him the basics of the Cao Daist creed, and instructed him to adopt the Divine Eye as a tangible representation of its existence. Posted back in Saigon soon afterwards, Ngo set about evangelizing, though according to French convert and chronicler Gabriel Gobron, the religion didn't gather steam until late in 1925, when Ngo was contacted by a group of mediums sent his way by the Cao Dai.

At this stage, **revelations** from the Cao Dai began to add further meat to the bones of the religion. Twice already, it informed its mediums, it had revealed itself to Mankind, using such vehicles as Lao Tzu, Christ, Mohammed, Moses, Sakyamuni and Confucius to propagate a range of systems of belief tailored to suit localized cultures. Such religious intolerance had resulted from this multiplicity, that for the **third alliance** it intended to do away with earthly messengers, and convey a universal religion via such unlikely spirit intermediaries as Louis Pasteur, William Shakespeare, Joan of Arc, Sir Winston Churchill and Napoleon Bonaparte. The revelations of these "saints" were received using a **planchette** (a pencil secured to a wooden board on castors, on which the medium rests his hand, sometimes known as a *corbeille à bec*).

Though a **fusion** of Oriental and Occidental religions, propounding the concept of a **universal god**, Cao Daism is primarily entrenched in Buddhism, Taoism and Confucianism, to which cause-and-effect creeds, elements of Christianity, Mohammedanism and spirituality are added. By following its five commandments – Cao Daists must avoid killing living beings, high living, covetousness, verbal deceit and the temptations of the flesh – adherents look to hasten the evolution of the soul through re-incarnation.

The religion was effectively **founded** in October 1926, when it was also officially recognized by the French colonial administration. Borrowing the structure and terminology of the Catholic Church, Cao Daism began to grow rapidly, its emphasis upon simplicty appealing to disaffected peasants, and by 1930 there were 500,000 followers. In 1927, Tay Ninh became the Cao Daists' Holy See; Ngo opted out of the papacy, and the first pope was **Le Van Trung**, a decadent mandarin from Cholon who had seen the error of his ways after being visited by the Cao Dai during a seance.

Inevitably in such uncertain times, Cao Daism developed a **political agenda**. Strongly anti-French during World War II, subsequently the Cao Daist militia turned against the Viet Minh, with whom they fought, using French arms, in the first Indochina War. By the mid-Fifties, the area around Tay Ninh was a virtual Cao Daist fiefdom; in *The Quiet American*, Graham Greene describes the Cao Dai militia as a "private army of 25,000 men, armed with mortars made out of the exhaust-pipes of old cars, allies of the French who turned neutral at the moment of danger". Even then, though, they were feuding with the rival Hoa Hao sect, and within a few years, their political clout had waned.

Post-liberation, the communist government confiscated all Cao Daist land, though it was returned ten years later. Today, the religion continues to thrive in its twin power bases of Tay Ninh District and the Mekong Delta.

them, the Chinese nationalist leader Sun Yat Sen holds an inkstone, a symbol of "Chinese civilization allied to Christian civilization giving birth to Cao Daist doctrine", according to a nearby sign.

Tourists are welcome to wander through the **nave** of the cathedral, as long as they remain in the aisles, and don't stray between the rows of **pink pillars**, entwined by green dragons, that march up the chamber. Cut-away **windows** punctuate the outer walls, their grillework consisting of the Cao Daist Divine Eye, surrounded by bright pink lotus blooms. Walk up the shallow steps that lend the nave its segmented, centipedal litheness, and you'll reach an **altar** that groans under its weight of its assorted vases, fruit, paintings and slender statues of storks. The **papal chair** stands at the head of the chamber, its arms carved into dragons; below it are six more chairs, three with eagle arms, and three with lion arms, for the cardinals. Dominating the chamber, though, and guarded by eight scary silver dragons, a vast, duck-egg-blue **sphere**, speckled with stars, rests on a polished, eight-sided dias; the ubiquitous Divine Eye peers through clouds painted on the front. You'll see more spangly stars and fluffy clouds if you look up at the sky-blue **ceiling**, in whose mouldings of lions and turtles, swallows have nested.

Services

Services are held daily at 6am, noon, 6pm and midnight; tours usually arrange their visit to coincide with the midday one. Tourists are shepherded past the traditional **band** that plays behind the front balcony, and up into the gods, from where they can look down on proceedings and take photographs. Most worshippers dress in white robes, though some dress in yellow, blue and red, to signify the Buddhist, Taoist and Confucian elements of Cao Daism. Priests don squared hats emblazoned, predictably enough, with the Divine Eye. At the start of a service worshippers' heads nod, like a field of corn in the breeze, in time to the clanging of a gong. Then a haunting, measured chanting begins, against the insect whine of the string band playing its own time. As prayers and hymns continue, incense, flowers, alcohol and tea are offered up to the Supreme Being.

travel details

Buses

It's almost impossible to give the frequency with which buses run. Though scheduled, long-distance public buses won't depart if empty. Moreover, private services, often minibuses or pick-ups, ply more popular routes such as the one to Vung Tau, and depart only when they have enough passengers to make the journey worthwhile. It's advisable to start your journey early – most long-distance departures leave between 5 and 9am, and few run after midday. Journey times can also vary; figures below show the normal length of time you can expect the journey to take.

Ho Chi Minh City to: Buon Me Thuot (16hr); Ca Mau (10hr); Can Tho (4hr); Chau Doc (8hr); Da Lat (8hr); Da Nang (26hr); Hanoi (49hr); Ha Tien (10hr); Hué (28hr); My Tho (1hr 30min); Nha Trang (11hr); Phan Thiet (5hr); Qui Nhon (18hr); Vung Tau (2hr).

Trains
Ho Chi Minh City to:
Da Nang (4 daily; 18hr 30min–25hr 10min); Dieu Tri (4 daily; 12hr 12min–16hr); Hanoi (3 daily; 40–44hr); Hué (4 daily; 22hr–29hr 30min); Muong Man (4 daily; 4hr 10min–4hr 50min); Nam Dinh (3 daily; 37hr 30min–41hr 30min); Nha Trang (4

daily; 8–11hr 10min); Ninh Binh (3 daily; 37–41hr);
Quang Ngai (3 daily; 19hr 40min); Thap Cham (4
daily; 7hr 20min– 8hr); Vinh (3 daily; 33–36hr).

Hydrofoils
Ho Chi Minh City to: Vung Tau (2 daily, when
services resume – see p.64).

Flights
Ho Chi Minh City to: Buon Me Thuot (2 daily;
50min); Da Lat (2 daily; 1hr 50min); Da Nang (5
daily; 1hr); Haiphong (2–3 daily; 2hr); Hanoi (9 daily;
2hr); Hué (3 daily; 1hr 40min); Nha Trang (2 daily;
50min); Phu Quoc (5 weekly; 50min); Plei Ku (1 daily;
1hr 15min); Qui Nhon (5 weekly; 1hr 10min).

CHAPTER TWO

THE MEKONG DELTA

Touring the orchards, paddy fields and swamplands of the **MEKONG DELTA**, you could easily be forgiven for thinking you've stepped onto the pages of a geography textbook. A comma-shaped flatland stretching from Ho Chi Minh's city limits southwest to the Gulf of Thailand, the delta is Vietnam's **rice bowl**, an agricultural wonderland capable of pumping out 38 percent of the country's annual food crop from a mere ten percent of its total land mass. Rice may be the delta's staple crop, but coconut palms, fruit orchards and sugar-cane groves also thrive in its nutrient-rich soil, and to witness these abundant harvests being tended by conical-hatted farmers is to glimpse one of Vietnam's most enduring images. To the Vietnamese, the region is known as *Cuu Long*, "Nine Dragons", a reference to the nine tributaries of the mighty **Mekong River** which dovetail across plains fashioned by millennia of flood-borne alluvial sediment. By the time it reaches Vietnam, the Mekong has already covered more than 4000km from its source high up on the Tibetan Plateau; en route it traverses southern China, skirts Burma (Myanmar), then hugs the Laos–Thailand border before cutting down through Cambodia and into Vietnam – a journey that ranks it as Asia's third-longest river, after the Yangtse and Yellow rivers. **Flooding** has always blighted the delta; ever since Indian traders imported their advanced methods of irrigation more than eighteen centuries ago, the remedy has been to score the landscape with canals in order to channel off excess water, but the rainy season still claims lives from time to time.

Surprisingly, agriculture gripped the delta only relatively recently. Under **Cambodian** sway until the close of the seventeenth century, the region was sparsely inhabited by the *Khmer krom*, or "downstream Khmers", whose settlements were framed by swathes of marshland. The eighteenth century saw the Viet **Nguyen lords** steadily broaden their sphere of influence to encompass the delta, though by the 1860s, **France** had taken over the reins of government. Sensing the huge profits to be gleaned from such fertile land, French *colons* spurred Vietnamese peasants to tame and till tracts of the boggy delta; and the peasants, realizing their colonial governors would pay well for rice harvests, were quick to comply. Ironically, the same landscape that had served the French so well also provided valuable cover for the Viet Minh resistance fighters who sought to overthrow them; as indeed it did later for the Viet Cong, who had well-hidden cells here – inciting the Americans to strafe the area with bombs and defoliants.

One of the most attractive aspects of the Mekong Delta is its **diversity**. Some visitors would single out its sweeping panoramas of paddy, fruit orchards and Khmer pagodas, others the friendliness of its people; but for most, it's the delta's skein of **waterways, canals and tributaries** that makes the region so special. It's difficult to overplay the influence of the river: the lifeblood of the rice and fruit crops grown here, it's also a crucial means of transportation, teeming with craft that range in size from impossibly delicate rowing boats to hulking sampans, and

PROVINCES

1 An Giang   7 Vinh Long
2 Dong Thap   8 Ben Tre
3 Long An   9 Soc Trang
4 Tien Giang   10 Tra Vinh
5 Kien Giang   11 Minh Hai
6 Can Tho

it forms a backdrop to everyday activities – some of the region's biggest markets are waterborne. One of the most enjoyable ways to experience riverine life is on a **boat trip**, though there's also much to be said for settling down at a waterfront café to watch the sunset while sipping at an iced coconut.

My Tho has traditionally been a first stop in the delta, and with good reason: near enough to Ho Chi Minh to be seen on a day-trip, the town affords an appetizing glimpse of the delta's northernmost tributary, the Tien Giang, and is well geared-up for boat trips. From My Tho, laid-back **Ben Tre** and the bounteous fruit orchards besieging it are only a hop and a skip away. **Cao Lanh** is strictly for bird enthusiasts but **Sa Dec**, with its timeless river scenes and riotously colourful flower markets, has a far more universal appeal; while just down the road, **Vinh Long** is another jumping-off point for boat trips.

Most visitors take a day or two out in **Can Tho**, taking advantage of its crop of decent hotels and restaurants to recharge batteries, before venturing out to the fascinating **floating markets** nearby. From Can Tho, there's something to be said for dropping down to the foot of the delta, where the swampland that surrounds **Ca Mau** can be explored by boat. Pulling up, en route, at the Khmer stronghold of **Soc Trang** is especially rewarding if your trip coincides with the colourful *Ghe Ngo Festival*, during which the local Khmer community takes to the river to stage spectacular longboat races. Northwest of Can Tho meanwhile, and a mere stone's throw from the Cambodian border, is **Chau Doc**, an ebullient town below which **Sam Mountain** provides a welcome undulation to the surrounding plains. A bustling fishing port due south of Chau Doc on the Gulf of Thailand, **Rach Gia** is the place to catch a boat to remote **Phu Quoc Island**, whose splendid beaches are set to promote it to the top drawer of tourism in future years. North of Rach Gia, **Ha Tien**, a delightful border town surrounded by Khmer villages, represents the end of the line – though before you get up this far, be sure to investigate the charming beach, accessed via a pagoda hewn into a rockface, at **Hon Chong**.

Given its seasonal flooding, **the best time to visit** the delta is, predictably enough, in the dry season, which runs from December to May.

Getting around the delta

Most visitors hurtle around on a **tour bus** out of Ho Chi Minh City, but this denies you the chance to sink into the beguilingly languid quality of life in the delta. With time in hand, it's far more satisfying to take **local transport** – not nearly as daunting a prospect as it is up the coast, since the number of settlements boasting hotels means journeys can be kept relatively short. Buses have to stop occasionally at the **ferries** which make road travel in the delta possible until the long-mooted bridges are constructed, though these enforced halts are enlivened by strolling hawkers. Locals do some of their travelling on the **passenger and cargo boats** that crawl around the delta's waterways, and some tourists have a wild time doing likewise. However, these decrepit vessels tend to be poorly maintained, and there have also been reports of travellers agreeing on a price, only to get ripped off once out on the water. For the determined, we've mentioned a few of the more accessible stopping points in this chapter, though remember that these boats run to the sketchiest of schedules.

Travelling by road, you'll encounter a complicated mesh of roads and ferry crossings as you progress through the delta. From Ho Chi Minh City, **Highway 1** bears southwest towards My Tho, from where a ferry crosses the uppermost strand of the **Tien Giang** to Ben Tre. Probing deeper into the delta from Ben Tre means hacking cross-country, so it's easier to return, via My Tho, to the highway, which pushes on west. Most tourists negotiate the main body of the Tien Giang on the **My Thuan ferry**, which is convenient for visting Sa Dec, Vinh Long or Tra Vinh; there's another, smaller ferry at **Cao Lanh**, if you want to make a bee-line for Long Xuyen and on towards the Cambodian border.

Both ferries deposit you on the "island" between the two channels, from where you'll need to traverse the **Hau Giang**: ferries cross to Long Xuyen or, further south, to Can Tho. At **Can Tho**, Highway 1 runs south to the remote mangrove swamps of Ca Mau, from where the only way out is to retrace your steps. A second road runs northwest from Can Tho to Long Xuyen, the eastern corner of the square of settlements formed in the delta's northwestern extremities by Chau Doc, Rach Gia and Ha Tien. From Chau Doc there are two alternative ways to reach the delta's northwestern coastline: Ha Tien is accessible by boat along border-hugging **Vinh Te Canal**, though most people backtrack through Long Xuyen and then forge across the somewhat grim road to Rach Gia.

My Tho and around

Southwest of Ho Chi Minh City, buses plying Highway 1 soon emerge from the city's unkempt urban sprawl and into the pastoral surrounds of the Mekong Delta's upper plains. The delta is too modest to flaunt its full beauty so soon, but ricefields stretching beyond the scruffy settlements draped along the highway hint tantalizingly at things to come, their burnished golds and brilliant greens broken only by the occasional white ancestral grave. Seventy kilometres out of Ho Chi Minh City, a left fork marks the turning to **MY THO**, an amiable market town that nestles on the north bank of the Mekong River's northernmost strand, the Tien Giang, or Upper River. My Tho's proximity to Ho Chi Minh City means that it soaks up much of the volume of tourism headed for the delta, resulting in a central jumble of hotels, restaurants and cafés that won't be to everyone's taste. Nevertheless, the town comes as a great relief after the onslaught of Ho Chi Minh city its uncrowded boulevards belying a population of around 150,000, and you can easily escape the central melee by hopping on to a boat.

My Tho's recent influx of visitors seems appropriate, given its history. Chinese immigrants fleeing Formosa (modern-day Taiwan) after the collapse of the Ming dynasty established the town in the late seventeenth century, along with a Vietnamese population keen to make inroads into this traditionally Khmer-dominated region. Two centuries later the French, wooed by the district's abundant rice and fruit crops, rated it highly enough to post a garrison here, and to lay a (now-defunct) rail line to Saigon; while the American War saw a consistent military presence in town. Today My Tho's commercial importance is as pronounced as ever, something a walk through the busy town market amply illustrates.

Arrival, information and accommodation

Buses terminate at Tien Giang bus station, 3km northwest of town, from where cyclos shuttle into the centre. Onward departures are from the same place, though with direct connections leaving before dawn, you'll probably need to take a bus to the My Thuan ferry (see p.124) and transfer onto a service along the highway. Cargo/passenger **boats** heading deeper into the delta use the jetty

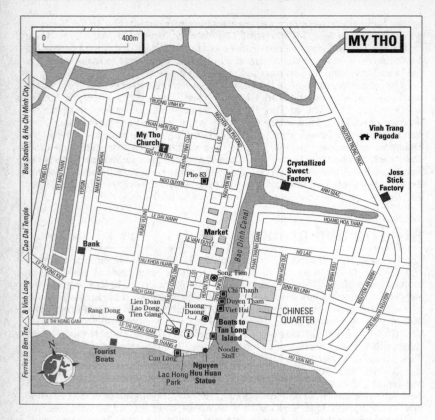

below Vong Nho Market, 200m west of the foot of Tran Hung Dao (departures to Vinh Long daily at noon; $1.50).

Cyclos are in plentiful supply around town, and a gaggle of Honda oms await custom at the junction of Trung Trac and Thu Khoa Huan, though for more flexibility you may consider renting a bicycle ($1 per day) from either the *Song Tien* or *Huong Duong* hotels (see below), or a car plus driver from *Tien Giang Tourist*, whose office is at no. 65, 30 Thang 4 (☎073/873184). The *State Bank*, two blocks north of here at Thu Khoa Huan's western end, is at present the only place in town that will **change** cash and travellers' cheques.

Accommodation

The *Lien Doan Lao Dong Tien Giang* (☎073/872166; ①), beside the GPO on 30 Thang 4, has spartan but light double rooms that can accommodate up to four people. The *Rang Dong* (☎073/874410; ②), 300m west along the street, is pricier but correspondingly smarter, its better rooms boasting air-con and hot water. Of two appreciably seedier hotels around the corner in Trung Trac, the six-storey *Song Tien* (☎073/872009; ①) is marginally the better bet, and a long-overdue

---

ACCOMMODATION PRICE CODES

All accommodation listed in this guide has been categorized according to the following scale:

① under US$10 (under 110,000 dong)　② US$10–15 (110–165,000 dong)
③ US$15–30 (165–330,000 dong)　④ US$30–75 (330–825,000 dong)
⑤ US$75–150 (825–1,650,000 dong)　⑥ over US$150 (over 1,650,000 dong)

Rates are for the cheapest available double or twin room; breakfast is not usually included. During holiday periods, rates are liable to rise, and proprietors may be less amenable to bargaining. Although the law requires prices to be quoted in dong, most hotels also give their rates in US$; payment can be made in either currency. *For a more detailed discussion of accommodation, see pp.31–34.*

---

should improve it considerably; its grotty near-neighbour, the *Huong Duong* (☎073/872011; ①), is strictly a last resort.

The town

The abiding reason for a trip to My Tho is to explore its surrounding waterways by boat (see "Around My Tho: boat trips on the delta" overleaf), but land-lubbers will get a working impression of the majestic Tien Giang by strolling along waterfront **30 Thang 4**. The river's relentless traffic – which ranges from elegant sampans to vast, lumbering junks, unpainted and crude – is best viewed from **Lac Hong Park**, at the street's eastern end. Also visible from here is the clot of cheery blue fishing vessels which moor at the mouth of the Bao Dinh Canal, while cargos are humped up and down precariously bowed gangplanks; feline eyes painted on their prows supposedly enable them to navigate. At night, the park's pine trees provide cover for young lovers; while men play shuttlecock football on the street above, under the intent gaze of a statue of nineteenth-century anti-French hero Nguyen Huu Huan, who studied in My Tho.

Follow the direction of the canal up past Trung Trac's restaurants and cafés, and you'll soon be gobbled up by My Tho's vast **market**. As well as the usual piles of fruit, cereals and tobacco, several stalls sell ships' chandlery, their heaped fishing nets almost indistinguishable from the fresh noodles on sale nearby. Practising Christians may want to stroll north of the market, to low-key **My Tho Church**, but others needn't bother: shaded by rose apple trees, its squat yellow frame harbours no stained glass and only the simplest of altars.

Over the canal
The lower of the two bridges now spanning the canal deposits you at the start of waterfront Phan Thanh Gian, home to My Tho's modest **Chinese Quarter**, though there's little to betray its existence other than a feverish sense of commerce. Shopfronts here are piled to the rafters with sugar-cane poles, watermelons and fish awaiting transportation up to Ho Chi Minh, as well as half-hatched eggs (containing chick embryos), a delicacy prized as the perfect complement to a *bia hoi*.

A cyclo journey east of Phan Thanh Gian, Nguyen Trung Truc's attractive **Vinh Trang Pagoda** (daily 7.30am–noon & 2–5pm), with its Rajah's palace-style front facade, has become rather a tourist trap. It's said that VC soldiers hid here in the

Sixties, but today it's home only to monks; the entrance, round to the right, dumps you in their dining room, flanked by the simple white cubicles where they sleep. The main chamber, beyond the miniature mountain to your left, is characterized by formidable darkwood pillars and tons of gilt woodwork; but of more interest are the eclectic influences at play in the pagoda's decor – classical pillars, Grecian-style mouldings of urns and bowls of fruit, and glazed tiles similar to Portuguese *azulejos*. Outside, the tombs of several monks stand near a pond patrolled by some truly gargantuan catfish, while the path outside and to the right of the ornate front gates wends its way through fruit gardens.

Perhaps more diverting, and certainly helping to justify the cyclo fare from the town centre, is the **joss stick factory** at the corner of Anh Giac and Nguyen Trung Truc, where sticks are made by rolling splinters of bamboo, first in a composite of scented sawdust and glue, and then in a yellow dye. Sacks of sawdust and bundles of drying sticks outside make the factory easy to spot. On the way back into town, look out for another cottage industry on Anh Giac. This one produces *mut*, or **crystallized sweets**, which are eaten at Tet: they're made by boiling ingredients such as ginger and gourd in huge vats; show interest, and you'll be offered some to taste.

Eating

A clutch of inexpensive **restaurants** huddle along Trung Trac's eastern side, of which the no-frills *Chi Thanh*, at no. 56, is far and away the best, its well-cooked Vietnamese food drawing nightly crowds. Otherwise, there's the friendly *Viet Hai* at no. 50, where great breakfasts, affordable shrimps and oysters, and truly exotic fruit salads are served up on a terrace built out over the channel on stilts. At night, the **noodle stall** that sets up between nos. 22 and 24 whips up the local speciality, *hu tieu My Tho* (spicy vermicelli soup with meat and seafood). Of the smattering of riverside restaurants along 30 Thang 4, the *Cuu Long* is as good as any, and a fine venue for catching a Mekong sunset.

If money is tight, you'd do well to make for the daytime **food stalls** at the top end of Nguyen Hue, or *Pho 83*, one block west on Le Loi, delivers tasty soups and *opla* (steak and eggs). Finally, for an after-dinner ice cream, cake or fresh coconut, duck into the *Duyen Tham*, next door to the *Chi Thanh* on Trung Trac – but check prices before ordering, as they've been known to scam tourists.

Around My Tho: boat trips on the delta

Taking a **boat trip** on the Mekong is the undoubted highlight of a stay in My Tho, but it's important to know first what your priorities are. Of the three nearby islands, Tan Long Island and Phung Island merit a visit, though you'll get more time on the water if you ask to explore the north coastline of Ben Tre Province, or just to idle along the river – in which case the Dong Tam snake farm provides an interesting enough focus. Whatever you do, it's worth making an **early start** to catch the river at its mistiest and most magical.

The tamest but easily the cheapest way of getting on to the water is to travel by **public ferry** to one of the islands; services to Phung Island use the Ben Tre Ferry Terminal, 300m west of Vong Nho Market, while those to Tan Long leave from opposite the *Huong Duong* hotel.

For a full-on tropical river experience, though, you'll want to **charter** a boat with driver. *Tien Giang Tourist* (see p.118) can arrange any trip you want, but the

ONG DAO DUA, THE COCONUT MONK

Ong Dao Dua, the Coconut Monk, was born Nguyen Thanh Nam in the Mekong Delta, in 1909. Aged nineteen, he travelled to France where he studied chemistry until 1935, when he returned home, married and fathered a child. Subsequently, he opted for a spiritual life, and during a lengthy period of meditation at Chau Doc's Sam Mountain (see p.145) devised a new religious sect, a fusion of Buddhism and Christianity known as **Tinh Do Cu Si**. By the Sixties, the sect had established a community on Phung Island, where the monk developed a cult of personality, lording it over his followers from a throne set into a man-made grotto modelled on Sam Mountain. The monk became as famous for his idiosyncrasies, as for his doctrine: his name, for instance, was coined after it was alleged he spent three years meditating and eating nothing but coconuts.

Unfortunately, the coconut monk never got to enjoy his "kingdom" for long: his belief in a peaceful reunification of North and South Vietnam (symbolized by the map of the country behind his grotto, on which pillars representing Hanoi and Saigon are joined by a bridge) landed him in the jails of successive South Vietnamese governments, and the communists were no more sympathetic to his beliefs after 1975.

Ong Dao Dua died in 1990.

touts along Trung Trac and 30 Thang 4 will undercut their prices substantially: $3–4 should get you a three-hour trip – time enough to explore the waterways along the coast of Ben Tre Province, and to land on an island in the river. There've been reports that the local **police** have become more zealous of late about tourists taking unofficial boats instead of those laid on by the tourist office – ask around in Ho Chi Minh before you set out.

The islands

Beyond its chaotic shoreline of stilthouses and boatyards, **Tan Long** ("Dragon Island") boasts bounteous sapodilla, coconut and banana plantations, as well as highly regarded longan orchards. The white glare you'll see as you approach is the reflection of sun-bleached seashells spread to bolster the shoreline.

Phung Island (daily 8am–7pm) is famed as the home of an offbeat religious sect set up three decades ago by the eccentric **Coconut Monk**, Ong Dao Dua (see box above), although there's not much left to see from his era, and only the skeleton of the open-air **complex** he established remains. Among its mesh of rusting staircases and platforms, you'll spot the rocket-shaped elevator the monk had built to whisk him up to his private meditation platform. Elsewhere are nine dragon-entwined pillars, said to symbolize the Mekong's nine tributaries, and betraying a Cao Daist influence. The Coconut Monk's story is told (in Vietnamese) on a magnificent **urn** which he is said to have crafted himself out of shards of porcelain from France, Japan and China. Beyond the urns stretch acres of **orchards**, whose fruits can be sampled at the several cafés dotted around the island – as can the acrid sticky-rice wine brewed locally.

The Ben Tre coastline

For more of an adventure, push on to the coastline of **Ben Tre Province**, south of My Tho (see over for more on this area), whose labyrinthine creeks afford marvellous scope for exploring. Gliding along these slender waterways, overhung by handsome waterpalm fronds which interlock to form a cathedral-like roof, it's easy to feel you're charting new territory. Swooping, electric-blue kingfishers and sumptuously coloured butterflies add to the romance. Boatmen usually incorporate stops at local coconut candy, rice wine and sugar-processing workshops into your trip. With time enough, it's even possible to take a boat to the **Dong Tam snake farm** (daily 7.30am–5pm; $1) 10km west of My Tho, where several varieties of snake including pythons and king cobras are bred and harvested to make medicines and tonic wines. Snake extract is said to be able to cure anything from rheumatism and headaches to insanity – something the poor monkeys, crocodiles and bears kept in squalor at the farm might suffer themselves. The snake farm can also be reached by heading west along My Tho's Le Thi Hong Gam – en route, you'll pass the *Tien Giang Brewery*, home of *BGI* beer.

Ben Tre and around

The few travellers who push on beyond My Tho into riverlocked **Ben Tre Province** are rewarded with some of the Mekong Delta's most breathtaking scenery. Famed for its fruit orchards and coconut groves (Vietnamese call it the "coconut island"), the province has proved just as fertile a breeding ground for revolutionaries, first plotting against the French, and later against the Americans, and was one of the ensuing areas seized by the Viet Cong during the Tet Offensive of 1968. Of the ensuing US bombing campaign on the provincial capital of **BEN TRE**, a US major was quoted as saying, "It became necessary to destroy the town in order to save it." Today, Ben Tre is a pleasant and industrious town displaying none of the wounds of its past, and is a world away from the tourist menus and boat-trip touts of nearby My Tho. Though rather short on sights, it's still a relaxing and friendly place to hole up for a couple of days, and a springboard for exploring the surrounding districts.

Once you've scanned the buzzing **town market**, you'll want to pass over the quaint bridge leading to the Ben Tre River's more rustic south bank, where scores of cross-eyed boats moor in front of jumbles of thatch houses. With a bicycle (bring one from My Tho, or ask at your hotel reception), you can capitalize upon the ample opportunities for exploring offered by the maze of dirt tracks on this side of the river. Before striking off, though, duck into the riverside **wine factory**, 450m west of the bridge, where fermenting *ruou trang* (Vietnamese rice wine) fizzes away in vast earthenware jars. A mountain of rice husks indicates the factory's location, though you'll find it easily if you follow your nose.

A side-trip to Cai Mon

Honda oms congregate outside the GPO in the centre of Ben Tre, and for $2.50 they'll whisk you off on a two-hour round-trip to the celebrated fruit orchards of **CAI MON**, to the southwest. Ten minutes' ride west of town a modest river is negotiated by the **Ham Luong Ferry**, after which a further five minutes reveals a right turn onto a red dirt track. Now the countryside unfurls grandly. Waxy green paddy fields stretch away to the horizon, tufted with "islands" of coconut trees; while along the road stand groves of bamboo, eucalyptus, and the grassy mop-tops of sugar-cane plants.

Twenty minutes beyond the ferry station, you'll reach the village of **BA VAP**, enveloped in the intoxicating aroma of coconuts being processed. Hinging this small town is a narrow river shaded by bowed water palms. Twenty-five minutes and a succession of rickety bridges later, the road reaches Cai Mon, a sleepy community whose extremely friendly residents make a living by cultivating fruit.

Hasten across the steep bridge ahead of you to the far bank of the tiny river threading the town, and you'll confront a vast plain of bounteous **orchards**, veined by mile after mile of narrow, duck-patrolled canals, and maze-like paths, along which kids run with homemade paper kites. March through May is high season for the huge variety of tropical fruits grown here, but whenever you go you're guaranteed a lush vista. As you walk, you'll be invited by local farmers into their thatched huts to taste their crops.

Practicalities

Ferries from My Tho disgorge their passengers 11km north of Ben Tre, from where a Honda loi is your best bet for reaching town: buses alighting from the ferry are cheaper, but terminate at the **bus station** 2km short of the town centre. As you run down Dong Khoi to the centre of town, look out for *Ben Tre Tourism* (☎075/829618), on your left, which is as helpful as any in the delta.

The tidy, riverside *Hung Vuong Hotel* (☎075/822866; ③) has the best lo-cation of Ben Tre's three **hotels**; if its enormous rooms are all full, check in at the poki-er *Ben Tre Hotel* (☎075/822223; ③), at the far end of town. Top of the price range is Hai Ba Trung's *Dong Khoi Hotel* (☎075/822240; ④), many of whose unfussy but reasonably well-appointed rooms overlook Truc Giang Lake.

There's no shortage of **places to eat** in town, if you don't fancy the cheery enough restaurants at the *Hung Vuong* or *Dong Khoi* hotels. The hulking great boat that holds the *Ben Tre Floating Restaurant* has seen better days, but remains a fine venue for a sunset drink – or dinner, if you can negotiate the menu, which is in Vietnamese only; main courses cost around $2. Better value for money is offered by the friendly *Nha Hang Truc Giang*, around the corner from the *Hung Vuong*, where plates of filling Vietnamese food cost $1; otherwise, the open-fronted *Dai Hue*, east of the market, knocks out decent steaks and local staples.

It's not unprecedented for travellers with their own transport to brave the knot of dirt tracks west of the town, and find their way to Vinh Long (see p.127) but by far the easiest means of **moving on** is to backtrack to My Tho.

West to the My Thuan ferry

The half-hour bus journey along Highway 1 from My Tho to the **My Thuan ferry** crossing – the first of the major cross-Mekong ferries, and the most common means of pushing further into the delta – is a bumpy and sporadically beautiful one that takes in expanses of longan orchards and picturesque river-hugging settlements. From one of these, **CAI LAY**, a minor track, strikes northwards, skirting the eastern edge of **Dong Thap Muoi**, or the **Plain of Reeds** (see "Cao Lanh", below). Today, the cajeput trees and waist-high grasses carpeting this large tract of marshland are home only to storks, cranes and herons, but formerly they harboured cells of guerrillas fighting successively against France and America – despite US bombing sorties out of nearby **MOC HOA**.

It was in the rice fields northeast of Cai Lay that the **Battle of Ap Bac** was fought, in January 1963. Ap Bac witnessed a heavily outnumbered group of 350 Viet Cong soldiers register a profound moral victory over the forces of the South Vietnamese Army (ARVN), over 150 of whom were left either wounded or killed by the confrontation. Ill-led and ill-organized, ARVN troops even fired on each other at one stage, while the communist guerrillas were able to down five helicopters, using only the most rudimentary of weapons. Before this, it had been assumed that South Vietnam could fight its own battles; the debacle at Ap Bac was instrumental in persuading US military observers that heightened American involvement was necessary in order to stamp out the communist threat.

Local buses out of My Tho offload at grubby **AN HUU**: to the northwest is Cao Lanh (see below), from where it's possible to connect with Long Xuyen and beyond. The more usual route, though, is to drop 4km south to the My Thuan ferry, best reached by xe lam. Long lines of shacks selling provisions, snacks and drinks are strung out along the approach to the ferry station, whose battalion of beggars and hawkers can make waiting for a ferry a stressful business. Once across the river, you can head west to the charismatic town of Sa Dec (p.132), or east to Vinh Long (p.126) and Tra Vinh (p.129).

Cao Lanh and around

Highway 30 peels off north from An Huu, rolling into modest **CAO LANH** 34km later. The town is no oil painting and little is gained from including it in your travel plans unless you're charmed by **wading birds**: its location beside the western edge of the Plain of Reeds makes Cao Lanh an ideal launching-pad for trips out to the herons and cranes that nest in the nearby swamplands. Coming from Ho Chi Minh, you'll pass the two great concrete tusks (intended to resemble lotus petals) of the **war memorial** as you veer onto the main drag, Nguyen Hue; one tusk bears a hammer and sickle, the other a Vietnamese red star. Way across on the southwestern outskirts of town, another concrete edifice, shaped like an open clam, marks the burial place of Ho Chi Minh's father, **Nguyen Sinh Sac**.

And that's about it, unless you're here for the birds. Of the 130 species nesting 45km northwest of Cao Lanh at the **Tam Nong Bird Sanctuary**, it's the **cranes**, with their distinctive red heads, that most visitors come to see. In flight above the marshland of the sanctuary, the slender grey birds reveal spectacular black-tipped wings. Cranes feed not from the water but from the land, so when the spate

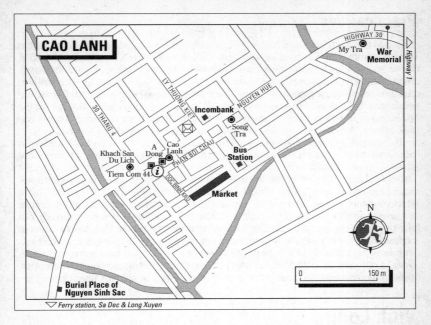

CAO LANH

HIGHWAY 30

My Tra   **War Memorial**

Highway 1

LY THUONG KIET

NGUYEN HUE

Incombank

Song Tra

Khach San Du Lich

A Dong

Cao Lanh

PHAN BOI CHAU

Bus Station

Tiem Com 44

NGOC BINH KIEU

Market

N

0   150 m

Burial Place of Nguyen Sinh Sac

▽ *Ferry station, Sa Dec & Long Xuyen*

season (Aug–Nov) waterlogs the delta, they migrate to Cambodia. You can learn more about them, and the terrain they favour, at the sanctuary's "Center for Environment Education and Crane Protection". To get the best view of the birds themselves, plan to be around either at dawn when they fly off in search of food, or at dusk when they return to roost. It's possible to reach Tam Nong by Honda om, though a boat trip ($30 for up to 17 people) arranged through the tourist office (see "Practicalities" overleaf) is a more special experience.

You'll also need to approach the tourist office if you want to take a trip out to the **Xeo Quit Tourist Jungle**, deep in the cajeput forest 20km southeast of Cao Lanh. The district's dense cover provided the perfect bolthole for Viet Cong guer-rillas during the American War, and from 1960 to 1975 the struggle against America and the ARVN was masterminded from here. The boggy nature of the terrain made a tunnel system similar to Cu Chi's (see p.107) unfeasible, so they made do with six submerged metal chambers sealed with tar and resin. Suspecting the base's existence, Americans bombed the area regularly, and even broadcast propaganda from the air to demoralize its occupants; but by developing a policy of "going without trace, cooking without smoke, speaking without noise", the cadres residing here escaped discovery throughout the war. The **boat trip** ($20 per boat) to Xeo Quit is a charming glide along eucalyptus-shaded canals teeming with freshwater fish and shrimps. Xeo Quit is often combined with a trip up to **Vuon Co Thap Muoi**, a bird garden 44km northeast of Cao Lanh whose bamboo and eucalyptus groves harbour herons, white storks and black ibises. Tens of thousands of wading birds nest here around hatching season, and at dawn you'll see them taking to the sky in their thousands to search for food. Prices for the combined trip are around the $30 mark (per boat).

Practicalities

Buses to and from Cao Lanh halt at the bus station, a few paces below the town centre; approach from Long Xuyen or beyond, and you'll cross the Tien Giang via the Cao Lanh ferry, around 4km southwest of town. Wherever you come from, be sure to change enough travellers' cheques before you leave, as the *Incombank* on Ly Thuong Kiet changes only dollars. Unusually, *Dong Thap Tourist*, based in the centre of town, are reasonably helpful and extremely friendly, and haven't yet priced themselves out of the independent travellers' market; as well as **boat trips** into the surrounding countryside (see above), they'll even organize **water-skiing trips** on the Mekong for you.

The tourist board-accredited *Song Tra* (☎067/852504; ③) is Cao Lanh's poshest **place to stay**, a smart white building supporting 52 cosy rooms; or there are cheery doubles with air-con and hot water at the less expensive *My Tra* (☎067/851218; ③), east of the town centre on Highway 30. Budget travellers will have to make do with grimy *Khach San Du Lich* (☎067/851214; ①), on 30 Thang 4; the cheaper rooms share truly horrid common toilets, so the extra few dollars for private facilities is money well spent. The in-house **restaurants** at the *My Tra* and the *Song Tra* are rather uncharismatic affairs, but Nguyen Hue has two decent restaurants: *Tiem Com 44*, where tasty yet inexpensive dishes such as chicken with lemongrass and chilli ($1.50) are taken in a large open courtyard; and the *A Dong*, a tidy *com* shop decked out with photos of Hong Kong movie stars and offering cheap and cheerful meals served over rice as well as *opla* for breakfast.

Vinh Long

Ringed by water and besieged by boats and tumbledown stilthouses, the island that forms the heart of **VINH LONG** has the feel of a medieval fortress. If you find yourself yearning for a peaceful backwater after the frenzy of the ferry crossing, first impressions will be a let-down: central Vinh Long is hectic and noisy, its streets a blur of buses and scooters. Make for the waterfront though, and it's a different story. Here, hotels, restaurants and cafés conjure a riviera atmosphere far quainter and more genuine than My Tho's. From here you can watch the **Co Chien River** roll by, dotted by sampans, houseboats, and the odd raft of river-weed.

Arrival, information and accommodation

Long-distance **buses** pull in at the provincial bus station, a couple of kilometres southwest of town on Nguyen Hue; you'll have to return here when it's time to move on, unless you're off to Sa Dec, which is served by the local station in the centre of town. If you are coming off the My Thuan ferry, and no bus marked Vinh Long or Tra Vinh is in sight, sharing a Honda loi or taking a xe lam is the best way to cover the 9km into town; either will deposit you beside the local station. If you've battled across from Ben Tre, you'll need to take a **ferry** from An Binh Island (see p.129), which will drop you 3km east of central Vinh Long.

Cuu Long Tourist at the top of 1 Thang 5 will arrange more leisurely **boat trips** on the Co Chien River – though at a price; you're better off speaking to the unofficial boatowners who approach you along the waterfront, though you'll have to take the ferry from Phan Boi Chau to Binh An and meet them there, since they're not supposed to take tourists.

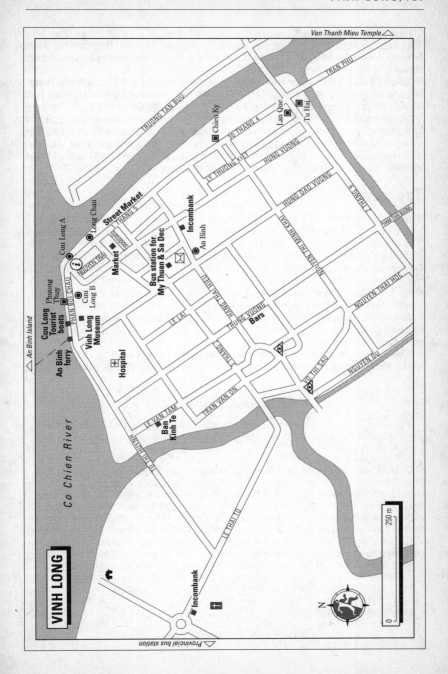

VINH LONG

Van Thanh Mieu Temple

Co Chien River

An Binh Island

Provincial bus station

250 m

The *Incombank* at the three-way roundabout west of town changes travellers' cheques, though for straight US currency transactions its Hoang Thai Hieu branch is more central. If you're headed for Tra Vinh, note that you can't change travellers' cheques there.

Most of Vinh Long's **accommodation** options are along 1 Thang 5: the down-at-heel *Long Chau* (☎070/823611; ①) boasts the cheapest river views in town; should its rooms prove too mucky, by-pass the fantastically overpriced *Cuu Long 'A' Hotel* (☎070/822494; ④) and make straight for the more modest *Cuu Long 'B'* (no phone; ②), whose cheery and reasonably appointed rooms command fine views of the Vinh Long riviera. Away from the river, the spick and span *An Binh* at 3 Hoang Thai Hieu (☎070/823190; ②) has a range of quarters to suit all pockets, though the cheaper rooms have shared facilities.

The town

The main reason for a trip to Vinh Long is for a taste of river life in the delta – other than An Binh Island (see opposite), Vinh Long isn't spoilt for attractions. The doors and shutters of **Vinh Long Museum**, facing the waterfront, were padlocked long ago but war enthusiasts can still amble past the tank, flamethrower, helicopter, planes and artillery left to rust under the unsightly plastic hangar in its open gardens. From here, you might walk west along colourful To Thi Huynh: there's a cache of impressive French colonial buildings on this side of town, none more eye-catching than Le Van Tam's **Ban Kinh Te**. Scanning this oddly shaped, yellow-wash mansion, with its red-tiled roof and shuttered windows topped by mouldings of garlands, it's easy to picture the ghosts of French *colons* and rice merchants in your mind's eye.

Thereafter, you'll have to journey 2km down the bumpy road that runs parallel to the Rach Long Canal and southeast of town, to the **Van Thanh Mieu Temple**,

---

PHAN THANH GIAN

Born in Vinh Long Province in 1796, the mandarin diplomat **Phan Thanh Gian** was destined to be involved in a chain of events that was to shape over a century of Vietnamese history.

On August 31, 1858, French naval forces attacked Da Nang, citing persecution of Catholic missionaries as their justification: the French colonial land-grabbing that would culminate, in 1885, in the total conquest of Vietnam, had begun. By 1861, the three eastern provinces of Cochinchina had been conquered by the **French Expeditionary Corps**, and although there were popular anti-French uprisings, Emperor Tu Duc sold out the following year, when the three provinces were formally ceded to the French by the **Treaty of Saigon**, which was signed by Phan Thanh Gian. A year later he had the opportunity to redress the damage it had done, when he journeyed to Paris as ambassador to Emperor Napoleon III, to thrash out a long-term peace – the first Vietnamese ambassador ever to be despatched to Europe.

However, attempts to claw back territory lost by the terms of the treaty failed, and by 1867 France moved to take over the rest of Cochinchina. Unable to persuade the spineless Tu Duc to sanction popular uprisings, Phan Thanh Gian embarked on a hunger strike in protest at French incursions, and Hué's ineffectuality. When, after fifteen days, he had still not died, he swallowed **poison**, and his place among the massed ranks of Vietnamese heroes was assured.

in search of diversion. This rather pokey temple is dedicated to Confucius –
unusually for southern Vietnam – and a heavily bearded portrait of him watches
over proceedings; the splendid blue robes he wears contrast starkly with the
mildewed and moth-eaten old canopies above him. Another temple in the compound honours local mandarin Phan Thanh Gian (see box on facing page), who
is pictured in red robes, flanked by slender storks. Fronting the temple are two
cannons that rained fire on the French in 1860.

An Binh Island

A five-minute ferry ride across the Co Chien River from the top of town accesses
a patch of the delta's most breathtaking scenery. Known by locals as **AN BINH
ISLAND**, in fact it's a jigsaw of bite-sized pockets of land, skeined by a fine web
of channels and gullies, eventually merging, to the east, with the province of Ben
Tre. This idyllic and fruitful landscape is criss-crossed by a network of dirt paths,
making it ideal for a morning's rambling.

A grove of longan trees a few paces north of the jetty shades sandy, century-old
Tien Chau Pagoda. Inside its harmonious rear chamber, monks sup tea against
the ghoulish backdrop of a mural depicting sinners being variously trampled by
horses, trumpeted at by elephants and devoured by snakes in the ten Buddhist
hells. One hundred metres east of the jetty, meanwhile, a truly hellish smell betrays
the location of a **fish sauce factory**. Fish too small to be sold off are chopped up at
the water's edge, before being fermented in huge barrels to produce *nuoc mam*, or
fish sauce. Look out, too, for the self-satisfied factory cat foraging for scraps.

These two diversions seen, strike off in any direction to explore the verdant
beauty of An Binh's orchards and gardens. As an alternative to following the
island's narrow tracks and single-log bridges, you could rent a **boat** out of Vinh
Long: with a vessel at your disposal, it's also possible to tootle along the river.

Eating and drinking

Eating is a down-to-earth affair in Vinh Long: the spotless *com* shop opposite the
Cuu Long 'A' serves tasty pork chops, and iced coconuts out of the fridge, until mid-
afternoon. At night, the stall next door to the *Long Chau*, selling chicken, shrimps or
pork on rice, soup and tea, all for less than $1, is hard to beat; the owner can also
rustle up an ice-cold *BGI*. East of the island, there's the hole-in-the-wall *Chieu Ky
Restaurant* where basic rice and soup meals are to be had. For a touch more class
though, you'll want to make for either the *Lan Que*, where locals flock for the fish
dishes, as well as for delicacies such as snake and turtle, or the simpler but more
upbeat *Tu Hai*; the two restaurants face each other on 2 Thang 9. The *Phuong Thuy*,
built out over the river, boasts the prime spot in town, but the food (a mix of
Vietnamese and Western) is only average and you'll become invisible to the staff as
soon as a tour bus arrives. There are basic **stalls** beside the covered market, on Bach
Dang, and a batch of equally basic **bars** along the central section of Trung Vuong.

Tra Vinh and around

It's only another 65km southeast across yawning flats of paddy fields to **TRA
VINH**, an outback market town whose broad, tree-lined streets and smattering of

colonial piles have yet to see tourists in any numbers. This region of the delta is Khmer country: as you get nearer to Tra Vinh, distinctive pagodas begin to appear beside the road, their steep horned roofs puncturing the sky.

Arrival, information and accommodation

Buses from Vinh Long and beyond hit the southwest corner of Tra Vinh, terminating 600m south of town on Chua Phung. The *Agribank*, one block west of the market at 70–72 Le Loi, will change cash (US$ only). Cargo/passenger **boats** to Ho Chi Minh depart twice weekly from the pier just above the bridge over the Tra Vinh River – contact the *Tra Vinh Tourist Company* at 999 Nguyen Thi Minh Khai for the current schedule.

The *Thanh Tra Hotel* (☎074/863621; ①) at the top of Pham Thai Buong is the town's finest place to **stay**: prices rise to ④, but even the basic rooms are dazzlingly clean. If it's full, you'll have to make do with the *Huong Tra* (☎074/862433; ①), two minutes' walk northeast of the *Thanh Tra* on Ly Thuong Kiet, or Le Thanh Ton's mildewy *Phuong Hoang Hotel* (☎074/862270; ①) – both are cheap and uninspiring, though $8 will at least secure you air-con and private bathroom.

The town

Most visitors come here to visit the storks at nearby Chua Hang (see opposite), though the town's low-key charm makes it an amiable enough place to while away a day or so. Unusually, Tra Vinh isn't ostensibly dominated by a branch of the Mekong – you'll have to journey a couple of hundred metres east of the 800-metre-square grid forming the town centre to find the river. A hike through the **market** to riverside Bach Dang makes the most engaging approach: the bridge 100m north of the fish market commands great views of the **Tra Vinh River**, whose eddying waters run canal-straight to the north. In places the river is almost corked by boats moored seven or eight deep, while boat-builders occupy several of the thatched stilthouses spilling off its east bank. Walk north of the town centre up Le Loi to the golden-roofed **Ong Met Pagoda**, and you're assured of a friendly reception from the monks studying at its English school. Beyond, on the left, is pretty **Tra Vinh Church**, a cream-coloured and buttressed construction, fronted by a statue of Christ taking refuge from the tropical sun in a niche above the front entrance, while waves of stonework ripple liquidly up its salmon-pink spire.

Ba Om Pond

Five kilometres southwest of town, a dirt track on the left after the second of two Khmer pagodas runs down to **Ba Om Pond**, beloved of Tra Vinh picnickers and courting couples. Along the trackway, a gaggle of cottage industries churn out **rice papers** for making spring rolls – go to any house fronted by thatch drying-frames, and you'll see puddles of rice gruel being steamed over a rice-husk fire, then dried and trimmed.

Despite the tourist board hyperbole this is a pond, plain and simple. Bordered by grassy banks, and shaded by aged trees whose roots clutch at the ground, Ba Om is a placid spot, seasonally cloaked by lotus blossoms that attract flocks of blackbirds in the late afternoon. The origin of Ba Om is clouded by time, but one version of events is enshrined in a quaint legend. Many centuries ago, the men and women of a village in the area were embroiled in an argument over which sex should shoulder marriage expenses. A race was decided upon to settle the dispute: women were to build a square pond, and men a round one, with the team managing the biggest pond by morning escaping marital expenses henceforth. Both teams dug all day and into the night, by which time it was clear that the men were winning. Ba Om, leader of the women, resorted to desperate measures. Setting up a lantern, she duped the opposing team into thinking the morning star had risen. While the men stopped digging and went to bed, the women continued, and the competition was won. To this day, the pond is square – and locals say that the town's male contingent has managed, on the whole, to keep its side of the bargain.

The area across the far side of the pond has been a Khmer place of worship since the eleventh century, and today it's occupied by **Ang Vuong Pagoda**. Steep-roofed, stained with age, and ringed by fragrant frangipani trees, the pagoda makes an affecting sight, especially when it echoes with the chants of its resident monks. Fronting it is a nest of stupas guarded by stone lions, while colourful murals inside depict events from the Buddha's life. In season, rice from the pagoda's paddy fields is heaped next to the altar, where it's guarded by an impressive golden Sakyamuni image and a host of smaller ones.

Stork spotting: Chua Hang and beyond

The sight of the hundred or so **storks** that nest in the grounds of **Hang Pagoda**, a Khmer pagoda around 6km south of town along Dien Bien Phu, is one which will long linger in the memory. The best time to catch these magnificent creatures is just before dusk, when they wheel and hover over the treetops, their snowy wings catching the evening's sunlight, before roosting for the night. It's a stirring sight, though one you'll appreciate more fully if you can shake off the saffron-robed monks that clamour to practise their English with you. Chua Hang itself – an arched stone gate to the left of the main road betrays the entrance to the compound – is nothing to write home about. Dominating is the inevitable **Sakyamuni statue**, this time hooped by a halo of fairy lights and flanked by murals of his life. There's no public transport to the pagoda, so you'll have to take a Honda om which will cost about $1 for the return trip.

For a real storkfest, **Giong Lon Pagoda**, 43km southeast of Tra Vinh, takes some beating. The number of storks in residence here approaches three hundred, but sadly the logistics of a trip out this far aren't in your favour, unless you take a Honda om all the way, which will cost around $6 (round-trip).

Eating

The *Thanh Tra* hotel's ground-floor **restaurant** is decent enough, or for a little more ambience, try the *Tuy Huong*, opposite the front of the market, where the speciality is delicious *nem nuong*, or fried spring rolls stuffed with barbecued pork. Otherwise, there's Tran Phu's smart *com* shop, the *Viet Hoa* – walk 120m south of the front of the market and turn right. Finally, **stalls** towards the eastern edge of the market hawk *pho* and *com* until the early evening.

Sa Dec

A cluster of brick and tile kilns announces your imminent arrival in the charming town of **SA DEC**, a little over 20km upriver of Vinh Long. French novelist Marguerite Duras lived here as a child, and decades later the town's stuccoed shophouse terraces, riverside mansions and remarkably busy stretch of the rumbling Mekong provided the backdrop for the movie adaptation of her novel *The Lover*.

Coming in from the bus station, the town's three main arteries – Nguyen Hue, Tran Hung Dao and Hung Vuong – branch off to your right. Duck straight down into Nguyen Hue, whose umbrella-choked ways hide the melee of Sa Dec's extensive riverside market. Further along the street, waterfront comings and goings are observed by rheumy old men playing chequers, and women squat on their haunches, selling fruit from wicker baskets. Ferries from the covered fish market cross to the childhood **home of Marguerite Duras** – hers is the nearest of the two villas that stand beside the place where boats drop you, and is now in use as a primary school. A crumbling old colonial villa that's been harshly treated by the tropical climate, its green shutters and red tiled roof are tired and faded, though the glazed bricks arching over its windows still glint defiantly in the sun.

Once you've explored the town, negotiate the venerable metal bridge that runs over the top of Nguyen Hue and across the river – its planks dance gaily on their sleepers under the impact of crossing traffic. At the far bank, climb down the steps to your left and follow the river road west and past Sa Dec's **Cao Dai temple**: after 25 minutes, a gaggle of cafés tells you you've hit **Qui Dong**, Sa Dec's famed flower village, where over a hundred farms cultivate a host of ferns, fruit trees, shrubs and flowers. Villagers are used to people strolling their regimented rows of blooms, which grow on raised bamboo platforms, tended by conical-hatted workers who wade, ankle-deep, through the mud ponds below. The 6000 hectares of **Tu Ton Rose Garden** get the lion's share of tourists visiting the village. In addition to the various breeds of roses cultivated here (among them the *Brigitte Bardot*, the *Jolie Madame* and the *Marseille*), over 580 species of plants are grown, ranging from orchids, marigolds and chrysanthemums, through to medicinal herbs and pines grown for export around Asia. Bear in mind that Qui Dong is overrun on Sundays by tourists from Ho Chi Minh City who come to pose for photos among the blooms; and that things get particularly busy and colourful in the run-up to Tet, as farms prepare to transport their stocks to the city's flower markets.

Practicalities

Buses terminate 300m southeast of the town centre: turn left out of the station and continue straight across the bridge. Take your pick from the two **hotels** in town, Hung Vuong's *Sa Dec* (☎067/861430; ②) or the better-value *Bong Hong* (☎067/861301; ①), below town on Lien Tinh. When it's time for **eating**, *Quan Com Thuy* and the neighbouring *Cay Sung* are both pleasant enough *com* shops offering the normal pork, fish and chicken on rice staples; you'll find them on the crossroads below the *Sa Dec*, which also has its own, rather glum, attached restaurant.

Can Tho

A population of around 310,000 makes **CAN THO** the delta's biggest city, and losing yourself in its commercial thrum for a few days is the perfect antidote to time spent as the centre of attention in less frequented towns. Approaching from the ferry terminal northeast of the city, first impressions are rather less than encouraging: Can Tho is a hefty settlement, but with the oppresive urban sprawl encasing the top of town negotiated, its breezy waterfront comes as a pleasant surprise.

At the confluence of the Can Tho and Hau Giang rivers, the city is a major mercantile centre and transport interchange. But Can Tho is no mere staging post. Some of the best restaurants in the delta are located here; what's more, the abundant rice fields of Can Tho Province are never far away, and at the intersections of the canals and rivers that thread between them you'll find several memorable floating markets. Can Tho was the last city to succumb to the North Vietnamese Army, a day after the fall of Saigon, on May 1, 1975 – the date that has come to represent the absolute reunification of the country.

Arrival, information and transport

Long-distance buses whisk you across the Hau Giang estuary and into the Mekong's transportational hub, Can Tho's **bus station**, 1200m northwest of town at the junction of Cach Mang Thang Tam and Hung Vuong. Most buses will terminate here, though local services from Vinh Long dump you on the north bank of the Hau Giang River at **Binh Minh**, from where you'll have to take a short **ferry** ride. The *Can Tho Tourist Company*, at 20 Hai Ba Trung, can help with **car and boat rental**, though for the latter, you'll do better to book an unofficial boat through one of the many touts prowling Hai Ba Trung. Finally, *Vietcombank* at 7 Hoa Binh will change cash and travellers' cheques.

Onward routes from Can Tho either veer up to Long Xuyen and the Cambodian border, or follow Highway 1 to Soc Trang and on to Ca Mau; there's a passenger/cargo **boat to Ca Mau** (see p.139), which departs from the jetty at the top of the market daily at 5pm.

Accommodation

Hai Ba Trung and Chau Van Liem together form the axis of Can Tho's healthy **hotel** scene; cyclo-drivers from either the bus or ferry station will take you from one hotel to another until you make your choice, in return for a modest commission from the reception desk.

Can Tho, 14–16 Hai Ba Trung (☎071/822218). Much effort has been put into this brand-new, 18-room hotel, resulting in agreeable rooms with marbled floors, sound paintwork and pleasing bathrooms. ②

Hao Hoa, 6 Hai Thuong Lang Ong (☎071/824836). Set back off Can Tho's main streets down a dirt track, this is a peaceful, quaint and low-priced hotel, though marred by the unlovely toilets in each room. ①

Hau Giang 'A', 34 Nam Ky Khoi Nghia (☎071/821806). Comfortable, if rather luridly decorated, rooms with air-con, hot water, satellite TV and breakfast included. ④

Hau Giang 'B', 27 Chau Van Liem (☎071/821636). Salubrious new place with light and quite spacious rooms, all with well-maintained facilities; air-con costs a few dollars more. ①

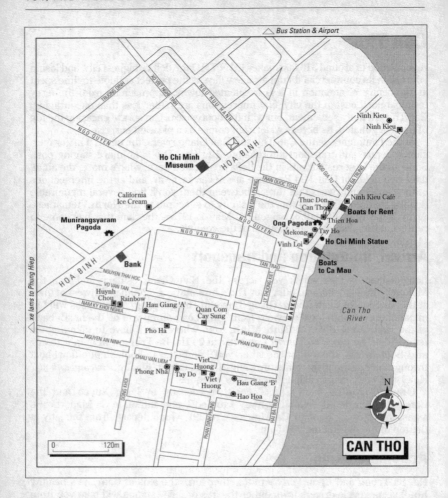

CAN THO

Ninh Kieu, 2 Hai Ba Trung (☎071/824583). Can Tho's smartest address boasts well-appointed rooms off coolly tiled halls; all rates are inclusive of breakfast, while an extra $6 secures a riverview suite. ③

Phong Nha, 75 Chau Van Liem (☎071/821615). Patronage by *Sinh Café* tour groups has left the *Phong Nha* more geared to travellers than most hotels; fan rooms with bathroom are tiny but adequate, and there are three cramped "corridor rooms" if every dollar counts. ①

Tay Do, 61 Chau Van Liem (no phone). Charmless but cheap, the dark and grubby rooms here have en suite showers, but toilets are down the corridor. ①

Tay Ho, 36 Hai Ba Trung (☎071/823392). Delightful, cottagey little hotel in an aged row of shophouses, with a riot of flowers spilling from its balcony; the cheapest rooms are claustrophobic and share communal toilets, so pay the extra $1 to upgrade. ①

Viet Huong, 35 Chau Van Liem (☎071/824832). Predictably grubby, but unbeatable value if you're penny-pinching; all rooms have toilets and their own balconies. ①

The city

Though its boat trips (see over) are undoubtedly Can Tho's star attraction, a handful of lesser diversions on dry land will help keep you amused in the meantime. Broad Hoa Binh is the city's backbone, and the site of the new **Ho Chi Minh Museum** (Mon–Sat 7–10.30am & 2–4.30pm), where yet more photographs and army ordnance (look out for a vicious homemade crossbow strung with hundreds of elastic bands) pertaining to the war have been dredged up and mounted or framed, above signs written solely in Vietnamese. If you've seen any of the museums in Hanoi or Ho Chi Minh, you'll know the plot by now; outside in the museum's grounds it's a familiar tale of burnt-out helicopters and rusting planes.

The 1946-built **Munirangsyaram Pagoda**, 250m south of the museum, warrants examination only if the more impressive Khmer pagodas around Tra Vinh or Soc Trang aren't on your itinerary. Entrance into the pagoda compound is through a top-heavy stone gate weighed down with masonry reminiscent of Angkor Wat. Don't be fooled by the false promise of the faded, three-headed snake bannisters that slither lithely up the steep steps fronting the pagoda – its upper hall is empty but for two statues of Sakyamuni, one seated, and the other reclining. Only fractionally more arresting is the main hall below, though the colourful rattan mats on the floor do at least testify to the continuing activity of its three remaining monks.

On the waterfront

Walking east of Munirangsyaram Pagoda for five minutes, along Nguyen Thai Hoc, deposits you bang in the middle of the city's **central market**, which swallows up the central segment of Hai Ba Trung. Fans of frenetic Asian markets will find much to enjoy here, with its makeshift stalls chock-a-block with exotic produce.

Once you've squeezed out of the top of the market, and past the troop of very vocal **baguette sellers** who tirelessly hawk their wares at the junction of Hai Ba Trung and Ngo Quyen, an imposing silver statue of a waving **Uncle Ho** announces the start of Can Tho's modest riviera. Your next stop, however, should be **Ong Pagoda**, a prosperous place financed and built late last century by wealthy Chinese townsman Huynh An Thai. Inside, a ruddy-faced Quan Cong presides, flaunting Rio Carnival-style headgear, and separated from proceedings by a tin-topped altar supporting several intricately painted incense urns. On his right is Than Tai, to whom a string of families come on the first day of every month, asking, not unreasonably, for money and good fortune. There's a small chamber dedicated to Quan Am to the left of the main hall; look out, too, for the counter selling incense sticks, where a **calligrapher** blithely daubs Chinese characters onto red prayer scrolls.

Waterfront cafés will rustle up a fresh coconut or a pot of green tea to clear the incense smoke out of your lungs, and from your deckchair you can watch the relentless sampan traffic of the Can Tho River gliding by.

Eating

Can Tho is well endowed with good, affordable **restaurants**, most of them serving Vietnamese food. Those along Hai Ba Trung target a primarily foreign market, while locals tend to fraternize the cluster of places along Nam Ky Khoi Nghia. An uninspiring selection of snacks are sold at the daytime **food stalls** at the upper end of the market, along Hai Ba Trung.

California Ice Cream, 18 Hoa Binh. Tiny ice-cream parlour that will satisfy even the sweetest tooth.

Huynh Chou, 54a Nam Ky Khoi Nghia. More corridor than restaurant, though if you can squeeze in, you'll be treated to the house speciality, superb *bun bo Hué* augmented with huge pieces of meat. 6am–10pm.

Mekong Restaurant, 38 Hai Ba Trung. Into its fourth decade and still hard to top for cheap, flavoursome Vietnamese meals – fried fish in sour sauce ($1) comes highly recommended. 7am–10pm.

Ninh Kieu Café, Hai Ba Trung. Romantic waterfront spot and cheaper than the restaurant (below) that shares its name, if you just want to watch the river roll by, over a drink. 10am–9.30pm.

Ninh Kieu, 2 Hai Ba Trung. Stylish riverside venue with a terrace that takes full advantage of its location. Steamboat for two comes to less than $4, or explore the mix 'n' match menu: combine your favourite vegetables and either meat or seafood, and choose how you want them cooked. 6am–9pm.

Pho Ha, 37 Nam Ky Khoi Nghia. Spit-and-sawdust noodle shop, with a gnarled tree growing up through the roof, and plates of refreshing mint leaves and beansprouts on each table. 6am–10pm.

Quan Com Cay Sung, 14b Nam Ky Khoi Nghia. Unprepossessing restaurant decorated with beer ads and bunting, but held in high regard by local gastronomes who savour its seafood and fried chicken. 6am–9pm.

Rainbow, 54 Nam Ky Khoi Nghia. Civilized, pleasing restaurant, where Chinese and Western dishes rub shoulders with American, Belgian and even Italian steaks; two people eat for $5 to $6. 10am–9.30pm.

Thien Hoa, 26 Hai Ba Trung. Yield to the hard sell of the proprietress, and you'll enjoy big-boy portions of sour soups and other Vietnamese food, either in the simple dining room or at a streetside table. 6am–midnight.

Thuc Don, *International Hotel*, 10–12 Hai Ba Trung. Characterless hotel restaurant specializing in the less appealing (to Western tastes) side – tortoise, snake and frog – of Vietnamese cuisine. 7am–10pm.

Viet Huong Bakery and Café, 37 Chau Van Liem. A good selection of freshly baked cakes, plus a wide-ranging breakfast menu embracing noodle soup and ham omelette. 6am–10pm.

Vinh Loi, 42 Hai Ba Trung. Hole-in-the-wall restaurant with a high reputation for its affordable Vietnamese dishes: a homemade *banh bao* makes a great snack, or try the *pork satty* – pork, spring onions and ginger combined to subtle effect. 24hr.

Around Can Tho: boat trips and floating markets

Every morning an armada of boats takes to the web of waterways spun across Can Tho Province, and makes for one of its **floating markets**. Lacking the almost staged beauty and charm of Bangkok's riverine markets, as snapshots of Mekong life these tableaux are still unbeatable. Everything your average villager could ever need is on sale, from haircuts to coffins, though predictably fruit and vegetables make up the lion's share of the wares on offer; each boat's produce is identifiable by a sample hanging off a bamboo mast in its bow. Among the flotilla of craft are ancient luggers piled so high they seem sure to sink; houseboats, with hangar-like arches of thatch covering their living quarters; and sampans, whose oarsmen and women stand up to strain against their scissor-oars. Few boats are painted, so photographers will have to rely on the cornucopia of fruit for splashes of colour.

Of the three major markets in the province, two are west of the city. First up, 7km out of Can Tho, is the modest **Cai Rang**, sited under the rusting hulk of Cai Rang Bridge, which dispels much of its magic; another 10km west and you're at larger **Phong Dien**. The appeal of these two is that they see relatively few tourists and so are correspondingly friendly; in all likelihood you'll be tossed fruits to sample from passing launches.

The real big daddy of Can Tho's markets, though, is **Phung Hiep**, 32km south of Can Tho, on the road to Soc Trang. Here you're guaranteed an extraordinary sight, as thousands of boats weave, jostle and bump along the water's edge, their owners shouting out to advertise their wares. The maelstrom is best viewed from Phung Hiep Bridge, which carries the main road across the river, and along which snake meat is sometimes laid out to dry. The town itself is a grubby place, its waterfront streets clogged with the overflow of stalls that the river has disgorged onto dry land. Along the main road that splits the town in two, look out for cages full of snakes whipping and arching furiously.

Practicalities

It's possible to visit all three of the floating markets around Can Tho – Cai Rang, Phong Dien and Phung Hiep – by boat, but with the round-trip to Phong Dien (passing Cai Rang) taking around five hours, and getting to Phung Hiep and back more like eight, you'd be wiser to go by **road**, and rent a sampan (approximately $1 an hour) on arrival if you want to join the melee. A Honda om ($3 return) is the safer bet for Phong Dien, while Phung Hiep is served by xe lams from Ly Tu Trong. However you travel, you'll need a really **early start**: any boat-owner who tells you the spectacle is just as impressive throughout the day is lying.

Soc Trang

Straddled across an oily branch of the Mekong, **SOC TRANG** lacks the panache of other delta towns. Scruffy and down at heel, the area is not without its offbeat attractions. On the 10th day of the tenth lunar month (Nov–Dec) the town springs to life, as thousands converge to see traditional Khmer boats (*thuyen dua*) racing each other during the **Ghe Ngo Festival**.

Khmer pagodas are ten-a-penny in this region of the delta; the distinctive feature of **Matoc Pagoda**, 2km south of town along Le Hong Phong, and then 800m down a track on the right, is that the trees surrounding it carry a vast community of golden-bodied fruit bats, which spectacularly take to the skies at dusk. Plan to get here around 5.30pm and as the drop in temperature wakes them, you'll see the bats spinning, preening and flapping their matt black wings – some have a span of 1.5m. At dusk they fly, clucking and squeaking, in search of fruit, only returning again at dawn. Khmer monks have worshipped at this site for four hundred years; the present pagoda is a hundred years old and fast going to seed, the murals on its front walls fading progressively to oblivion. Inside, brighter murals bearing the names of the Khmer communities around the world that financed them recount the life of the Buddha, though the first thing that will strike you is the disturbingly life-like **statue** of a revered monk in front of them – even his spectacles have been added.

If Matoc Pagoda fires an interest in all things Khmer, you might venture into the **Khmer Museum** (Mon–Sat 7–11am & 1–5pm), whose low-key exhibits include stringed instruments made of snakeskin and coconut husks, and some wonderfully colourful food covers, shaped like conical hats, but with a stippled surface. From the museum, cross the street to **Kleang Pagoda**, a fine Khmer pagoda surrounded by a two-tiered terrace. The doors and windows are adorned with traditional Khmer motifs in dazzling greens, reds and golds, while inside is a wonderfully reposeful golden Sakyamuni statue, whose peace is disturbed every hour, on the hour, by a clock that plays Dvorak's *New World Symphony* at varying speeds. Around his head spins a wheel of fairy lights. Both the museum and Kleang Pagoda are at the eastern end of Nguyen Chi Thanh, at the top of town.

Practicalities

The waterway running roughly west to east splits Soc Trang in two, with most of the town nestling on its south bank. The town's spine is Hai Ba Trung, which runs across the water, before becoming Tran Hung Dao on the southern outskirts. The **bus station** is north of the river, on Nguyen Chi Thanh. Long-distance buses leave in the early hours, so unless you're up with the lark, ask your cyclo driver to carry on a few hundred metres west of here, to where Hung Vuong hits Highway 1, and wave down a passing bus. *Soc Trang Tourist* is across the road from the bus station at 131 Nguyen Chi Thanh (☎079/853498); its staff, though, are a sleepy-headed bunch.

Avoid the temptation to **stay** in the unsavoury *Tay Nam Hotel* opposite the bus station and head instead for Tran Hung Dao's excellent *Khanh Hung Hotel* (☎079/821026; ②), where all rooms have air-con and satellite TV. Otherwise, the 19-room *Phong Lan* (☎079/821619; ③) on the south bank of the river at 124 Dong Khoi is fine – some rooms have a balcony over the river and the management sometimes agrees to a discount. When it's time to **eat**, *Quan Com Hung*, north of the river on Hai Ba Trung, serves generous portions of *com*, and has a fuller menu in Vietnamese; or there's a fascinating restaurant at the *Phong Lan* hotel – waiters produce a menu from a restaurant in Philadelphia, you choose, and they give it their best shot.

Bac Lieu

Beyond Soc Trang the landscape becomes progressively more waterlogged and water palms hug the banks of the waterways that criss-cross it. A little over 40km southwest of Soc Trang, Highway 1 dips south towards the crown of **BAC LIEU**, before veering off west to Ca Mau. An unremarkable town geared around shrimp farming, oyster gathering and salt production, Bac Lieu may not be able to boast sights to set the pulse racing, but with the only places to stay between Soc Trang and Ca Mau it's worth keeping in mind as a staging-post.

The **bus station** is 1.5km north of town, and cyclos shuttle back and forth to the centre. Of the two **hotels** on central Hoang Van Thu, an air-con room at the *Rang Dong* (☎078/822437; ②) is your better option; in the cheaper rooms you'll have to run the gauntlet of some archaic communal washing facilities. The neighbouring *Bac Lieu* (☎078/822621; ③) is kept in a slovenly state: mid-range rooms are adequate if overpriced, but the cheapest ones are truly squalid. There's a **restaurant** below the *Bac Lieu*, where, happily, standards are higher than upstairs, while along the road that leads to the bus station are a number of *banh bao* and baguette stalls, and *com* shops such as the clean and pleasant *Minh Thanh*, at 8 Tran Phu.

Ca Mau and around

With its left shoulder braced against the Bac Lieu Canal, the main road now trundles westwards towards the **Ca Mau Peninsula**. This far south, waterways are the most efficient means of travel – a point pressed home by the slender ferries moored in all the villages the road passes. Much of this pancake-flat region of the delta is composed of silt deposited by the Mekong, and the swamplands covering portions of it are home to a variety of wading birds. In addition to rice cultivation, shrimp farming is a major local concern – from the bus you're sure to spot shrimp ponds, demarcated by mud banks that have been baked and cracked crazily by the sun.

Vietnam's southernmost town of any size, **CA MAU** is a town with few redeeming features, and one which has changed little since 1989 when travel writer Justin Wintle described it as a "scrappy clutter...a backyard town in a backyard province". Unless you intend to explore its surrounding mangrove or cajeput forests (see below), don't waste your time coming down to Ca Mau. The town centre is banked against the narrow Ca Mau River, which snakes through it as though trying to wriggle free before the encroaching stilthouses squeeze the life from it; lurking along its north bank is the rag-tag squall of the **market**, a shantytown of canvas and sacking.

Around Ca Mau: swampland and bird-spotting

The **marshes** circling Ca Mau form one of the largest areas of swampland in the world. The Ca Mau Peninsula was a stronghold of resistance against France and America, and for this it paid a heavy price, as US planes dumped millions of gallons of Agent Orange defoliant over it to rob guerrillas of jungle cover. Further damage has been done to the swamp by the burgeoning shrimp-farm industry, but great swathes still remain, comprising vast mangrove and cajeput forests inhabited by sea birds, wading birds, waterfowl and honey bees, attracted by the mangrove's blossoms.

The swamplands can be explored through judicious use of public ferries and private boats (see "Into the swamps", over, for the low-down). Heading by ferry for **NAM CAN**, you'll drift past intensive shrimp farming, and around the settlement itself, there's dense **mangrove forest** to explore by chartered boat. The prime destination for birdspotters is **DAM DOI**, where you can charter a launch and strike off to one of two **bird sanctuaries** – Vuon Chim Dam Doi, or smaller but better Vuon Chim Tan Tien, the latter attracting as many as one hundred species in the wet season (Aug–Nov). The place to go to see the elegant trees of the **cajeput forest** is **U MINH**: the slender white trunks of the cajeput thrive in U Minh's shallow, marshy waters, and gliding through them in a boat is a truly tranquil experience. What's more the ferry ride to U Minh makes a cheap and interesting river trip even if you can't run to the extra expense of chartering a boat at the other end. Lining the ferry route are water palms, modest groves of cajeput, and fish traps consisting of triangles of bamboo sticks driven into the riverbed. Once at U Minh, there are several cheery com shops and a picturesque market to occupy you until the return journey.

Practicalities

Central Ca Mau lies north of the river, along the stretch of Ly Bon running southwest to northeast between Ngo Quyen and Phan Ngoc Hien. On arrival at the **bus** station 2km southeast of town, ask a xe dap loi driver to take you to the junction of Phan Ngoc Hien and Ly Bon. *Minh Hai Tourist* is near here, at 17 Nguyen Van Hai, while the Ca Mau branch of *Vietcombank* is a couple of minutes' walk away at 3 Ly Bon, and will **exchange** travellers' cheques. With so few serviceable roads around Ca Mau, locals rely on **ferries** to get around. From Boat Station A (*Ben Tau A*), 1km west of the centre, boats leave for points north; while vessels heading south depart from Boat Station B, 2km over the river and south of town. Ferries on the peninsula can be flagged down in the same way as buses.

Ca Mau's **hotels** aren't up to much. The *Ca Mau Hotel*, 20 Phan Ngoc Hien (☎078/831165; ③), is presently being restored, and worth checking out; otherwise, there are clean but unexciting rooms at near-neighbour the *Sao Mai Hotel* (☎078/831035; ②), or, if that's too pricey, try the *Tan Hung Guesthouse*, 11 Nguyen Van Hai (☎078/831622; ①), whose dark, cobwebbed fan rooms share unsavoury toilets.

It's much the same story with the town's **restaurants**. The *Trieu Chau*, 19 Nguyen Van Hai, is the best of a bad bunch, and its steamboats come recommended. Also passable is the *Hong Ky* restaurant, across the street – a hole-in-the-wall venue churning out filling Vietnamese dishes. Otherwise, there's a *bun bo Hué* stall below the *Tan Hung* at night; or else check out the **stalls** towards the southwestern end of Ly Bon.

Into the swamps

Unless you can afford a private vessel chartered through the local tourist office, the only way to access Ca Mau's swamps is to take a **public ferry** to an outlying settlement, and **rent a boat** there.

Given the relative slowness of ferries, this means rising early, though if you go to **Nam Can** (ferry from Boat Station B), you can get a head start by staying at the *Nam Can Hotel* (☎078/877039; ②). At Nam Can jetty, $10 should buy you three hours' touring around the mangrove swamps: tell boatmen you want to see "rung duoc". Boats (for **Dam Doi** (for the bird sanctuaries) also leave from Station B. To get to **U Minh**, catch a ferry at Boat Station A; and to explore further, ask boatmen at U Minh's jetty to take you to "Rung U Minh Ho" or tell them you want to see cajeput forest, "rung tram".

Long Xuyen

The road northwest of Can Tho, meanwhile, runs into **LONG XUYEN** some 60km later. Vietnamese towns don't come much more dull than Long Xuyen, but its location at the junction of the two main routes to the delta's northwestern corner means you may well end up here.

Dominating town is the spire of the ugly concrete **cathedral**, shaped like two upstretched arms whose hands clasp a cross. Numerous tiny portals shed light on the anaemic interior, illuminating gilt stations of the cross and another giant pair of hands over the altar, this one clutching a globe. Long Xuyen makes much of being the birthplace of Ton Duc Thang, successor to Ho Chi Minh as president of the Democratic Republic of Vietnam; a visit to his birthplace on **My Hoa Hung Island** provides an excuse for a trip on the Hau Giang, while a gallery in the **An Giang Museum** (Tues & Thurs 8–10am, Sun 8–10am & 6–8pm; $1), at 77 Thoai Ngoc Hau, houses such artefacts as the leg irons he wore in Con Dao Prison and

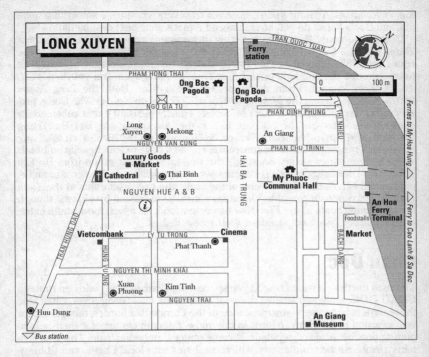

his prime ministerial bicycle. A large linga takes centre stage in the Oc Eo culture room (see box on p.151 for more on the ancient port of Oc Eo), among whose exhibits are an elegant wooden Buddha, so decayed it now resembles the running flesh of a golem; and a stone cairn, in which the ashes of the dead would have been deposited. The third gallery's rag-tag display of weaponry, scraps from American planes and pictures of Uncle Ho will induce a profound sense of *déjà vu*. Hurry past Long Xuyen's unsightly **market** and up to the western ends of Le Minh Nguon and Le Thi Nhieu, where cyclos whizz by and there's a real hotbed of commerce. En route, you'll pass the dragon-stalked roofs of the grandest building in town, **My Phuoc Communal Hall**.

Practicalities

Buses from Can Tho and Chau Doc screech to a halt a few hundred metres south of town, on Tran Hung Dao – coming from Chau Doc, yell for the driver to stop as you pass the cathedral. From Sa Dec and Cao Lanh you'll reach town via the An Hoa **ferry**; while services from Ho Chi Minh City come either through Can Tho or – more usually – Cao Lanh, and await passengers at the riverside end of Nguyen Hue for the return journey.

Passenger/cargo **boats** for Sa Dec (daily at noon) and Rach Gia (daily at 8am) depart from Long Xuyen's other ferry station, across the river and north of town. For what it's worth, *An Giang Tourism* is at 83–85 Nguyen Hue B; more usefully, the *Vietcombank*, 1 Hung Vuong, changes travellers' cheques – something none of Chau Doc's banks do yet, so plan ahead if that's your next destination.

Unless you count the cheap but truly unspeakable **rooms** at the grotty *Phat Thanh Hotel*, 2 Ly Tu Trong (☎076/852708; ①), a surgically clean billet at the *Huu Dung*, 283a Tran Hung Dao (☎076/853882; ②), represents the best value in town – though the similarly priced *Kim Tinh*, at 39 Nguyen Trai (☎076/853137; ①), is more central. From there, prices take a hike. Both the *Long Xuyen* (☎076/852927; ③) and the *Mekong* (☎076/852365; ③), on Nguyen Van Cung, profess to be classy hotels, but don't be fooled: equally pleasant – and substantially cheaper – rooms can be had, at either the *An Giang*, 40 Hai Ba Trung (☎076/852297; ②), or the *Xuan Phuong*, 68 Nguyen Trai (☎076/852041; ②). Long Xuyen isn't renowned for its **restaurants**, so you'll have to lean heavily on hotels when hunger pangs strike. Boasting "the well known cook group from Ho Chi Minh City", the *Long Xuyen*'s restaurant serves specialities such as snake, turtle, pigeon and eel. At the cheaper end of the scale, the two restaurants at the *Xuan Phuong* can rustle up passable Vietnamese meals, steaks and breakfasts, though the tiny dining room at the *Kim Tinh* has better food. As usual, **food stalls** in the central market knock out standard Vietnamese dishes.

Chau Doc

The road northwest from Long Xuyen splices huge expanses of paddy en route to **CHAU DOC**. Snuggled against the west bank of the Hau Giang River, Chau Doc these days falls on the Vietnamese side of the Cambodian border, though until it was awarded to the Nguyen lords in the mid-eighteenth century for their help in putting down a localized rebellion, it came under Cambodian rule. The area sustains a large Khmer community, which combines with local Chams and Chinese to form a diverse social melting-pot. Just as diverse is Chau Doc's religious make-up: as well as Buddhists, Catholics and Muslims, the region supports an estimated 1.5 million devotees of the indigenous Hoa Hao religion (see box opposite). Forays by Pol Pot's genocidal Khmer Rouge into this corner of the delta led to the Vietnamese invasion of Cambodia in 1978. Today, there's no such danger, and Chau Doc is a bustling, friendly town deserving a prominent place on your Mekong Delta itinerary.

The road from Long Xuyen runs out at Chau Doc, but rather than retracing your steps, a more exciting alternative is to follow the Vinh Te Canal that defines the border with Cambodia to Ha Tien, from where you can loop back via Rach Gia. It's also possible to take advantage of the occasional bus service to Triton (see p.147) and catch a bus out to the coast from there.

Arrival, information and transport

Buses offload southeast of town, on Le Loi, from where xe dap lois run into town. (Travelling south towards Long Xuyen, you might well see locals strapping cartons of contraband *Hero* cigarettes around their waists and limbs with elastic bands – you may be pressed to hide some, but if you don't get involved, there'll be no anxious moments at the police checkpoint en route.) If you're carrying travellers' cheques, make sure you change sufficient **money** in Long Xuyen; the *Incombank* on Nguyen Huu Canh changes US dollars – cash only.

THE HOA HAO RELIGION

Sited 20km east of Chau Doc, the diminutive village of Hoa Hao lent its name to a unique religious movement at the end of the 1930s. The **Hoa Hao Buddhist sect** was founded by the village's most famous son, Huynh Phu So. A sickly child, Huynh was placed in the care of a hermetic monk under whom he explored both conventional Buddhism and more arcane spiritual disciplines. In 1939, at the age of twenty, a new brand of Buddhism was revealed to him in a trance. Upon waking, Huynh found he was cured of his congenital illness, and began publicly to expound his breakaway theories, which advocated purging worship of all the clutter of votives, priests and pagodas, and paring it down to simple unmediated communication betwen the individual and the Supreme Being. The faith has a fairly strong **ascetic** element, with alcohol, drugs and gambling all discouraged. Peasants were drawn to the simplicity of the sect, and by rumours that Huynh was a faith healer in possession of prophetic powers; soon the Hoa Hao was a force to be reckoned with.

Almost immediately, the Hoa Hao developed a **political agenda**, and established a **militia** to uphold its fervently nationalist, anti-French and anti-communist beliefs. The Japanese army of occupation, happy to keep the puppet French administration it had allowed to remain nominally in charge of Vietnam on its toes, provided the sect with arms. For themselves, the French regarded the Hoa Hao with understandable suspicion: Huynh they labelled the "Mad Monk", imprisoning him in 1941 and subsequently confining him to a psychiatric hospital – where he promptly converted his doctor. By the time of his eventual release in 1945, the sect's uneasy alliance with the Viet Minh, which had been forged during World War II in recognition of their common anti-colonial objectives, was souring, and two years later Viet Minh agents assassinated him. The sect battled on until the mid-Fifties when **Diem's purge** of dissident groups took hold; its guerrilla commander, Ba Cut, was captured and beheaded in 1956, and by the end of the decade most members had been driven underground. Though in the early Sixties some of these resurfaced in the Viet Cong, the Hoa Hao never matched its early dynamism, and any lingering military or political presence was erased by the communists after 1975.

Today there are thought to be somewhere approaching 1.5 million Hoa Hao worshippers in Vietnam, concentrated mostly around Chau Doc. Some male devotees still sport the distinctive long beards and hair tied up in a bun that originally identified a Hoa Hao adherent.

Chau Giang is reached by **ferry** from the jetty opposite the GPO, and Con Tien Island from the one at the end of Thuong Dang Le.

Around 400m up Tran Hung Dao from the Con Tien jetty, a narrow concrete path marked "Ben Tau Ha Tien" signals the departure point for the passenger/cargo **boat** along the Vinh Te Canal to Ha Tien (daily 4am; $4.50).

Accommodation

Despite its limited number of **hotels**, Chau Doc's range of accommodation still runs from windowless hovels, up to presentable quarters with riverview, air-con and TV. All establishments bar one, the *Hang Chau*, are in the centre of town.

Chau Doc, 17 Doc Phu Thu (☎076/866484). No frills, but perfectly habitable if you don't mind the low-key massage parlour downstairs; even the cheapest rooms boast toilet and shower. ①

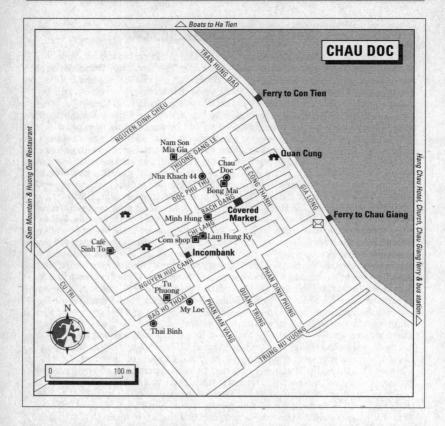

Hang Chau, 32 Le Loi (☎076/866196). A little over 300m east of the town centre, Chau Doc's swankiest hotel offers a range of mod-cons, and a free breakfast; give the riverside bungalows a miss, though. ③

My Loc, 51 Nguyen Van Thoai (☎076/866455). A fresh lick of paint wouldn't go amiss here; still, the place is geared to tourists, and a simple breakfast is thrown in for good measure; $2 extra gets you air-con. ①

Nha Khach 44, 44 Doc Phu Thu (☎076/866540). Bright corridors, sizeable and freshly painted rooms and amiable staff make this first choice in the budget range; a couple of extra dollars secure a huge room that sleeps four, and there are bikes for rent. ①

Thai Binh Hotel, 37 Nguyen Van Thoai (☎076/866221). Sleepy, family-run establishment, whose rooms – open-topped boxes, some sharing common toilets – are basic but unbeatable value; one deluxe room sleeps eight people. ①

The town

First stop should be the venerable **covered market**, a colonial relic running between Quang Trung and Le Cong Thanh. The red roof tiles may have long since faded and begun to slough off, but it still catches the eye, due in part to the cast-iron fans above both entrances, topped by metal mouldings of lion's heads with red flowers in their teeth. Inside, brick pillars, blackened like chimney stacks, support its cobwebbed, vaulted ceiling. More colonial reminders are on parade on nearby Doc Phu Thu, whose grand **shophouse terraces** flaunt arched upper-floor windows, and awnings propped up by decorous wrought-iron struts.

A grand, four-tiered gateway deep in the belly of the open market announces **Quan Cong Temple**. Beyond a courtyard that doubles as a playground to Chau Doc's most mischievous kids, two rooftop dragons oversee its entrance and the outer walls' vivid murals, their baubled whiskers bouncing in the wind. Tread carefully inside: two roving tortoises have been granted the freedom of the pagoda, at whose head is the familiar red visage of Quan Cong, sporting green robe and bejewelled crown, and surrounded by a rhinestone-studded red velvet canopy. In comparison, the lofty chambers of nearby **Chau Phu Temple** seem devoid of character; fans of gilt woodwork will find much to divert them, but others should head northwest up Tran Hung Dao, where long boardwalks lead to sizeable **stilthouse communities**.

Across the river

Once you've exhausted the town, you might venture to one of two settlements a stone's throw away across the Hau Giang River. Closest is **Con Tien Island**, whose stilthouse sprawl can be explored from the jetty at the eastern end of Thuong Dang Le. Ferries leave regularly, but if you charter your own boat you can enjoy the river at your leisure, and stop off at one of the **fish-farm houses** floating on oil drums out on the river, above nets of fish that are fed through a hatch in the floor.

Opposite the GPO, and past a gaggle of hawkers selling Cambodian cigarettes, a second jetty strikes out past a cluster of bobbing houseboats; from here, you can access Cham-dominated **Chau Giang District**. Turn right when you dock, and you'll discover kampung-style wooden houses, sarongs and white prayer caps that betray the influence of Islam, as do the twin domes and pretty green and white minaret of the **Mubarak Mosque**. Just beyond the mosque, another ferry delivers you back to the west bank, setting you down just below the *Hang Chau*. While you're down this way you might visit the yellow-washed stucco walls and distinctive dome of **St Laurence's Church**, which was established by a French missionary late last century. Beside it, Saint Joseph presides over a pretty garden, while statues of two local Catholic martyrs oversee the courtyard.

Sam Mountain

Arid, brooding **Sam Mountain** rises dramatically from an ocean of paddy fields 5km southwest of Chau Doc. More hill than mountain, it's known as Nui Sam to Vietnamese tourists, who flock here in their thousands to worship at its clutch of pagodas and shrines. A trip out to the mountain has become *de rigueur* for visitors to town, but it's a distinctly tacky experience. From town, a road runs bowling-alley-straight to the foot of the mountain, hemmed in to the left by a canal lined with eucalyptus and *vo* (retractable fishing nets), and to the right by a spine of stilthouses. An arm of karaoke-belching cafés reaches out to greet you as you near the foot of the mountain.

Sam doesn't believe in saving the best until last: ahead, as you approach from town, is kitsch, 1847-built **Tay An Pagoda**, the pick of the bunch, its frontage awash with portrait photographers, beggars, joss stick vendors and bird-sellers (liberating a caged bird is believed to bring good fortune). Tourist blurb describes its style as "Hindu-Islamic", and certainly the central tower is reminiscent of a minaret. Guarding the pagoda are two elephants, one black, one white, and a shaven-headed Quan Am Thi Kinh. The number of gaudy statues inside exceeds two hundred: most are of deities and Buddhas, but an alarmingly lifelike rendering of an honoured monk sits at one of the highly varnished tables in the rear chamber. Also in this room is an incongruous poster of Europe's nineteenth-century kings; while to the right of it an annexe houses a goddess with a thousand eyes and a thousand hands, on whose mound of heads teeters a tiny Quan Am.

Ba Chua Xu Temple, 50m beyond Tay An, honours Her Holiness Lady of the Country, a stone statue said to have been found on Sam's slopes early last century. The present building, with its four-tiered, glazed green tile roof, dates only from 1972; inside, the Lady sits in state in a marbled chamber, resplendent in red gown and peacock feathers. Glass cases in corridors either side of her are crammed to bursting with splendid garb and other offerings from worshippers, who flood here between the 23rd and 25th of the fourth lunar month, to see her ceremonially bathed and reclothed.

Having toured its religious sites, it'd be a shame not to head **up the mountain** itself – the track originates beyond a large, mustard-coloured school, 1km around Sam in a clockwise direction. After fifteen minutes, a sharp turn and a looming Tyrannosaurus Rex (one of several plastic creatures, among them rhinos, elephants and zebras, inhabiting a tacky park) give notice of an **observatory** that affords peerless views of the patchwork of fields below. There's a marked contrast between the lush paddy fields – scored by hundreds of waterways, like scratches on a school desk – and the barren mountain, on whose slopes cacti and scuttling scorpions thrive. Another twenty minutes to the top, but don't feel you have to go all the way, if you've had your fill of views – "military zone no picture" is daubed in red on a boulder at the peak. From here, Vietnamese soldiers keep a sharp eye on the Cambodian border, their barracks and the hilltop café making unlikely bedfellows.

Xe dap lois and xe lams cover the 5km to Sam, but if you rent a bike from *Nha Khach 44* (see "Accommodation", p.144), you can potter along the tracks at will.

Eating

Chau Doc has more **places to eat** than most Mekong Delta towns: it's mostly Vietnamese food that's available, though if you're crying out for a steak, or eggs for breakfast, you'll find somewhere that can oblige. Most of the recommendations below are in the town centre – there's a further glut of places on the road ringing Sam Mountain, though none are particularly outstanding and their prices are over the odds. A snack at one of the **stalls** that set up at the front of the market, along Gia Long, won't break the bank if you're strapped for cash.

Bong Mai, 17 Doc Phu Thu. Given the pristine white colonial mansion housing this place, the bare dining room is a let-down; besides Western and Eastern breakfasts and the more conventional Vietnamese staples, there's snake and tortoise on the menu.

Café Sinh To, Bach Dang. Fruit-juice bar that sets up nightly in front of the town basketball court: if you can stomach the unrelenting disco beat, get set for sugar-cane juice and sublime sapodilla shakes.

Huong Que, 53/4 Nui Sam. A Vietnamese menu and no spoken English make ordering tricky at this streetside outfit, betrayed by a *Tiger Beer* sign 1km west of town, but unsurpassed views over the paddy fields behind amply reward perseverance.

Lam Hung Ky, 71 Chi Lang. Smiles are few and far between, but the imaginative menu, featuring dishes like beef with bitter melon and black beans, more than compensates; a full meal, including a beer, will come to around $2.50.

Minh Hung, covered market, Chi Lang. The pick of a number of nocturnal restaurants which haul in passing tourists – their generous steamboat fills a gap.

Nam Son Mia Gia, 100 Thuong Dang Le. Spick and span roadside eating house serving wonderfully tasty *hu tieu*; a little pricier than normal, but worth it.

Tu Phuong Restaurant, 76 Nguyen Van Thoai. Sour soups and pork on rice doled out in clean but unfussy surrounds.

Southwest to Ba Chuc

With your own transport, or the services of a Honda om driver, it's possible to explore the sweep of staggeringly beautiful countryside southwest of Chau Doc. Refugees fleeing Pol Pot's Cambodia boosted the Khmer populace here in the late Seventies, and Khmer Rouge forays after them led to numerous indiscriminate massacres; a grisly memorial to one such massacre, at the village of Ba Chuc (see below), lends a tragic focus to a trip through the region.

With Sam Mountain rounded, the road is marshalled ahead by lush paddy fields etched by an intricate canal system. Beyond a left fork at **NHA BANG**, the variable road chicanes through gently sloping hills, some dark and littered with scree, others green and wooded. There's a timeless grandeur to the scenery, here: distant waterways are lined by spiky *thot not* trees, whose fronds are clustered like firework flashes, and whose fruits, reminiscent of coconuts roasted in a fire, yield a handful of transparent, edible seeds; and you're likelier to see cattle- and horse-drawn carts than cars or trucks. In time, darker skins, red-and-white checked turbans and horned temples indicate you're in Khmer territory. As you hit **TRITON**, a dirt track to your right signals the way to Ba Chuc, but carry on into Triton town for a drink, and to see the fine Khmer pagoda that stands proudly to the right of the road, beyond the bus station.

You'll know you're upon **BA CHUC**, when you notice graceful glades of bamboo flanking the road. Scoot through the town's tatty main drag and bear right, and you'll quickly spot the **memorial** to the thousands who died in 1978's massacre, standing peacefully in a field (the return trip by Honda om should cost around $7–8). An unattractive pink concrete canopy fails to lessen the impact of the eight-sided memorial: behind its glass enclosure, the bleached skulls of the dead of Vietnam's own "killing fields" are piled in ghoulish heaps, grouped according to age to underline the infancy of many of the dead. The bare wooden table that suffices as a shrine bristles with joss-stick stems. To the right of the memorial is **Tam Buu Pagoda**, where a horrific montage of photos shows buckled, abused corpses scattered around both its walls and those of nearby **Phi Lai Pagoda**.

Rach Gia

Roughly 11km below Long Xuyen the road that connects **Kien Giang Province** with the rest of Vietnam shoots off southwest towards the coast, chased all the way by the Rach Soi Canal. Pending repair work, this stretch of road is the worst in the delta and occupants of settlements bordering it are forced to drape canopies

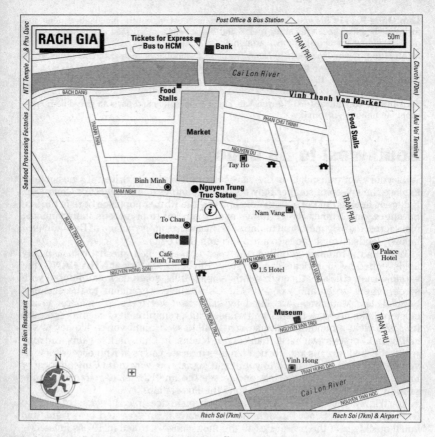

fashioned from empty cement sacks over doors and windows, to keep at bay the gagging fug of dust thrown up by passing traffic.

Three hours after leaving Long Xuyen you'll reach the thriving port of **RACH GIA**, which teeters precariously over the Gulf of Thailand. Rach Gia is home to a community of almost 150,000 people, who eke out a living through rice cultivation in the surrounding fields, or by tapping the gulf's rich vein of seafood. A small islet in the mouth of the Cai Lon River forms the hub of town, but the urban sprawl spills over bridges to the north and south of it and onto the mainland. At first sight, Rach Gia is a noisy, claustrophobic, and not immediately likeable place, its central area shoehorned tightly between Le Loi and Tran Phu. Given time though, its nautical charm can work quite a spell on visitors.

Arrival, information and accommodation

Buses from points north pull up 500m above town, at 30 Thang 4's Noi Tinh Station. Arrivals from Long Xuyen and beyond hit the coast at Rach Soi, 7km southeast of Rach Gia. Some continue on into town, dropping you outside the *Palace Hotel*; others terminate at Rach Soi, from where a xe lam or Honda om will get you to the centre. Arriving at the **airport** (flights from Ho Chi Minh), you'll need to catch a xe lam to Rach Soi, and then another into Rach Gia.

When you're ready to **move on**, xe lams heading back to Rach Soi can be picked up on Tran Phu, though if you're taking one of the four nightly **express buses to Ho Chi Minh**, you'll board in town: buy tickets in advance from the building marked "Toc Hanh", opposite the **GPO** at 20, 30 Thang 4, or from the booth beside the **telecom centre** just north of town. Nearby is the *Vietcombank*, where you can **exchange** travellers' cheques as well as cash – a priority if you're pushing on to Ha Tien or the Hon Chong Peninsula. **Boats** out of Rach Gia depart from one of two sites. Ferries bound for Phu Quoc Island (see p.151) depart daily at 7am from a quay 200m west of the Nguyen Trung Truc Pagoda; tickets are about $4. From Mui Voi ("Elephant's Nose") terminal, at the eastern end of town, passenger/cargo boats leave for Ha Tien and Long Xuyen (both trips cost under $1). If you're doing a circuit that includes Phu Quoc Island, check out the twice-weekly **flight** from Ho Chi Minh City that calls at Rach Gia before proceeding to Phu Quoc and then heading home. For tickets or information, contact either the airport (☎077/864326), or *Kien Giang Tourism* – which can also arrange boat **excursions** around Rach Gia – at 12 Ly Tu Trong (☎077/862081).

Accommodation

As far as **accommodation** goes, the cheery new *Palace Hotel* (☎077/863049; ①) takes some beating; its handful of endearing little top-floor garrets, which share a spruce communal bathroom, are real bargains. Otherwise, the central *To Chau* (☎077/863718; ②) is clean and habitable – ask for one of the rooms with hot water – as is the nearby *Binh Minh* (☎077/862154; ①). Surly staff and pokey rooms characterize the *1.5* (May 1) *Hotel* (☎077/862103; ②), on Nguyen Hung Son, though its pricier rooms are very pleasant.

The town

Once you've seen the wartime souvenirs and Oc Eo relics – shards of pottery, coins and bones – of the pedestrian **museum** at 21 Nguyen Van Troi (variable opening hours), and dived through the lively **markets**, you've pretty much bled Rach Gia town dry of sights. Walk west along **Bach Dang** for a few hundred metres, though, and the town springs spectacularly to life. To your right is the upper channel of the Cai Lon River, choked by an armada of blue fishing boats, on each of whose red-painted decks sits a "lifeboat" coracle. Boats are decked out as for a parade, their masts and rigging traced with bunting and colourful flags, under which cooks squat, preparing food for their crews. The **shoreline** is a hive of activity: men and women darn and fold nets; charcoal sellers hawk their wares to ships' captains; and roadside cafés heave with fishermen – many of whom have seen the bottoms of a few *BGI* bottles – awaiting the next tide.

Turn onto the dirt track to your right, 50m after Bach Dang veers left onto Hoang Dieu: past the boats laid up for repainting, and the chickenwire frames pegged with drying fish, you'll reach Rach Gia's **seafood processing factories**. In corrugated iron sheds around here, conical-hatted women squat over buckets of octopus and squid, which they scrape clean for export to other Asian countries, receiving less than $1.50 a day for their trouble.

There's another flotilla of fishing boats one block south, beyond the *Hoa Bien Restaurant*. Rowing-boat **ferries** thread these waters, taking fishermen back to their boats – take one yourself, and you may be invited onto a ship. Sunsets over distant **Turtle Island** (so-called because its dual humps look like a turtle's head and shell) are breathtaking viewed from the makeshift cafés around here.

Nguyen Trung Truc Temple

Of Rach Gia's handful of pagodas, only the **Nguyen Trung Truc Temple**, at 18 Nguyen Cong Tru, is really worth making an effort to see. From 1861 to 1868, Nguyen Trung Truc spearheaded anti-French guerrilla activities in the western region of the delta: a statue in the centre of Rach Gia depicts him preparing to unsheathe his sword and harvest a French head. In 1861, Nguyen masterminded the attack that culminated in the firing of the French warship *Esperance*. For this and other events, he became a wanted man, and was forced to retreat to Phu Quoc, from where he continued to oversee the campaign. Only after the French took his mother hostage in 1868 and threatened to kill her did he turn himself in, and in October of the same year he was executed by a firing squad in the centre of Rach Gia. Defiant to the last, his final words could have been lifted from a Ho Chi Minh speech: "So long as grass still grows on the soil of this land, people will continue to resist the invaders."

The riotous colour scheme of the temple roof, with its lurid pink tiles rising to powder-blue crests that are stalked by dragons made of porcelain shards, is plainly visible from a distance. Inside, a portrait of Nguyen in black robe and hat provides the main chamber with its centrepiece. Before it stands a framed poster of other nineteenth-century anti-colonialists – Ky Con, Ham Nghi, Duy Tan, Phan Chu Trinh among them – which reads like a Vietnamese street directory. Two darkened paintings above the front doors, one of which depicts the firing of the *Esperance*, continue the anti-colonial theme. Up at the main altar, the brass urn labelled "Anh hung N.T.T." and flanked by slender storks standing on two cheeky-looking yellow turtles, is said to hold the ashes of Nguyen Trung Truc himself.

Inland to the Oc Eo ruins

Think hard before making a trip to the ancient **ruins of Oc Eo**, 12km east of Rach Gia. Time and museum curators have conspired to strip this former outpost of the Funan Empire (see box on facing page) down to its pilings, and there's now so little to see here that even the provincial tourist office advises against the excursion. If you are still tempted but don't want to shell out dollars galore for a boat through the tourist office in Rach Gia (see p.149), take the boat from Mui Voi Station to Long Xuyen as far as Tan Hoi village ($1 round-trip), then walk to Vong The village.

Eating

When it's time to **eat**, the seafront *Hoa Bien* claims the best site in town and is famed locally for its excellent seafood, though there are several more affordable options, like the venerable *Nam Vang*, where dusty jars of mysterious wines line the back wall, and homemade *banh bao* are served from a Pisa-like tower of bamboo steaming-baskets. Nearby *Tay Ho* is another winner, but don't expect everything on the menu to be available; or there's the *Vinh Hong*, where the essential ingredients of its seafood dishes eye you warily from tanks mounted on the walls. To round off

OC EO AND THE FUNAN EMPIRE

Between the first and sixth centuries, the western side of the Mekong Delta, southern Cambodia and much of the Gulf of Siam's seaboard came under the sway of the Indianized **Funan Empire**, an early forerunner of the great Angkor civilization. The heavily romanticized annals of contemporary Chinese diplomats describe how the Funan Empire was forged when an Indian Brahmin visiting the region married the daughter of a local serpent-god; and how the serpent rendered the region suitable for cultivation by drinking down the waters of the flood-plains. Such fables are grounded in truth: Indian traders would have halted here to pick up victuals en route from India to China, and would have disseminated not only their Hindu beliefs, but also their advanced irrigation and wet-rice cultivation methods.

One of Funan's major trading ports, **Oc Eo**, was located east of Rach Gia. In common with other Funan cities, Oc Eo was ringed by a moat and consisted of wooden dwellings raised off the ground on piles. Judging by the discovery of Persian, Egyptian, Indian and Chinese artefacts and even a gold coin depicting the Roman Emperor Marcus Aurelius at Oc Eo sites, the port must have played host to an intriguing diversity of traders from around the world.

The Funan Empire finally disappeared in the seventh century, when it was absorbed into the adjacent **Chen La** Empire (see p.59).

a meal, head for the *Café Minh Tam*, where fruit cocktails and ice cream come with sugar-coated cream crackers and a sprinkling of nuts and sultanas.

Phu Quoc Island

It's a little under 120km from Rach Gia to **PHU QUOC ISLAND**, which rises from its slender southern tip like a genie released from a bottle. Stranded just off the southern coast of Cambodia in the Gulf of Thailand, the island – which spans 46km from north to south – is classed as a district of Kien Giang Province, though it's also claimed by Cambodia, which calls it Kho Tral. Phu Quoc's isolation made it an attractive hiding place for two of the more famous figures from Vietnam's past. Nguyen Anh holed up here while on the run from the Tay Son Brothers in the late eighteenth century (see p.413), and so too, in the 1860s, did Nguyen Trung Truc (see facing page). Today, over 40,000 inhabitants and a sizeable population of indigenous Phu Quoc dogs dwell on the island, which is famous throughout Vietnam for its black pepper and its fish sauce (*nuoc mam*), graded like olive oil. At present, Phu Quoc crops up only rarely on tourists' agendas, but with Singaporean entrepreneurs fast hatching plans to capitalize on its lush forests and fine beaches and turn it into a resort island, this looks set to change.

After you've explored one of the *nuoc mam* factories in Duong Dong, and promenaded along its waterfront (at its busiest and most colourful during the squid and cuttlefish season, normally between Jan and May), you'll want to take a Honda om further afield. Unspoilt beaches ring Phu Quoc, but the best of them all is **Bai Kem**, a few kilometres northeast of An Thoi quay – the name means "ice-cream beach", an alluring reference to its soft, white sand. **Ham Ninh Beach**, further up the east coast, also comes recommended, and with $40 to spend on chartering a boat from An Thoi, you might take the three-kilometre trip to **Tham Island**, where there's fine swimming and snorkelling. If beaches don't appeal there are two cleansing hot springs in the centre of the island – ask your Honda driver for **Suoi Da Ban** or **Suoi Chanh**; the forested mountains nearby can be explored, but the three northernmost peaks on the island are off-limits owing to their proximity to Cambodia.

Practicalities

Unless you arrive on a flight from Ho Chi Minh via Rach Gia (see p.149), your boat will dock at **An Thoi Quay**, at the south of the island. From here, a bus connects with the island's only settlement of any size, **DUONG DONG**, which lies halfway up its west coast. Here you'll find the only **hotel** on the island that accepts foreigners, the state-run *Huong Bien* (☎077/846113; ②), as well as a branch of *Kien Giang Tourist* (☎077/846138).

Hon Chong Peninsula

After a little over two hours the road running northwest of Rach Gia to Ha Tien hits **BA HON**, a pretty settlement from where a left turn leads, after around 10km, to the **Hon Chong Peninsula**. A string of offshore isles has earnt this region the monicker "mini-Ha Long", but it's as a coastal resort that it draws tourists. Sadly, Hon Chong is living on borrowed time, as Swiss investors are looking to finance a cement factory here. But in the meantime its calm waters and secluded, palm-fringed beaches make the peninsula far and away the best spot for relaxation in the delta.

Though described as being in the peninsula's main settlement of **BINH AN**, the area's two places to stay in fact lie a couple of kilometres south of the village's core, though all bus and Honda om drivers will know where to drop you. Rooms are spacious and salubrious at the *Binh An Guesthouse* (☎077/854332; ①) but the *Hon Trem Guesthouse* (☎077/854331; ①), formerly reserved for high-ranking communist cadres, can claim the better location, and rents out bikes.

The **beach** in front of the *Binh An Guesthouse* is fine for sunbathing, but too spongy for swimming. Things are better nearer the *Hon Trem*; but the most spectacular beach lies 1.5km further south. After passing cacti, tamarind and *thot not* trees, the coastal track peters out at a towering cliff, into which **Sea and Mountain Pagoda** ("Hai Son Tu"), has been hewn: a low doorway leads from its outer chamber to a grotto in the cliff's belly, where statues of Quan Am and several Buddhas are lit by gas lamps. The cramped stone corridor that runs on from here makes as romantic an approach to a beach as you could imagine. As you hit the sand, the twin peaks of **Father and Son Isle** ("Hon Phu Thu") rear up in front of you; if they look familiar it's because they feature on the logo of *Kien Giang Tourism*. The beach itself is a little gem, its clean sand and placid waters disturbed only by the odd bobbing fishing boat. For a small fee, kids armed with torches will take you round nearby **Diamond Cave** and point out strangely shaped stalactites supposed to resemble monkeys, eagles and Buddhas.

Food couldn't be fresher than at beachfront *Quan Kim Cuong*, where fruits of the sea are bought off fishermen on the beach right in front of you. At the *Hoa Cuc*, the better of the two restaurants at the entrance to the cave, you can grill your own prawns, turning them with chopsticks – but you'll miss the sunset from here.

Boatmen and women will approach you on the road to take you to the surrounding islands, though this will set you back at least $20 for the day. If you're still keen, your best bet is to head for the caves and monkey-infested forests of **Nghe Island**, an hour and a half away. Best of the area's handful of grottoes is **Hang Tien Grotto**, known locally as Ca Sau Grotto, and reached by sampan from the centre of Binh An. Nguyen Anh (later to become Gia Long) hid here while on the run after the Tay Son Rebellion, and locals have dubbed its stone plateaux as his throne, sofa, bed and so on.

A **bus** from Binh An leaves from Rach Gia daily at 9am, returning at 4am the next morning; or take a Honda om ($1.50) from Ba Hon to the main Rach Gia–Ha Tien road and wave down a bus there.

Ha Tien

Past the turning to the Hon Chong Peninsula, buses whizz over a bridge spanning an estuary crammed with blue fishing boats, and continue up to the far north-western corner of the delta. Beyond Ba Hon, the road is funnelled by the coastline to the left and vast tracts of water palm to the right, towards dusty but endearing **HA TIEN**, 93km northwest of Rach Gia. Lapped by the Gulf of Thailand, and only a few kilometres from the Cambodian border, Ha Tien has a real end-of-the-line feel, despite a thriving population of around 90,000. This atmosphere of remoteness is accentuated by the aged pontoon bridge you need to cross to reach the town proper.

Many visitors find Ha Tien, with its shuttered terraces, crumbling colonial buildings and ubiquitous mats of seafood drying in the sun, the quaintest and most beautiful town in the delta; it's also one of the few with a substantial recorded history. Founded with the permission of the Cambodian lords who then ruled this region, by Chinese immigrant **Mac Cuu** in 1674, the town quickly thrived, capitalizing on its position astride the trade route between India and China. By the turn of the century, Siam (later Thailand) had begun to eye the settlement covetously, and Mac Cuu was forced to petition Hué for support. The resulting alliance, forged with Emperor Minh Vuong in 1708, ensured Vietnamese military back-up, and the town prospered further. Mac Cuu died in 1735, but the familial fiefdom continued down seven generations, until the French took over in 1867. Subsequently, the town became a resistance flashpoint, with Viet Minh holing up in the surrounding hills, and even sniping on French troops from the **To Chau Mountain**, to the south.

Once you've dipped into Ben Tran Hau's lively waterfront **market** and examined the fishing boats unloading below the common land to the west of it, you've pretty much exhausted the sights of Ha Tien. Walk up Mac Thien Tich and west along Mac Cuu though, and a temple dedicated to Mac Cuu stands at the foot of the hill where he and his relatives lie buried in semicircular Chinese graves; beyond courtyard walls as fiery red as the dragons on its roof, three electric "incense" sticks glow constantly before Mac Cuu's funerary tablet, keeping the memory of Ha Tien's founding father alive. Mac Cuu's actual **grave** is uppermost on the hill, daubed with a yin and yang symbol, and guarded by two swordsmen, a white tiger and a blue dragon. From this vantage point, there are good views from the hill over the mop tops of the coconut trees below and down to the river.

Further up Mac Thien Tich, meanwhile, is mellow **Tam Bao Pagoda**, set in tree-lined grounds dominated by an attractive lotus pond and a huge statue of Quan Am. Out the back of this gaudy yellow pagoda, said to have been founded

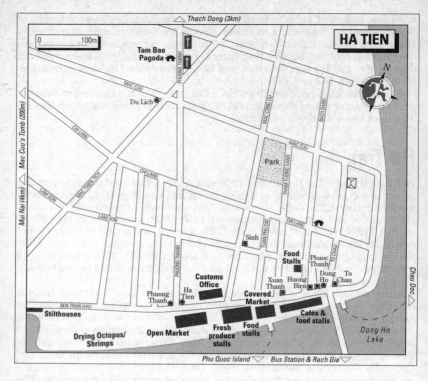

by Mac Cuu himself, is a pretty garden tended by the resident nuns, its colourful flowers interspersed with tombs. In the rear chamber of the pagoda, a statue of the goddess with a thousand hands and a thousand eyes sits on a lurid pink lotus; behind her are photos and funerary tablets remembering the local dead, while rudimentary drawings of the ten Buddhist hells hang to the left of her.

Biking around Ha Tien

A full day can be spent **biking** through the countryside around Ha Tien, with a convenient circular route northwest of town meaning you won't need to back-track; bikes can be rented at either the *To Chau* or *Du Lich* hotels (see "Practicalities" opposite).

Strike off west along Lam Son, and you'll soon be touring through magical coun-tryside, peopled by ducks, pigs, and children riding their pet buffaloes. Endless rice fields, coconut groves and swathes of water palm hem in the track as it kinks gently around low-lying hills towards the Cambodian border. A **war cemetery** serves as a landmark 2.5km from town, and from here it's another 1.5km to the first of two marked turnings to **Mui Nai** – "Stag's Head Peninsula", though you'd be hard pressed to see the silhouette of a stag's head in of any of the surrounding hills. The turning leads past a picturesque village to a peaceful, dark-sand cove.

If you hadn't already guessed this was Khmer country, **Mui Nai Pagoda**, just beyond the turning, leaves you in no doubt. Given its unremarkable fittings, though, sneaking past the aggressive geese that patrol the pagoda's yard represents an unnecessary risk. Several hundred metres further on is the second Mui Nai turning, from which a track leads past two brick kilns weathered like aged Cham towers, to the best stretch of beach in the area. An undeniably pleasant – if not idyllic – 400-metre curve of sand, shaded by coconut palms and backed by lush green hills, the beach offers reasonable swimming in its clean but shallow waters. There's nowhere to stay, but a handful of cafés and restaurants means you can spend a full day here – pick of the bunch is the cheery red-brick *Sao Bien Seafood Restaurant*.

You'll see the 48-metre-high granite outcrop housing **Thach Dong**, or Stone Cave, long before you reach it; 3–4km past Mui Nai, the track hits a sealed road, and a right turn (a sign reading "Frontier Area" makes a left turn impossible) deposits you at its base. A **monument** shaped like a defiant clenched fist and commemorating the 130 people killed by Khmer Rouge forces near here in 1978 marks the entrance (daily 7am–6pm) to Thach Dong, beyond which steps lead up to a **cave-pagoda** that's home to a colony of swooping, squeaking bats. Its shrines to Quan Am, Buddha et al are unremarkable, and its walls graffiti-ed, but balconies hewn out of the side of the rock afford great views over the hills, paddy fields and sea below; look to your right and you're peering into Cambodia.

From here, another 3km brings you to journey's end.

Practicalities

Buses terminate below the southern end of the pontoon bridge that links Ha Tien with the rest of Vietnam, from where it's a short walk up to town. Street names count for more than numbers here, the most important being waterfront Ben Tran Hau, from where **ferries** depart for Chau Doc and Phu Quoc Island, daily at 6am and 9am, respectively – but heed the warning below.

Across the street, Ha Tien's two best **accommodation** options square up to each other at the southern end of To Chau. First stop should be the recently revamped *Dong Ho Hotel* (☎077/852141; ③), which has greater finesse than the high-ceilinged rooms and communal facilities of the *To Chau* (☎077/852148; ①), opposite. Further west along Ben Tran Hau are the *Ha Tien* (no phone; ①) and the *Phuong Thanh* (☎077/852152; ①), both cheap but uninspiring, with surly staff, and big bare rooms sharing toilets and facilities, while rooms at Mac Thien Tich's grim *Du Lich Hotel* (☎077/852169; ②) are an insult, but depending on the extent of the *Dong Ho*'s overhaul, could still boast the only en suite facilities in town.

The *Phuoc Thanh*, at the eastern end of Ben Tran Hau, is the best **restaurant** in town, serving Vietnamese favourites such as spring rolls and *lau* off fine porcelain plates and bowls. Also good is the *Huong Bien,* two doors west of the *Phuoc*

BOATS TO CHAU DOC AND PHU QUOC ISLAND

At the time of writing, the local **police** were consistently stopping Westerners from taking public ferries from Ha Tien to **Chau Doc** and **Phu Quoc Island**. While this situation may change, we recommend you plan on getting to Phu Quoc Island from Rach Gia, and on finding an alternative route to Chau Doc. There doesn't seem to be a problem on **arrival** from either place.

Thanh – and its main rival. Otherwise, give the fly-blown *Xuan Thanh* a miss, and cross the street to the gaggle of **cafés and food stalls** on the waterfront, some of which keep a few simple *com* dishes on the go. Up into town, there's only a limited menu at Lam Son's friendly *Sinh* – locals are more interested in adding to the collection of empty snake-wine jars and dusty beer bottles along the back wall.

travel details

Buses

*It's almost impossible to give the **frequency** with which buses run. Though scheduled, long-distance public buses won't depart if empty. It's advisable to start your journey early – most long-distance departures leave between 5 and 7am, and few run after midday. **Journey times** can also vary; figures below show the normal length of time you can expect the journey to take.*

Ca Mau to: Bac Lieu (2hr); Can Tho (6hr); Ho Chi Minh City (11hr); Long Xuyen (8hr); Soc Trang (3hr 30min).

Can Tho to: Bac Lieu (4hr); Ca Mau (6hr); Chau Doc (3hr 40min); Ha Tien (7hr); Ho Chi Minh City (5hr); Long Xuyen (2hr); My Tho (3hr).

Chau Doc to: Ca Mau (9hr 40min); Can Tho (3hr 40min); Ho Chi Minh City (8hr 40min); Long Xuyen (1hr 40min).

Ha Tien to: Can Tho (7hr); Ho Chi Minh City (13hr); Long Xuyen (6hr); Rach Gia (4hr).

Long Xuyen to: Ca Mau (1hr 40min); Ha Tien (6hr); Ho Chi Minh City (7hr).

My Tho to: Can Tho (3hr); Cao Lanh (3hr); Cholon, Ho Chi Minh (2hr); My Thuan ferry (1hr 30min).

Vinh Long to: Sa Dec (1hr); Tra Vinh (2hr).

Boats

See "Getting around the delta", p.116, for more on the various craft that ply the delta's waterways.
Rach Gia to: Phu Quoc (1 daily; 10hr).

Flights

Phu Quoc to: Ho Chi Minh City (2 weekly; 50 min); Rach Gia (2 weekly; 30min).

Rach Gia to: Ho Chi Minh City (2 weekly; 2hr); Phu Quoc (2 weekly; 30min).

CHAPTER THREE

THE SOUTHERN AND CENTRAL HIGHLANDS

Vietnam's altitudinous midriff isn't the first region of the country that most tourists think to visit. And yet, after a hot and sticky stint labouring across the coastal plains, the **southern and central highlands**, with their host of ethnic minorities, mist-laden mountains and crashing water-falls, can provide an enjoyable contrast to the Tropics. Pinpointing the appeal of the area isn't easily done: travel can be a headache, and roads at times impassable; local tourist authorities have been known to raise a fuss about tourists travelling independently; and there are no really heart-stopping sights. For all that, the high-lands retain the elusive allure inherent in such simple pleasures as inhaling their invigoratingly chill airs; walking or cycling with a spray of mist on your face; and sipping at a piping hot coffee in a streetside café. What's more, despite being cocooned in colourful woolly jumpers, scarves and bobble hats, the highlanders exude a warmth and a sincerity unsurpassed elsewhere in the country, making a trip here doubly appealing.

Bounded to the west by the Cambodian border, and ranged out over the lofty peaks and broad plateaux of the **Truong Son Mountains**, the southern and central highlands stretch from the base of Highway 1 right up to the bottleneck of land that squeezes past Da Nang towards Hanoi and the north. The destructive slash-and-burn method of cultivation that once characterized the region's agriculture has now been all but phased out, and today its fertile red soils yield considerable **natural resources**, among them coffee, tea, rubber, silk and hardwood. Not all of the highlands, though, have been sacrificed to plantation-style economies of scale – or to the toxic flames of the napalm that US planes emptied over swathes of the region. Tracts of primeval forest still thrive, where **wildlife** as dramatic as elephants, bears, gibbons and tigers have survived the days when this area of Vietnam was famed as a happy hunting-ground for Saigon's idle rich and Hué's idle royal.

Of the highlands' 2.5 million inhabitants, many belong to the **ethnic minorities** that live on its plateaux, struggling to maintain their identities in the face of persistent pressure from Hanoi to assimilate. The French knew them as **montagnards** (or *Moï*, meaning "savages", if they were feeling less charitable), and the name, meaning "mountain folk", has stuck – though *montagnards* themselves would reject the suggestion of unity implicit in this generic term. The peoples of the central highlands – the Bahnar, Ede, Jarai, Sedang, Koho and Mnong are the largest – belong to one of two ethno-linguistic groups, Mon-Khmer or Malayo-Polynesian. Perhaps because of the substantial numbers of *montagnards* forced into labour on French plantations in colonial days, Viet Minh agents mined a rich

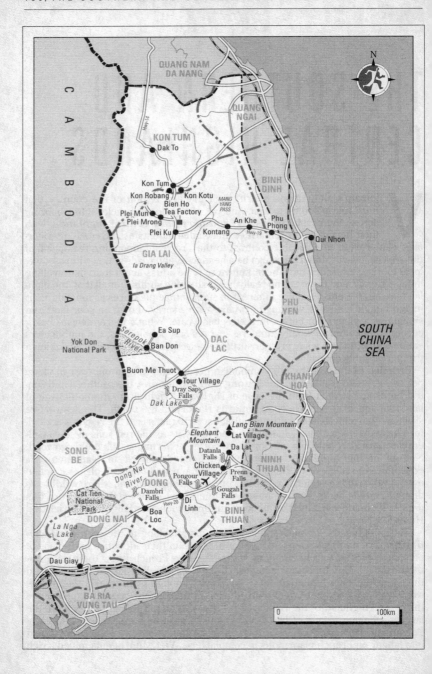

vein of anti-colonial feeling. Years later the highlands were deemed of sufficient strategic importance for several American army bases to be erected here, and *montagnard* conscripts put their knowledge of the upper plateaux to work for the forces of the South. For their pains, the minorities' villages were parcelled into strategic hamlets, and their land was devastated by carpet bombing.

Post-war, the communists proved unsympathetic to the *montagnards*' wish to retain their cultural identity. The rebel organization, **FULRO** (United Front for the Liberation of Oppressed Races; see p.439), which had emerged in the Sixties to uphold tribal rights, was weakened and ultimately extinguished by the government. Hanoi, for over a decade, followed a policy of **forced assimilation**, drawing together numerous villages into new settlements where they could be more closely monitored. Recently, the **liberalization** of *doi moi* has led to a positive shift in attitudes towards the minorities, and moves to preserve their unique cultures have gained extra impetus from their appeal to tourists. Whether these measures have come in time, though, remains to be seen.

Visiting one or other of the highlands' many minority villages independently can be difficult (see p.382 for some tips on village etiquette): you'll need either to go through a local tourist office (and pay handsomely for the privilege) or else arrange a Honda om.

For most of the tourists who ascend to these altitudes, the main target is **Da Lat**, an erstwhile French mountain retreat that looks more romantic in direct proportion to the heaviness of the mists draped across it. Visitors are often disappointed by Da Lat, however. The only settlement of any size in the region, it falls short of the idyll promised by many guidebooks, thanks to some dreary architecture and drearier tourist trappings. That said, the city is not without its charms, among them some beguiling colonial buildings, picturesque bike rides and a market overflowing with delectable fruits and vegetables. Above Da Lat, the **central highlands** harbour a series of gritty towns whose reputations rest less on tourist sights than on the villages and open terrain that ring them. Sensitive to the minority rights issue, the Vietnamese authorities opened this region to foreigners only in 1993, and the majority of tourists remain too intent on the beckoning charms of Highway 1 to drop by its main towns, **Buon Me Thuot**, **Plei Ku** and **Kon Tum**.

At present, the favoured way of seeing the highlands is on a minibus **tour** out of Hanoi or Ho Chi Minh City, but if the breakneck pace of a tour isn't to your taste, it's eminently possible to swing through these regions independently. You needn't travel far from the coast **to reach Da Lat**: perfectly good roads shoot up from the east side of Ho Chi Minh and Phan Rang. The best way of **pushing on from Da Lat** to the more northerly towns, until the new road linking Da Lat with Buon Me Thuot is finished, is to effect an S-shaped route, leapfrogging down to Nha Trang, then up to Buon Me Thuot, and then down again from Plei Ku to Qui Nhon. With your own transport, it *is* possible to push directly on from Da Lat to Buon Me Thuot along **Highway 27**, which links Buon Me Thuot to Highway 20, somewhere south of Chicken Village (see p.174) – though this road is dodgy, especially in the rainy season, and public buses prefer to loop around the coast to get to the central highlands. If you want to make life harder for yourself, you can even follow the high road from **Ho Chi Minh** straight up via Song Be Province **to Buon Me Thuot** – though buses spurn this bad road.

Once up in the central highlands, you've no option, other than expensive tourist office tours, than to travel by Honda om. Your highland experience will vary enormously depending upon **when you visit**. The dry season runs from November through to April; to see the region at its atmospheric best, though, you're better going in the wet season, May to October, although the rain can cause problems: some less polished roads will be awash and you could have trouble getting out to some less accessible villages.

DA LAT AND THE
SOUTHERN HIGHLANDS

The conical-hatted tappers that work the regimental avenues of the rubber plantations around **Dau Giay**, 67km east of Ho Chi Minh, have long since ceased to bat an eyelid at the scores of minibuses that hurtle past them to **Da Lat and the southern highlands**. As the road – **Highway 20** – starts its ascent, the rubber trees coralling its traffic occasionally peel away to permit tantalizing views of the valleys below. Tourist buses out of Ho Chi Minh invariably screech to a brief halt on the causeway traversing **La Nga Lake**, from where the wood and thatch **houseboats** cast adrift on its waters are only a zoom lens away. Locals use curious foot-powered rowing boats to access their homes, under which lie fish-farms similar to those at Chau Doc (see p.145). East of La Nga, Highway 20 drags its heels through wooded slopes, whose gentle peaks are almost invariably draped with torn-tossed clouds. The slopes' verdant greens are flecked only occasionally by the red-tiled roofs of farmsteads and the roving figures of grazing cattle.

In time these hills yield to the tea, coffee and mulberry plantations of the **Bao Loc Plateau**. If you want to make a pitstop between Ho Chi Minh and Da Lat, your best bet is the plantation-town of **Bao Loc**, as more diminutive **Di Linh**, 35km further on, is bereft of hotels. Unless you're effecting a very roundabout route to Phan Rang, **Da Lat** signposts journey's end.

Bao Loc to Da Lat

The terrain around the mid-sized settlement of **BAO LOC** resembles a sheet of paper that's been first crumpled, and then flattened out again. The plains pinched between the low ridges of the Bao Loc Plateau provide rich agricultural pickings: as well as **tea** and **coffee**, locals cultivate the mulberry bushes off whose leaves **silkworms** feed. The area's main attraction, until access to nearby **Cat Tien National Park**'s wild cats, elephants and monkeys is improved, is the reasonably impressive, 25-metre drop of **Dambri Waterfall** (daily 7am–5pm; $1), some 18km out of town. The fall features on many a Ho Chi Minh City tour agenda, but a Honda om from Bao Loc will also get you there; if you've reached Bao Loc under your own steam, follow the road that strikes north from beside the post office, veer left at the first two forks – the first is signposted by two burnt-out helicopters – and then follow the signs. The road to the fall bisects rolling countryside carpeted by coffee and mulberry plantations, and passes cottage silk farms whose whereabouts are betrayed by the bamboo baskets of mulberry leaves outside them. From the entrance to Dambri, a five-minute hike through the forest encircling the fall hauls you up to the viewpoint, where only some ugly spider's-web fencing stands between you and a precipice over which a torrent tumbles in the rainy season.

Accommodation in Bao Loc boils down to the ropey partitioned rooms at the *Bao Loc* (☎063/864107; ①), and the infinitely more appealing *Seri* (☎063/864150; ③), a sizeable place with IDD and exchange facilities. Both are on Highway 20 as it courses through town (first up, coming from Ho Chi Minh, is the *Bao Loc*, followed, 600m later, by the *Seri*), and both have in-house **restaurants**; or explore one of the several stalls and restaurants between the *Bao Loc* and the GPO.

More hummocky tea plantations abound along the road around quaint **DI LINH**. Aged shuttered terraces mingle with more faceless buildings here, to create the feel of a provincial French hamlet; the pretty old **church** puts the icing on the cake. Around 25km beyond Di Linh, pine trees begin to feature in the landscape; at this point you'll see signs for two of the region's most impressive waterfalls, **Pongour** to the left, and **Gougah** to the right. The final ten-kilometre stretch of road into Da Lat cuts through heavily wooded slopes.

Da Lat and around

Hinged by the Cam Ly River, and nestled at an elevation of around 1500m among the pitching hills of the **Lang Bian Plateau**, the city of **DA LAT** is Vietnam's premier hill station, a beguiling amalgam of mazy cobbled streets, picturesque churches, bounteous vegetable gardens and crashing waterfalls, all suffused with the intoxicating scents of pine trees and wood-smoke. The city's more fanciful historians swear its name is an acronym of the Latin, *dat aliis laetitium aliis temperiem*, "offering pleasure to another and freshness to another", though a far likelier derivation renders it as the stream ("da") of local hilltribe, the Lat.

It was Dr Alexander Yersin who first divined the therapeutic properties of Da Lat's temperate climate on an exploratory mission into Vietnam's southern highlands, in 1893; his subsequent report on the area must have struck a chord, for four years later Governor-General Paul Doumer of Indochina ordered the founding of a convalescent hill station, where Saigon's hot-under-the-collar *colons* could recharge their batteries, enjoy the bracing alpine chill, and perhaps even partake in a day's game-hunting. The city's Gallic contingent had to pack up their winter coats after 1954's Treaty of Geneva, but by then the cathedral, train station, villas and hotels had been erected, and the French connection well and truly forged. By tacit agreement during the American War, both Hanoi and Saigon refrained from bombing the city and it remains much as it was half a century ago.

It's important to come to Da Lat with no illusions. With a population of 135,000, Da Lat is anything but an idyllic backwater: sighting its forlorn architecture for the first time in the 1950s, Norman Lewis found the place "a drab little resort" and today its colonial relics and pagodas stand cheek by jowl with some of the dingiest examples of East European construction anywhere in Vietnam. Moreover, attractions here pander to the domestic tourist's predilection for such tat as swan-shaped pedal-boats and pony-trek guides in full cowboy gear, while at night the city can be as bleak as an off-season ski resort. Despite all this, Da Lat remains a quaint colonial curio, and a welcome tonic to heat-worn tourists – all in all, a great place to chill out, literally and metaphorically.

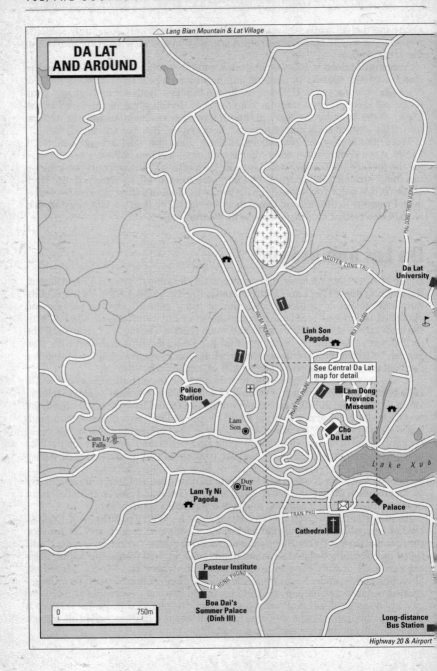

DA LAT
AND AROUND

△ Lang Bian Mountain & Lat Village

PHU DONG THIEN VUONG

NGUYEN CONG TRU

Da Lat
University

HAI BA TRUNG

Linh Son
Pagoda

BUI THI XUAN

See Central Da Lat
map for detail

Police
Station

PHAN DINH PHUNG

Lam Dong
Province
Museum

Lam
Son

Cho
Da Lat

Cam Ly
Falls

L a k e   X u a

Duy
Tan

Lam Ty Ni
Pagoda

Palace

TRAN PHU

Cathedral

Pasteur Institute

LE HONG PHONG

Boa Dai's
Summer Palace
(Dinh III)

Long-distance
Bus Station

0   750m

Highway 20 & Airport

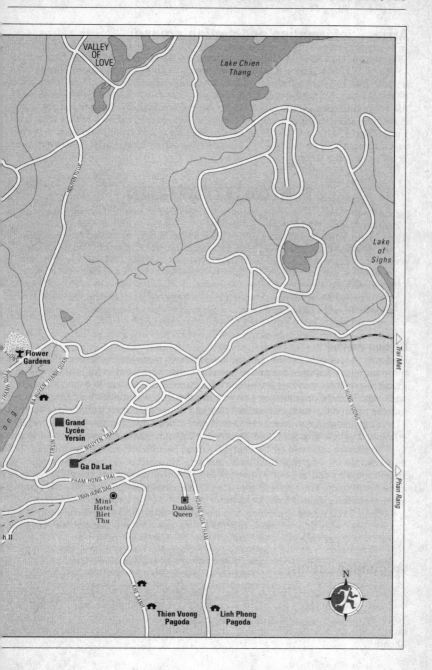

Arrival, information and getting around

Buses from Ho Chi Minh, Nha Trang and elsewhere arrive at Da Lat Bus Station (☎063/822479), 1.5km south of the city on 3 Thang 4, from where Honda oms trundle into the centre. Modest **Lien Khuong Airport** (☎063/843379) is 29km below the city, off the road to Ho Chi Minh: *Lam Dong Tourist Co* buses ($2) ply the route into town, while a taxi or Honda om will cost $6. As usual, there's precious little **information** to be had from the local tourist office – in this case *Lam Dong Tourist*, 4 Tran Quoc Toan (☎063/822125) – and unless you want a permit to see the Lat Village (see p.173), you're better off seeking practical advice at your hotel's reception desk.

LEAVING DA LAT BY BUS

Lam Dong Tourist has recently taken to insisting that all tourists **leaving Da Lat for Ho Chi Minh or Nha Trang** by bus do so on special tourist services, priced $10 and $8 respectively, and a booth has been set up at the bus station to enforce the rule. Honda om drivers will tell you if the scam is still being worked. If it is, simply wait outside the station gate, flag down a bus going in the direction you want, and pay the local fare. Should you decide to comply and simply pay extra for a tourist bus, tickets are sold at most of the central hotels; and *Sinh Café* has a daily trip down to the Pham Ngu Lao area of Ho Chi Minh City leaving from *Mini-hotel Pensée 6*, at 6, 3 Thang 4.

Getting around

Da Lat is too hilly for cyclos, and the horse-drawn carts that were one of the city's more attractive features are pretty much a thing of the past, so for journeys of any distance you'll have to rely on Honda oms (sometimes known here as "Simsons") and taxis. **Honda oms** are ten-a-penny, but the drivers with the best English tend to hang around the budget hotels. A day-long tour of the area weighs in at around $7 – English-speaking drivers brandish itineraries taking in pagodas, waterfalls, ethnic villages, a silk farm and an incense factory. **Taxis** congregate beside the food market at the base of Le Dai Hanh, and two blocks above the cinema, but they operate on a turn-by-turn basis and will be reluctant to leave the queue for smaller fares; a full day costs upwards of $12. Otherwise, *Lam Dong Tourist* (see above) will rustle you up a car plus driver for a whopping $25, but be sure you get someone who speaks a little English.

Cycling is the most charming way to tour central Da Lat and the immediate vicinity, and with this in mind, several hotels are now renting out **bicycles** for around $1.50 per day; see "Accommodation", below, for details.

Accommodation

Enduringly popular with both Western and domestic tourists, Da Lat has a predictably wide range of places to stay, from cheap, grimy billets, to the former summer residence of the governor-general of Indochina. However, if your visit coincides with a Saturday night or **public holiday**, either arrive early or book ahead.

ACCOMMODATION PRICE CODES

All accommodation listed in this guide has been categorized according to the following scale:

① under US$10 (under 110,000 dong) ② US$10–15 (110–165,000 dong)
③ US$15–30 (165–330,000 dong) ④ US$30–75 (330–825,000 dong)
⑤ US$75–150 (825–1,650,000 dong) ⑥ over US$150 (over 1,650,000 dong)

Rates are for the cheapest available double or twin room; breakfast is not usually included. During holiday periods, rates are liable to rise, and proprietors may be less amenable to bargaining. Although the law requires prices to be quoted in dong, most hotels also give their rates in US$; payment can be made in either currency.
For a more detailed discussion of accommodation, see pp.31–34.

The densest concentrations of **budget hotels** lie on the web of roads around the cinema and along Phan Dinh Phung; check that prices include hot water – a luxury in most of Southern Vietnam, but a necessity in Da Lat. Several cut-price **guesthouses** operate along Nguyen Chi Thanh; presently they only accept Vietnamese guests, but if money is tight, taking a minute to check the current situation could pay dividends – look for the words "nha nghi". A couple of **classier hotels** operate downtown, but there are many more out in the open spaces south and west of the city centre; if you really want to push the boat out, it's sometimes possible to rent one of the colonial villas along Tran Phu and Tran Hung Dao – enquire at *Lam Dong Tourist* for details.

Cam Do, 81 Phan Dinh Phung (☎063/822732). Salubrious rooms, some sharing outside washing facilities, others boasting a hot bath; laundry and bike-rental services are available, and there's a café downstairs. ②

Dinh II, 12 Tran Hung Dao (☎063/822092). Built as a summer palace for Jean Decoux, Governor-General of Indochina during World War II, and later occupied by President Diem's brother, there's no doubting *Dinh II*'s pedigree. Rooms, however, are comfortable but not cosy: all in all, rather like sleeping in a museum – and pricey. ④

Duy Tan, 83, 3 Thang 2 (☎063/823564). Mid-range motel-style joint, ten minutes' walk from the city centre, featuring smart but slightly characterless rooms; insist on being berthed on the upper floor, or you'll front onto the car park. ④

Hoa Binh, 64 Truong Cong Dinh (☎063/822787). Only recently open to foreigners, a standard budget hotel where the cheapest rooms share outside facilities; an extra $2 buys you a good view of the busy square below, and there are bikes for rent. ①

Hoang Hau Villa, 8a Ho Tung Mao (☎063/821431). Just below the GPO, an appealing mini-hotel with well-appointed rooms, some overlooking the lake. Recommended – but book ahead. ③

Lam Son, 5 Hai Thuong (☎063/822362). After the quaint lobby, the *Lam Son*'s adequate but shabby rooms are disappointing; at least their wooden wall panels add a little warmth. Downstairs there's a bar and restaurant. ②

Mimosa, 170 Phan Dinh Phung (☎063/822656). One of Da Lat's cheaper options, and a popular backpacker haunt, its unremarkable rooms all have hot water; the café downstairs will rustle up decent enough snacks, but head across the road to the *Mekong* (see "Restaurants", p.171) for breakfast. ②

Mini-Hotel Biet Thu, 28 Tran Hung Dao (☎063/822764). Spurn the modern annexe, and opt for a room with a view over the surrounding countryside in the quaint auberge-style house; all 11 rooms have hot water, and guests have access to a charmingly moth-eaten sitting room with open fire. ③

Ngoc Lan, 42 Nguyen Chi Thanh (☎063/822136). Soccer-pitch-sized rooms in this central hotel offer "every modern comfort" and bird's eye views of Lake Xuan Huong. ④

Palace, 2 Tran Phu (☎063/822203). Extensive renovations to Da Lat's most splendid colonial pile should be finished by the time you read this, and prices will probably be in the region of ⑤ or ⑥.

Phu Hoa, 16 Tang Bat Ho (☎063/822194). A lick of paint wouldn't go amiss in this aged, 42-room hotel, and the staff are less than friendly, but room-rates are low, bedrooms presentable, and the location couldn't be more central; taking one of several rooms with 3 double beds makes sense if you're in a group. ②

Thanh Binh, 40 Nguyen Thi Minh Khai (☎063/822909). Great views over the market are the reward for booking into a front room at the no-frills *Thanh Binh*; hot water is available, but the cheapest rooms share a bathroom. ①

Thanh The, 118 Phan Dinh Phung (☎063/822180). Rooms are nothing to write home about in this rambling hotel, but on the plus side, there's constant hot water, and the singles are a good deal. ②

Thuy Tien, 7, 3 Thang 2 (☎063/822482). There's no lift here, so rooms get cheaper as they get higher; if you can ignore the sickly hues of the decor, rooms are comfortable and welcoming, with modern bathrooms. ③

The city

Central Da Lat forms a rough crescent around the western side of man-made **Lake Xuan Huong**, created in 1919 when the Cam Ly River was dammed by the French, who named it the "Grand Lac". The city escaped bomb damage, and a French influence is still plainly evident when meandering the tangle of its central area, whose twisting streets and steps, lined with stone buildings rising to red-tiled roofs, cover a hillock defined by the streets of Le Dai Hanh and Phan Dinh Phung. Your first stop, though, should be at the market, **Cho Da Lat**, a reinforced concrete eyesore whose underbelly reveals a staggering range of fruit and vegetables. Strawberries, beetroot, fennel, avocados, blackberries and cherries grown in the market gardens surrounding the city are all sold here, along with a riot of flowers. Artichoke teabags, with their "propitious functions for liver, bile" and their "diuretic" properties, make quirky **souvenirs**, and candied Da Lat strawberries are also sold at many stalls. The market's upper level, linked by a raised walkway to the top of Le Dai Hanh, is pale and pasty by comparison, though a dig through its household goods unearths such buyables as water-gourds, lacquerware, and hilltribe backpacks and fabrics. **Montagnards**, decked out in their distinctive apparel and carrying their chattels in decorated backpacks, are a fairly common sight at the market, especially early in the morning when they come to trade with stallholders.

A ten-minute hike down Phan Boi Chau and left up Ly Tu Trong deposits you before the ground-floor gallery of the self-effacing **Lam Dong Province Museum** (daily 8–11.30am & 2–4pm), home to a reasonably engaging accumulation of *montagnard* odds and ends. A few artefacts stand out from the mass of water gourds, tribal dress, jewellery and pottery, among them textiles whose designs incorporate planes and helicopters spied from the forest by their wartime weavers; and a huge lithophone, made from volcanic rock, that looks as if it's been nabbed from the set of *The Flintstones*. There's a token nod to Ho Chi Minh upstairs, beside such oddities as Emperor Bao Dai's Havana cigar box and a copy of *Playboy* intended, presumably, to highlight the dissolute ways of the Americans and the South Vietnamese Army. More prosaically, the museum's hilltop setting

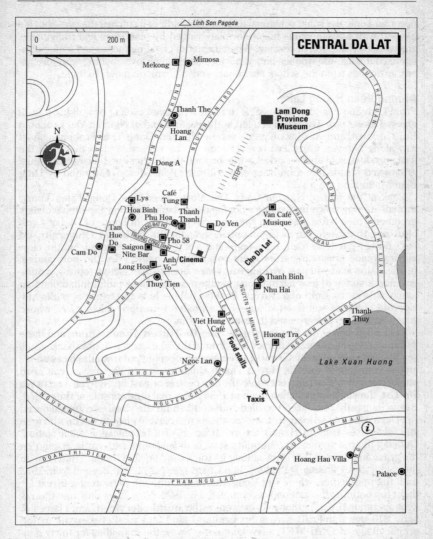

CENTRAL DA LAT

Linh Son Pagoda

Mekong • Mimosa

Thanh The

Hoang Lan

Dong A

Lam Dong Province Museum

Café Tung

Lys

Hoa Binh

Phu Hoa

Thanh Thanh

Do Yen

Van Café Musique

Tan Hue Do

Pho 58

Cam Do

Saigon Nite Bar

Anh Vo

Cinema

Long Hoa

Cho Da Lat

Thuy Tien

Thanh Binh

Nhu Hai

Thanh Thuy

Viet Hung Café

Huong Tra

Ngoc Lan

Lake Xuan Huong

Food stalls

Taxis

Hoang Hau Villa

Palace

affords marvellous views of the city and surrounding countryside – great for catching your bearings. If the museum is closed, scout around the building for the janitor, who'll unlock it for you.

As the crow flies, it's no distance from the museum to **Linh Son Pagoda**, on Nguyen Van Troi, but to reach it you'll have to drop down a flight of steps to the area above the **cinema** (its name, *Rap 3/4*, recalls the city's liberation on April 3, 1975) and bear right along Nguyen Van Troi. There's nothing in this low, yellow-washed pagoda that you won't have seen elsewhere – the main chamber boasts minimal decor and only the squat octagonal turret to the right of it catches the eye – but it's blessed with a harmonious hilltop location, ringed by pine trees and frangipanis, and worth a visit if you're passing. When they aren't tending the tea and coffee plantations out back, the woollen-hatted novices based here love chatting with foreigners, as do kids from the school next door, so don't bank on much solitude.

Around Xuan Huong Lake

From Linh Son Pagoda, it's possible to make a pleasant cycling or walking tour of glassy **Lake Xuan Huong**. Turn left at the eastern end of Nguyen Van Troi onto Bui Thi Xuan, and you'll soon reach serene **Nguyen Cong Tru**. Probing a short way along Nguyen Cong Tru reveals some of the vegetable plots that yield the fresh produce sold at the market, while beyond the horticulture, a large Buddhist **graveyard** stands like a housing estate in the middle-distance, framed by Lang Bian Mountain (see p.173).

Back at the foot of Nguyen Cong Tru, flower-lined Phu Dong Thien Vuong threads its way down to the lake's northeastern bank, skirting the immaculately groomed green baize lawns and twee, peach-coloured clubhouse of Da Lat's **golf club** and, to the left, the Swiss mountain-style chalets of **Da Lat University**. Da Lat's **flower gardens** (daily 6am–6pm) stand at the base of the road, but the cloying fragrance emanating from them reaches you halfway up the golf course. Inside, paths lead you past hydrangeas, roses, orchids, poinsettia, topiary, a nursery, and a series of less harmonious monkey cages whose pitiful inhabitants go totally wild at the sight of a banana. Besides bobble hats and trinkets, **stalls** outside the entrance sell knotted lumps of a golden fern fibre called *cu ly*, whose coagulant properties are used to staunch bleeding.

Take a left below the flower gardens onto **Ba Huyen Thanh Quan**, and trace its broad arc past cows and horses and around the lake. As you double back, you'll see the slate belfry of the **Grand Lycée Yersin** peeping out from the trees above and to your left. Where Ba Huyen Thanh Quan turns into Yersin, you can head one of two ways: west, and back into the city centre; or east up Nguyen Trai to **Ga Da Lat**, the city's train station, built in 1938 and a real time capsule of the period. Below its gently contoured red-tiled roof and behind the slender, multi-coloured Art Deco windows striping its front facade, its marble and glass ticket booths (one still advertises trips to Hanoi) are reminiscent of a provincial French station. Outside, the rail yard is in a charming state of dilapidation, with cattle grazing on the grass and flowers that grow among its tracks and ancient trains. Trains ran on the rack railway linking Da Lat to Thap Cham (see p.202) and beyond from 1933 until the mid-Sixties, when Viet Cong attacks became too persistent a threat for them to continue; the station was completed in 1938. Nowadays only one train is kept operational, and enthusiasts may enjoy the **shuttle service** (7am, 11am, 1 & 5pm; $10 per trainload) across horticultural land and market gardens to the orbital village of **TRAI MET**, a few kilometres away; the train idles for thirty minutes in this unremarkable hamlet before returning to Da Lat.

Tran Hung Dao and beyond

By retracing your steps down Nguyen Trai and ascending Pham Hong Thai you reach **Tran Hung Dao**, the central segment of Da Lat's southern rim, from where two slender roads wiggling south offer cyclists pleasant detours out into the countryside. The first, **Hoang Hoa Tham**, targets colourful **Linh Phong Pagoda**, which is fronted by a gateway bearing a fierce, panting dragon-face with protruding eyes. Behind its gaudy yellow doors, blue ceramic roof dragons and pillbox-red pillars etched with Chinese inscriptions, the pagoda itself is something of a disappointment. However, its tranquil location affords peerless views of the culti-vated and wooded valley below, from where threads of smoke rise from wood-fires.

Much the same is true of **Khe Sanh**, almost immediately opposite you as you access Tran Hung Dao. This time, the focus of the detour is **Thien Vuong Pagoda**, remarkable for its trio of four-metre-tall, caramel-coloured sandalwood statues (Sakyamuni, in the centre, rubs shoulders with the Goddess of Mercy and the God of Power) imported from Hong Kong in 1958; and for the huge **statue of Buddha** seated on a lotus, 100m up the hill above the pagoda. Stalls near Thien Vuong hawk the usual candied strawberries, artichoke tea and *cu ly* to the Vitenamese tourists who flock here.

The movers and shakers that once maintained **villas** in Da Lat preferred to site their homes along the city's bottom lip, rather than in the maws of its central area; the villas survive today and their timberwork, slated roofs and pastel hues lend an air of some distinction to Tran Hung Dao. You'll pass below one of the more impressive examples, **Dinh II** (daily 7–11.30am & 1.30–4.30pm), once the resi-dence of the French governor-general of Indonesia, at the street's western end. A light brown, angular lump of a building softened by bay windows, portholes and balconies, its contents resemble the tired stock of a secondhand furniture shop, and not even the contemporary art for sale around the walls can make a trawl through the interior worthwhile.

Tran Phu and around

West of Dinh II, Tran Hung Dao segues into **Tran Phu**, which cradles two of the city's most memorable French-era buildings. First up is the unfussy **Palace Hotel**. The social heart of colonial-era Da Lat following its construction in the Twenties, the *Palace* is blessed with wonderful prospects of Lake Xuan Huong below and, once renovations are over – probably early in 1997 – enjoying a long cool drink overlooking its flawlessly manicured lawns is sure to be *de rigueur* on a trip to the city. Across the road, Da Lat's dusty pink **cathedral**, consecrated in 1931 and completed eleven years later, is dedicated to Saint Nicholas, protector of the poor; a statue of him stands at the opposite end of the nave to the simple altar, with three tiny children loitering at his feet. Light streaming in from the cathe-dral's seventy stained-glass windows, mostly crafted in Grenoble, teases a warm, sunny glow from the mellow pink of the interior walls, and picks out the flam-boyant colours of the fresh-cut flowers adorning the nave. Of the cathedral's unspectacular fittings, the **collage** beside the altar is perhaps the most interest-ing. Depicting Vietnam's Catholic martyrs, it was made using waste paper to reflect the renewal of the Catholic Church in Vietnam; bones of some of these martyrs are kept under the altar itself.

Bao Dai's Summer Palace

The nautical portholes punched into its walls, and the mast-like pole sprouting from its roof give **Dinh III** (daily 7.30am–noon & 1.30–5pm; $1), erstwhile sum-mer palace of Emperor Bao Dai, the distinct look of a ship's bridge. Compared to the *Mimosa* or the *Phu Hoa*, the palace, which is reached by bearing left onto Le Hong Phong 500m west of the cathedral, and then left again when you see the wide mansion housing the **Pasteur Institute** to your right, is indeed palatial – but don't expect Buckingham Palace. The palace was erected between 1933 and 1938 to provide Bao Dai with a bolthole between elephant-slaughtering sessions, and its mustard-coloured bulk, etched with stark white grouting, is set amid charming rose and pine **gardens** marred somewhat by an unsightly cluster of hideous artificial toadstools. Past the two large blue metal lanterns flanking the front entrance, the first room to your right is Bao Dai's **working room**, modestly dominated by a bust of the man himself, and home both to the imperial motorbike helmet, and to a library that effortlessly spans Bibles, an edition of Shakespeare and Charlotte Bronte's *Shirley*. Buffalo horns in the **reception room** were bagged by Bao Dai himself, on one of his hunting forays into the forests around Da Lat; his queen preferred more sedate pastimes, and would have tinkled on the piano here. The palace's most elegant common room is its **festivities room** or dining room, though eyeing the dark wooden chairs and dining table, and catching an acrid whiff of polish in this dark, echoing room, it's hard to imagine the royal revelries that would have gone on here.

Royal ghosts are far easier to summon upstairs, where the musty **imperial bedrooms** seem just to have had the dust-sheets whipped back for another royal season. Princes and princesses all had their quarters, as did the queen, whose chamber features a chaise longue that looks rather unnervingly like a dentist's chair. But the finest room, predictably enough, went to Bao Dai, who enjoyed the luxury of a balcony for his "breeze-getting and his moon-watching". Out on the landing, look out for a bizarre mini-sauna, labelled a *Rouathermique* – of a similar vintage to the Peugeot taxis in town.

Lam Ty Ni Pagoda

Dropping in at **Lam Ty Ni Pagoda**, north of Le Hong Phong on Thien My, represents one of the unlikeliest and most delightful attractions of a stay in Da Lat. The pagoda is home to Vien Thuc, the so-called "mad monk" of Da Lat, whose two huge dogs alert him to guests' arrival at the front gate. Poet, gardener, builder and artist, Vien Thuc is a monk of all trades, but his proudest achievement is his painting – which started out as finger-daubing on the walls of the pagoda he entered at the age of ten. His studio, a warren of lean-tos behind the pagoda, is stacked to the rafters with over 80,000 delicious soups of abstract watercolour, boasting names like "Golden Dragon Swimming in the River Milky Way" and "Blue Music in the Bosom of a Human World". Vien Thuc relishes visitors and as he gives the full conducted tour in English, words tumble from him, followed by lunatic and hooting laughter. All his pieces are for sale, and it's hard not to succumb to his patter: Vien Thuc closes deals with what the *New York Times* called "the skill of a car dealer". And don't worry if you find yourself short on dollars – the gleaming white training shoes protruding incongrously from beneath the monk's robes were received in exchange for one of his works.

If he ever lets you get that far, you'll find that the **pagoda** bears Vien Thuc's unmistakeable hallmark. His paintings flank the walls, and the canopy around the altar depicting birds carrying Buddhist *sutras* is also his handiwork.

Cam Ly Falls

The closest of the area's many waterfalls are the tame **Cam Ly Falls** (daily 7am–6pm), reached by tracing Tran Phu until it becomes bumpy Hoang Van Thu, and then continuing on for 1200m, with the Cam Ly River and the vegetable plots banking it to your right. Beyond a guardian yellow stone lion at the entrance with luscious red-stained lips, the falls are pretty enough, though hardly compelling, their several slender channels of water running under a picturesque blue bridge before threading across a broad, smooth plateau down to a rather unkempt pool. Visitors can ride the ponies grazing on the grassland bordering the falls for a fistful of dollars.

Eating, drinking and nightlife

Da Lat has a broad range of **restaurants** serving Vietnamese, Chinese, French and even *montagnard* cuisines. The majority are situated either along Phan Dinh Phung, or near to the cinema in the city centre. **Foodstalls** are also abundant. *Pho*, *com* and the like are bashed out at the covered food market at the base of Le Dai Hanh; there are one or two vegetarian stalls here, signposted as *com chay*. But the stalls pitched on the steps running down from the cinema and across to the market offer the most **exotic dishes**: snails, quail's eggs and shellfish all boil away here in huge, steaming cauldrons. More stalls proliferate up the steps opposite the *Cam Do* hotel. Finally, if you are taking a bike out for the day, you could stop by at the central market and make up a **picnic** of bread, cheese and cake, complemented by fresh strawberries, raspberries or cherries.

For most locals, nightlife means a cup of coffee in one of the city's atmospheric **cafés**. That said, the city now boasts two proper **bars**, one of which has copied Ho Chi Minh City's winning formula of loud music and pool tables.

Restaurants

Anh Vo, 15 Truong Cong Dinh. Run by an adorable French-speaking hostess, a charming place that knocks up the best steak in town, as well as *la lot*: onions, garlic and minced beef wrapped in leaves. A glass of port-like mulberry wine rounds off a meal in civilized fashion. 7am–10pm.

Dankia Quan, 5 Yen The (☎063/821225). The full-on *montagnard* dining experience: seated on cushions in grass-roof huts, guests choose from bat, deer, snake and wild boar, washed down with copious amounts of *ruou can*, the local rice wine. For less adventurous eaters, the cook runs to chicken and beef; phone ahead. 9am–11pm.

Do Yen, 7 Khu Hoa Binh. If you can decipher its cramped, photocopied type, the intriguing menu here includes such temptations as beef and vine leaves on skewers, fillet of turbot with cashew nuts, and chateaubriand with anchovies; main courses are around $1.50. 9am–9pm.

Dong A, 82 Phan Dinh Phung. Inexpensive workaday dishes with rice, soups, and a limited menu of vegetarian options, in simple surroundings. 10am–10pm.

Hoang Lan, 118 Phan Dinh Phung. Next door to the *Thanh The* hotel, a bare but reputable restaurant where Vietnamese and Chinese cuisines share top billing; the Vietnamese meat and vegetable soup, *ta pin lu*, is worth investigating. 7am–9pm.

Huong Tra, 1 Nguyen Thai Hoc. The commanding views of the lake below have made this a prosperous restaurant; if rabbit, deer and wild boar don't grab you, there are generous European and veggie selections to fall back on. 7am–9pm.

Long Hoa, 3 Thang 2. Decent and filling Vietnamese food and steaks – kick off with a strawberry wine aperitif; for dessert, a sublime homemade yoghurt takes some beating. Two can dine for $6; recommended. 7.30am–9.30pm.

Lys, 117a Hoang Van Thu. Low-key restaurant serving from a limited roll-call of passable Vietnamese meals; the spring rolls are good. 10am–10pm.

Mekong, 239b Phan Dinh Phung. Cosy joint whose selection of well-cooked, affordable – and mainly Vietnamese – dishes also features such unlikely bed-fellows as Korean *kimchi* and (unmissable) *beef Napoleon* – fried eggs on steak served with a baguette. 6.30am–10pm.

Nhu Hai, 40–41 Nguyen Thi Minh Khai. Meals are filling and affordable in this terrific open-fronted joint, but it's the range of exotic fruits that lingers in the memory. 6am–10pm.

Pho 58, 58 Tang Bat Ho. The speciality here is steamy bowls of tasty *pho* that fill a gap. 7am–10pm.

Tan Hue Do, 48–50 Phan Dinh Phung. Cheery, but slightly pricey bistro, cooking up Vietnamese and Chinese dishes of decent quality; start with a chrysanthemum or watercress soup, and for a main course, try the chicken in minced meat sauce. 9am–9pm.

Thanh Thanh Restaurant, 4 Tang Bat Ho (☎063/821836). Refined, friendly and popular, this is far and away Da Lat's best restaurant; sugarcane prawns are tasty and fun, and the Vietnamese special salad (shrimps, peanuts, lotus gourd, pork and herbs, eaten with prawn crackers) is superb. 6.30am–10pm.

Thanh Thuy Restaurant, Nguyen Thai Hoc. Another lake-view address, though dishes like grilled bear or sauteed porcupine are hardly designed to tickle Western palates. 6am–11pm.

Cafés and bars

Café Tung, 6 Khu Hoa Binh. Leather upholstery, dark varnished wood and covers of old 45s by Nancy Sinatra and Jacques Brel on the walls: truly a café lost in time. 6.30am–10pm.

Da Lat by Night, 42 Nguyen Chi Thanh. Within the *Ngoc Lan* hotel, this is a passable enough bar unless the karaoke kicks in. 5pm–1am.

Saigon Nite Bar, 45 Truong Cong Dinh. Da Lat's first Western-style bar comes complete with pool table, deafening music and inflated prices. 8am–2am.

Van Café Musique, 19 Phan Boi Chau. An irresistible hybrid of Vietnamese café life and Western music, hung with lovingly framed posters of Michael Jackson, the Bee Gees and Abba, and currently *the* place for teenage coffee abuse in Da Lat. 7am–10.30pm.

Viet Hung Café, 7 Nguyen Chi Thanh. An amiable café that rustles up beers as well as ices and yoghurts; the gaily lit terrace's pint-sized tables overlook busy Le Dai Hanh. 8am–10pm.

Listings

Hospital *Lam Dong Hospital* is at 4 Pham Ngoc Thach (☎063/822155).

Police 9 Tran Binh Trong (☎063/822460).

Post office 16 Tran Phu (Mon–Sat 7am–6pm), with a *poste restante* service.

Tourist office *Da Lat Tourist* is at 4 Tran Quoc Toan (☎063/822125).

North of Da Lat: lakes, hilltribes and Lang Bian Mountain

Of the several tourist spots secreted about the undulating slopes above Da Lat, the closest to the city is *Ho Thanh Tho*, the **Lake of Sighs** (daily 7am–5pm), 5km northeast of the city centre beyond a broad swathe of open fields. The lake's melancholy name pays lip service to the sorry tale of Hoang Tung and his sweetheart Mai Nuong, who held trysts here until his call-up to join Quang Trung's war against the Chinese (see p.181). One version has him neglecting to tell her of his departure, while another describes how she heard a mistaken rumour of his death; whatever the reason, Mai Nuong drowned herself in the lake, and since then the pine trees around it are said to have sighed in vicarious grief. Nowadays, romance is at a premium, as more and more of the land around the lake is sliced up for cultivation, and the sighing pines are felled. Soon all that will be left will be the tourist tack – souvenir shops, merry-go-rounds, paddle boats and rides on horses led by Da Lat "cowboys" sporting hats and fake guns – that has grown up here.

Thung Lung Tinh Yeu, the **Valley of Love** (daily 6am–5pm), offers more of the same kitsch diversions as the Lake of Sighs. The valley's still waters and wooded hills are actually quite enticing and, were it not for the music blasting from souvenir stalls at the entrance, and the buzzing of rented motorboats, *Lam Dong Tourist*'s brave assertion that the valley "makes sense for you, poetically and romantically" might actually hold water. It's said that Bao Dai and his courtiers used to hunt here in the Fifties, though a damming project in 1972 flooded part of the valley and created **Lake Da Thien**.

If you bother to travel up to the Valley of Love, you'll be aware of the twin peaks of 2160-metre-high **Lang Bian Mountain** looming above you to the north. Inevitably, a schmaltzy legend has been concocted to explain the mountain's formation. The story tells of two ill-starred lovers, a Lat man called Lang and a Chill girl named Bian, who were unable to marry because of tribal enmity. Brokenhearted, Bian passed away, and the peaks of Lang Bian are said to represent her breast heaving its dying breath. Bian's death seems not to have been wholly in vain: so racked with guilt was her father, that he called a halt to tribal unrest by unifying all of the local factions into the Koho.

It's possible to **climb** up to the canopy of pines at the top of Lang Bian Mountain from where, it's said, you can see the coast on a clear day. The four-hour ascent begins at the nine hamlets of **Lat Village**, 12km north of Da Lat along Xo Viet Nghe Tinh. The village's thatch-roofed, bamboo stilthouses are occupied by Chill and Ma, but mostly Lat, groups of Koho peoples eking out a living growing rice, pulses and vegetables. *Lam Dong Tourist* require you to buy a **permit** ($5) to visit either village or mountain, so if you just want to get a flavour of minority village life you'll do almost as well by going to Chicken Village (see over) or one of any number of other settlements that Honda drivers can recommend. If you *do* decide to go to Lat or climb Lang Bian, the total amount you end up paying depends upon the mood of *Lam Dong Tourist*'s staff. At best, you'll only have to pay for the permit, and can then either hire a Honda driver, or cycle; at worst, you'll have to fork out $10 a day for an official guide ($15 if you plan to climb Lang Bian), and $20 for a car. Regulations, though, are in a state of flux, so check the latest when you arrive.

South along Highway 20

As Highway 20 to Ho Chi Minh drops southward from the city limits of Da Lat and down dramatic **Prenn Pass** (which affords splendid views of the pine forests and valleys below) it weaves past several sights of varying levels of interest.

Datanla Falls

First up, halfway down the pass, are the **Datanla Falls** (6am–4pm), signposted on the right of the road as *Thac Datanla*, around 5km out of Da Lat. In Koho, *datanla* means "water under leaves", and that pretty much sums up the place: from the car park, it's a five-minute walk down to the falls, probing some splendidly lush forest. The falls themselves are unthrilling, their muddy waters cascading onto a plateau spanned by a cute wooden footbridge that provides a hackneyed photo-opportunity. A couple of hundred metres before Datanla is the right turn to **Lake Tuyen Lam** (6am–4pm), presently being turned into a ghastly park in the Valley of Love mould, as if another were needed.

Prenn Waterfall

Prenn Pass levels out around the entrance to the **Prenn Waterfall** (7am–5pm). A major attraction for Vietnamese tourists, the fall sees a veritable convoy of buses roll into its car park, harried by a stampede of cigarette and chewing-gum vendors. Unlike Datanla, the attraction here is the waterfall itself, which thunders over a wide overhang and into the broad pool below. By following the path that circles the pool, you can walk right behind the fall, look out through the curtain of water, and feel its refreshing spray on your face. During the monsoon, rainfall churns the fall's broad, roaring flush into a milky tangerine colour. Back up at the car park, the *Prenn Restaurant* is on hand to cater for hungry visitors.

Chicken Village

None of the Koho residents of **Chicken Village** (ask Honda drivers for *Lang Con Ga*), 18km from Da Lat, seem sure of the origins of the five-metre-high cement cockerel that stands proudly on a plinth in the midst of their dwellings, its mouth open as if in mid-squawk. Some say praying to it is supposed to ensure a good harvest; others attach the inevitable slushy love story to the edifice. Whatever the truth, strolling around this pleasing hamlet gives visitors a taste of the daily life of a minority community. Known by its residents as *Klong*, the village is a composite of modern homesteads made of zinc and timber, and more traditional thatched wattle and daub huts. Dotting it are copses of coffee plants, cotton trees and bamboo. Approaching from Da Lat, two rows of golden thatched barns to your right tell you you're nearing the village. A kilometre later, a group of Koho women by the roadside sell traditional textiles which they weave painstakingly themselves on a rudimentary loom that they need to be strapped into. From here, it's a ten-minute stroll through the village to the infamous chicken, beyond which you can take a walk up into the layered hills, often skimmed by dappled clouds, casing the village.

THE CENTRAL HIGHLANDS

North of Da Lat, the yawning plateaux of the **central highlands** are worth visiting for their minority peoples. First up on the region's checklist of towns is **Buon Me Thuot**, an unlovely place that's the gateway to Ede longhouses, elephant-back rides and some truly beautiful scenery. From Buon Me Thuot, Highway 14 probes further north to **Plei Ku**, where there's more scope for witnessing everyday life in Jarai villages. With Plei Ku seen off, there's a directional choice between dropping back down to Qui Nhon and continuing your coastal odyssey, or really milking the highlands dry of sights by carrying on up to **Kon Tum** and visiting a Bahnar tribal **rong**, or communal hall. A high road links Kon Tum with Highway 1 near Hoi An, but for ease of travel, you're better of dropping back to Plei Ku and continuing on from there.

Buon Me Thuot and around

Without the added incentive of its outlying minority villages, **BUON ME THUOT** would have little to offer. Of the precious few that do make the onerous journey up from the coast's well-trodden tourist trail, many erroneously expect a quaint longhouse community, and for them the town's central sprawl of buildings splayed across an unlovely grid of streets, can only disappoint. Seeing **longhouses** and traditional **minority communities** – of which most around these parts comprise Ede people – necessitates a day-trip out to **Tour**, **Ban Don**, or some other outlying *montagnard* village, though enough Edes have by now been assimilated into Buon Me Thuot's population of around 70,000 for a public-address system to relay the news across the town in Ede, daily at dusk.

Sited 160km west of Ninh Hoa, Buon Me Thuot is both administrative centre to Dak Lak Province, and the western highlands' unofficial capital. During French colonial times, the town developed on the back of the coffee, tea, rubber and hard-wood crops that grew so successfully in its fertile red soil, and was the focal point for the **plantations** that smothered the surrounding countryside. Plantation-owners and other *colons* would amuse themselves by picking off the **elephants, leopards and tigers** once prevalent in the area; and Bao Dai himself enjoyed bagging game so much, that he had a house built some way south of the town on **Dak Lake**, and connected by a private track to his summer palace in Da Lat. In later years Americans superseded the French, but they were long gone by the time the North Vietnamese Army (NVA) swept through in March 1975, making Buon Me Thuot the first "domino" to fall in the Ho Chi Minh Campaign. More recently, natural resources have made the town a comparatively affluent community, as evidenced by the number of Hondas and jeeps buzzing its streets.

The town

Central Buon Me Thuot can't throw up much of interest for tourists, but if bad weather consigns you to a day's idling, you could always pass by the Russian-made **tank** at the town's epicentre – the first to arrive on Liberation Day – to the **Dak Lak Museum**, at 1 Doc Lap (Tues, Thurs & Fri 7–11.30am & 2–4.30pm). The museum's motley collection of minerals, hardwoods, and photos of local sights such as rubber plants and plantations, and the Dray Sap Falls (see over), are severely yawn-inducing, but infinitely less offensive than the glass cabinet containing a mock-up of the local wildlife, in which a stuffed deer, lizard, and anteater are joined by a mounted hog's head propped up against a tree. Of considerably more interest are the exhibits pertaining to local minority peoples, among them a scale model of an Ede longhouse, rice-wine jars, grave statues of peacocks and tusks, and instruments for taming elephants, such as vicious mahouts' spikes, and two horribly thorny harnesses.

Once you've seen the museum that's about it for the town centre, though you could check out **BUON KO SIER**, an Ede community 2km beyond the *Saigon Moi* eating house. When Norman Lewis visited Buon Me Thuot in 1950, he was informed by a Monsieur Doustin that he had arrived in an "anthropologist's paradise", but "one that was passing away before your very eyes". Today that's more true than ever: while some villages are fading out, others are being swallowed up by the major highland towns, with Buon Ko Sier a case in point. Buon Me Thuot

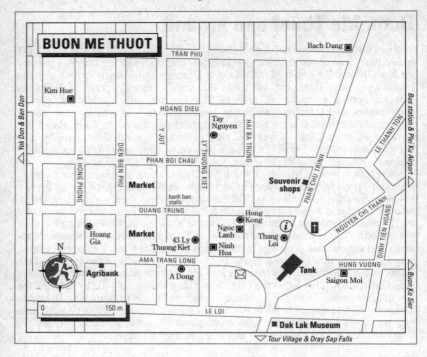

has encroached to such an extent that the village now effectively forms no more than a district, yet so long as you don't mind the urban backdrop it's still a convenient way of witnessing a longhouse community going about its daily routines. For more information about the village, ask for Mr Ysang Mlo, who speaks English and French.

Practicalities

Buon Me Thuot's **bus station** (☎050/852603) is 2km above town on Nguyen Chi Tranh. The **airport** is a few kilometres back off the road towards Ninh Hoa: *Vietnam Airlines* (☎050/855055), at 158 Nguyen Chi Thanh, has an airport shuttle from their office ($2).

Of Buon Me Thuot's **places to stay**, none really stands out until the renovations at the *Thang Loi* are finished. The cheapest beds in town are at the *A Dong* (☎050/853710; ①) on Ama Trang Long, though the spartan rooms sharing bathrooms here are blighted by early morning street noise. The lacklustre rooms in Hai Ba Trung's *Hong Kong* (☎050/852630; ②) at least enjoy a relatively quiet location; or there's the *Tay Nguyen* (☎050/852250; ③) on Ly Thuong Kiet, run by surly staff and offering standard rooms that are way overpriced (air-con is a whopping $10 extra). Le Hong Phong's *Hoang Gia* (☎050/852161; ②) has relatively cheery rooms, all with private bathroom, off a maze of stairs, but some are very boxlike, so look at a range before choosing; and there are basic fan rooms with shared facilities at 43 Ly Thuong Kiet (☎050/853921; ②).

When it's time to **eat**, *Saigon Moi*, a no-frills roadside eating house on Hung Vuong, serves stuffed tofu and prawns as well as flavoursome *com suon* and excellent *thit kho tau* (slow-boiled pork and eggs). The *Ninh Hoa* on Ly Thuong Kiet is famed locally for its fine *nem* (spring rolls); or try out one of the several *banh bao* (dumpling) stalls that set up in the town centre at night. With its classical columns, chandeliers and upper-floor terrace, the *Bach Dang* on Phan Chu Trinh is an altogether swisher oasis, and the revolving centres on the tables ensure you don't miss anything; or there's the dependable *Kim Hue* on Hoang Dien, where the wide-ranging Vietnamese menu runs to snails, frog and duck. Finally, Hai Ba Trung's *Ngoc Lanh* cooks tasty food from its simple menu, and the staff are very friendly.

Tour village and the Dray Sap Falls

The splendid Dray Sap Falls are accessed by heading southwest out of Buon Me Thuot along Doc Lap. Before them, 14km out of town, a track to the left of the road runs into serene **TOUR VILLAGE**, one of the biggest minority villages in the area, where four hundred Edes share fifteen stilted wooden longhouses. Eyeing the wood-smoke that billows out of these longhouses, and the chickens and geese scooting around their stilts, it's difficult not to be struck by the village's almost primeval aspect: although sheets of corrugated iron have recently insinuated themselves into Tour's architecture, its residents still live very much as they have done for centuries, sustained by their maize, corn, peanut and cashew crops.

Visitors are often invited to take tea with the village's **headman**, a white-haired gentleman called Enor. French-speaking Enor used to be vicar in the former Protestant church (now schoolhouse) in the middle of the village until the government outlawed services here, fearing that large gatherings would encourage FULRO activism. While Tour's residents are more than happy to let you look inside their longhouses, a token gift is much appreciated – cigarettes, sweets, salt and sugar will all be well received.

The Honda om return trip to Tour costs around $2 but you'll need to add half that again if you wish to continue on to crescent-shaped **Dray Sap Falls** (7am–6pm), 20km from Buon Me Thuot. Almost 15m high and over 100m wide, the falls aren't called Dray Sap, or "waterfall of smoke", for nothing: a fug of invigorating spray sags the air, though to feel it on your face you'll need to clamber through bamboo groves and over rocks to the right of the pool formed by the falls. With a little effort, you can climb up to the top of the falls, but for safety's sake, don't overstep the red line.

Yok Don National Park and Ban Don

Exit west out of Buon Me Thuot along Phan Boi Chau, and 37km later you'll arrive at the entrance to Vietnam's largest wildlife preserve, the **Yok Don National Park**, whose 58,000 hectares lie nestled into the hinge of the Cambodian border and the **Serepok River**. Make the trip early in the morning, and you'll see the minority peoples who reside along the dusty, pot-holed road leaving their split bamboo thatch houses for work in the fields, carrying their tools in raffia backpacks.

Over sixty species of animals, including tigers, leopards and bears, and around two hundred types of birds, from peacocks to hornbills, populate Yok Don Park; but **elephants** are what it is best known for. Elephant-hunters have found rich pickings in the region's lush forest for centuries, and today an elephant-back ride is the park's main attraction. For $20 an hour (less if you haggle), two can lumber around the park's eastern edge by elephant; while $240 buys a three-day, two-night safari deep into the forest, a trip best saved for the dry season, when the park's wildlife ups sticks and makes for **Yok Don Mountain** in search of food and water, and your chances of glimpsing something interesting improve. If all you're after is a brief stroll around the park HQ, a guide costs $5 for a morning and $10 for a full day – but don't expect to stumble across any very exciting wildlife. For **bookings** or enquiries, phone the park HQ (☎050/853110) and ask for either Mr Ly or Mr Luong.

The three sub-hamlets that comprise the quietly fascinating village of **BAN DON** lie 2km beyond Yok Don's park HQ on the bank of the crocodile-infested Serepok. Khmer, Thai, Lao, Jarai and Mnong live in the vicinity, though it's the **Ede** who are again in the majority. They adhere to a matriarchal social system, whereby a groom takes his bride's name, lives with her family and, should his wife die subsequently, marries one of her sisters so that her family retains a male workforce. Houses around the village, a few of which are longhouses, are built on stilts, and some are decorated with ornate woodwork. As you explore, you are bound to be welcomed in somewhere to share tea or rice wine ($2.50 a jar). If you contrive to get yourself invited to a party, bear in mind that the women drink first, then the village elder, and finally the other guests.

Ban Don village boasts a long and distinguished tradition of elephant-taming; indeed, elephants are still caught and trained to this day, and remain very much a part of the workforce. Beyond its final sub-hamlet stands the tomb of the legendary **Khonsonuk** (1850–1924), the greatest elephant-catcher of them all, whose lifetime tally of 244 included an auspicious white elephant which he presented to the King of Siam (later to become Thailand). Locals will gladly point you towards the graveyard where he lies; Khonsonuk's is the square tomb, and the pointed one in front is his nephew's, also a prodigious elephant hunter. Elephant riders, or mahouts, still come to make offerings here before venturing out to tame wild elephants. Other tombs nearby are adorned with wooden carvings of peacocks standing on tusks – both considered as expensive items to take into the next life.

Dak Lak Tourist would have you believe that you have to take a tour through them to visit Ban Don ($15 excluding transport), but in fact you'll do far better taking a Honda om ($8–10), and hiring a guide ($5 for a half-day) from the Yok Don Park HQ – where you must stop in any case, to pay a "formality before entrance" fee of $2. If your trip engenders a huge interest in all things Ede, enquire back at HQ about the Ede cultural programme ($45 per group), an enjoyable three hours of dance, music and wine; for a further $2.50 a head you can sleep off your rice-wine head at a local longhouse.

If tour groups and Honda oms both sound beyond your means, you could reach Ban Don by opting for a **bus** (8am & noon) to **EA SUP**; buses leave from beside no. 200 Phan Boi Chau.

Plei Ku and around

North of Buon Me Thuot, Highway 14 rocks and rolls over the hills and plains of the **Dak Lak Plateau**, passing rubber plantations, hardwood forests and the corrugated leaves of coffee plants on its way to **PLEI KU**. The band of peaks to the west of the highway, and the rugged terrain buttressing them, constituted one of the American War's major combat theatres. It was an NVA (North Vietnamese Army) attack on Plei Ku, in February 1965, that elicited the "Rolling Thunder" campaign (see p.421); and the war's first conventional battle of any size was fought in the **Ia Drang Valley**, southwest of Plei Ku, eight months later. Hundreds of Americans died at Ia Drang, but many times more communists perished, spurring America to claim the victory by dint of a higher body count. A decade later, in March 1975, Plei Ku was abandoned when NVA troops overran Buon Me Thuot. As the South's commanding officers flew by helicopter to safety, 200,000 Southern soldiers and civilians were left to make their own way down to the coast, hounded at every step by NVA shells.

So little of Plei Ku was left standing by these last days of the war, that a near-total reconstruction was required. The Nineties reincarnation that you'll see, stacked up the side of a gentle slope, lacks any charm; yet if you can turn a blind eye to its drabness and lack of architectural finesse, you'll find it an extraordinarily friendly frontier town, and the perfect antidote to the bustle of Buon Me Thuot. Lower in altitude and blessed with a more clement temperature than Da Lat, Plei Ku is nevertheless equally prone to the ravages of the **monsoon**, which annually stirs its roads into a soup.

Barring an early morning stroll along central, east–west **Tran Phu**, where hawkers sell eggplants, shallots, parsnips and garlic, and into the adjacent town market, there's little to do in Plei Ku, so you'll need to head out of town for your thrills. This far north in the highlands, the **Jarai** and, to a lesser extent, the **Bahnar**, outnumber the Ede, and from Plei Ku it's possible to venture out and visit their villages. Plei Ku's tourist board is notoriously defensive of the region's more interesting settlements and doesn't approve of individuals making forays into the wilds. However, touring by Honda om we encountered no problems.

Practicalities

Plei Ku's long-distance **bus station** sits above the three-way crossroads 600m southeast of town. From here, it's a short Honda om trip into town along Hung Vuong, Plei Ku's southern limit, from which its main roads shoot north; when you see a broad flight of steps cut into the middle of the road you'll know you've reached northbound Le Loi, to all intents and purposes the town's eastern extent. **Buses to Kon Tum** (gateway to Bahnar villages) terminate and originate east of the market, on open ground beside the intersection of Le Lai and Tran Phu. The tourist office, in the *Pleiku Hotel* (see below), can arrange for you to stay in a minority village if money is no object, and there's a US Army map of the region on the wall which warrants a look if you're passing.

Far and away the best **place to stay** in town is the intriguingly named *Movie Star Hotel* (☎059/824626; ②) on Vo Thi Sau, whose light spacious rooms with fan and hot water are preferable to the jaded *Pleiku Hotel* (☎059/824628; ②) across town on Le Loi, where at least you can change currency. The *Hung Vuong*

(☎059/824270; ②) at the junction of Hung Vuong and Le Loi, has spotless rooms and staff that bend over backwards to be of help, but its more expensive rooms aren't worth the extra; or there's the *Yaly Hotel* (☎059/824843; ③) opposite the GPO at the junction of Hung Vuong and Tran Hung Dao, where prices drop according to how many flights of stairs you have to climb – the air-con rooms with hot water on the top floor are a steal. Bargain-basement lodgings are available at *Thanh Huong* (☎059/823557; ①) on Tran Phu, as long as you can stomach dank rooms with stained walls.

There are no outstanding **places to eat** in Plei Ku, though there's a decorous little restaurant in the ground floor of the *Movie Star Hotel* and another decent enough place upstairs at the *Yaly Hotel*. For a cheaper snack, delve into the central market and try out one of its gaggle of *pho* stalls.

The Jarai villages

Once past the *Pleiku Hotel* and out of town, Le Loi probes the coffee, tea and rice crops that hem the road to Kon Tum. Tourists are welcome to drop by the **Bien Ho Tea Factory**, 14km north of Plei Ku, and discover how tea leaves are dried and processed, though most push on to the left turn, 2km further north, that heads off to the **Yaly Falls** – a route which offers the chance to explore traditional minority life. Impressive as they are, the falls themselves are being sacrificed to make way for a new hydroelectric dam, but the road to them is still interesting, passing through several Jarai villages, and yielding peerless views across the plain it bisects, on which rice, maize and rubber are grown. You'll see Jarai people sauntering along the road, carrying their effects in backpacks; some of the women wear horizontally striped, multi-coloured skirts.

First stop, several kilometres up the Yaly road, is **PLEI MRONG**, which can be explored by following the dirt tracks that vein it. Of the countless Jarai houses you'll see here, some have walls crafted from earth and straw, others are made from split bamboo, while still others are more conventional edifices, with raised front porches under which wood is stacked to keep dry. Longhouse life seems to be fading out around these parts, and very few such houses can now be seen. An intriguing ethnic tradition which does still exist is the planting, on graves, of **hardwood statues** representing the dead buried beneath. There is a graveyard at Plei Mrong (ask to see the *nha mo*), but it's better to push on to **PLEI MUN**, whose graveyard has several wonderful carvings. In the past the Jarai would stick bamboo poles through the earth and into a fresh grave, through which to "feed" the dead.

Downhill to Qui Nhon

As recently as four decades ago, tigers stalked the upper reaches of **Highway 19** from Plei Ku down to Qui Nhon, known as the **Mang Yang Pass**. Norman Lewis, travelling here in the Fifties, found a French military outpost commanded by "a slap-happy sergeant from Perpignan, a cabaret-Provençal, who roared with laughter at the thought of his isolation, and poured us out half-tumblers of Chartreuse". The fort may have gone, but scores of **Bahnar settlements** speckle the route as it snakes its way through a majestic blister of hills and down to the coast. Around 33km out of Plei Ku you'll see a *rong* (communal house) in the distance, but hold on for another 12km until you reach the Bahnar district of **Kontang**, just north of the road, where four villages each have an impressive *rong*.

For the most spectacular panoramas, you'll need to wait until you're 65km out of Plei Ku, and then the countryside slowly begins to level out. Shortly after scruffy **AN KHE**, a kink in the highway leads you round onto the **An Khe Pass**, from where you are able to see the coastal plain yawning magnificently below you, embroidered by the Ha Giao River. By the time you've passed through **VINH SON**, and traversed the bridge that crosses to more sizeable **PHU PHONG**, 50km from Qui Nhon, you're down in the paddy of the coastal plain. Phu Phong lies under the jurisdiction of **Tay Son District** whose most famous sons, the Tay Son brothers, engineered a popular uprising that succeeded in unifying Vietnam for the first time, in the 1770s. Sickened by the land-grabbing and hunger afflicting their countrymen, Nguyen Nhac, Nguyen Lu and Nguyen Hue in 1771 mustered a peasant army, in order more volubly to express their anger. The army exceeded all expectations: by 1788 it had defeated the Trinh Dynasty to the north and the Nguyen dynasty to the south, and Nguyen Hue had proclaimed himself Emperor Quang Trung of Vietnam – an assertion to which he lent further weight a year later when he unceremoniously booted the Chinese out of northern Vietnam at the battle of Dong Da. Quang Trung's death in 1792 denied the brief Tay Son dynasty of his charismatic leadership, and ten years later French-backed Nguyen Anh of the Nguyen dynasty seized back power. Despite its brevity, the Tay Son period is recalled as a prosperous one when economic reforms were set in place, and education encouraged. The brothers' escapades are celebrated a three-kilometre Honda om ride from Phu Phong, at the **Quang Trung Museum** (7.30–11.30am & 2–4.30pm; $2), whose mediocre ensemble of weapons, clothes and armour is really only worth a visit if you're around for the *Dong Da Festival*, at which demonstrations are staged of the **martial arts** taught here throughout the year.

Beyond Phu Phong, countless brick kilns pepper the landscape, their rippling roofs seeming to melt in the heat. Qui Nhon itself is covered in *The South-Central Coast* chapter, on p.216.

Kon Tum and the Bahnar villages

Some 49km north of Plei Ku, northbound Highway 14 crosses the Dakbla River and runs into the southern limits of diminutive **KON TUM**, a sleepy, friendly town which serves as a springboard for jaunts to its outlying **Bahnar villages**. Under the guise of Phan Dinh Phung the highway forms the western edge of town; running east above the river is Nguyen Hue, and between these two axes lies the town centre. In common with Buon Me Thuot and Plei Ku, Kon Tum had a hard time of it during the American War, and yet a stroll along Nguyen Hue still reveals a handful of red-tile terraces of shophouses left over from the French era, their low, bowed roofs blackened with age, as well as two churches. At the base of Tran Phu stands the grand, white-washed bulk of **Tan Huong Church**; further east is the so-called **Wooden Church**, built by the French in 1913, and lovingly restored to its highly varnished prime in the mid-Nineties. A statue of Christ stands behind glass over the front entrance; below him, a stained-glass window neatly fuses the classic Christian symbol of the dove with images of local resonance – a Bahnar village and an elephant. In the grounds, a statue of the nineteenth-century French bishop who established the diocese of Kon Tum stands before a scale model of a communal house.

Kon Kotu

There are dozens of Bahnar villages encircling Kon Tum. At some, such as **KON ROBANG**, 2km west of Phan Dinh Phung along Ba Trieu, the village *rong,* or communal house, has been robbed of much of its drama by an aluminium roof; others are simply too far away to be easily reached. Fortunately, there is one village that's both fascinating and accessible: **KON KOTU**, a timeless community only 4 or 5km east of Kon Tum. A kilometre or so east of the bus station, Nguyen Hue veers northeast; another 500m later, and the *Paradis Café* to your left is the signal to turn right onto a track that strikes past stilt villages, cassava and sugar-cane plantations, as it spears the Bahnar heartland. The track crosses a suspension bridge to the south bank of the river, at which point you'll have to veer left (east) for 3 to 4km to reach the village – a stretch that becomes a quagmire during the wet season. All the dwellings in Kon Kotu are made of bamboo and secured with rattan string, but it's the village's immaculate *rong* that commands the most attention. The *rong* is used as a venue for festivals and village meetings, and as a village court at which anyone found guilty of a tribal offence has to ritually kill a pig and a chicken, and must apologize in front of the village. No nails were used in the construction of the bamboo walls, floor, and impossibly tall thatch roof of this lofty communal hall.

Practicalities

Kon Tum's **bus** station is on your left, as you cross the bridge into town. From there, it's a 250-metre walk east along Nguyen Hue to the foot of Le Hong Phong, and another 150m to Tran Phu; both run up into the town centre. **Currency exchange** is possible at the *Agribank* on Tran Phu.

Several affordable **places to stay** are located around town. North of the centre on Ba Trieu, the government-run *Quang Trung* (☎060/862703; ③) has rather cheerier rooms (some with air-con and hot water) than its austere reception would suggest, though Tran Phu's *Guesthouse 90* (☎060/862853; ②), housed in a yellow colonial villa, is a homelier choice. Otherwise you'll have to make do with one of the slovenly and overpriced rooms down the road at *Nha Khach 946* (☎060/862610; ②) or a hutch-like partition room, sharing bathroom, at the *Hiep Thanh Guesthouse* (☎060/862403; ①), below the market at 34 Le Hong Phong. A classier hotel, the *Dakbla*, is currently under construction opposite the bus station and beside the river.

When it's time to **eat**, the hygienic *Dakbla Restaurant*, 100m east of the bus station, is a safe bet; a magnet for local students of English, it serves standard *com* and *pho* dishes from an English menu. Failing that, *Quan Nem 99* on Le Hong Phong is decent enough, and the *My Tam*, further up the road, boils up a wicked *pho*.

On from Kon Tum to Da Nang

Until the rumoured improvements to the Kon Tum–Quang Ngai road materialize, most visitors to Kon Tum are backtracking to Plei Ku and dropping down to Qui Nhon in order to continue their tour. Actually, onward travel from Kon Tum to Da Nang along **Highway 14** is possible with your own transport, but be warned that

VIETNAM'S REAL-LIFE KURTZ

The Sedang played their part in one of colonial Vietnam's oddest interludes and one which mirrored events in Joseph Conrad's novella, *Heart of Darkness*, in which a mysterious voyager named Mr Kurtz proclaims himself as a king far up the Belgian Congo – a story later plundered by Francis Ford Coppola for his film *Apocalypse Now*.

The career of opportunist French rogue, **Marie-David de Mayréna**, was a chequered one. After a stint with the French Army in Cochinchina in the mid-1860s, he made his way back to Paris, only to return to the East after failing as a banker. Back in Vietnam by the 1880s, he established himself as a planter around Ba Ria, but another change of course came when the governor sent him to explore the highlands in 1888. Of the hundred or so porters and soldiers that accompanied him, only one, a Frenchman named Alphonse Mercurol, remained by the time he reached Kon Tum. Through the contacts of the French missionaries based there, Mayréna was able to arrange meetings with local tribal chiefs; soon, the leaders fell under the spell of his "blue eyes" and "bold, confident stare", and he conspired to proclaim himself **King Marie I of Sedang**. Mercurol acquired the title of marquis of Hanoi. For three months, Mayréna ruled from a straw hut flying the national flag (a white cross on a blue background, with a red star in the centre) legislating, creating an army and even declaring war on the neighbouring Jarai people.

Ultimately, however, Mayréna was more interested in money than in altruistic sovereignty. Within months he decamped, and set off to get some mileage from his "title". In his book, *Dragon Ascending*, Henry Kamm quotes an erstwhile manager of Saigon's *Continental*, where Mayréna boarded on credit with assorted courtiers: "Alas, when, several days later, Mayréna moved out of the hotel, nothing was left to Laval [the then hotel manager] as payment for his services, except for a decoration, that of the National Order of the Kingdom of the Sedangs, which the king gave him before departure". Returning to Europe, Mayréna capitalized yet further upon circumstances, selling fictitious titles, positions and mining concessions to raise cash. Inevitably, cracks began to appear in his story, and he fled back to southeast Asia in 1890. Mayréna died in penury on Malaya's Tioman Island, supposedly of a snake bite.

the road is in a sorry state of repair, especially in the wet season, and a good motorcycle or four-wheel-drive jeep is essential. Around 45km north of Kon Tum is the district of **Dak To**, which witnessed some of the most sustained fighting of the American War; to the west of the road to Dak To is **Rocket Ridge**, a brow of hills that earnt its name from the heavy bombing – napalm and conventional – it received during this time. This far north you're in **Sedang** territory, and with a little exploration you should be able to find some Sedang longhouses; if you're up here, you should try to visit **DAK RE**, where there's a spectacular *rong*. Beyond here, the route takes you through wonderfully verdant countryside – though on a progressively worsening surface – before Highway 14 eventually rejoins Highway 1 some 20km south of Da Nang, at **DIEN BAN**.

Da Nang and its surroundings are covered in *The Central Provinces* chapter, starting on p.223.

travel details

Buses

*It's almost impossible to give the **frequency** with which buses run. Though scheduled, long-distance public buses won't depart if empty. Moreover, private services, often minibuses or pick-ups, ply more popular routes, and depart only when they have enough passengers to make the journey worthwhile. It's advisable to start your journey early – most long-distance departures leave between 5 and 9am, and few run after midday. **Journey times** can also vary; figures below show the normal length of time you can expect the journey to take.*

Buon Me Thuot to: Da Nang (21hr 30min); Ho Chi Minh City (16hr 30min); Nha Trang (5hr 30min); Plei Ku (5hr 30min).

Da Lat to: Buon Me Thuot (10hr 30 min); Da Nag (21hr); Ho Chi Minh City (7hr 30min); Nha Trang (5hr); Phan Rang (2hr).

Plei Ku to: Buon Me Thuot (5hr 30min); Da Nang (14hr); Kon Tum (1hr); Qui Nhon (5hr).

Trains

Da Lat to: Trai Met (4 daily; 40min).

Flights

Buon Me Thuot to: Da Nang (3 weekly; 1hr 20min); Hanoi (3 weekly; 3hr 30min); Ho Chi Minh City (1 daily; 50min).

Da Lat to: Ho Chi Minh City (3 weekly; 50min); Hué (3 weekly; 1hr 20min).

Plei Ku to: Da Nang (3 weekly; 50min); Hanoi (4 weekly; 4hr 15min); Ho Chi Minh City (4 weekly; 1hr 15min).

CHAPTER FOUR

THE SOUTH-CENTRAL COAST

O nce you've dusted off the grime of Ho Chi Minh City and Bien Hoa, you're ready to head up the elongated flatlands that comprise Vietnam's **south-central coast**. Extending from the wetlands of the Mekong Delta right the way up to the central provinces (see p.223), and bounded by the South China Sea to the east, and the bulk of the Truong Son mountain range to the west, the south-central coast is braced by the twin backbones of **Highway 1** and the pan-Vietnam **rail** line. In some places, the mountains' rugged crests stoop right down to peer into the turquoise shallows of the sea; at these points along the coast, both highway and rail line scythe through the heights, across precipitous passes that afford truly bewitching views of the countryside below.

Sea-fishing provides a living for a considerable percentage of the region's population. Captivating fleets of fishing-boats jostle for space in the cramped ports and estuaries of the coastal towns, awaiting the turn of the tide; and fish and seafood drying along the road are a common sight. The farmers who till the region's soils have tended to leave rice-growing in the capable hands of the Mekong Delta, and the crops you are likeliest to see here are coconut and rubber **plantations**, shrimp farms, wintry salt flats and fruit **orchards**.

Historically, this swathe of Vietnam was the domain of the Indianized trading empire of **Champa**. Courted in its prime by seafaring merchants from around the globe, Champa was steadily marginalized from the tenth century onwards by the unswerving march south of the Vietnamese. These days a few enclaves living around **Phan Thiet** and **Phan Rang** are all that remain of the Cham people; but the gnarled remnants of the **towers** with which they once punctuated the countryside, and which reached their apogee within the natural bowl of hills cupping the majestic **My Son** system (covered in *The Central Provinces* chapter, see p.238), recall Champa's erstwhile magnificence. The power struggles of the Chams and Vietnamese were still fairly recent history when the **French** took advantage of factional strife in Hué's royal court, following the passing of the Emperor Tu Duc in 1883, to sidle into the region, seize it and declare it as the French Protectorate of Annam. Many a Vietnamese peasant was consigned to a cheerless life of forced labour in the **plantations** the French subsequently established. The **American War** brought still further social dislocation. Hundreds of thousands of villagers were uprooted from their homes and boxed up in strategic hamlets. Their lands were rendered "free-fire zones" and bombed pancake-flat by planes making sorties out of the US army bases that peppered the region.

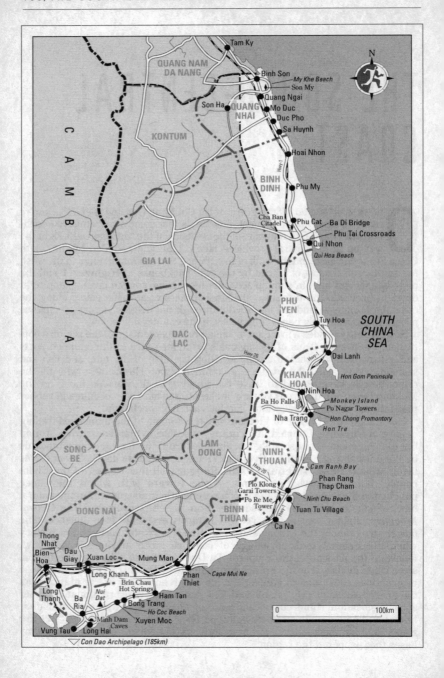

N

Tam Ky

QUANG NAM
DA NANG

Binh Son
My Khe Beach
Son My
Quang Ngai
Son Ha
QUANG Mo Duc
NHAI Duc Pho
Sa Huynh

KONTUM

Hoai Nhon

Hwy 1

BINH
DINH Phu My

C A M B O D I A

Cha Ban
Citadel Phu Cat Ba Di Bridge
Phu Tai Crossroads
Qui Nhon

GIA LAI Qui Hoa Beach

PHU
YEN

DAC
LAC Tuy Hoa SOUTH
CHINA
SEA

Hwy 26 Hwy 1 Dai Lanh

KHANH Hon Gom Peninsula
HOA

Ninh Hoa
Ba Ho Falls Monkey Island
Po Nagar Towers
Nha Trang Hon Chong Promontory
SONG Hon Tre
BE LAM
DONG

NINH
THUAN
Cam Ranh Bay
Hwy 20

Plo Klong
Garai Towers Phan Rang
DONG NAI Thap Cham
Po Re Me Ninh Chu Beach
Tower Tuan Tu Village
BINH
THUAN Ca Na

Thong
Nhat
Bien Dau
Hoa Giay Xuan Loc Mung Man
Long Khanh Cape Mui Ne
Long Phan Thiet
Thanh Brin Chau
Ba Hot Springs
Ria Nui Ham Tan
Dat Bong Trang
Minh Dam Ho Coc Beach
Vung Tau Caves Xuyen Moc
Long Hai

▽ Con Dao Archipelago (185km)

0   100km

Strung out between raucous Ho Chi Minh and the cultural showpieces of Hué and Hoi An, and serving as a springboard for travel in the central highlands, this section of the coastline is inevitably perceived as a rather dull interlude between more rewarding destinations. While sites of considerable interest and beauty do exist along this portion of coast, most tourists are merely **passing through**; nonetheless, all but the hardiest of travellers will need to work at least one pitstop into their itinerary. For this, you'll have to juggle tranquil beaches – and there are some real peaches on offer – with more cultural pursuits.

Coming from Ho Chi Minh, there's an early choice to be made. Highway 1 has to wait until it reaches Phan Thiet to see the South China Sea, but you needn't: from Bien Hoa, a minor road drops down to **Vung Tau**, once a French seaside resort, and still boasting the winning combination of sun, sea and sand. Two more beaches, **Long Hai** and **Ho Coc**, lie just a day-trip's distance around the coast; while to the south, the former French prison island of **Con Dao** can be reached either by ship or by helicopter. With tourism still in its infancy across Vietnam, few beaches further along the south-central coast have a developed tourist trade as yet. **Mui Ne**, a short hop from the jolly fishing town of **Phan Thiet**, is a notable exception, and the single set of bungalows above its aquamarine waters won't be alone for long. Those for whom a day sunbathing is a day wasted will prefer to make a little more headway, and rest up at grisly **Phan Rang**, site of the most southerly of the many **tower complexes** erected by the once-mighty empire of **Champa** (see box on p.204).

The beach at **Ca Na** isn't in the same league as Mui Ne, but its location just beyond the hard shoulder of the highway makes it a convenient short-term staging-post. If you press on to **Nha Trang**, however, you have the best of both worlds: arresting Cham towers, attractive municipal beach and a brisk trade in snorkelling trips. Other, more secluded, beaches that warrant an expedition include **Doc Let** and **Sa Huynh**; while for a little more civilization, **Qui Nhon** makes a useful halt above Nha Trang. The scars of war tend not to intrude too much along this stretch of the country, though many visitors make time to visit **Quang Ngai**, where Vietnam's south-central arc of coastline culminates, and to wander the sombre site of the notorious **My Lai** massacre perpetrated by US forces in 1968.

Vung Tau and around

From **Bien Hoa**, just outside Ho Chi Minh, Highway 51 drops southward via modest **Long Thanh** (famed locally for its impressive **fruit market**) to **Ba Ria**. From there, a dog-legged road ventures out across the swampland and shrimp farms of the **Vung Tau Peninsula** to Vung Tau itself, home of the most southerly beaches on the eastern Vietnamese coast.

With every passing day, a little more of the charm ebbs from **VUNG TAU**, "The Bay of Boats", located some 125km southeast of Ho Chi Minh City on a hammerheaded spit of land jutting into the mouth of the Saigon River. Once a thriving riviera-style beach resort, the city is now a shadow of its former, quaint self, its several strips of sand looping out from a city centre that lacks any real finesse. As Vung Tau's **offshore oil** industry and steadily growing port have bloated the city into a more business-oriented conurbation, tourism has been

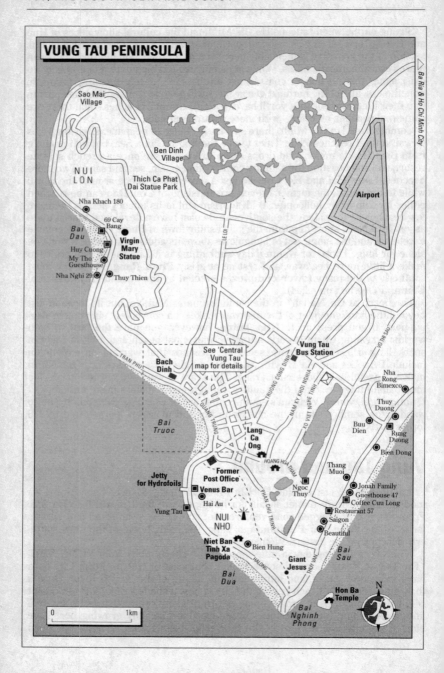

VUNG TAU PENINSULA

Sao Mai Village

Ben Dinh Village

NUI LON

Thich Ca Phat Dai Statue Park

Airport

Nha Khach 180

69 Cay Bang

Bai Dau

Virgin Mary Statue

Huy Cuong

My Tho Guesthouse

Nha Nghi 29

Thuy Thien

LE LOI

Ba Ria & Ho Chi Minh City

TRAN PHU

Bach Dinh

See 'Central Vung Tau' map for details

QUANG TRUNG

Vung Tau Bus Station

TRUONG CONG DINH

NAM KY KHOI NGHIA

VO THI SAU

VO VIET NGHE TINH

Nha Rong Bimexco

Thuy Duong

Buu Dien

Rung Duong

Bien Dong

Bai Truoc

Lang Ca Ong

HOANG HOA THAM

Thang Muoi

Jetty for Hydrofoils

Former Post Office

Venus Bar

Hai Au

Vung Tau

NUI NHO

PHAN CHU TRINH

Ngoc Thuy

Jonah Family

Guesthouse 47

Coffee Cuu Long

Restaurant 57

Saigon

Beautiful

Niet Ban Tinh Xa Pagoda

Bien Hung

HALONG

Giant Jesus

THUY VAN

Bai Sau

Bai Dua

Hon Ba Temple

Bai Nghinh Phong

N

0   1km

forced to take a back seat. With Hanoi planning more fully to exploit the area's mineral wealth, this trend looks set to accelerate. That said, as a retreat from the frenzy of Ho Chi Minh, Vung Tau is worth considering. On a sunny **Sunday**, when the stripey deckchairs and beach umbrellas are out and locals come in their droves, its beachfronts still manage to affect a certain charm. Downtown Vung Tau nestles between two diminutive peaks, **Nui Lon** ("Big Mountain") to the north, and **Nui Nho** ("Small Mountain") to the south. Roads loop around both, and these **circuits** take in all of the city's **beaches** – hushed, northerly **Bai Dau**, blustery **Bai Dua**, and **Bai Sau**, or "Back Beach", which has the city's best sands. Between them runs **Bai Truoc** ("Front Beach"), Vung Tau's skinny municipal beach.

Portuguese ships are thought to have exploited the city's deep anchorage as early as the fifteenth century. By the turn of this century, French expats, who knew the place as *Cap Saint-Jacques*, had adopted it as a retreat from the daily rig-marole of Saigon, and set to work carving colonial villas into the sides of Nui Lon and Nui Nho. Shifts in Vietnam's political sands duly replaced French visitors with American GIs. With them gone, and the communist government in power, the city became a favoured launchpad for the vessels that spirited away the **boat people** (see p.426) in the late Seventies. Today, Western oil-workers nurturing the city's burgeoning oil industry are a common sight around town, and a slather of bars and massage parlours have sprung up to cater for them.

Vung Tau didn't have a monopoly on French holidaymakers out of Saigon. Many preferred to push on past Ba Ria to more intimate **Long Hai**, a likeable resort town that's just 20km around the coast. Presently a well-kept secret among domestic tourists, Long Hai moves at a considerably slower pace than Vung Tau – but if it's real seclusion you crave, get yourself down to the virgin sands of won-drous **Ho Coc Beach**, around 50km east of Ba Ria.

Arrival and getting around

Arriving by bus, you'll disembark in the square below the cathedral on Tran Hung Dao if you're in a **minibus**; and at Vung Tau Bus Station, at the northeastern end of Nam Ky Khoi Nghia if you're in a **public bus**. Either way, a gaggle of cyclo dri-vers will be on hand to ferry you to a hotel. **Hydrofoils** from Ham Nghi in down-town Ho Chi Minh dock opposite the *Hai Au Hotel* (see over), just south of the city centre on Ha Long. Once in Vung Tau, your choices for **getting around** are pretty limited: cyclos are, of course, ubiquitous, though if you need a lift along bumpy Tran Phu to Bai Dau, a Honda om is more practical. There are no taxis, but plenty of bicycles or mopeds for rent; prices are $1/$7 a day respectively (see "Listings", p.195, for details of outlets).

Accommodation

An abundance of **hotels** and **guesthouses** operate in Vung Tau. Bai Sau boasts the most varied lodgings, from comfortable hotels to cheap dives, and even one or two beach hut set-ups that allow you quick and easy access to the city's best strip of beach. Classier places have so far tended to concentrate – and prices take a corresponding hike – in the central area; while for peace and quiet, you'd do well to make for one of a cluster of guesthouses and hotels up on Bai Dau.

Bai Sau (Back Beach)

Beautiful Hotel, 100–102 Thuy Van (☎064/852177). Friendly place with appealingly fresh and modern rooms with IDD and satellite TV. ④

Bien Dong, 3 Thuy Van. Shaded by trees and just above the beach, the 10 cheery blue huts comprising the *Bien Dong* boast bathroom, fan and mozzie nets – good value. ①

Buu Dien, 1 Le Hong Phong (☎064/859792). Nearby construction threatens to rob the *Buu Dien* of its commanding seaviews but rooms should remain bright, well appointed and welcoming. ③

Guesthouse 47, 47 Thuy Van (no phone). Cheap but cheerless waterfront guesthouse, its dark, barracks-like rooms all fitted with showers. ①

Jonah Family, 29 Thuy Van (no phone). Makeshift rooms in this beachside outfit could stand a little grooming, but the owners are friendly and helpful to a fault. ①

Nha Rong Bimexco, Thuy Van (☎064/859916). Peacefully sited in the pine groves up at the far northeastern end of Thuy Van, the 50 tidy and solid huts here have garnered good reports; air-con is available for an extra $3, and there are some 4-bed rooms. ②

Saigon, 72 Thuy Van (☎064/852317). Not blessed with Bai Sau's best strip of beach yet still a reliable and good-value base, kept spick and span by an army of cleaners, and close to inexpensive restaurants; rooms have inside bathroom, and there are bikes for rent. ②

Thang Muoi, 4–6 Thuy Van (☎064/852665). With its wide variety of rooms, all of them clean and capacious, the motel-style *Thang Muoi* is sure to have accommodation to suit you; the spacious grounds reveal a garden café. ②

Thuy Duong, 4 Thuy Van (☎064/852635). Choose between a no-frills, stripey hut beside the beach, or swisher lodgings inland and across the road. ①

Bai Truoc (Front Beach), the city centre and Bai Dua

Bien Hung, 62 Ha Long (☎064/856019). Three hillside villas framed by frangipanis house the *Bien Hung*'s 17 rooms, making this a wonderfully quiet and relaxing spot for holing up with a good book; below, the hotel's small restaurant knocks out reasonable breakfasts and snacks. ②

Hai Au, 100 Ha Long (☎064/856178). Splendid isolation above Bai Dua lends this mid-range hotel an appeal its facilities don't particularly merit. ③–④

Palace, 11 Nguyen Trai (☎064/856411). Slightly more dated than the *Royal* maybe, but rooms at the *Palace* approach the same high standards, and staff are extremely attentive; not all rooms overlook the sea, so ask. Breakfast is thrown in, and bikes and motorbikes are available for rent. ④

Rang Dong, 5 Duy Tan (☎064/852133). Gloomy rooms and foreboding corridors characterize this bleak and unkempt hotel, but it's still one of the city centre's cheaper options, and even economy rooms have air-con and hot water. ②

Royal, 48 Quang Trung (☎064/859852). Charming and modern hotel with all the trimmings – and good facilities for business travellers; many of its rooms boast delightful seaviews. ④

Song Hong, 12 Hoang Dieu (☎064/852137). Competitively priced, despite its recent upgrade – the 3 budget rooms with air-con and satellite TV are unbeatable value. ③

Bai Dau

My Tho Guesthouse, 47 Tran Phu (no phone). A gem of a place run by a charming and attentive couple who'll rustle up hearty meals on request: choose between big, unfussy rooms fronting the beach, and smaller but cheaper internal rooms; a terrace upstairs lends itself to sunbathing. ①

Nha Khach 180, 180 Tran Phu (☎064/858553). Pleasingly well-groomed operation, substantially pricier than its competition, but worth the extra if you crave a few creature comforts. ③

Nha Nghi 29, 29 Tran Phu (no phone). The cheapest of the spartan but tolerable rooms in this grim concrete block have no sea views, so shell out a little extra for a better outlook. ①

Thuy Thien, 96 Tran Phu (no phone). Another functional place offering very good value, as long as you don't expect too much luxury. ①

The city

Scouting around central Vung Tau unearths precious little to see or do. Apart from a handful of box-like, louvred villas at Tran Hung Dao's northern end and a few colonial piles along waterfront Quang Trung, French ghosts have been all but laid to rest, while the litter- and rubble-strewn town beach, labelled Coconut Beach in colonial times but now referred to, somewhat more prosaically, as Bai Truoc or **Front Beach**, offers little by way of consolation. A skinny strip of sand, ribbed by a strip of souvenir shops, bars and restaurants, only at dawn and dusk does it muster any charm, when fishermen dredge its shallows, gaily lit fishing-boats unload their catches and coracles bob to and from the shore.

A welcome slice of history survives on the southern slope of Nui Lon, where the red-tile roof of imposing **Bach Dinh** (daily 7–11.30am & 1.30–5pm; $2) peeps out from behind a vanguard of frangipani and bougainvillea, above the northern extent of Quang Trung. Built at the end of the nineteenth century, it long served as a holiday home to Vietnam's political players, hosting such luminaries as Paul Doumer, Governor-General of Indochina (for whom it was originally erected), emperors Thanh Thai and Bao Dai, and President Thieu. Recently the villa has fallen on hard times, but the front facade's classical busts, and the mosaics under the eaves still catch the eye. Inside you can thrill to the building's collection of "valuable antique items", excavated from a seventeenth-century shipwreck off Con Dao; among the exhibits are such unmissables as "dry burned fruits", "beard-tweezers" and "pieces of stone in the ship". A snakeskin-patterned bannister leads up to the first floor's fancily tiled chambers, whose Cambodian Buddhist statuary and shards of old pottery are eclipsed by the commanding views of Front Beach's broad sweep.

Around Nui Nho

The foot of Quang Trung is the starting-block for the six-kilometre circuit of **Nui Nho**. From there, the exposed coastal road, Ha Long, loops around the southside of the mountain. Not far past the former post office, a pretty pink villa marked "53/2 Ha Long" signposts the left turn up to Vung Tau's **lighthouse**, whose construction, in 1910, seems to have been based on a child's sketch of a space-rock-

HOTELS
1 Palace 3 Royal
2 Rang Dong 4 Song Hong

RESTAURANTS
A Abeille D'or F Oasis
B Hue Anh G Thanh Lich
C Huu Nghi H The Frenchie
D Ma Maison I Thuan Ky
E Moby Dick's J Whispers
  Bar

Bach Dinh

Bakery

Vung Tao
Commercial
Bank

Pharmacy

Vicarrent

Vietcombank

Cathedral

Minibus
Stop

*Bai
Truoc*

Vietnam
Airlines

Con Dao
Transportation

**CENTRAL
VUNG TAU**

N

Statue of
Tran Hung Dao

▽ *Bai Dua & Back Beach*

et. Off-limits in the days when the French retained a strong military presence in the city, it's now accessible and affords panoramic views of the peninsula.

The most noteworthy of several pagodas strung along this stretch of coastline is **Niet Ban Tinh Xa Pagoda**, a modern and multi-level complex fronted by a structure resembling a high-rise dovecote. The pagoda's main claims to fame are its 5000kg bronze bell (struck by the red log suspended beside it), and a twelve-metre-long reclining Buddha whose feet bear the requisite 108 auspicious marks. Matters spiritual, though, have long since been superseded by matters commercial, and touts striving to offload joss sticks and seashells are far more vocal than the pagoda's monks.

A composite of shingle, dark sand and rocks, it's no wonder **Bai Dua**, south of Niet Ban Tinh Xa, was dubbed "Roches Noires" by the French: if you want a swim or a sunbathe, hold on until you round the promontory. Meanwhile, a gruelling fifteen-minute hike from the southwestern tip of Nui Nho brings you to Vung Tau's own little touch of Rio, its 33-metre-high **Giant Jesus** (daily 7.30–11.30am & 1.30–5pm). Cherubs wielding harps and trumpets herald your final approach to the outstretched arms of the city's most famous landmark; climb the steps inside the wind-buffeted statue and you can perch, parrot-like, on Jesus's shoulder, from where you'll enjoy truly giddying views of the surrounding seascape. A depressing menagerie of monkeys, rabbits and snakes lurk behind Jesus's back; walk beyond them, and you'll eventually reach the lighthouse.

Immediately around the headland is the sweet, sandy cove of **Bai Nghinh Phong**, and beyond that, **Hon Ba Temple** marooned a little way out to sea on a tiny islet. Only at low tide will you be able to reach the island – and even then you'll feel like a latter-day Moses as you negotiate its shingly causeway, waves lashing the rocks either side of you. The temple itself is diminutive and unremarkable, but from between the frangipanis and coconut trees shading the island, there are good views back toward Jesus and Bai Sau.

If swimming and sun-seeking brought you to Vung Tau, make a bee-line for the yellow sands of **Bai Sau**, a beach in the classic sense of the word, far and away Vung Tau's widest, longest and best. Backed by ugly block-buildings, and a little unkempt, it's not exactly a tropical paradise, though on Sundays, cluttered with deckchairs and umbrellas, and the pineapple- and banana-sellers out in force, it's pleasant enough. Lower down, a squall of construction sites blot the landscape, so opt for the dunier and generally more appetizing strip up near the turning onto Le Hong Phong.

There's no need to backtrack around Nui Nho to reach the city centre, as Hoang Hoa Tham cuts around the north side of the mountain. En route, you might check out **Lang Ca Ong**, or Whale Temple. According to Cham folklore, the whale was a sacred creature, and protector of seafarers; at Lang Ca Ong, this tradition is preserved, and at the **Whale Festival**, held on the sixteenth day of the eighth lunar month, local fishermen make offerings to the world's largest mammal. Three glass cabinets behind the altar are filled with the bones of whales washed up on the shore; judging by some of the skulls, though, a few dolphins seem to have been thrown in for good measure.

Bai Dau and beyond

North of Bach Dinh, Quang Trung becomes Tran Phu and skirts the western skirts of Nui Lon en route to sleepy **Bai Dau**, the most hassle-free of all Vung Tau's beaches. Barring the odd restaurant, there's very little action here, but heavy stone walls forming a bluff against the sea, and the blue-shuttered buildings that line them lend it a distinctly Mediterranean ambience. The actual beach is short, dark and slightly pebbly but perfectly suited to swimming and lounging. An outsized statue of Mary with Child will, when finished, compete with Front Beach's Giant Jesus.

With a rented bicycle (see p.195) it's possible to trace Tran Phu's circumnavigation of Nui Lon, and to visit the delightful fishing village of **Sao Mai**, set appealingly against the backdrop of the mountain's lush green slopes. Aged, paved paths pilot you down among the waterfront's weatherbeaten shuttered houses where fish hang out on lines to dry, coracles lean up against walls, and leaf-roofed stilthouses teeter over the shore. Further clockwise, Sao Mai blends into bigger **Ben Dinh**, which runs it a distant second in the charm stakes, but boasts a busy quayside, littered with huge wicker baskets of nets and old ropes, where blue and red boats bob, waiting for the next tide. Unexceptional **Thich Ca Phat Dai Statue Park** (daily 7am–5pm; $1.50) mounts the slope of Nui Lon a little beyond Ben Dinh. Among its Buddhist monuments is an exhibit room (7.30–11am & 2–4.30pm) displaying photographs and relics from Con Dao Prison (see p.197).

Eating and drinking

Vung Tau supports a marginally more cosmopolitan span of **restaurants** than your average Vietnamese town; French cuisine weighs in particularly heavily, but it's also possible to find spaghetti bolognaise and burgers. Menus are far more traditional once you leave the central area, but there are two approximations of travellers' cafés on Back Beach. For a light snack, check out the **bakery** at 214 Bacu. In addition, a few **bars** have sprung up on Front Beach, wise to the demand for cold beer.

Front Beach and Bai Dua

Abeille D'Or, 12 Nguyen Trai (☎064/856004). Decor may be low-key, but subtly washed walls, dicky-bowed waiters, picturesque setting in an aged terrace and a range of authentic and well-prepared French dishes – at prices a notch below *Ma Maison* – conspire to create a pleasing dining experience.

The Frenchie, *Grand Hotel*, 26 Quang Trung (☎064/856164). Minty walls, well-laundered tablecloths and fresh-cut flowers create a favourable dining ambience in this tidy French-run bistro, whose blackboard menu's mish-mash of cuisines, from fondue to shepherd's pie, squarely targets local expats; their "business lunch" ($8) offers soup, main course, dessert, beer and coffee. 11.30am–1.30pm & 6.30–10pm.

Hue Anh, 446 Truong Cong Dinh. Chicken with plum is boney but delicious and the diced beef is also good, but big-boy portions are guaranteed whatever your choice in this popular and central restaurant; two eat for $8, whether in the bamboo-encased dining room or out on the garden terrace. 9am–10pm.

Huu Nghi, 14 Tran Hung Dao. Cavernous Chinese and Vietnamese restaurant where a menu of phone directory proportions embraces everything from ducks' feet to pigeon; customers choose from small, medium or large portions. 8.30am–9pm.

Ma Maison, 89 Tran Hung Dao (☎064/852014). Refined French restaurant, lent character by crisp white tablecloths and terracotta floor tiles and graced by well-prepared dishes such as roasted duck and lamb chops in garlic and parsley sauce, and desserts like *crêpe suzette* and soufflé with Grand Marnier, for which you can expect to pay through the nose; two can spend up to $50 on a meal.

Moby Dick's Bar, 23 Quang Trung. With excellent music, affordable beer, and a loyal expat clientele, it's no surprise that *Moby Dick's* is often still going at dawn – but be sure to avoid the drab front bar and head for the back room. 5pm–early hours.

Oasis, 1 Le Loi. Hard to beat for bulky platefuls of such Western favourites as burger with fries. 11.30am–2pm & 6–10pm.

Thanh Lich, 11 Quang Trung. One of the homelier, more reasonable options on central Vung Tau's main drag of cafés and restaurants, marred only by the constant droning muzak. Meals on rice start at $1 and there are filling breakfasts, too. 6am–1am.

Thuan Ky, 90 Trung Nhi. Huge, and hugely popular two-floored *com* and *pho* shop, slap-bang in the centre of the city.

Venus Bar, 15 Ha Long. Pavement tables exploit the refreshing sea breeze wafting past this tackily cosy café-bar, below the *Hai Au* hotel on the headland over Bai Dua; beer is $1.50, cocktails $4. 6pm–2am.

Vung Tau, 150 Ha Long (☎064/856577). The emphasis is squarely on seafood in this upmarket Vietnamese/Chinese restaurant housed in a custom-built circular building set over the sea, though the menu still yields many affordable fish, beef and pork dishes – or settle for a sunset aperitif. 9am–10pm.

Whispers, 438 Truong Cong Dinh (☎064/858762). Formerly Vung Tau's branch of *Apocalypse Now Bar*, but now no less bland than the several other expat bars around this area; still, worth it if you hanker for cold beer and a pool table. 6pm–2am.

Back Beach

Coffee Cuu Long, 57 Thuy Van. Another restaurant in the *Restaurant 57* mould: fortifying breakfasts, cheap and cheerful meals (sizzling fish in hot pot with hot pepper is a winner), bikes for rent, and good advice. 5.30am–10.30pm.

Ngoc Thuy, 63 Hoang Hoa Tham. Stilthouse restaurant, suspended over an emerald lake and reached by a boardwalk, but otherwise ordinary; main dishes from $1.50. 11am–11pm.

Restaurant 57, 48a Thuy Van. Once you've polished off the (recommended) grilled prawns, or a "wholeday" breakfast, chat to the friendly owner who is a font of local knowledge; bikes and motorbikes are available for rent. 6am–10pm.

Rung Duong, 2 Thuy Van. Seafood gets top billing in this hexagonal restaurant, set back 50m from the beach; prices are slightly over the odds. 8am–10pm.

Bai Dau

69 Cay Bang, 69 Tran Phu. A little pricey but popular with locals who are moved to travel out of town for seafood overlooking the beach at sunset.10am–8pm.

Huy Cuong, 57 Tran Phu. More modest and rustic than the *Cay Bang*, yet still able to match its fine views; main courses (crab, fish, shrimps) start around $1. 7am–9pm.

Listings

Banks and exchange *Vietcombank*, 27–29 Tran Hung Dao (closed Thurs pm), changes travellers' cheques and advances cash on *Visa* and *Mastercard*; *Vung Tau Commercial Bank*, 59 Tran Hung Dao, will swap dollars for dong.

Bicycle and moped rental Thuy Van's *Restaurant 57* and *Coffee Cuu Long* have both bicycles and mopeds for rent, as does the *Palace* hotel, while the nearby *Saigon* hotel has only bicycles; on Bai Dau, go to the *My Tho Guesthouse*.

Boats to Con Dao Islands *Con Dao Transportation*, 430 Truong Cong Dinh (☎064/852399), arranges 1 or 2 trips weekly, taking 12hr to reach Con Son (see p.197), and costing $115 (return) per person.

Bus station North of the city centre, on Nam Ky Khoi Nghia.

Car rental Car rental plus driver can be arranged at *Vicarrent*, 46 Tran Hung Dao (☎064/852400).

Hospital *Le Loi Hospital*, 22 Le Loi (☎064/852667), has an outpatients' clinic for foreigners.

Hydrofoil Hydrofoils ($6–12 one way) to Ho Chi Minh City depart from the jetty opposite the *Hai Au Hotel* daily at 4pm.

Pharmacy 62 Tran Hung Dao.

Post office The GPO at 45 Le Hong Phong offers full postal services and 24-hr IDD.

Vietnam Airlines Booking office above the *Lotus Restaurant* at 59 Quang Trung (☎064/856099).

Around Vung Tau: Long Hai

Apart from its pretty, yellow-washed, and twin-towered church, **Ba Ria** has nothing worth seeing, but with buses leaving for points east of Vung Tau from the station beside the market, on the western outskirts of town, you may still have cause to linger here.

The right turn at a forked road a couple of kilometres east of Ba Ria gives, 12km later, onto the frontage of the modest resort of **LONG HAI**, located 20km around the coast from Vung Tau below a wall of impressive mountains. Once a lure for French holidaymakers, and with a splendidly distinguished colonial-era hotel to prove it, Long Hai is a drowsy and relaxing holiday resort. Sands here, while not perfect, are arguably more enticing than those at Vung Tau; dunes fringe the town's eastern extreme; while to the west stands a fishing village, complete with stilthouses, a huge flotilla of fishing boats, and assorted coracles sporting brightly coloured flags. Long Hai's single tourist sight – though not a very attractive one – is the **Lady Temple**, a great, ugly hunk of grey concrete facing out to sea from just above the town, within which spanking new effigies of deities are lined up on smartly tiled mantels.

Long Hai is served by **buses** from Ho Chi Minh's Mien Dong Station; coming from Vung Tau, you'll need to take a bus to Ba Ria and then change. A huge, domed mansion, set amid frangipanis, the *Palace Hotel* (☎064/868364; ③), from the outside at least, is a gem of a **place to stay**, though its eighteen big, woody rooms are clean but overpriced and cheaper ones have fan only. There are similar rooms at the nearby *Rang Dong* (☎064/868356; ③); or try the *Long Hai* (☎064/868010; ③), where all rooms have hot water and air-con. At the other end of the scale, there are box-like rooms, sharing common facilities, at the *Hai Au* (☎064/868429; ①). All four hotels are on the main drag, parallel to the beach. The *Palace* and the *Hai Au* both have reasonable **restaurants**, but if you want to venture out, head for the *Hang Duong*, south of the *Palace*, and near the beach.

Beyond Long Hai

Trace the road hugging the coast east of Long Hai, and after a few kilometres and several waterfront **seafood restaurants**, you'll find the signposted left turn that runs up to the elevated **Minh Dam caves** (7am–4.30pm; $1.50), a communist bolthole from 1948, from where you'll enjoy prodigious views of the rice fields that quilt the coastal plain stretching to the horizon to the northeast, and of the boulder-strewn coastline below. Reached by scrambling up steps hewn into the rock, and alarmingly rickety bamboo ladders, the caves are really more like gaps between piled boulders; yet with a little imagination it's still possible to picture Viet Minh and Viet Cong soldiers lounging, cooking and sleeping here. Regular skirmishes took place on the mountainside – bullets have left pockmarks on some of the rocks, and joss sticks are still lodged in crevices in memory of the troops who fell here.

The road linking this stretch of coast to Ba Ria loops up to the marketplace in little Dat Do, a genial one-horse town 25km east of Ba Ria. (A couple of kilometres up the road striking northward from beside the town's post office, the hillock to your right, **Nui Dat**, was the site of an Australian hilltop base between 1966 and 1972, though there's nothing to see now save a communist memorial that's been planted pointedly on the summit.) East of Dat Do, the road from Ba Ria pushes past groves of bamboo, eucalyptus and coconut and through **XUYEN MOC**, before reaching diminutive **BONG TRANG**, from where a five-kilometre-long dirt track leads to **Ho Coc Beach**. Ho Coc is a spellbinding, five-kilometre stretch of wonderfully golden sand, dotted with coracles and deckchairs, lapped by clear waters and backed by fine dunes. Bungalows on the beach are supposedly on the way, but until they materialize you'll have to make do with one of five **rooms** with outside bathroom at the *Ho Coc Bungalows* (electricity only at night; ①), a few hundred metres back up the track; there's a decent **restaurant** on the beach. **Buses** from Ho Chi Minh and Ba Ria trundle as far as Xuyen Moc, from where you'll need to take a Honda om.

The area's final attraction of note, **Brin Chau Hot Springs** (7am–4.30pm; $1), are 10km further east, and a devil to get to unless you're on a motorbike or Honda om. The sulphurous waters bubbling hellishly in the streams and wells here vary greatly in temperature. Old people soothe their aching limbs in the 42°C stream, while elsewhere, visitors boil eggs sold on-site to make up ad hoc picnics. Your admission fee entitles you to bathe in the murky **swimming pool**, though renting your own **mini-pool** (from $3 an hour) is a much more civilized option. Reached by braving a precarious network of thin bamboo poles that pass as bridges, all pools have deckchairs and sun umbrellas. The on-site **guesthouse** (no phone) has fan rooms (②), or air-con for $5 more; and there are bungalows (also ②) featuring toilets but no en suite washing facilities. The complex also features a fairish **restaurant**. A Honda om from Xuyen Moc to Brin Chau costs $3 return.

The Con Dao Archipelago

Cast adrift in the South China Sea some 185km south of Vung Tau, the dozen or so islands of the **Con Dao Archipelago** are actually far closer to the base of the Mekong Delta, yet the helicopters and ships linking them with the mainland leave from Vung Tau. Had the **fortified outpost** established here by the British East India Company in 1703 flourished, **CON SON**, by far the largest of the islands, could by now have been a more diminutive Hong Kong or Singapore, given its strategic position on the route to China. Such, though, was not its fate. Within three years the Bugis mercenaries (from Sulawesi) drafted in to construct and garrison the base had murdered their British commanders, and put paid to this early experiment in colonization. Known then as Poulo Condore, Con Son was still treading water when the American sailor John White spied its "lofty summits" a little over a century later, in 1819. White deemed it a decent natural harbour, though blighted by "noxious reptiles, and affording no good fresh water".

The island finally found its calling when the French chose it as the site of a **penal colony** for anti-colonial activists, decades later. Con Son's savage regime soon earnt it the nickname, "Devil's Island". Prisoners languished in squalid pits called "tiger cages", which featured metal grilles instead of roofs, allowing guards to tower above and intimidate them. As the twentieth century progressed the colony developed into a sort of unofficial "revolutionary university". Older hands instructed their greener cell-mates in the finer points of Marxist-Leninist theory, and the terrible conditions they had to endure only helped reinforce these lessons.

Modern-day inhabitants live by fishing, growing cashews, peanuts and teak, and the more exotic pursuits of diving for pearls and collecting swallows' nests. Ringed by coral, and boasting dense patches of forest and fine beaches where turtles lay their eggs, Con Son is sure to become a tourist destination in the future. Until then getting here is rather too time-consuming a business to be a viable proposition, and anyone simply interested in prison life on the island would do better to settle for the mocked-up tiger cages at Ho Chi Minh's War Crimes Museum (see p.82), or the tiny gallery of photographs in Vung Tau's Thich Ca Phat Dai Statue Park (p.193). Should you decide to trek out to Con Son, you'll find a **museum** that sketches out the struggle against the French, as well as the prison itself.

To visit the island, contact *Vietnam Airlines*, who lay on regular helicopter trips; or *Con Dao Transportation*, who run one or two boats a week (see "Listings", p.195, for details).

The coastal road to Nha Trang

Highway 1 marches east from Bien Hoa, passing through **Thong Nhat, Gau Diay** (from where Highway 20 shoots up to Da Lat), and untold acres of rubber plantations before reaching **Xuan Loc**, 78km from Ho Chi Minh. It's 100km from Xuan Loc's orbital town of **Long Khanh** to the flamboyant fishing community of **Phan Thiet**; for the last fifty, the horizon is blistered by the foot of the Truong Son mountain range, which escorts the highway on its laborious ascent to Hanoi. The first of the scores of weathered towers left by the ancient kingdom of **Champa** stand just outside Phan Thiet, but the town's fishing fleet and the fine sands of nearby **Cape Mui Ne** are far more beguiling. There's another chance to take a dip in the South China Sea a little further north at **Ca Na**, but if you are keen to see some *serious* Cham towers, beat a hasty path straight to **Phan Rang**, an undistinguished town salvaged by the impressive **Po Klong Garai Complex** nearby. From Phan Rang, Highway 1 ploughs through sugar-cane plantations, salt flats and shrimp farms on its way into **Nha Trang**.

Phan Thiet – and Cape Mui Ne

A sea change in travellers' attitudes towards **PHAN THIET** is in the offing as more and more foreigners happen upon its hidden charms, and this friendly fishing town now looks set to become one of the stepping stones between Ho Chi Minh and Hanoi. Bunched around the Ca Ty River, and a bolthole for one of Vietnam's most impressive fishing armadas, the town is also blessed by its proximity to wonderful **Cape Mui Ne**, a 21-kilometre-long arc of fine sand that's attracting a lot of interest among developers.

The territory around Phan Thiet once came under Cham sway, but it's the years of French occupation that are recalled by the town's **architecture** – quaint colonial villas season the main streets, some decorated with glazed ceramic tiles, others with bas relief flowers, most with louvred windows and colonnaded facades. **Tran Hung Dao Bridge**, over which the town's main drag vaults the river, yields views of a fleet of fishing boats that might have bobbed straight off a Hans Kemp postcard. Turn left off the bridge's southwestern end and stroll along Trung Trac, and you'll soon plunge into the thick of things at the wharfside **fish market**. Be prepared for a major sensory assault: the market is enveloped by a stench as heady as any produced at the *nuoc mam* factories that proliferate around this region of Vietnam. Packed close with hoary fishermen, fishwives and shoppers arguing the toss around great, fly-blown wicker baskets of seafood, there's a jamboree atmosphere every morning, though especially between June and October, when daily catches reach a peak. North of the bridge, fishermen in coracles and with miners' lamps strapped to their heads try their luck at a little night fishing after dusk.

In the other direction, Trung Trac skirts the town centre en route to the sedate riverside position occupied by the **Ho Chi Minh Museum** (Tues–Sun 7.30–11am & 1.30–4.30pm). Wending its way through Ho's life from his early days abroad up to his death in 1969, it's essentially rather a flat museum, though it's leavened somewhat by memorabilia such as his white tunic, walking stick, sandals and metal helmet, and an offbeat action shot of him playing volleyball. The rows of varnished wooden desks and tables in the charismatic **Duc Thanh School** (same

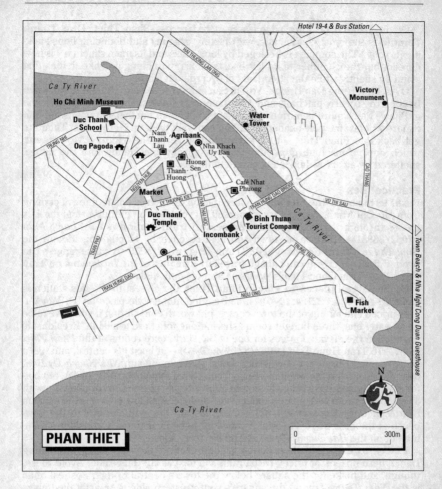

Hotel 19-4 & Bus Station

Ca Ty River

Ho Chi Minh Museum

Duc Thanh
School

Victory
Monument

Water
Tower

Nam
Thanh
Lau

Agribank

Ong Pagoda

Nha Khach
Uy Ban

Huong
Sen

Thanh
Huong

Market

Café Nhat
Phuong

Duc Thanh
Temple

Binh Thuan
Tourist Company

Incombank

Ca Ty River

Phan Thiet

Town Beach & Nha Nghi Cong Duan Guesthouse

Ngu Ong

Fish
Market

Ca Ty River

N

PHAN THIET

0   300m

hours) next door have remained unchanged since Ho's brief spell as a teacher here, and effortlessly conjure another age. A couple of hundred metres south of here on Tran Phu, **Ong Pagoda** also merits a browse: of its four chambers, only the middle two are of interest – access is through the alley dividing them, whose entrance is spanned by a huge bat decked with fairy lights. Turn right and Quan Cong lords it from beneath a roof groaning under the weight of some huge incense spirals. Led by a goggle-eyed attendant at the front of the room, his horse stares across at the largest dragon-dance head you'll ever see. More incense spirals congest the left-hand chamber, home to **Me Sanh**, to whom women come to pray for children – something that's certainly worked for the fecund female statues, laden with children, that flank the chamber.

Of the handful of other pagodas scattered across Phan Thiet, **Duc Thanh Temple** is the most charismatic, with flexing dragons and flouncing lions stalking its roofs. The complex is besieged by long grass and its main sanctuary is now derelict but the chamber to its left boasts an array of china doll-like deities that stand by silently while the attendants play cards out front.

Over Tran Hung Dao Bridge, Vo Thi Sau stikes off to the right and to the **town beach**. The scruffy patch of sand it hits supports some shanties that house some of Phan Thiet's more penurious inhabitants, but 700m northeast it opens out into a more wholesome pine-shaded spot. You can walk back up Nguyen Tat Thanh to get back into Phan Thiet – turn left when you reach the **Victory Monument**, which depicts machine gun-toting patriots gazing expectantly into the future, sheltered by an arrow-headed concrete umbrella.

Practicalities

Buses terminate at the **bus station** a couple of kilometres north of town; coming from Ho Chi Minh, you can save yourself a cyclo fare by getting off as the bus passes through the town centre. The nearest **train station** is *Ga Muong Man* (☎062/868814), 10km from town and best reached by Honda om, though the *Binh Thuan Tourist Company* at 82 Trung Trac (☎062/821394) can arrange a car. Around the corner you can change travellers' cheques at the *Incombank* on Tran Hung Dao; Tran Quoc Tuan's *Agribank* accepts only dollars.

Of the several **places to stay** in Phan Thiet, the closest to the bus station is *Hotel 19-4* (☎062/822194; ①–③), a bedraggled motel-style place on Tu Van Tu, over-priced and far out of the town centre, but worth considering if you have to be on an early bus; three budget rooms sharing one toilet are available. Breakfast is included in the elevated prices for one of the stark, bare rooms at the *Phan Thiet Hotel*, 276 Tran Hung Dao (☎062/821694; ③–④) – at least it's central, and has a well-groomed restaurant downstairs. Local government-run *Nha Khach Uy Ban*, over the river from the water tower, on Trung Trac (☎062/822219; ①–②), is a better deal: choose from a range of simple but well-equipped rooms, or make do with a very basic room with shared toilet in the annexe. Also low priced is the spartan *Nha Nghi Cong Duan* (☎062/821395; ②), just off the grubbier end of the town beach at the base of Vo Thi Sau. If you want to be near the sea, consider splashing out on the *Hai Duong Resort* at Mui Ne (see below).

Places to eat are thickest on the ground north of the river along Tran Hung Dao, where dozens of pricey restaurants vie for passing bus trade. Avoid these, though, and make for the square below the town's central bridge. Poshest of all is the *Nam Thanh Lau* on the square's southwestern side, a smartly tiled place whose upper-floor terraces overlook the square; the seafood is great, but portions aren't over-generous. Across the square are two simple but friendly *com* shops: the *Huong Sen*, with its turquoise-washed walls and aged fittings; and the *Thanh Huong*, where bargain meals of, say, grilled shrimps or barbecued pork on rice include iced tea. Once you've dined, clear your palate with an ice cream or yoghurt from one of two cafés round the corner on Kim Dong; or a coffee overlooking the river from the terrace upstairs at Trung Trac's *Café Nhat Phuong*. The beachfront *Doi Duong* café/*com* shop also enjoys a good location.

East to Mui Ne

At the head of every Phan Thiet itinerary should be the jaunt out east along Thu Khoa Huan towards **Cape Mui Ne** – a trip rewarded by mile after mile of palm-shaded golden sand, lapped by clear waters. The beach commences soon after you've crossed Ke Bridge and passed the **Phu Hai Cham towers**, a pair of gnarled towers dating from the eighth century, but lacking the high definition and sandstone ornamentation of others upcountry. At first the beach is rocky – the finest portion commences around 12km out of Phan Thiet, after which the coconut trees that have thus far formed a guard of honour over the road give way to the impressive red dunes for which this area is famous.

Until recently, the sands out to Mui Ne had to be visited as a day-trip out of Phan Thiet (a Honda om should cost around $1–1.50 each way), but the opening of the French-run *Hai Duong Resort* (☎062/848401, fax 823590; ④) has changed all that. The resort comprises fifteen tasteful bungalows set just above the sand, and complete with verandahs, Cham-style fabrics and purring air-con, plus a smart terrace bar-restaurant in the reception lodge offering set Vietnamese and French meals, as well as pool and darts. The resort, which also has provision for windsurfing, sailing, mountain-biking and motorbiking, is 12.5km from Phan Thiet, in Ham Tien Village. If you're coming from Ho Chi Minh, they'll arrange for you to be met off the *Sinh Café* minibus to Nha Trang; on the way back they'll get the southbound service to stop for you.

Ca Na

Highway 1 ducks inland above Phan Thiet. Hemmed in by paddy fields and eucalyptus trees, in season it's also strung with stalls doing a roaring trade in the other-worldly **dragon fruits** (see p.38) that grow in this neck of the woods. You'll see orchards of the cactus that bears them set back from the road, their fronds hanging like dreadlocks from the levelled tree stumps on which they bloom. By the time you coast down into **CA NA**, a little over 100km northeast of Phan Thiet as the crow flies, you're tightly sandwiched between hills, scattered with bleached boulders, and the choppy, turquoise waters of the South China Sea. Hardly more than a wide spot in the road, Ca Na is nevertheless reasonably well equipped for feeding and watering passing tourists and, with time in hand, you might choreograph your ascent of the country to allow an overnight stay. Given its proximity to the highway, Ca Na is a more relaxing place than it has any right to be, and is actually surprisingly peaceful. Beyond the coracles parked along the beach the water is fairish, and snorkelling is a possibility, though you'd be wise to ask locals where to wade in as the coral here is razor sharp. If you crave a little more solitude, a spine of decent dunes back up another good stretch of sand a couple of kilometres south; while a five-minute walk north of the resort area is Ca Na Village itself, characterized by the blue fishing boats so typical of coastal Vietnam.

There are only two **places to stay** at Ca Na. The *Hai Son* (☎068/861322; ②) is showing signs of age, but has clean simple rooms, some with back doors onto the beach. Otherwise the *Ca Na* (☎068/861320; top end of ②), 150m up the beach, is run along the same lines, and also has three smart rooms in a bungalow set out on the sand. Both have their own **restaurants** – prices at the *Ca Na* are consistently a little cheaper – or else there's the enticingly named *Ca Na Transport Café*, tucked between them, which has a booth selling biscuits, nibbles and drinks in addition to a menu that's identical to the *Ca Na* hotel's. As you'd imagine, fresh seafood is the order of the day here.

Phan Rang and around

The numerous vine trellises that abut the highway are the biggest surprise of the journey between Ca Na and Phan Rang. Grapes are a speciality of **Ninh Thuan Province** (of which Phan Rang is the capital) and the vineyards in which they grow lend the area a faintly Mediterranean tang. **PHAN RANG** itself is an unsettling and an unlovely place. With Highway 1 muscling through it under the guise of Thong Nhat, the rumpus of horns and engines is relentless from dawn to dusk, and your nerves will be shot after just a day here. Phan Rang's western limits have fused with the neighbouring town of **THAP CHAM**, whose name, meaning "Cham Towers", gives a clue to the real reason for stopping here. This region of Vietnam once comprised the Cham kingdom of Panduranga, and of the nearby Cham remnants, none are better preserved than those at **Po Klong Garai**. If ancient ruins aren't your thing, you might still have cause for a night in Phan Rang, as beyond Thap Cham, Highway 20 claws its way uphill **to Da Lat** (see p.161), the most direct route into the highlands if you're travelling south from Nha Trang.

Arrival, information and accommodation

Arriving in Phan Rang by **bus** you'll be dropped at the bus station 300m north of the *Thong Nhat* hotel; **trains** pull in 7km northwest of town at *Ga Thap Cham*. The **tourist office** on the corner of Nguyen Trai, at 404 Thong Nhat, can arrange trips out to the surrounding countryside, but at a price, so you may prefer to use Honda oms. As for changing **money**, the *Agribank* just above the *Huu Nghi* hotel on Thong Nhat accepts dollars but not travellers' cheques.

Inexpensive **places to stay** in Phan Rang are insalubrious, to say the least: rooms at the *Huu Nghi* (☎068/822721; ②), at 334 Thong Nhat, are set behind foreboding sheet metal doors and double as stables for the local cockroach population, while the *Huu Nghi II* (☎068/822592; ②), its sister hotel up at no. 194 is equally slummy. For more comfort, head for the smart *Thong Nhat* (☎068/827202; ④) at no. 99, or the less intimate *Ninh Thuan* (☎068/827100; ③) on Le Hong Phong. Alternatively you could avoid the town completely and run for the beach, where the *Ninh Chu* (☎068/873944; ③–④) has polished rooms in the tidy main block, and an ugly cluster of concreted "bungalows" on the beach; the *Babon Guesthouse* (☎068/873021; ①) around the beach is less expensive but rooms have only fans, and facilities are shared.

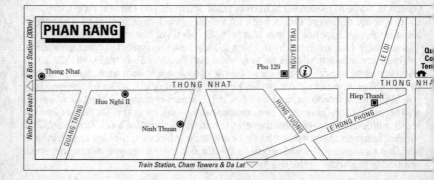

The town

Though their kingdoms may have fractured long ago, many thousands of Chams still live in the province, and an introduction to their ways may be gleaned from Phan Rang's pink and grey **Cham Collectives Display Museum** (Mon–Sat 7–11am & 1.30–5pm). To reach the museum, walk east off Thong Nhat at the tourist office, and then left along the track beside 17 Nguyen Trai. The collection is a rag-tag one in which shards of pottery and items of jewellery stand shoulder to shoulder with a Cham typewriter and a copy of a statue of Shiva, all displayed with little pizzazz.

Otherwise, forays into the town centre are limited to peeking into Thong Nhat's impressive **Quan Cong Temple**, now fast approaching its 150th birthday. Its faded, pink-wash walls rise to three consecutive roofs, each draped upon huge red wooden piles imported from China, and laden with fanciful figurines and dragons. Quan Cong is at the head of the third and final chamber, framed by ornate gilt woodwork and rows of pikes. Chams sometimes come to shop at the **market** immediately below the pagoda but for closer encounters, you'll need to venture out to Tuan Tu (see over).

Chams and Cham towers

Elevated with fitting grandeur on a granite mound known as Trau Hill, the **Po Klong Garai Cham towers** (daily 7am–6pm) are far worthier of your time than anything in the town centre. Dating back to the turn of the fourteenth century and the rule of King Jaya Simharvarman III, the complex comprises a *kalan*, or sanctuary, a smaller gate tower and a repository, under whose boat-shaped roof offerings would have been placed. It's the 25-metre-high *kalan*, though, that's of most interest. From a distance its stippled body impresses; up close, a bas-relief of six-armed Shiva cavorts above doorposts etched with Cham inscriptions and ringed by arches crackling with stonework flames, while other gods sit cross-legged in niches elsewhere around the exterior walls. In days gone by, the statue of Shiva's bull Nandin that stands in the vestibule would have been "fed" by farmers wishing for good harvests, and even now it gets a feed at the annual **Kate Festival** – the Cham New Year, and a great spectacle if you're here around October-time. Push deeper into the *kalan*'s belly and there's a *mukha-linga* fashioned in a likeness of the Cham king, Po Klong Garai, after whom the complex is named. On the eve of the festival, there's traditional Cham music and dance at the complex, followed, the next morning, by a lively procession bearing the king's raiments to the tower.

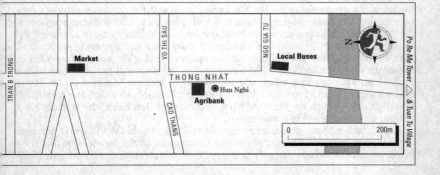

THE KINGDOM OF CHAMPA

The weathered but beguiling **towers** that punctuate the scenery upcountry from Phan Thiet to Da Nang are the only remaining legacy of **Champa**, an Indianized kingdom that ruled parts of central and southern Vietnam for over fourteen centuries. In 192 AD, Chinese annals reported that a man named Khu Lien (later to be titled King Sri Mara) had gathered together a chain of coastal chiefdoms in the region around Quang Tri in defiance of the expansionism of the Han Chinese to the north, and established an independent state which the Chinese referred to as **Lin Yi**. Subsequently, Champa unified an elongated coastal strip from Phan Thiet to Dong Hoi, and by the end of the fourth century legacy of Champa comprised four provinces: **Amaravati**, around Hué and Da Nang; **Vijaya**, centred around Qui Nhon; **Kauthara**, in the Nha Trang region; and **Panduranga**, which corresponds to present-day Phan Thiet and up to Phan Rang. The unified kingdom's first capital, established in the fourth century in Amaravati, was **Simhapura** ("Lion City"); nearby, just outside present-day Hoi An, **My Son**, Champa's holiest site, was established (see p.238).

Concertinaed between the Khmers to the south and the clans of the Vietnamese (initially under Chinese rule) to the north, Champa's history was characterized by consistent **feuding with the neighbours**. Between the third and fifth centuries, relations with the **Chinese** followed a cyclical pattern of antagonism and tribute, culminating in the 446 AD sacking of Simhapura when the Chinese made off with a fifty-tonne, solid-gold Buddha statue. Wars raged with the **Khmers** in the twelfth and thirteenth centuries, one fateful retaliatory Cham offensive culminating in the destruction of Angkor. With the installation on Champa's throne of war-mongering **Binasuor** in 1361, three decades of Cham expansionism ensued; upon his death in 1390, though, the Viets regained all lost ground, and soon secured the region around Indrapura. In a decisive push south, the Viets, led by **Le Thanh Tong**, overran Vijaya in 1471; Champa shifted its capital south again, but by now it was becoming profoundly marginalized. For a few centuries more, the Cham kings still claimed nominal rule of the area around Phan Rang and Phan Thiet, but their claws

To reach the complex, take the road to Da Lat for 7km then veer north for a further 500m (approximately $2–3 return by Honda om from Phan Rang). On your way back down Trau Hill, look above the arched stone gateway below the complex and you'll spot **pill-box defences**, established by the French to protect trains pulling out of the station below from Viet Minh attack.

If Po Klong Garai doesn't slake your thirst for Cham towers, you could make the trickier journey out to **Po Re Me Tower**, built at the turn of the sixteenth century during the final phase of Cham tower architecture. Like its near-neighbour, the tower (which draws its name from the last Cham king) enjoys a fine hilltop location, though its four storeys tapering to a *linga* are sturdier and less finished than Po Klong Garai. Its highpoint is the splendid and gaily painted bas-relief in the *kalan*'s interior, depicting Shiva manifest in the image of moustachioed King Po Re Me, waggling her arms, and watched over by two Nandins. Po Re Me is also a focus of Cham festivities during the Kate Festival. To reach the tower, follow Highway 1 south for 8km and then bear west at Hau Sanh; the track is hard to find, so a Honda om is a wise move.

There's still a Cham presence around Phan Rang. **Tuan Tu Village** is home to more than a thousand Chams, whom you'll recognize by the headcloths that they favour over conical hats. Largely muslims, they maintain an unpretentious, 1966-

had been blunted. In 1697, the last independent Cham king died, and what little remained of the kingdom became a Vietnamese vassal state. **Minh Mang** dissolved even this in the 1820s, and the last Cham king fled to Cambodia. Most of the estimated 100,000 **descendants** of the Cham Empire reside around Phan Rang and Phan Thiet, though there are also tiny pockets in Tay Ninh and Chau Doc.

Champa's **economy** hinged around agriculture, wet-rice cultivation, fishing and maritime trade, which it carried out with Indians, Chinese, Japanese and Arabs through **ports** at Hoi An and Qui Nhon. Exposure to Indian traders in the fourth century had a particularly strong influence upon the kingdom's culture, agriculture and religion. Though Buddhism took hold for a time in the ninth century, **Hinduism** was very much the dominant religion in Champa, until Islam started to make in-roads in the second half of the fourteenth century. Orthodox Hindu gods, and in particular Shiva, were fused with past kings, in accordance with the belief that kings were *devaraja* – reincarnations of deities.

To honour their gods, Cham kings sponsored the construction of the **religious edifices** that still stand today. The typical Cham **temple complex** is centred around the **kalan**, or sanctuary, normally pyramidal inside, and containing a linga, or phallic representation of Shiva, set on a dais that was grooved to channel off water used in purification rituals. Having first cleansed themselves and prayed in the **mandapa** or meditation hall, worshippers would then have proceeded under a **gate tower** and below the kalan's (normally) east-facing vestibule into the sanctuary. Any ritual objects pertaining to worship were kept in a nearby repository room, which normally sported a boat-shaped roof.

Cham towers crop up at regular intervals, all the way up the coast from Phan Thiet to Da Nang, but many of them are inaccessible, and many more so weathered as to be of only fleeting interest. A handful of sites representing the **highlights** of what remains of Champa civilization would include:

Po Klong Garai towers (p.203)	**Thap Doi towers** (p.217)
Po Re Me Tower (p.204)	**My Son** (p.238)
Po Nagar towers (p.211)	

built mosque free of any trappings, not even a minaret. More enjoyable than the village itself is the trip out, though, which leads you through cacti, rice paddies and vineyards along a track that's often congested by bullock carts. Tuan Tu is 3 or 4km along a track that veers east after the BP service station, 350m below the bridge at the bottom of town; the Honda om fare shouldn't be more than $1 round-trip.

Ninh Chu Beach

A more indolent alternative to trekking around Phan Rang's Cham towers is to visit **Ninh Chu Beach**, a narrow, but reasonably clean, semi-circle of sand that's at least soft, if not exactly golden. Unless you come on a Sunday, when ranging hordes of teenagers won't leave you alone for a moment, it's a quiet enough spot for a dip and a sunbathe. To reach Ninh Chu, turn onto Nguyen Van Troi just above the bus station and immediately to the right of the post office, and carry on for 5km.

Eating and drinking

Far and away the best **place to eat** is the *Hiep Thanh*, 18a Le Hong Phong, with soft music, tablecloths and competitive prices; their *nem* (interestingly translated as "kebab and pork pie boiled") is a tasty starter, then try lotus sprouts with shredded chicken – best sprinkled with a squeeze of fresh lemon. Otherwise, the *Thong Nhat* and *Ninh Thuan* hotels have their own restaurants and the *Ninh Cuu* boasts both restaurant and beach-view coffee shop. Budget *com* and *pho* is on hand at the *Nam Thanh*, immediately above Quan Cong Temple on Thong Nhat; and *Pho 129*, above the tourist office on Thong Nhat, is always packed in the morning.

Nha Trang and around

From Phan Rang, the highway pushes on against a consistent backdrop of first sugar-cane plantations, then toothpaste-white salt flats and shrimp farms, on its way to the city of **NHA TRANG**. Nestled below the bottom lip of the Cai River, some 260km north of Phan Thiet, Nha Trang has earnt its place on Vietnam's tourist mainline partly on merit and partly due to its location. Much has changed here since the days when the Chams knew the area as *Eatrang*, the "river of reeds", and the city now supports a population approaching 300,000. By the time the Nguyen lords wrested this patch of the country from Champa in the mid-seventeenth century, the intriguing **Po Nagar Cham towers** had already stood, stacked impressively on a hillside above the Cai, for over 700 years. They remain Nha Trang's most famous image, yet it's the **coastline** that brings tourists flocking: boasting the finest **municipal beach** in Vietnam, Nha Trang offers splendid scope for mellowing out on the sand, with hawkers on hand to supply paperbacks, fresh pineapple and massage. **Scuba-diving** classes are available here, and several local companies offer popular day-trips to Nha Trang's **outlying islands** that combine island visits and **snorkelling** with an onboard feast of seafood.

Nha Trang is much more than a dozy backwater, however. The **downtown area**, which swirls aound **Cho Dam** ("central market"), its colourful epicentre, heaves with life; while the route up to the Po Nagar towers escorts you past the city's huge and photogenic **fishing fleet**. These, and other lesser sites around the city, are best seen by renting a **bicycle** for the day.

Should none of this appeal, Nha Trang is still a convenient **staging-post** on the long haul between Hanoi and Ho Chi Minh, and blessed with a crop of decent **restaurants** and **hotels**.

Arrival and getting around

Nha Trang's **long-distance bus station** sits 1km west of the city centre at 58, 23 Thang 10, with the **train station** (ticket office daily 7.30–11am & 2–4.30pm; ☎058/822113) a few hundred metres east along Thai Nguyen, a continuation of the same road; both are a short cyclo journey from central Nha Trang. Flights into the city land at the **airport** just below town; again, hop into a cyclo to get to a hotel.

Nha Trang isn't a very large city, so **walking** can be an effective means of covering ground – especially if a daily pilgrimage to the municipal beach marks the extent of your peregrinations. Should you plan to stray a little further afield, **bicycle rental** is the most efficient and enjoyable way to go. Bicycles are available for rental ($1 per day) at most of the city's hotels, though less active souls will always find **cyclos** and **Honda oms** aplenty. Fully fledged **car** tours of the region can be arranged through the provincial tourist board, *Khanh Hoa Tourism*; while a number of operators offer day-trips to the islands off Nha Trang – see box on facing page for details.

All the companies below offer day-long **boat trips** ($7 a head) to a selection of the **islands** off Nha Trang (see p.213); trips include **snorkelling** and an impressive seafood lunch on board, as well as island stops. In addition, all bar one sell tickets for tourist **minibuses** to Ho Chi Minh, Da Lat, Hoi An and Da Nang.

Khanh Hoa Tourism, 1 Tran Hung Dao (☎058/822753). Car tours, boat trips to outlying islands and vehicle rental; can also book train, air or public bus tickets. 7–11.30am & 1.30–5pm.

Let's Tour, 18 Tran Phu (☎058/824579), with another office right by the municipal beach. City tours minibus tickets and *Mama Hanh* boat trips to the nearby islands. 7.30–11.30am & 2–10pm.

Mama Linh, 38 Tran Phu (☎058/026693). Highlands tours, boat trips and minibus tickets. 7am–10pm.

Sinh III, 46 Tran Phu (☎058/825064). Boat trips and minibus bookings. 7am–10pm.

Vinagen, opp. *Manila Hotel*, Tran Phu (☎058/823591). Incorporating *Lang's Boat Trips*, and offering half-day trips up the Cai River and longer forays to the central highlands. 6am–midnight.

Accommodation

The fact that Nha Trang is chock-full with hotels doesn't seem to be discouraging developers, and the city's already varied choice of **accommodation** looks set to increase exponentially. Even so, it's worth bearing in mind that the city draws Vietnamese as well as foreign tourists, and that you could have difficulties finding a room to your taste over public holidays. Equally, remember that in many hotels, opting for a cheaper room consigns you to a dingy annexe far from the main building, and you may well judge the extra few dollars' upgrading cost as money well spent.

Bai Duong, Hon Chong Beach (☎058/831015). Sleepy seaside hotel that's signposted 300m north of the turning to Hon Chong Promontory: bargain-priced but shipshape doubles with fan and private bath, or several smarter rooms in a fancy new villa; there's also an adjoining restaurant. ②–③

Bao Dai's Villas, Tran Phu (☎058/881049). Once holiday-homes to the emperor of Vietnam, 5 villas set in extensive and well-kept gardens; the swish bed-chambers of Bao Dai and his queen are good for a splurge, but other rooms aren't so charismatic, and all are inconveniently placed way down the beach from the city. ③–④

Duy Tan, 24 Tran Phu (☎058/822671). Rooms in this large, modern and extremely bright hotel are well appointed and tasteful – and some have seaviews – but overpriced; avoid the gloomy annexe. ③

Grand, 44 Tran Phu (☎058/822445). August colonial pile set amid palms and frangipani – though you'll need to pay the top rate of ③ to graduate from the grottier annexe. Rooms in the main building are spacious, if rather tired. ②–③

Guesthouse 6, 6 Tran Phu (☎058/822706). Immediately above the Pasteur Institute at the quieter end of Tran Phu, a delightful sky-blue villa with just 4 spick and span rooms, 2 of which sleep up to 8. ②

Guesthouse 78, 78 Tran Phu (☎058/826342). Motel-style place offering characterless but pristine doubles with attached bathroom and air-con, and no-frills fan rooms sharing bathroom in a grungier annexe. ①–②

Hai Yen, 40 Tran Phu (☎058/822828). Plays second fiddle to the nearby *Vien Dong* (see p.210), but rooms are still well fitted and comfy, and there are a handful of budget rooms. Hairdresser, souvenir shop, tourist information and currency exchange downstairs. ②–③

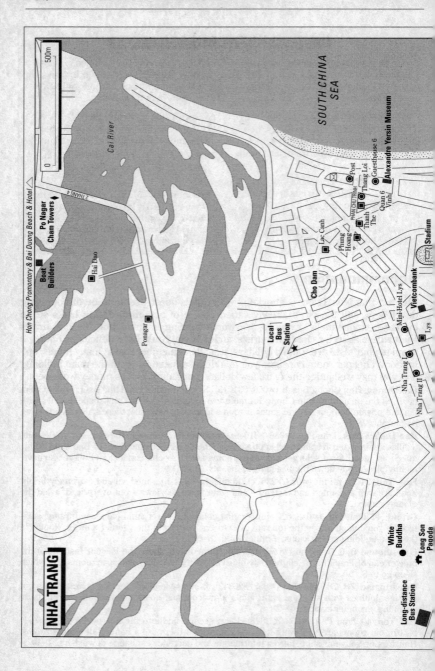

SOUTH CHINA SEA

N

Municipal Beach

Coconut Cove

Municipal Beach

Nha Trang Sailing Club

Guesthouse 78

Bao Dai's Villas & Cau Da Wharf

Let's Tour

Mama Linh

Let's Tour

Hai Yen

Khanh Hoa Tourism

Viragen

War Memorial

TRAN PHU

Duy Tan

Grand

Sinh III

Restaurant 46

Vietnam Airlines

TRAN HUNG DAO

NGUYEN CHANH

Hung Dao

Vien Dong

Lizard

QUANG TRUNG

LE THANH TON

Quan Nem Ngoc Tien

Banana Split 60

Nha Trang Cathedral

NGUYEN TRAI

Train Station

LE HONG PHONG

DONG NAI

Hung Dao, 3 Tran Hung Dao (☎058/822246). Perennial backpackers' stamping ground, its 70 rooms are unglamorous but inexpensive and secure, and all have private bathrooms; some rooms in the annexes out front suffer noise from early-morning bus departures. ①

Mini-Hotel Lys, 62 Hoang Van Thu (☎058/821305). Situated opposite the *Lys Restaurant* near the city centre, a backstreet concern whose amicable nature and competitive prices compensate for the breathtakingly gaudy decor in its 7 rooms. ①

Nha Trang I, 129 Thong Nhat (☎058/822224). Good-value budget hotel with tidy rooms, attached bathroom and either fan or air-con, and great city- and seaviews from its top-floor restaurant. ①

Nha Trang II, 21 Le Thanh Phuong (☎058/822956). Faceless but sanitary rooms with attached bathrooms, some with air-con ($4 extra): a passable fall-back. ①

Post Hotel, 2 Le Loi (☎058/821252). Slighty oppressive rooms peeling off utilitarian corridors belie this hotel's posh white facade, but have all mod-cons; seaviews cost an extra $6. Top end of ③

Thang Loi, 4 Pasteur (☎058/822241). Light, spacious, cheerily painted en suite rooms handily placed just east of the city centre. ③

Vien Dong, 1 Tran Hung Dao (☎058/821606). Professionally run operation counting swimming pool, tennis courts, satellite TV, currency exchange and a decent restaurant among its amenities. Rooms in the main building are unfussy but welcoming and scrupulously clean, but those in the poolside annexe are less polished. ③

The city centre

The disorienting knot of roads constituting **central Nha Trang** hugs the southern lip of the Cai River. Its beating heart is the hectic central market, semi-circular **Cho Dam**, which stands on land reclaimed from the Cai; the market positively churns with life from morning to night. Most new arrivals in the city, however, make a beeline for its **municipal beach**, a grand six-kilometre scythe of soft yellow sand lapped by rolling waves, whose upper extent lies five minutes' stroll east of the market. The tourists that descend on the beach in numbers every day are promptly besieged by traders hawking massages, tropical fruits, T-shirts and paperbacks, though it's possible to escape their clutches by taking a boat trip (see p.207) – alternatively you can sunbathe undisturbed at the pool in the *Vien Dong Hotel* ($1.50 per day for non-residents). Locals are wise enough to wait until the hour before dusk to do their bathing, at which time the surf is peppered with squealing, splashing kids. The Americans sought wartime R&R on the beach, and contemporary accounts describe the cyclo races they held along the wide, palm-lined **corniche**, Tran Phu. Upgrading presently underway along placid Tran Phu promises to reinject a spot of colonial dash into the beachfront, and to showcase architectural leftovers like the eye-catching facade of the *Grand Hotel*.

The Alexandre Yersin Museum

There are oodles of waterfront cafés to duck into along Tran Phu when the sun reaches its zenith. Alternatively, you could dart up to the top of Tran Phu and into the Pasteur Institute, where the **Alexandre Yersin Museum** (Mon–Sat 1.30–4.30pm) profiles the life of the Swiss-French scientist who transformed Da Lat, and who settled in Nha Trang in 1893 after travelling to southeast Asia as a ship's doctor. By the time of his death in 1943, Yersin had become a local hero, thanks not to his greatest achievement – the discovery of a plague bacillus in Hong Kong in 1894 – but rather to his educational work in sanitation and agriculture, and to his ability to predict typhoons and thus save the lives of fishermen.

Yersin's desk is here, with his own French translations of Horace still slotted under its glass top; so, too, are the barometers and telescope he used to forecast the weather, and a model boat presented to him by grateful fishermen. But it's the doctor's library, where French, English, Latin and Vietnamese tomes cover a giddying span of subjects from medicine to horticulture, astrology to bacteriology, that conveys most strongly Yersin's insatiable thirst for knowledge. The institute (which Yersin himself set up in 1895) is still active today, and you'll see white-coated technicians buzzing about.

Along Thai Nguyen

Thread your way southwest from the Pasteur Institute, and after a few minutes you'll hit Thai Nguyen, home to two of Nha Trang's lesser sights. Presiding over the street's eastern end, stolid, grey-brick **Nha Trang Cathedral** casts its shadow over the head of a sloping cobbled track that peels up and round to its front doors from Nguyen Trai. Under the lofty, vaulted ceilings within the cathedral's dowdy exterior, vivid stained-glass windows depict Christ, Mary, Joseph, Joan of Arc and Saint Theresa. If you feel as if you're being watched as you climb up to the cathedral, it's probably the disconcerting effect of the huge white Buddha-image seated on a hillside above **Long Son Pagoda**, 800m west along Thai Nguyen. A narrow lane leads to the 1930s-built pagoda, which replaced a simpler thatched-roof construction that stood nearby. An impressive, 700-kilogram bronze Buddha stands at the head of the altar, and there are the usual capering dragons on the eaves, but it's the huge **White Buddha**, 152 steps up the hillside behind, that's the pagoda's greatest asset – and Nha Trang's most recognizable landmark. Crafted in 1963 to symbolize the Buddhist struggle against the repressive Diem regime, around its lotus-shaped pedestal are carved images of the monks and nuns that set fire to themselves in protest, among them Thich Quang Duc (see box on p.83).

North to the Po Nagar Cham towers

North of the city centre along 2 Thang 4, two bridges whisk you safely over the **Cai River**, affording wonderful views en route of Nha Trang's immense fishing fleet. Massed palm trees riot to the west of Ha Ra Bridge, while to the east, tumbledown stilthouses teeter over the estuary. The lion's share of the city's flotilla of cheery blue-and-red fishing boats harbour east of Xom Bong Bridge; from this vantage point you'll spy fishermen scrubbing down decks and getting things shipshape before the next tide. Scissor-boats and coracles glide between this congregation of vessels, and balanced precariously on a boulder in the water is a small joss-house where fishermen make offerings prior to setting sail.

Xom Bong Bridge deposits you slap bang in front of the entrance to Nha Trang's most gripping attraction, the **Po Nagar Cham Towers** (daily 7.30am–5pm), just 1.5km north of the city centre. Of the estimated ten towers or *kalan*, constructed by the Hindu Chams (see p.204 for more on the Cham civilization) on Cu Lao Hill between the seventh and twelfth centuries, only four remain, their baked red bricks weathered so badly through the centuries that they now resemble rotting teeth bared to the sky. Even so, this complex of age-old towers affects a mystique that transcends its shambolic, neglected appearance – and represents very big business for the gaggles of irresistible young postcard-sellers who counter rebuffs with a plaintive "Maybe later?" Visitors to the complex now approach the towers via a curling flight of steps swarming with beggars, but Cham worshippers would have entered the *mandapa*, or meditation and offerings hall, whose stone pillars are still visible on the hillside; and from there they would have mounted a set of steps directly up to the main tower.

The complex's largest and most impressive tower is the 23-metre-high **northern tower**, built in 817 by Harivarman I and dedicated to Yang Ino Po Nagar, tutelary Goddess Mother of the Kingdom and a manifestation of Uma, Shiva's consort. Time has taken its toll on this square-shaped tower rising to a coned, three-storey roof, but the lotus-petal and spearhead motifs that embellish it are still intact, as is the lintel over the outer door, on which a lithe four-armed Shiva dances, flanked by musicians, on the back of an ox; the two sandstone pillars supporting this lintel bear spidery Cham inscriptions. Inside, a vestibule tapering to a pyramidal ceiling leads to the main chamber, whose sooty darkness takes a little getting used to. The golden statue that originally stood in here was pilfered by the Khmers in the tenth century and replaced by the black stone statue of Uma still here today – albeit minus its head, which was plundered by the French, and now resides in a Parisian museum. The ten arms of cross-legged Uma are nowadays obscured by a gaudy yellow robe and a doll-like face has been added. Po Ino Nagar is still worshipped as the protectress of the city, and the statue bathed during the **Merian Festival** each March.

Possessing neither the height nor the intricacy of the main *kalan*, the **central tower** has been badly eroded. The tower is dedicated to the god Cri Cambhu, and sees a steady flow of childless couples pass through to pray for fertility at its linga. The main chamber is crammed with such paraphernalia as candle sticks, incense urns and flower vases, and its weighty stone altar has been given a glass top and draped with cloth. The **southern tower** is the smallest of the four; viewed from the west it has a certain crumbling beauty, its sloping trunk vaguely recalling the Sphinx.

Graffiti artists seem to have targeted the **northwest tower** for particular attention, but beneath its boat-shaped roof, vague, half-formed statues in relief are still visible, among which the most recognizable is a huge elephant on the western facade, whose serpentine trunk and tusks are now blackened with age. Climb the **granite boulders** behind this tower, and there are great views back over the Cai River to Nha Trang and the endless coconut palms west of it – a more interesting alternative to nosing through the dreary on-site **museum** (daily 7.30am–5pm); if you can be bothered, you might breeze through the complex's museum, though its handful of modest stone statues and grainy old photographs can't hold a light to Da Nang's (see p.246), and there aren't even any signs in English.

Hon Chong Promontory and Beach

Press on beyond the Cham towers, and 400m later you'll confront a roundabout where a board promoting the *Hon Chong Hotel* (open only to Vietnamese) signposts the ten-minute slog on foot to **Hon Chong Promontory**, a finger of granite boulders dashed by the sea in a spume of spray. It's quite possible to clamber down to the rocks, the largest of which is said to bear a handprint, left, if you believe the local folklore, by a clumsy giant who slipped and fell while ogling a bathing fairy. The headland above the rocks makes a refreshingly blustery venue for a fresh coconut bought at one of the stalls in the shanty town of cafés and souvenir stalls here. Looking northwest you'll spot **Nui Co Tien**, or the Heavenly Maid Mountains, so-called because their three ridges resemble the head, breasts and legs of a woman. Immediately up the coast from the promontory is **Hon Chong Beach**, scruffier and shinglier than the city beach, but more secluded.

South to Cau Da Wharf

Six kilometres south of Nha Trang, the **Oceanographic Institute** (daily 7.30am–noon & 1–4.30pm), housed in a mustard-washed colonial mansion and established in 1923, boasted as many as 60,000 exhibits until a recent shake-up radically diminished its collection. What remains in this offbeat museum's sombre chambers and corridors, is a veritable Frankenstein's lab of pickling jars and glass cases yielding preserved crustaceans, fish, seaweeds and coral. It's hard to get too excited about the assemblage, though if you've been out snorkelling you might spot some recent acquaintances in its twenty or so tanks of primary-coloured live fishes. Entry is past three large open ponds in the forecourt, home to horseshoe crabs, turtles and baby sharks. A cluster of **souvenir shops** over the road from the entrance hawks an ecologically unsound stock of dried seahorses, conches, shell jewellery and stuffed animals. Beyond them is **Cau Da Wharf**, the jumping-off point for the mini-archipelago off Nha Trang.

The islands

Perhaps the single greatest pleasure of a stay in Nha Trang is a **day-trip to the islands** speckling the adjoining waters. Some are just a stone's throw away, others require several hours of boating. Independent travel out to sea is a pricey business, as you'll have to charter your own boat from **Cau Da Wharf** (prices start at $50 per boat per day); fortunate, then, that several companies in Nha Trang (see box on p.207 for details) offer day-trips to a selection of islands, which include a stop for snorkelling and a sumptuous seafood lunch on board – all for around $7 per person.

The closest of the islands to Cau Da, **HON MIEU**, is actually served by a local ferry (15min; $1 return) which docks at **Tri Nguyen**, a colourful if not particularly picturesque fishing village. From Tri Nguyen, a walk of only a few minutes brings you to **Tri Nguyen Aquarium** – in fact not an aquarium at all, but rather a series of saltwater ponds constructed back in 1971 for breeding and research purposes. If the sight of all the fishes, crabs, turtles and baby sharks on display makes you come over a little peckish, you might consider a seafood feast at the restaurant built over the ponds. Afterwards, check out the shingly beach south-east of the aquarium at **Bai Soai**.

The shallows that ring **HON TAM**, 2km southeast of Mieu and plainly visible from Bai Soai, presently afford good snorkelling, although with boat anchors daily damaging the coral, this may not be the case for long; the pricey *Tam Seafood Restaurant* provides sustenance onshore.

Meaning "Bamboo Island", **HON TRE** has been compared to a crocodile crawling in a vast lake. Its cliffs lend a welcome dash of drama to this, the largest of Nha Trang's islands, and offset the fine white sand of its beach, **Bai Tru**. It says much about the beauty of Bai Tru, located 45 minutes from Cau Da by motorboat at the northwest corner of the island, that there are plans to upgrade it into a resort. Two smaller isles hover off Hon Tre's southern coast. The first, **HON MOT** (One Island) has a stony beach but good snorkelling; the other is **HON MUN**, or Black Island, named after the dark cliffs that rear up from it. Caves within these cliffs harbour salangenes, whose **nests**, made from saliva, are harvested and then sold on – at thousands of dollars per kilo – for use in birds' nest soups, aphrodisiacs and tonics. There's no beach to speak of on Mun, but some great coral; watch out for sea-urchins, though.

Eating and drinking

Finding a decent place to **eat** presents no problem in Nha Trang. Beachfront Tran Phu is awash with breezy café-restaurants where parched and hungry sunbathers can adjourn for a bite to eat. Nha Trang's heavyweight restaurants are inland in the city centre and on Phan Chu Trinh, where a cluster of seafood operations grapple nightly for the passing tourist trade. For night-time **drinking**, there are only two options – one slick, the other rowdier.

Banana Split 60, 60 Quang Trung. Delicious ice creams on central Nha Trang's main drag. 7am–11pm.

Coconut Cove, opposite *Hai Yen Hotel,* Tran Phu. More laid-back, less windswept than most of its beachfront competition, and a fair stab at desert-island decor; the eclectic (and a little pricey) menu spans Vietnamese dishes, sandwiches, salads and even pizzas. 7am–midnight.

Grand Hotel Restaurant, *Grand Hotel*, 44 Tran Phu. Located under the arched verandah of Nha Trang's most splendid colonial mansion, this hotel restaurant offers affordable, if slightly lacklustre, meals. Check out the grilled tuna or go for one of several hearty breakfasts. 5am–9pm.

Hai Dao, 304, 2 Thang 4. Accessed by a rickety wooden bridge, this secluded restaurant is perched on an isle in the Cai River with views of Nha Trang's Cham towers and riverbank boat-builders; grilled cuttlefish with citronella and pimento comes recommended, or try the chicken with onions in lemon sauce. 8am–10pm.

Lac Canh, 11 Hang Ca. A grubbily charismatic hole-in-the-wall joint with a vanguard of streetside tables; some bridle at its brusque staff, and at the eye-watering smoke off the cooked-at-table barbecues for which the place is locally famed, but the food compensates for these discomforts. 10am–2pm & 4–9.30pm.

Lizard, 2 Hung Vuong. Nha Trang's trendiest bar-restaurant: gorge on delicious shrimps in a coconut milk hotpot, or beef grilled at table and rolled in rice paper, then shift to the well-stocked bar and pick some sounds from the stack of CDs. 7am–10pm (food); 5pm–midnight (bar).

Lys, 117a Hoang Van Thu. Enormously popular family-run restaurant, thanks to specialities like deer, wild pig, and duck cooked in wine. The quaintly fusty street-level room does a tasty line in breakfast *pho* and *bun bo Hué* 5.30am–10pm.

Nha Trang Sailing Club, 72–74 Tran Phu. Draws a well-heeled expat crowd to its refined beachfront bar, many of whom decamp to the restaurant across the club compound, where the Western menu assuages any post-G&T hunger pangs; pumpkin soup makes an ambrosial starter. 6am–10pm.

Phung Hoang, 12 Phan Chu Trinh. Touts outside Phan Chu Trinh's seafood restaurants clamour for your patronage; you could do far worse than the *Phung Hoang*, especially if you plump for its tamarind-roasted crab. 10.30am–11pm.

Ponagar, 284, 2 Thang 4 (☎058/023992). If you can tolerate the arctic air-con, you can choose from small, medium or large dishes of well-prepared Vietnamese food, or phone ahead to do battle with a succulent, roasted whole baby pig ($20). 6am–10pm.

Quan 6 Vinh, 7 Le Loi. If it's *com tam* you're after, 9 out of 10 locals will point you to this no-frills foodstop, actually a courtyard draped with plastic sheeting. 5am–3pm.

Quan Nem Ngoc Tien, 8 Le Thanh Ton. Cavernous corner-restaurant that does a roaring night-time trade in more-ish *nem*, cooked out front on satay-style charcoal barbecues. 3pm–midnight.

Restaurant 46, 46 Tran Phu. High-calibre seafood, best savoured al fresco at one of the many tables mustered out on the forecourt. 10am–2pm & 5–10pm.

Thanh The Restaurant, 3 Phan Chu Trinh. Another bright, open-fronted seafood restaurant on Phan Chu Trinh; the shrimps grilled with garlic won't disappoint. 8am–11pm.

Listings

Airlines *Vietnam Airlines*, 91 Nguyen Thien Thuat.

Bank *Vietcombank*, 17 Quang Trung, changes cash and travellers' cheques, and can also advance cash against *Visa*, *Mastercard* and *JCB* cards.

Car rental *Khanh Hoa Tourism*, outside the *Vien Dong* hotel on Le Thanh Ton, can arrange a car plus driver for you; rates are around $35 a day.

Hospital Nha Trang's hospital is below the city stadium, on Yersin.

Post office Nha Trang's GPO, 2 Tran Phu (daily 7am–9pm), has fax and IDD facilities; you can also post letters and make international calls at the smaller *Post & Telecommunications Service Center* opposite the *Vien Dong*, at 50 Le Thanh Ton.

Tour operators See box on p.207.

Around Nha Trang

Above Nha Trang, Highway 1 marches northward, scattering several noteworthy attractions in its wake. The most practical means of exploring this area is to rent a motorbike out of Nha Trang; alternatively, you could catch a service from the local bus station in Nha Trang and return on one of the numerous buses plying the highway at your day's end.

Following the main road running north from the Cham towers and over the **Ru Ri Pass**, after 14km you'll see a track to your right that terminates, in a few hundred metres, at the jetty for departures to **Monkey Island**. Predictably enough, the island plays host to a sizeable colony of inquisitive monkeys, and a boat trip to see them is great fun – especially if you've got kids with you. The return boat trip costs $2 a head and takes an hour or so, but only sets off when there are ten takers. Great therapeutic properties are attributed to the waters of the three pools at **Ba Ho Falls**, the lowest of which is 5km further up the highway and a couple of kilometres' stroll west. From there, pick your way up through lush forestry to the second pool (described in the local tourist literature, with a typically overblown sense of romance, as a mirror "by sheer negligence left behind by a certain fairy") and the third. To access the track to the falls – which make a relaxing spot for an amble, picnic and swim – take a bus headed for Hinh Hoa district from Nha Trang's local station, telling the driver where you wish to alight.

With the left turn to Buon Me Thuot (see p.175) behind you, next up is splendid **Doc Let Beach**, 10km down a road peeling off east along Hon Khoi Peninsula and signposted on the highway, 38km north of Nha Trang. You'll be keen to linger at Doc Let: its pine trees, toothpaste-white sands and high dunes are currently the perfect recipe for a lazy day's beach-bumming, though plans are afoot to develop a resort here.

North to Son My

Most tourists leapfrog the four-hundred-plus kilometres of coastline between Nha Trang and Hoi An on a tour bus, and it's hard to fault their decision. Swathes of splendid coastline *do* exist along this stretch of the country, but none have been exploited to any extent as yet: get a taster 83km past Nha Trang at the tiny fishing village of **DAI LANH**, whose appeal lies in the fact that there's absolutely nothing to do. With its patchwork of clay tile roofs and modest fleet of blue fishing boats, the village dots the "i" of the kilometre-long beach curving around Vung Ro Bay, a beach whose pine trees and searing white sands are hemmed between the clear, turquoise waters of the South China Sea and a mantle of green mountains. Sadly, although there are several eating options in the village there's presently nowhere to stay – if you are desperate, you could feasibly kip down on the sand causeway linking the foot of the beach with thirty-kilometre-long **Hon Gom Peninsula**.

Beyond here, you'll have to wait until **Sa Huynh** to settle in and enjoy beach-life to the hilt. The most major settlement along the route, **Qui Nhon**, has little to recommend it, though if you are heading **up Highway 19 to Plei Ku** (see p.180) you might be glad of a night here to break up the journey; the most memorable of the many **Cham sites** scattered around the city are rather too remote to be of relevance to any but the most determined of aficionados.

The one stop between Nha Trang and Hoi An that many visitors feel compelled to make is **Quang Ngai**, from where you can reach **Son My Village**, site of one of the war's most dastardly incidents, the My Lai massacre.

Qui Nhon and around

Try as it may, **QUI NHON**, a mid-sized seaport set on a narrow stake of land harpooning the South China Sea, can't quite cut it as a beach resort. As elsewhere in Vietnam, times are changing and the local tourist authorities are wising up to what's required if foreigners are to come in numbers; but for now, the city remains very much the poor relation to glossier Nha Trang. Qui Nhon's origins lie in the Cham migration south, at the start of the eleventh century, under pressure from the Vietnamese to the north. The empire they established in the area, they named Vijaya ("Victory"); its epicentre was the citadel of Cha Ban (see p.219), and Qui Nhon – then known as Sri Bonai – developed into its thriving commercial centre. Centuries later, the Tay Son Rebellion boiled over in this neck of the woods; and during the American War the city served as a US port and supply centre, and was engorged by refugees from the vicious bombing meted out to the surrounding countryside – you can still spot the remains of a US air base below town en route to the *Hai Au Hotel*. Yet for all its historical resonance, there's nothing here to set pulses racing and, unless you've developed an inordinate interest in **Cham towers**, you'll only be here to refuel and sleep. One potential saving grace could come if your visit coincides with a performance of *Tuong*, or **Vietnamese classical opera**: Qui Nhon is considered the cradle of *Tuong*, and the tourist office can provide details of events at the *Tuong Theatre*, 828 Nguyen Thai Hoc. Otherwise, check out **Quang Trung Park**, where impromptu performances are sometimes held.

Arrival and information

Qui Nhon's **long-distance bus station** is a several-kilometre cyclo or (preferably) Honda om ride west of the city centre, at 71 Lam Son. If you miss your bus
and it's time to move on, make your way out to Phu Tai Crossroads (see p.219)
and wave down a bus there; services to Phu Tai, Ba Di Bridge (from where all
buses to Plei Ku depart) and for all other destinations within Binh Dinh Province,
operate out of the **local bus station** on Pham Hong Thai. Buses from here also
make the twelve-kilometre run to Dieu Tri, the site of the nearest mainline **train
station**; and to the **airport**, 35km to the north in Phu Cat District. Train tickets
can be booked at Qui Nhon's branchline station below Tran Hung Dao; while
Vietnam Airlines (☎056/823125) is at 2 Ly Thuong Kiet, and operates a shuttle
bus ($1.50) connecting with all arrivals and departures. *Binh Dinh Tourist*
(☎056/822524), beside the *Qui Nhon Hotel* at 10 Nguyen Hue, can provide basic
local **information**, and can arrange tours and car rental; the *Vietcombank*, 152 Le
Loi, will **exchange** dollars and travellers' cheques.

Accommodation

Of the many **places to stay** in Qui Nhon most are, to say the least, of under-
whelming quality. The city's two brightest hotels are the modern but secluded
Hai Au (☎056/846473; ③) at 489 Nguyen Hue; and the *Qui Nhon*, 8 Nguyen Hue
(☎056/822401; ③), which is similar in quality, but has the added advantage of
being plumb in the centre of the town's best strip of beach. Backpackers tend to
bunch at the *Dong Phuong*, 39 Mai Xuan Thuong (☎056/822915; ②): cheap but
cockroach-ridden, and with a stairwell that acts as an echo-chamber for noise
from the ground-floor restaurant, it's still marginally more appealing than the
grubby rooms of the rambling *Huu Nghi*, at 210 Phan Boi Chau (☎056/822152;
①). The *Phuong Mai* (☎056/822921; ②) at 136 Nguyen Hue is another grimy
address though at least it can boast a waterfront location, and a few rooms with
seaviews. The *Peace Hotel*, 361 Tran Hung Dao (☎056/822900; ②), has all the
charm of a prison and should be investigated only as a last resort.

The city and beaches

Central Qui Nhon is almost bereft of interest, though at a push you could drop by
well-maintained **Long Khanh Pagoda** at 141 Tran Cao Van. The present sanctuary was built on the site of an eighteenth-century pagoda founded by a Chinese
trader, and stands amid grounds dominated by a tall, white Buddha and two tur-
rets – one containing a drum, the other a giant bell. On the back wall of the main
sanctuary, and below its varnished wooden roof, a Bodhi tree mural provides an
appropriate backdrop for the large copper Buddha sitting in meditative pose on
the altar; below him is a portrait of many-armed Chuan De. The room behind the
pagoda's courtyard contains an intriguing statue of a fabulous thousand-eyed and
thousand-handed Buddha, with the white figure of Avalokitesvara perched on its
head.

The most accessible of all the Cham monuments around Qui Nhon are the
Thap Doi or "Double towers", 2km west of town. The shabby backstreet setting
does nothing to enhance the towers, so it's a testament to their grandeur that your
first sight of them still stops you in your tracks. Square-trunked, and rising to
stubby roofs sprouting fringes of vegetation, both date from around the end of the
twelfth century. Time has weathered them, but embellishments such as sand-

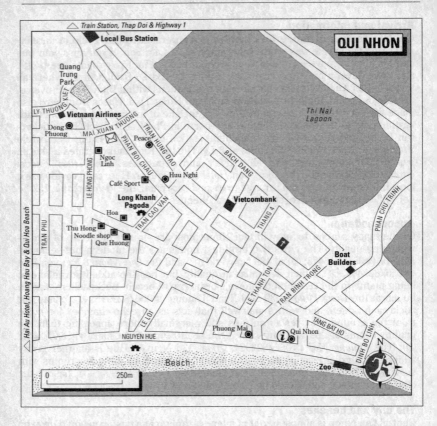

stone pilasters, spearhead-shaped arches and the remnants of sandstone statues of winged Garuda, the vehicle of Vishnu, still remain. To reach Thap Doi, head west out of town along Tran Hung Dao, and veer north when street numbers reach the 900s.

The strand of **beach** in front of the *Qui Nhon Hotel* is the best in town: fairly wide, and passably clean, it still doesn't see many tourists, so you can expect your presence to draw a crowd. The square nets of numerous **fish traps** are draped over the water just offshore; watching over them from the distant tip of the promontory that shelters the city, is a huge statue of Quang Trung. Monkeys, snakes, bears, pelicans and tortoises are kept in truly rancid conditions at the waterfront **zoo**, a short walk east of the *Qui Nhon*.

From the central area, coastal Nguyen Hue slopes away southwest, reaching the pebbly inlet of **Hoang Hau Bay** (daily 7am–7pm), a five-kilometre Honda om or cyclo ride later. Its name translates as "Queen's Bay", and it was said to be a favourite spot of Bao Dai's consort, but if you are looking for some peace and quiet, press on for a further 3 or 4 kilometres to the region's cleanest and most attractive stretch of sand, three-kilometre-long **Qui Hoa**.

Eating and drinking

When it comes to **eating**, you could do far worse than Tang Bat Ho's *Thu Hong*, a bright and breezy, open-fronted joint with a wide menu of standard Vietnamese dishes. Indeed, there are several congenial venues along Tang Bat Ho: *nem*-lovers should make for the *Hoa* at no. 124; while there's good Hanoi-style noodles on offer in the unmarked shophouse opposite at no. 261 and simple *com* meals are the order of the day at the friendly *Que Huong*, on the corner at no. 125. Ignore the surly staff at Le Hong Phong's vaguely Mediterranean *Ngoc Lin*: the food there is filling, reasonable, and not at all bad. The roasted shrimps are tasty, as is the "fried meat-pie and shrimp" (spring rolls). There are several cafés around the waterfront war memorial, but if it's a **drink** you're after, far better to go to Phan Boi Chau's *Café Sport*, a perennial favourite among local smoochers, and capable of knocking up a mean hot chocolate.

North to Sa Huynh

Ten kilometres northwest along Qui Nhon's feeder road, the throng of cafés and restaurants operating around **Phu Tai Crossroads** heralds your arrival at the junction with Highway 1. From here it's another 9km north to **Ba Di Bridge** (Cau Ba Di), where highways 1 and 19 meet, and buses await fares to Plei Ku. (Clearly visible from Ba Di Bridge, the **Banh It** Cham towers, known locally as *Thap Bac*, cut a dash on a hilltop over the river, and can be accessed by a road off to the right above the bridge; their site yields tremendous views of the surrounding countryside, but the towers themselves are unremarkable.)

North of Ba Di, Highway 1 rushes on apace towards Sa Huynh. If you are travelling under your own steam you could visit the last vestiges of **Cha Ban Citadel**, the erstwhile capital of Vijaya, 1km west of the highway and around 27km north of Qui Nhon. This site constituted the epicentre of Champa from the early eleventh century until 1471, when Le Thanh Ton finally seized it, killing 50,000 Chams in the process. The Tay Son brothers renamed the site Hoang De and made it their base in the mid-1770s (see p.181) but it's been neglected since then, and now all that remains, apart from its several-kilometre-long square protective wall, is **Canh Tien Tower**, a rectangular brick and sandstone tower framed by sandstone pilasters below a crenellated roof.

After racing across terrain whose fertile soil supports huge coconut plantations and through **Phu Cat**, **Phu My** and **Hoai Nhon**, small towns that saw great suffering in the war, the highway nears the coast at **SA HUYNH**, a pleasing fishing backwater perched on a broad curve of palm-fringed, golden sand. With its offing speckled with scores of blue fishing boats, sleepy Sa Huynh makes a convenient and relaxing staging-post en route from Nha Trang to Hoi An, and the roaring of its excitable surf masks the noise of traffic from the road. The best way to enjoy the town's deserted beach is to make for its sole **place to stay**, the laid-back *Sa Huynh Hotel* (☎055/860311; top end of ②; reservations advised), 2km below town, whose sixteen simple rooms are set in billet-style blocks above the fringe of the beach. Seafood features prominently on the reception lodge **restaurant**'s limited but affordable menu; or there's a gaggle of *com* **stalls** sniffing out passing trade on the highway behind and above the hotel.

Shrimp farms, salt flats and vast expanses of paddy characterize the countryside above Sa Huynh. Once past **Duc Pho**, an R&R base for the Viet Minh in the late Forties, and the tobacco plantations of **Mo Duc**, you quickly hit Quang Ngai.

Quang Ngai and around

Slender **QUANG NGAI**, clinging to the south bank of the Tra Khuc River some 130km south of Da Nang, is about as pleasant as you could expect of a town skewered by Vietnam's main highway. The area's long tradition of resistance against the French found further focus during American involvement, for which the reward was some of the most extensive bombing meted out during the war: by 1967, American journalist Jonathan Schell was able to report that seventy percent of villages in the town's surrounding area had been destroyed. A year later, the Americans turned their focus upon **Son My Village**, site of the infamous My Lai massacre (see box below), whose moving memorial garden and museum are the only justifications for a stopover in this workaday settlement.

Son My Village

From the stele immediately to your right over the bridge at the top of Quang Ngai, it's 12km east to **SON MY**, the site of an infamous massacre of civilians by American soldiers in early 1968 that is remembered at the **Son My Memorial Park** (daily 7am–6pm; $2) in the village's sub-hamlet of Tu Cung. Pacing through this peaceful and dignified place, set within a low perimeter wall surrounded by ricefields, you'll be accompanied by a feeling of blanched horror, and a palpable

---

THE MY LAI MASSACRE

The massacre of civilians in the hamlets of **Son My Village**, the single most shameful chapter of America's involvement in Vietnam, began at dawn on March 16, 1968. US Intelligence suggested that the 48th Local Forces Battalion of the NVA, which had taken part in the Tet Offensive on Quang Ngai a month earlier, was holed up in Son My. Within the task force assembled to flush them out was Charlie Company, whose First Platoon, led by Lieutenant William Calley, was assigned to sweep through **My Lai 4** (known to locals as **Tu Cung Hamlet**). Recent arrivals in Vietnam, Charlie Company had suffered casualties and losses in the hunt for the elusive 48th, but always inflicted by snipers and booby traps. Unable to contact the enemy face-to-face in any numbers, or even to distinguish civilians from Viet Cong guerrillas, they had come to feel frustrated and impotent. Son My offered the chance to settle some old scores.

At a briefing on the eve of the offensive, GIs were glibly told that all civilians would be at market by 7am and that anyone remaining was bound to be an active VC sympathizer. Some GIs later remembered being told not to kill women and children, but most simply registered that there were to be no prisoners. Whatever the truth a massacre ensued, whose brutal course Neil Sheehan describes with chilling understatement in *A Bright Shining Lie*:

The American soldiers and junior officers shot old men, women, boys, girls, and babies. One soldier missed a baby lying on the ground twice with a .45 pistol as his comrades laughed at his marksmanship. He stood over the child and fired a third time. The soldiers beat women with rifle butts and raped some and sodomised others before shooting them. They shot the water buffalos, the pigs, and the chickens. They threw the dead animals into the wells to poison the water. They tossed satchel charges into the bomb shelters under the houses. A lot of the inhabitants had fled into the shelters. Those who leaped out to escape the explosives were gunned down. All of the houses were put to the torch.

sense of the dead all around you. Wandering the garden, visitors effect a ghoul-ish dot-to-dot of the visible scars left by the atrocities that took place here – bullet holes in trees; foundations of homes burnt down, each with a stone tablet record-ing its family's losses; and blown-out bomb shelters. After skirting three haunting statues of bodies on the brink of death, the path through the centre of the garden ends at a large, Soviet-style statue of a woman cradling a baby amid the fallen, rais-ing her right fist in defiance. Once you've seen the garden, step inside the second of two buildings on its western flank. Here, beyond a plaque recording the names of the dead, family by family, and a montage of rusting hardware, a grisly **photo-graph gallery** documents the events of March 16, 1968, from snaps of American helicopters disgorging GIs in the paddy outside the hamlet, to spine-chilling intru-sions into the villagers' last moments of life. Perhaps more affecting, though, are simpler relics – the teapot top of Mr Nguyen Gap, and a plate broken by a bullet as Mrs Nguyen Thi Doc and her family were breakfasting – which help lend a human face to the residents of the village. **Buses** for Son My leave occasionally from the bus station in Quang Ngai, but the most efficient means of reaching the village is by Honda om.

In stark contrast, secluded **My Khe Beach**, 3km east of My Lai, is several kilo-metres long and very good for swimming. Hamlets stand along the back of the beach, while fishing boats are moored off it.

In all, the Son My body count reached 500, 347 of whom fell in Tu Cung alone. Not one shot was fired at a GI in response, and the only US casualty was thought to have deliberately shot himself in the foot to avoid the carnage. The 48th battal-ion never materialized. The military chain of command was able temporarily to suppress reports of the massacre, with the army newspaper, *Stars and Stripes*, and even the *New York Times* branding the mission a success. But the awful truth sur-faced in November 1969, through the efforts of former GI Ronald Ridenhour and investigative journalist Seymour Hersh, and the incontrovertible evidence of the grisly colour slides of army photographer Ron Haeberle. Laughably, when the mas-sacre did finally make the cover of *Newsweek* it was under the headline "An American Tragedy" – an angle which, as John Pilger pointed out, "deflected from the truth that the atrocities were, above all, a *Vietnamese* tragedy".

Of 25 men eventually charged with murder at the massacre, or for its subse-quent suppression, only Lieutenant William Calley was found guilty, though he had served just three days of a life sentence of hard labour when Nixon intervened and commuted it to house arrest. Three years later he was paroled.

It is all too easy to dismiss Charlie Company as a freak unit operating beyond the pale. A more realistic view may be that the very nature of the US war effort, with its resort to unselective napalm and rocket attacks, and its use of body counts as barometers of success, created a climate in which Vietnamese life was cheap-ened to such an extent that a My Lai became almost inevitable. If indiscriminate killing from the air was justifiable, then random killing at close quarters was only taking this methodology to its logical conclusion.

Michael Bilton and Kevin Sim, whose *Four Hours in My Lai* remains the most complete account of the massacre, conclude that "My Lai's exposure late in 1969 poisoned the idea that the war was a moral enterprise". The mother of one GI put it more simply: "I gave them a good boy, and they made him a murderer".

Practicalities

The junction of Quang Trung (Highway 1) with westward-pointing Hung Vuong effectively forms central Quang Ngai. **Trains** arrive 3km west of town along Hung Vuong, while the **bus** station is a little over 500m south of the centre, and 50m east of Quang Trung on Le Thanh Ton. For what it's worth, you'll find *Quang Ngai Tourist* 150m north of Hung Vuong at 310 Quang Trung; the post office is 300m west of the highway, on Hung Vuong.

First choice among the handful of **places to stay** in town is one of the twenty rooms, all with hot water, in Hung Vuong's clean and friendly *Kim Thanh Hotel* (☎055/823471; ①). A few metres west, the *Vietnam* (☎055/823610; ②) is rather grimier, but still adequate; or try the *Song Tra* (☎055/822664; ②–③), beside the bridge at the top of town: the place is rarely full and bargaining has been known to knock several dollars off the price of a room. The *Song Tra's* indifferent **restaurant** is sometimes enlivened by live music at night; otherwise, head for one of two tidy enough *com* shops – the *Mimosa* and the *Bac Son* – next door to the *Kim Thanh* in town; or for either the *Long Hue* or the *Thien Tue* restaurants, secreted around the corner from the post office – turn left at the sign for the *Long Hue*, at 93 Phan Ding Phung.

travel details

Buses

*It's almost impossible to give the **frequency** with which buses run. Though scheduled, long-distance public buses won't depart if empty. Moreover, private services, often minibuses or pick-ups, ply more popular routes, and depart only when they have enough passengers to make the journey worthwhile. Highway 1 sees a near-constant stream of buses passing through to various destinations, and it's possible to flag something down at virtually any time of the day. Off the highway, to be sure of a bus it's advisable to start your journey early – most long-distance departures leave between 5 and 9am, and very few run after midday. **Journey times** can also vary; figures below show the normal length of time you can expect the journey to take.*

Ba Di Bridge (Qui Nhon) to: Plei Ku (5hr).

Ba Ria to: Xuyen Moc (1hr).

Nha Trang to: Buon Me Thuot (5hr 30min); Da Lat (7hr); Da Nang (16hr); Hanoi (38hr); Ho Chi Minh City (11hr); Hué (17hr).

Phan Rang to: Da Lat (2hr 40min); Ho Chi Minh City (8hr); Nha Trang (3hr); Phan Thiet (3hr 30min).

Phan Thiet to: Ho Chi Minh City (4hr); Nha Trang (6hr 30min).

Quang Ngai to: Da Nang (4hr); Nha Trang (12hr).

Qui Nhon to: Da Nang (9hr); Nha Trang (7hr); Quang Ngai (5hr).

Vung Tau to: Ba Ria (40min); Da Lat (8hr 30min); Ho Chi Minh City (2hr); Hué (29hr); Nha Trang (12hr)

Trains

Dieu Tri to: Da Nang (4 daily; 5hr 45min–7hr 30min); Ho Chi Minh City (4 daily; 12hr 50min–16hr); Hué (4 daily; 9–11hr); Nha Trang (4 daily; 4hr 40min–5hr 30min).

Muong Man to: Da Nang (4 daily; 20hr 50min–22hr 30min); Ho Chi Minh City (4 daily; 4hr 10min–4hr 50min); Hué (4 daily; 24hr 20min–26hr 50min); Nha Trang (4 daily; 5hr–5hr 40min).

Nha Trang to: Da Nang (4 daily; 10hr 30min–12hr 10min); Hanoi (3 daily; 28hr–33hr 30min); Ho Chi Minh City (4 daily; 8hr–11hr 10min); Hué (4 daily; 13hr 40min–16hr 30min).

Thap Cham to: Da Nang (4 daily; 13hr 20min–14hr 40min); Ho Chi Minh City (4 daily; 7hr 20min–8hr); Hué (4 daily; 16hr 50min–19hr); Nha Trang (4 daily; 2hr– 2hr 30min).

Boats

Vung Tau to: Con Son (1–2 weekly; 12hr).

Flights

Nha Trang to: Da Nang (2 weekly; 1hr); Hanoi (5 weekly; 2hr 30min); Ho Chi Minh City (1 daily; 50min).

Qui Nhon to: Da Nang (3 weekly; 40min); Ho Chi Minh City (2 weekly; 1hr).

CHAPTER FIVE

THE CENTRAL PROVINCES

Vietnam's narrow waist comprises a string of provinces squeezed between the long, sandy coastline and the formidable barrier of the **Truong Son Mountains**, which mark the border between Vietnam and Laos. Ragged spurs sheer off the Truong Son range towards the South China Sea, cutting the coastal plain into isolated pockets of fertile rice-land. For much of Vietnam's early history one of these spurs, the thousand-metre-high Hoanh Son Mountains north of Dong Hoi, formed the cultural and political divide between the northern, Chinese-dominated sphere and the Indianized Champa kingdom to the south. As independent Vietnam grew in power in the eleventh century, so its armies pushed southwards to the next natural frontier, the Hai Van Pass near Hué. Here again, the Cham resisted further invasion until the fifteenth century when their great temple complex at My Son was seized and their kingdom shattered.

Since then other contenders have battled back and forth over this same ground, among them the Nguyen and Trinh lords, whose simmering rivalry ended in victory for the southern Nguyens and the emergence of **Hué** as the nation's capital in the nineteenth century. The Nguyen dynasty transformed Hué into a stately imperial city, whose palaces, temples and grand mausoleums now constitute one of the highlights of a visit to Vietnam, despite the ravages they suffered during successive wars. In 1954 Vietnam was divided at the Seventeenth Parallel, only 100km north of Hué, where the Ben Hai River and the **Demilitarized Zone (DMZ)** marked the border between North and South Vietnam until reunification in 1975. Though there's little to see on the ground these days, the desolate battlefields of the DMZ are a poignant memorial to those, on both sides, who fought here and to the civilians who lost their lives in the bitter conflict.

Da Nang and nearby **China Beach** are other evocative names from the American War, but the region also has more to offer. The compact, riverside town of **Hoi An**, with its core of traditional, wood-built merchants' houses and jaunty Chinese Assembly Halls, is a particularly captivating place. Inland from Hoi An, the Chams' spiritual core, **My Son**, survives as a haunting array of overgrown ruins in a hidden valley, while the coast here presents a succession of empty, white-sand beaches, that are among the finest inVietnam. Finally, if you're heading **overland to Laos**, the only functioning border gate for foreigners is at Lao Bao, along Highway 9 from **Dong Ha**.

All these highlights lie in the southernmost of the central provinces. In stark contrast, the more northerly provinces suffer a particularly hostile climate, and

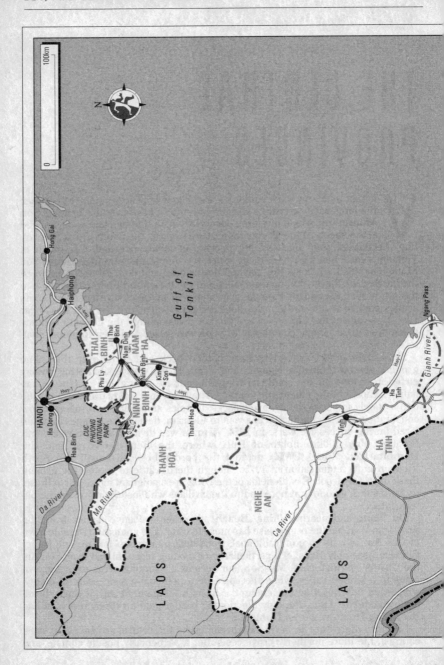

100 Rough Guides*

100% Reliable

Stay in touch with us!

ROUGH*NEWS* is Rough Guides' free newsletter. In three issues a year we give you news, travel issues, music reviews, readers' letters and the latest dispatches from authors on the road.

I would like to receive ROUGH*NEWS*: please put me on your free mailing list.

NAME ....

ADDRESS ....

Please clip or photocopy and send to: Rough Guides, 1 Mercer Street, London WC2H 9QJ, England or Rough Guides, 375 Hudson Street, New York, NY 10014, USA.

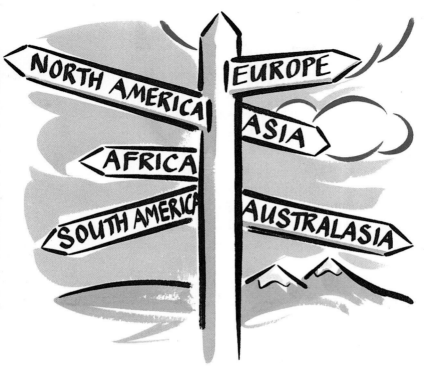

Travel the world
HIV *Safe*

Travel *Safe*

HIV, the virus that causes AIDS, is worldwide.

You're probably aware of the dangers of getting it from unprotected sex, but there are many other risks when travelling.

Wherever you're visiting it makes sense to take precautions. Try to avoid any medical or dental treatment, but if it's necessary, make sure the equipment is sterilised. Likewise, if you really need to have a blood transfusion, always ask for screened blood.

Make sure your travelling companions are aware of the risks and the necessary precautions. In fact, you should take your own sterile medical pack, available from larger high street pharmacies.

Remember, ear and body piercing, acupuncture and even tattoos could be risky, because they all involve puncturing the skin. And although you might not normally consider any of these things now, after a few drinks - you never know.

Of course, the things that are dangerous at home are just as dangerous when you travel. So don't inject drugs or share works.

Avoid casual sex and always use a good quality condom when having sex with a new partner (and each time you have sex with them).

And it's not just a gay disease' either. In fact, worldwide, it's most commonly transmitted through sex between men and women.

For information in the UK:

Ring for the TravelSafe leaflet on the Health Literature Line freephone 0800 555 777, or pick one up at a doctor's surgery or pharmacy.

Further advice on HIV and AIDS: National AIDS Helpline: 0800 567 123. (Cannot be reached from abroad).

The Terrence Higgins Trust Helpline (12 noon–10pm) provides advice and counselling on HIV/AIDS issues: 0171 242 1010.

MASTA Travellers Health Line: 0891 224 100.

Travel *Safe*

Travel the world HIV *Safe*

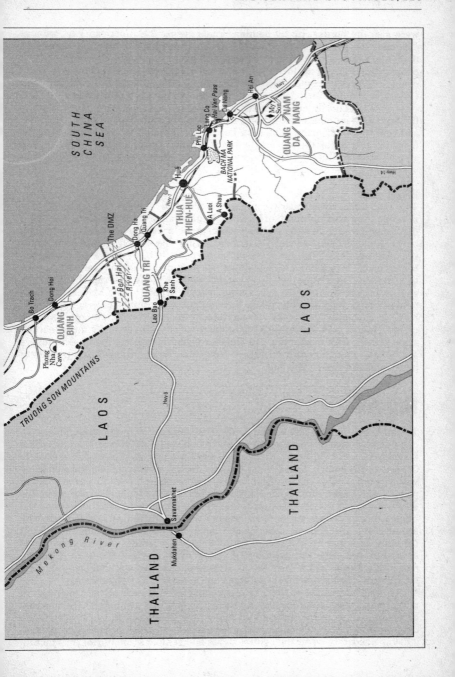

were also the hardest hit by bombing raids during the American War; without exception the towns here are post-war reconstructions with little to recommend them other than as overnight stops on the long haul north. In fact, from Hué most people skip straight up to Hanoi, but if you're travelling overland, there are a couple of places en route which warrant a stop. First of these is the **Phong Nha Cave**, the mouth of an extensive underground river system near Dong Hoi. Then right up in the north, and within easy striking distance of Hanoi, **Ninh Binh** is the base for a number of attractions, from engaging river-trips to ancient temples and reserves of primary rainforest. For those travelling by car or minibus, the usual place to break the journey between Hué and Hanoi is **Vinh**, though if you stop off at Dong Hoi for the caves, you should be able to press on to Ninh Binh in a long day.

When to go

This region has a particularly complicated climate as it forms a transitional zone between the north and south of Vietnam. In general, **around Da Nang and Hué** the rainy season lasts from September to February, with most rain falling between late September and December; during this season it's not unusual for road and rail links to be cut. Hué suffers particularly badly and, even during the "dry season" from March to September, it's not uncommon to have several days of torrential rain, giving the city an annual average of 3m. Overall, the best time to visit this southern region is in spring, from February to late May, before both temperatures and humidity reach their summer maximum (averaging around 30˚C), or just at the end of the summer before the rains break. The region **north of the Hoanh Son Mountains** experiences a drier climate and a more marked rainy season, with September and October again the wettest months. Summers are hot and dry, though from July to November typhoons can bring periods of heavy rain and severe flooding.

Hoi An

The approach to **HOI AN** across sandy scrub land and through straggling, modern outskirts may be disappointing, but its ancient core is a rich architectural fusion of Chinese, Japanese, Vietnamese and European influences dating back to the sixteenth century. In its heyday the now drowsy channel of the Thu Bon River was a jostling crowd of merchant vessels representing the world's great trading nations, and there's still a compelling sense of history in the mellow streets of this small, amiable town. Hoi An's most noteworthy monuments are the 200-year-old homes of prosperous Chinese merchants whose descendants, surrounded by astonishing collections of antiques and family memorabilia, continue to inhabit the cool, dark houses. Between their sober wooden facades, riotous confections of glazed roof-tiles and writhing dragons mark the entrances to **Chinese Assembly Halls**, which form the focal point of civic and spiritual life for an ethnic-Chinese community that constitutes one quarter of the population.

Hoi An is now firmly on the tourist agenda and for some is already too much of a trap, with its proliferating souvenir stalls, art galleries and hotels. The majority of visitors pause only briefly, but it takes time to tune in to the town's subtle charms, which are as much about human encounters as ancient vestiges. At least a day is needed to cover the central sights and sample some of Hoi An's mouthwatering speciality dishes, and by then most people are hooked. It's easy to spend longer, taking day-trips to the atmospheric Cham ruins of **My Son** or some of the other sights closer to town (see "Around Hoi An", p.236), biking out into the surrounding country or opting for a leisurely sampan ride on the Thu Bon River.

Some history

For centuries Hoi An played an important role in the maritime trade of southeast Asia, going back at least to the earliest days of the Champa Kingdom in 2 AD. But things really took off in the mid-sixteenth century when Chinese, Japanese and European vessels ran with the trade winds to congregate at a port then called Fai Fo. Its annual spring fair grew into an exotic showcase of world produce: from southeast Asia came silks and brocades, ivory, fragrant oils, fine porcelain and a cornucopia of medicinal ingredients; while the Europeans brought their textiles, weaponry, sulphur, lead – and the first Christian missionaries in 1614. During the four-month fair merchants would rent lodgings and warehouses; many went on to establish a more permanent presence through marriage to a Vietnamese woman, renowned for their business acumen. Tax collectors arrived to fill the imperial coffers, and the town swelled with artisans, money-lenders and bureaucrats as trade reached a peak in the seventeenth century.

Commercial activity was dominated by Japanese and Chinese merchants, many of whom settled in Fai Fo, where each community maintained its own governor, legal code and strong cultural identity. But in 1639 the Japanese Shogun prohibited foreign travel and the "Japanese street" dwindled to a handful of families, then to a scattering of monuments and a distinctive architectural style. Unchallenged, the Chinese community prospered, and its numbers grew as every new political upheaval in China prompted another wave of immigrants to join one of the town's self-governing "congregations" organized around a meeting hall and place of worship.

In the late eighteenth century silt began to clog the Thu Bon River just as markets were forced open in China, and from then on the port's days were numbered. Although the French established an administrative centre in Fai Fo, and even built a rail link from Tourane (Da Nang), they failed to resuscitate the economy and when a storm washed away the tracks in 1916 no one repaired them. The town, renamed Hoi An in 1954, somehow escaped damage during both the French and American wars and retains a distinctly antiquated air in its narrow streets of wooden-fronted shophouses topped with moss-covered tiles.

Arrival, information and getting around

Most people **arrive** in Hoi An by car, or by Honda om **from Da Nang** (30km), which serves as Hoi An's nearest airport and train station; local buses drop you 1km west of the town centre. For local **information** the best place to head for is *Tourist Office of Hoi An* at 12 Phan Chu Trinh (☎051/861982), who also provide knowledgeable guides at excellent rates ($5 for a 2-hr city tour; $3–5 per hour for My Son and elsewhere). Otherwise, try one of the many private tour agencies springing up all over town (see "Listings", p.236): most offer similar services – tours, transport, rail and air tickets – but prices vary so it's worth shopping around.

Almost every guesthouse, restaurant or booking office has well-priced **bicycles** for rent (less than $1 per day), or can arrange **motorbikes** at around $4–6 per day – a popular way to visit My Son (see p.238). While bikes are recommended for touring the outlying districts, Hoi An's central sights are all best approached **on foot**, especially since **traffic restrictions** apply in the core streets of Tran Phu, Nguyen Thai Hoc and Bach Dang. The regulations are part of a much-needed effort to save the old town from the worst effects of fame: cars and large motorbikes are prohibited from the above three streets, motorbikes of any size are forbidden on the Japanese bridge, while pedal-bikes must be pushed across the bridge and in the vicinity of the market. However annoying it may be to see locals apparently flouting the law – some will be authorized users – it's not worth risking a fine of up to $20.

Accommodation

The number of **hotels** in Hoi An mushroomed in recent years until the local government put a block on new developments in the centre – too late to prevent some eyesores in the old streets. The good news is that prices of accommodation have come down and standards have risen, most places will bargain and there's no longer a shortage of beds in peak season; the bad news is that touts, usually gangs of children, have made an appearance. Nearly all Hoi An's hotels are within easy walking distance of the centre, if not actually on Tran Phu Street itself.

Binh Minh, 12 Thai Phien (☎051/861943). One of the newer hotels whose cheaper rooms are fair value. On the northern outskirts of town. ②

Guesthouse 92, 92 Tran Phu (☎051/861331). An old, state-run guesthouse right in the heart of things. Small, spartan rooms but clean and with views over the old town from the third floor. ②

Hoi An, 6 Tran Hung Dao (☎051/861373, fax 861636). A state-run, colonial-style hotel and former billet for US Marines which was the mainstay of Hoi An accommodation until mini-hotels came on the scene. It provides a one-stop tourist service including restaurant, exchange, information office, bike rental and onward transport. Its 100-plus rooms come in 4 different categories from shared bathroom with cold water in courtyard blockhouses, to spacious suites with fridge and telephone. Despite its age all rooms are well maintained, if sparsely furnished. ①–②

Huy Hoang, 73 Phan Boi Chau (☎051/861453). Right beside the Cam Nam Island bridge, this place is recommended for its riverfront terraces, though its rooms are also good value, including a 5-bed dormitory. ②

ACCOMMODATION PRICE CODES

All accommodation listed in this guide has been categorized according to the following scale:

① under US$10 (under 110,000 dong)   ② US$10–15 (110–165,000 dong)
③ US$15–30 (165–330,000 dong)   ④ US$30–75 (330–825,000 dong)
⑤ US$75–150 (825–1,650,000 dong)   ⑥ over US$150 (over 1,650,000 dong)

Rates are for the cheapest available double or twin room; breakfast is not usually included. During holiday periods, rates are liable to rise, and proprietors may be less amenable to bargaining. Although the law requires prices to be quoted in dong, most hotels also give their rates in US$; payment can be made in either currency.

For a more detailed discussion of accommodation, see pp.31–34.

Pho Hoi and **Fai Fo**, 7/2 Tran Phu (☎051/861633). Two neighbouring hotels under the same owner, located down an alley beside the Coconut Milk Café. You'll find some of Hoi An's cheapest accommodation but their plumbing gets a mixed reception. ①–②

Thanh Binh, 1 Le Loi (☎051/861740). A shiny bright hotel offering good value. ①

Thien Trung, 63 Phan Dinh Phung (☎051/861720). Large, comfortable rooms at affordable prices though a bit of a way from town. ①–②

Thuy Duong, 11 Le Loi (☎051/861574). Clean 4-berth rooms and a central location make this a favourite with budget travellers. Its new annexe at 68 Huynh Thuc Khang (☎051/861394), near the bus station, offers equal value though it's a fair walk from the centre. ①

Trade Union Guesthouse (*Khach San Du Lich Cong Doan*), 50 Phan Dinh Phung (☎051/861899). Fourteen rooms in a bungalow-style guesthouse set back from the road. Clean, friendly and inexpensive. ②

Vinh Hung, 143 Tran Phu (☎051/861621, fax 861893). Highlights of the *Vinh Hung* are its location and top-notch foyer occupying a well-restored, old shophouse. Sadly, the rest of the house is beyond repair so rooms are mostly in a modern, comfortable extension and are expensive for what you get. ②

The town

The **historic core** of Hoi An consists of just three short streets running parallel to the river. Tran Phu is the oldest and even today is the principal commercial street, running from Hoi An's most famous monument, the Japanese Covered Bridge, in the west to the market in the east. One block south is Nguyen Thai Hoc, with a fine array of wooden townhouses, traditional pharmacists and an overspill of galleries and antique shops. Finally comes riverfront Bach Dang, site of the ferry station and a line of attractive, waterside cafés. Just north of this central core are a scattering of sights, including two of the less-visited merchants' houses that shouldn't be overlooked.

Japanese Covered Bridge

The western extremity of Tran Phu is marked by a small, arched bridge of red-painted wood, popularly known as the **Japanese Covered Bridge**, which has been adopted as Hoi An's emblem. It was known to exist in the mid-sixteenth century, and has subsequently been reconstructed several times to the same simple design. According to local folklore, the bridge was erected after Japan suffered a series of violent earthquakes which geomancers attributed to a restless monster lying with its head in India, tail in Japan and heart in Hoi An. The only remedy was to build a bridge whose stone piles would drive a metaphorical sword through the

Hoi An now has a **ticket scheme** in operation, covering its more famous sights. A **combined ticket** ($5) allows access to four places: the temple on the Japanese Covered Bridge; the Historical and Cultural Museum (including Chua Ong); one of the participating Chinese Assembly Halls; and one of the participating merchants' houses or family chapels. If you want to visit more houses or halls in the scheme, you can buy **extra tickets** at $1 per sight. Tickets are **on sale** at four outlets: the *Tourist Office of Hoi An* (see p.227); 52 Nguyen Thi Minh Khai; 19 Nhi Trung, 5 Hoang Dieu (all marked on the map over the page). These offices are **open** from 6am to 6pm, as are the sights included in the scheme. For sights not in the ticket scheme, we've given details of opening hours in the accounts below.

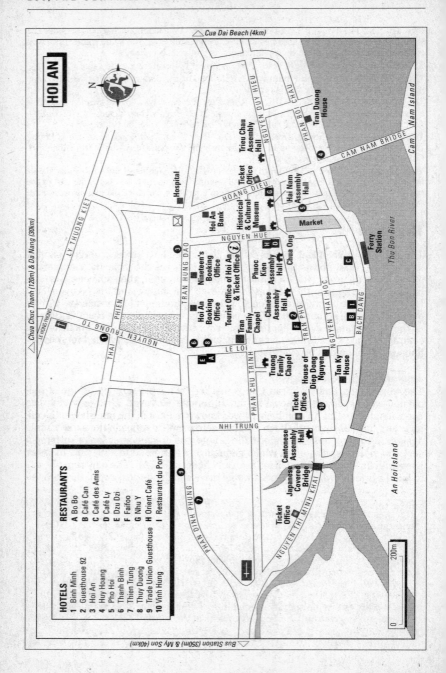

HOI AN

△ Cua Dai Beach (4km)

△ Chua Chuc Thanh (120m) & Da Nang (30km)

Cam Nam Island

Cam Nam Bridge

Thu Bon River

An Hoi Island

Trieu Chau Assembly Hall

Tran Duong House

Hospital

Hoi An Bank

Ticket Office

Historical & Cultural Museum

Hai Nam Assembly Hall

Market

Ferry Station

Nineteen's Booking Office

Tourist Office of Hoi An & Ticket Office

Phuoc Kien Assembly Hall

Chua Ong

Hoi An Booking Office

Tran Family Chapel

Chinese Assembly Hall

Truong Family Chapel

House of Diep Dong Nguyen

Tan Ky House

Ticket Office

Cantonese Assembly Hall

Japanese Covered Bridge

Ticket Office

NGUYEN DUY HIEU
PHAN BOI CHAU
HOANG DIEU
NGUYEN HUE
TRAN HUNG DAO
LY THUONG KIET
LE HONG PHONG
THAI PHIEN
NGUYEN TRUONG TO
LE LOI
TRAN PHU
NGUYEN THAI HOC
BACH DANG
PHAN CHU TRINH
NHI TRUNG
PHAN DINH PHUNG
NGUYEN THI MINH KHAI

△ Bus Station (350m) & My Son (40km)

HOTELS
1 Binh Minh
2 Guesthouse 92
3 Hoi An
4 Huy Hoang
5 Pho Hoi
6 Thanh Binh
7 Thien Trung
8 Thuy Duong
9 Trade Union Guesthouse
10 Vinh Hung

RESTAURANTS
A Bo Bo
B Café Can
C Café des Amis
D Café Ly
E Dzu Dzi
F Faifoo
G Nhu Y
H Orient Café
I Restaurant du Port

0   200m

beast's heart, and fortuitously provide a handy passage across the muddy creek. Inside the bridge's narrow span are a collection of stelae and four statues, two dogs and two monkeys, usually said to record that work began in the year of the monkey and ended in that of the dog. The small **temple** suspended above the water is a later addition dedicated to the Taoist god Tran Vo Bac De (Emperor of the North), a favourite of sailors as he controls wind, rain and other "evil influences".

Four hundred metres north of the bridge, at the west end of Phan Dinh Phung, an equally mysterious **shrine** nestles among the giant buttress roots of an ancient banyan tree. Locals say this shrine, which also honours the Emperor of the North, helps protect the bridge from floods, but no one's yet been able to fathom the strange symbols inscribed on the stone stele, alongside a constellation map of the navigational North Star.

The Chinese Assembly Halls

Historically Hoi An's ethnic Chinese population organized themselves according to their place of origin (Fujian, Guangdong, Chaozhou or Hainan). Each group maintained its own Assembly Hall as both community centre and house of worship, while a fifth hall also provided assistance to all the local groups and to visiting Chinese merchants. The most populous group hales from Fujian, or Phuoc Kien, and their **Phuoc Kien Assembly Hall**, at 46 Tran Phu, is a suitably imposing edifice, kicking-off with an ostentatious, triple-arched gateway added in the early 1970s. The hall started life as a pagoda built in the late seventeenth century when, so it's said, a Buddhist statue containing a lump of gold beached-up on the river bank. Almost a century later, the Chinese took over the decaying structure and rededicated it as a temple to Thien Hau, Goddess of the Sea and protector of sailors. She stands, fashioned in 200-year-old papier mâché, on the principal altar flanked by her two assistants, green-faced Thien Ly Nhan and red-faced Thuan Phong Nhi, who between them can see or hear any boat in distress over a range of a thousand miles. A second sanctuary room behind the main altar shelters a deity favoured by couples and pregnant women: the awesome Van Thien and her aides, the "twelve heavenly midwives", who decide the fundamentals of a child's life from conception onwards, including the fateful matter of gender. On the way out of the temple, take a look at the entrance porch decorated with colourful wooden friezes and delicate motifs in stone.

It's worth strolling out to **Trieu Chau Assembly Hall**, on the far eastern edge of town at 157 Nguyen Duy Hieu. Built in 1776 by Chinese from Chaozhou, or Trieu Chau, it's renowned for its remarkable display of woodcarving. In the altar-niche sits the gilded Ong Bon, a general in the Chinese Navy believed to hold sway over the wind and waves, surrounded by a frieze teeming with bird, animal and insect life so real you can almost hear it buzz. Moving back, the altar table itself depicts life on land and in the depths of the ocean, while panels on either side show two decorative ladies of the Chinese court modelling the latest Japanese hair fashions. On the way to Trieu Chau hall, you'll pass **Hai Nam Assembly Hall** (not covered by ticket scheme; 7–11.30am & 2–5pm), founded by the Chinese community from Hainan, or Hai Nam, and also noted for its ornately carved, gilded altar table – though its unusual history is more intriguing. In 1851 a Vietnamese general plundered three merchant ships, killing 107 passengers, after which the vessels were painted black to imply they were pirate ships. A lone survivor revealed the crime to King Tu Duc, who promptly condemned the gen-

---

UNRAVELLING THE ARCHITECTURAL FEATURES OF HOI AN

You can't walk far in Hoi An without confronting a **mythical beast** with fish's body and dragon's head; though they're found all over northern Vietnam they seem to have struck a particular chord with Hoi An's architects. One of the most prominent examples tops a weather vane in the Phuoc Kien Assembly Hall, but there are plenty of more traditional representations about, carved into lantern brackets, beam ends, or forming the beams themselves. The **carp** symbolizes prosperity, success and, in this form metamorphosing into a **dragon**, is a reminder that nothing in life comes easily. To become a dragon, and thereby attain immortality, a fish must pass through three gates – just as a scholar has to pass three exams to become a mandarin, requiring much patience and hard work.

Another typical feature of Hoi An's architecture are "**eyes**" watching over the entrance to a house or religious building. Two thick, wooden nails about 20cm in diameter are driven into the lintel as protection against evil forces, following a practice that originated in the pagodas of northern Vietnam. Assembly Halls offer the most highly ornamented examples: that of Phuoc Kien consists of a yin and yang with two dragons in obeisance to the sun, while the Cantonese version is a fearsome tiger. The **yin and yang** symbol became fashionable in the nineteenth century and is the most commonly used symbol on houses, sometimes set in a chrysanthemum flower, such as at the Tan Ky House, or as the octagonal talisman representing eight charms.

---

eral to death and ordered that the booty be returned to the victims' families. When the hall was built, later in the century, it was dedicated to the unlucky passengers' memory.

Just east of the Japanese bridge you can't miss the **Cantonese Assembly Hall**, its gaudy entrance-arch a recent embellishment to the original late-seventeenth-century hall built by immigrants from Guangdong. Though there's nothing of particular merit here, it's an appealing place, mostly because of its plant-filled courtyard, ornamented with dragon and carp carvings (see box above). The main altar is dedicated to the red-faced Quan Cong, a Chinese general of the Han dynasty revered for his loyalty, honesty and exemplary behaviour. Lastly, plum in the centre of town is the **Chinese Assembly Hall**, or *Chua Ba* (not covered by ticket scheme; 7–11.30am & 2–5pm), built in 1740 as an umbrella organization for all Hoi An's ethnic-Chinese population. Thien Hau graces the altar but the hall is nowadays used mainly as a language school where local ethnic-Chinese children and adults come to learn their mother-tongue; the school was closed in 1975 and only permitted to re-open in 1990.

The merchants' houses

The majority of Hoi An's original wooden buildings are found along Tran Phu and south towards the river, which is where you'll find the most well-known merchants' house, at 101 Nguyen Thai Hoc. The **Tan Ky House** is a beautifully preserved example of a two-storey, late eighteenth-century shophouse, amalgamating Vietnamese, Japanese and Chinese influences in an architectural style typical of Hoi An. The present house was built by a second-generation member of the Tan Ky family, who fled China as political refugees in the late sixteenth century, and took eight years to complete. The long, narrow building has shop space at the front, a tiny central courtyard and direct access to the river at the back, from where merchandise would be hauled upstairs to storerooms safe above the floods. The house, wonderfully cluttered with the accumulated property of seven generations grown wealthy from trading silk, tea and rice, is constructed of dark hardwoods, including termite-resistant jackfruit for its main columns. The skill of local wood carvers is evident throughout, but most stunning is the inlay work: look out for two hanging poem-boards on which mother-of-pearl brush-strokes form exquisitely delicate birds in flight. Guides, speaking French and English, are on hand to answer questions but at times the house is completely overwhelmed with visitors – far better to come back, if you can, at a quieter time (early or late in the day) to appreciate the weight of history here. Diagonally across Nguyen Thai Hoc, at no. 80, is the **house of Diep Dong Nguyen**, built at the end of the last century for a Chinese merchant and later converted into a pharmacy (not covered by ticket scheme; daily 8am–noon & 2–4.30pm; small donation expected). This one's also a must for antique-connoisseurs: the glass medicine cases downstairs and the library upstairs are stuffed full of family heirlooms.

On the face of it Phan Chu Trinh, one block north of Tran Phu, is an unspectacular road but it hides two captivating "family chapels", again houses built by wealthy Chinese merchants but to a design reflecting their spiritual rather than predominantly commercial focus. Here the central element is an imposing sanctuary room in which stands the ancestral altar, under the guardianship of the family head. On Phan Chu Trinh itself is the 200-year-old **Tran Family Chapel** within a walled compound on the junction with Le Loi. Over homemade lotus flower tea and sugared coconut you learn about the building and family traditions, going back thirteen generations (300 years) to when the first ancestor settled in Hanoi. The move to Hoi An came, so the story goes, when one son married a Vietnamese woman and such was the parental disapproval that he fled southward to make his fortune trading silk, pepper and ivory in Hoi An; miraculously, all was forgiven and the whole family turned up on the doorstep. Succeeding generations continued to shine, with two mandarins to their credit – their portraits and accoutrements, bearing the imperial insignia, are displayed in the reception room. On the altar itself oblong, wooden funerary boxes contain a name-tablet and biographical details of deceased family leaders and their wives – carved lotus blossoms indicate adherents of Buddhism. Each year the entire family, in the Tran case more than eighty people, gather round the altar to venerate their ancestors and discuss family affairs.

The smaller but more elaborate **Truong Family Chapel** is hidden down an alley beside Pho Hoi Restaurant at 69 Phan Chu Trinh (not covered by ticket scheme; 7.30am–noon & 2–5pm; small donation expected). The Truong ancestors, like many ethnic-Chinese now in Hoi An, fled China in the early eighteenth century following the collapse of the Ming dynasty. The ground-breaking ceremony took place in 1840 at the auspicious moment of 5am on the 5th day of the eleventh lunar month – that is, on the hour of the cat and day of the cat, in the month and year of the mouse. In the late nineteenth century, family members made their first pilgrimage back to Fujian, returning to Hoi An with an unwieldy souvenir of four finely carved wooden partitions for their sanctuary room. This family also embraces two mandarin forefathers and cherishes gifts from the Hué court, but more intriguing is an inscribed panel bestowed by Emperor Bao Dai on the wife of the fifth generation who, widowed at 25 years old and with three children, nevertheless remained faithful to her dead husband.

Around the market

The north side of the market square is dominated by the colourful frontage of **Chua Ong**, a seventeenth-century pagoda-temple conversion dedicated to General Quan Cong. Exit through the back of the temple and you find Hoi An's **Historical and Cultural Museum**, attractively housed in another former pagoda. Apart from the copies of ancient maps of Fai Fo, the primary appeal of this small, informative museum is its quiet courtyard and carved, wooden door panels, depicting the four sacred animals: crane, dragon, turtle and the mythical kylin.

Hoi An **market** itself retains the atmosphere of a typical, traditional country market despite the number of tourists. Like most, it's best in the early morning, especially among the riverfront fresh-food stalls. Look out for tiny preserved tangerines, a regional speciality, amid neat stacks of basketware, bowl-shaped lumps of unrefined cane-sugar, liniments, medicinal herbs and every variety of rice. Wandering down through the market square brings you out by the ferry docks and Bach Dang Street, which regularly disappears each autumn under the swollen **Thu Bon River**. The floods are bad news for Hoi An's ancient buildings, occasionally precipitating the collapse of weakened roofs and walls, and eating into the fabric as pollution levels increase. The worst flood in recent years was in 1964 when the water rose over 2m, but for the most part you can go dry-shod along Bach Dang and watch the river-scene from beneath the cheery awning of a waterside café.

From the market, walk east along the river and you come to Phan Boi Chau Street, where the town takes on a distinctly European flavour – louvred shutters, balconies and stucco – in what was the beginnings of a **French quarter**. The interiors of these late-nineteenth-century townhouses are characterized by vast, high-ceilinged rooms and enormous roof-spaces, markedly different from the Chinese abodes. If you're interested to see inside one, take a brief tour round **Tran Duong House**, at no. 25, the home of an enterprising man who owns a smattering of period furniture (small donation expected).

Eating

Hoi An has a fine choice of **restaurants** at which you can sample an array of local speciality dishes (see box on facing page). In the evenings tables and chairs line Bach Dang, looking more Mediterranean than Vietnamese, while Tran Phu has no shortage of popular outlets, spreading up Nguyen Hue near the market. There's also a growing number of cheaper restaurants on Le Loi, which is becoming something of a backpacker centre. Better-known places tend to fill up quickly in the evening and at weekend lunchtimes when tourist numbers swell with Da Nang day-trippers.

Bo Bo, 18 Le Loi. Good music, a jocular host and cheap prices justify *Bo Bo*'s popularity, though the food is average – the normal range of pancakes, pastas and pizzas, plus a number of local dishes. Ask about the restaurant's name.

Café Can, 74 Bach Dang. A welcoming restaurant offering Hoi An specialities and an excellent-value seafood-menu – 4 courses for $3. The food tastes even better when you're sitting under an umbrella beside the Thu Bon River though, as with all these waterside places, you're a target for kids hawking postcards and gum.

Café des Amis, 52 Bach Dang. The café is legendary among French travellers for its charming Francophone proprietor and his "Vietnamese cuisine plus imagination". There's no menu and no choice, but it's all great – vegetarian and seafood specialities in huge quantities – and

---

HOI AN SPECIALITIES

Hoi An has excellent food of all kinds, including a number of tasty specialities to sample. Most famous is *cao lau*, a mouthwatering bowlful of thick rice-flour **noodles**, bean sprouts and pork-rind croutons in a light soup flavoured with mint and star anise, topped with thin slices of pork and served with grilled rice-flour crackers or sprinkled with crispy rice-paper. Legend has it that the genuine article is cooked using water drawn from one particular local well. Lovers of **seafood** should try the delicately flavoured steamed manioc-flour parcels of finely diced crab or shrimp called *banh bao* (or *banh vac*), translated as "white rose". Lemon, sugar and *nuoc mam*, complemented by a crunchy onion-flake topping, add extra flavour. To fill any remaining gaps, there's even a special Hoi An **cake**, *banh it*, made by steaming green-bean paste and strands of sweetened coconut in a sticky rice-flour dough – one portion goes a long way.

---

you won't get the same meal twice. Prices range from $2 to 5 per person, excluding drinks, depending on how many courses you manage. Get there early to be sure of a table.

Café Ly, 22 Nguyen Hue. *Café Ly* is often packed out but its reputation is well deserved. Some swear this is the best *cao lau* and *banh bao* in town.

Dzu Dzi, 12 Le Loi. Just as friendly and popular as its neighbour, *Bo Bo*, and offering similar food.

Faifoo, 104 Tran Phu. Vietnamese specialities rub shoulders with spaghetti and guacamole on the illustrated and annotated menu.

Nhu Y, 2 Tran Phu. Great food and fair prices draw people back to the friendly *Nhu Y*. Speciality of the house is marinated fish grilled with saffron in banana leaf; the *hoanh thanh* (won ton) is also a good choice.

Orient Café, 20 Nguyen Hue. A reliable place for tasty vegetarian dishes at regular prices.

Restaurant du Port, 70 Bach Dang. An atmospheric restaurant in a delightful riverside location, this place gets lots of recommendations, especially for its fish in lemon sauce or fish wrapped in banana leaf; squid stuffed with pork, shrimp and lemongrass is also worth a try.

72 Tran Phu Street. During the winter months this small, nameless street kitchen gives you a mound of ingredients and a crash course in how to eat *banh xeo*, an egg, shrimp and pork pancake which you roll in rice-paper with selected greens.

Shopping

With the influx of tourists, Hoi An's craft industries have revived and the town's becoming a centre for **arts** and antiques, though by no means everything is genuine and there's plenty of second-rate stuff. Dedicated browsers will find galleries and shops along Tran Phu and Nguyen Thai Hoc occupy an hour or two, while just over the Japanese bridge a cluster of old houses doubling as showrooms are also worth a look. If you're keen on the local **stone-carvings** then buy them here – they're generally better quality than at the Marble Mountains or in Da Nang. The other bargain in Hoi An is **silk** and tailoring, with prices comparable with those in Hanoi or Ho Chi Minh City. You'll find silk shops all along Tran Phu but the original outlet was the market, where even now rows of tailors sit at sewing machines next to rainbow-coloured stacks, and for a few dollars will knock-up beautiful garments in a matter of hours. At Thanh Ha **pottery** village near Hoi An (see p.237) you can buy sturdy, hand-thrown pots or perhaps a clay money-jar in pleasingly simple designs.

Listings

Banks and exchange *Hoi An Bank*, at 4 Hoang Dieu, and *Hoi An Hotel*, exchange dollar notes and travellers' cheques.

Ferries From the market end of Bach Dang, small ferry boats depart for villages along the Thu Bon River.

Post office The GPO at 5 Tran Hung Dao boasts *poste restante* in addition to the usual services.

River trips Along Bach Dang, sampan-owners tout excursions on the river at $1 an hour, or you can take a boat out to the craft villages and downstream as far as the Cua Dai estuary (see pp.237–238). Starting prices vary from $5 to $8 per hour for an 8-person boat, but it's worth bargaining.

Tour agencies Best of the bunch seems to be *Hoi An Booking Office* (also known as *Hai's Café*; ☎051/861928), at 23 Tran Hung Dao, though *Nineteen's Booking Office* (☎051/861937), a few doors down at no. 19, also gets good recommendations.

MOVING ON FROM HOI AN

Onward transport is a highly organized business in Hoi An, with **cars** and tourist **minibuses** vying to take you **to Hué** (at about $5 per person), **Nha Trang** ($10–15 per person) and so on. The epicentre of all this activity is the *Hoi An Hotel*, 6 Tran Hung Dao, where you can sign-up for your chosen destination, day of travel and even mode of transport (depending on what's passing through town); alternatively, try guesthouses, restaurants or one of the **tour agencies** listed above.

Any of these places will also be able to help with transport up the coast **to Da Nang**; by far the best way to get there is by **hired car** ($8–10) or **Honda om** ($2–3), particularly as you can then stop off at the Marble Mountains and Non Nuoc beach (see p.250) en route. Local **buses** plying between Hoi An and Da Nang are very much a last resort: ancient, colourful pick-ups, stuffed to the gunnels, leave Hoi An bus station every three hours or so, taking up to two hours to cover the 30km ($1–2; services stop around 4 or 5pm).

Around Hoi An

One of Hoi An's attractions is to bike out along meandering paths to a nearby village, or hop on a sampan to one of the islands of the Thu Bon River, just for the ride. There are a couple of **pagodas** to head for just north of Hoi An, or the white expanse of **Cua Dai Beach** is an easy bike ride out to the east. River tours take you to low-lying, estuarine islands and the craft villages along their banks, while it's also now possible to visit the distant **Cham Islands**, renowned for their sea swallows' nests. Turning inland, Hoi An makes a good base from which to visit the sacred heartland of the ancient Champa kingdom, **My Son**. Despite extensive war-damage and the rough ride out there, the sanctuary is well worth devoting a day to, a mystical place which still bears witness to the once-vibrant Cham civilization. Finally, heading north, both China Beach and the Marble Mountains (see p.250) are convenient stops on the road to Da Nang, or can be covered on an easy day's outing from Hoi An.

Pagodas and beaches

A popular bike ride takes you along the sandy tracks north of Hoi An, into an area studded with graves and nurseries growing miniature tangerines. The final destination is two small pagodas whose main attraction is their quiet gardens of wizened trees, orchids and bougainvillea. **Chua Chuc Thanh** (or *Nam Thanh*) was founded in 1454 by Minh Hai, Hoi An's first Buddhist monk; his renovated stupa is the tallest in the enclosure. To get there, turn right off Le Hong Phong just after the open-air theatre and follow a dirt road about 120m straight to the pagoda. **Chua Phuoc Lam** is 300m west of Chuc Thanh, past an obelisk and over a small canal. The pagoda garden is full of frangipani trees and moss-covered memorials, many of them decorated with a mosaic of pottery fragments and antique glazed dishes.

Alternatively, **Cua Dai Beach** is a pleasant four-kilometre bike ride heading due east along Tran Hung Dao, quickly leaving Hoi An behind for empty roads and rice fields. The beach is long, clean and white, coracles bob offshore and cold beers are on sale, though you'll probably want to walk some way up the beach away from the notoriously aggressive beach attendants who rent out deck chairs. It's not surprising, given the popularity of Hoi An and the beach's natural appeal, that Cua Dai is earmarked for hotel development.

Islands

A group of mountainous islands lying 10km offshore are clearly visible from the coast near Hoi An. *Cu Lao Cham* or the **Cham Islands** are inhabited by fishermen, the navy and collectors of highly prized birds' nests. Cham islanders have been harvesting sea swallows' nests since the late sixteenth century and today the government-controlled trade contributes greatly to the local economy, with prices up to $2500 per kilo for the culinary delicacy, which is also attributed with extraordinary medicinal virtues. So each spring, when thousands of the tiny birds nestle among the islands' caves and crevices, villagers build bamboo scaffolding or climb up ropes to prize the diminutive structures, about the size of a hen's egg, off the rock. Three thousand people live on the main island, where there's no electricity, but until 1995 even Vietnamese people weren't allowed to visit because of the naval base. Now you can take a boat trip out to the main island (2hr each way), to swim, wander round the fishing village or climb in the mountains. As yet there are no hotels or other facilities on the islands, and the day-trips are aimed at tour parties ($140 for a 12-person boat). However, individual tours are planned, and will probably cost around $20 per person for a minimum of three people; ask at the *Tourist Office of Hoi An* (see p.227) for the latest.

Specialist **craft villages** inhabited by skilled artisans, developed around Hoi An during the sixteenth and seventeenth centuries. The work of one famous community of stone and woodcarvers, from *Kim Bong* village, can be seen throughout Hoi An. Most carpenters have moved out of the village but a handful remain on **Cam Kim Island**, building fishing boats or crafting furniture for export. The large island is a ten-minute ride from the Hoi An ferry station (see "Listings", on facing page) heading west up the river; you'll find one of the few surviving boatyards right beside the island's jetty. In the same direction, **Thanh Ha** is a pottery village where you can see pots hand-thrown and then fired in brick kilns. Both these and other craft villages can be visited on a **river tour from Hoi An**; either approach the boatmen direct, or go through a tour agency (see "Listings", p.236, for details of river trips and tour agencies).

My Son

Vietnam's most evocative Cham site, **MY SON** (daily 7.30am–5.30pm; $2), lies 40km southwest of Hoi An, in a bowl of lushly wooded hills towered over by aptly named Cat's Tooth Mountain. The track out to the site strikes west from Highway 1 at Duy Xuyen. It's quite possible to rent a **motorbike** in Hoi An or Da Nang and travel to My Son independently. Given the treacherous state of the track, however, unless you are a competent rider, taking a **tour** (about $7 per person; see p.236 and p.250 for agencies) is much the better way to see the place. My Son may be no Vietnamese Angkor Wat, but it richly deserves its place on the tourist map. The near-tangible sense of faded majesty that hangs over its mouldering ruins is enhanced by the vegetation rioting over the extant towers, by the assorted *lingam* and Sanskrit stelae strewn around, and by its isolated rural setting, whose peace is broken only by the wood gatherers who trace the paths around the surrounding coffee and eucalyptus glades.

Excavations at My Son have revealed that Cham kings were buried here as early as the fourth century, indicating that the site was established by the rulers of the early Champa capital of **Simhapura** (sited some 30km back towards the highway, at present-day Tra Kieu); see box on p.204 for more on the **Kingdom of Champa**. The stone towers and sanctuaries whose remnants you see today were erected between the seventh and thirteenth centuries, with successive dynasties adding more temples to this holy place, until in its prime it comprised some seventy buildings. The area was considered the domain of gods and god-kings, and living on-site would have been an attendant population of priests, dancers and servants.

The inventory of My Son's elegant assembly of ruins, compiled by the French archeologists who discovered them late last century, gathered all its buildings into distinct groups, prosaically labelled A, B, C, and so forth. Within these groups, each monument was given its own number. The Chams' fine **masonry** skills – instead of mortar, they used a resin mixed with ground mollusc shells and crushed bricks, which left only hairline cracks between brick courses – ensured that the passing of the centuries left much for the French to admire. But after the Viet Cong based themselves here in the Sixties, many unique buildings were pounded to oblivion by American B52s, most notably the once-magnificent A1 Tower. Craters around the site, now full of water and blanketed with lilies, testify to this tragic period in My Son's history.

While we've outlined a handful of the site's particularly noteworthy edifices below, you'll get most out of My Son simply by wandering at your leisure – but don't stray far from the towers, as **unexploded mines** may still be in the ground.

Groups B and C

Once you've rounded the corner from the traders who harangue you to buy their fake Cham statuettes and overpriced drinks at the **entrance**, it's a ten-minute hike to the first of My Son's edifices. Of all the groupings of ruins at My Son, those labelled B, C and D most warrant your attention: viewing these, it's possible, with a little stirring of the imagination, to visualize how a functioning temple complex would have appeared in My Son's heyday.

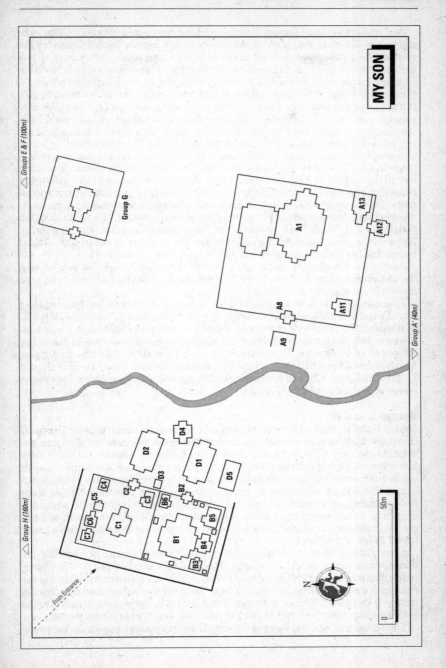

Archeologists regard **Group B** as the spiritual epicentre of My Son. Of the central **kalan**, **B1**, only the base remains, along with a *lingam* discovered under the foundations a few years ago; but stone epitaphs found nearby reveal that it was dedicated to the god-king Bhadresvara, a hybrid of Shiva and fourth-century King Bhadravarman, and erected in the eleventh century, under King Harivarman IV. Fortunately, other elements of Group B have fared rather better, particularly **B5**, the impressive **repository-room**, boasting a bowed, boat-shaped roof still in reasonably good nick. Votive offerings and other ritual paraphernalia would have been stored in B5's chimney-shaped interior, whose extravagant masonry is pitted by bulletholes from skirmishes between GIs and VC guerrillas. The outer walls support ornate columns and statues of deities, and, on the western side, a bas-relief depicting two elephants with their trunks entwined around a coconut tree. The carving of Vishnu sitting below the thirteen heads of the snake-god Naga that adorned the roof of **B6** was an early casualty of war, but the oval **receptacle** for the holy water used in purification rituals and statue-washing ceremonies is still intact inside. The two smaller temples flanking B1's south-side, **B3** and **B4**, would have been dedicated to Skanda and Ganesha, the children of Shiva; while posted around the complex are the remains of seven tiny shrines honouring the gods of the elements and of the points of the compass.

East of the foundations of B1, and precisely aligned with it, is D1 (see below), the **mandapa**, where the priests would meditate prior to proceeding through the (now-ruined) gate **B2**, to worship.

A similar pattern is at work next door in **Group C**, a complex quite distinct from B, and originally separated from it by a wall. This time the central *kalan*, **C1**, is standing and fairly well preserved, though the statue of Shiva that it was built to house long since went to Da Nang's museum, leaving only its base in place. The statues of standing gods around the walls have been allowed to stay, though, as has the carved lintel that runs across the entrance. As with Group B, C1 is aligned both with its gate, **C2**, and its mandapa, **D2**, outside which stands an impressive statue of Vishnu's vehicle, **Garuda**.

Groups D and A

East of B and C, the two long, windowed meditation halls that comprise **Group D** have now both been converted into modest **galleries**. **D1** contains a *lingam*, the remains of a carving of Shiva, and some statues of cows; while in **D2** you'll see a fine frieze depicting many-armed Shiva dancing, and, below the steps up to its eastern entrance, a statue of Garuda. The ground between these two galleries was named the **Court of Stelae** by early archeologists, a reference to the stone tablets, etched with Sanskrit script, that litter it. As well as these stelae, altars and statues of deities would have stood in the court, though all that remain of these are their plinths, on whose sides are sculpted images of dancing women, arms raised to carry their gods.

Bomb damage was particularly cruel in the vicinity of **Group A**, reducing the once-spectacular *kalan*, **A1**, to a heap of toppled columns and lintels that closely resembles a collapsed hall of cards. Unusually, A1 was constructed with an eastern and a western entrance; within, a huge *lingam* base is ringed by a number of detailed, 15cm-high figures at prayer. You'll pass **A9**, the mandapa, and **A8**, the gate, en route from B, C and D; **A11** would have been the repository-room.

The remaining bits and bobs of **Group A'** are presently too overgrown to see.

Other groups

The remains of hilltop **Group G**, 60m north of Group A, have only recently been prised out of the undergrowth. The main *kalan* is badly weathered, but you can still pick out lion faces, sporting toothsome fangs and bulbous eyes, carved into its sides. A *lingam* stands at the *kalan*'s southwestern corner, with breasts around its base; while a horned gargoyle stands sentry at the southeastern corner. From Group G, a path leads on to **groups E and F**, though bomb damage was bad here, and only a handful of *lingam* and stelae, and a rounded *lingam* base, have survived. Odd walls and piles of bricks are all that remain of **Group H**.

Da Nang

Sitting on the southerly curve of a vast, well-protected bay, **DA NANG** has developed into central Vietnam's dominant port and its fourth-largest city. The real spur to this growth came in the American War when the neighbouring airbase spawned the greatest concentration of US military personnel in South Vietnam. But walking around central Da Nang today, it's the earlier, French presence which is more apparent, in the leafy boulevards and some classy, colonial edifices along the elegant, riverfront promenade. Considering its size (over 400,000 in population), its history and the fact that this is a major transport hub, offering air connections as well as road and rail links, Da Nang is an unexpectedly relaxed, amiable place.

Though Da Nang harbours few specific sights of its own, beyond the **Cham Museum** with its unique collection of Cham sculpture, the city makes a reasonable base for exploring this stretch of coast, offering a less atmospheric but also less touristy alternative to Hoi An. Some of Vietnam's best **beaches** are to be found only a few kilometres from the city (see "Around Da Nang", p.250), while, further afield, My Son (see above) and Hoi An itself can be covered on day-trips.

Some history

During the sixteenth and seventeenth centuries trading vessels waiting to unload at Fai Fo (Hoi An) often sheltered in nearby Da Nang Bay, until Hoi An's harbour began silting-up and Da Nang developed into a major **port** in its own right. After 1802, when Hué became capital of Vietnam, Da Nang naturally served as the principal point of arrival for foreign delegations to the royal court. The new emperor, Gia Long, had earlier promised France a concession at Da Nang (which the French called **Tourane**) in return for their help in gaining the throne, but it didn't become a reality until 1888 after the French had repeatedly attacked the port.

In 1954 Vietnam was effectively partitioned at the Seventeenth Parallel only 200km north of Da Nang, from where bombing sorties could easily reach into communist-held territory or strike westwards to the Ho Chi Minh Trail. The city grew rapidly around the South Vietnamese airbase and then mushroomed after 1965 when America entered the war in earnest, heralded by the arrival of the first American combat troops on March 8, 1965. An advance guard of two battalions of Marines waded ashore at Red Beach in Da Nang Bay, providing the press with a photo opportunity that included amphibious landing craft, helicopters and young Vietnamese women handing out garlands – not quite as the generals had envisaged. The Marines had come to defend Da Nang's massive **US Air Force base**;

as the troops flew in so the base sprawled. Eventually Da Nang became "a small American city", as journalist John Pilger remembers it, "with its own generators, water purification plants, hospitals, cinemas, bowling alleys, ball parks, tennis courts, jogging tracks, supermarkets and bars, lots of bars". For most US troops the approach to Da Nang airfield formed their first impression of Vietnam, and it was here they came to take a break from the war at the famous **China Beach**.

At the same time the city swelled with thousands of **refugees**, mostly villagers cleared from "free-fire zones" but also people in search of work – labourers, cooks, laundry staff, pimps, prostitutes and drug pushers, all inhabiting a shantytown called Dogpatch on the base perimeter. Da Nang's population rose inexorably: 20,000 in the 1940s, 50,000 in 1955 and, some estimate, a peak of one million during the American years. North Vietnamese mortar shells periodically fell in and around the base, but the city's most violent scenes occurred when two South Vietnamese generals engaged in a little power struggle. In March 1966 Vice Air Marshal Ky, then prime minister of South Vietnam, ousted a popular Hué overlord, General Thi, following his open support of Buddhist dissidents. Demonstrations spread from Hué to Da Nang where troops loyal to Thi seized the airfield in what amounted to a **mini-civil war**. After much posturing Ky crushed the revolt two months later, killing hundreds of rebel troops and many civilians. In the preceding chaos, the beleaguered rebels held forty Western journalists hostage for a brief period in Da Nang's largest pagoda, Chua Tinh Hoi, while streets around filled with Buddhist protestors.

When the North Vietnamese Army finally arrived to **liberate** Da Nang on March 29, 1975, they had less of a struggle. Communist units had already cut the road south and panic-stricken South Vietnamese soldiers battled for space on any plane or boat leaving the city, firing on unarmed civilians; many drowned in the struggle to reach fishing boats, while planes and tanks were abandoned to the enemy. Da Nang had been all but deserted by South Vietnamese forces, leaving the mighty base to be "taken by a dozen NLF cadres waving white handkerchiefs from the back of a truck", according to John Pilger. After 1975 thousands of refugees were sent back to their native villages or packed-off to reclaim agricultural land. Da Nang's army faction still wields considerable power but under a newly appointed, dynamic city administration their grip is beginning to weaken, as evidenced by a more liberal outlook, less suspicion of foreigners, and an upbeat local economy.

Arrival, information and getting around

Da Nang's smart new **airport** is only 3km southwest of the city. Outside the terminal taxis and motorbikes compete for passengers at around $5 for a taxi and $1–2 by Honda om into the centre. The **train station** lies 2km west of town at 122 Hai Phong, while long-distance **buses** arrive at Lien Tinh bus station, 33 Dien Bien Phu, 1km further out. Local buses from Hoi An – colourful, top-heavy pick-ups – pull in to a central bus station opposite Con Market at the west end of Hung Vuong.

Danang Tourist is the largest and most upmarket of the three main **tour agencies** (see "Listings", p.250), though *Danatours* offers slightly better deals aimed at the budget traveller. Both these offices and *Vietnamtourism* can help with various day-trips, and provide a basic **information** service. **Exchange facilities** are available at *Vietcombank*, 104 Le Loi, including credit-card transactions and travellers' cheques, with a more limited operation for the northern hotels at *VID*

Public Bank, 2 Tran Phu. The main **post office** overlooks the river at 60 Bach Dang, but cross the Le Duan junction to find *poste restante* at no. 62, announcing "foreign services post office". Bookstalls along the riverfront here sell Da Nang **maps**, English-language newspapers and a few tourist guides.

Da Nang is big enough and its sights sufficiently spread out to make walking round town fairly time consuming. Several hotels and tour agents offer **bicycle rental** at $1 per day, otherwise there's no shortage of cyclos or Honda oms. **Car rental** ($20–30 per day) and self-drive **motorbikes** ($5–7) are available from tour agencies and from almost every hotel, restaurant, café, cigarette vendor – you name it. Try the gentlemanly, English-speaking Mr Hai (☎051/824809), who has a solid reputation for price and reliability; find him at the far north end of Yen Bai, down an alley beside no. 6/8 . The *Travel Shop* at the *Hoai Huong Guesthouse* (see below) also offers competitive rates. From opposite the junction of Bach Dang and Phan Dinh Phung, small passenger **ferries** shuttle across the Han River to Son Tra peninsula, providing a short cut for cyclists on the way to My Khe Beach.

Accommodation

Although many of Da Nang's hotels are geared to the business market and tour groups, so many new hotels have opened that there's now a **glut** and off-season bargaining is possible. Furthermore, **mini-hotels** have recently eased in at the cheaper end to give a reasonable spread of accommodation. Hotels are found scattered throughout central Da Nang, though more expensive places tend to concentrate on or near Bach Dang, which the authorities plan to transform into a tourist boulevard. Most, but by no means all, of the prostitutes that used to hang around Da Nang hotels, especially those on Dong Da, have been moved on.

Bach Đang, 50 Bach Dang (☎051/823649, fax 821659). Seven floors on the riverfront with good views, while behind lurks an old guesthouse with more character, big balconies, bigger baths but no view. All rooms are comfortably furnished, and boast satellite TV. ④

Binh Duong, 32 Tran Phu (☎051/827666, fax 827666). An expanding private mini-hotel catering mostly for long-term rentals but worth trying if you want all the trimmings – IDD, satellite TV etc. Cheaper rooms are cramped and a little overpriced but it's friendly and clean. ③

Da Nang, 3–5 Dong Da (☎051/821986, fax 823431). A 4-block, 200-room complex created out of the old Da Nang and Marble Mountains hotels, formerly US Army officers' billets. Now in mid-renovation to 3-star level but for the moment its range of well-appointed rooms offer good value. The hotel is a bit out of the way, but it's served by a clutch of cafés opposite and there's reasonably priced transport for hire at reception. ①–②

Hoai Huong Guesthouse, 105 Tran Phu (☎051/824874). A central location plus some of the cheapest rooms in Da Nang make this a popular venue, where cold water and some partition walls are acceptable at these rates. It's also clean and friendly with well-priced transport downstairs in the *Travel Shop*. ①

Hung Vuong Mini-hotel, 95 Hung Vuong (☎051/823967, fax 824023). *Danatours* offers a few inexpensive rooms in their French-era building right in the middle of town. Rooms are big and basic but well swept, quiet and come with hot water plus air-con. ①

Hung Vuong, 123 Nguyen Chi Thanh (☎051/829099, fax 822037). A more modern and upmarket *Danatours* establishment whose good-value rooms all come with hot water, air-con and telephone. Central and well cared for. ②–③

Marco Polo, 11c Quang Trung (☎051/823295, fax 827279). Da Nang's most glitzy hotel by a long chalk, owned by Hanoi's Royal Hotel Group. Their smallish, standard rooms are decorated to international standards, while executive suites boast 3 rooms, 2 TVs, 3 telephones, 2 fridges and a huge price tag. ⑤

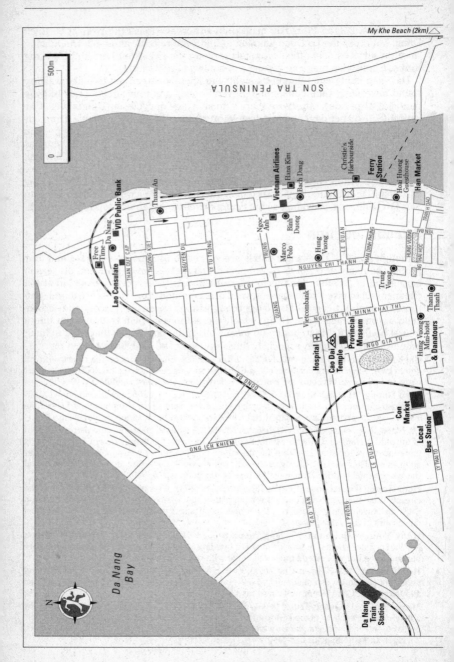

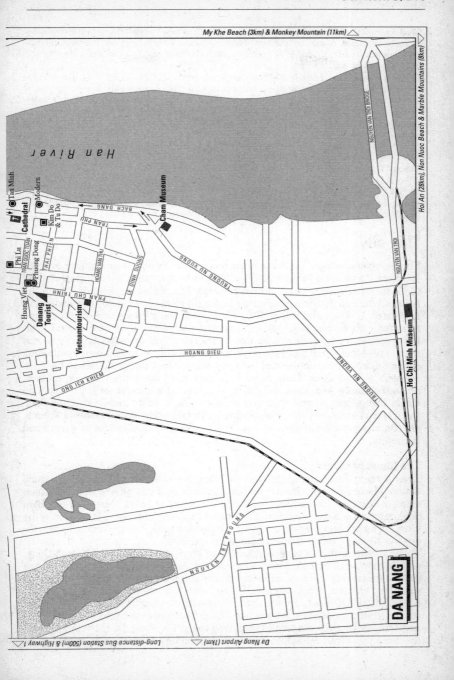

My Khe Beach (3km) & Monkey Mountain (11km)

Han River

Hoi An (28km), Non Nuoc Beach & Marble Mountains (8km)

NGUYEN VAN TROI BRIDGE

NGUYEN VAN TROI

Tan Minh

Modern

Cathedral

Kim Do & Tu Do

Phi Lu

Phuong Dong

TRAN QUOC TOAN

THAI PHIEN

Huong Viet

Danang Tourist

Vietnamtourism

BACH DANG

TRAN PHU

Cham Museum

HOANG VAN THU

LE DINH DUONG

PHAN CHU TRINH

DUONG TRAN PHU

TRUONG NU VUONG

HOANG DIEU

ONG ICH KHIEM

TRUONG NU VUONG

Ho Chi Minh Museum

NGUYEN TRI PHUONG

DA NANG

Long-distance Bus Station (500m) & Highway 1

Da Nang Airport (1km)

Modern, 182 Bach Dang (☎051/820113, fax 821842). A new riverfront hotel with views from its more expensive rooms and the third-floor restaurant. Even bottom-end rooms, some with no window, get IDD, TV, fridge and immaculate bathrooms, and you may get a discount rate from the helpful staff. ③

Phuong Dong (*Orient Hotel*), 93 Phan Chu Trinh (☎051/821266, fax 822854). The lobby of this central hotel maintains an off-putting gloom while rooms are slowly being rejuvenated. Top category rooms, aimed at long-term rentals, are more spacious and offer river views. Standard rooms come with all the trimmings but are small and dingy for the price. ④

Tan Minh, 142 Bach Dang (☎051/827456, fax 830172). Reservations are a must for this popular hotel at the south end of Bach Dang, handy for the Cham Museum. The spotlessly clean, homely mini-hotel is topped by a panoramic fifth-floor restaurant. All rooms have air-con, telephone and fridge. Bike rental available. ②–③

Thanh Thanh, 50 Phan Chu Trinh (☎051/830684, fax 829886). A big hotel, of 53 rooms, offering cheap rates for the city centre, with a choice of cold water and fan, or hot water and air-con. The bathrooms are run-down but otherwise it's reasonably spruce. ②

Trung Vuong, 118 Nguyen Chi Thanh (☎051/834159). Despite the off-putting exterior the Trung Vuong's refurbished rooms aren't bad value. Very central. ②

The city

The elongated oval of Da Nang occupies a small headland protruding into the southern curve of Da Nang Bay. The city faces east, fronting onto Bach Dang and the Han River, across which the narrow Son Tra peninsula shelters it from the South China Sea. Its streets follow a rough grid-plan, dissected by two main thoroughfares, Le Duan and Le Loi/Phan Chu Trinh. Hung Vuong and streets around form the commercial heart of Da Nang, running between the two central **markets**: sprawling, oppressive Cho Con in the west and orderly Cho Han by the river. Two blocks south of Han market, past the soft, salmon-mousse cathedral, colonial Da Nang is represented by a few wooden and stucco houses at the eastern end of Tran Quoc Toan. From here turn right along the river for 750m to reach the **Cham Museum**, the city's prime tourist attraction, or left to stroll up **Bach Dang**, past several cluttered ship chandlers. In its middle reaches Bach Dang is a pleasant, riverfront boulevard with a collection of well-restored French-era administrative buildings now occupied by People's Committees or earmarked for hotels.

The Cham Museum

Even if you're just passing through Da Nang, try to spare an hour for the small **Cham Museum** (daily 7am–6pm; $2), particularly if you plan to visit the Cham ruins at My Son (see p.238). Note that the small booklet, "Museum of Cham Sculpture in Da Nang" (Foreign Languages Publishing House; $1) on sale at the kiosk, is an academic work, outlining the historical background and Cham artistic development, rather than a guide to the exhibits.

The museum sits in a garden of frangipani trees at the south end of Bach Dang, and its display of graceful, sometimes severe, terracotta and sandstone figures gives a tantalizing glimpse of an artistically inspired culture that ruled most of southern Vietnam for a thousand years (see box on p.204 for more on the Kingdom of Champa). In the late nineteenth century French archeologists started collecting statues, friezes and altars from once-magnificent Cham cities and sanctuaries dotted around the hinterland of Da Nang. In 1916 they opened the museum in an attractive, open-sided building whose design incorporates

Cham motifs; though this is undoubtedly the most comprehensive display of Cham art in the world, it's said many of the best statues were carried off into European private collections.

Exhibits are grouped according to their place of origin in four rooms starting from the left as you enter: sculpture from My Son (4–11C) in the left wing; Tra Kieu (Simhapura; 4–10C) in the connecting building, with the Dong Duong pieces (Indrapura; 8–10C) in an annexe behind; and finally, sculpture from Binh Dinh Province (11–15C) occupies the right wing. Recurring images in Cham art are lions, elephants and Hindu deities, predominantly Shiva (founder and defender of Champa) expressed either as a vigorous, full-lipped man or as a *lingam*, but Vishnu, Garuda, Ganesha and Nandi the bull are also portrayed. Buddhas feature strongly in the ninth-century art of Indrapura, a period when Khmer and Indonesian influences were gradually assimilated. But the most distinctive icon is Uroja, a breast and nipple that represents the universal "mother" of Cham kings.

The first two rooms demonstrate Cham art at its height. A massive, square altar pedestal (late seventh century) from the religious centre of My Son is considered a masterpiece of early Cham craftsmanship, particularly its frieze depicting jaunty dancing-girls, and a soulful flute player. However, experts and amateurs alike usually nominate two lithe dancers with Mona Lisa smiles, their soft, round bodies seemingly clad in nothing but strings of pearls, as the zenith of Cham artistry. The piece, displayed in the second room, also features two musicians on a fragment of capital produced by Tra Kieu sculptors in the late tenth century, just before Cham art, and the Champa kingdom, started to decline. A monumental, seventh-century altar dominates the Tra Kieu room; scenes of Princess Sita's wedding from the Hindu epic *Ramayana* decorate the pedestal frieze.

As the Viets pushed south during the eleventh century so the Chams retreated, and their sculptures evolved a bold, cubic style. Though less refined than earlier works, the chunky mythical animals from this period retain a distinctive, playful charm and a pleasing solidity.

Other museums

None of Da Nang's three other museums need take up much of your time. The small **Ho Chi Minh Museum**, is worth a quick look only if you'll miss Hanoi's more modern version. Photos and documents predominate but the museum does boast a faithful replica of Ho's stilthouse – even down to the works of Lenin on Ho's desk. The same compound contains a much larger museum relating the history of the **5th Military Zone Army**. Huge swathes of the four floors' exhibits are incomprehensible, despite the chaperone-guide, but coverage of the American War and anti-Pol Pot campaigns in Cambodia liven things up a bit, as does a forecourt stuffed with weaponry captured in various wars or abandoned in 1975. Find the two museums 1km south of the Cham Museum and west of the Han River bridge at 10 Nguyen Van Troi (Tues–Sun 7.30–11am & 1.30–4.30pm; $1 fee covers admission to both museums).

A colonial building with a US helicopter out front buried among boscage houses the **Provincial Museum**, *Bao Tang Quang Nam–Da Nang*, at 24 Le Duan (Tues–Sun 7–11am & 1–3pm; $1). It inevitably covers much the same ground as those above, though devotes more space to the region's ethnic minorities and is better supplied with English translations. Parts of the museum are closed, and opening times are largely theoretical while it undergoes a very plodding renovation, but rooms completed so far, such as the American War display, are promising. If workmen ever get up to the top floors it'll be worth taking a look at the ethnic minority exhibition, highlight of which is a beautifully melodic water harp made by Sedang people. The twenty-metre-long harp is constructed of bamboo sections strung together and weighted with stones. When placed in a stream the flow stirs the bamboo to create a haunting sound believed to ward off wild beasts and evil spirits.

Cao Dai Temple

Da Nang's **Cao Dai Temple**, built in 1956, is Vietnam's second most important after Tay Ninh (see p.110), where an elderly archbishop, assisted by seventeen priests, ministers to a congregation said to number 50,000. The temple is a smaller, more simple version of Tay Ninh, dominated inside by the all-seeing eye of the Supreme Being and paintings of Cao Dai's principal saints, Lao-tzu, Confucius, Jesus Christ and Buddha. Services were banned between 1975 and 1986 and the building locked up, but now adherents gather to worship four times a day (6am, noon, 6pm, midnight). The occasional tourists that do turn up receive a warm welcome from priests keen to explain the religion's history and its colourful intricacies (see box on p.111 for more on these tenets).

Eating

Da Nang has no shortage of places to eat, ranging from foodstalls to full-blown, top-notch restaurants, and a couple of decent local beers – *Da Nang Export* and *Bière la Rue* – to quaff as sundowners at a Bach Dang drinks stand. Fruitful hunting grounds for local restaurants and **foodstalls** are along Ly Tu Trong, the southern end of Nguyen Thi Minh Khai, and streets around the *Phuong Dong Hotel* crossroads. There's another clutch opposite the *Trung Vuong Hotel* on Nguyen Chi Thanh; try no. 125 for a filling breakfast omelette or a beef steak (*bittet*) with warm bread. **Cafés** and cake shops dot Phan Chu Trinh south of the junction with Hung Vuong, or head for a small stall at 56 Nguyen Thi Minh Khai near the *Hung Vuong Mini-hotel*, for a delicious, iced glass of *chè xavan*. This Lao variant of the traditional Vietnamese "sweet soup", brought back from Savannakhet by the friendly patron, includes potato, mushroom and coconut – it tastes a lot better than it sounds.

Christie's Harbourside, 9 Bach Dang. Comfy rattan chairs, satellite TV, book exchange *and* great views of river-life from this breezy, New Zealand-run café-restaurant perched over the Han River. Not the cheapest place in town but ample portions of comfort food – lasagne, fish and chips, toasted sandwiches – plus a number of well-prepared Vietnamese dishes and lots of fresh seafood.

Free Time, 6 Dong Da. The best of several small café-bars lined up opposite the *Da Nang Hotel*. American-inspired decor with rattan seating, bar stools and good music. The food's reasonable, a mix of Western and local fast-food dishes, and not overpriced.

Hana Kim, 7 Bach Dang. Da Nang's plushest dining, on the riverbank opposite the *Bach Dang Hotel*, in elegant air-con rooms or outside terraces. Prices are high but not unaffordable, offering a menu of Western and Asian foods, with fish specialities.

Huong Viet, 77 Tran Quoc Toan. A popular, mid-range restaurant on the corner with Phan Chu Trinh. The dining area consists of several small rooms while the extensive menu offers traditional Vietnamese dishes; the steamed fish is especially recommended.

Kim Do, 174 Tran Phu. One of Da Nang's most well-known restaurants, serving a broad range of good-quality Vietnamese cuisine. Comfortable, air-con dining to soothing music with attentive service, though a bit soulless for some. The quality is good but prices are high and it possibly doesn't deserve its fulsome reputation.

Ngoc Anh, 30 Tran Phu (☎051/822778). Arrive early or make a reservation for one of the tables in a shaded, garden courtyard, or you'll be stuck in a characterless air-con room. Generous portions of tasty sour soups and seafood specialities at manageable prices; try stuffed crabs, fresh prawns or the more modest seafood noodles.

Phi Lu, 249 Nguyen Chi Thanh. Moderate prices, friendly staff – and even a stab at interior decoration – make this place popular among locals, but tables begin to come free around 7.30–8pm. Serves a limited range of Chinese food plus Vietnamese-French dishes from an English menu.

Tu Do, 172 Tran Phu. This highly rated open-air restaurant packs more atmosphere than neighbouring *Kim Do* thanks to the vivacious Mr Ky aided by his attentive colleagues, backed up by great local cuisine at moderate prices. Not the place for a quiet, cosy meal, however.

Listings

Airlines *Vietnam Airlines*, 35 Tran Phu (☎051/821130).

Banks and exchange *Vietcombank*, 104 Le Loi; *VID Public Bank*, 2 Tran Phu.

Hospital *Benh Vien C*, 76 Hai Phong, opposite the Cao Dai Temple (☎051/821118).

Immigration police 71 Le Loi. The place to go if you've lost your passport or have similar difficulties.

Nightlife Talk of the town is the new *Royal Palace Dancing* next to the *Royal Hotel* offering live music (6pm–2am; $3). *Da Nang Hotel* also hosts live bands, popular with a young local crowd, though the drinks are pricey (8–11pm; $3); and opposite is the *Harmony Hotel*'s disco and karaoke rooms (8.30–11pm; $2).

Post office Main office at 60 Bach Dang, *poste restante* at no. 62; other branches at 56 Hung Vuong and 8 Phan Chu Trinh.

MOVING ON FROM DA NANG

Heading on **up the coast to Hué** it's a difficult choice between road and rail over the dramatic Hai Van Pass. If you plump for **train**, the early morning service (6am) is faster; ask for seats on the right, looking east, for the best views as the train hugs the cliff. Highway 1 winds much higher but keeps more inland and clouds often shroud the top; **buses** for Hué leave from the main Lien Tinh bus station or, preferably, hire a car and driver ($20–30) or Honda om ($10) for the three- to four-hour trip so you can stop to enjoy the scenery.

Motorbikes wait outside Da Nang train station to whisk you off to **Hoi An** or **Non Nuoc** (for the Marble Mountains and beach): a one-way ride out to Hoi An (45min) should cost $4–5 with a bit of bargaining, plus a touch more if you want to visit Non Nuoc en route; the same journey by taxi or hire car will come in at around $15. Local buses run out to Hoi An from a bus station opposite Con market but are way too overcrowded to be a comfortable, or safe, proposition; buses leave roughly every three hours and the journey takes between one and a half and two hours ($1–2).

The only land crossing **into Laos** open to foreigners is Lao Bao border gate, west of Dong Ha (see p.288 for details). At present the *Lao Consulate* in Da Nang, located at 12 Tran Quy Cap (☎051/821208; Mon–Fri 8–11.30am & 2–4.30pm), issues only seven-day transit visas ($25; allow 2 working days); see p.349 for information on regular tourist visas. Da Nang tour agencies (see over) can help with changing your visa exit-point. An **overnight bus** service runs from Da Nang's Lien Tinh bus station direct to Savannakhet four times a week (Mon, Wed, Thurs and Sun; 6–7hr; $8).

Silks and tailoring Outlets line Hung Vuong and Phan Chu Trinh streets. Try *Hanh Silk Shop* at 91 Phan Chu Trinh, or the state silk company, *Silkco*, at 38 Quang Trung.

Taxi Metred taxis are operated by *MASCO* (☎051/825555).

Tour agencies *Danatours*, 95 Hung Vuong (☎051/823993, fax 824023); *Danang Tourist*, 92a Phan Chu Trinh (☎051/821423, fax 821560); *Vietnamtourism*, 158 Phan Chu Trinh (☎051/822990, fax 822999).

Around Da Nang

Beaches are mostly what's around Da Nang, from Red Beach (Nam O) in the north where the first US Marines came ashore, down the broad, bleached-white fringe of **China Beach**, and continuing all the way south through **Non Nuoc** to Hoi An. Of all the beaches in Vietnam, these are the most coveted by international resort developers and terrain is already being carved up, boding ill for this empty, attractive coastline. A note of warning, however: there's a powerful undertow off this coast and when the northeast, winter monsoon blows up, riptides become particularly dangerous. Beach guards operate during certain hours at resorts, where flags indicate safe swimming areas. Best months on the beach are April to August, with peak season for local holidaymakers in July and August.

Heading south down the coast, past old US installations occupied these days by the People's Army, a group of abrupt hills constitute the coast's other main tourist attraction, usually a stop on the trip to Hoi An: the **Marble Mountains**. The five limestone and marble knobbles are peppered with sacred caves, wrapped in legend – and liberally sprinkled with souvenir stands, litter and hawker hordes. For generations Non Nuoc village at the mountains' base has resonated with the chink of stone-masons chiselling away at religious statues, memorials and imitation Cham figures. Further south still, both Hoi An (p.226) and My Son (p.238) can also be visited on day-trips from Da Nang. Up the coast from Da Nang, Highway 1 zigzags over the **Hai Van Pass**, affording sweeping views of the bay and north to the brilliant white sands of **Lang Co** beach. Both these places make an easy day's excursion from Da Nang, or can be covered conveniently on the road to Hué.

South of Da Nang

Long, lumpy Son Tra peninsula, tipped by **Monkey Mountain**, shelters Da Nang and its port from the worst winter monsoons. The peninsula's seaward side provides the city with its nearest unpolluted beach, My Khe, the original **China Beach**; its rival to the south, the quieter **Non Nuoc Beach**, also claims the same soubriquet. If you're heading for Non Nuoc, or down the coast to Hoi An, the honeycomb cave-shrines of the **Marble Mountains**, just back from the beach, are worth a quick trot round in passing.

Monkey Mountain and China Beach

A low-lying neck of land forms the Han River's east bank and then rises 700m in the north to rolling Nui Tien Sa, dubbed **Monkey Mountain** on account of its wildlife population. Monkeys still inhabit the promontory, which is mostly a restricted military area. At present you can follow the busy road out to Tien Sa docks, 15km from central Da Nang by motorbike ($6 by Honda om), past an

Export Processing Zone and nineteenth-century European graves. A few people with their own transport have made it past the military for a panorama from Tien Sa's first cluster of observatories, but otherwise, skirt round the northern tip where you can scramble down to coves and beaches in several places. Tien Sa means "descending angels", a reference to heavenly creatures who apparently would often alight on the summit for a game of chess.

Da Nang's nearest beach resort, My Khe, lies at the southern end of the peninsula and 7km southeast of the centre, close enough to fill with Da Nang townspeople at dawn and dusk though largely empty during the day. My Khe is better known as **China Beach** where US servicemen were helicoptered in for R&R during the American War. To reach My Khe from Da Nang cross Nguyen Van Troi bridge – two-wheelers are restricted to the small, ex-railway bridge built in 1906 – and head east straight over the crossroads. Pedal-bikes can take a shortcut via the Han River ferry (last ferry 9pm), from where it's 2km across the peninsula. Just behind My Khe beach the former Vietnamese Military Guest House and VIP villas have reopened as *My Khe Hotel* (☎051/836125, fax 836123; ②–③) offering **accommodation** in a quiet corner of bougainvillea and palm gardens, plus bike and motorbike rental. The hotel's best asset is its location and a reasonable restaurant, though evening stalls selling ultra-fresh seafood along the seafront are more popular; a Honda om will cost around $1 for the ride from Da Nang.

The Marble Mountains

Turn right over Nguyen Van Troi bridge for the road to Hoi An, an unattractive stretch of storage tanks and scrubby, post-war wasteland, which leads to Vietnam's most southerly limestone outcrops, known as the **Marble Mountains**. Despite all the fuss, only one of the mountains' caves rates above ordinary, while the self-appointed, souvenir-selling guides, although occasionally entertaining and knowledgeable, make the whole experience too much hassle for some people. A torch is useful for exploring the caves.

The simplest way of covering the 12km to the Marble Mountains and Non Nuoc **from Da Nang** is by **car**, **Honda om** ($5 return-trip) or **bicycle**. Just past the first mountain turn left at a T-junction and find Thuy Son staircases on your left after a few hundred metres. Da Nang city **buses** run infrequently out to Non Nuoc (7am–5pm), heading down Phan Chu Trinh with a stop outside the *Danang Tourist* office in central Da Nang and terminating at the Non Nuoc T-junction. Finally, if you can face the scrum, Hoi An-bound **pick-ups** will drop you off at Non Nuoc; if you're pressing on from here, Hoi An is another 20km down the coast from Non Nuoc – take a Honda om ($3 one-way) or squeeze back on a passing local bus.

Local **mythology** tells of the Turtle God hatching a divine egg on the shore from which emerged a nymph as the shell cracked into five pieces, represented by the five small mountains. Historically, Cham people came here to worship their Hindu gods and then erected Buddhist altars in the caves, which became places of pilgrimage, drawing even the Nguyen kings to the sacred site. When Ho Chi Minh died, marble from these mountains was used for his mausoleum in Hanoi; quarrying has since been banned. In Vietnamese the mountains are named Ngu Hanh Son, meaning the five ritual elements: Thuy Son (water mountain) and Moc Son (wood) to the east of the road; Tho Son (earth), Kim Son (gold or metal) and Hoa Son (fire) to the west.

The highest, at 107m, and most important mountain is **Thuy Son** (6am–5.30pm; $2). Two staircases, built for the visit of Emperor Minh Mang, lead up its southern flank; an anticlockwise circuit is recommended, starting at the easterly steps which give expansive views over Non Nuoc Beach, the Cham Islands and north to Monkey Mountain. Near the top stands Linh Ung Pagoda behind which lurks the first of Thuy Son's warren of **cave pagodas**, in this case occupied by tenth-century Cham Hindu altars and two Buddhas, one sitting and one reclining. Continuing uphill, past another viewpoint, brings you to the hollow summit surrounded by jagged rocks with grottoes in every direction. Pass through a narrow defile, under a natural rock-arch and you enter the ante-chamber to Thuy Son's most impressive cave; turn left in front of the sandstone Quan Am statue, down steep, dark steps into the eerie half-light and swirling incense of **Huyen Khong Cave**. Straight ahead across the thirty-metre-high cavern is a large, seated Buddha while small altars and temples around venerate Hindu, Buddhist, Taoist and Confucian deities. Locals will point out stalactites resembling wrinkled faces and so on, but the cave's best feature is its roof through whose lacework openings midday sunlight streams like spotlights. A wall-plaque commemorates a deadly accurate women's Viet Cong guerrilla unit, based here during the American War, which destroyed 19 planes with just 22 rockets.

Backtracking to the main path, take a right at the T-junction to reach the westerly staircase passing recently renovated Tam Thai Pagoda, still lived in by monks, on your way back to **NON NUOC** village. Since the fifteenth century,

Non Nuoc has been inhabited by stone carvers, who coax life out of the local white, grey and rose marble. Nowadays workshops generally churn out mass-produced souvenirs using marble imported from Thanh Hoa Province but it's fascinating to watch the masons at work – just follow your ears.

Non Nuoc Beach

Follow the paved road east from Thuy Son Mountain for about 500m, round a dog-leg and you emerge at **Non Nuoc Beach**, promoted locally as "new China Beach". It's huge, empty, covered in clean, fine white sand and far enough from Da Nang to leave you unpestered (see "The Marble Mountains", opposite, for details of transport from Da Nang). Not that it's hassle-free: you pay a nominal charge to use the beach and parking attendants here have a bad reputation for tampering with motorbikes. Flags indicate safe areas where swimming is permitted between 6am and 6.30pm in summer (March to Aug) and 7am to 5.30pm the rest of the year. There's a cluster of cafés, restaurants and souvenir stalls beside the car park and **hotel** complex of *Non Nuoc Seaside Resort* (☎051/836216, fax 836335; ③). The hotel's three, 1970s blocks set among gardens are surprisingly smart inside with four grades of room, from fan only up to air-con plus sea- view balconies, but they're all spacious, airy and well-scrubbed. Non Nuoc's a popular overnight stop for tour groups and recently hosted Vietnam's first **surfing** competition.

If the resort is too expensive or touristy for your tastes, head back to the dog-leg where several mini-hotels and cafés have sprouted up. Avoid the overpriced places beside the road and turn down the sandy track towards the beach to find two tiny **guesthouses**: *Hai Hoa* (☎051/836603; ①) and *Hoa's Place* (☎051/836188; ①). This is cold-water and fan accommodation but both are clean, good value and offer a basic menu; *Hoa's Place* has the edge for its friendly welcome. If these are full, the cheapest alternative back on the road is *Xuan Thu* (no phone; ②); *Anh Thuan* **restaurant** next door serves cheap and cheerful fare. All these places can help arrange a Honda om to Hoi An or Da Nang; count on $2–3 in either direction for a one-way journey.

North of Da Nang: Hai Van Pass and Lang Co

Thirty kilometres north of Da Nang, beyond a region of grave-pocked, sandy desolation, the first and most dramatic of three mountain spurs off the Truong Son Range cuts across Vietnam's pinched central waist. This thousand-metre-high barrier forms a climatic frontier blocking the southward penetration of cold, damp winter airstreams which often bury the tops under thick cloudbanks and earn it the title **Hai Van**, or "Pass of the Ocean Clouds". These mountains once formed a national frontier between Dai Viet and Champa, and Hai Van's continuing strategic importance is marked by a succession of forts, pill-boxes and ridge-line defensive walls erected by Nguyen dynasty Vietnamese, French, Japanese, and American forces. Highway 1 grinds over the col at nearly 500m above sea level, among advertising hoardings and a scrum of vendors torn between truckers and tourists. From the top there are superb views, weather permitting, south over the sweeping curve of Da Nang Bay, with glimpses of the rail lines looping and tunnelling along the cliff.

Descending again into warmer air, a much-photographed, white-tipped spit of land comes into view round a hairpin bend, jutting into an aquamarine lagoon strung with fishing nets like spiders' webs; the lagoon's oyster-beds provide mother-of-pearl for Vietnam's artisans. **LANG CO** village hides among coconut palms ·on the sandy peninsula, its presence revealed only by a white-spired church. The original bridge spanning Lang Co lagoon has the dubious distinction of being the Viet Minh bomb squads' first target in 1947 and its ruined piles are still visible. Now the village makes a popular lunch-stop on the road between Da Nang and Hué, followed by a quick swim from the narrow beach, marred by a string of electricity pylons. Lang Co's beach **hotel**, *Nha Nghi Du Lich* (☎054/874426; ②), provides basic facilities – no hot water or daytime electricity – but non-residents can pay a nominal fee for a swimming ticket and deck-chairs; find it north of the village near the Petrolimex filling station. *Quan Thuy* **restaurant** beside the hotel-turning serves excellent seafood – crab is the local speciality – though there's plenty to choose from all along the highway; check prices before ordering. The only off-road eating is at the hotel's slightly more expensive café-restaurant. Lang Co lies about 40km north of Da Nang, 65km from Hué; the train station is on the lagoon's western side, or buses will drop you off anywhere on the highway.

Hué

Unlike Hanoi, Ho Chi Minh and most other Vietnamese cities, **HUÉ** somehow seems to have stood aside from the current economic frenzy and, despite its calamitous history, has retained a unique cultural identity. It's a small, peaceful city, full of lakes, canals and lush vegetation, all celebrated in countless romantic outpourings by its much-esteemed poetic fraternity. Since the early nineteenth century, when Hué became the capital of Vietnam, it has also been a city of scholars, and today boasts no fewer than five universities. Though it's considered overly highbrow by the rest of the country, there's a discernible touch of refinement in the Hué air, and an easygoing tolerance that stems from a long tradition of popular Buddhism. More recently, French culture has left a strong impression on Hué, which is perhaps the most Francophile of all Vietnamese cities.

Hué repays exploration at a leisurely pace, and contains enough of historical interest to swallow up three days with no trouble at all. The city divides into three clearly defined urban areas, each with its own distinct character. The nineteenth-century walled **citadel**, on the north bank of the Perfume River, contains the once-magnificent **Imperial City** as well as an extensive grid of attractive residential streets and prolific gardens. Across Dong Ba Canal to the east lies **Phu Cat**, the original merchants' quarter of Hué where ships once pulled in, now a crowded district of shophouses, Chinese Assembly Halls and pagodas. What used to be called the **European City**, a triangle of land caught between the Perfume River's south bank and the Phu Cam Canal, is now Hué's modern administrative centre, where you'll also find most hotels and tourist services. Pine-covered hills, scattered with tombs and secluded pagodas, form the city's southern bounds, where the Nguyen emperors built their palatial **Royal Mausoleums**. And through it all meanders the Perfume River, named somewhat fancifully from the tree-resin and blossoms it carries, passing on its way the celebrated, seven-storey tower of **Thien Mu Pagoda**. If you can afford the time, cycling out to **Thuan An Beach** and **Thanh Toan Covered Bridge** are enjoyable excursions from Hué, while this is also the main jumping-off point for day-tours of the DMZ (see p.279).

With all this to offer, Hué is inevitably one of Vietnam's pre-eminent tourist destinations. The choice and standard of accommodation are generally above average, as are its restaurants serving the city's justly famous speciality foods. Nevertheless, the majority of people pass through Hué fairly quickly, partly because high entrance fees make visiting more than a couple of the major sights beyond many budgets, and partly because of its troublesome **weather**. Hué suffers from the highest rainfall in the country, mostly falling over just three months from October to December when the city regularly floods for a few days, though heavy rain is possible at any time of year.

Some history

Hué was part of the Kingdom of Champa until 1306 when territory north of Da Nang was exchanged for the hand of a Vietnamese princess under the terms of a peace treaty. The first Vietnamese to settle in the region established their administrative centre near present-day Hué at a place called Hoa Chan, and then in 1558 Lord Nguyen Hoang arrived from Hanoi as governor of the district, at the same time establishing the rule of the Nguyen lords over southern Vietnam, which was to last for the next two hundred years. In the late seventeenth century the lords moved the citadel to its present location where it developed into a major town and cultural centre, **Phu Xuan**, which briefly became capital under the Tay Son emperor, Quang Trung (1788–1801). But it was the next ruler of Vietnam, Emperor Gia Long, founder of the Nguyen dynasty, who literally put Hué on the map after 1802 when he sought to unify the country by moving the capital, lock, stock and dynastic altars, from Thang Long (Hanoi) to the renamed city of **Hué**. Gia Long owed his throne to French military support but his Imperial City was very much a Chinese concept, centred on a Forbidden City reserved for the sovereign, with separate administrative and civilian quarters.

The Nguyen emperors (see box over the page) were Confucian, conservative rulers, generally suspicious of all Westerners, who were nevertheless unable to withstand the power of France. In 1884 the French were granted land northwest of Hué citadel, and they then seized the city entirely in 1885, leaving the emperors as nominal rulers. Under the Nguyens, Hué became a famous centre of the arts, scholarship and Buddhist learning, but their extravagant building projects and luxurious lifestyle demanded crippling taxes.

Hué ceased to be the capital of Vietnam when Emperor Bao Dai abdicated in 1945; two years later a huge fire destroyed many of the city's wooden temples and palaces. By the early twentieth century the city was engulfed in social and political unrest led by an anti-colonial educated elite, which simmered away until the 1960s. Tensions finally boiled over in May 1963 when troops fired on thousands of Buddhists peacefully demonstrating against the strongly Catholic regime of President Ngo Dinh Diem. The protests escalated into a wave of self-immolations by monks and nuns until government forces moved against the pagodas at the end of the year, rounding-up the Buddhist clergy and supposed activists in the face of massive public demonstrations.

During the 1968 **Tet Offensive** Hué was torn apart again when the North Vietnamese Army (NVA) held the city for 25 days. Communist forces entered Hué in the early hours of January 31, hoisted their flag above the citadel and found themselves in control of the whole city bar two small military compounds.

THE NGUYEN DYNASTY

In 1802 Prince Nguyen Anh, one of the southern Nguyen lords, defeated the Tay Son dynasty with the help of a French bishop, Pigneau de Behaine. When Nguyen Anh assumed the throne under the title Emperor Gia Long he thus founded the Nguyen dynasty, which ruled Vietnam from Hué until the abdication of Emperor Bao Dai in 1945. Eleven of the Nguyen emperors are buried in Hué while Bao Dai still lives in Paris; it remains to be seen whether he will be allowed to join his ancestors.

Gia Long	1802–1820	
Minh Mang	1820–1841	(fourth son of Gia Long)
Thieu Tri	1841–1847	(eldest son of Minh Mang)
Tu Duc	1847–1883	(second son of Thieu Tri)
Duc Duc	1883	(eldest adopted son of Tu Duc, reigned 3 days; dethroned)
Hiep Hoa	1883	(brother of Tu Duc, reigned 4 months; died from suspected poisoning)
Kien Phuc	1883–1884	(adopted son of Tu Duc; reigned 6 months)
Ham Nghi	1884–1885	(younger brother of Kien Phuc; exiled to Algeria, where he is buried)
Dong Khanh	1885–1889	(elder brother of Ham Nghi and Kien Phuc)
Thanh Thai	1889–1907	(son of Duc Duc; exiled to Réunion)
Duy Tan	1907–1916	(son of Thanh Thai; exiled to Réunion)
Khai Dinh	1916–1925	(son of Dong Khanh)
Bao Dai	1926–1945	(son of Khai Dinh)

Armed with lists of names, they began searching out government personnel, sympathizers of the Southern regime, intellectuals, priests, Americans and foreign aid workers. Nearly 3000 bodies were later discovered in mass graves around the city – the victims were mostly civilians who had been shot, beaten to death or buried alive. But the killing hadn't finished: during the ensuing counter-assault as many as 5000 North Vietnamese and Viet Cong, 384 Southern troops and 142 American soldiers died, plus at least another thousand civilians. Hué was all but levelled in the massive firepower unleashed on NVA forces holed-up in the citadel but it took a further ten days of agonizing, house-to-house combat to drive the communists out, in what Stanley Karnow described as "the most bitter battle" of the entire American War. Seven years later, on March 26, 1975, the NVA were back to liberate Hué in its pivotal position as the first major town south of the Seventeenth Parallel.

The mammoth task of **rebuilding** Hué has been going on now for twenty years but received a boost in 1993 when UNESCO listed Hué as a World Heritage Site, which served to mobilize international funding for a whole range of projects, from renovating palaces to the revival of traditional arts and technical skills. Then in 1995 the Vietnamese government recognized Hué's growing economic importance by granting it independent city status, almost on a par with Hanoi and Ho Chi Minh City.

Arrival, information and getting around

Flights arriving at Hué's **Phu Bai Airport**, 15km southeast of the city, are met by an airport bus ($1) which takes you to central hotels, and by metered taxis (around $7). The **train station** lies about 1500m from the centre of town at the far western end of Le Loi, a boulevard running along the south bank of the Perfume River. Note that trains out of Hué get booked-up, especially sleepers to Ho Chi Minh City and Hanoi, so make onward travel arrangements as early as possible (ticket office open daily 7.30–11am & 1.30–4pm). Hué has two long-distance **bus stations**: services from the south pull into An Cuu station, 1km southeast of the centre, while buses from Hanoi and the north dump you at An Hoa station, 4km northwest on Highway 1 ($2–3 by cyclo).

The most prominent of Hué's two state-run **tourist offices** is *Thua Thien–Hué Tourism* at 9 Ngo Quyen (☎054/822990), while *Hué Tourist Company* at 1 Truong Dinh (☎054/823577) also provides guides and transport though it deals mainly with pre-booked tours. Bookstalls on Le Loi sell city **maps** and English-language guidebooks to Hué's monuments. The main **post office** is at 8 Hoang Hoa Tham, and offers *poste restante* facilities, while the newsstand next door sells Vietnamese English-language papers. A couple of doors closer to the river you'll find *Vietcombank* at 6 Hoang Hoa Tham, for **exchange** of cash and travellers' cheques.

Even Hué's wide avenues become crowded during rush hour (7–9am & 4–6pm), but generally the most enjoyable way of **getting around** the city's scattered sights – and especially of touring the Royal Mausoleums – is by **bicycle**. Most hotels and guesthouses, plus a few cafés, offer rental of bikes (at less than $1 per day) and **motorbikes** ($6–10 a day). The same places can usually help with **car rental** ($20–30 per day), or try the tour agents listed on p.278. Hué has no shortage of cyclos and also boasts a metered **taxi** service (*Hué* or *ATC Taxi*, ☎054/833333).

Accommodation

The majority of accommodation in Hué is located south of the Perfume River, where the **top-class** establishments overlook the river while **budget hotels** and **guesthouses** are scattered in the streets behind. A few hotels have opened-up within the citadel's southwest quadrant, though as yet you'll find better value south of the river. Despite the recent additions there's still a serious **room-shortage** in the peak months for local tourism (July and Aug) when the rates given below may increase by up to a third.

All the following places to stay are marked on the map on p.276.

A Dong, 1b Chu Van An (☎054/824148, fax 823858). A clean, efficient mini-hotel at the north end of town offering reasonable rates. *A Dong 2* is a sister-establishment two blocks west. ④

Ben Nghe, 4 Ben Nghe (☎054/823687). Slightly run-down guesthouse but with some of the cheapest beds in central Hué, with a pleasant courtyard garden. Generally clean, spartan rooms, some with shared bathroom and all with hot water. ①

Binh Minh, 12 Nguyen Tri Phuong (☎054/825526, fax 828362). Bright, welcoming hotel with a good restaurant. This popular place has 22 rooms across the spectrum, with facilities ranging from fan and no window, to TV, IDD phone and balcony. ③

Century Riverside Inn, 49 Le Loi (☎054/823390, fax 823399). A slick, international hotel on the banks of the Perfume River with swimming pool, bar, post office and souvenir shops. Comfortable but a touch characterless. ④

ACCOMMODATION PRICE CODES

All accommodation listed in this guide has been categorized according to the following scale:

① under US$10 (under 110,000 dong)   ② US$10–15 (110–165,000 dong)

③ US$15–30 (165–330,000 dong)   ④ US$30–75 (330–825,000 dong)

⑤ US$75–150 (825–1,650,000 dong)   ⑥ over US$150 (over 1,650,000 dong)

Rates are for the cheapest available double or twin room; breakfast is not usually included. During holiday periods, rates are liable to rise, and proprietors may be less amenable to bargaining. Although the law requires prices to be quoted in dong, most hotels also give their rates in US$; payment can be made in either currency.
For a more detailed discussion of accommodation, see pp.31–34.

Dong Loi, 11a Pham Ngu Lao (☎054/822296, fax 826234). A deservedly popular hotel across from the *Century*, with helpful staff and 37 well-kept rooms at a variety of prices. An added bonus is its pre-1975 US Army jeep, available for hire, that will appeal to nostalgia buffs. ①

Dong Phuong, 26 Nguyen Tri Phuong (☎054/825333). A popular, friendly mini-hotel offering good-value rooms and a recommended restaurant. ②

Hoa Hong, 46c Le Loi (☎ & fax 054/824377). A successful private hotel with helpful staff and good facilities that's recently added another 70 rooms round the corner at 1 Pham Ngu Lao, just back from the riverfront. ③

Huong Giang, 51 Le Loi (☎054/822122, fax 823102). Hué's second most classy hotel, originally built in 1962 but well renovated, stands on the riverbank next door to its rival, the *Century*. The *Huong Giang*'s a more homely establishment, with well-priced rooms at the lower end and a relaxed, garden-style top-floor restaurant. Imperial meals are offered in the downstairs dining area. ③–④

Kinh Do, 1 Nguyen Thai Hoc (☎054/823566, fax 823858). A pleasant, older hotel in the mid-range on a quiet back street. Rooms don't quite live up to the attractive, flower-decked exterior, but are comfortable and well furnished, if slightly overpriced. ③

Kylin, 58 Le Loi (☎054/826575, fax 826596). This smart, new hotel just behind the *Huong Giang* offers large, well-decorated rooms with satellite TV as standard. It also boasts a restaurant serving Hué specialities and a roof-top bar with river views. ④

Le Loi Hué 2, 2 Le Loi (☎054/824668, fax 824527). A big hotel of unattractive concrete blocks but the closest to the train station and with fair prices. Well kept for its age, with a good café-restaurant and reasonably priced tours. ②

Le Loi Hué 5, 5 Le Loi (☎054/822155, fax 828816). The former Government Guesthouse, with peaceful gardens overlooking the river and 16 huge rooms, some with balconies and a certain antique charm. ③

Mimosa, 46/6 Le Loi (☎054/828068, fax 823858). The best value of several guesthouses on a quiet alley behind the *Century*. Hot water and air-con come as standard. ②

Mini-hotel 18, 18 Le Loi (☎054/823720). Small, well-run hotel offering a warm welcome and good-value, no-frills rooms in a converted villa, located near *Phu Xuan* Bridge. ②

Morin, 30 Le Loi (☎054/823039, fax 825155). The former *Frères Morin* Hotel, now resurrected by *Saigon Tourist*, offering upmarket accommodation in a prime location. ④–⑤

Thanh Loi, 7 Dinh Tien Hoang (☎054/824803, fax 825344). One of the few hotels north of the river. Its top-floor rooms offer the best value, affording views of the flag tower. ②

Thuan Hoa, 7 Nguyen Tri Phuong (☎054/822553, fax 822470). A big, state-run hotel that's been refurbished to a reasonable standard and kitted-out with rattan furnishings. All rooms come with en suite bathrooms, IDD phones, TV and air-con; dancing, tennis, sauna and massage are also on offer. ③

Tourist Villas, 9 Ly Thuong Kiet (☎054/825163, fax 825814). *Hué Tourist Co* owns 6 villas along this road, each a converted colonial house consisting of 4 rooms, plus cheaper rooms in a block behind. The villas have marginally more atmosphere than the average hotel room, and small gardens. Find them at nos. 9, 16, 5, 11, 14, 7 Ly Thuong Kiet (in descending price-order), or try the head office at no. 9. ①–②

Truong Tien, 8 Hung Vuong (☎054/823127, fax 825910). A spruce hotel offering well-priced rooms, all with bathrooms and some with air-con. Tour booking office. ①

The citadel

Hué's days of glory kicked off in the early nineteenth century when Emperor Gia Long laid out a vast **citadel**, comprising three concentric enclosures, ranged behind the prominent **flag tower**. Within the citadel's outer wall lies the **Imperial City**, containing administrative offices, parks and dynastic temples, with the royal palaces of the **Forbidden Purple City** at its epicentre. Though wars, fires, typhoons, floods and termites have all taken their toll, it's these imperial edifices, some now restored to their former magnificence, that constitute Hué's prime tourist attraction. Apart from a couple of **museums**, there are no specific sights in the outer citadel, but it's a pleasant area to cycle round, especially the northern sector where you'll find many lakes and the prolific gardens for which Hué is famed.

In accordance with ancient tradition the citadel was built in an **auspicious location** chosen to preserve the all-important harmony between the emperor and his subjects, heaven and earth, man and nature. Thus the complex is oriented southeast towards the low hummock of Nui Ngu Binh ("Royal Screen Mountain"), which blocks out harmful influences, while to either side two small islands in the Perfume River represent the Blue Dragon's benevolent spirit in balance with the aggressive White Tiger. Just in case that wasn't protection enough, the whole 520 hectares is enclosed within seven-metre-high, twenty-metre-thick brick and earth walls built with the help of French engineers, and encircled by a moat and canal. Eight villages had to be relocated when construction began in 1805 and over the next thirty years tens of thousands of workmen laboured to complete more than 300 palaces, temples, tombs and other royal buildings, some using materials brought down from the former Imperial City in Hanoi.

The flag tower and the sacred cannons

The citadel's massive, ten-kilometre-long perimeter wall has survived intact, as has its most prominent feature, the **flag tower**, or *Cot Co* (also known as *Ky Dai*, "the King's Knight"), which dominates the southern battlements. The tower is in fact three squat, brick terraces topped with a flag-pole first erected in 1807, where the yellow-starred Viet Cong flag flew briefly during the 1968 Tet Offensive. Ten gates pierce the citadel wall: enter through Ngan Gate, east of the flag tower, to find a grassy parade ground and the nine **sacred cannons**, which were cast in the early nineteenth century of bronze seized from the Tay Son army. The cannons represent the four seasons and five ritual elements (earth, fire, metal, wood and water); originally they stood in front of Ngo Mon Gate, symbolizing the citadel's guardian spirits.

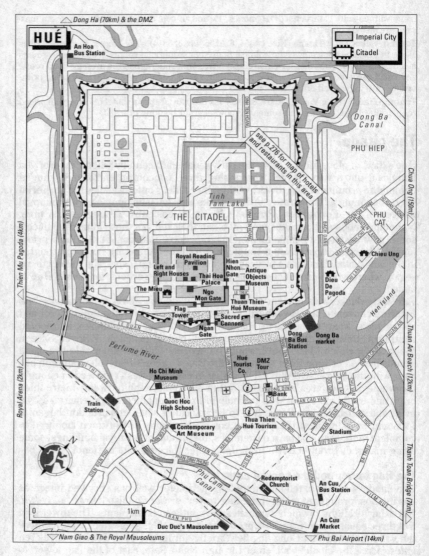

The Imperial City

A second moat and defensive wall inside the citadel guard the **Imperial City** (daily 7am–5.30pm; $5 plus extra for video cameras, guide $3), which follows the same symmetrical layout about a north–south axis as Beijing's Forbidden City. The city, popularly known as *Dai Noi* ("the Great Enclosure"), has four gates – one in each wall – though by far the most impressive is south-facing **Ngo Mon**, the Imperial City's principal entrance. In its heyday the city must have been truly awe-inspiring, a place of glazed yellow and green roof-tiles, pavilions of rich red and gilded lacquer, and lotus-filled ponds – all surveyed by the emperor with his entourage of haughty mandarins. However, many of its buildings were badly neglected even before the battle for Hué raged through the Imperial City during Tet 1968, and by 1975 a mere twenty out of the original 148 were left standing among the vegetable plots. But those that have been restored are stunning, in particular **Thai Hoa Palace** and the Nguyen emperors' dynastic temple, **The Mieu**. Others, such as the charming Royal Reading Pavilion and an overgrown octagonal pavilion, are less formal mementoes of the dynasty. The rest of the Imperial City, especially its northern sector, is a grassed-over expanse full of birds and butterflies where you can still make out foundations and find bullet pock-marks in the plasterwork of ruined walls.

NGO MON GATE

In 1833 Emperor Minh Mang replaced an earlier, much less formidable gate with the present dramatic entrance-way to the Imperial City, **Ngo Mon** ("the Noon Gate"), considered a masterpiece of Nguyen architecture. Ngo Mon has five entrances: the emperor alone used the central entrance paved with stone; two smaller doorways on either side were for the civil and military mandarins, who only rated brick paving, while another pair of giant openings in the wings allowed access to the royal elephants. The bulk of Ngo Mon is constructed of massive stone slabs, but perched on top is an elegant pavilion called the **Five Phoenix Watchtower** as its nine roofs are said to resemble five birds in flight when viewed from above. Note that the central roof, under which the emperor passed, is covered with yellow-glazed tiles, a feature of nearly all Hué's royal roofs. Emperors used the watchtower for two major ceremonies each year: the declaration of the lunar New Year; and the announcement of the civil service exam results, depicted here in a lacquer painting. It was also in this pavilion that the last Nguyen emperor, Bao Dai, abdicated in 1945 when he handed over to the new government his symbols of power – a solid gold seal weighing ten kilos and a sheathed sword encrusted with jade.

THAI HOA PALACE

Walking north from Ngo Mon along the city's symmetrical axis, you pass between two square lakes and a pair of *kylin*, mythical dew-drinking animals that are harbingers of peace, to reach **Thai Hoa Palace** ("the Palace of Supreme Harmony"). Not only is this the most spectacular of Hué's palaces, its interior glowing with sumptuous red and gold lacquers, but it's also the most important since this was the throne palace, where major ceremonies such as coronations or royal birthdays took place and foreign ambassadors were received. On these occasions the emperor sat on the raised dais, wearing a golden tunic and a crown decorated with nine dragons, under a spectacular gilded canopy. He faced south across the **Esplanade of Great Salutations**, a stone-paved courtyard where the mandarins stood, civil mandarins to the left and military on the right, lined-up in their appointed place beside eighteen stelae denoting the nine subdivided ranks. A French traveller in the 1920s witnessed the colourful spectacle, with "perfume-bearers in royal-blue, fan-bearers in sky-blue waving enormous yellow feather fans, musicians and guardsmen and ranks of mandarins in their curious hats and gorgeous, purple-embroidered dragons, kow-towing down, down on their noses amidst clouds of incense – and all in a setting of blood-red lacquer scrawled with gold".

The palace was first constructed in 1805, though the present building dates from 1833 when the French floor tiles and glass door panels were added, and was the only major building in the Imperial City to escape bomb damage. Nevertheless, the throne room's eighty ironwood pillars, swirling with dragons and clouds, had been eaten away by termites and humidity and were on the point of collapse when rescue work began in 1991. During the restoration every column, weighing two tonnes apiece, had to be replaced manually and then painted with twelve coats of lacquer, each coat taking one month to dry. Behind the throne room a souvenir shop now sells imitation imperial artefacts and tapes of Hué folksongs where once the emperor prepared for his grand entrance.

THE FORBIDDEN PURPLE CITY

From Thai Hoa Palace the emperor would have walked north through the Great Golden Gate into the third and last enclosure, the **Forbidden Purple City**. The ten-hectare city, enclosed by a low wall, was reserved for residential palaces, living quarters of the state physician and nine ranks of royal concubines, plus kitchens and pleasure pavilions. Many of these buildings were destroyed in the 1947 fire, leaving most of the Forbidden Purple City as open ground, a "mood piece", haunted by fragments of wall and overgrown terraces.

However, a handful of buildings remain, including the restored **Left House** and **Right House** facing each other across a courtyard immediately behind Thai Hoa Palace. Civil and military mandarins would spruce themselves up here before proceeding to an audience with the monarch. Of the two, the Right House (actually to your left – the names refer to the emperor's viewpoint) is the more complete with its ornate murals and two gargantuan mirrors in gilded frames, a gift from the French to Emperor Dong Khanh. Walking northeast from here you pass behind the Royal Theatre, built in 1826 and now under restoration, to find the **Royal Reading Pavilion**, an appealing, two-tier structure surrounded by bonsai gardens. The pavilion was built by Minh Mang and then restored by Khai Dinh, who added the kitsch mosaics; inside are more souvenir sellers and photos of Hué monuments. The only other building left standing near here is an octagonal pavilion, originally one of a pair, where the emperor came to listen to music and commune with nature.

THE ANCESTRAL ALTARS

The last cluster of sights are in the southwest corner of the Imperial City and best approached from the south. Head back to Ngo Mon Gate, turn right along the ramparts and walk through *Hien Lam Cac* ("Pavilion of Everlasting Clarity"), a graceful three-storey structure with some notable woodwork, to emerge among the **Nine Dynastic Urns**. Considered the epitome of Hué craftsmanship, the bronze urns were cast during the reign of Minh Mang and are ornamented with scenes of mountains, rivers, rain clouds and wildlife, plus one or two stray bullet-marks. Each urn is dedicated to an emperor: the middle urn, which is also the largest at 2600 kilos, honours Gia Long. They stand across the courtyard from the long, low building of **The Mieu**, the Nguyens' dynastic temple erected in 1821 by Minh Mang to worship his father. Since then altars have been added for each emperor in turn, except Duc Duc and Hiep Hoa who reigned only briefly; those of the three anti-French sovereigns – Ham Nghi, Thanh Thai, and Duy Tan – had to wait until after Independence in 1954. Each altar table is equipped with a sleeping mat, pillows and other accoutrements, together with photos of the later monarchs, while the shrine behind holds funeral tablets for the emperor and his wife or wives. Anniversaries of the emperors' deaths are still commemorated at The Mieu, attended by members of the royal family in all their finery.

Follow the path round to the west of The Mieu, past a 170-year-old pine tree trained in the shape of a flying dragon, and cross into the next compound to find **Hung Mieu**. This temple is dedicated to the Nguyen ancestors and specifically to the parents of Gia Long, and is distinguished by its fine carving.

The museums

Instead of leaving the Imperial City via Ngo Mon Gate, cut east to exit via the only other gate in use, the well-preserved *Cua Hien Nhon* ("Gate of Humanity"). From here it's a short walk to the **Hué Museum of Antique Objects**, at 3 Le Truc (7.30–11am & 2–4pm; $2), which boasts an interesting display of former royal paraphernalia with limited English descriptions. Its most valuable exhibits are a collection of inlay-work poems composed by various monarchs, and some lively paintings on glass which adorn the ironwood columns. But the museum's greatest asset is the building it's housed in, **Long An Palace**, built in 1845 inside the Imperial City and then moved to its present location in 1909 to become the National University Library before Khai Dinh turned it into a dynastic museum in 1923. The palace was renovated in 1995 and decorated with rich browns, highlighting the wealth of exhibits decorated with mother-of-pearl inlay.

Bao Tang Thuan Thien–Hué, the Provincial Museum, lies directly across Le Truc Street (daily except Thurs 7–11am & 1.30–5pm; $1.50). In fact this is three museums in one: archeological and ethnographic exhibits in the central building; outstanding achievements of local industry, agriculture and other success stories to the west; and the well-presented "Museum of the Resistance against US invaders (1954–75)" to the east. This last section occupies just three small rooms but it's packed with information, much of it in English, about the war in Hué. Photos, documents and original film-clips cover both the Buddhist demonstrations in 1963 and the 1968 battle, including footage of the National Liberation Front flag being hoisted above the citadel. There's even a diorama of the battle with English commentary and sound-effects. But don't ignore the other two buildings: take a look at the Ede funeral statues, full of personality, in the ethnography display; and the excellent scale model of the citadel in its heyday that resides in the provincial section.

Phu Cat and Phu Hiep

Hué's civilian and merchant quarter grew up alongside the citadel on a triangular island now divided into **Phu Cat** and **Phu Hiep** districts. This part of town has a completely different atmosphere: it's a lively, crowded, dilapidated area centred on Chi Lang Street which still boasts some single-storey, wood and red-tiled houses as well as more ornate, colonial-era shophouses. These districts were once home to the Chinese community and five **Assembly Halls** still stand along Chi Lang, though most are badly neglected. Old trees shade the Dong Ba Canal on the island's eastern border, where Bach Dang Street was the site of anti-government demonstrations in the 1960s, centred around **Dieu De Pagoda**. There's nothing compelling to draw you onto the island, particularly if you've already seen the Chinese temples of Hoi An and Ho Chi Minh City, but the area provides a bustling contrast to the otherwise sedate streets of Hué.

The Chinese Assembly Halls

Chinese immigrants to Hué settled in five congregations around their separate **Assembly Halls**, of which the most interesting is **Chua Ong**, opposite 224 Chi Lang (daily 8–11am & 2–5pm). Founded by the Phuoc Kien (Fujian) community in the mid-1800s and rebuilt several times since, the most recent restorations came after 1968 when Viet Cong troops hit a US munitions boat on the river nearby and destroyed the pagoda plus surrounding houses. Surprisingly, there's no Buddha on the main altar but instead several doctors of medicine, along with General Quan Cong to the right and Thien Hau to the left, both protectors of sailors. The story goes that Quan Cong sat on the main altar until a devastating cholera epidemic in 1918 when he was displaced by the doctors, and the outbreak ended soon after. Of the other halls, **Chieu Ung**, opposite no. 154, is worth dropping in to. It's badly decayed but the gilded altar displays some skilled carpentry. This pagoda was also founded in the nineteenth century by ethnic Chinese from Hai Nam, and has been rebuilt at least twice since.

The European city

Although the French became the de facto rulers of Vietnam after 1884, they left the emperors in the citadel and built their administrative city across the Perfume River on the south bank. The main artery of the **European city** was riverside Le Loi where the French Resident's office stood, together with other important buildings such as **Quoc Hoc High School** and the *Frères Morin* hotel. Residential streets spread out south of the river as far as the Phu Cam Canal, and were linked to the citadel by Clemenceau Bridge, renamed Trang Tien Bridge after 1954. Apart from the high school, the only major sight is the **Ho Chi Minh Museum**, not just the obligatory gesture in this case as Ho actually did spend much of his childhood in Hué. The extraordinary, tiered spire of the **Redemptorist Church** dominates the southern horizon with its improbable blend of Gothic and Cubism created by a local architect in the late 1950s. The church caters to some of Hué's 20,000 Catholics and is interesting to view in passing, though the interior is less striking. Admirers of modern Vietnamese art should call in at the **Museum of Contemporary Art**, 1 Pham Boi Chau – in fact a gallery devoted to the works of Diem Phung Thi, who was born in Hué in 1920. The old villa provides the perfect setting for her chunky "modules" developed from Chinese calligraphy.

The Ho Chi Minh Museum

Ho Chi Minh was born near Vinh in Nghe An Province (see p.292) but spent ten years at school in Hué (1895–1901 and 1906–1909) where his father worked as a civil mandarin. The small **Ho Chi Minh Museum** at 7 Le Loi (Mon–Sat 7.30–11.30am & 2–4.30pm) presents these years in the context of the anti-French struggle and then takes the story on to Independence. The most interesting material consists of family photos and rare glimpses of early-twentieth-century Hué. You can still see the house where Ho lived for a time with his father in Duong No village on the way to Thuan An Beach (see p.279), but the primary school he attended near Dong Ba market no longer exists.

Quoc Hoc High School

Ho Chi Minh was the most famous student to attend **Quoc Hoc High School**, which stands almost opposite his museum on Le Loi. The school was founded in 1896 as the National College, dedicated to the education of royal princes and future administrators who learnt about the history of their European "motherland" – all in French until 1945. Ho studied here for at least a year before being expelled for taking part in anti-government demonstrations. Other revolutionary names that appear on the roster are Prime Minister Pham Van Dong, General Giap and Party Secretary Le Duan, while former president of South Vietnam Ngo Dinh Diem was also a student. Even during the 1960s Quoc Hoc had a justly earned reputation for breeding dissident intellectuals and after reunification in 1975 some staff were sent for "re-education".

Nam Giao, Van Mieu and the Royal Arena

For the most part the Nguyen emperors lived their lives within the citadel walls but on certain occasions they emerged to participate in important rituals at symbolic locations. Today these places are of interest more for their history than anything much to see on the ground, though the mouldering **Royal Arena** still hints at past spectacles. As all three places are located on the outskirts of Hué, they are best covered in combination with other sights, as suggested below.

Nam Giao

First and foremost in the ceremonial and religious life of the nation was **Nam Giao** ("Altar of Heaven"), where the emperor reaffirmed the legitimacy of his rule in sacred rituals, held here roughly every three years from 1807 to 1945. The ceremonies were performed on a series of hill-top terraces, two square-shaped and one round, symbolizing heaven, man and earth. Before each occasion the monarch purified himself, keeping to a strict regime of vegetarian food – and no concubines for several days. He then carried out the sacrifices, with the assistance of some 5000 attendants, to ensure the stability of both the country and the dynasty. Nam Giao is 3km south of central Hué at the end of Dien Bien Phu Street, en route to the Royal Mausoleums.

Van Mieu

Confucianism had been the principal state religion in Vietnam since the eleventh century and the Nguyens were a particularly traditional dynasty. Early in his reign, in 1808, Gia Long dedicated a national temple to Confucius, **Van Mieu**, or the Temple of Literature, to replace that in Hanoi. Nothing much remains of the complex, beyond a collection of stone stelae recording successful candidates in the mandarinal examinations. In this case there are 32 stelae listing the names of 297 doctorates from exams held between 1822 and 1919. Two other stelae under small shelters record edicts from Minh Mang and Thieu Tri banning the "abuse of eunuchs and royal maternal relatives". The complex may well be more interesting when its reconstruction is finished, but for the moment you get a fine view of the royal landing stage and temple gate passing by on a Perfume River boat trip (see box over the page). Alternatively, Van Mieu is only 500m by road west of Thien Mu Pagoda (see p.267).

The Royal Arena

On the opposite bank of the Perfume River stands the **Royal Arena**, or *Ho Quyen*, where the emperors amused themselves with fights between elephants and tigers. Not that this was entirely sport: elephants symbolized the unequalled might of the sovereign while tigers represented rebel forces, and the arena was built on the site of an old Cham fort just to underline the message of imperial power. It was, apparently, a pretty one-sided fight which the elephant was never allowed to lose, and contemporary accounts suggest that in later years the tigers were tied to a stake and had their claws removed. Originally the contests were held on open ground in front of the citadel but after a tiger attacked Minh Mang they were staged in the arena from 1830 until the last fight in 1904.

The Royal Arena still exists almost in its original state, though the royal pavilion has rotted away and the recent addition of a concrete stage blocks off some of the tiger cages. For the best view, climb up the overgrown staircase on the north wall to where the emperor would have sat facing south over the small arena only 44m across. After they died, the elephants were worshipped nearby in a small temple, **Long Chau Dien**, which stands to the west of the arena, although almost completely hidden by undergrowth and with only a couple of elephant statues to see: follow the path round the arena's south side to find the temple, overlooking a small lake. The Royal Arena is 4km from central Hué, taking Bui Thi Xuan along the Perfume River's south bank through Phuong Duc, a famous metal-casting village. At no. 198 Bui Thi Xuan, turn left up a dirt track and take the left fork after 20m to see the arena's brick steps in front of you. If you want to combine the arena with the Royal Mausoleums (see p.268), you can use a rough backroad from Phuong Duc village, though this takes you up steeper inclines than the main route to the mausoleums, via Dien Bien Phu Street.

The Perfume River

A boat-trip on the **Perfume River** is one of the city's highlights (see box below), puttering in front of the citadel on a misty Hué morning, past row-boats loaded with vegetables heading for Dong Ba market, workmen with bamboo baskets ducking down to dredge the shallow banks for building sand, and all the slow bustle of river-life. A sizeable number of people still live in boats on the Perfume River

---

BOAT TRIPS ON THE PERFUME RIVER

A day's boating on the Perfume River is a good way to soak up some of the atmosphere of Hué and do a little gentle sightseeing off the roads. The standard **boat trip** takes you to Thien Mu Pagoda, Hon Chen Temple and the most rewarding mausoleums, usually those of Tu Duc, Khai Dinh and Minh Mang. However, if you want to visit some of the others or spend more time exploring, it's usually possible to take a bicycle on the boat and cycle back to Hué, though double-check this when you book the trip. Most tour agents (see "Listings", p.278) and hotels offer river-tours at between $4 and $6 per person, plus $1 for lunch cooked on board, which is generally excellent. If you'd rather do it independently, the same agents can arrange charter boats at $20–25 for the day, or go direct to the boatmen beside the Dap Da causeway, where the going rate should be around $2–3 per hour.

and the waterways of Hué, such as the Dong Ba and Phu Cam canals, despite government efforts to settle them elsewhere. Leaving the city behind, the first distinctive feature heading upstream is the tower of **Thien Mu Pagoda** which played a prominent role in the founding of Hué and in Vietnam's more recent history, but which is also famous for the natural beauty of its setting. Then where the river loops south among low pine-clad hills, **Hon Chen Temple** harks back to the earlier Cham rulers of this region. On either bank, mostly hidden from view, reside the Royal Mausoleums (see over), a few of which are within fairly easy reach of the river.

Thien Mu Pagoda

Two closely related legends recount the history of **Thien Mu Pagoda**, also known as *Linh Mu* ("Pagoda of the Celestial Lady"), which stands on the site of an ancient Cham temple. In 1601 Lord Nguyen Hoang left Hanoi to govern the southern territories. Upon arriving at the Perfume River he met an elderly woman who told him to walk east along the river carrying a lighted incense stick and to build his city where the incense stopped burning. Later Lord Hoang erected a pagoda in gratitude to the lady, whom he believed to be a messenger from the gods, on the site where they met. Another version has the white-haired lady, dressed in a red tunic with green trousers, appearing on a small hill shaped like a dragon's head and resting on a dragon's vein, and predicting that a lord would build a pagoda on the site and bring everlasting prosperity to the country. In either case Nguyen Hoang is credited with founding the pagoda in 1601, making it the oldest in Hué.

During the 1930s and 1940s Thien Mu was already renowned as a centre of Buddhist opposition to colonialism and then in 1963 it became instantly famous when one of its monks, the Venerable Thich Quang Duc, burned himself to death in Saigon, in protest at the excesses of President Diem's regime (see box on p.83). The monk drove down from Thien Mu in his powder-blue Austin car, which is now on display just behind the main building with a copy of the famous photograph that shocked the world. Thien Mu has continued to be a focus for Buddhist protest against repression and a sore spot for the government.

Despite its turbulent history, the pagoda is a peaceful place where the breezy, pine-shaded terrace affords wide views over the Perfume River. Approaching by either road or river you can't miss the octagonal, seven-tier brick **stupa**, built by Emperor Thieu Tri in the 1840s, in which each tier represents one of Buddha's incarnations on earth. Two **pavilions** to either side respectively shelter a huge bell, cast in 1710, weighing over 2000 kilos and said to be audible in the city, and a large stele erected in 1715 to record the history of Buddhism in Hué. Walk inland to find the main sanctuary (Buddhist services daily at 5.30pm), fronted by a gilded Maitreya Buddha.

While most people arrive at Thien Mu Pagoda by tour-boat, it's also within cycling distance of Hué (6km; 30min). Follow Le Duan (Highway 1) south from the citadel as far as the train tracks and then just keep heading west along the river where the road eventually gets quieter. If you've got time there's a pleasant **cycle ride** on from Thien Mu, past Van Mieu (see p.265) along an empty country lane beside the river. On the way back to Hué, stop for a bite to eat at the excellent *Huyen Anh* restaurant (see p.277) in **Kim Long** village.

Hon Chen Temple

From Thien Mu boats continue westwards for a while, passing Van Mieu on the right, and then head south to stop at the rocky promontory of **Hon Chen Temple**, named Temple of the Jade Bowl after the concave hill under which it sits ($2, video camera $6). Again it's the scenery of russet temple roofs among towering trees that is memorable, though the site has been sacred since the Cham people came here to worship their divine protectress Po Nagar, whom the Vietnamese adopted as Y A Na, the Mother Goddess. Emperor Minh Mang restored Hon Chen Temple in the 1830s but it was Dong Khanh who had a particular soft-spot for the goddess after she predicted he would be emperor. He enlarged the temple in 1886, declared himself Y A Na's younger brother and is now worshipped alongside his favourite goddess in the main sanctuary, **Hue Nam**, up from the landing stage and to the right. Of several shrines and temples that populate the hillside, Hue Nam is the most interesting, particularly for its unique nine-tier altar table and a small, upper sanctuary room accessible via two steep staircases.

Festivals at Hon Chen were banned between Independence and 1986 but have now resumed, taking place twice yearly in the middle of the third and seventh lunar months. The celebrations, harking back to ancient rituals, include trancedances performed by mediums, usually females dressed in brightly coloured costumes, who are transported by a pulsating musical accompaniment.

Hon Chen Temple is 9km from Hué and is only accessible from the river. If you don't want to take a **tour**, go to Minh Mang **ferry** station by road and hire a **sampan** to head 4km back towards Hué; expect to pay a couple of dollars per person for the return ride.

The Royal Mausoleums

These wise kings of Annam, who make death smile.

Charles Patris, late 1800s

Unlike previous Vietnamese dynasties, which buried their kings in the ancestral village, the Nguyens built themselves magnificent **Royal Mausoleums** in the valley of the Perfume River among low, forested hills to the south of Hué (see map on p.280). For historical reasons only seven mausoleums were built, but each one is a unique expression of the monarch's personality, usually planned in detail during his lifetime to serve as his palace in death. It is here more than anywhere else in Hué that the Nguyen emperors excelled in achieving a harmony between the works of man and his natural surroundings and, along with the Imperial City, these are Hué's most rewarding sights.

It often took years to find a site with the right aesthetic requirements that would also satisfy the court cosmologists charged with interpreting the underlying supernatural forces. Artificial lakes, waterfalls and hills were often added to improve the geomantic qualities of the location, at the same time creating picturesque, almost romantic, **garden settings** for the mausoleums, of which the finest ex-amples are those of Tu Duc and Minh Mang. Though the details vary, all the mausoleums consist of three elements: a **temple** dedicated to the worship of the deceased emperor and his queen; a large, stone **stele** recording his biographical details and a history of his reign, usually written by his successor; and the royal **tomb** itself. The main temple houses the funeral tablets and possessions of the royal couple, many of which have been stolen, while nearby stand ancillary buildings where the emperor's concubines lived out their years. In front of each stele-house is a paved courtyard, echoing the Imperial City's Esplanade of Great Salutations where officials and soldiers lined-up to honour their emperor, but in this case the mandarins, horses and elephants are fashioned in stone; military mandarins are easily distinguished by their sword, whereas the civil variety clutch sceptres. Obelisks nearby symbolize the power of the monarch and lastly, at the highest spot, there's the royal tomb enclosed within a wall and a heavy, securely fastened door. Traditionally the burial place was kept secret as a measure against grave-robbers and enemies of the state, and in extreme cases all those who had been involved in the burial were killed immediately afterwards.

Visiting the mausoleums

The mausoleums are intoxicating places, occasionally grandiose but more often achieving an elegant simplicity, where it's easy to lose yourself wandering in the quiet gardens. Of the seven, the contrasting mausoleums of Tu Duc, Khai Dinh and Minh Mang are the most attractive and well preserved, as well as being easily accessible. These are also the three covered by the boat trips, so they can get crowded; don't let this put you off – but if you do want something more off the beaten track then those of Gia Long, Dong Khanh and Thieu Tri are worth calling in on. Finally, Duc Duc's temple is in a sad state but his mausoleum is the closest to Hué, and is still tended by members of the royal family. Even if time allowed, however, you probably won't want to visit all the mausoleums at a **ticket price** of $5 a pop for the first three and $2 for Thieu Tri's and Dong Khanh's, though Gia Long's and Duc Duc's are free. The mausoleums are **open** from 7.30am to 4.30pm every day, but note that it's best to avoid weekends if possible when they're at their busiest.

To get to the mausoleums you can either rent a **bicycle** or **motorbike** for the day (see "Arrival, information and getting around", p.257), or take a Perfume River boat trip (see box on p.266). On a **boat tour**, you'll face a couple of longish walks, while with your own wheels you'll have to negotiate your own ferry crossings, but will have more time to explore, and won't be restricted to the main three mausoleums; a good compromise is to take a bike onboard a tour boat and cycle back to Hué from the last stop.

The Mausoleum of Tu Duc

Emperor Tu Duc was a romantic poet trying to rule Vietnam at a time when the Western world was challenging the country's independence. Although he was the longest reigning of the Nguyen monarchs, he was a weak ruler who preferred to hide from the world in the lyrical pleasure gardens he created. The **Mausoleum of Tu Duc** is the most harmonious of all the mausoleums, with elegant pavilions and pines reflected in serene lakes. The walled, twelve-hectare park took only three years to complete (1864–67), allowing Tu Duc a full sixteen years for boating and fishing, meditation, drinking tea made from dew collected in lotus blossoms, and composing some of the 4000 poems he is said to have written, besides several important philosophical and historical works. Somehow he also found time for 50-course meals, plus 104 wives and a whole village of concubines living in the park, though – possibly due to a bout of smallpox – he fathered no children. Perhaps it's not surprising that Tu Duc was also a tyrant who pushed the 3000 workmen building his mausoleum so hard that they rebelled in 1866, and were savagely dealt with.

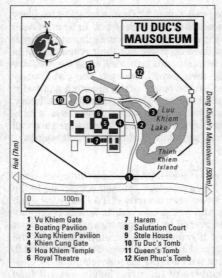

TU DUC'S MAUSOLEUM

N

Dong Khanh's Mausoleum (500m)

Hué (7km)

Luu Khiem Lake

Thinh Khiem Island

0   100m

1 Vu Khiem Gate
2 Boating Pavilion
3 Xung Khiem Pavilion
4 Khien Cung Gate
5 Hoa Khiem Temple
6 Royal Theatre
7 Harem
8 Salutation Court
9 Stele House
10 Tu Duc's Tomb
11 Queen's Tomb
12 Kien Phuc's Tomb

Entering by the southern gate, **Vu Khiem**, brick paths lead beside a lake covered in water-lilies and lotus to a small three-tiered **boating pavilion** which looks across to larger **Xung Khiem Pavilion**, where Tu Duc drank wine and wrote poetry; *khiem*, meaning "modest", appears in the name of every building. From the lake, steps head up through a triple-arched gateway, the middle door painted yellow for the emperor, into a second enclosure containing the main temple, **Hoa Khiem**, which Tu Duc used as a palace before his death. The royal funeral tablets here are unusual in that Tu Duc's, bearing a dragon, is smaller than the phoenix-decorated tablet of the queen. Behind the temple find the colourful **royal theatre**, while the crumbling edifices opposite were once quarters for Tu Duc's numerous concubines.

The second group of buildings, to the north, is centred on the emperor's tomb, preceded by the salutation court and stele-house. Tu Duc's stele, weighing twenty tonnes, is by far the largest; unusually, Tu Duc wrote his own eulogy, running to over 4000 characters to elucidate all his difficulties. Behind the stele is a kidney-shaped pond, representing the crescent moon, and then a bronze door leading into a square enclosure where the severe tomb shelters behind a screen adorned with the characters for longevity. Emperor Kien Phuc, one of Tu Duc's adopted sons, is also buried here, just north of the lake.

Tu Duc's Mausoleum is 7km from central Hué **by road**. From the **boat** jetty, it's a 2km walk from the river on a roughish path, or there might be a **Honda om** waiting on the river bank.

The Mausoleum of Khai Dinh

By way of a complete contrast the **Mausoleum of Khai Dinh** is a monumental confection of European Baroque, highly ornamental Sino-Vietnamese style and even incorporates elements of Cham architecture. Its most attractive feature is the setting, high up on a wooded hill, but it's worth climbing the 130-odd steps to take a look inside the sanctuary itself, still in its original state. Khai Dinh was the penultimate Nguyen emperor and his mausoleum is a radical departure from his predecessors, with neither gardens nor living quarters and only one main structure. Khai Dinh was also a vain man, a puppet of the French very much taken with French style and architecture, and though he only reigned for nine years it took eleven (1920–31) to complete his mausoleum, and it cost so much he had to levy additional taxes for the project.

The approach is via a series of grandiose, dragon-ornamented stairways leading first to the salutation courtyard, with an unusually complete honour-guard of mandarins, to the stele-house. Climbing up a further four terraces brings you to the **principal temple**, built of reinforced concrete with slate roofing imported from France, whose extravagant halls are a startling contrast to the blackened exterior. Walls, ceiling, furniture, everything is decorated to the hilt, writhing with dragons and peppered with symbolic references and classic imagery such as the Four Seasons panels in the ante-chamber. Most of this lavish display, not as garish as it might sound, is worked in glass and porcelain mosaic – even the central canopy, which looks like fabric though it's actually made of cement. A life-size gilded bronze statue of the emperor holding his royal sceptre sits under the canopy while his altar table and funeral tablet is up on the mezzanine floor behind. Before leaving, take a look at the portrait on the incense-table in the ante-chamber: Khai Dinh was a particularly flamboyant dresser and it's rumoured that he brought back a string of fairy lights from France and proceeded to wear them around the palace, twinkling, until the batteries ran out.

Khai Dinh's Mausoleum is 10km from Hué **by road**. Arriving **by boat**, it's a 1500-metre walk on a paved road, heading eastwards with a giant Quan Am statue on your right until you see the mausoleum on the opposite hillside.

The Mausoleum of Minh Mang

Court officials took fourteen years to find the location for the **Mausoleum of Minh Mang** – for which the mandarin responsible was awarded two promotions – and then only three years to build (1841–43), using 10,000 workmen. Minh Mang, the second Nguyen emperor, was a capable, authoritarian monarch who was selected for his serious nature and distrust of Western religious infiltration. He was also passionate about architecture – it was Minh Mang who completed Hué citadel after Gia Long's death – and designed his mausoleum along traditional Chinese lines, with all the principal buildings symmetrical about an east–west axis. But the mausoleum's stately grandeur is softened by fifteen hectares of superb landscaped gardens, almost a third of which is taken up by lakes reflecting the handsome, red-roofed pavilions.

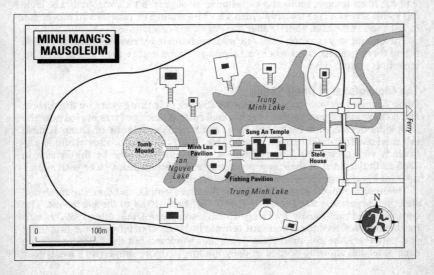

Inside the mausoleum a processional way links the series of low mounds bearing all the main buildings. After the salutation courtyard and stele-house comes the crumbling **principal temple** (*Sung An*), where Minh Mang and his queen, who died at seventeen, are worshipped. Despite this early loss, Minh Mang managed to father 142 children with his 33 wives and 107 concubines. The only point of interest about the temple itself is that local Christians vandalized it in 1885 as a protest against Minh Mang's virulent anti-Catholicism. Continuing west you reach **Minh Lau**, the elegant, two-storey "Pavilion of Pure Light" standing among clouds of frangipani trees, symbols of longevity, while beyond two stone-gardens trace the Chinese character for long life. From here the ceremonial pathway crosses a crescent lake and ends at the circular burial mound.

To reach Minh Mang's Mausoleum from Khai Dinh's, follow the **road** west until you hit the Perfume River (1500m) and turn left along the bank, looking out on your left for the village post office, opposite which you'll find **sampans** to take you across the river ($2 return per person). The entrance is then a couple of hundred metres' walk on the other side through a barrage of souvenir sellers. Note that this is also where you'll pick up sampans for Gia Long's Mausoleum and the Hon Chen Temple (see p.268).

The Mausoleum of Gia Long

As the first Nguyen ruler, Gia Long had his pick of the sites and he chose an immense natural park 16km from Hué on the left bank of the Perfume River. Unfortunately the **Mausoleum of Gia Long** was badly damaged during the American War and is only now being restored so there's not a great deal to see beyond some fine carving and a double-tomb with pitched roofs housing Gia Long and his wife. However, this is the least visited of Hué's mausoleums and is recommended for the boat trip and the peaceful stroll through sandy pine forest – though some visitors complain of attracting a convoy of persistent soft-drink sellers for the duration of the two-kilometre walk. You approach the complex from the north to find the main temple, tomb and stele-house all aligned on a horizontal axis, looking south across a lake towards Thien Tho Mountain. The mausoleum was begun in 1814 and completed shortly after the emperor's death in 1820.

The easiest way to reach Gia Long's Mausoleum is **by road** as far as the Minh Mang **ferry** station, from where a **sampan** (20min each way) costs around $5, including waiting time.

The Mausoleum of Dong Khanh

Dong Khanh died suddenly at the age of 25 after only three years on the throne, and so never got round to planning his final resting place but was buried near the temple he dedicated to his father. As a result the **Mausoleum of Dong Khanh** is a modest affair built in open countryside, but it has a rustic charm and is particularly well preserved. Dong Khanh was put on the throne by the French in 1885 as titular head of their new protectorate. He was a pliant ruler with a fondness for French wine, perfume and alarm clocks.

The mausoleum consists of two parts: the main temple, and then the tomb and stele in a separate, walled enclosure on a slight rise 100m to the northwest. The complex was built mostly by Dong Khanh's son, Khai Dinh, after 1889, though has been added to since. The **main temple** holds most of interest: the first thing you notice are the coloured-glass doors and windows, but the faded murals on each side wall showing scenes of daily life are far more attractive. Twenty-four glass-paintings, illustrated poems of Confucian love, hang on the temple's iron-wood columns and, at either end of the first row, are two engravings of Napoleon and the Battle of Waterloo. The three principal altars honour Dong Khanh with his two queens to either side, while his seven concubines have a separate altar in the back room. Finally, don't miss the altar to Y A Na in a small side-chamber, off to the right as you enter: Dong Khanh often consulted the goddess at Hon Chen Temple (see p.268) and dedicated an altar to her after she appeared in a dream and foretold that he would be emperor.

Dong Khanh's Mausoleum is only 500m from Tu Duc's; follow the **road** round to the southeast or take a **short-cut** over the hill by **footpath** from between the refreshment stalls, forking left twice before you see Dong Khanh's tomb on your right and the temple straight ahead behind some trees.

The Mausoleum of Thieu Tri

Emperor Thieu Tri was the son of Minh Mang and shared his father's aversion to foreign influences – it's said he destroyed anything Western he found in the imperial palaces – and his taste in architecture. The **Mausoleum of Thieu Tri** follows the same basic pattern as Minh Mang's though without the attractive walled gardens, and is split into two sections placed side by side. As it's also smaller it took less than a year to build (1847–48), but its most distinctive feature is that it faces northwest, a traditionally inauspicious direction, and many people believed that this was the reason the country fell under the French yoke a few years later. The complex is currently being restored and there's little to justify the trek out here. The main temple contains numerous poems, in mother of pearl or painted on glass, since Thieu Tri was a prolific poet who would pen a stanza or two at a moment's notice.

To get here from Hué follow the **road** towards Khai Dinh's Mausoleum but after Cau Lim Bridge, branch right beside a faded sign saying "Lang Thieu Tri" opposite the Social Welfare School; the mausoleum is 6km from the centre of Hué.

The Mausoleum of Duc Duc

Three emperors are buried at the **Mausoleum of Duc Duc** which, although it's the closest to Hué, is rarely visited because of its bad state of decay. The temple, built in 1899, is on the point of collapse though the walled compound where Duc Duc is buried with his wife is still intact, while emperors Thanh Thai and Duy Tan are interred in a separate row of graves behind the main temple. Duc Duc was forced to resign by his senior courtiers after a mere three days as emperor in 1883 and died a year later in prison, while his son, Thanh Thai, was also removed in 1907 after a suspected anti-French conspiracy. The French then put Thanh Thai's eight-year-old son, Duy Tan, on the throne but he fled the palace nine years later amid another revolutionary plot, and was eventually exiled with his father to the French territory of Réunion in the Indian Ocean. Duy Tan died in a World War II plane crash in 1945, fighting on the side of the Allies, but Thanh Thai was allowed back to Vietnam in 1947 and died in Saigon in the 1950s. Descendants of the imperial family, two French-speaking nephews of Bao Dai, still live in the temple buildings and possess a historic collection of family photos including some of the funeral of Thanh Thai.

Find the mausoleum down **Tan Lang Lane** (opposite 36 Tran Phu), 100m along on the right; someone will show you around for a small donation.

Tu Hieu Pagoda

While you're out exploring the mausoleums it's worth making a short detour to visit **Tu Hieu Pagoda**, buried in the pine forests northwest of Tu Duc's Mausoleum. Although it's not the most famous pagoda in Hué, Tu Hieu is one of the most attractive, and it does have an imperial link since this is where royal eunuchs retired to and were worshipped after their deaths. The pagoda was founded in 1843 and still houses an active community of forty monks who extend a warm welcome to their occasional visitors. The main altar is dedicated to Sakyamuni, with the Buddhist trinity sitting up above, while a secondary shrine room behind contains altars to several famous mandarins and the eunuchs. Between the two buildings is a small courtyard festooned with orchids and a hundred-year-old star-fruit vine. To find the pagoda, take the road towards Tu Duc's Mausoleum from the Nam Giao T-junction and near the top of the hill look out for two tall columns announcing "Tu Hieu". Turn right here down a dirt road and then fork left to reach the pagoda's triple-arched gate behind which lies a peaceful, crescent-moon lake.

Eating

It's not only Hué people who say their cuisine is the best in Vietnam, combining as it does special dishes originating from the imperial kitchens, vegetarian meals prepared with exquisite care in the pagodas, and simple but delicious "frugal meals" which are the essence of Hué home-cooking; see the box opposite for more on Hué's **speciality foods**.

Much of the local cuisine originated from **imperial meals**, which involved many elaborate dishes presented like works of art before the royal family. Some of the large hotels, such as the *Huong Giang*, now stage "royal meals" for tourists, including traditional music and the opportunity to embarrass yourself in imperial togs. All this frivolity doesn't come cheap though – the food is rich and plentiful, but at $80 for two it's really aimed at tour groups and business entertaining. An interesting and cheaper alternative, though without the music, is available at *79 Phan Dinh Phung* which until 1980 was the home of Emperor Bao Dai's mother, the wife of Khai Dinh. The house is now a small museum with a few pieces of royal furniture plus a stack of family photos, and makes an unusual dining room. Imperial meals here cost $10 per head or less, depending on the number of people; you need to book at least two or three days ahead. If you just fancy a **snack**, an unmarked stall at the west end of Nguyen Tri Phuong (tucked behind an ancient banyan tree opposite the entrance to Le Loi school) cooks up some of the best *banh khoai* in town. For spicy *bun bo*, join breakfasting locals (before 8am) on Pham Hong Thai Street – the stall at no. 5 is worth a look. Or, for something sweet, try Hué's most famous *chè* outlet down the alley at 17 Hung Vuong, where for next to nothing you can have a refreshing **drink** made from green bean and coconut (*chè xanh dua*), fruit (*chè trai cay*) or, if you're lucky, lotus seed (*chè hat sen*).

Most of the places listed below (and marked on the map on p.275) are found **south of the Perfume River**, near the hotels and guesthouses, but a few restaurants now opening up **in the citadel** make convenient lunch-stops or are worth an excursion in their own right. Several of the smaller hotels serve decent food, usually all day, and there's no shortage of cafés or cheap and cheerful local hostelries scattered throughout the city.

HUÉ SPECIALITIES

One good argument for staying in Hué an extra couple of days is its many speciality food, best sampled at local stalls and street kitchens. The most famous Hué dish is *banh khoai*, a small, crispy yellow **pancake** made of egg and rice-flour, fried up with shrimp, pork and bean sprouts and eaten with a special peanut and sesame sauce (*nuoc leo*), plus a vegetable accompaniment of star-fruit, green banana, lettuce and mint. Hué is also well known for its **noodles** and has its own spicy version of the rice-noodle soups, called *bun bo, bun ga* or *bun bo gio heo* depending on the meat used – beef, chicken or beef and pork – and flavoured with citronella, shrimp and basil.

There are even special **snacks**, usually eaten around four or five in the afternoon. Order *banh beo* and you get a whole trayful of individual dishes containing a small amount of steamed rice-flour dough topped with spices, shrimp flakes and a morsel of pork crackling; add a little sweetened *nuoc mam* sauce to each dish and tuck in with a teaspoon. *Banh nam*, or *banh lam*, is a similar idea but spread thinly in an oblong, steamed in a banana leaf and eaten with rich *nuoc mam* sauce. Manioc flour is used instead of rice for *banh loc*, making a translucent parcel of whole shrimps, sliced pork and spices steamed in a banana leaf, but this time the *nuoc mam* is pepped up with a dash of chilli. Finally, *ram it* consists of two small dollops of sticky rice-flour dough, one fried and one steamed, to dip in a spicy sauce.

One Hué dish that most people steer clear of, for fear of health repercussions, is *com hen* whose main ingredient is a small **shellfish** of the mussel family (*hen*) dredged up from around the Perfume River's Hen Island and further down the estuary. It's a popular and very tasty breakfast dish in summer, the main *hen* season, but can occasionally be found at other times of year in early morning stalls on Pham Hong Thai and at the west end of Truong Dinh. *Com hen* is complicated to prepare, but its main constituents are *hen*, rice vermicelli noodles, shrimp sauce and chilli.

Am Phu ("Hell"), 35–37 Nguyen Thai Hoc. Moderate prices and good cooking have made *Am Phu* very popular with locals and foreigners alike. The limited menu covers traditional Vietnamese dishes such as beef dipped in vinegar, boiled shrimp or the recommended *nem lui*, grilled pork sausages ready to wrap in rice paper and dunk in a thick, spicy peanut-sesame sauce.

Banh Beo Ba Cu, 93/5 Phan Dinh Phung. A locally famous establishment where you can sample *banh beo*, *banh loc* and *banh nam* at lunchtime or in the afternoon, up until around 5pm; or try the equally popular outlet at no. 93/9. To find both places, walk up the narrow lane opposite 142 Nguyen Hue.

Banh Beo Ba Do, 9 Nguyen Binh Kiem. Some Hué people swear this small restaurant in Phu Cat district serves the best *banh beo* etc in town. They sell out quickly so get there before 5pm.

Café Cheo Leo, 51 Ong Ich Khiem. This outdoor café is set beside the citadel walls in a beautiful garden belonging to a well-known, classical musician. The music of choice on the café's sound system is Vietnamese pop, but the family are willing to show their small collection of traditional instruments to interested visitors.

Café 3, 3 Le Loi. A cheap and cheerful streetside café opposite the *Le Loi Hué Hotel*, serving the standard range of Western and Vietnamese dishes, from spring rolls to fruit shakes.

Chao Ga, 3 Ly Thuong Kiet. This small no-nonsense restaurant ladles out filling bowls of chicken soup, *chao ga*, made with rice, lotus seed, pulses and sizeable chunks of meat.

Co Do, 4 Ben Nghe. Well-prepared food and cheap prices attract a mixed crowd to this small restaurant offering a limited menu of tasty dishes. Lemongrass and chilli are the predominant flavours, accompanying squid, chicken or shrimps, while their fried squid with vegetables is also recommended.

Dong Phuong, 26 Nguyen Tri Phuong. Local specialities plus the usual Western-Vietnamese menu are on offer in this hotel restaurant. Don't be put off by the lack of atmosphere; the food's good and the prices are fair.

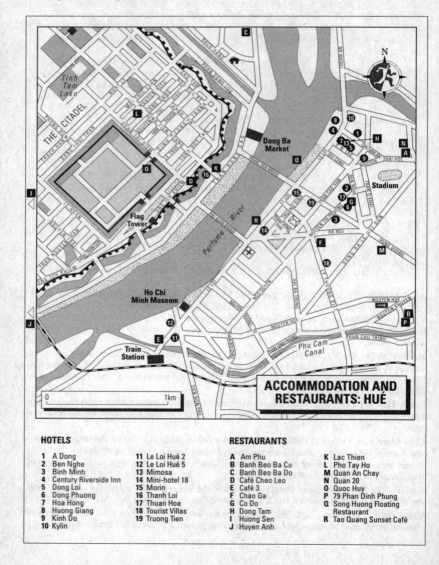

ACCOMMODATION AND
RESTAURANTS: HUÉ

HOTELS

1   A Dong
2   Ben Nghe
3   Binh Minh
4   Century Riverside Inn
5   Dong Loi
6   Dong Phuong
7   Hoa Hong
8   Huong Giang
9   Kinh Do
10 Kylin
11 Le Loi Hué 2
12 Le Loi Hué 5
13 Mimosa
14 Mini-hotel 18
15 Morin
16 Thanh Loi
17 Thuan Hoa
18 Tourist Villas
19 Truong Tien

RESTAURANTS

A   Am Phu
B   Banh Beo Ba Cu
C   Banh Beo Ba Do
D   Café Cheo Leo
E   Café 3
F   Chao Ga
G   Co Do
H   Dong Tam
I   Huong Sen
J   Huyen Anh
K   Lac Thien
L   Pho Tay Ho
M   Quan An Chay
N   Quan 20
O   Quoc Huy
P   79 Phan Dinh Phung
Q   Song Huong Floating
    Restaurant
R   Tao Quang Sunset Café

Dong Tam Vegetarian Restaurant, 48/7 Le Loi. Best at lunch-time when the food's freshest and you can take advantage of the garden courtyard. *Dong Tam* is run by a Buddhist family who offer a short menu including vegetarian *banh khoai* and good-value combination plates, *com dia*, of rice plus selected dishes.

Huong Sen, 42 Nguyen Trai. A moderately expensive floating restaurant on a lake northeast of the Imperial City. It's breezy and pleasant at any time of day but most seductive in the evening – remember the mosquito repellent.

Huyen Anh, 207 Kim Long, Kim Long village. A riverside restaurant with a garden terrace, on the road to Thien Mu Pagoda. Specialities are an excellent *banh cuon*, a fresh (unfried) spring roll eaten with peanut sauce, and a noodle dish called *bun thit nuong* – rice-flour noodles served with grilled pork and peanuts plus a salad of shredded banana bud, lettuce and mint.

Lac Thien, 6 Dinh Tien Hoang. Hué's two most famous restaurants, run by a family of deaf-mutes, stand next door to each other just outside the citadel walls. There's little to choose between them: both have lots of atmosphere, good prices and the food's fine, catering to the tourist trade with Hué specialities, noodle soups and banana pancakes.

Pho Tay Ho, 15 Dinh Tien Hoang. In the early morning this place in the citadel is packed out with locals slurping a breakfast bowl of *pho*. It's run by Hanoians who know how to produce a mean *pho bo*, with big chunks of succulent beef.

Quan An Chay, 41 Hung Vuong. A good-value vegetarian restaurant with some interesting variations. Try the *sup nam*, fresh mushroom soup, *banh cuon* spring roll, or *mi can bop*, a salad of wheat-flour "can" (a sort of shredded chicken-substitute) and onions. A rival vegetarian place at no. 44 is also popular.

Quan 20, 20 Ba Trieu. The speciality here is eel, *luon*, which is considered a male food and needs lots of beer to wash it down; if you go in the evening it's a lot quieter. The inexpensive menu is not restricted to eel, but at least try a bowl of eel soup.

Quoc Huy (formerly *Ong Tao 2*), 43 Dinh Cong Trang. The main attraction here is the setting, in the shaded courtyard of Trieu Temple, just inside the Imperial City's Hien Nhon gate. However, the food is also well presented, mostly traditional Vietnamese dishes such as grilled beef wrapped in mint, and surprisingly affordable.

Song Huong Floating Restaurant, just east of Trang Tien Bridge. Not the best quality food, but this place is recommended for an early evening beer.

Tao Quang Sunset Café, opposite 18 Le Loi. A cheaper alternative to the *Song Huong* for a quiet drink is this appropriately named, no-frills riverside café.

Entertainment and shopping

Under the Nguyen emperors Hué was the cultural and artistic as well as political capital of Vietnam. A rich tradition of dance and music evolved from popular culture, from the complex rituals of the court and from religious ceremonies. Though much of this tradition has been lost over the last fifty years, considerable effort has gone into reviving **Hué folksongs**, *Ca Hué*, which you can now sample, drifting down the Perfume River on a balmy Hué evening. If you want something a bit more upbeat, then try one of Hué's **nightclubs**, all of which have live music: best in town is at the *Dong Da Hotel*, 15 Ly Thuong Kiet (8pm–midnight; $3); or try the *Ngoc Anh Nightclub* next to the *Thuan Hoa Hotel* (8–11pm; $5).

Royal patronage nurtured not only fine cuisine and the performing arts but also highly skilled artisans whose descendants today are working to restore the imperial palaces or turning their skills to create **handicrafts** for the tourist trade.

Hué folksongs

Historically the Perfume River was a place of pleasure where prostitutes cruised in their sampans and artists entertained the gentry with poetry and music. While the former officially no longer exist, today's **folksong** performances are based on the old traditions, eulogizing about the city's beautiful scenery or the ten charms of a Hué woman – including long hair, dreamy eyes, flowing *ao dai*, and a conical hat – while she waits for her lover beside the river. Another popular strain is an improvised courtship song between a boy and girl, and occasionally you'll hear hypnotic, blues-like music, *Chua Van*, which accompanies the dance-trances at Hon Chen Temple, or the rhythmic chants of sampan rowers. The instruments themselves are intriguing, particularly the percussion section of four bone-china coffee cups and a wooden instrument garnished with old coins. To hear the folksongs, go to the kiosk next to *Song Huong Floating Restaurant*, where they organize boats most evenings and may be able to put together a group if you want to share the expense. An hour's performance costs $30, which includes a boat for up to ten people, plus six musicians (three singers and three instrumentalists); unfortunately the introductory talk is usually given only in Vietnamese.

Shopping

Hué's commercial life centres on the rambling **Dong Ba Market**, a huge covered market at the southeast corner of the citadel. Fruit, fish and vegetable vendors overflow into the surrounding spaces while in the downstairs hall you'll find Hué's contribution to the world of fashion, the *non bai tho* or **poem hat**. These look just like the normal conical hat but have a stencil, traditionally of a romantic poem, inserted between the palm fronds – and only visible when held up to the light. The market is within walking distance of the centre, but a more enjoyable way to get there is to hop on one of the sampans that shuttle back and forth from beside the Dap Da causeway.

The east end of Le Loi, opposite the two big hotels, has become the main location for souvenir and **crafts** shops, but there a couple of more interesting outlets worth seeking out: hand-sewn embroideries are produced at a small shop, *Cam Chau* at 6a Hung Vuong; over in the citadel, the *Gallery of Traditional Lacquer*, at 15a Dinh Tien Hoang, sells woodcarvings, ceramics, fine arts and lacquerware. The gallery also doubles as a studio, run by artist Do Ky Hoang, where you can see the painstaking work that goes into creating a lacquer painting.

Listings

Airlines *Vietnam Airlines*, in the *Thuan Hoa Hotel* at 7 Nguyen Tri Phuong (7–11am & 2–5pm).

Airport bus MASCO airport bus ($1) leaves from their office at 12 Ha Noi (☎054/825640), or will collect you from your hotel for an extra $1.

Bank and exchange *Vietcombank*, 6 Hoang Hoa Tham, accepts cash and travellers' cheques.

Hospital Hué Central Hospital is at 16 Le Loi (☎054/822325).

Immigration police, 45a Ben Nghe. If you lose your passport, this is the place to head for. To get your visa exit-point changed, though, you'll have to go to Da Nang.

Post office The GPO at 8 Hoang Hoa Tham offers a *poste restante* service.

Taxi For a metered taxi call *Hué Taxi*, also known as *ATC Taxi* (☎054/833333).

Tours and onward transport For tours of Hué and the surrounding sights, try hotels and guesthouses or one of the following: *Café 3*, 3 Le Loi; *DMZ Tour*, 26 Le Loi; *Le Loi Hotel*, 2 Le Loi; *Thua Thien–Hué Hotel & Service Co*, 2 & 8 Hung Vuong; or *Thua Thien–Hué Tourism*, 9 Ngo Quyen. These same places can also help arrange onward transport by tourist minibus or hired car to Hoi An, Da Nang, Hanoi and so forth, or try *ATC Tourist Co.*, 44 Le Loi.

Around Hué

With so much to discover in Hué itself most people don't get out to visit the surrounding districts. The usual excursion is a bike ride to **Thuan An Beach**, which can be combined with the attractive **Thanh Toan Brick Bridge**, though in both these cases it's the travelling as much as the getting there that makes it worthwhile. Heading inland, **Bach Ma National Park** contains some of the most lush vegetation in the whole of Vietnam and an old French hill station which is earmarked for tourist development in the near future. Further afield, one of the most popular excursions from Hué is a whirlwind day-trip round the **DMZ** (see p.283), a tour offered by most agents, though *DMZ Tour* are the real specialists in this field, with offices in Hué at 26 Le Loi and in Dong Ha inside the *Dong Ha Hotel*.

Thuan An Beach

Northwest of Hué the Perfume River ends in a vast estuary lagoon, sheltered by a long sandy spit with **Thuan An Beach** at its northern end. It was here that Rear-Admiral Courbet landed a thousand members of the French Expeditionary Force in August 1883, which ultimately persuaded the Vietnamese monarchs to recognize the French Protectorate. Nowadays Thuan An is a quiet place where residents of Hué come to escape the summer heat, and there are grand plans for resort hotels along the beach. Already there a few **places to stay**, of which the smartest is the small *Khach San Tan My* (☎054/866033; ④), run by Hué's *Huong Giang Hotel*, or try the newer *Duong Hai* (☎054/866115; ②).

Thuan An is 14km from Hué by road, through flat rice country and via a causeway which floods easily in the monsoon season (late Sept to early March), when the sea here also gets very rough. On the way you pass through Duong No village, 8km outside Hué, where Ho Chi Minh once lived with his father. It's a pleasant **cycle** ride or, alternatively, you can take a local **bus** from Hué's Dong Ba bus station, beside Dong Ba Market on the river's north bank, for the thirty-minute ride, but note that the last bus back leaves around 4pm. If you have your own transport, you'll have to pay a nominal **parking fee** at the beach.

Thanh Toan Covered Bridge

In the mid-eighteenth century Tran Thi Dao, the wife of a senior mandarin, paid for a covered bridge to be built over a canal, for which generosity she was deified in 1925 by Emperor Khai Dinh. The arched wooden bridge has been rebuilt several times, with the somewhat gaudy mosaics a recent addition. Though in itself not particularly spectacular, **Thanh Toan Covered Bridge**, *Cau Ngoi Thanh Toan*, makes a pleasant excursion off into the side roads and along tree-fringed canals. To get there, take Kiem Hué lane between nos. 119 and 117 Ba Trieu Street, or turn left off Hung Vuong Avenue beside An Cuu bridge to follow Phu Cam Canal east, then ask for directions along the way; the bridge is 8km east of Hué.

Bach Ma National Park

Well off the beaten track, **Bach Ma National Park** ($1, payable at entrance station) is being developed as an ecotourism destination, and dedicated ornithologists and botanists may want to make the effort to get here for the chance of seeing some of the 150 bird species and more than 500 species of flora in the park's

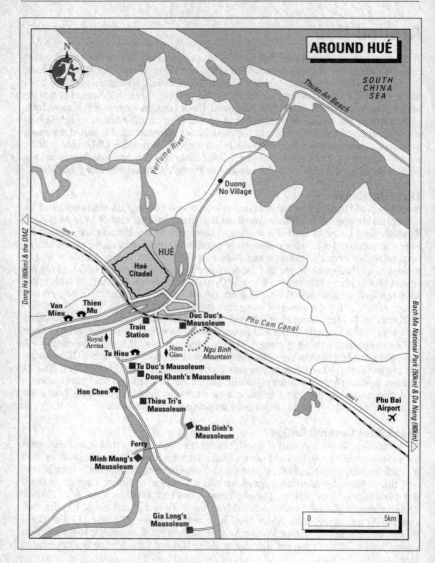

AROUND HUÉ

SOUTH CHINA SEA

Thuan An Beach

Perfume River

Duong No Village

HUÉ

Hué Citadel

Dong Ha (60km) & the DMZ

Hwy-1

Van Mieu

Thien Mu

Train Station

Duc Duc's Mausoleum

Phu Cam Canal

Royal Arena

Tu Hieu

Nam Giao

Ngu Binh Mountain

Tu Duc's Mausoleum

Dong Khanh's Mausoleum

Hon Chen

Thieu Tri's Mausoleum

Khai Dinh's Mausoleum

Ferry

Hwy-1

Phu Bai Airport

Bach Ma National Park (50km) & Da Nang (90km)

Minh Mang's Mausoleum

Gia Long's Mausoleum

0   5km

25,000 hectares of evergreen forests. Bach Ma highlands were once the location of a French summer resort, where Emperor Bao Dai also kept several luxury villas. The hundred-odd buildings, tennis courts and rose-beds are now in ruins but Hué People's Committee is repairing the road and has plans to refurbish some of the villas for tourist accommodation.

You'll need your own **transport** to get here: 60km south of Hué, turn west off Highway 1 in Phu Loc town opposite the post office, past the district secondary school and then drive for another 3km until you see the distinctive, white **park headquarters** building on top of a small hill to the right. The **guesthouse** (☎054/871328; ①) here has ten simple rooms. There are a couple of basic, inexpensive **eating** places near the park entrance, and a restaurant and bar are planned for the near future. You could also bring your own food from markets in Hué or Phu Loc, and you can buy a certain amount of fresh produce from villagers at Bach Ma.

Several **nature trails** are being created – leading to beautiful waterfalls and surrounded by stunning mountainscapes. Until construction of a second guesthouse at the top of the mountain is completed, you must be prepared to walk 16km up from the guesthouse to reach the trailheads and then to camp out in the park. Although it's not a requirement, it's definitely a good idea to take a **guide** (around $5 per day) when you're walking in the park, principally for your own safety – it's easy to get lost – though few of the guides speak any English. Note that it's normal "forest etiquette" to share drinks, meals and carrying the loads. If you want to make a positive contribution to the onerous task of **reforestation**, the park has a programme whereby you can buy a sapling for $1 and help plant it in one of the denuded areas of the park.

Dong Ha and the DMZ

Quang Tri and Quang Binh, the two provinces either side of the **DMZ** (Demilitarized Zone), were the most heavily bombed and saw the highest casualties, civilian and military, American and Vietnamese, during the American War. Names made infamous in 1960s and 1970s America have been perpetuated in countless films and memoirs: Camp Carroll, The Rockpile, Hamburger Hill and Khe Sanh. For some people the DMZ will be what draws them to Vietnam, the end of a long and difficult pilgrimage; for others it will be a bleak, sometimes beautiful, place where there's nothing particular to see but where it's hard not to respond to the sense of enormous desolation. Most visitors take an organized trip out of Hué (see p.278 for recommended operators), visiting all the major sites in a long day, but it's also possible to use **Dong Ha** as a base or cover a more limited selection on the drive north. From Dong Ha the old French road, Highway 9, runs parallel to the DMZ on its way west to the **Lao Bao** border gate, the only land-crossing into Laos from Vietnam.

Quang Tri

American troops weren't the first to suffer heavy losses in this region: during the 1950s French soldiers dubbed the stretch of Highway 1 north of Hué as *la rue sans joie*, or "street without joy", after they came under constant attack from elusive Viet Minh units operating out of heavily fortified villages along the coast. Later, in the 1972 Easter Offensive, communist forces overran the whole area, capturing **QUANG TRI** town, some 60km from Hué, from the South Vietnamese Army (ARVN) and holding it for four months while American B-52s pounded the township and surrounding countryside, before it was retaken at huge cost to both sides as well as to hapless civilians caught up in the battle. Quang Tri was simply wiped off the map and though a town of sorts has risen in its stead, known officially as **Trieu Hai**, you could be forgiven for missing it. Keep your eyes peeled for one of its few identifying features, the small, pockmarked shell of **Long Hung Church** to the east of the road, 55km from Hué, kept as a memorial to victims of 1972. Soon after, a track on the opposite side of the highway leads 4km south to the more impressive ruin of **La Vang Church**, beside which stands an extraordinary monument of Alice-in-Wonderland mushrooms supposedly representing the apparition of the Virgin Mary to persecuted Catholics on this spot in 1798. Back on the highway, road and railway share a bridge over the Quang Tri River from where it's only another 13km to the town of Dong Ha, which took over as provincial capital when Quang Tri ceased to exist.

Dong Ha

As a former US Marine Command Post and then ARVN base, **DONG HA** was also obliterated in 1972 but unlike Quang Tri it has bounced back, thanks largely to its administrative status and location at the eastern end of Highway 9 which leads through Laos to Savannakhet on the Mekong River (see p.288 for details of cross-border travel). The future looks rosy as well: discussions with landlocked Laos are under way to establish a deep-water harbour at Cua Viet and develop markets along the border. As the closest town to the DMZ, Dong Ha also attracts a lot of tourist traffic though few people choose to stay here, preferring the comfort and facilities of Hué.

Dong Ha is a two-street town: Highway 1, known here as Le Duan Avenue, forms the main artery as it passes through on its route north, while Highway 9 takes off inland at a central T-junction. The town's **bus station** is located on this junction, while its **train station** lies 1km south towards Hué and just west of the highway. An impressive new market and bridge over the Cua Viet River, 1km beyond the bus station, mark Dong Ha's northern extremity, where a road branches left to find the **post office** (spot the tell-tale radio mast) and the remains of Dong Ha's own memorial, a collection of three US tanks rotting beside the post office junction. **Information**, expensive car rental and guides can be found at either the helpful *DMZ Tour* (☎053/853047), linked to the Hué company of the same name and based in the *Dong Ha Hotel*, or at the state-owned *Quang Tri Hotel and Tourism Co*, 135 Le Duan (☎053/852927). In theory you can only visit the DMZ with a local guide, but this is recommended anyway as most sites are unmarked and, more importantly, they know which paths are safe – local farmers are still regularly being killed or injured by unexploded ordinance in this area. The tour fee includes a "permit" ($1–2), that you're supposed to have before setting off into the wilds.

Accommodation and eating

Budget travellers looking for **accommodation** should head straight for *Nha Tro Hai Ly* (no phone; ①), a small but acceptably clean place with cold water and negotiable prices tucked down a lane right across from the bus station. Alternatively, the slightly aged but well-kept *People's Committee Guesthouse* (*Nha Khach UBND Thi Xa Dong Ha*; ☎053/853373; ①) is a longer trek but offers a range of rooms at reasonable prices: walk left out of the bus station onto Le Duan for about 400m and take the first left, Le Quy Don, to find the guesthouse up on the right-hand side. On the same road but closer to the highway is Dong Ha's top address, the bungalow-style *Ngan Ha Guesthouse* (☎053/852806; ③) at 2 Le Quy Don, with comfortable, well-furnished rooms. For something in the middle range, ignore the damp *Dong Ha Hotel* (☎053/852292; ①) next to the bus station and take Highway 1 south towards Hué for about 600m to reach *Buu Dien Tinh Guesthouse* (☎053/854417; ②–③), offering twelve good-value rooms set round a quiet courtyard.

Dong Ha's two best **restaurants**, the *Hiep Loi* and *Tan Chau*, are located next to each other on the intersection of highways 1 and 9. Both are popular but the *Tan Chau* just wins out with its traditional music and family altar in the main room; it also serves huge piles of piping hot food at good prices. Otherwise the *Dong Ha Hotel* has a decent restaurant where tour groups usually stop, and there's no shortage of no-nonsense street kitchens serving *com* and *pho* all along Le Duan.

The DMZ and around

Under the terms of the 1954 Geneva Accords, Vietnam was split in two along the Seventeenth Parallel, pending elections intended to re-unite the country in 1956. The demarcation line ran along the Ben Hai River and was sealed by a strip of no-man's-land 5km wide on each side known as the Demilitarized Zone, or DMZ. All communist troops and supporters were supposed to regroup north to the Democratic Republic of Vietnam, leaving the southern Republic of Vietnam to non-communists and various shades of opposition. When the elections failed to take place the Ben Hai River became the de facto border until 1975.

In reality both sides of the DMZ were anything but demilitarized after 1965, and anyway the border was easily circumvented – by the Ho Chi Minh Trail to the west (see box on p.286) and sea routes to the east – enabling the North Vietnamese to by-pass a string of American firebases overlooking the river. One of the more fantastical efforts to prevent communist infiltration southwards was US Secretary of Defence Robert McNamara's proposal for an electronic fence from the Vietnamese coast to the Mekong River, made up of seismic and acoustic sensors which would detect troop movements and pinpoint targets for bombing raids. Though trials in 1967 met with some initial success, the "McNamara Line" was soon abandoned: sensors were confused by animals, especially elephants, and could be triggered deliberately by the tape-recorded sound of vehicle engines.

Nor could massive, conventional bombing by artillery and aircraft contain the North Vietnamese, who finally stormed the DMZ in 1972 and pushed the border 20km further south. Exceptionally bitter fighting in the territory south of the Ben Hai River (I Corps Military Region) claimed more American lives in the five years leading up to 1972 than any other battle zone in Vietnam. Figures for North Vietnamese losses during that period are not known, but it's estimated that unexploded devices lurking in the DMZ have, since 1975, been responsible for up to 9000 deaths and injuries. So much fire-power was unleashed over this area, including napalm and herbicides, that for years nothing would grow in the impacted, chemical-laden soil, but the region's low, rolling hills are now mostly reforested with a surprising green sea of pine, eucalyptus and acacia.

Some civilians north of the DMZ managed to escape the onslaught by relocating their villages into tunnels deep underground, of which the most famous are

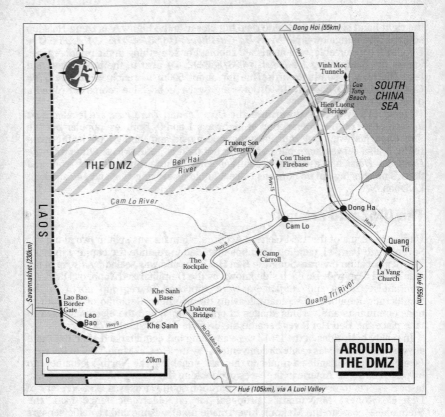

Map legend and labels:
- △ Dong Hoi (55km)
- N
- Hwy 1
- Vinh Moc Tunnels
- Cua Tung Beach
- SOUTH CHINA SEA
- Hien Luong Bridge
- Truong Son Cemetry
- Con Thien Firebase
- THE DMZ
- Ben Hai River
- Cam Lo River
- Hwy 15
- Dong Ha
- Cam Lo
- Hwy 1
- Quang Tri
- LAOS
- △ Savannakhet (230km)
- Hwy 9
- Camp Carroll
- The Rockpile
- La Vang Church
- Quang Tri River
- Hué (55km) ▷
- Lao Bao Border Gate
- Khe Sanh Base
- Lao Bao
- Hwy 9
- Khe Sanh
- Dakrong Bridge
- Ho Chi Minh Trail
- 0   20km
- **AROUND THE DMZ**
- ▽ Hué (105km), via A Luoi Valley

those of Vinh Moc. Unlike the Cu Chi tunnels, near Ho Chi Minh City (see p.107), these tunnels were built primarily for civilian use and have been preserved in their original form. Apart from Vinh Moc, the area's main sights lie south of the Ben Hai River. Even in a long day it's not possible to cover everything but most of the places described below are included on organized tours from Hué. If you have limited time then the Vinh Moc tunnels should be high on your list, along with a drive up Highway 9 to Khe Sanh, both for the scenery en route and the sobering battleground itself.

Hien Luong Bridge and the Vinh Moc Tunnels
A mere 15km north of Dong Ha, Highway 1 drops down into the DMZ, running between paddy fields to **Hien Luong Bridge** and the Ben Hai River, which lies virtually on the Seventeenth Parallel. Until it was destroyed in 1967, the original bridge was painted half red and half yellow as a vivid reminder that this was a physical and ideological boundary separating the two Vietnams. The present iron-girder bridge was reconstructed in 1973 and officially re-opened in 1975 as a symbol of reunification, though it still represents an important psychological barrier between north and south.

One kilometre north of the Ben Hai River, 22km from Dong Ha, a signpost indicates a right turn to an amazing complex of tunnels where over a thousand people sheltered, sometimes for weeks on end, during the worst American bombardments. A section of the **Vinh Moc Tunnels** has been restored and opened to visitors as a powerful tribute to the villagers' courage and tenacity, with a small museum at the entrance providing background information (daily 7am–5pm; $1.50 including English-speaking guide and flashlight, $5 for video camera). Although not recommended for the claustrophobic, the tour only takes around fifteen minutes and these tunnels were built taller (the ceiling is almost 2m high in places) than those of Cu Chi. Vinh Moc lies about 16km from Highway 1 on a twisting, unmarked route that takes you north beside the coast through stands of casurina; note that the last few unpaved kilometres become impassable in heavy rains, and there's a small road-toll for cars and motorbikes.

When American bombing-raids north of the DMZ intensified in 1966 the inhabitants of Vinh Linh district began digging down into the red laterite soils, excavating more than fifty tunnels over the next two years. Although they were also used by North Vietnamese soldiers, the tunnels were primarily built to shelter a largely civilian population who worked the supply route from the Con Co Islands lying just offshore. Five tunnels belonged to Vinh Moc, a village located right on the coast where for two years 250 people dug more than 2km of tunnel, which housed all 600 villagers over varying periods from early 1967 until 1969, when half decamped north to the relative safety of Nghe An Province. The tunnels were constructed on three levels at 10, 15 and 20–23m deep – though nowadays you can't visit the lowest level – with good ventilation, freshwater wells and, eventually, a generator and lights. The underground village was also equipped with school, clinics, and a maternity room where 17 children were born; each family was allocated a tiny cavern, the four-person space being barely larger than a single bed. Safe from bomb attacks but only able to emerge at night to tend the fields and vegetable plots, the greatest problem was lack of fresh air and sunlight, especially for young children who would sit in the tunnel mouths whenever possible. In 1972 the villagers of Vinh Moc could finally abandon their underground existence and rebuild their homes, rejoined by relatives from Nghe An a year later.

Con Thien Firebase and the Truong Son Cemetery

The American front line comprised a string of firebases set up on a long, low ridge of hills looking north across the DMZ and the featureless plain of the Ben Hai River. The largest was **Con Thien Firebase**, first established by the Special Forces (Green Berets) and then handed over to the Marines in 1966, from where their big guns could reach far into North Vietnam. In the lead up to the 1968 Tet Offensive, as part of the NVA's diversionary attacks, the base became the target of prolonged shelling, followed by an infantry assault during which it was briefly surrounded. The Americans replied with everything in their arsenal, including long-range strafing from gunships in the South China Sea and carpet-bombing by B-52s. The North Vietnamese were forced to withdraw temporarily, but then completely overran the base in the summer of 1972.

In the last twenty years the pulverized land has struggled back to life and now has a veneer of green, mostly scrubland and tussocks of invasive "American grass", but crops such as manioc, sweet potato and rubber trees have recently managed to survive. From the ruined lookout post on Con Thien's highest point you get a great view over the DMZ and directly north to what were enemy positions, chillingly close on the opposite bank of the Ben Hai River. Otherwise there's nothing to see apart from the odd, casually placed boot or Claymore mine, some scraps of netting and tattered camouflage clothing washed out by the rains.

To reach Con Thien, drive west on Highway 9 from Dong Ha as far as Cam Lo town (11km) and then turn north on Highway QL15, following signs to the Truong Son Cemetery. The base is roughly 9km out of Cam Lo and 1km east of the road on an unmarked, winding path which it's best to tackle in the company of a guide.

THE HO CHI MINH TRAIL

At the end of its "working" life, the Ho Chi Minh Trail had grown from a rough assemblage of animal tracks and **jungle paths** to become a highly effective **logistical network** stretching from near Vinh, north of the Seventeenth Parallel, to Tay Ninh Province on the edge of the Mekong Delta. Initially it took up to six months to walk the trail from north to south, most of the time travelling at night while carrying rations of rice and salt, medicines and equipment; in four years one man, Nguyen Viet Sinh, is reputed to have carried more than 50 tonnes and covered 40,000km, equivalent to walking round the world. By 1975, however, the trail – comprising at least three main arteries plus several feeder roads leading to various battlefronts and totalling over **15,000km** – was wide enough to take tanks and heavy trucks, and could be driven in just one week. It was protected by sophisticated anti-aircraft emplacements and supported by regular service stations (fuel and maintenance depots, ammunition dumps, food stores and hospitals), often located underground or in caves and all connected by field telephone. Eventually there was even an oil pipeline constructed alongside the trail to take fuel south from Vinh to a depot at Loc Ninh. All this absorbed thousands of men and women in maintenance work, as engineers, gunners and medical staff, while as many as 50,000 Youth Volunteers repaired bridges and filled in bomb craters under cover of darkness.

The trail was conceived in early 1959 when **General Giap** ordered the newly created Logistical Group 559 to reconnoitre a safe route by which to direct men and equipment down the length of Vietnam in support of communist groups in the south. Political cadres blazed the trail, followed in 1964 by the first deployment of 10,000 regular troops, and culminating in the trek south of 150,000 men in preparation for the **1968 Tet Offensive**. It was a logistical feat that rivalled Dien Bien Phu (see pp.392–393) in both scale and determination: this time it was sustained over fifteen years and became a symbol to the Vietnamese of both their victory and their sacrifice. For much of its southerly route the trail ran through **Laos** and **Cambodia**, sometimes on paths forged during the war against the French, sometimes along riverbeds, and always through the most difficult, mountainous terrain plagued with leeches, snakes, malaria and dysentery.

On top of all this, people on the trail had to contend with almost constant bombing. By early 1965 **aerial bombardment** had begun in earnest, using napalm and defoliants as well as conventional bombs, to be joined later by carpet-bombing B-52s. Every day in the spring of 1965 the US Air Force flew an estimated three hundred bombing raids over the trail and in eight years dropped over two million tonnes of bombs, mostly over Laos, in an effort to cut the flow. Later they experimented with seismic and acoustic sensors to eavesdrop on troop movements and pinpoint targets, but the trail was never completely severed and supplies continued to roll south in sufficient quantities to sustain the war.

Six kilometres further along the same road you come to the **Truong Son War Martyr Cemetery**, dedicated to the estimated 25,000 men and women who died on the Truong Son Trail, better known in the west as the Ho Chi Minh Trail (see box on facing page). Many bodies were never recovered but a total of 10,036 graves lie in the fourteen-hectare cemetery among whispering glades of evergreen trees. Graves are arranged in five geographical regions, subdivided according to native province, and centred round memorial houses listing every name and grave number in the sector. Each headstone announces *liet si* ("martyr"), together with as many details as are known: name, date and place of birth, date of enrolment, rank, and the date they died.

Khe Sanh

Continuing west on Highway 9, you pass the turning south to another US Marines base, **Camp Carroll**, now a pepper farm, and begin to climb into the foothills of the Truong Son range. Where the road veers off south, a sheer-sided isolated stump 230m high dominates the valley: the **Rockpile**. For a while American troops, delivered by helicopter, used the peak for directing artillery to targets across the DMZ and into Laos, but the post was abandoned after 1968. The highway continues over a low pass and then follows a picturesque valley past the Dakrong Bridge, which carries a spur of the Ho Chi Minh Trail, before climbing among ever-more forested mountains to emerge on a windswept plateau that was the site of a pivotal battle in the American War.

The **battle of Khe Sanh** was important not because of its immediate outcome, but because it attracted worldwide media attention and, along with the simultaneous Tet Offensive, demonstrated the futility of America's efforts to contain their enemy. In 1962 an American Special Forces team arrived in Khe Sanh town to train local Bru minority people in counterinsurgency and then four years later the first batch of Marines were sent in to establish a forward base near Laos, to secure Highway 9 and to harass troops on the Ho Chi Minh Trail. Skirmishes around Khe Sanh increased as intelligence reports indicated a massive build-up of North Vietnamese Army (NVA) troops in late 1967, possibly as many as 40,000, facing 6000 Marines together with a few hundred South Vietnamese and Bru. Both the Western media and American generals were soon presenting the confrontation as a crucial test of America's credibility in South Vietnam and drawing parallels with Dien Bien Phu (see pp.392–393); as US President Johnson famously remarked, he didn't want "any damn Dinbinfoo".

The NVA attack came in the early hours of January 21, 1968 when rockets raining in on the base added to the terror and confusion by striking an ammunition dump, gasoline tanks and stores of tear gas. There followed a seemingly endless, nerve-grinding NVA artillery barrage, when hundreds of shells fell on the base each day, interspersed with costly US infantry assaults into the surrounding hills. In an operation code-named "Niagara", General Westmoreland called in the air battalions to silence the enemy guns and break the siege by unleashing the most intense bombing-raids of the war: in nine weeks nearly 100,000 tonnes of bombs pounded the area round the clock, averaging one airstrike every five minutes, backed up by napalm and defoliants. Unbelievably the NVA were so well dug in and camouflaged that they not only withstood the onslaught but continued to return fire, despite horrendous casualties, estimated at 10,000. On the US side around 500 troops died at Khe Sanh (although official figures record only 248 American deaths, of which 43 occurred in a single helicopter accident), before a relief column broke through in early April, seventy-odd days after the siege had begun. Meanwhile NVA forces gradually pulled back and by the middle of March had all but gone, having successfully diverted American resources away from southern cities prior to the Tet Offensive. Three months later the Americans also quietly withdrew, leaving a plateau that resembled a lunar landscape, contaminated for years to come with chemicals and explosives; even the trees left standing were worthless because so much shrapnel was lodged in the timber.

Today, the former Marines base at Khe Sanh is one of the few places around the DMZ where vegetation still won't grow and where white phosphorus continues to smoulder in the summer sun. The terrain is pock-marked with shallow holes left by scrap-metal hunters, and children run up to offer fistfuls of bullets or "genuine" dog-tags. Guides point out trenches and craters, difficult to distinguish from the scars of erosion, and the red gash of the airstrip, but nothing else remains: when American troops were ordered to abandon Khe Sanh, everything was blown up and bulldozed flat. The only memorial is a drab concrete panel describing the siege – made even more poignant by the hauntingly beautiful mountains all around.

PRACTICALITIES

The town of **KHE SANH** (now officially rechristened **Huang Hoa**) is a bleak, one-street settlement, its frontier atmosphere reinforced by the smugglers' trail across the border to Laos, only 19km away. To find **the base**, fork right beside a three-legged monument on the town's eastern outskirts, follow the road for 2km and then turn right beside a house where an unmarked path strewn with bullets leads off among coffee bushes struggling to survive in the hostile soil.

There are two basic **guesthouses** on Khe Sanh's dusty main street (Highway 9): *Mien Nui Guesthouse* (☎053/880237; ①) in the centre of town under the radio mast is marginally the better, where it's worth paying the extra dollar for their bigger rooms; 1km further west find the slightly cheaper but more run-down *Huong Hoa Guesthouse* (☎053/880536; ①). Opposite the *Mien Nui*, and about 20m west, are a few wooden shacks which serve as pretty good **restaurants** – try the *Quan Am*, identifiable by a painted fish. At 450m above sea-level, Khe Sanh is frequently shrouded in fog and mornings can be cold, making the warm bread rolls with spicy meat and veg fillings sold at roadside stalls a particularly welcome breakfast. The **bank** next to the *Huong Hoa* will change dollar notes but at poor rates.

ACROSS THE BORDER INTO LAOS

Lao Bao border crossing is the only land route open to foreigners between Vietnam and Laos, though most of the traffic consists of local tradespeople bringing in cigarettes, clothes and electrical goods. It's an attractive ride up from Khe Sanh, through misty mountains on a reasonable road, and the crossing is hassle-free beyond having to walk a kilometre between inspection posts; see p.249 for information on **visas**.

The quickest way to reach the border from Khe Sanh is **by Honda om** ($1–2; 30min). Local **buses** from Khe Sanh or Dong Ha take you only as far as Lao Bao village, where you can pick up a **motorbike** for the final 3km. On the Laotian side of the border, buses leave for Savannakhet, from where there are connections north to Vientiane by road, river (both unpredictable during the rains) and air, or you can head straight over the Mekong River to Mukdahan in Thailand.

Entering Vietnam from Laos, buses down to Khe Sanh leave from Lao Bao village roughly every thirty minutes, according to demand; some go straight through to Dong Ha, or you may have to change at Khe Sanh.

Buses either stop on the highway or leave from Khe Sanh bus station, an open field across from the *Mien Nui*, with frequent departures for Lao Bao and the Laotian border (see box on facing page), and for Dong Ha in the opposite direction; change in Dong Ha for Hué.

The A Luoi Valley – and Hamburger Hill

Tours of the DMZ usually take a short deviation at the **Dakrong Bridge**, roughly 9km east of Khe Sanh, to follow a spur of the **Ho Chi Minh Trail** (see box on p.286) feeding in from Laos – unconvincing in its tarmacked state and totally denuded of forest cover – and to visit the **minority villages** (see *Contexts*, p.438, for more on Vietnam's ethnic minorities). Closest of several Bru villages is Mit (jackfruit) village, 200m south of the river and up a path to the right, where a collection of distinctive "turtle carapace" thatched stilthouses shelter under jackfruit trees laced with pepper vines. The immaculately swept village seems to be populated mostly by diminutive, pot-bellied pigs and pipe-smoking old ladies with filed and lacquered teeth. Small communities of Ta-Oi live further from the bridge, sporting earlobe-stretching jewellery; the Ta-Oi, unlike the Bru, supported the North Vietnamese during the American War and helped maintain the Ho Chi Minh Trail.

Keep heading south on this little-travelled backroad, a rough track that becomes impassable in rains, and eventually you reach **A Luoi** township (nearly 100km from the bridge). Stands of rare primary forest in the A Luoi Valley somehow missed being drenched with chemicals during the war, in stark contrast to the so-called "Agent Orange Museum" of A Shau Valley on the Lao border south of A Luoi. One of the small hills dotting A Shau Valley was the scene of a gruelling fight in May 1969: around 700 lives (70 American and approximately 633 NVA) were lost in nine days on the slopes of Ap Bia hill – better known to cinema audiences as **Hamburger Hill** (see p.465). After failing several times to dislodge the estimated 1200 North Vietnamese troops holed-up in concrete bunkers on top of Ap Bia, the Americans built a road west from Hué to the valley and tried again with five battalions plus massive air support. Against such odds the North Vietnamese fought their way out to Laos, and then one month later the Americans also withdrew, provoking intense public criticism at home.

Dong Hoi to Ninh Binh

North of the DMZ, Vietnam shrinks to a mere 50km wide and is edged with sand dunes up to 80m high, marching inland at a rate of 10m per year despite efforts to stabilize them with screw-pine and cactus. The narrow coastal plain is walled-in by the jagged Truong Son Mountains and drained by short, flood-prone rivers. But one of these rivers, the Son, has created an extensive underground drainage system which constitutes one of the few sights of any note in the region. **Phong Nha Cave**, where the river emerges, has recently been rediscovered and already attracts a steady stream of travellers, mostly on excursions from Hué or the nearby town of **Dong Hoi**. There's little else to tempt the tourist on the route north and most people push straight through to Ninh Binh or even Hanoi. Those travelling by road usually overnight in **Vinh**, where there's the opportunity to visit **Ho Chi Minh's birthplace** in the nearby village of Kim Lien. For motorcyclists and others in need of alternative accommodation, both **Ha Tinh** and **Thanh Hoa** furnish the basic requirements, but hold no particular interest otherwise.

Dong Hoi and Phong Nha Cave

The first town of any size north of the Seventeenth Parallel is **DONG HOI** and, as such, it was flattened in the American War's bombing raids. The town has risen from its ashes to become a provincial capital of 20,000 people – built on a grand scale with well-ordered streets, massive theatre hall and an attractive riverfront boulevard – though bereft of any particular sights. Those tourists that do stop in Dong Hoi are usually heading for the **Phong Nha Cave**, a genuinely impressive cave system.

The town

Dong Hoi is slowly gearing up for tourist traffic as Phong Nha begins to attract more interest. The town centre is a crossroads beside the landmark **post office** radio mast: south of this junction Highway 1 is named Quang Trung, becoming Ly Thuong Kiet to the north; Tran Hung Dao leads west to the **train station**, 3km out of town, while east takes you 50m to the Nhat Le Estuary and riverfront Quach Xuan Ky. There's no long-distance **bus station** in Dong Hoi – just go out on the highway and flag one down. The provincial **tourist office**, *Quang Binh Tourism*, is located behind the Dong Hoi Hotel on the left of the highway as you come in from Dong Ha; they offer affordable car rental and guides but you're probably better off talking to English-speaking staff at one of the hotels first of all. The only **bank** that handles foreign exchange (cash and travellers' cheques) is at 46 Quang Trung, next to a brightly painted monument marking Dong Hoi's southern extremity, said to be a gateway of the eighteenth-century citadel. Opposite the monument, Me Suot Street leads down to a lively, riverside fish **market** and an area of covered stalls where vendors sell ice-cold glasses of sweet-bean *chè*.

Accommodation and eating

If you're staying the night in Dong Hoi, ignore **hotels** on the main highway and turn east at the post office crossroads to find Dong Hoi's two top hotels: the clean and comfortable *Huu Nghi* (☎052/822567, fax 822463; ③) at 22 Quach Xuan Ky, on the corner where road and river meet; and the *Phuong Dong* (☎052/822276, fax 822404; ②), one block south at no. 20 – a big, friendly place with a selection of rooms to suit all budgets. Both of these are quiet, have decent restaurants and can help arrange tours to Phong Nha. The only other hotel worth trying is the *Phuong Nam* (☎052/823194, fax 823306; ③), on the main highway at 26 Ly Thuong Kiet, which offers small, well-kept rooms. If you get stranded at the train station, there are a couple of *nha tro* (**dormitories**) immediately outside, where you can find a bed for a dollar or two.

Dong Hoi's most popular **restaurant** is the *Anh Dao*, on the main street at 56 Quang Trung, run by a Hué emigrant. For off-the-highway eating, *Nha Hang Hanoi* serves home cooking, including baked rice in terracotta pots; find it just behind the *Phuong Dong Hotel*, along a dirt track linking with Quang Trung. Hué specialities, such as *banh beo* and *banh khoai*, are available at a strip of small restaurants near the market; walk north from the market on riverside Quach Xuan Ky and take the first left, Co Tham. And look out for signs announcing the **local speciality** of *chao luon*, a thick eel soup sold at roadside restaurants.

Phong Nha Cave

Since time immemorial the underground river emerging at **Phong Nha Cave** has held a mystical fascination for the local population. The earliest-known devotees were ninth- and tenth-century Cham people, followed by Vietnamese who petitioned the **guardian spirits** during periods of drought, with great success by all accounts. When Europeans started exploring the caves earlier this century it's said the rain-maker took everlasting umbrage; undeterred, by the 1950s tunnels 2km long had been surveyed and the number of visitors warranted a small hotel. Due to the intervening wars, when Phong Nha provided safe warehousing, nothing further happened until a British expedition was allowed to investigate in 1990 and began pushing upriver, eventually penetrating deep into the limestone massif. What they discovered is a **spelunker's delight**: 8km of underground waterway, vast chambers full of magical rock formations and intriguing side-channels waiting to be explored. For the less intrepid, tour boats take you the first kilometre or so (1–2hr) between rippling walls of limestone, certainly far enough to be awed by the scale of Phong Nha and its immense multi-coloured stalactites and stalagmites. Note, though, that **after heavy rain** the water-level may be too high to venture further than the cave mouth.

To **get to the cave**, Dong Hoi's big hotels and *Quang Binh Tourism* can help with car rental ($30 per day), or alternatively it's a long xe om ride ($10–12 return, including waiting time). Some Hué tour agents already offer Phong Nha excursions, but at five hours on the road each way it's too far for a comfortable day-trip and most overnight in Dong Hoi anyway. Once you've got transport sorted out, finding the cave isn't difficult: take Highway 1 north for 15km to Bo Trach village where a signpost indicates a left to Phong Nha, heading west on a mostly unpaved road until you reach Son Trach village 40km later (90min). From here you travel on by boat ($6 per person), an attractive, forty-minute trip meandering up the peaceful Son River. Torches or caving lamps would come in handy.

Over the Ngang Pass to Vinh

A few kilometres north of Dong Hoi, Highway 1 grinds to a halt at a ferry across the turbulent Gianh River which formed the boundary between the southern Nguyen and the northern Trinh lords during the seventeenth and eighteenth centuries. The region around the **Ngang Pass** is empty, wild country where a handful of beggars along the road indicate that you are about to enter Vietnam's poorest provinces, Ha Tinh and Nghe An. Summer droughts and winter flooding, exacerbated by typhoons from September to December, cause frequent food shortages, high levels of malnutrition and even occasional famines.

The region's few bright spots are areas of exceptionally dense highland forests on the border with Laos, harbouring **rare species** such as the Asian elephant and tiger. Since 1992 scientists have identified two new species of mammal (previously known only to local hunters) in these hills: the elusive **saola ox** and the more numerous **Giant Muntjac** deer. The government has enlarged the area of local nature reserves to almost 160,000 hectares and is implementing a programme to protect the highly vulnerable mammals. Breeding more commonplace species of deer is big business in Nghe An as young antlers fetch high prices for their medicinal properties.

Highway 1 rumbles into the large featureless city of **HA TINH**, 150km north of Dong Hoi. The rail tracks, forced inland by the Hoanh Son mountains, bypass Ha Tinh to rejoin the coast at Vinh but train travellers need not feel left out – there's nothing to stop for in Ha Tinh and most tourists head straight on to Vinh's greater choice of hotels. If you do need **accommodation**, the most central choice is *Binh Minh Hotel* (☎039/856825; ③) located on the main highway opposite the post office radio mast; take a room at the back if possible. A quieter alternative is the *Huong Sen Hotel* (no phone; ③), a couple of blocks east of the post office. As there's no handy bus station, just flag down **buses** going your way on the main street which, in typical fashion, is lined with cheap **eating** houses.

Vinh and around

Just 47km further north, **VINH** is a sprawling grey city with a sad past, sitting astride Highway 1 – which throws up dust and a steady trickle of tourists breaking their journey between Hué and Hanoi. Soviet-style apartment blocks and socialist town planning on a grand scale may hold a certain historical interest, but there's nothing attractive about the town and for most people its saving grace is a selection of reasonable-standard hotels. Nevertheless, the province of Nghe An savours its proud history, having spawned a wealth of revolutionary figures, many of them enshrined in street names: Le Hong Phong, Nguyen Thi Minh Khai, Phan Boi Chau, and top of the list, Ho Chi Minh. **Ho's birthplace** and childhood home are found in **Kim Lien** village, 14km from Vinh, a place of pilgrimage for Vietnamese, though rather sterile for most foreign visitors. **Cua Lo** beach resort lies 19km north of the city, comprising a straggle of overpriced hotels beside a long, unspoilt beach with good white sand but too much rubbish to make you want to linger.

Arrival and information

Vinh's main axis is Highway 1, renamed in the centre as Quang Trung and then Le Loi streets. Heading up Quang Trung, after about 500m you'll find **tourist information** in the *Kim Lien Hotel*, followed by the **bus station** 1km further on. Continue north to the *Huu Nghi Hotel* crossroads and turn left for Vinh **train station**, 1km west at the end of Phan Boi Chau (ticket-office hours 7.30–10.30am, 2–4.30pm & 8–9.30pm), and right at the crossroads for **Vietcombank**. The main **post office** is nearly a kilometre east of the *Kim Lien Hotel* beside the unmissable radio tower. Car rental in Vinh is available at all the main hotels, and you can pick up xe om at the two stations or at the southern end of Quang Trung, in front of Vinh market.

The city

Vinh has fared particularly badly in this century. As an industrial port-city dominating major land routes whose population was known for rebellious tendencies, the town became a natural target during both French and American wars. In the 1950s French bombs destroyed large swathes of Vinh, after which the Viet Minh burnt down what remained rather than let it fall into the hands of their enemy. Then the rebuilt town was flattened once again in American air-raids of the 1960s and 1970s. Reconstruction proceeded slowly after 1975, mostly financed by East Germany, and the city still feels half-completed. Vinh's smartest building is the shocking pink, colonial-era **Nghe Tinh Soviet Museum** (daily 7.30–11.30am & 1.30–4.30pm), celebrating a mass uprising against French rule in the 1930s (see

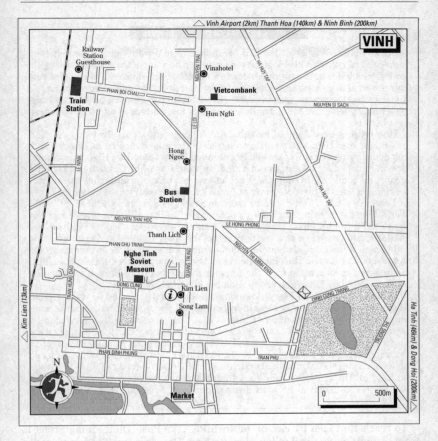

Contexts, p.416). The recently refurbished museum relates the causes, development and aftermath of the uprising, but is really only for the specialist.

Kim Lien: Ho Chi Minh's birthplace

Ho Chi Minh was born in 1890 in Hoang Tru village, **KIM LIEN** commune, 14km west of Vinh. The two simple houses made of bamboo wattle and palm-leaf thatch are 1959 reconstructions, now surrounded by fields of sweet potatoes. Ho's birthplace is said to be the hut by itself on the left as you approach, while behind stands the brick-built family altar. At the age of six, Ho moved 2km west, to what is now called Sen (Lotus) village, to live with his father in very similar surroundings. The two Sen houses are also replicas, built in 1955, with nothing much to see inside, but the complex is peaceful and alive with dancing butterflies. A **museum** nearby (daily summer 7.30–11am & 2.30–5pm; winter 8.30–11.30am & 2–5pm) illustrates Ho's world travels with many photos you've probably seen before – the difference being that some here are originals.

THE LIFE OF HO CHI MINH

So inextricably is the life of **Ho Chi Minh** intertwined with Vietnam's emergence from colonial rule that his biography is largely an account of the country's struggle for independence in the twentieth century. As Ho adopted dozens of pseudonyms and never kept diaries, uncertainty clouds his public life and almost nothing is known about the private man beneath the cultivated persona of a celibate and aesthete totally dedicated to his family – a concept that embraced all the Vietnamese people.

Ho's **origins** were humble enough, born Nguyen Sinh Cung, the youngest child of a minor mandarin who was dismissed from the imperial court in Hué for anti-colonialist sympathies. For a while Ho attended Hué's Quoc Hoc High School until he was expelled for taking part in a student protest and left Vietnam in 1911 on a steamship bound for France. Then began several years of **wandering the world**, including a spell in the dockyards of Brooklyn and as pastry chef under Escoffier in London's Carlton Hotel, before returning to France in the aftermath of World War I, to earn his living retouching photographs. In Paris, Ho became an increasingly active **nationalist**, going by the name Nguyen Ai Quoc ('Nguyen the Patriot'), and caused quite a stir during the Versailles Peace Conference when he published a petition demanding democratic constitutional government for Indochina. For a while Ho joined the French Socialists, but when they split in 1920 he defected to become one of the founder members of the French Communist Party, inspired by Lenin's total opposition to imperialism.

Ho's energetic role in French communism was rewarded when he was called to Moscow in 1923 to begin a career in **international revolution**, and a year later he found himself posted to southern China as a Comintern agent. Within a few months he had set up Vietnam's first Marxist-Leninist organization, the Revolutionary Youth League, which attracted a band of impassioned young Vietnamese eager to hear about the new ideology. But in 1927 Chiang Kai-Shek, leader of the Chinese nationalists, turned against the communists and Ho was forced to flee. For a while he lived in Thailand, disguised as a Buddhist monk, before turning up in Hong Kong in 1930 where he was instrumental in founding the **Vietnamese**

To reach Kim Lien by **car or motorbike**, take Phan Dinh Phung Street in front of Vinh market and follow signs to Nam Dan on a tree-lined road until a hoarding welcomes you to "Ho Chi Minh's native land". Turn left here for Ho's birthplace or follow signs straight on for "Lang Sen" to find the museum beside a car park and Ho's father's house a little further back, down a path beside a small lotus pond. By **public transport**, take one of the Nam Dan-bound pick-ups waiting on Phan Dinh Phung and ask to be dropped off at the Kim Lien junction, from where it's a walk of 1500m to the village.

Accommodation and eating

Because it's such a transport hub, Vinh has a large number of **hotels**, which means places are willing to bargain, though in some cases the cheapest rooms are not available to foreigners. The main drawback is that many hotels sit right on the highway, so wherever possible go for a room at the back. Ignoring several grotty, socialist-style places, there's still a reasonable choice among those listed below.

Communist Party. By now the French authorities had placed a death sentence on Ho's head, for insurrection, and while in Hong Kong he was arrested on trumped-up charges, released and then re-arrested before finally escaping with the help of prison hospital staff, who managed to persuade everyone, including the French police, that Ho had died of tuberculosis.

Ho disappeared again for a few years while the fuss died down, before reappearing on China's southern border in the late 1930s. From here he re-entered Vietnam for the first time in thirty years, in early 1941, wearing Chinese-style tunic, rubber-tyre sandals and carrying just a small rattan trunk plus his precious typewriter. He was aged 51, had dysentery, malaria and tuberculosis, and was about to embark on the most momentous task of his life. In the mountains of northern Vietnam Ho, now finally known as Ho Chi Minh (meaning "he who enlightens"), was joined by Vo Nguyen Giap, Pham Van Dong and other young militants. Together they laid the groundwork for the anticipated national uprising, establishing a united patriotic front, the League for the Independence of Vietnam – better known by its abbreviated name, the **Viet Minh** – and training the guerrilla units that would eventually evolve into the Vietnamese People's Army. But events conspired against Ho: in 1942 he was arrested as a Franco-Japanese spy when he crossed back into China to raise support for the nationalist cause, and languished for more than a year in various prisons, writing a collection of poetry later published as the "Prison Diary".

Meanwhile, however, events were hotting up, and when the Japanese occupation of Vietnam ended in August 1945 the Viet Minh were ready to seize control. Ho Chi Minh, by this time seriously ill, led them to a brief period in power following the August Revolution, and then ultimately to Independence in 1954. For the next fifteen years, as **president of the Democratic Republic of Vietnam**, Uncle Ho took his country along a sometimes rocky socialist path, continually seeking reunification through negotiation and then war. But he didn't live to see a united Vietnam: early in 1969 his heart began to fail and on September 2, Vietnam's National Day, he **died**. Since then, myth and fact have converged in a cult placing Ho Chi Minh at the top of Vietnam's pantheon of heroes, true to Confucian tradition – though against Ho's express wishes.

There's less of a choice when it comes to **places to eat**. Both the *Huu Nghi* and *Kim Lien* hotels have decent and inexpensive if rather soulless dining rooms. For more atmosphere try street kitchens around the major junction south of the bus station. The *Railway Station Guesthouse* has an open-air café which makes a pleasant place to wait for your train.

Hong Ngoc, 86b Le Loi (☎038/842165, fax 841229). Just north of the bus station find 6 floors of pure ostentation at the "Ruby Hotel" financed from the gem mines of Nghe An. Prices start high but you might get a bargain with bath, TV, fridge and air-con. A new extension opposite offers slightly cheaper rates. ②–③

Huu Nghi, 41 Le Loi (☎038/842492, fax 842813). At 9 storeys, the "Friendship Hotel" is Vinh's tallest building and vies with the *Kim Lien* for best-hotel title. Its communal spaces are dingy but rooms are well furnished. ③

Kim Lien, 12 Quang Trung (☎038/844751, fax 843699). The *Huu Nghi*'s arch rival opened in 1990 to commemorate the anniversary of Ho Chi Minh's hundredth birthday – and is perhaps marginally better, but there's little to chose between them. ③

Railway Station Guesthouse, (☎038/842764). Situated above a café in the northeast corner of the station forecourt is this friendly, basic guesthouse. The drawback is the station loudspeakers. ①

Song Lam, 8 Quang Trung (☎038/840603). A new hotel, south of the *Kim Lien*, offering small, well-scrubbed rooms at good prices. ②

Thanh Lich, Quang Trung, near the bus station (☎038/844961). A small, neatly kept bungalow hotel that's worth a look. It's set back from the highway and offers air-con, hot water and TV as standard. ②–③

Vinahotel, 9 Nguyen Trai (☎038/846989, fax 844819). Twenty well-furnished rooms above a *Vinamilk* shop. Very fair prices and all rooms face away from the highway. ②

Thanh Hoa

North of Vinh the narrow waist of Vietnam begins to open out towards the northern delta, entering the region known to the French as Tonkin. It's only a short haul to the town of **THANH HOA** which produces good beer, but there's not a lot else to the place. The province was home to an impressive number of Vietnamese kings, of whom the most illustrious was **Le Loi**, born here in 1385. Delving further back, the Ma River Valley has yielded rich archeological evidence of Neolithic settlement, notably some of the glorious Bronze Age drums found at **Dong Son village**, northwest of Thanh Hoa, but there's precious little to see nowadays. The only other notable site is **Ham Rong Bridge**, or "Dragon's Jaw", which spans the Ma River 3km north of town, and gained almost mythical status during the American War. US bombers tried for three years to destroy the heavily defended, 160-metre-long road and rail link. Around seventy aircraft were lost, more than against any other single target in the north, and the land around was bombed into a moonscape. Eventually, a laser-guided bomb found its target in May 1972, but the victory was short-lived as the NVA immediately rigged up a pontoon bridge and had a permanent structure in place soon after. The name Dragon's Jaw refers to a sinuous, nine-peaked ridge of hills – the dragon – to the west of the river, which holds in its mouth an isolated hump on the east bank called *Nui Ngoc*, or "Ruby Mountain".

Most people either press on to Hanoi, only 150km to the north, or make Ninh Binh their next stop. If you do need to overnight, Thanh Hoa has several decent hotels (see below), which are in general preferable to the concrete blocks of **Sam Son** beach resort, 16km to the southeast.

Practicalities

Thanh Hoa is a large town with no focal point and almost no landmarks apart from a huge **post office** where Highway 1 crosses Le Loi. About 400m north of this is another major junction where Phan Chu Trinh leads west past several **banks** to Thanh Hoa's impressive **train station**. Or continue on Highway 1 to find the northern **bus station** 300m further on. Inconveniently, buses heading south depart from Nga Ba Voi bus station, 3km down the highway. **Thanh Hoa Tourism** is located in the *Thanh Hoa Hotel* compound, on the left as you come up from Vinh.

The big, state-run *Thanh Hoa* (☎037/852517, fax 853963; ②) is where most people stay since it offers a wide choice of **accommodation**, clean rooms and good value. Heading north from here, look out on the right for the glitzy five-storey *Ngan Hoa* (☎037/851421; ④), about 600m from the *Thanh Hoa* and just off the highway on Nguyen Trai; this is a welcome newcomer boasting the works, including satellite TV and VCR in its top-flight suites. There's another clutch of more modest hotels east of the train station on Phan Chu Trinh: *Nha Khach Sao Mai* (☎037/852851; ②) is an older place but still popular, while closer to the station is the small, friendly *Khach San Ba Dinh* (☎037/824156; ①). Finally, imme-diately behind (south of) the *Ba Dinh*, lies the bright and welcoming *Hotel Binh Minh* (☎037/852088; ③), with a pleasant garden courtyard but higher room rates.

Both the *Thanh Hoa* and *Binh Minh* have recommended **restaurants**, or otherwise try local joints such as the *Minh Lien* or *Dalan*, near where Phan Chu Trinh meets Highway 1. **Food stalls** also gather around this junction, along Phan Chu Trinh and on the main highway near the *Thanh Hoa Hotel*.

Ninh Binh and around

The provincial capital **NINH BINH** is another dusty town straddling Highway 1, no more attractive than those to the south but slightly smaller and with sugar-loaf hillocks encroaching on the western horizon. While the town itself has nothing to detain you, the surrounding hills shelter the area called **Tam Coc–Bich Dong** where sampans slither through the limestone tunnels of "Ha Long Bay on land" and one of Vietnam's ancient capitals, **Hoa Lu**, represented by two darkly atmospheric dynastic temples. Both places can be tackled in one day, using either car or motor-bike, though Hoa Lu also makes a pleasant, more leisurely excursion by bicycle. To the east, the stone mass of **Phat Diem Cathedral** wallows in the rice fields, an extraordinary amalgam of Western and Oriental architecture that still shepherds an active Catholic community. Further afield, **Cuc Phuong** is one of Vietnam's more accessible national parks and contains some magnificent, centuries-old trees. These last two sights are more distant, and consequently off the main tourist route: the cathedral requires a half-day outing, while Cuc Phuong is possible as a long day-trip.

Hanoi is only 90km (2hr) away and the Hoa Lu/Tam Coc–Bich Dong circuit makes a popular and inexpensive day-tour out of the capital but, with more time, you could take advantage of Ninh Binh's hotels and services to explore the area at a more leisurely pace.

The town

Two radio masts provide convenient landmarks in **Ninh Binh**: the taller stands over the post office in the south, while the shorter signals the northern extremity 2km away up Highway 1 (Tran Hung Dao). Exactly half-way between the two, Le Hong Phong shoots off east at a major junction, taking traffic to join the Nam Dinh road. The town claims just two sights of its own: to the east a dismembered church spire bears witness to American bombing raids of the late 1960s, while 1km to the north a picturesque little pagoda nestles at the base of Non Nuoc Mountain. This knobbly outcrop – no more than 60m high – is noted for an eminently missable collection of ancient poetic inscriptions and views east over a power station to the graphically named "sleeping lady mountain".

Arrival and information

Ninh Binh's refreshingly spruce, well-organized **bus station** lies 100m south of the post office, across the small Lim Bridge and beside a busy crossroads. To find the **train station**, head one block north on Le Dai Hanh and turn right opposite the Huong Gia Hotel; the pint-size station is then 200m east past the ruined church. From either station, the "centre" of town is a one-kilometre xe om ride away. The **tourist office** resides in the Ninh Binh Hotel beside the Lim Bridge, with a second office just north of the *Hoa Lu Hotel* at the top end of town; both offer tours and guides. Alternatively, your hotel or guesthouses can oblige – staff at both the *Thuy Anh* and *Hoa Lu* are particularly knowledgeable about the area. All these places can help with **transport**, whether it's cars, motorbikes or bikes, though guesthouses and smaller hotels usually offer cheaper rates. You can **exchange** cash at *Agribank*, immediately south of the *Hoa Lu Hotel*, and at *Vietincombank* located behind the State Bank two blocks north of the post office on Tran Hung Dao; *Vietincombank* also takes travellers' cheques.

Accommodation and eating

The standard and range of **hotels** in Ninh Binh has improved dramatically as ever greater numbers of tourists are discovering this accessible province. Almost all accommodation is strung along the main highway – you won't have any trouble finding them but you might have trouble sleeping. Note that the bus station's loudspeakers start up at 4am, so ignore the adjacent guesthouses and head for one of the places listed below.

Ninh Binh has a more limited choice of **eating** places: best for both value and quality is the *Thuy Anh Hotel* which serves a fixed, evening menu of home cooking – order in advance – and can provide snacks at other times of day. *Than Thuy* operates a similar system and is worth trying; otherwise, check out restaurants along Highway 1 just south of the Lim Bridge. In the evenings a furniture store next to the *Star Hotel* turns out excellent *chao ga* (rice and chicken) and *nem* (spring rolls) over streetside braziers.

Hoa Lu, Tran Hung Dao (☎030/871217, fax 871200). Top of the range and favourite of tour groups, this hotel is beside Highway 1 on the town's northern edge. Best value are its mid-price, older rooms situated behind a new four-storey building. ③

Queen, Hoang Hoa Tham (☎030/871874). This small, popular mini-hotel is just 30m straight in front of the train station. It's fairly basic but clean enough and sports a pleasant roof-top eating area. ①–②

Song Van, Le Hong Phong (☎030/871974, fax 872608). A four-storey hotel off the main highway which is beginning to look a bit jaded. Its standard rooms are reasonably comfortable, with air-con and telephone, and it also offers three 5-bed dorms. ③

Star, Tran Hung Dao (☎030/871602, fax 871200). Under the same ownership as the *Thuy Anh*, but offering cheaper accommodation maintained to an equally high standard. Rooms are small but come with bathrooms and air-con as standard. ①–②

Thanh Thuy, Le Hong Phong (☎030/871811). If you're looking for real budget accommodation, then try this tiny no-frills guesthouse, 20m east of Highway 1. Cheaper rooms have partition walls and a shared bathroom. ①

Thuy Anh, Truong Han Sieu (☎030/871602, fax 871200). This welcoming hotel offers the best-value accommodation in town. Though small, it boasts a range of well-furnished rooms whose immaculate bathrooms make up for lack of space; not surprisingly it's often full. Find it 300m north of the post office and tucked down a side-street opposite the *Star*. ②

Tam Coc–Bich Dong

The film *Indochine* put **Tam Coc–Bich Dong**, 9km southwest of Ninh Binh, firmly on the map for French tour groups and you're more likely to find the hawkers here speaking French than English. Despite the sometimes overwhelming numbers it's hard not to be won over by the mystical, watery beauty of the area, which is a miniature landlocked version of Ha Long Bay. The three-hour sampanride is a definite highlight, meandering among dumpling-shaped, karst hills in a flooded landscape where river and fields merge serenely into one. Journey's end is **Tam Coc**, three long, dark tunnel-caves (the longest over 120m) eroded through the limestone hills with barely sufficient clearance for the sampan in places. Ducking down as the boat scrapes under low-slung, stone bridges and through the dripping caves is all part of the fun, and though embroideries and soft drinks are hawked at the half-way stage, the selling is fairly low-key.

If you have time, follow the road another 2km beyond the boat dock (see below) to visit the cave-pagoda of **Bich Dong**, or the "Jade Grotto" ($1). Stone-cut steps, entangled by the thick roots of banyan trees, lead up a cliff-face peppered with shrines to the cave entrance, believed to have been discovered by two monks in the early fifteenth century. The cave walls are scrawled with graffiti but the three Buddhas sit unperturbed on their lotus thrones beside a head-shaped rock which bestows longevity if touched. A second entrance opens out higher up the cliff, from where steps continue to a viewpoint over the water-logged scene, while on the rock face above two giant characters declare "Bich Dong". The story goes that these were engraved in the eighteenth century by the father of Nguyen Du (author of the classic *Tale of Kieu*), who was entrusted with construction of the complex.

Practicalities

The easiest and most enjoyable way to reach Tam Coc–Bich Dong is to rent a **bicycle** or **motorbike** (respectively $1 and $6 for a day from most guesthouses in Ninh Binh); the turning, signed to "Bich Dong", is 4km south of the Lim Bridge on Highway 1, before the cement factory. Hiring a **xe om** for the excursion from Ninh Binh will cost about $4 including waiting time.

To avoid the crowds it's best to set off either **early** in the morning or **late** in the afternoon (boats run between 6.30am and 5pm), but whatever the time you'll still have to endure the scrum of boat-owners eager for business. Fortunately **tickets** are fixed-price ($2 per person) and are on sale beside the **boat dock** in **Van Lam village**, a collection of restaurants and cafés around the car park where tour groups usually take lunch.

Hoa Lu

Thirteen kilometres northwest of Ninh Binh, **Hoa Lu**, site of the tenth-century capital of an early, independent Vietnamese kingdom called Dai Co Viet, makes another rewarding excursion. The fortified royal palaces of the Dinh and Le kings are now reduced to archeological remains but their dynastic temples, seventeenth-century copies of eleventh-century originals, still rest quietly in a narrow valley surrounded by wooded, limestone hills. Though the temple buildings and attractive walled courtyards are unspectacular, the inner sanctuaries are compelling – mysterious, dark caverns where statues of the kings, wrapped in veils of pungent incense, are worshipped by the light of candles.

First stop at the site should be the more imposing **Den Dinh Tien Hoang**, furthest from the ticket barrier, dedicated to King Dinh Tien Hoang (also known as Dinh Bo Linh) who seized power in 968 AD and moved the capital south from Co Loa in the Red River Delta to this secure valley far from the threat of Chinese intervention. Dinh Tien Hoang's gilded effigy can be seen in the temple's second sanctuary room, flanked by his three sons. The king was born near Hoa Lu, the illegitimate son of a provincial governor, and was known as a reforming monarch who ruled with a firm hand; he is reputed to have placed a bronze urn and caged tiger in front of his palace and decreed that "those who violate the laws will be boiled and gnawed". But in 979 an assassin, variously rumoured to be a mad monk or a palace hitman, killed the king and his two eldest sons as they lay in a drunken sleep.

In the anarchy that followed, Le Hoan, commander of Dinh Tien Hoang's army and supposed lover of his queen (whom Le Hoan later married), wrested power and declared himself King Le Dai Hanh in 980. The second temple, **Den Le Dai Hanh**, is dedicated to his Early Le dynasty which itself spiralled into chaos 25 years later while the king's three sons squabbled over the succession. Le Dai Hanh is enshrined in the temple's rear sanctuary with his eldest son and Queen Duong Van Nga. On the way out, look up at the roof beams of the temple porch, decorated with polychrome carvings of dragons and lotus flowers in lively contrast to the simple, restrained interior.

After visiting the two shrines, energetic types could climb the steps of "Saddle Mountain" (*Nui Ma Yen*), opposite the temples, for a panoramic view of Hoa Lu and its surroundings. It's also possible to take a **boat trip** (2–3hr; $1.50 per person) punting along the Sao Khe River into a landscape similar to Tam Coc though with only one tunnel-cave and not so beguiling. However, if you're averse to crowds, a point in its favour is that few people come this way and you glide along the channels virtually undisturbed among kingfishers and dragonflies; if you do get this far, don't bother with the walk to Dong Am Tien, a mosquito-ridden cave pagoda.

Practicalities

The quickest way out to Hoa Lu is to rent a motorbike for the day or take a xe om ($4–5 for the round-trip), but if time allows this is definitely one to do by **bicycle**. After the first five unnerving kilometres on Highway 1, it's a pleasant ride on paved back-roads west of the highway, following signs to Truong Yen village and Hoa Lu (13km in total). And you can then cycle back through some great scenery following dirt-tracks along the Sao Khe River: take the paved road heading east directly in front of the temples and then turn right over the bridge (allow at least 1hr to cover the 12km to Ninh Binh).

Hoa Lu is just as popular as Tam Coc and the temples can be swamped, particularly mid-morning and early afternoon when tour groups arrive from Hanoi. The hawkers can also be just as enthusiastic, if not plain aggressive, though fortunately they aren't allowed to pursue you into the temples. **Admission** to the complex is $1.

Phat Diem

Strike east from Ninh Binh and there's no mistaking that you've stumbled on a Christian enclave, where church spires sprout out of the flat paddy land on all sides and it's said that 95 percent of the district's population attend church on a regular basis. These coastal communities of northern Vietnam were among the first to be targeted by Portuguese missionaries in the sixteenth century; this area owes its particular zeal to the Jesuit Alexandre de Rhodes who preached here in 1627. The greatest monument to all this religious fervour is the century-old stone cathedral, **Phat Diem** (7.30–11.30am & 2.30–5pm), situated some 30km from Ninh Binh in **Kim Son village**.

The first surprise is the cathedral's monumental **bell-pavilion**, whose curved roofs and triple gateway could easily be the entrance to a Vietnamese temple save for a few tell-tale crosses and a host of angels. The structure is built entirely of dressed stone, as is the equally impressive cathedral facade sheltering in its wake; both edifices rest on hundreds of bamboo poles embedded in the marshy ground. Behind, the tiled double-roof of the **nave** extends for 74m, supported by 52 immense ironwood pillars and sheltering a cool, dark and peaceful sanctuary. The **altar** table is chiselled from a single block of marble, decorated with elegant sprays of bamboo, while the altar-piece above glows with red and gold lacquers in an otherwise sober interior. Twelve priests conduct daily services here for a diocese that musters 140,000 Catholics.

The cathedral was conceived and designed by Father Tran Luc, whose tomb lies behind the bell-tower, and was more than ten years in the preparation, as stone and wood were transported from the provinces of Thanh Hoa and Nghe An, though it apparently took a mere three months to build in 1891. During the French War, the Catholic Church formed a powerful political group in Vietnam, virtually independent of the French administration but also opposed to the communists. The then bishop of Phat Diem, Monseigneur Le Huu Tu, was outspokenly anti-French and an avowed nationalist but as his diocese lay on the edge of government-held territory, the French supplied him with sufficient arms to maintain a militia of 2000 men in return for containing Viet Minh infiltration. However, in December 1951 the Viet Minh launched a major assault on the village and took it – with suspicious ease for French tastes, who felt the Catholics were withholding information on enemy activities in the area, if not actually assisting them. When paratroops came in to regain control the Viet Minh withdrew, taking with them a valuable supply of weapons. The author Graham Greene was in Phat Diem at the time, ostensibly on an assignment for *Life Magazine*, and watched the battle from the bell-tower of the cathedral – later using the scene in *The Quiet American*.

Practicalities

Frequent public **buses** depart from Ninh Binh bus station for the hour's journey **to Kim Son**; otherwise it's near enough to reach by rented **motorbike**, or the return trip by **xe om** will cost $6. If you're riding here yourself, take the road heading die-straight east from Ninh Binh's Lim Bridge and, when you get to Kim Son village, 100m after passing an elegant covered bridge take a right turn to the cathedral; follow the compound wall anticlockwise to reach the entrance.

Cuc Phuong National Park

In 1962 Vietnam's first national park was established around a narrow valley between forested limestone hills on the borders of Ninh Binh, Thanh Hoa and Hoa Binh provinces, containing over 200 square kilometres of mountain rainforest. Unless you have sufficient time to walk into the park interior, to overnight in Muong villages, and to experience the multi-layered forest, there's little specific to divert you to **Cuc Phuong**. Nevertheless the park is well set up for tourism and sees a steady stream of visitors, attracted principally by the easy access to impressively ancient trees. The most enjoyable time for walking in the park is October to January, when mosquitoes and leeches take a break and temperatures are relatively cool – but this is also peak season. Flowers are at their best during February and March, while April to May are the months when lepidopterists can enjoy the "butterfly festival" as thousands of butterflies colour the forest.

Even now the park has not been fully surveyed but is estimated to contain approximately 250 **bird species** and more than sixty **mammal species**, some of which were first discovered in Cuc Phuong, such as red-bellied squirrels and a fish that lives in underground rivers. Several species of bat and monkey, including the seriously endangered *Delacour langur*, inhabit the park, while tigers and leopards roam its upper reaches. Hunting has taken its toll, though, and you're really only likely to see butterflies, birds and perhaps a civet cat or a tree squirrel, rather than the more exotic fauna. What you can't miss is the luxuriant **vegetation** including thousand-year-old trees (living fossils up to 70m high), tree ferns and kilometre-long corkscrewing lianas, as well as a treasure-trove of medicinal plants.

Of several **walks** in the park the shortest and most popular starts at Car Park A, one hour's drive (20km) from the park gate (see below). For seven steamy kilometres (roughly 2hr) a well-trodden path winds through typical rainforest to reach the magnificent **cho xanh tree**, a 45-metre-high, thousand-year-old specimen of *Terminalia myriocarpa* – its dignity only slightly marred by a viewing platform. Dropping back down to the flat, take a left turn at the unmarked T-junction to bring you back to the road higher up at Car Park B. This second car park is also the start of the "Adventurous Trail", a fifteen-kilometre hike through the park to Muong villages noted for their gigantic wooden water-wheels, for which you'll need a guide ($5 per day) plus a night's accommodation at the top ($8, excluding food).

Much is made of Cuc Phuong's **prehistoric caves**, the most accessible of which is Dong Nguoi Xua, only 300m from the road, 7km from the park gate. Joss sticks burn in the cave mouth near three tombs estimated to be over 7000 years old but there's nothing else to see and the site isn't well tended.

Practicalities

Cuc Phuong **park gate** lies 45km (one and a half hour's drive) north and west of Ninh Binh; head north on Highway 1 for 10km to find the sign indicating "Cuc Phuong" to the left. There are no public buses so you'll either have to rent a **car** or **motorbike** in Ninh Binh, or haul out there with a **xe om** ($8–10 for the round-trip); note that beyond the gates it's a fairly rough, unmetalled road which becomes impassable in heavy rains. Visiting the park is also feasible as a day-trip out of Hanoi – an option offered by several tour agencies (see p.347).

Entry **tickets** are on sale at the headquarters beside the gate ($5, including guide), where you can also arrange **accommodation** (℡030/866085; ③), ranging from unexpectedly comfortable, if somewhat expensive, bungalows and bamboo chalets to a basic hostel, located either at the headquarters or in the interior. Be aware that Cuc Phuong is some way above the plains and winter nights can get chilly.

Nam Dinh and the Keo Pagoda

Instead of bashing straight on to Hanoi from Ninh Binh, Highway 10 takes you northeast via Nam Dinh and Thai Binh to Haiphong, from where you can travel on to Ha Long Bay (see *Haiphong and the Northern Seaboard* chapter, starting on p.369). The route isn't stunning, on a slow road with three ferry crossings (allow a total of 5–6hr driving time), but it traverses some typical delta country and passes close by a handsome example of traditional Vietnamese architecture, the Keo Pagoda. It was in this region, around Nam Dinh, that the famous Magnum Agency photographer **Robert Capa**, best known for his images of the Spanish Civil War, died in May 1954. Flown in by *Life Magazine* to film the death throes of French Indochina after the fall of Dien Bien Phu, Capa was accompanying French soldiers on a mission in the Red River Delta when, to get a better shot of the convoy, he stepped off the road – and onto a land-mine.

If you need to change buses or otherwise break the journey then you'll end up in the large, industrial city of **NAM DINH**, which nevertheless has a certain appeal as a city off the main tourist trail – its wide tree-lined streets come as a pleasant surprise. Placed firmly in the delta, a mere 6km south of the Red River, the city is spattered with lakes, canals and open green spaces, principally **Ho Vi Xuyen**, a lake northeast of the centre near where you'll find a modest choice of hotels.

Practicalities

Nam Dinh is on the mainline to Hanoi and its **train station** is a couple of kilometres west of the centre along Tran Phu Street. The vast but well-ordered **bus station** is virtually the same distance out to the northwest on Dien Bien Phu Street. **Tourist information** is available at either the *Son Nam Hotel*, or at *Nam Ha Tourism*, 115 Nguyen Du, on opposite sides of the lake; both provide car rental, guides and the usuals.

Ignore the grotty *Vi Hoang Hotel* next to *Nam Ha Tourism* and head straight for two **hotels** across the lake on Le Hong Phong, both popular places that soon fill up: the clean and friendly *Son Nam* on the corner (☎035/848920, fax 848915; ③), and the no-frills *Nha Nghi Du Lich Cong Doan* just up the lake (☎035/844307; ②). The final possibility is the *Nam Ha Rest House* one block north of the lake at 386 Han Thuyen (☎035/849723; ③), offering well-priced, refurbished rooms.

For **eating**, try the restaurant next to the *Vi Hoang Hotel*, or the *Thanh Nam* round the corner on Mac Thi Buoi, where you'll also find a few other cafés and local restaurants to chose from.

Keo Pagoda

Confusingly there are two pagodas with the same name on opposite banks of the Red River but the **Keo Pagoda** you want is 10km southwest of Thai Binh town in Vu Thu District, Thai Binh Province. This was the original pagoda, erected in the eleventh century on the river's north bank, but after it was destroyed by floods in 1611 its replacement took 21 years to complete and a substitute was built across in Nam Ha Province, on what was considered a less vulnerable spot. Since the seventeenth century there have been many reconstructions, each faithfully preserving the pagoda's distinct architectural features, of which the most notable is a magnificent three-storey, wooden **bell-tower** containing two bronze bells cast in 1687 and 1796. Unfortunately you can't climb the bell-tower but the walled compound, standing on its own amid a sea of paddy, contains a whole cluster of impressive wood and tile buildings. Although this is a Buddhist foundation, its main altar is dedicated to the eleventh-century monk **Minh Khong**, who was a gifted healer much venerated by the Ly kings and today still attracts a lively community of worshippers.

From Nam Dinh follow Highway 10 until you're nearly into Thai Binh town and take a paved road off to the right. The pagoda's not an easy one to find so ask at each junction: there are no signs to indicate the turnings and the route is fairly tortuous, though it passes through an interesting succession of delta villages. Some people visit Keo as a day-trip out of Hanoi but, at around 100km (3hr), it's debatable whether it's worth a special journey. When you get there, there's an **entry fee** of $2.

travel details

Buses

*It's almost impossible to give the **frequency** with which buses run. Though scheduled, long-distance public buses won't depart if empty. Moreover, private services, often minibuses or pick-ups, ply more popular routes, and depart only when they have enough passengers to make the journey worthwhile. Highway 1 sees a near-constant stream of buses passing through to various destinations, and it's possible to flag something down at virtually any time of the day. Off the highway, to be sure of a bus it's advisable to start your journey early – most long-distance departures leave between 5 and 9am, and very few run after midday. **Journey times** can also vary; figures below show the normal length of time you can expect the journey to take.*

Da Nang to: Dong Ha (5hr); Hoi An (1hr 30min–2hr); Hué (3–4hr); Nha Trang (16hr); Quang Ngai (5hr); Qui Nhon (11hr).

Dong Ha to: Hué (2hr 30min); Dong Hoi (2hr 30min); Khe Sanh (2hr 30min).

Dong Hoi to: Dong Ha (2hr 30min); Hué (5hr); Vinh (6hr).

Hoi An to: Da Nang (1hr 30min–2hr); Quang Ngai (4hr).

Hué to: Dong Ha (2hr 30min); Dong Hoi (5hr); Da Nang (3–4hr).

Khe Sanh to: Dong Ha (2hr 30min); Lao Bao (40min).

Nam Dinh to: Haiphong (4–5hr); Hanoi (3hr); Ninh Binh (1hr).

Ninh Binh to: Haiphong (5–6hr); Hanoi (3hr); Kim Son (Phat Diem) (1hr); Nam Dinh (1hr); Thanh Hoa (2hr).

Thanh Hoa to: Hanoi (4–5hr); Ninh Binh (2hr); Vinh (4hr).

Vinh to: Dong Ha (9hr); Dong Hoi (6hr); Hué (11hr); Ninh Binh (6hr); Thanh Hoa (4hr).

Trains

Da Nang to: Hanoi (3 daily; 17–21hr); Ho Chi Minh City (3–4 daily; 19–26hr); Hué (3–4 daily; 3–4hr); Nha Trang (3–4 daily; 10–14hr).

Dong Ha to: Dong Hoi (2 daily; 2hr); Hanoi (2 daily; 15–16hr); Hué (2 daily; 1hr 30min).

Dong Hoi to: Dong Ha (2 daily; 2hr); Hanoi (3 daily; 11–13hr); Hué (2 daily; 3hr 30min–4hr); Ninh Binh (2 daily; 9–10hr); Vinh (2 daily; 5hr).

Hué to: Da Nang (3–4 daily; 3–4hr); Dong Ha (2 daily; 1hr 30min); Dong Hoi (3 daily; 3–4hr); Hanoi (3 daily; 14–17hr); Ho Chi Minh City (3–4 daily; 22–31hr); Nha Trang (3–4 daily; 13–19hr); Ninh Binh (2 daily; 13–15hr).

Nam Dinh to: Hanoi (5 daily; 2–3hr); Ninh Binh (4 daily; 30min–1hr).

Ninh Binh to: Dong Hoi (2 daily; 10–11hr); Hanoi (4 daily; 2hr 30min–4hr 30min); Hué (2 daily; 13–15hr); Vinh (2 daily; 4hr 30min).

Thanh Hoa to: Hanoi (5 daily; 4–6hr); Ninh Binh (4 daily; 1hr 30min–2hr); Vinh (3 daily; 3–4hr).

Vinh to: Dong Ha (2 daily; 7–8hr 30min); Dong Hoi (2 daily; 5–6hr); Hanoi (3 daily; 7–8hr 30min); Hué (2 daily; 8hr 30min–10hr); Ninh Binh (2 daily; 4hr 30min).

Flights

Da Nang to: Buon Me Thuot (3 weekly; 1hr 15min); Haiphong (3 weekly; 1hr); Hanoi (3 daily; 1hr 10min); Ho Chi Minh City (3 daily; 1hr 10min); Nha Trang (3 weekly; 1hr 20min); Vinh (3 weekly; 1hr 10min).

Hué to: Da Lat (3 weekly; 1hr 20min); Hanoi (2 daily; 1hr 30min); Ho Chi Minh City (2 daily; 1hr 50min).

Vinh to: Da Nang (3 weekly; 1hr 10min); Hanoi (3 weekly; 50min).

CHAPTER SIX

HANOI AND AROUND

The Vietnamese nation was born among the lagoons and marshes of the Red River Delta around 4000 years ago and for most of its independent existence has been ruled from **Hanoi**, Vietnam's small, elegant capital lying in the heart of the northern delta. The region is steeped in the past and, while it lacks the bustling river-life and rich physical beauty of the Mekong Delta, there's a wealth of historical and spiritual sights to explore – despite innumerable wars and a sometimes hostile natural environment that's only partly been tamed by an elaborate, centuries-old network of canals and embankments.

Given the political and historical importance of Hanoi and its burgeoning population of one million, it's a surprisingly **low-key city**, with the character of a provincial town – quite unlike brash, young Ho Chi Minh City. Its central district is a mellow area of tree-fringed lakes and shaded avenues of classy, French villas dressed-up in jaded stucco. Despite first impressions, though, Hanoi is bursting at the seams, and nowhere is this more evident than in the vibrant, intoxicating tangle of streets known as the **Old Quarter**, the city's commercial heart since the fifteenth century. Delving back even further, a handful of Hanoi's more than six hundred temples and pagodas hail from the original, eleventh-century city, most notably the **Temple of Literature** which encompasses both Vietnam's foremost Confucian sanctuary and its first university. Many visitors, however, are drawn to Hanoi by more recent events, seeking answers among the exhibits of the **Army Museum** and in **Ho Chi Minh's Mausoleum** to the extraordinary Vietnamese tenacity displayed during the wars of this century.

Modern Hanoi is peppered with building sites, foreign goods are flooding the markets, satellite dishes are sprouting from flashy new rooftops and motorbikes are the most common mode of transport, altering the face of a city where roundabouts, traffic lights and insistent horns were unknown until 1994. The authorities are trying to temper this anarchy with a flurry of laws and a masterplan of urban development which aims to ease the congestion by creating satellite towns. For all that, the city has not completely lost its old-world charm nor its distinctive character, and certainly life here proceeds at a more gentle pace than in Ho Chi Minh City. Hanoians are well known for being reserved, but they are also said to be less corrupt and more hospitable than southerners. Cut off from the non-communist world for two decades, the city may be short on high-standard services, but foreign travellers are still regarded with a genuine, open curiosity.

Hanoi, somewhat unjustly, remains less popular than Ho Chi Minh City as a jumping-off point for touring Vietnam, but provides a convenient base for **excursions** to Ha Long Bay, and to Sa Pa and the northern mountains (see chapters 7 and 8, respectively). There are also a few attractions much closer at hand, predominantly religious foundations such as the **Perfume Pagoda**, with its spectacular setting among limestone hills. In the historical realm, dynastic temples mark where the Bronze Age Dong Son culture gave rise to the proto-Vietnamese king-

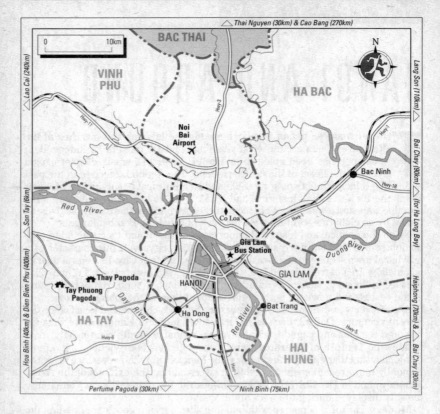

Thai Nguyen (30km) & Cao Bang (270km)

BAC THAI

VINH PHU

HA BAC

Noi Bai Airport ✈

Bac Ninh

Lao Cai (240km)

Lang Son (110km)

Bai Chay (90km) (for Ha Long Bay)

Hwy-3

Hwy-1

Hwy-11

Red River

Co Loa

Gia Lam Bus Station ★

Duong River

Son Tay (6km)

GIA LAM

Thay Pagoda

Tay Phuong Pagoda

HANOI

Ha Dong

Bat Trang

Red River

Day River

HA TAY

Hwy-6

HAI HUNG

Hoa Binh (40km) & Dien Bien Phu (400km)

Haiphong (70km) & Bai Chay (90km)

Hwy-5

Hwy-1

Perfume Pagoda (30km) ▽   ▽ Ninh Binh (75km)

doms of Van Lang and then Au Lac, ruled from the spiral-shaped citadel of **Co Loa** just north of today's capital. The Red River Delta's fertile alluvial soil supports one of the highest rural population densities in southeast Asia, living in bamboo-screened villages dotted among the paddy fields. Some of these communities have been plying the same trade for generations, such as ceramics, carpentry or snake-breeding, and while the more successful **craft villages** are becoming commercialized it's possible, with a bit of effort, to get well off the beaten track to where Confucianism still holds sway.

The **best time to visit** Hanoi is during the three months from October to December, when you'll find warm, sunny days (25–30°C) and levels of humidity below the norm of eighty percent, though it can be chilly at night. From January to March cold winds from China combine with high humidity to give a fine mist which often hangs in the air for days. During this period temperatures hover around 20°C but may plunge as much as ten degrees in a few hours. March and April usually bring better weather, and swathes of electric-green rice seedlings, before the extreme summer heat arrives in late April, accompanied by monsoon storms which peak in August and can last until early October, causing serious flooding throughout the delta.

HANOI

When Tang Chinese armies invaded Vietnam in the seventh century they chose a small, **Red River fort** as capital of their new protectorate named, optimistically, *Annam*, the "Pacified South". Two centuries later the rebellious Vietnamese ousted the Chinese from their "Great Nest", *Dai La*, in 939 AD. After that the citadel lay abandoned until 1010 when **King Ly Thai To**, usually credited as Hanoi's founding father, recognized the site's potential and established his own court beside the Red River, envisaging a great commercial centre "where men and wealth from all four points of the compass could gather". It seems the omens were on his side for, according to legend, when the king stepped from his royal barge onto the riverbank a golden dragon flew up towards the heavens. From then on **Thang Long**, "City of the Soaring Dragon", was destined to be the nation's capital, with only minor interruptions, for the next eight hundred years.

Ly Thai To and his successors set about creating a city fit for "ten thousand generations of kings", choosing auspicious locations for their temples and palaces according to the laws of geomancy. They built protective dykes, established a town of artisans and merchants alongside the **Imperial City**'s eastern wall, and set up the nation's first university, in the process laying the foundations of modern Hanoi. From 1407 the country was again under Chinese occupation but this time only briefly before the great hero **Le Loi** retook the capital in 1428. The Le dynasty kings drained lakes and marshes to accommodate their new palaces as well as a growing civilian population, and towards the end of the fifteenth century Thang Long was enjoying a **golden era** under the great reformer, King Le Thanh Thong. Shortly after his death in 1497, however, the country dissolved into anarchy, while the city slowly declined until finally Emperor Gia Long moved the royal court to Hué in 1802.

By the 1830s Thang Long had been relegated to a provincial capital, known merely as *Ha Noi* or "City within the River's Bend", and in 1882 its reduced defences offered little resistance to **attacking French forces**, led by Captain Rivière. Initially capital of the French Protectorate of Tonkin, a name derived from *Dong Kinh* meaning "Eastern Capital", after 1887 Hanoi became centre of government for the entire Union of Indochina. Royal palaces and ancient monuments made way for grand residences, administrative offices, tree-lined boulevards and all the trappings of a **colonial city**, more European than Asian. It seems to have been a congenial place in its heyday: Joleaud-Barral, a French geographer visiting Hanoi in the 1890s, enthused "at Singapore, at Saigon, one exists; at Hanoi, one lives". However, while the French erected fine buildings and a modern infrastructure, the Vietnamese community lived a largely separate, often impoverished existence, creating a seed-bed of insurrection.

During the 1945 August Revolution thousands of local nationalist sympathizers spilled onto the streets of Hanoi and later took part in its defence against returning French troops, though they had to wait until 1954 for their city finally to become the **capital of an independent Vietnam**. Hanoi sustained more serious damage during air raids of the American War, particularly the infamous Christmas Bombing campaign of 1972 (see box on p.334). Since then political isolation together with lack of resources have preserved what is essentially the **city of the 1950s**, somewhat faded, a bit battered and very overcrowded. Until two years ago, sleepy was the adjective most frequently applied to Hanoi, but the city, like the rest of Vietnam, is struggling to reinvent itself as a dynamic, international capital. The big question now is how much of central Hanoi will survive the onslaught of modernization.

Arrival and information

It's a 45-minute ride into central Hanoi from **Noi Bai airport**, 40km away. *Vietnam Airlines* runs a **minibus** (tickets on sale inside the airport building; $4) which drops you outside its main office on Hoan Kiem Lake, convenient for most central hotels and guesthouses. Metered **taxis** cost between $25 and $30 for the ride into town, or you should be able to get an unmetered car for $15; when negotiating make it clear your price is for the car and not per person. Note that taxis can only carry three people officially, though some may be persuaded to take four for a little extra. As neither of the airport's two **exchange** bureaux offer particularly good rates, it's best to pay the fare in dollars and change your money in Hanoi.

Hanoi's **train station** is roughly 1km west of centre, on Le Duan Avenue. Arriving from Ho Chi Minh City and all points south you exit the station onto Le Duan. However, trains from the east and north (the Chinese border and Haiphong) pull into platforms at the rear of the main station, bringing you out among market stalls on a narrow street called Tran Quy Cap. There are a few places to stay within a short walk of the station (see p.316 for details) that are useful if you arrive late or have an early start; otherwise, pick up a cyclo or xe om to the centre of town (the fare should be less than $1).

Hanoi's three public **bus stations** are all located several kilometres from the centre, and you'll need to catch a city bus or hop on a cyclo or xe om (see box on facing page for an idea of fares). Long-distance buses **from the south** terminate at **Giap Bat station** (☎864 1467), 6km south of town on Giai Phong Avenue. Services **from the northeast** (Haiphong, Bai Chay and Cao Bang) arrive at **Gia Lam station** (☎827 1529), 4km away on the east bank of the Red River. Finally, buses **from the northwest** (Son La, Dien Bien Phu and Lao Cai) use **Kim Ma station** (☎845 2846), located at the junction of Giang Vo and Kim Ma, 2km west of the centre. However, some buses, particularly **private services**, venture further into central Hanoi and may drop you at a more convenient, though unofficial and unpredictable, "bus stop". Note that buses **from Hoa Binh** sometimes terminate in Ha Dong, a suburb of Hanoi 10km from the centre; jump on one of the waiting city buses for the forty-minute ride into town.

Information

For **information**, try one of the big state-run agents, such as *Vietnamtourism* at 30a Ly Thuong Kiet (☎826 4154, fax 825 7583) or *Vinatour*, 54 Nguyen Du (☎825 2986, fax 825 2707), though they'll probably be more interested in signing you up for a tour. You might have more luck scouring noticeboards in the travellers' cafés around Hoan Kiem Lake – *Green Bamboo* is conveniently placed just a couple of minutes' walk from where the *Vietnam Airlines* bus stops.

Hanoi **maps** are available from bookshops, stalls and hawkers on Trang Tien and in front of the GPO: *Vinatour's* city map provides the clearest and most useful coverage, while *Vietnamtourism*'s map, with a country map on the reverse side, is also passable. Both the English-language journals, *Vietnam Investment Review* and *Vietnam Economic Times*, publish useful city listings including a limited selection of **what's on** plus restaurants, clubs and bars.

> The **telephone code** for Hanoi is ☎04.

Options for **moving on** from Hanoi are detailed on pp.348–349.

City transport

Getting around **on foot** is the best way to do justice to Hanoi's central district, especially the congested streets of the Old Quarter, taking an occasional **cyclo** ride or xe om to scoot between places. Bear in mind, though, that traffic discipline is an unfamiliar concept in Hanoi: teenagers on their new Suzuki choppers ride without fear, and everyone drives without looking. Despite the chaotic traffic, **bicycle** is still a popular way to get around and can be fun – for those with strong nerves. If you prefer something solid between you and the maelstrom, and don't mind the expense, there are now several **taxi** and **car-rental** companies operating in Hanoi. Finally, painfully slow **city buses** serve a limited number of routes and are mostly useful for getting out to the long-distance bus stations.

Cyclos and taxis

Hanoi **cyclos** are wider than the Ho Chi Minh City version, so can take two people at a squeeze. Always establish terms before setting off; you might want to write down the figures, making it clear whether you're negotiating in dollars or dong, for one person or two, just one way or for a return journey. You can also hire a cyclo

---

FARES AROUND TOWN

Costs of local transport, excluding taxis, are extremely low and are usually paid in dong.

Cyclos and xe oms

Expect to pay a minimum of 5000d per kilometre for a cyclo or xe om ride within central Hanoi. Below are some **sample fares** for one person travelling by cyclo or xe om; note that cyclo drivers charge a little extra for luggage. (Centre in this case means around Hoan Kiem Lake.)

Train station to south Hoan Kiem Lake: 5–7000d.
Train station to Cau Go, the Old Quarter: 7–10,000d.
Giap Bat bus station to centre: 15,000d by xe om; 25,000d by cyclo.
Gia Lam bus station to centre: 10–15,000d by xe om only.
Centre to Ho's Mausoleum: 10–12,000d.
Ho's Mausoleum to the Temple of Literature: 5–7000d.
Centre to the *Hanoi Hotel*, Giang Vo: 10–15,000d.

Buses

Hanoi's one-way traffic system means that bus **routes** are complicated, but all the useful buses stop on Trang Tien, beside the Opera House, from where they run as follows:

to *Gia Lam* bus station (25min)
to *Giap Bat* bus station (30min), with a stop near the train station on Tran Hung Dao
to *Ha Dong* (40 min) via Trang Thi (stop opposite *Vietnam Airlines*) and Nguyen Thai Hoc (stop near the Temple of Literature).

The standard **fare** is 2000d.

HANOI

N

Gia Lam Bus Station (1km) & the northeast

Bat Trang Village (7km)

Red River

Red River

0   1km

Thang Loi Hotel, Kim Lien Pagoda & Ho Tay Peninsula

Long Bien Bridge

Chuong Duong Bridge

HOAN KIEM DISTRICT

State Bank

History Museum

LY THAI TO

TRAN QUANG KHAI

TRAN NHAT DUAT

THE OLD QUARTER

Hoan Kiem Lake

YEN PHU

Green Bamboo

Vietnam Airlines

HANG TRONG

HAI BA TRUNG

TRAN HUNG DAO

Hanoi Station

Hui Nghi

Thang Long

Truc Bach Lake

Quan Thanh Temple

Army Museum

LY NAM DE

HOANG DIEU

DIEN BIEN PHU

TRAN QUY CAP

Yen Phu Temple

Tran Quoc Pagoda

NGHI TAM

YEN PHU

KIM LIEN

QUAN THANH

BAC SON

LE HONG PHONG

NGUYEN THAI HOC

Temple of Literature

HUNG VUONG

PHAN DINH PHUNG

HOANG HOA THAM

THUY KHUE

Presidential Palace

Ho Chi Minh's Mausoleum

Ho Chi Minh's Museum

DOI CAN

BA DINH DISTRICT

West Lake

Kim Ma Bus Station

KIM MA

GIANG VO

Swedish Clinic

VAN PHUC

KIM MA

Giang Vo Lake

Hanoi Hotel

Heritage Hotel

Noi Bai Airport (37km)

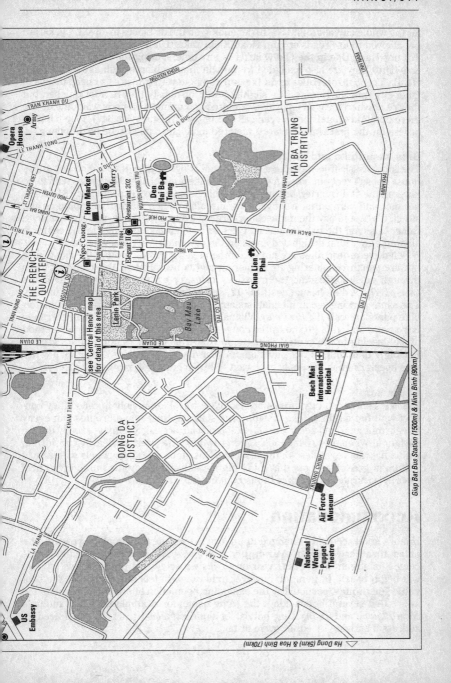

for the whole day, at around $6–10 depending on the distances involved. Cyclos are not allowed to use roads around Hoan Kiem Lake (Dinh Tien Hoang and Le Thai To) nor Hang Dao in the Old Quarter at any time. During the rush hour (7–9am & 4–6pm) they are also excluded from main thoroughfares such as Le Duan and Hai Ba Trung. **Motorbike taxis** (xe om) compete with cyclos as a cheap means of inner-city transport; prices are slightly lower, obviously they're a lot quicker, but they're nowhere near as enjoyable. Metered and unmetered **taxis** wait outside the more upmarket hotels or you can call one up (see "Listings", p.347). Flag-fall is $2 or less for the first 2km and fares, metered in dollars, can also be paid in dong.

Bike, motorbike and car rental

The most hassle-free way to get about Hanoi is by **bicycle**. If your hotel or guest-house doesn't rent out bikes, try one of the outlets given on p.346. Prices tend to be lower in the Old Quarter, but are not exorbitant anywhere; expect to pay $1 or less per day, and bargain for a longer-term discount. When leaving your bike on the street, it's best to pay the minuscule charge at a supervised bike park (*gui xe dap*), rather than run the risk of deflated tyres or a stolen bike. Parking in the centre is allowed only within designated areas on the pavement – in theory anyway.

Self-drive **motorbikes** are not recommended for getting around the city centre but are worth considering for exploring sights near Hanoi. You can rent them through guesthouses and the travellers' cafés, or try the smaller tour agencies (see p.347). A day's rental costs $6–12, depending on the size and make of bike. The same parking recommendations apply as for pedal bikes; supervised motor-bike parks are called *gui xe may*. Virtually every tour agency will gladly arrange **car rental** and, though the traffic congestion makes this a cumbersome method of sightseeing in the central districts, for day-trips out of Hanoi it offers greater flexibility than tours. Prices average $35 per day for a car plus driver; as few dri-vers speak English, you may also want to hire a guide for another $15 a day.

City buses

Hanoi's snail-paced **city buses** are useful to travellers mainly because they con-nect with the far-flung long-distance bus stations. Buses on all routes run every fifteen minutes between 5am and 5.30pm, and are fairly empty except during rush-hour when they're hideously overcrowded. The fares are heavily subsidized, with a flat rate regardless of the distance. Bus stops are white panels with routes written in green, but note that route numbers displayed on the buses aren't nec-essarily accurate, so check with the conductor.

Accommodation

Hanoi's hotel scene has changed dramatically over the last couple of years, to the extent that there's now an **oversupply** at all levels. As a host of new luxury hotels comes on stream in the next year or so, it's expected that prices at this top end will begin to fall. In general, however, mid-range hotels still represent the best **value for money**, particularly the exploding population of private mini-hotels. Be aware that several hotels adopt the same name, for example there are multiple *Nam Phuong* and *Thang Long* hotels, let alone *Especen* 1 to 11, so you'll need an address if arriving by either cyclo or taxi.

ACCOMMODATION PRICE CODES

All accommodation listed in this guide has been categorized according to the following scale:

① under US$10 (under 110,000 dong)   ② US$10–15 (110–165,000 dong)

③ US$15–30 (165–330,000 dong)   ④ US$30–75 (330–825,000 dong)

⑤ US$75–150 (825–1,650,000 dong)   ⑥ over US$150 (over 1,650,000 dong)

Rates are for the cheapest available double or twin room; breakfast is not usually included. During holiday periods, rates are liable to rise, and proprietors may be less amenable to bargaining. Although the law requires prices to be quoted in dong, most hotels also give their rates in US$; payment can be made in either currency. *For a more detailed discussion of accommodation, see pp.31–34.*

The city's most sought-after addresses are in the **French Quarter**, favoured for its somewhat quieter streets and open space. Here you'll also find many of the echoing, old state hotels, but very little in the bargain stakes. The best place to look for budget accommodation is among the the hustle and bustle of Hanoi's **Old Quarter**, where the travellers' cafés and a number of cheap hotels provide basic facilities. In the vicinity there's a good choice of mini-hotels offering a range of reasonable-value rooms, while a couple of Hanoi's top hotels also squeeze onto the outer edges. Sandwiched between the French Quarter and the Old Quarter is an up-and-coming area to the **west of Hoan Kiem Lake**, concentrated along Hang Trong and Nha Chung streets. Hotels here are reasonably priced for their standard and their location, with most of the central attractions easily walkable.

Within a radius of 500m of the **train station** are a few, fairly expensive business hotels, a better range of middle-price establishments and a couple of places aimed at budget travellers. These are handy if you need to be near the station, but other districts offer more attractive surroundings.

Hotels in the **outer districts** tend to be big, new international-style hotels catering to business visitors and tour groups. Nevertheless, there are some more modest establishments on the fringes of the city centre, including a fast-growing group in an interesting area to the east of Truc Bach Lake and another to the south in Hai Ba Trung District. Staying at any of these out-of-centre hotels, though, you'll be reliant on taxis or cyclos for transport.

The French Quarter

All the following hotels and guesthouses (except the Army – see below) are marked on the map on p.314.

Army, 33c Pham Ngu Lao (☎825 2896, fax 825 9276). A well-equipped, central and popular hotel set among trees on a quiet backstreet (see map on pp.310–311), near the History Museum. This place offers better-value accommodation than the MOD Palace next door, though you might want to take advantage of the latter's pleasant, open-air restaurant. ④

Artistic (*Nha Khach Van Nghe Si*), 22a Hai Ba Trung (☎825 3044, fax 824 3919). Tucked at the end of a long alley is a peaceful, shaded courtyard and this well-maintained, reasonably priced hotel. Rooms are sparsely furnished, and tiny at the cheaper end, but adequate. ②

Dan Chu, 29 Trang Tien (☎825 4937, fax 826 6786). This old French hotel retains some period flavour in its open corridors, courtyard, wooden fittings and good-sized bathrooms.

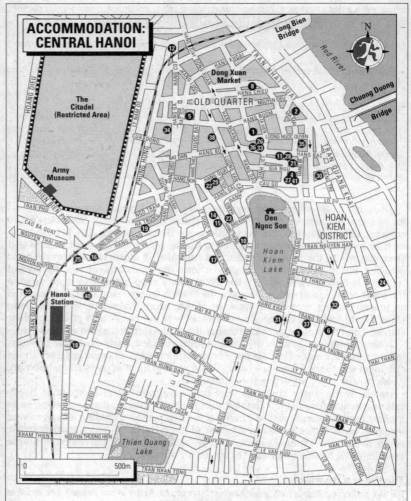

ACCOMMODATION:
CENTRAL HANOI

ACCOMMODATION

1	A Dong	12	Galaxy	23	Nam Phuong	34	Thanh Ha
2	Anh Dao	13	Green Bamboo	24	New Tong Dan	35	Thanh Long
3	Artistic	14	Hang Trong	25	New World	36	Thuy Nga
4	Binh Minh	15	Ho Guom	26	Ngoc Minh II	37	Trang Tien
5	Continental	16	Hoang Cuong	27	Orchid	38	Venus
6	Dan Chu	17	Hotel Mini	28	Queen Café	39	Victory
7	De Syloia	18	Khach San 30–4	29	Real Darling Café	40	Villa Bleue
8	Dong Xuan	19	Kinh Do II	30	Royal	41	Violet
9	Eden	20	Lotus	31	Sofia		
10	Especen Head Office	21	Mai Phuong	32	Sofitel Metropole		
11	Especen 4	22	My Lan	33	Ta Hien		

Air-conditioning, IDD, TV, and minibar come as standard, though cheaper rooms are small and lack windows. It's spruce, efficient and inevitably popular. ⑤

De Syloia, 17a Tran Hung Dao (☎824 5346, fax 824 1083). A stylish, international hotel with a mock colonial facade and 8 floors of impeccably furnished rooms, some a touch on the small side. It boasts a top-class restaurant, health club and the works. ⑤

Eden, 78 Tho Nhuom (☎824 5273, fax 824 5619). An unusual palm-house atrium and quality wood furnishings give a touch of character to this efficient business hotel. The rooms themselves are bland but comfortable. Downstairs is a good, café-style restaurant and a popular bar. ④

Lotus, 42v Ly Thuong Kiet (☎826 8642). A popular guesthouse with the cheapest beds in the French Quarter, consisting of bunks squeezed in a stuffy corridor and 5 cramped rooms. Nevertheless, this place is popular for its location and homely atmosphere. Look out for a tiny sign on the wall among a row of stationers. ①

New Tong Dan, 210 Tran Quang Khai (☎825 2219, fax 825 5354). A friendly, laidback place on a busy road offering cheapish accommodation on the area's northern extremity. The rooms are simply furnished, though all have air-con, telephone and hot water. It's worth paying a few dollars extra for the quieter rooms at the back. ②–③

Sofia, 6 Hang Bai (☎826 6848). As the name suggests, this is a relic of communist days, but the place has been successfully refurbished. Rooms are generally small but fitted out with bathroom, telephone and TV, offering reasonable value for the location. ③

Sofitel Metropole, 15 Ngo Quyen (☎826 6919, fax 826 6920). Hanoi's top hotel, built in 1911, was patronized by Graham Greene and Somerset Maugham. The whole place was gutted for a refit to international, 4-star standards in the early 1990s and a new wing has been added. Bedrooms are tastefully characterless and the cheapest are decidedly small. Despite the whopping price tag (from $250), it's still difficult to get a reservation. ⑥

Trang Tien, 35 Trang Tien (☎825 6115, fax 825 1416). Once a favourite of budget travellers, this place is overpriced even for such a prime location. Its big, spartan rooms are much in need of renovation, and you may be able to bargain them down. ③

The Old Quarter and west of Hoan Kiem Lake

All the following hotels and guesthouses are marked on the map opposite.

A Dong, 46 Luong Ngoc Quyen (☎825 6948, fax 828 2601). A spread of acceptable accommodation, on a quiet backstreet. ①–②

Anh Dao, 37 Ma May (☎826 7151, fax 828 2008). Good-value middle-market place on an interesting street. IDD, satellite TV and air-con are standard. ③

Binh Minh, 50 Hang Be (☎826 7356, fax 824 7183). Its good location, fair prices and relaxed atmosphere make this old hotel a popular first-stop for many travellers. A wide range of rooms are on offer, including some that are dingy and just adequate at the cheaper end. They can also help with tours and transport. ②

Continental, 24 Hang Vai (☎828 2897, fax 828 2989). A smart, medium-sized hotel, with good-value rooms at a variety of prices, all equipped with air-con, satellite TV and IDD phone. ③

Dong Xuan, 3 Thanh Ha (☎825 3290). It's worth searching out this homely, cheap hotel in a colourful area just south of Dong Xuan market. Rooms are better than at many budget places. ②

Especen Hotels, 79e Hang Trong (☎826 6856, fax 826 9612; ②–④). A group of 11 private mini-hotels owned by *Especen Tourist Company*, mostly located in the Old Quarter. They offer reliable budget and intermediate accommodation, though rooms are sometimes overpriced. Cheapest in the vicinity is **No 4** at 16 Trung Yen (☎826 1512; ②), down a back-alley past *pho* stalls and traditional medicine shops; rooms are uninspiring but fulfil the basic needs.

Galaxy, 1 Phan Dinh Phung (☎828 2888, fax 828 2466). New luxury hotel on the Old Quarter's northern fringe. Its 50 tastefully decorated rooms and professional service justify the 3-star prices. ⑤

Green Bamboo, 42 Nha Chung (☎826 8752, fax 826 4949). There's a handful of comfortable rooms at this doyen of the travellers' cafés, but they're often booked-out. ②

Hang Trong, 54 Hang Trong (☎825 1346, fax 826 7120). A small, popular hotel with well-equipped rooms at a good price for the area. ③

Ho Guom, 76 Hang Trong (☎825 2225, fax 824 3564). A surprisingly smart but low-key business hotel tucked off the main street. The simply decorated, light rooms make a pleasant change though cheaper rooms are cramped. ④

Hotel Mini, 24 Nha Chung (☎826 9823, fax 825 0099). Very mini mini-hotel with quirky decor but clean rooms – and a great roof-top room with views over town. ②

Mai Phuong, 32 Hang Be (☎826 5341). This friendly hotel offers a few cheap rooms maintained to reasonable standards. Fair prices mean that it's often full. ①

My Lan, 1 Hang Hom (☎826 0880, fax 828 5871). Choose between three grades of accommodation, from cheap windowless affairs to spacious rooms with balcony, at this clean, well-placed mini-hotel. Standard equipment at all levels includes TV, telephone and air-con. ②

Nam Phuong, 16 Bao Khanh (☎825 8030, fax 825 8964). One of a group of reasonably priced hotels sharing the same name. This one offers basic rooms in an excellent location near Hoan Kiem Lake. ②

Ngoc Minh II (*Ocean Hotel*), 47 Luong Ngoc Quyen (☎826 8459, fax 828 3184). This small, well-kept hotel boasts 7 uncluttered rooms of generous proportions, all with satellite TV and IDD phones. ③

Orchid, 28 Cau Go (☎824 9571). A welcoming, family-run guesthouse found at the far end of the entrance hall. Its handful of rooms are big and bright. ②

Queen Café, 65 Hang Bac (☎826 0860, fax 825 0000). Up there on the backpacker circuit for its well-maintained dormitory accommodation plus a few small, partitioned rooms. ①

Real Darling Café, 33 Hang Quat (☎826 9386, fax 825 6562). The dormitory beds and basic double rooms here are well known as the cheapest accommodation in town, so reservation is a must. ①

Royal, 20 Hang Tre (☎824 4230, fax 824 4234). One of Hanoi's swisher hotels, incongruously located on a grey backstreet. It boasts a business centre, satellite TV, in-house movies, IDD, expensive restaurants, plus nightclub, and plans are afoot for another 70 rooms, tennis court and swimming pool. ⑥

Ta Hien, 22 Ta Hien (☎825 5888). Popular budget hotel with 11 small rooms above a busy café. The rooms are basic but clean, all with bathrooms and some with air-con, while those upstairs are less stuffy. ①–②

Thanh Ha, 34 Hang Ga (☎824 6496, fax 828 2248). A well-run hotel providing good value accommodation over on the west edge of the Old Quarter. Facilities are standard for a mid-range hotel, including TV, air-con and IDD phone. ③

Thanh Long Guesthouse, 73 Ma May (☎824 4425). A few clean rooms at reasonable prices on a quiet street. Cheapest rooms come with air-con and bathroom but no window. ②

Thuy Nga, 24c Ta Hien (☎826 6053, fax 828 2892). A smart-looking mini-hotel whose rooms are well-priced if rather small, and stuffed with ornate wooden furniture. ②

Venus, 10 Hang Can (☎826 1212, fax 824 6010). Well-rated friendly hotel, where above average furnishings and lowish prices make up for being on the main drag. ③

Violet, 18 Cau Go (☎824 7386, fax 824 7386). Moderate hotel on a lively street offering good accommodation. Cheaper rooms are rather box-like, but all come with TV and telephone. ②

Around the train station

All the following hotels are marked on the map on p.314.

Hoang Cuong, 15 Nguyen Thai Hoc (☎826 9927, fax 822 0060). The best value among a group of hotels by the rail lines on busy Nguyen Thai Hoc. Generous-sized rooms and, surprisingly, not too noisy once you're inside. ③

Khach San 30–4, 115 Tran Hung Dao (☎826 0807, fax 825 2611). Directly opposite the station is this unprepossessing hotel offering the cheapest accommodation in the area. Inside the rooms aren't too bad, and even the shared bathrooms are clean and have hot water. ①

Kinh Do II, 120b Hang Bong (☎828 5150, fax 828 3315). This mid-range hotel is on a quiet alley right on the edge of the Old Quarter. Its rooms are well furnished and reasonably priced, all with satellite TV, IDD and air-con. ③

New World, 12 Dinh Ngang (☎824 4163, fax 824 4409). One of several moderate hotels along a short street. This one offers a range of well-equipped rooms. ②–③

Victory, 9, 225 Street (☎825 8725, fax 826 0539). A well-run old hotel that's popular despite its location. Rooms are comfortably furnished and clean. ③

Villa Bleue, 82 Ly Thuong Kiet (☎824 7712, fax 824 5676). This French-era villa makes a better-value business hotel than the neighbouring *Saigon Hotel*. Fourteen spacious rooms with wooden furniture and bags of character. ④

The outer districts

All the following hotels are marked on the map on pp.310–311.

Elegant II, 107 Trieu Viet Huong (☎822 7637, fax 822 9621). Best value of several small business hotels along an attractive, tree-lined road. Front rooms are big and light, while those on the back are less generous but still comfortable. Ornate, dark-wood furniture, satellite TV and IDD. ④

Hanoi, D8 Giang Vo, Ba Dinh District (☎845 2270, fax 845 9209). This expensive 10-storey hotel just off Giang Vo will eventually be joined by other top-class establishments. In the meantime it's surrounded by depressing apartment blocks, though inside all is air-conditioned, international efficiency: business centre, hairdressers, bank, plush restaurant and nightclub. ⑥

Heritage, 80 Giang Vo, Ba Dinh District (☎834 4727, fax 835 1458). Further out along Giang Vo, near the TV tower, this upmarket business hotel offers better value than much of the competition. It's built to an unusual, low-level design, is immaculately kept and offers international standards. ⑤

Huu Nghi (*Friendship*), 23 Quan Thanh (☎845 3182, fax 845 9272). A reliable, well-run older hotel sitting on a busy intersection southeast of Truc Bach Lake. Its 38 rooms are of a reasonable size, with the standard furnishings. ④

Merry, 5 Thi Sach, Hai Ba Trung District (☎822 8242, fax 822 8279). This place lives up to its name with friendly staff and light, bright rooms. Two blocks east of Hom market in a lively area with a village atmosphere. ④

Thang Loi, Yen Phu (☎826 8211, fax 825 2800). This airy, Cuban-designed hotel opened beside West Lake in 1976, following Fidel Castro's visit to Hanoi, and is in remarkably fine condition. Rooms, half with lake view, are in 2 single-storey wings plus in newer bungalows and villas. Restaurants, business centre, hairdresser, tennis, sauna and swimming pool (open to non-residents in the summer) are all on site; 5km from the centre but still popular. ⑤

Thang Long, 5 Nguyen Bieu (☎823 1437, fax 823 1436). Spruce hotel near Truc Bach Lake, well-positioned on a peaceful, tree-lined street. Not cheap but one of the area's best, with rooftop bar and 18 well-appointed rooms, some with balconies. It's often full, despite being a bit on the expensive side. ④

The city

Hanoi **city centre** is a compact area neatly bordered by the Red River embankment in the east and by the rail line to the north and west. Its present-day hub and most obvious point of reference is **Hoan Kiem Lake** which lies between the cramped and endlessly diverting **Old Quarter** in the north, and the tree-lined boulevards of the **French Quarter**, arranged in a rough grid system, to the south. West of this central district, across the rail tracks, some of Hanoi's most impressive monuments occupy the wide, open spaces of the former **Imperial**

City, grouped around Ho Chi Minh's Mausoleum on Ba Dinh Square and extending south to the ancient, walled gardens of the Temple of Literature. A vast body of water confusingly called **West Lake** sits north of the city, harbouring a number of interesting temples and pagodas, but attractive villages that once surrounded West Lake are disappearing fast, making way for international conference centres and upmarket residential areas.

The major tourist sights are nearly all located within the central and western districts; to do both areas justice takes at least two full days. Each district can be covered comfortably on foot, though a bike or cyclo helps over longer distances. Seeing the more far-flung sights of West Lake and the outskirts could occupy a further two to three days, depending on how many more pagodas and temples you can take.

Central Hanoi

The commercial core of Hanoi is **Hoan Kiem District**, home to the city's banks, airlines and the GPO, plus most of the hotels, restaurants, shopping streets and markets. But there's a lot more to the area: the **History Museum** boasts some of Vietnam's most valued archeological finds, while the **temples** here date back to the earliest days of the city. Though you'll want to spend time on these individual sights, it's the abundant streetlife and architectural wealth that give the area its special allure.

Around Hoan Kiem Lake

Early morning sees **Hoan Kiem Lake** at its best, stirring to life as walkers, joggers and *tai chi* enthusiasts limber up in the half-light. Space is at a premium in this crowded city and the lake's strip of park meets multiple needs, at its busiest when lunch-hour hawkers, beggars and shoeshine boys are out in force, and easing down slowly to evenings of old men playing chess and couples seeking twilight privacy on benches half-hidden among the willows. The lake itself is small – you can walk round it in thirty minutes – and not particularly spectacular, but to Hanoians this is the soul of their city.

A squat, three-tiered pavilion known as the **Tortoise Tower** ornaments a tiny island in the middle of *Ho Hoan Kiem*, "Lake of the Restored Sword". The names refer to a legend of the great Vietnamese hero, Le Loi, who led a successful uprising against the Chinese in the fifteenth century. Tradition has it that Le Loi netted a gleaming sword while out fishing in a sampan and when he returned as King Le Thai To, after ten years of battle, wanted to thank the spirit of the lake. As he prepared the sacrifice there was a timely peal of thunder and the miraculous sword flew out of its scabbard, into the mouth of a golden turtle (turtle and tortoise are the same word in Vietnamese) sent by the gods to reclaim the weapon. A few, hardy turtles do still live in the lake, but the one you're most likely to see is a well-varnished specimen captured in 1968. It's now preserved and on view on a second island accessible via the striking **The Huc Bridge**, an arch of red-lacquered wood poetically labelled the "place where morning sunlight rests". Beside the bridge stands a nine-metre-high obelisk, the **Writing Brush Tower**, on which three outsized Chinese characters proclaim "a pen to write on the blue sky". Crossing over to the island you find the secluded **Den Ngoc Son**, "Temple of the Jade Mound", sheltering among ancient trees (daily 7.30am–5pm; $1). This small temple was founded in the fourteenth century and is dedicated to an eclectic

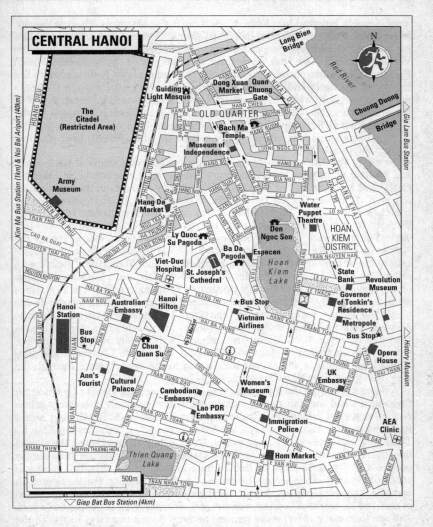

group: national hero General Tran Hung Dao, who defeated the Mongols in 1288, sits on the principal altar; Van Xuong, God of Literature; physician La To; and a martial arts practitioner, Quan Vu. The temple buildings date from the 1800s and are typical of the Nguyen dynasty; inside, take a look at the prominent dragon heads, carved with bulbous noses and teeth bared in manic grins. The giant turtle, over two metres long, resides in a room off the first sanctuary hall, while another building houses a small, antiques shop.

A good way to get your bearings in Hanoi is to make a quick circuit of **Hoan Kiem Lake**; a pleasant walk at any time of year, and stunning when the flame trees flower in June and July. In the 1960s these paths, like many others in the city, were studded with hundreds of individual air-raid shelters – concrete-lined holes big enough for one person, topped with a manhole cover. Heading south from the Writing Brush Tower, you can't miss the stony-faced, grey marble **Hanoi People's Committee** building, about halfway down the lake. Just to its south lies the green oblong of **Indira Gandhi Park** which marks the French Quarter's northern extremity, where the cream of colonial society would gather in the 1890s for weekly concerts held in the bandstand. The next block is occupied by the **General Post Office**, opposite which stands a small, brick tower, all that remains of an enormous pagoda complex, Chua Bao An, after French town-planners cleared the site in 1892.

Rounding the lake's southern tip, past the tiny souvenir shops of Hang Khay, and heading up its west shore, you might want to take a detour to **St Joseph's Cathedral** at the far end of Nha Tho ("Big Church") Street, on the way passing the arched entrance to Ba Da Pagoda, which houses an impressive array of Buddhas. Hanoi's neo-Gothic cathedral was constructed in the late 1880s, partly financed by two lotteries, and though the exterior is badly weathered its high-vaulted interior is still imposing. Among the first things you notice inside are the stained-glass windows, most of which are French originals. Other points of interest are the dozens of votive plaques, inscribed in Latin, French and Vietnamese, around the Chapel of the Virgin Mary on the north aisle, and a black marble tomb on the opposite wall where the last cardinal of Vietnam was buried in 1990, since when the politically sensitive post has remained vacant. Over the tomb stands one of several statues commemorating martyred Vietnamese saints, in this case André Dunglac who was executed in 1839 on the orders of the fervently anti-Christian Emperor Minh Mang. The cathedral's main door is open during services – the celebration of Mass was allowed to resume on Christmas Eve 1990 after a long hiatus; at other times walk round to the side entrance through the grey, iron gates at 40 Nha Chung (closed 1–2pm).

Walking north from the cathedral along Ly Quoc Su brings you to **Ly Quoc Su Pagoda**, a small and uninspiring pagoda but with a genuinely interesting collection of statues. Ly Quoc Su (sometimes also known as Minh Khong) was a Buddhist teacher, healer and royal advisor who cured the hallucinating King Ly Than Tong from believing he was a tiger. Quoc Su's image resides on the altar of this thirteenth-century temple – when it later became a pagoda they simply popped a trinity of Buddhas up behind him. In front of the altar, two groups of statues face each other across the prayer floor: four secular, female figures sit opposite three perfectly inscrutable mandarins of the nineteenth century, clothed in rich, red lacquer and bearing symbols of their rank. Against the pagoda's back wall are four much older, stone figures, perhaps dating from the 1500s. To the right of the altar sits Tu Dao Hanh (see "Thay Pagoda", p.351) accompanied by his charming mother, who both have unusually distinctive faces, while to the left of the altar is Tu Dao Hanh's white-bearded teacher beside an unknown tantric monk.

From Ly Quoc Su retrace your steps to Hoan Kiem Lake and continue northwards to where *Thuy Ta Café* offers respite from the traffic and a particularly fine place to relax, downing a beer while the sun sets over Den Ngoc Son on the opposite bank.

The Old Quarter

A distinctively ugly office block with turtles pinned to its sides dominates the northern end of Hoan Kiem Lake. Walk behind this onto Cau Go and suddenly you're in the tumultuous streets of the **Old Quarter**. Hanoi is the only city in Vietnam to retain its ancient, merchants' quarter, a congested square kilometre which was closed behind massive ramparts and heavy, wooden gates until well into the nineteenth century. Apart from one gate, at the east end of Hang Chieu, the walls have been dismantled but a glance at the map reveals the quarter's jigsaw of narrow streets with evocative names (see box below). There are few compelling sights in the quarter; the best approach is simply to dive into the backlanes, fascinating at any time of day but taking on a special atmosphere as the evening traffic dies down, stalls blaze with colour and everyone comes out to relax and gossip under dim street lights.

Everything spills out onto pavements which double as workshops for stonecarvers and tin-smiths, and as display space for merchandise ranging from pungent therapeutic herbs and fluttering prayer flags to ranks of Remy Martin and shiny-wrapped chocolates. With so much to attract your attention at ground level

---

WHAT'S IN A NAME?

The Old Quarter's street names date back five centuries to when the area was divided among 36 artisans' guilds, each gathered around a temple or a *dinh* (communal house) dedicated to the guild's patron spirit. Even today many streets specialize to some degree, and a surprising number are still dedicated to the original craft or its modern equivalent. The most colourful examples are Hang Quat, full of bright red banners and lacquerware for funerals and festivals, or Hang Ma, where paper products have been made for at least five hundred years, and now gaudy tinsel dances in the breeze above brightly coloured votive objects, which nowadays include model TVs, dollars and cars to be offered to the ancestors. A selection of the more interesting streets with an element of specialization are listed below.

Street name	Meaning	Modern speciality
Hang Bac	Silver	Jewellers, funeral tablets
Hang Bo	Bamboo baskets	Haberdashers, jewellers
Hang Bong	Cotton	Copper wire
Hang Buom	Sails	Imported foods, confectionery
Hang Chieu	Mats	Mats, ropes, screens
Hang Dau	Cooking oil	Shoes
Hang Dieu	Pipes	Cushions, mattresses
Hang Duong	Sugar	Clothes
Hang Gai	Hemp goods	Silks, tailors, souvenirs
Hang Hom	Wooden chests	Glue, paint
Hang Luoc	Combs	Metal goods
Hang Ma	Paper votive objects	Paper goods
Hang Non	Conical hats	Formica ware
Hang Quat	Ceremonial fans	Religious accessories
Hang Thiec	Tin goods	Tin goods, mirrors
Hang Vai	Fabrics	Bamboo ladders
Ha Trung	Drum skin	Bag menders, upholsterers
Lan Ong	Herbal medicines	Traditional medicines, towels

it's easy to miss the **architecture**, which reveals fascinating glimpses of the quarter's history starting with the fifteenth-century merchants' houses otherwise found only in Hoi An (see p.226). Hanoi's aptly named **tube-houses** evolved from market stalls into narrow shops of a single storey, no higher than a passing royal palanquin, under gently curving, red-tiled roofs. Some are just 2m wide, the result of taxes levied on street-frontages and of subdivision for inheritance, while behind stretches a succession of store rooms and living quarters up to 60m in length, interspersed with open courtyards to give light and air. Nowadays, the majority of facades bear distinctly European touches – faded wooden shutters, sagging balconies and rain-streaked moulding – dating from the early 1900s when the streets were widened for pavements. Certain occupants were either too wealthy or influential to be shifted and you can find their houses still standing out of line at the west end of Hang Bac and on Ma May. In fact these two streets contain a wealth of interesting detail typical of the quarter's patchwork architecture: simple one-storey shophouses, some still sporting traditional wood-panel doors; elaborate plaster-work and Art Deco styling from colonial days; and Soviet-chic of the 1960s and 1970s, each superimposed on the basic tube-house design.

Walk north up Ma May to Hang Buom, past an attractive row of tube-houses at nos. 10–18, and you reach the quarter's oldest and most revered place of worship, **Bach Ma Temple** (daily 7.30–11am & 2–6pm). The temple was founded in the ninth century and later dedicated to the White Horse (*Bach Ma*), the guardian spirit of Thang Long who posed as an ethereal site-foreman and helped King Ly Thai To overcome a few problems with his citadel's collapsing walls. The present structure dates largely from the eighteenth century and its most valuable relic is the yellow-clad, copper statue of Bach Ma on the main altar, here in his original incarnation as the earth god Long Do. A festival-float representation of the horse stands to one side and, in front of the altar, two charismatic, red-cloaked guardians flaunt an impressive array of lacquered gold dentures. As you explore the quarter you'll come across a great many other sacred sites – temples, pagodas, *dinh* and venerable banyan trees – hidden among the houses. One of the more surprising is the **Guiding Light Mosque** on Hang Luoc, which was built in 1903 by an Indian Islamic community of traders and civil servants, and now serves Hanoi's one hundred or so Muslims as the only mosque in northern Vietnam.

One block east of the mosque, the city's largest covered market, **Dong Xuan**, occupies a whole block at the far north end of Hang Dao. Originally built in 1889, the market is under reconstruction following a fire in 1994, but by the time you read this its three floors should be back in business, packed with everything from karaoke machines to *nuoc mam* fish sauce. Head one block east again from Dong Xuan and you find two ramps taking bikes and pedestrians up onto **Long Bien Bridge**, originally named Paul Doumer Bridge in honour of the governor-general of Indochina in its inaugural year, 1902. Until Chuong Duong Bridge was built in the 1980s, Long Bien was the Red River's only bridge and therefore of immense strategic significance. During the American War this was one of Vietnam's most heavily defended spots, which American bombs never managed to knock out completely. If you have time, take a bicycle ride across the 1700-metre span of iron lattice-work, but spare a thought for the maintenance staff: in the 1960s, perhaps the last time it was done, it took a hundred workers five years to repaint the bridge.

Cutting back southwards, it was at 48 Hang Ngang that Ho Chi Minh drafted the Declaration of Independence for the Democratic Republic of Vietnam in 1945. The house where he lived for those heady months is now the **Museum of Independence** (daily 7am–5pm). A small exhibition downstairs shows yet more photos of Uncle Ho with beaming children, but it's worth taking a look at the two first-floor rooms where he slept, wrote and debated, which are sparsely furnished with oversized, Western period furniture. From here it's only a couple of minutes' walk down to Hoan Kiem Lake, passing through the traditional street market selling fresh meat, fish and vegetables under an improvised canopy of low-slung sacks that clots the lanes just behind Cau Go. This southern edge of the Old Quarter, particularly Hang Gai, is where you'll find the biggest concentration of souvenir shops, but before leaving the old streets completely take a quick detour up **To Tich**, a short lane of wood-turners and small restaurants serving fragrant skewers of grilled pork or steaming bowls of *pho*, to walk among **Hang Quat's** bright red prayer flags.

The French Quarter

After the hectic streets of the Old Quarter, the grand boulevards and wide pavements of Hanoi's **French Quarter** to the south and east of Hoan Kiem Lake are a welcome relief. Again it's the architecture here that's the highlight, with a few specific attractions spread over a couple of kilometres, so you might want to explore by bicycle or cyclo. The first French concession was granted in 1874, an insalubrious plot of land on the banks of the Red River, southeast of where the Opera House stands today. Once in full possession of Hanoi, after 1882, the French began to create a city appropriate to their new protectorate, starting with the area between the old concession and the train station, 2km to the west. Gradually elegant villas filled plots along the grid of tree-lined avenues, then spread south in the 1930s and 1940s towards what is now Lenin Park.

In the process of building their capital the French destroyed many ancient Vietnamese monuments, including one of Hanoi's oldest pagodas, Bao Thien, which was demolished to make way for the cathedral. They were replaced, however, with some fine, Parisian-style buildings such as the stately **Opera House** (now officially known as the Municipal Theatre), at the eastern end of Trang Tien. Based on the Neo-Baroque Paris Opéra, complete with ionic columns and grey slate tiles imported from France, the theatre was erected on reclaimed land and finally opened in 1911 after ten years in the making. It was regarded as the jewel in the crown of French Hanoi, the colonial town's physical and cultural focus, until 1945 when the Viet Minh proclaimed the August Revolution from its balcony. After Independence, audiences were treated to a diet of socialist realism and revolutionary theatre, surrounded by crystal chandeliers and sweeping staircases. Now the building is closed while air-conditioning, new sound-systems and a larger stage are installed as part of a $20 million face-lift, scheduled for completion in late 1997.

One block east of the Opera House is Hanoi's **History Museum**, at 1 Trang Tien (Tues–Sun 8–11.45am & 1.15–4pm; $1). Buried among trees and facing the river, the museum isn't immediately obvious, but its architecture is unmissable – a fanciful blend of Vietnamese palace and French villa which came to be called "Neo-Vietnamese" style. The museum was founded in the 1930s by *l'Ecole Française d'Extrême Orient*, but after 1954 changed focus to reflect Vietnam's evolution from Paleolithic times to Independence. Exhibits, including many plaster reproductions, are arranged in chronological order on two floors: everything downstairs is pre-1400, while the second floor takes the story up to August 1945.

Unfortunately the English labelling is sporadic and the museum booklet is none too helpful.

On the ground floor, the museum's prize exhibits are those from the **Dong Son culture**, a sophisticated Bronze Age civilization which flourished in the Red River Delta from 1200 to 200 BC. The display includes a rich variety of implements, from arrowheads to cooking utensils, but the finest examples of Dong Son creativity are several huge, ceremonial bronze drums, used to bury the dead, invoke the monsoon or celebrate fertility rites. The remarkably well-preserved **Ngoc Lu Drum** (first on the left) is the highlight, where advanced casting techniques are evident in the delicate figures of deer, birds and boats ornamenting the surface. Other notable exhibits include a graceful Amitabha Buddha of the eleventh century, a gold-inscribed lacquered board from the same period – a poem by King Ly Thuong Kiet, regarded as the first declaration of Viet independence – and a group of five wooden stakes from the glorious thirteenth-century battle of the Bach Dang River (see p.365).

The museum's second floor is dominated by a three-metre-tall stele inscribed with the life story of Le Loi, who spearheaded the resistance against the Chinese occupation in the fifteenth century, but the most interesting exhibits here relate to the nineteenth-century Nguyen dynasty and the period of French rule. A series of ink-washes depicting Hué's Imperial Court in the 1890s are particularly eye-catching, as are several rare, early 1900s photos of Hué citadel in all its magnificence. But outside the citadel walls the country was again in turmoil, culminating in the struggle for independence led by Ho Chi Minh; the evidence of royal decadence and French brutality gathered here alone explains the strength of popular support for the nationalist cause.

The story continues at the **Museum of Vietnamese Revolution**, one block north at 25 Tong Dan (Tues, Fri & Sat 8–11.30am, Wed, Thurs & Sun 8–11.30am & 1.30–4.30pm), housed in a classic colonial building that started life as a customs house. This museum catalogues the "Vietnamese people's patriotic and revolutionary struggle" from the early years of this century to post-1975 reconstruction. Much of the tale is told through original documents, including the first clandestine newspapers and revolutionary tracts penned by Ho Chi Minh. Unfortunately there are no English explanations and there's little here that isn't better presented at other museums.

Back at the Opera House, walking two blocks north on Ly Thai To brings you to the junction with Ngo Quyen, dominated by two very different buildings. The imposing Art Deco structure with a circular portico, once the French Bank of Indochina, now houses the **State Bank** and central *Vietcombank* in its lofty halls. Diagonally opposite stands one of Hanoi's most attractive colonial edifices, the immaculately restored **Residence of the Governor of Tonkin**, constructed in 1918; it's now known as the State Guest House and used for visiting VIPs. Unfortunately you can't get inside but as you peer in take a closer look at the elegant, wrought-iron railings, pitted with bullet-mark souvenirs of the 1945 Revolution. More recently the building's terraces appeared in the film *Indochine* (see p.466). In comparison, the bright, white Neo-Classical facade of the **Metropole** – nowadays, *Hotel Sofitel Metropole* – just south on Ngo Quyen, verges on the austere. The Metropole opened in 1911, the same year as the Opera House, and soon became one of southeast Asia's grand hotels. Even during the French War Bernard Fall, a journalist killed by a landmine near Hué in 1967, described the hotel as the "last really fashionable place left in Hanoi", where the barman "could produce a reasonable facsimile of almost any civilized drink except water". After Independence it re-emerged as the *Thong Nhat* or Reunification Hotel, but otherwise stayed much the same, including en suite rats and lethal wiring, until 1990 when Pullman-Sofitel gutted and restored the place, creating one of the first international class hotels in Hanoi, but destroying much of its character in the process. Not that anyone's complaining too much – the Metropole is one of Vietnam's biggest money-spinners.

Trang Tien, the main artery of the French Quarter, is still a busy shopping street where you'll find bookstores and art galleries, as well as cafés and a couple of hotels. After a lot of controversy, the site of the state-run General Department Store, a prime piece of real estate on the corner with Hang Bai, is being redeveloped as the Hanoi Plaza, eight storeys of shops, apartments and offices due for completion by mid-1998. South of Trang Tien you enter French Hanoi's principal residential quarter, consisting of a grid of shaded boulevards whose distinguished villas are much sought after for restoration as embassies, offices or as desirable, expatriate residences. These houses, which like those of the Old Quarter have survived largely due to lack of money for redevelopment, run the gamut of early-twentieth-century European architecture from elegant Neo-Classical through to 1930s Modernism and Art Deco, with an occasional Oriental flourish.

To take a swing through the area, drop down Hang Bai onto Ly Thuong Kiet and start heading west. Just round the corner from Hang Bai, the informative ethnic-minority room on the fourth floor of Hanoi's revamped **Women's Museum**, at 36 Ly Thuong Kiet (Mon–Sat 8–11.30am & 1.30–4pm), is well designed and worth a quick look, especially if you're heading out to the northern mountains. A few hundred metres further on, you cross Quang Trung, where dozens of roadside barbers' shops create a black carpet, before arriving at the southern entrance of Cho 19–12 (19 December Market), a short, covered street of stalls selling predominantly vegetables and meat, including the tortured carcasses of roast dog. The next block west from here was once home to the French-built Hoa Lo ("furnace") prison, nicknamed the **Hanoi Hilton** by American PoWs in wry comment on its harsh conditions and often brutal treatment. The jail became famous in the 1960s when American prisoners, mostly pilots and crew members, were shown worldwide on televized propaganda campaigns. Used as a prison until 1994, the site is being redeveloped as a high-rise hotel and conference centre due for completion in 1997. Stretches of wall and a few cells will be incorporated into a museum to commemorate American PoWs as well as Vietnamese convicts from an earlier war: the French incarcerated many nationalist leaders here, including Do Muoi, who escaped in 1945 and became general secretary of the Communist Party nearly fifty years later.

At the next junction west on Ly Thuong Kiet, turn left down Quan Su to find the arched entrance of **Chua Quan Su**, the Ambassadors' Pagoda (daily except Sat 8.30–11.30am & 1.30–4pm), founded in the fifteenth century as part of a guest-house for ambassadors from neighbouring Buddhist countries, though the current building only dates from 1942. Nowadays Quan Su is one of Hanoi's most active pagodas: on the first and fifteenth days of the lunar month worshippers and mendicants throng its forecourt while inside a magnificent iron lamp, ornamented with sinuous dragons, hangs over the crowded prayer-floor and ranks of crimson-lacquered Buddhas glow through a pungent haze of burning incense. The compound, shaded by ancient trees, is home to various research institutions and is a centre of Buddhist learning, hence the classroom in the backyard.

Ho Chi Minh's Mausoleum and around

Hanoi's most important cultural and historical monuments are found in the district immediately west of the Old Quarter, where the Ly kings established their Imperial City in the eleventh century. The venerable **Temple of Literature** and the picturesque **One Pillar Pagoda** both date from this time, but nothing else remains of the Ly's vermilion palaces, whose last vestiges were cleared in the late nineteenth century to accommodate an expanding French administration. Most impressive of the district's colonial buildings is the dignified Residence of the Governor-General of Indochina, now known as the **Presidential Palace**. After 1954 some of the surrounding gardens gave way in their turn to Ba Dinh parade ground, the National Assembly Hall and two great centres of pilgrimage: **Ho Chi Minh's Mausoleum** and **Museum**. The **citadel** encloses a restricted military area right in the city: its most famous feature is the **Cot Co Flag Tower** which dominates the extreme southwest corner, next to one of Hanoi's most rewarding museums, the **Army Museum**. Although there's a lot to see in this area, it's possible to cover everything described below in a single day, with an early start at the mausoleum and surrounding sites, leaving the Army Museum and Temple of Literature until later in the day.

Ba Dinh Square and Ho Chi Minh's Mausoleum

The wide, open spaces of **Ba Dinh Square**, 2km west of Hoan Kiem Lake, are the nation's ceremonial epicentre. It was here that Ho Chi Minh read out the Declaration of Independence to half a million people on September 2, 1945, and here that Independence is commemorated each National Day with military parades. The National Assembly Hall, venue for Party congresses, stands on the square's east side, while the west is dominated by the severe, grey bulk of **Ho Chi Minh's Mausoleum** (April–Oct Tues–Thurs & Sat 7.30–10.30am, Sun 7.30–11am; Nov–March Tues–Thurs & Sat 8–11am, Sun 8–11.30am; closed Mon & Fri). In the tradition of great communist leaders, when Ho Chi Minh died in 1969 his body was embalmed, though not put on public view until after 1975. The mausoleum is probably Hanoi's most popular sight, attracting crowds of visitors, from school parties to ageing confederates, all come to pay their respects to "Uncle Ho".

Foreign visitors to the mausoleum must leave bags and cameras at the Hung Vuong Street reception centre before crossing over to an assembly point opposite, from where you'll be escorted by soldiers in immaculate white uniforms. Busiest times for local tour parties are weekends and national holidays; though foreigners are given priority, it's best to visit on a weekday if you can. Respectful behaviour is requested, which means removing hats and keeping silence within the sanctum, and there's talk of reimposing the dress code – no shorts or vests. Note that each year the mausoleum closes for two months while Ho goes to Moscow for maintenance, usually between September and November.

Inside the building's marble entrance hall Ho Chi Minh's most quoted maxim greets you: "nothing is more important than independence and freedom". Then it's up the stairs and into a cold, dark room where this charismatic hero lies under glass, a small, pale figure glowing in the dim light, his thin hands resting on black covers. Despite the rather macabre overtones, it's hard not to be affected by the solemn atmosphere, though in actual fact Ho's last wish was to be cremated and his ashes divided between the north, centre and south of the country, with each site marked only by a simple shelter. The grandiose building where he now lies seems sadly at odds with this unassuming, egalitarian man.

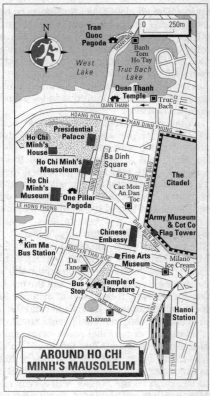

AROUND HO CHI MINH'S MAUSOLEUM

The Presidential Palace and Ho Chi Minh's house

Follow the crowd on leaving Ho's mausoleum and you enter the **Presidential Palace** via its side gate. The palace was built in 1901 as the humble abode of the governor-general of Indochina – all sweeping stairways, louvred shutters and ornate wrought-iron gates of the Belle Epoque – and these days is used to receive visiting heads of state. It's closed to the public but you can admire the outside as you walk through the palace gardens to **Ho Chi Minh's house** (Tues–Sun 8–11am & 2–4pm). After Independence in 1954 President Ho Chi Minh built a modest dwelling for himself behind the palace, modelling it on an ethnic minority stilthouse, a simple structure with open sides and split-bamboo screens. The ground-level meeting area is equipped with desk, telephones and table used by Ho and the politburo, while his study and bedroom upstairs are said to be just as he left them, sparsely furnished, unostentatious and very highly polished. Apparently Ho lived here for the last eleven years of his life, even during the American War, tending his garden and fish-pond; tradition has it that he died in the small hut next door.

The One Pillar Pagoda

Close by Ho's stilthouse, the **One Pillar Pagoda** rivals the Tortoise Tower as a symbol of Hanoi. It is the most unusual of the hundreds of pagodas sponsored by devoutly Buddhist Ly dynasty kings in the eleventh century, and represents a flowering of Vietnamese art. The tiny, wooden sanctuary, dedicated to Quan Am whose statue nestles inside, is only 3 square metres in size and is supported on a single column rising from the middle of an artificial lake, the whole structure designed to resemble a lotus blossom, the Buddhist symbol of enlightenment. In fact this is by no means the original building – the concrete pillar is a real give-away – and the last reconstruction took place after departing French troops blew up the pagoda in 1954.

The pagoda's origins are uncertain but a popular legend recounts that it was founded in 1049 by King Ly Thai Tong, an ardent Buddhist with no male offspring. The goddess Quan Am appeared before the king in a dream, sitting on her lotus throne and holding out to him an infant boy. Soon after, the king married a village girl who bore him a son and heir, and he erected a pagoda shaped like a lotus blossom in thanks. The fact that King Ly Thai Tong already had a son born in 1022, six years before he came to the throne, gives greater credence to a less romantic version. According to this story, King Ly Thai Tong dreamt that Quan Am invited him to join her on the lotus throne. The king's advisors, deeming this an ill omen, advised him to found a pagoda where they could pray for their sovereign's longevity.

Whatever the truth, most people find the pagoda an anti-climax – partly because of its size and the concrete restoration work, and partly because of the overpowering presence of Ho Chi Minh's Museum. Behind the pagoda grows a **bo tree**, said to be an offshoot of the one under which the Buddha gained enlightenment, which was presented to Ho Chi Minh when he visited India in 1958. Before leaving the pagoda garden, take a look in the small building in the southwest corner: through the door is a delightfully intimate courtyard full of potted plants and bonsai trees, where a monk sometimes practises acupuncture.

Ho Chi Minh's Museum

The gleaming white building just 200m west of the One Pillar Pagoda is **Ho Chi Minh's Museum** (Tues–Sun 8–11am & 1.30–4pm), built with Soviet aid and inaugurated on May 19, 1990, the hundredth anniversary of Ho's birth. The museum celebrates Ho Chi Minh's life and the pivotal role he played in the nation's history; not surprisingly, this is also a favourite for school outings. Exhibits around the hall's outer wall focus on Ho's life and the "Vietnamese Revolution", in the context of socialism's international development, including documents, photographs, and a smattering of personal possessions, among them a disguise Ho adopted when escaping from Hong Kong (see p.294 for more on Ho's life story). Running parallel on the inner ring are a series of heavily metaphoric "spatial images", six tableaux portraying significant places and events, from Ho's birthplace in Nghe An to Pac Bo cave and ending with a symbolic rendering of Vietnam's reunification. Most exhibits are labelled in English but low lighting and tiny lettering make them hard to read. Go in for the surreal nature of the whole experience, but don't expect to come away having learnt much more about Ho Chi Minh.

The Army Museum and the Cot Co Flag Tower

From Ho Chi Minh's Museum head back east past Ba Dinh Square to Dien Bien Phu, a road lined with gnarled trees and gloomy colonial offices interspersed with gingerbread villas. Around 500m from the square, Lenin's statue stands opposite a white, arcaded building, the **Army Museum** (Tues–Sun 8–11.30am & 1.30–4.30pm; $1, plus extra for cameras). If you have the time or energy for only one museum in Hanoi, then this should be it. Not only does it cover an important period of Vietnamese history but it's also comparatively well laid out and provides a fair amount of English explanation. While ostensibly tracing the story of the People's Army from its foundation in 1944, in reality the museum chronicles national history from the 1930s to the present-day, a period dominated by the French and American wars, though it's noticeably quiet on China and Cambodia.

The museum courtyard is full of weaponry: pride of place goes to a Russian MiG 21 fighter, alongside artillery from the battle of Dien Bien Phu (see box on pp.392–393), anti-aircraft guns from the American War, and the mangled wreckage of a B-52 piled against a tree. The exhibition proper starts on the museum's second floor which runs chronologically from the 1930 Nghe Tinh Uprising, through the August Revolution, to the "People's War" against the French, culminating in the decisive victory at Dien Bien Phu. Unfortunately video presentations, giving the context for each period, are only shown to groups of ten or more, but you might be lucky enough to coincide with a tour. Some of the photo-stacks are interesting: the third room, covering the early French War, features photos of battle-scarred streets of Hanoi in the late 1940s. But the museum's highlight is the hall devoted to the **battle of Dien Bien Phu**, particularly its diorama of the unfolding battle; if there's enough demand they'll show an English-language version of the accompanying video. Despite the heavy propaganda overlay, the archive footage is fascinating, including Viet Minh hauling artillery up mountain slopes and clouds of French parachutists. Naturally, General Giap and Ho Chi Minh make star appearances – after the ubiquitous still images, it's a shock to see Ho animated. In contrast, the refurbished American War room, in a back hall, is a disappointing collection of equipment, medals and battle flags erratically labelled in English.

Within the Army Museum compound stands the 33-metre-high **Cot Co Flag Tower**, one of the few remnants of Emperor Gia Long's early-nineteenth-century citadel, where the national flag now billows in place of the emperor's yellow banner. In 1812 Vietnamese architects added several towers to the otherwise European-designed citadel, and when the French flattened the ramparts in the 1890s they kept Cot Co as a handy look-out post and signalling tower. From the top you can see Hanoi's first high-rise developments broaching the tree-line and the metal arches of Long Bien Bridge off to the east, or look down into today's citadel, a military barracks harbouring relics of the fifteenth-century Imperial City which are not open to the public. If the tower is locked, ask at the museum entrance.

National Fine Arts Museum
From the Army Museum follow Hoang Dieu Avenue south, past the Chinese Embassy, and turn right on Cau Ba Quat to find a three-storey colonial block with chocolate-brown shutters, the **National Fine Arts Museum** (Tues–Sun 8am–noon & 1–4pm; $1). The collection here is a real mish-mash of exhibits starting with a disappointing display of faded artefacts from various ethnic minorities, dusty Dong Son drums, replica Buddhas and so on. The saving grace is a selection of arhats from the Tay Phuong Pagoda (see p.352) but even these fail to inspire in such a drab environment. The two lower floors are of greater interest, comprising a selection of folk art and handicrafts including some fine wood-block prints, and an exhibition tracing the technical evolution of lacquer painting. Connoisseurs of contemporary Vietnamese art shouldn't miss the new gallery, in a separate block to the side, where works of twentieth-century artists demonstrate an evolution from solidly European style through Socialist Realism to the emergence of a distinct, Vietnamese school of art.

The Temple of Literature
Across busy Nguyen Thai Hoc Avenue is Hanoi's most revered temple complex, the **Temple of Literature** or **Van Mieu**, both Vietnam's principal Confucian sanctuary and its historical centre of learning (daily 8am–6pm; $1). The temple is also one of the few remnants of the Ly kings' original city and retains a strong sense of harmony despite reconstruction and embellishment over the nine hundred years since its dedication in 1070.

Entry is through the two-tiered Van Mieu Gate on Quoc Tu Giam. The temple's ground plan, modelled on that of Confucius's birthplace in Qufu, China, consists of a succession of five, walled courtyards. The first two are havens of trim lawns and noble trees separated by a simple pavilion; entry to the third is via the imposing *Khue Van Cac*, a double-roofed gateway built in 1805, its wooden upper storey ornamented with four radiating suns. Central to the third courtyard is the Well of Heavenly Clarity – a walled pond – to either side of which stand the temple's most valuable relics, 82 stone **stelae** mounted on tortoises. Each stele records the results of a state examination held at the National Academy between 1442 and 1779, though the practice only started in 1484, and gives brief biographical details of successful candidates. It's estimated that up to thirty stelae have gone missing or disintegrated over the years, but the two oldest (exams of 1442 and 1448) occupy centre spot on opposite sides of the pond.

Passing through the Gate of Great Success brings you to the fourth courtyard and the main temple buildings. Two pavilions on either side once contained altars dedicated to the 72 disciples of Confucius, but now house administrative offices, a bookshop and small museum. The exhibits are mostly post-eighteenth century, including 1920s photos of the temple and students' textbooks, ink stones and other accoutrements, such as a wine gourd for the fashion-conscious nineteenth-century scholar. At Tet this courtyard is the scene of life-size chess games using people as pieces on the square paving stones.

The temple's **ceremonial hall**, a long, low building whose sweeping, tiled roof is crowned by two lithe dragons bracketing a full moon, stands on the courtyard's north side. Here the king and his mandarins would make sacrifices before the altar of Confucius, accompanied by booming drums and bronze bells. These days

---

BECOMING A MANDARIN

Examinations for admission to the **imperial bureaucracy** were introduced by the Ly kings in the eleventh century as part of a range of reforms which served to underpin the nation's stability for several centuries. Vietnam's exams were based on the Chinese system, though included Buddhist and Taoist texts along with the Confucian classics. It took until the fifteenth century, however, for academic success, rather than noble birth or patronage, to become the primary means of entry to the civil service. By this time the system was open to **all males**, excluding "traitors, rebels, immoral people and actors", but in practice very few candidates outside the scholar-gentry class progressed beyond the lowest rung.

First came **regional exams**, *thi huong*, after which successful students (who could be any age from 16 to 61) would head for Hanoi, equipped with their sleeping mat, ink stone and writing brush, to take part in the second level *thi hoi*. These **national exams** might last up to six weeks and were as much an evaluation of poetic style and knowledge of the classic texts as they were of administrative ability; it was even felt necessary to ban the sale of strong liquor to candidates in the 1870s. Those who passed all stages were granted a doctorate, *tien si*, and were eligible for the third and final test, the *thi dinh* or **palace exam**, set by the king himself. Some years as few as three *tien si* would be awarded whereas the total number of candidates could be as high as six thousand, and during nearly three hundred years of exams (1076–1779) only 2313 *tien si* were recorded. Afterwards the king would give his new mandarins a cap, gown, parasol and a horse on which to return to their home-village in triumphal procession.

recitals of traditional music echo among the magnificent ironwood pillars (daily 9am–5pm; donation requested). Directly behind the ceremonial hall lies the **temple sanctuary**, at one time prohibited even to the king, where Confucius sits with his four principal disciples, newly decorated in vivid reds and golds.

The fifth and final courtyard used to house the **National Academy**, regarded as Vietnam's first university, which was founded in 1076 to educate princes and high officials in Confucian doctrine. Later the academy held triennial examinations to select the country's senior mandarins (see box on facing page), a practice that continued almost uninterrupted until 1802 when Emperor Gia Long moved the nation's capital to Hué. In 1947 French bombs destroyed the academy buildings, leaving a few traces visible among the weeds.

West Lake

Back in the mists of time a gifted monk returned from China, bearing quantities of bronze as a reward for curing the emperor's illness. The monk gave most of the metal to the state but from a small lump he fashioned a bell, whose ring was so pure it resonated throughout the land and beyond the mountains. The sound reached the ears of a golden buffalo calf inside the Chinese imperial treasury; the creature followed the bell, mistaking it for the call of its mother. Then the bell fell silent and the calf spun round and round, not knowing which way to go, until it trampled a vast hollow which filled with water and became **West Lake**, *Ho Tay*. Some say that the golden buffalo is still there, at the bottom of the lake, but can only be retrieved by a man assisted by his ten natural sons.

More prosaically, West Lake is a shallow lagoon left behind as the Red River shifted course eastward to leave a narrow strip of land, reinforced over the centuries with massive embankments, separating the lake and river. The lake was traditionally an area for royal recreation or spiritual pursuits, where monarchs erected summer palaces and sponsored religious foundations, among them Hanoi's most ancient pagoda, **Tran Quoc**. In the seventeenth century villagers built a causeway across the lake's southeast corner, creating a small fishing lake now called **Truc Bach**. Feet-rowing fishermen still eke a living from these two lakes despite mounting pollution levels.

West Lake District, nicknamed Hanoi's Beverley Hills, is fast becoming a fashionable residential area, earmarked for ambitious hotel and conference developments, parks and exclusive lakeside clubs, but for the moment a bike-ride up the lake's east shore makes a pleasant excursion with one or two sights to aim for. Alternatively, the more southerly attractions of the causeway, described below, are only about 500m north of the Presidential Palace and can easily be combined with a visit to the monuments around Ba Dinh Square.

The causeway and Truc Bach Lake

The name **Truc Bach** derives from an eighteenth-century summer palace built by the ruling Trinh lords which later became a place of detention for disagreeable concubines and other "errant women" who were put to work weaving fine white silk, *truc bach*. The palace no longer exists but eleventh-century **Quan Thanh Temple** still stands on the lake's southeast bank, erected by King Ly Thai To and dedicated to the Guardian of the North, Tran Vo, who protects the city from malevolent spirits. Quan Thanh has been rebuilt several times, most recently in 1893, along the way losing nearly all its original features, but it's worth wandering into the quiet, dilapidated courtyard to see the **statue** of Tran Vo, cast in black bronze in 1677 and seated on the main altar. The statue, over 3m high and weighing 4 tonnes, portrays the Taoist god accompanied by his two animal emblems, a serpent and turtle. The shrine room also boasts a valuable collection of seventeenth- and eighteenth-century poems and parallel sentences (boards inscribed with wise maxims and hung in pairs on adjacent columns), some of intricate, mother-of-pearl inlay work. On the way out, look up at the second storey of the main gate to see a large bronze bell, also cast in 1677.

The gate of Quan Thanh is just a few paces south of the **causeway**, Thanh Nien Street, an avenue of flame trees that is a popular picnic spot in summer when a cooling breeze comes off the water and hawkers set up shop along the grass verges. Where the road bears gently right look for a small memorial on the Truc Bach side, which is dedicated to teams of **anti-aircraft gunners** stationed here during the American War. In particular the memorial commemorates the downing of Navy Lieutenant Commander John McCain, who parachuted into Truc Bach Lake in October 1967 and survived more than five years in the Hanoi Hilton to become US senator for Arizona, and a strong supporter of normalization between America and Vietnam.

Continuing along the causeway you come to Hanoi's oldest religious foundation, **Tran Quoc Pagoda**, occupying a tiny island in West Lake (Mon–Sat 7–11.30am & 1.30–6pm, Sun & national holidays 7am–6pm). The pagoda's exact origins are uncertain but it's usually attributed to the sixth-century Early Ly dynasty during a brief interlude in ten centuries of Chinese domination. A stone stele of 1639 records that in the early seventeenth century, when Buddhism was enjoying a revival, the pagoda was moved from beside the Red River to its present, less vulnerable location. You can see the stele standing just outside the front doors, but entry is via the back of the pagoda, along a narrow, brick causeway lying just above the water, past a collection of imposing, brick stupas. The sanctuary's restrained interior and general configuration are typical of northern Vietnamese pagodas though there's nothing inside of particular importance.

Around West Lake

The east side of West Lake is experiencing rapid urbanization but it does have a sprinkling of mildly interesting, far-flung sights that are best tackled by bike or car. In contrast, its north side remains largely a region of farmland and villages. It's possible to circumnavigate the lake by bicycle, a total of roughly 13km. To start off, take Yen Phu Avenue, halfway up the Red River embankment from the causeway, rather than compete with the ferocious stream of trucks and buses along the top road, Nghi Tam.

Not far along Yen Phu an arch on the left, inscribed "Lang Yen Phu", marks the entrance to a narrow lane, down which **Yen Phu Temple** is worth a quick detour for its massive entrance hall and a jolly group of statuettes making offerings before the altar. Continuing along the main road, past unusually ostentatious villas – fantasy houses combining a touch of Spanish hacienda with a slice of French chateau – you get an idea of the pace of development in this district, which for a while outstripped any attempt at planning or design controls. The most notorious example was illegal construction-work along Nhgi Tam, just east of here, which caused cracks up to 200m long in the city's thousand-year-old flood defences. After a much publicized enquiry, in which a few heads rolled, some offending structures were torn down, though new ones seem to be going up right next door.

About 1km from the causeway, just past the long, low blocks of the *Thang Loi Hotel* are the red-tiled roofs of **Kim Lien Pagoda**, whose best attributes are its elaborately carved entrance arches and unplastered brick walls dating from an eighteenth-century rebuild. In spring, the gardens around here are full of blossoms for Tet celebrations, but judging from the pace of encroaching apartment blocks it's hard to believe that the nurseries of Nghi Tam flower village, much vaunted in the tourist literature, will survive much longer. The next left turn takes you out along the **Ho Tay Peninsula** to a quiet but isolated hotel, Ho Tay Villas, from where a dirt track leads down to a row of lakeside restaurants and **Phu Tay Ho**. This temple is dedicated to Thanh Mau, the Mother Goddess, who appeared as a beautiful girl to a famous scholar out boating on the lake in the seventeenth century. She refused to reveal her name, just smiled enigmatically, recited some poetry and disappeared. But when the scholar worked out her identity from the poem, local villagers erected a temple where they still occasionally worship the goddess in trances – as at Hon Chen Temple in Hué (see p.268). Phu Tay Ho attracts few tourists and the petitioners here are mostly young people asking for favours by burning their fake dollars under the banyan trees; according to Chinese belief, the bats depicted on the temple's unusually exuberant facade are symbolic of five wishes – for longevity, security, success, happiness and health.

The southern districts

South of the French Quarter colonial villas gradually give way to fairly ordinary, urban blocks, while west of Le Duan (Highway 1) the city quickly dissolves into suburban villages. Pockets of high-rise development are beginning to sprout along the major thoroughfares dissecting these **southern districts**, particularly around Giang Vo's pioneering *Hanoi Hotel*. But it's not all city sprawl: remnants of farmland interspersed with numerous lakes relieve the congestion. The area's few attractions are widely scattered and wouldn't appear on anyone's must-see list but, for those with more time, exploring the outskirts adds an insight into everyday life, away from the tourist sights.

Between Le Duan and the Red River lies **Hai Ba Trung District**, named after an ancient temple which is also the area's principal tourist sight. **Den Hai Ba Trung** honours two heroic sisters who led the first popular rebellion against Chinese occupation and set up a short-lived, independent kingdom in 40 AD (see pp.409–410). When the rebellion collapsed, the Trung sisters threw themselves into a river to escape capture, so that when two stone figures washed up on the banks of the Red River several centuries later, they were taken to be the petrified bodies of the two heroines. A shrine was built on the site in 1142 before being moved to its present location in the nineteenth century. Unfortunately, the temple authorities are reluctant to admit foreigners at present, though you might gain admittance on the first and fifteenth days of the lunar month, or during the temple festival held in February (on the fifth and sixth days of the second lunar month), when the statues are washed in water brought from the Red River and dressed in new robes.

Chua Lien Phai, "Pagoda of the Lotus Sect", is tucked away in a tangle of narrow alleys amongst a crush of one-storey houses 1km southwest of Den Hai Ba Trung. The most interesting thing about Lien Phai is the story of its foundation by Lord Trinh Thap who dug up a lotus-root-shaped rock in his back garden. Convinced this was a sign from Buddha, he shaved his head and trans-

---

THE CHRISTMAS BOMBING

In December 1972 President Nixon ordered intensive bombing raids on Hanoi and Haiphong, targeting transport arteries, power stations, factories and military installations, in the hope of influencing the Paris peace negotiations. This controversial "Christmas Bombing" inflicted considerable damage to civilian districts, causing an estimated 1300 deaths in Hanoi, where districts southwest of the train station were the worst hit. More than two hundred people died in and around Kham Thien Street on December 26, but the most infamous strike was that on Bach Mai hospital in which, miraculously, only eighteen people were killed though seven bombs fell on the cardiology unit alone. At the time the North Vietnamese feared Hanoi would be wiped off the map and even laid out plans for a new capital; in the event, central Hanoi survived relatively unscathed.

---

formed his palace into the Lotus Pagoda, where his ashes were buried in 1734. The monks get few visitors, so you're likely to receive a warm welcome to their secluded courtyard. The pagoda isn't easy to find: turn down an alley beside 182 Bach Mai and keep heading west until you see a stupa and stele to you right. The pagoda is then straight ahead behind a brick-walled enclosure; ring the bell to be let in.

North of Lien Phai Pagoda, **Lenin Park** has been created out of an expanse of swamp that doubled as Hanoi's rubbish tip prior to 1960. It's green, peaceful and has some wonderful trees, but apart from the annual Tet flower festival it's a bit featureless and appears to be settling slowly back into the marsh, giving the concrete benches a curious incline.

Immediately west of the park, across Le Duan in **Dong Da District**, is an area of tightly packed one- and two-storey houses that suffered particularly badly during the 1972 "Christmas Bombing" (see box above). Vietnamese forces did manage to wreak some revenge, destroying between fifteen and twenty B-52s during the December raids, and you can see one of the planes that brought down an American bomber in the **Air Force Museum**, about 1km west of Bach Mai on Truong Chinh (daily 7.30–11am & 1.30–5pm). Since the Vietnamese Air Force was only established in 1959 the museum deals mainly with the American War, plus some coverage of the anti-Pol Pot campaign and action against China in 1979. Its most interesting exhibits are photos of heroic aircrews and of early efforts to keep airfields open and the force's few planes operational. You can also see Uncle Ho's plush red velvet flight seat taken from a MiG 4 helicopter, one of several aircraft languishing outside.

Eating

In recent years eating in Hanoi has become an easier and far more enjoyable experience, in terms of both choice and quality. Though Hanoi can't compare with the sophistications of Ho Chi Minh City, it boasts an increasing number of top-quality **restaurants**, mostly found in the new hotels or around the French Quarter, though a few are now also popping up at less prestigious addresses; check *Vietnam Investment Review* or *Vietnam Economic Times* for the latest newcomers. There's no shortage, either, of local **coffee houses**, serving thick, strong coffee and sometimes a range of pastries or other snacks. More recent arrivals are the **ice-cream parlours**, catering to all tastes, from green tea flavour to young rice or rum 'n' raisin.

Even though this is the capital city, you still need to **eat early**: whatever the advertised closing time might be, local places stop serving around 8pm and peak time is 7–7.30pm, while Western-style restaurants and top hotels tend to allow an extra hour or two.

Food stalls and street kitchens

For sheer value for money your best option is to eat either at the rock-bottom, stove-and-stools **food stalls** or at the slightly more upmarket **street kitchens**. These places provide basic rice and noodle dishes, including two Hanoi **specialities**: the ubiquitous *pho* noodle soup and *bun cha*, small barbecued pork burgers served with a small bowl of rice noodles, which makes a tasty snack. Something else you might want to nibble at are *banh gio*, fried pastries filled with vermicelli, minced pork and mushrooms, and eaten with a thin sweet sauce, parsley and chilli; to sample them, join the crowd at a stall nestling under a giant banyan tree beside the entrance to Ly Quoc Su Pagoda.

You'll find food stalls and street kitchens scattered throughout the city, though with a greater concentration in the **Old Quarter** and the streets **west of Hoan Kiem Lake**. While the stalls are, by their nature, itinerant, street kitchens are more permanent operations – even so, the majority are unnamed and often have no recognizable addresss. The list of streets below should point you in the right direction; all fall within the area covered by the map on p.337, with the exception of Nghi Tam Avenue, which takes you out north of the city beside the Red River.

Dinh Liet Street. This Old Quarter street is famous for its early-morning *pho* kitchens, while a couple of places also serve excellent *my van than* (won ton soup) at any time of day.

Hang Hanh Street, at the northeast corner of Hoan Kiem Lake. Choose from several kitchens serving wholesome bowls of piping-hot *bun* and *pho* soups, particularly at breakfast-time.

Ly Thai To Street, at the intersection with Lo Su. Chickens' feet are the delicacy at these eating houses, but a wide variety of more palatable fare is also on offer including fried rice and noodle dishes, *bun cha*, *ga tan* and more. Liveliest in the evenings.

Nghi Tam Avenue. If you want to sample dog meat (*thit cho*), a northern speciality eaten mostly in winter, then head out of Hanoi on the Red River dyke. Nghi Tam has dozens of places to choose from and, as they've all copied successful names (notably "An Thu"), the best thing is just to look for the busiest. Fido comes served-up as stew, steaks, sausages or soups, and actually tastes pretty good. Even with a few jars of *bia hoi*, prices are still moderate.

Ngo Hang Bong. An alley at the far west end of Hang Bong, beside the Kinh Do Hotel, lined with local establishments dishing up a variety of foods including *chao* – thick, rice soups topped with shredded chicken or lightly cooked beef.

To Tich Street, on the southern fringes of the Old Quarter. A lively little lane which boasts a selection of soup and rice kitchens.

Tong Duy Tan Street. At the north end of Ngo Hang Bong is this street packed with local eateries specializing in *ga tan*, Chinese-style chicken broth brewed from medicinal herbs, pulses, plums and lotus seed. Touts here can be pushy.

Restaurants

At the inexpensive end of the scale are the stalwart **travellers' cafés**, offering a limited selection of foods, often imitation Western dishes of variable quality but at low cost, at all hours of the day; they tend to work better as a meeting place than a gourmet dining experience. Moving up a step you find a growing number of moderately priced Western-style **restaurants** which serve a range of cuisine, from classic Vietnamese dishes to salads, pizzas and hamburgers for the homesick. Top-notch places are on the increase, too, as Hanoi challenges Ho Chi Minh's culinary supremacy.

When it comes to number and variety of budget and mid-price eating places the **Old Quarter** takes some beating, while Hanoi's glitziest dining rooms tend to be located in the **French Quarter**. Here several moderately priced restaurants are charmingly housed in renovated colonial villas; there's also a smattering of less formal, local eating places and cafés to suit more modest budgets. Further out of the centre, there are a few places **around Ho Chi Minh's Mausoleum** that come in useful for a respite from sightseeing – and one or two way down in **the southern districts** which merit a special trip.

Finally, restaurants tend to be small: in the listings below, we've given phone numbers for places where it's advisable to make **reservations**.

The Old Quarter and west of Hoan Kiem Lake
All the following restaurants are marked on the map opposite.

Baan Thai, 3b Cha Ca. Excellent food makes up for the lack of atmosphere in this restaurant catering to Hanoi's Thai community. Not spicy enough for some, but the fish in coconut and chilli is recommended, or try some Thai noodles.

Bittet, 51 Hang Buom. Hidden down a long, dark passage at the back of a tube-house is this small and inexpensive restaurant serving *bittet* – a corruption of the French *biftek*. Steak and chips with lashings of garlic are the house speciality.

Cha Ca La Vong, 14 Cha Ca. *Cha ca* means fried fish, and that's all they serve in this famous restaurant, home of the dish's creator in the late nineteenth century. The food's tasty and well presented – cooked with fresh dill over a clay brazier on your table and eaten with cold rice noodles, chilli and peanuts. The portions are small but that hasn't dented its reputation.

Five Royal Fish, 16 Le Thai To. Mediocre hamburgers, sandwiches and Vietnamese standards served on a shaded terrace with fine views over Hoan Kiem Lake. Cheap for the location and popular with tourists and businesspeople.

Green Bamboo, 42 Nha Chung. This travellers' café is clean, bright and spacious, serving better-quality food – at slightly higher prices – than the rest, and also running an embryonic book exchange.

Hoang Nam, 39d Hang Hanh. Tucked away on the corner of a quiet backstreet, in a tiny, courtyard full of plants. Good music, pleasant atmosphere and an extensive choice of traditional dishes at reasonable prices. No relation to...

Hoang Nam, 46 Hang Vai. A bright, clean establishment with soothing music and French-Vietnamese menu. Try steamboat (*lau*), shrimp on cauliflower or something more adventurous such as barbecued venison with citronella. Verging on expensive but good quality and relaxing ambience.

Huyen Dung, 4 Ly Thai To. Join the locals on wooden benches for a good fry-up. Sausage, eggs, steak and chips on sizzling hotplates, or omelette and warm rolls. Great for a cheap, filling breakfast, or for refuelling later in the day.

Lonely Planet Café, 33 Hang Be. Spick and span travellers' café that's bursting at the seams some evenings; the food is cheap and cheerful.

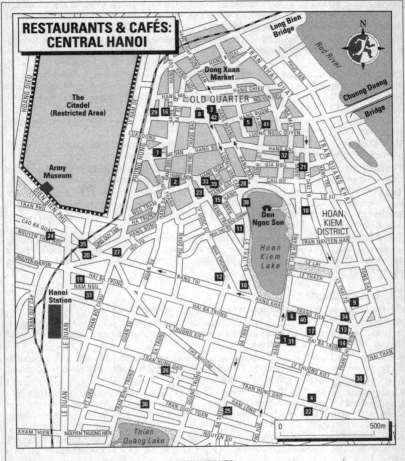

RESTAURANTS & CAFÉS: CENTRAL HANOI

RESTAURANTS

1 Al Fresco	15 Hoang Nam (Hang Hanh)	29 Piano Restaurant
2 Art Café	16 Hoang Nam (Hang Vai)	30 Quan Hué
3 Baan Thai	17 Huong Lan	31 Quan Sake
4 Le Bistro	18 Huyen Dung	32 Queen Café
5 Bittet	19 Indochine	33 Real Darling Café
6 Bodega Café	20 Kinh Do Café	34 Restaurant 006
7 Café Quynh	21 Lonely Planet Café	35 Restaurant 3
8 Cha Ca La Vong	22 Memory Café	36 Restaurant 75
9 Club Opera	23 Mickey Fast Foods	37 Tam Tu
10 Fanny	24 Milano Ice Cream	38 Thuy Ta Café
11 Five Royal Fish	25 Mother's Pride	39 Tourist Café
12 Green Bamboo	26 Nang Tam	40 Trang Tien Hotel
13 Gustave's	27 Ngu Thien Hué	41 Truong Tho
14 Hoa Sua	28 No Noodles	42 Tuyet Nhung

Mickey Fast Foods, 37 & 39 Hang Manh. Despite the name this is a decent restaurant and *bia hoi* place where smartly turned out waiters serve a wide range of affordable Vietnamese dishes plus pizzas and salads for the homesick.

No Noodles, 51 Luong Van Can. Warm, crunchy baguettes stuffed with a variety of scrumptious fillings to eat in or take away. Chicken Tandoori hits the spot after a week or two on *pho*. 10am–9pm.

Piano Restaurant, 50 Hang Vai (☎823 2423), with a sister-establishment round the corner at 93 Phung Hung. A Hanoi institution run by a musical family who dish up Mozart classics and refined Vietnamese-Chinese cuisine to expats and tourists. High prices and erratic quality don't deter the faithful.

Queen Café, 65 Hang Bac. Grungy dining-room decor, but a loyal following for its rice platters, chips and cheap beers.

Real Darling Café, 33 Hang Quat. Despite (or perhaps because of) the dingy interior and predictable menu of Western favourites, this place is busy from dawn to dusk.

Tourist Café, 6 To Tich. This friendly, unpretentious café serves excellent breakfasts such as toasted sandwiches or muesli with yoghurt, and is well placed for watching streetlife.

Truong Tho, 11 Ha Tien. One of a clutch of moderately priced restaurants on this street serving Vietnamese special foods, *dac san*. There's little to chose between them for decor or price but *Truong Tho* has the edge on quality and a friendly reception. Others to try along here are nos. 13 and 17.

Tuyet Nhung, 17 Cha Ca. Those with strong taste-buds might want to try *tinh ca cuong*, essence of bug. This popular local restaurant is one of the last places in Hanoi to make authentic *ca cuong*, a hot sauce somewhat like chilli, made from an insect and eaten with steamed rice pancakes.

The French Quarter
All the following restaurants are marked on the map on p.337.

Al Fresco, 23l Hai Ba Trung. Relaxed, Australian-run place with a pleasant, back balcony on the first floor. The menu is good-quality, American international (burgers, salads, nachos and pizzas), all served in hefty portions.

Le Bistro, 34 Tran Hung Dao. Justly rated restaurant in a mellow villa with a French-Vietnamese menu. Service tends to the erratic at busy times, but quality food, good atmosphere and moderate prices more than make up for it.

Club Opera, 59 Ly Thai To(☎826 8802). Separate Asian and European restaurants in a revamped villa. Toasted sandwiches, burgers and steaks tempt the lunchtime crowd downstairs, while upstairs offers relaxed evenings with some of Hanoi's best Vietnamese cooking. Prices are surprisingly affordable.

Gustave's, 17 Trang Tien (☎825 0625). Named after Gustave Eiffel of tower fame. This very Parisian first-floor restaurant, light and airy yet formal, serves a lunchtime set menu plus expensive à la carte of French cuisine and crêpes. Jazz piano or French favourites nightly in the bar (7.30–11pm).

Hoa Sua (*La Boulangerie*), 6 Phan Chu Trinh (☎824 0448). Excellent, French-style food – vegetable terrine, quiche and salad, chocolate profiteroles – created by trainee chefs and served in the garden and front room of a villa. *Hoa Su* is rumoured to be moving to larger premises on Tho Nhuom Street, near the *Eden Hotel*. For the moment, reservations are essential at lunchtime. 8am–7pm.

Huong Lan, 20 Ngo Quyen. Excellent Vietnamese cuisine at moderate prices is the main attraction at this second-floor restaurant; try to get a table out on the balcony for more atmosphere. As you leave, it'll be hard to resist a Baskin-Robbins ice cream from next door.

Indochine, 16 Nam Ngu (☎824 6097). Food and decor of unusual quality make this restaurant a favourite of the expat community, though at busy times service can be slow. Well-presented Vietnamese specialities, from hot and sour soups to steamed fish and prawn on sugar cane, served either in the tastefully decorated colonial house or its courtyard. Reservations are essential in the evenings. Live Vietnamese folk music Mon, Wed, Fri & Sat from 7.30pm.

Memory Café, 33b Tran Hung Dao. Flowers and classical music make this small, friendly café opposite *Le Bistro* a popular venue. Standard snack menu, but recommended for its fruit-shakes and yoghurts.

Mother's Pride, 53 Ba Trieu (☎822 8055). Malay curries and Singaporean specialities rub shoulders with toasted sandwiches and ice cream. Clean, bright and popular, with only a handful of tables.

Nang Tam, 79a Tran Hung Dao (☎826 6140). Small, elegant vegetarian restaurant named after a Vietnamese Cinderella-character. *Goi bo*, a main-course salad of banana flower, star fruit and pineapple, is recommended. No MSG used.

Ngu Thien Hué, 58 Trang Thi. Hué specialities are the order of the day in this unfussy restaurant. Its two extensive, set-menus offer a good value sampler of Hué dishes, including *banh beo* and *banh khoai*.

Quan Hué, 6 Ly Thuong Kiet. The more highly rated of two restaurants serving Hué cuisine on opposite sides of the street. This one gets votes for open-air seating and reasonable prices. If you can't get to Hué, try one of these.

Quan Sake, 23d Hai Ba Trung, with *Quan Sake II* at 43b Ngo Quyen. This authentic, tiny Japanese restaurant evokes downtown Tokyo with its informal, intimate atmosphere. Set menus provide the best deal, and the tempura is especially recommended.

Restaurant 006, 6 Trang Tien. A well-rated Vietnamese restaurant on the main drag. Forget the decor, but the food comes up trumps, though you might want to steer clear of the house speciality – "carp from the immortal oven" – that comes out alive.

Restaurant 3, 3 Dien Bien Phu. Cheap, traditional Vietnamese place beside the train tracks, where the remnants of Hanoi's expat Russian community come to croon melancholy songs. Beware large quantities of MSG in the soups, though.

Restaurant 75, 75 Tran Quoc Toan. Well-rated Vietnamese food and a warm welcome are assured at this converted villa on the southern edge of the district. Eating here won't break the bank, either.

Tam Tu, 84 Ly Thuong Kiet. Cheap and cheerful Thai food, including green curries and *pad thai* fried noodles, served-up in a warren of small rooms. Friendly service and good portions compensate for claustrophobia.

Around Ho Chi Minh's Mausoleum

All the following restaurants are marked on the map on p.327.

Banh Tom Ho Tay, 1 Thanh Nien. On the causeway near Tran Quoc Pagoda, facing over Truch Bach Lake is this reasonably priced open-air restaurant. Sample the local speciality, *banh tom*, small cakes of fried battered prawns, or stop for a drink in the lakeside garden. Floating restaurants tethered to the causeway's west bank offer *banh tom* at higher prices.

Cac Mon An Dan Toc, 36 Dien Bien Phu. Cheap, no-frills restaurant in the backyard of a villa, cooking-up rustic fare for a mostly local crowd. No English spoken and no menu, so see what you recognize in the kitchen – not all of it is chickens' testicles. Baked rice is served in country-style, earthenware bowls.

Da Tano, 10 Hang Chao (☎823 4850). Moderately expensive Italian restaurant near the Temple of Literature, with good views from the fourth floor and an authentic flavour.

Khazana, 27 Quoc Tu Giam (☎843 3477). Hanoi's first Indian restaurant boasts a genuine tandoor oven and serves tasty, northern dishes in very small quantities; lunchtime buffets are better value at $10 a head.

Truc Bach, 1 Nguyen Bieu (☎825 6945). An attractive, shaded terrace on the south side of Truc Bach Lake, popular with Vietnamese business diners. Traditional Vietnamese foods and excellent steamed fish. Moderate prices but occasionally grumpy service.

BUYING YOUR OWN FOOD: MARKETS AND MINI-MARKETS

With so much fresh fruit, bread and take-away food available in the **markets** or hawked on the streets, especially in the Old Quarter, it's easy to prepare excellent do-it-yourself meals. You can buy milk, yoghurt and cheeses other than the ubiquitous *La Vache Qui Rit* at some of Hanoi's new **mini-markets**, which also sell imported foodstuffs – if you're prepared to pay the huge mark-ups for your favourite brand-names.

Markets
Cho Dong Xuan, Dong Xuan Street. Hanoi's biggest covered market, originally built in 1889, is under reconstruction after a fire. By the time you read this its three floors should be back in action.

Cho Hom, Pho Hué. Dong Xuan's closest rival , with foodstuffs downstairs.

Cho Hang Da, Hang Da Street. A small covered market with a ground-floor dry-goods section heavy with aromatic mushrooms and the sharp smell of dried fish, while stalls outside sell imported foods.

Cho 19–12, between Hai Ba Trung and Ly Thuong Kiet. A one-street, fresh-food market.

Mini-markets and provisions stores
BS Minimarket, 66 Ba Trieu. Hanoi's best selection of Western comestibles is tellingly located opposite the French Embassy.

Eurofood, 65 Hang Trong. Wel provisioned with dairy products, wines, and tinned goods.

FBS International, Kiosk 3, Pho Hué. Cheese, crisps, soft drinks and biscuits on sale in a store just outside Hom market.

Kotobuki, Kiosk 4, Pho Hué. Next door to *FBS* is one of a chain of Japanese-run bakeries, selling quality cakes and confectionery.

Viet Hoa, 59 Hai Ba Trung. Bread, cheese and other essentials, plus a range of wines from $5 upwards.

The southern districts
Both the following restaurants are marked on the map on pp.310–311.

Ngoc Cuong, 14 Nguyen Binh Kiem. Well-established, friendly and very busy *com binh dan* place. Serves lunches only (until 1.30pm), but get there just after 1pm to avoid the worst crush.

Restaurant 202, 202 Pho Hué (☎825 9487). A busy multi-storey restaurant with several small rooms, offering French-Vietnamese food at moderate prices. Popular with tour groups and businesspeople; reservations recommended at peak times. Crab with garlic is a perennial favourite.

Coffee houses, patisseries and ice-cream parlours

There's little to choose between Hanoi's hundreds of coffee houses, offering minimum comfort but great coffee. Several are also popular patisseries, while there's also a growing number of outlets selling fresh milk, yoghurts and ice cream. *All the following places are marked on the map on p.337.*

Art Café, 57 Hang Non. A refined, upmarket café with gingham tablecloths, potted palms and artworks which stays open until late. It serves delicious drinks, fresh fruit juices and a short-order menu at prices a little above average.

Bodega Café, 57 Trang Tien. Ice creams to take-away or eat in, and a range of pastries and pies sold outside the *Bodega Hotel*'s downstairs café.

Café Quynh, 46b Bat Dan. A fairly ordinary coffee house frequented by artists and with an attractive French-era facade. Photos of film-actress owner, Nhu Quynh, star of *Cyclo* (see p.466), adorn the walls.

Fanny, 48 Le Thai Tho. Immaculate ice-cream parlour serving French-style ices and sorbets beside Hoan Kiem Lake. High prices are offset by good presentation, art-gallery ambience and the widest choice of flavours in Hanoi.

Gustave's, 17 Trang Tien. On the ground floor of this elegant restaurant is a comfortable coffee-bar, ideal for watching life pass by on Trang Tien, though prices are over the odds.

Hoa Sua (*La Boulangerie*), 6 Phan Chu Trinh. Croissants, pain-au-chocolat and other succulent French pastries to eat in the garden café or take-away. Also serves French-inspired full meals at lunchtime (see p.338). 8am–7pm.

Kinh Do Café, 252 Hang Bong. "Café 252" became famous after Catherine Deneuve complimented the patron on his yoghurts. Fresh milk, fruit juices, sandwiches, or freshly baked cakes are sold to a mixed crowd of suited businessmen, backpackers and Hanoians. Rival cafés along the street are almost as good and a little cheaper. 7am–11pm.

Milano Ice Cream, 20 Nguyen Thai Hoc. Handy for a quick fix of cooling ice cream on the trek round Ho's Museum and the Temple of Literature. Choose from jackfruit, mango or cream and egg among other flavours.

Thuy Ta Café, on the northwest bank of Hoan Kiem Lake. Recommended for an afternoon tea or an evening beer – remember the mosquito repellent. Also serves ice creams and snacks, and plans are afoot for an upstairs restaurant.

Trang Tien Hotel, 35 Trang Tien, with another branch at 38 Le Thai To. You'll find crowds gathering in the evening in front of the hotel for the best, local-style ice cream in Hanoi.

Nightlife and entertainment

For a capital city, Hanoi is pretty sleepy: most **bars**, outside the big hotels, have swept-up by midnight and **nightclubs** don't stay open much later. Things have perked up a little recently, however, following the influx of tourists and businesspeople with money to spend. A few pioneering bars claim to keep pouring till sunrise or at least till the last customer leaves, while one or two swish clubs have invested in imported sound-and-light systems. Check in the English-language press for the latest additions.

As for **traditional entertainment**, a performance of the water puppets, Vietnam's charming contribution to the world of marionettes, should be high on everyone's itinerary. However, there's little else on offer in the cultural sphere just yet, apart from a few groups playing traditional music at some of Hanoi's main tourist sights. Very occasionally, events are listed in the English-language press, but are more likely to be announced on street banners or outside the venues themselves, so you'll have to ask around to see if there's anything interesting happening.

Bars and pubs

Hanoi doesn't have a great choice of **bars**: characterless hotel bars or cafés and pseudo-pubs which double as restaurants, plus the occasional, dedicated drinking hole. The liveliest venues are *bia hoi* outlets which have exploded over the city selling pitchers of the local brew (see box over). Young Hanoians out on the town prefer intimate cafés and karaoke bars, though the more affluent might make it into a Western-style bar.

Apocalypse Now, 338 Ba Trieu. Sister-establishment to the original bar in Ho Chi Minh City that's seething on Friday and Saturday nights – even though it's inconveniently located out in the southern boondocks. Dark, apocalyptic decor and great music. 7pm–late.

Blue Bar, 57 Ly Thai To. Next to *Club Opera* is this tiny, dark billiards bar with MTV. Until 2–3am.

The Emerald, 53 Hang Luoc. An Irish pub-restaurant in the Old Quarter with predictably green decor, Bass on draught – at a price – and Jameson Irish Whiskey on request. It's mostly frequented by visiting businessmen but the homespun food attracts the occasional tourist. Until midnight.

The Flagon Café, 36 Lo Su. Sample authentic rice wine (*ruou can*) at this second-floor café-bar in the Old Quarter with rustic decor and a street-front terrace. Limited evening snacks (noodles, sandwiches and spring rolls) and a mixed clientele. All day.

The Gold Cock, 5 Bao Khanh. Very popular with both locals and expats, for its central location and cheapish drinks. Until midnight.

Green Bamboo, 42 Nha Chung. The second-floor *Starlight Bar* draws the crowds with its cheap drinks and billiards until 2am.

The Polite Pub, 5 Bao Khanh. Stylish decor and a touch more atmosphere than its neighbour, the *Gold Cock*, but still an inexpensive place to drink, mixing some of the best margaritas in town. 5pm–midnight.

The Pub, 52 Ly Thuong Kiet. Reasonable attempt at a British pub with some local touches – try the "Hanoi Hilton" cocktail. Serves bar-snacks with chips all day. 8am–midnight.

Sofitel Metropole, 15 Ngo Quyen. *Bar Le Club* is classy but the poolside *Bamboo Bar* has more appeal. Jazz evenings in *Le Club* (Mon & Wed 6–8pm, Fri 10pm–midnight) and traditional folk music (Sat & Sun 5–6pm).

Tin Tin, 14 Hang Non. Narrow, Old Quarter bar which keeps its regulars despite its dingy decor. Cheap drinks, music videos and food on offer from 7am until midnight.

BIA HOI BARS

Beer drinking tends to be an all-male preserve in Vietnam but don't be put off; **bia hoi** outlets are usually fun, friendly and cheap. Some serve excellent **food** at lunchtime or in the evening. The Old Quarter and streets west of Hoan Kiem Lake are happy hunting grounds, or try one of the selection below.

18 Bao Khanh. Small, traditional outlet just west of Hoan Kiem Lake.

Bao Quoc, 25 Tong Dan. Popular lunchtime beer garden and restaurant beside the Opera House.

36 Bat Dan. Unusually large venue on the Old Quarter's west side, with interesting local restaurants in the surrounding streets.

18 Le Hong Phong. Quench your thirst after Ho's Mausoleum.

57 Ly Thai To. Another well-patronized lunchtime venue, beside the *Blue Bar*.

11 Ma May. Tiny place on a quiet back street in the Old Quarter which pours a reliable beer.

34 and 34a Phan Chu Trinh. Two smarter outlets next door to each other on the junction with Ham Long. Also recommended for excellent food served in their upstairs restaurants.

20 Tong Dan. Pleasant beer garden in the grounds of a villa behind the State Bank.

Clubs

Nearly all Hanoi's top hotels squeeze in a **nightclub**, complete with handkerchief-size dance floor and live band, to tempt their free-spending guests. Ahead by a long way for music and ambience is the *Royal Palace Nightclub* (8pm–2am; $5) in the *Royal Hotel*, where a Filipino band plays live. Some of the best venues coming on stream, however, are reincarnated cinemas: real elbow-room and better prices, a-buzz with expats, business visitors and a sprinkling of rich Vietnamese on Friday and Saturday nights. Of these, Hanoi's most sophisticated venues so far, in terms of atmosphere and equipment, are *Centropell*, at 46 Hang Cot (7.30pm–2am; $2–5), and *Metal* at 57 Cua Nam. *Queen Bee*, with its big dance floor and live band, is way out at 42 Lang Ha (8pm–12.30am; $3–5), but still draws the punters. Finally, when the *Palace Dance Hall,* once heaving with trendy young Hanoians, re-opens it should be worth checking out; find it at 40 Nha Chung, next door to *Green Bamboo*.

Traditional entertainment

While in Hanoi you should devote an hour one evening to the **water puppets**, *mua roi nuoc* – literally, puppets that dance on the water – a uniquely Vietnamese artform which originated in the Red River Delta (see p.448 for more background). Traditional performances consist of short scenes depicting rural life or historic events accompanied by mood-setting musical narration. Hanoi's three puppet troupes present an updated repertoire and use modern stage-effects to create an engaging spectacle. Though these shows are largely put on for tourists, you can't help but admire the artistry and be charmed by the puppets' antics.

By far the most popular group, and the most polished, is the **Thang Long Water Puppet Troupe** which was established in 1960 and has toured internationally. They give nightly performances, kicking-off with a short musical recital, at the small, air-conditioned *Kim Dong Theatre*, 57 Dinh Tien Hoang (☎825 5450; 8pm; tickets $2–4, plus extra for camera and video). The **National Water Puppet Theatre**, 32 Truong Chinh (☎853 4545; Tues, Thurs, Sat & Sun 7.45pm; $3), is a smaller and less sophisticated set-up, but is rather a long way out of town for most people. However, if they ever revive performances on the outdoor lake, it will definitely be worth the effort. **Song Ngoc Water Puppet Troupe** is the only group unsubsidized by the state and currently performs in a dinky, mobile pool beside the Temple of Literature while their normal home, *Hong Ha Theatre* at 51 Duong Thanh (☎825 2803), is being renovated. They suffer from makeshift props and poor-quality recorded music but the outdoor setting is at least traditional; entry is via the Temple of Literature and short performances take place according to demand ($2).

At present water-puppet theatres are about the only places in Hanoi show-casing Vietnamese **traditional music**, though small ensembles do play folk music every afternoon at the Temple of Literature (2–5pm) and the Ho Chi Minh Museum (8.30–11am & 1.30–4.30pm) for a small donation. On extremely rare occasions you might catch a **Cheo** performance (see p.447) at *Kim Ma Theatre*, 199b Son Tay (☎825 7403) or at the *Cheo Club*, 15 Nguyen Dinh Chieu (☎826 7361); ask locally if there are any shows in the offing.

Shopping and markets

When it comes to shopping, Ho Chi Minh City may have a greater choice but Hanoi generally wins on prices. Specialities of the region are embroideries, inlay work, sandalwood carvings and lacquer, and the best streets to browse are around the southern edge of Hoan Kiem Lake and Hang Gai in the Old Quarter. Until recently the **Government Department Stores** – branches at the south end of Dien Bien Phu (by the rail line), and at the north end of Hoan Kiem Lake on Dinh Tien Hoang – were a showcase of all that was *not* available in other shops. Although they're now finding it hard to compete with the rash of new outlets, these stores have fixed prices and are a useful first stop to check the going rate of basic items such as toiletries, stationery and some foodstuffs before you hit the markets.

Hanoi has over fifty **markets**, half of them street markets, and most selling predominantly foodstuffs (see "Buying your own food", p.340); for a greater variety of wares, try **Cho Hom**, on Pho Hué, which has clothing upstairs, and a supermarket selling mostly household goods and toiletries. What's more, all around Hom market are **specialist shopping streets**: Tran Nhan Tong focuses on jeans and shirts, while Phung Khac Khoan, off Tran Xuan Soan, is a riot of colourful fabrics.

Fabrics, handicrafts and souvenirs

Compared with Thailand, Vietnamese **silk** is slightly inferior quality but prices are lower and the tailoring is still great value, with awesome delivery times. So many silk shops are concentrated on Hang Gai, at the southern edge of the Old Quarter, that it's now referred to as "Silk Street". The best-known shop along here is *Khai Silk* at 96 Hang Gai (with a branch at 121 Nguyen Thai Hoc) but browse the street first and have a look in *Kenly* at no. 102, recommended for its tailoring, and *Le Minh* at no. 79, which stocks the largest selection of colours. Most bigger outlets have English- and French-speaking staff, accept credit cards and offer ready-made items as well as tailoring. If you want to order an *ao dai*, tailors round the corner on Luong Van Can are popular with the discriminating Vietnamese woman.

Embroideries and drawn threadwork make eminently packable souvenirs and you'll find better quality and prices here than in Ho Chi Minh City. Standard designs range from traditional Vietnamese to Santa Claus and robins, but you can also take along your own artwork for something more unique. Both *Tan My* and *Tuyet Lan*, next door to each other at 65 & 66 Hang Gai, have a reputation for quality and design. There's strong competition, however, and prices tend to drop as you go west – where *Phuc Thanh* at 8 Hang Bong is recommended.

One of the most interesting places to look for souvenirs is *Hoa Sen Gallery*, at 61 Quan Su, a non-profit-making outlet which sells **ethnic minority crafts** as part of income-generating projects in the villages. There's lots of information in English, everything's priced and there's even a catalogue if you want to order from a range of fabrics, bags, cushions and clothes. The gallery also stocks a jolly collection of **water puppets**, each hand-crafted by a master-puppeteer working with Hanoi street children. In a similar vein *Craft Link* has recently opened at 43 Van Mieu, selling mainly Black Thai products.

Other popular souvenirs are embroidered and printed **T-shirts**; although the selection is limited, you'll find no shortage of places to buy them, notably on Hang Gai and at the top end of Ly Quoc Su. Most galleries and souvenir shops sell hand-painted **greetings cards**, usually scenes of rural life or famous beauty spots painted on paper or silk; the best are unbelievably delicate and sell for next to nothing. Shops along Hang Khay are crammed with boxes, tables and other goods covered with **mother-of-pearl inlay**, and also sell **silver items**, both plated and solid silver – where you might find some genuinely old jewellery or the odd antique **watch**. Otherwise, Trang Tien has the biggest concentration of **antiques** shops, although most items on display won't be particularly old and those that are it's illegal to export anyway (see *Basics*, p.49).

For more unusual mementos, have a look at the traditional Vietnamese **musical instruments** on sale at two shops at the east end of Hang Non. A small shop at 53 Hang Bong supplies Communist Party **banners and badges** as well as Vietnamese flags. If you're into **army surplus** gear, hit the stretch of Le Duan south of the train station – for those nifty camouflage boxer-shorts.

Art galleries

Art galleries have traditionally concentrated on Trang Tien but increasingly artists are opening their own galleries, and one or two small, private concerns have now appeared on the scene. There's a run-down of the more interesting outlets below.

Art Inheart, 28 Nha Tho. An eclectic mix of art on sale beside the cathedral.

Ba Kieu Temple, 59 Dinh Tien Hoang. This former temple beside Hoan Kiem Lake makes great exhibition space, including eye-catching works from minority artists.

Bell Gallery, 66 Hang Trong. Lacquer paintings and photos are the speciality in this tiny gallery squeezed between two buildings.

Mai Gallery, 3b Phan Huy Chu. This small gallery tucked down an alley displays a broad range of artists.

Mai Hen-Anh Ken Gallery, 99 Nguyen Thai Hoc. A famous painting couple share wall-space in their second-floor gallery, at the back of the courtyard.

Nguyen Thang, 1 Trang Thi. First-floor, studio-gallery run by war-veteran artist Nguyen Thang.

Red River Gallery, 71a Nguyen Du. The first international-class gallery to open in Hanoi puts on revolving exhibitions of up-and-coming artists.

Salon Natasha, 30 Hang Bong. Tiny, avant-garde gallery where it's all happening.

Listings

Airlines *Aeroflot*, 4 Trang Thi (☎825 6742); *Air France*, 1 Ba Trieu (☎825 3484); *Cathay Pacific*, 27 Ly Thuong Kiet (☎826 7298); *China Southern Airlines*, Room 102 Binh Minh Hotel, 27 Ly Thai To (☎826 9233); *Japan Airlines*, 1 Ba Trieu (☎826 6693); *Lao Aviation*, 41 Quang Trung (☎826 6538); *Malaysia Airlines*, Hotel Sofitel Metropole, 15 Ngo Quyen (☎826 8820); *Pacific Airlines*, 100 Le Duan (☎851 5356); *Singapore Airlines*, 17 Ngo Quyen (☎826 8888); *Thai International*, 25 Ly Thuong Kiet (☎826 6893); *Vietnam Airlines*, 1 Quang Trung for domestic and international services (☎829 2118), and with sales agents at 60 Nguyen Du (☎825 5194) and 30a Ly Thuong Kiet (☎826 9130).

Alliance Française 42 Yet Kieu (☎826 6970; Mon–Sat 8am–noon & 2–6pm). Cultural programme of films, concerts and exhibitions, plus library, journals and TV room. Membership $2 (2 photos and proof of identity required).

Banks and exchange *Vietcombank* head office is at 47–49 Ly Thai To, for all services including cash withdrawals on credit cards and telegraphic transfers. Sub-office at 78 Nguyen Du and branches at 42a Ly Thuong Kiet and 50 Trang Tien. Other banks with counter facilities are: *ANZ Bank*, 14 Le Thai To; *Asia Pacific Bank*, Van Phuc; *Bank of America*, 27 Ly Thuong Kiet; *Citibank*, 17 Ngo Quyen; *Crédit Lyonnais*, 10 Trang Thi; *Indovina*, 88 Hai Ba Trung; *Standard Chartered*, 27 Ly Thai To; *VID Public Bank*, 194 Tran Quan Khai. Unusually persistent money changers around the GPO offer suspiciously high rates; they are running a scam and are best avoided.

Bike rental Try the following for cheap rates (around $1 per day) and reliable machines: in the Old Quarter, 31 and 33 Ta Hien; in the French Quarter, go down the alley beside the *Bodega Hotel* on Trang Tien, or to *Memory Café* at 33 Tran Hung Dao.

Bike repair You'll find someone to repair pedal-bikes on virtually every street corner. For motorbikes, try Phu Doan, just behind the cathedral, or Thinh Yen at the south end of Pho Hué, where you can also buy locally made helmets ($40).

Books and bookshops Apart from small outlets in top-class hotels, Trang Tien is the main area for books, with several state-run bookshops plus stalls selling English-language publications on Vietnam, including photocopies of out-of-print editions together with pirated guides and phrasebooks. Kids also peddle books, postcards and maps here and around Hoan Kiem Lake. The government publishing house, *The Gioi Publishers* (formerly *Foreign Languages Publishing House*), has an outlet at 46 Tran Hung Dao. Otherwise, the best-stocked shops are *Hanoi Bookshop*, 34 Trang Tien; *Fahasa*, 22b Hai Ba Trung; *Xunhasaba*, 32 Hai Ba Trung. *Green Bamboo*, at 42 Nha Chung, also has a book exchange.

Car rental Try *ATC* (☎826 4007), *Fuji Cab* (☎825 5452), *Mansfield TOSERCO* (☎826 9444), *Vicarrent* (☎825 9027), or tour agents listed on facing page.

Cinema Asian and Western films, in either English or Vietnamese language, are screened nightly at *Fansland*, 84 Ly Thuong Kiet (☎825 7484). Vietnamese films plus the occasional Hollywood epic show at *New Age Cinema*, 45 Hang Bai (☎824 5376). Tickets sell out quickly, so book ahead.

Courier Services *DHL* has its main office at 49 Nguyen Thai Hoc (☎826 7020), and a more useful branch office in the GPO (☎825 7124); *TNT* is at 23 Trang Thi (☎825 7750).

Embassies and consulates *Australia*, 66 Ly Thuong Kiet (☎825 2763); *Belgium*, 48 Nguyen Thai Hoc (☎823 5005); *Cambodia*, 71 Tran Hang Dao (☎825 3788); *Canada*, 31 Hung Vuong (☎823 5432); *China*, 46 Hoang Dieu (☎823 5569); *Denmark*, 19 Dien Bien Phu (☎823 1888); *Finland*, B3b Giang Vo (☎825 6754); *France*, 57 Tran Hung Dao (☎825 2719); *Germany*, 29 Tran Phu (☎845 3836); *Israel*, 68 Nguyen Thai Hoc (☎826 6919); *Italy*, 9 Le Phung Hieu (☎825 6246); *Laos*, 40 Quang Trung (☎826 8724); *Myanmar (Burma)*, A3 Van Phuc (☎825 3369); *Netherlands*, D1 Apt 105, Van Phuc (☎843 0605); *New Zealand*, 32 Hang Bai (☎824 1481); *Singapore*, 41–43 Tran Phu (☎823 3966); *Sweden*, 2 Road 358, Van Phuc (☎825 4824); *Switzerland*, 77b Kiem Ma (☎823 2019); *Thailand*, 63–65 Hoang Dieu (☎823 5092); *UK*, 16 Ly Thuong Kiet (☎825 2349); *USA*, 7 Lang Ha (☎843 1500). For information on visas to China and Laos, see p.349.

Emergencies Dial ☎14 in case of fire or ☎15 for an ambulance; better still, get a Vietnamese-speaker to call on your behalf.

Export licences for antiques and other items of "cultural or historical significance" are issued at 51 Ngo Quyen (Mon–Sat 8–11.30am & 1.30–4.30pm); the office is first on the left inside the gates.

Friends of Hanoi is an Australian foundation set up to co-ordinate conservation work, raise funds and conduct restoration projects in the city. Memberships are available at 90 Tho Nhuom (☎824 6895, fax 824 6890).

Helicopters *Northern Flight Service* run a weekly jaunt out to Ha Long Bay, using Russian choppers. If that doesn't put you off, the price might: $175 for the return trip. Departures every Sunday at 8am, back at 4.15pm. Contact *Hotel Sofitel Metropole* on ☎826 6919, ext 8015.

Hospitals and clinics The emergency assistance company, *AEA International* at 4 Tran Hung Dao, provides routine care to members and travellers (☎821 3555; 9am–6pm; $65 consultation fee). Alternatively, there's the *Swedish Clinic*, 358 Van Phuc, opposite the Swedish

Embassy (☎845 2464; Mon & Fri 9–11.30am & 1.30–4.30pm, Tues–Thurs 1.30–4.30pm; $90 consultation fee), which offers a 24-hr service and dental care. Of the major **hospitals**, *Bach Mai (International) Hospital* on Giai Phong has English-speaking doctors, but go to the Intensive Care Unit (☎869 3525; $10–20) rather than the International Department. *Viet–Duc Hospital*, 40 Trang Thi (☎825 3531; $10–25) also offers 24-hr emergency services, surgery, intensive care and has English-speaking doctors.

Immigration police In emergencies, such as lost or stolen passports, and for information on visa extensions or change of exit point contact the *Immigration Department of Police* at 40 Hang Bai (Mon–Sat 8–11.30am & 1.30–4pm). Their branch office at 89 Tran Hung Dao (Mon–Sat 8am–12.30pm & 1–5pm) may also be able to help.

Language courses The *Vietnamese Language Centre* of Hanoi Foreign Language College, 1 Pham Ngu Lao (☎826 2468), offers practical instruction for groups or individuals from $5 per hour. The centre also arranges exchanges.

Laundry Most hotels and guesthouses have a laundry service, while top hotels now offer dry cleaning. Alternatively, try one of the following low-priced laundries (*giat la*): 59 Hang Be; 39 Ma May; 17 Trang Thi; 55 Nguyen Du.

Left luggage *Real Darling Café*, at 33 Hang Quat, runs a left-luggage service for a small fee.

Newspapers and magazines Foreign-language papers and magazines are on sale at book-shops listed opposite, at stalls on Trang Tien or outside the GPO, and in top-class hotels of which the *Metropole's* boutique offers the best selection. Hawkers also peddle secondhand magazines around Hoan Kiem Lake.

Pharmacies Both *AEA* and the *Swedish Clinic* (see "Hospitals and clinics" above) have pharmacies. Of the local retail outlets *Nguyen Luan* at 3 Trang Thi stocks the widest selection of imported medicines. Traditional medicines can be bought on Lan Ong, or there's a small clinic at 27 Dinh Tien Hoang, under the Daewoo building.

Post office The GPO occupies a whole block at the south end of Dinh Tien Hoang. International postal services, including parcel dispatch (7am–noon & 1–8pm) and *poste restante*, are located in the southernmost hall; next entrance up is for telephone and fax services (6am–10pm); finally, the main entrance leads to general mail services and money exchange (cash only). Useful sub-post offices are at 66 Trang Tien, 66 Luong Van Can, 18 Nguyen Du, D2 Giang Vo and at Hanoi train station.

Sports Some big hotels open their facilities to non-residents: for tennis and swimming try the *Hanoi Hotel* or *Thang Long Hotel*. The north's first golf course (18 holes; open to non-members on weekdays) is 45km west of Hanoi at *King's Island Golf Resort*; information and memberships from 4 Tran Hung Dao (☎826 0342). The exclusive *Hanoi Club* at 76 Yen Phu (☎823 8115) is soon to open beside West Lake, offering all sorts of goodies – squash, wind-surfing, gym plus bars and restaurants – to members and guests only.

Taxis To call a metered cab use one of the following numbers, listed in descending price order and level of reliability: *Hanoi Taxi* (☎853 5252); *Red Taxi* (☎835 3686); *CP Taxi* (☎824 1999); *PT Taxi* (☎853 3171).

Tour agencies The travellers' cafés organize bargain-basement tours and fulfil a multitude of other functions, including car rental, visa services and airport transport. Though *Green Bamboo* is the most upmarket, there's little to choose between the big four: *Green Bamboo*, 42 Nha Chung (☎826 8752, fax 826 4949); *Lonely Planet*, 33 Hang Be (☎825 0974, fax 825 0000); *Queen*, 65 Hang Bac (☎826 0860, fax 825 0000); and *Real Darling*, 33 Hang Quat (☎826 9386, fax 825 6562). Reliable mid-price private agents include *Ann's Tourist*, 26 Yet Kieu (☎822 0018, fax 822 9403) and *Especen Tourist Company*, 79e Hang Trong (☎826 6856, fax 826 9612), while an interesting addition to the scene is state-run *Educulture Tours* at 14b Phan Chu Trinh (☎825 1551, fax 826 2468), whose profits are ploughed back into preservation projects. So far they run a Red River boat tour, not stunningly exciting though it does include Bat Trang pottery village, and are planning guided cyclo tours around the Old Quarter and French streets of Hanoi. Of the big, government agencies try *Vietnamtourism*, 30a Ly Thuong Kiet (☎826 4154, fax 825 7583) or *Vinatour*, 54 Nguyen Du (☎825 2986, fax 825 2707): their tours cover the whole country, but are the most expensive.

MOVING ON FROM HANOI

For addresses and telephone numbers of airlines and foreign embassies in Hanoi, see "Listings", p.345; sample fares to and from stations are given in the box on p.309.

PLANES

Minibuses to the airport leave from outside *Vietnam Airlines* at 1 Quang Trung every thirty minutes from 5am to 5pm: buy your tickets inside the office at least a day in advance ($4). Tour operators and hotels will arrange a car for about $15–20, or call up a taxi (see "Listings", previous page) at around $25–30. If you want to split the fare, sign up at one of the travellers' cafés for a shared car or minibus at $4–5 per person. Note that there's an **airport tax** of $1.50 levied on domestic flights, and $7 on international departures. **Flight enquiries** should be directed to the office of the relevant carrier (see "Airlines" p.345).

TRAINS

Tickets and **information** are available at the window marked "Booking Office for Foreigners" (daily 7am–7.20pm) in the main station building facing onto Le Duan, where you'll also find English timetables posted on a pillar. It's best to make onward travel arrangements early, especially for sleeping berths to Hué and Ho Chi Minh City as these sell out several days in advance. Note that services **to the east and north** , including destinations in **China** (see below for more on travel to China), leave from a back station, *Ga Tran Quy Cap*, whose entrance is off Tran Quy Cap Street; any tickets remaining on the day of travel for these trains are also sold here.

BUSES

Hanoi's three long-distance bus stations all serve different destinations: for points **south**, head for Giap Bat station, 6km south of town on Giai Phong; eastbound services for **Haiphong**, **Bai Chay** (for **Ha Long Bay**) and **Cao Bang** leave from Gia Lam station, 4km from the centre; and buses to **Son La**, **Dien Bien Phu**, **Lao Cai**, and the northwest in general, use the Kim Ma station, just 2km out at the junction of Giang Vo and Kim Ma. It's advisable to check at the station a day or two before you want to travel, especially for destinations north and west of Hanoi where public services are crumbling in the face of independent operators. Often these private buses, which aren't always entirely legal, hang around outside the appropriate station, though they may simply fill up outside the driver's house or on a backstreet – someone at the station should know the latest situation. For public buses it's best to buy your ticket at the bus station in advance.

Among the more established **private services** are hordes of minibuses running out to Bai Chay (for **Ha Long Bay**) which gather in the early morning south of the Opera House at the junction of Hai Ba Trung and Le Thanh Tong ($4–5). A rival group have started congregating at the north end of Tran Quang Khai, near the Royal Hotel, but the scene is constantly evolving, so check locally for the latest. There's also a privately run tourist bus making the trek down **to Hué** every few days; details are available from Hanoi tour agencies.

TRAVEL TO CHINA AND LAOS

Land border crossings are now open between Vietnam and its northern neighbours. Visa regulations and entry formalities change frequently, so check the current situation with the relevant embassy. Note that if you leave by one of these land crossings you need to get the **exit point** changed on your **Vietnam visa** *after* you've got the relevant entry visa for China or Laos (see *Basics*, p.12, for more on this procedure).

Into China

At the time of writing the **China** border is open to foreigners at Lao Cai, Dong Dang and Mong Cai. **Train services** between Hanoi and Beijing (58hr) have restarted, leaving Hanoi on Tuesdays and Fridays at 11pm, and Beijing on Mondays and Fridays. Fares are quoted in Swiss francs, in accordance with international rail agreements, and payments are calculated using exchange rates posted at stations. **Visas** are issued by the Chinese Embassy Consular Section (☎823 5569; Mon–Fri 8.30–11am) on Tran Phu, round the corner from the main embassy building at 46 Hoang Dieu. A one-month tourist visa takes five working days to process and costs around $30–40, payable in dollars only.

Into Laos

The only land crossing into **Laos** at the moment is via Lao Bao border gate, near Dong Ha (see p.288). The Lao Embassy in Hanoi at 40 Quang Trung (☎826 8724; Mon–Fri 8.30–11am & 2.30–4pm) issues seven-day transit **visas** within three working days (limited to one province; $25). Full one-month tourist visas are easier and cheaper to arrange in Bangkok: in Hanoi you'll be directed to a tour agent, such as *Vietnamtourism* (30a Ly Thuong Kiet; ☎826 4154, fax 825 7583) or *Hanoi Youth Tourism Company* (14a Phan Chu Trinh; ☎826 3077, fax 824 6463), where you'll pay $90–100 for only a two-week visa which takes seven working days to process; for all visas, payment is required in dollars. This visa can be extended to a month in Laos but you'll need the appropriate Laotian agent's address from the embassy.

ORGANIZED TOURS

Tour agencies in Hanoi can put together **individual programmes** including vehicle rental, guide and accommodation, or whatever combination you want. This is a useful option to consider for touring the **northern provinces** where travelling by public transport can be difficult and you'll have more freedom with your own vehicle.

Otherwise, organized **tours** following a **fixed itinerary** are often the cheapest and easiest way of exploring further afield. Tours can be arranged at the travellers' cafés or through *Especen*: they all offer the same basic destinations at a fairly standardized price, but remember to check what the extra costs will be – and you'll save a lot of time traipsing around Hanoi in the early morning if you take a tour with just one pick-up point. By far the most popular of the **day-trips** on offer are the Perfume Pagoda ($17) and Hoa Lu ($15). **Longer excursions** to Ha Long Bay start at $24 for a two-day tour, rising to $36 for three days cruising round the bay plus a visit to Cat Ba National Park. The most tempting option in Sa Pa is **trekking**, since this is difficult to organize independently: the standard two-day trek, travelling by train and overnighting in a minority village costs around $60 per person; or there's a four-day programme that takes in Sa Pa's weekend market and a couple of nearby villages. Finally, **Mai Chau** trips offer a night in a stilthouse as part of a two-day excursion ($22–25).

Recommended tour agencies are listed on p.347; see *Basics*, p.30, for provisos and tips on signing up for a tour in Vietnam.

AROUND HANOI

The **Red River** slides across its delta like a "great warm stream of tomato soup", as the journalist James Cameron put it, along the way feeding brick kilns, rich farmland and the country's most densely populated provinces. Though the northern delta barely makes it above sea-level, it's been canalized and cultivated for so many centuries that there's little water in evidence. The landscape is criss-crossed with ancient dykes, averaging a massive 14m high, and is studded with temples, pagodas, churches, family graves, communal houses and all the other leftovers of successive generations.

At least one journey out of Hanoi into delta country is recommended for the experience, though, apart from the dramatic **Perfume Pagoda**, there are no absolutely compelling sights. Among dozens of historic buildings the most strongly atmospheric are the **Thay Pagoda** and **Tay Phuong Pagoda**, buried deep in the delta, as well as **Keo Pagoda** (see *The Central Provinces* chapter, p.303), all of which are fine examples of traditional Vietnamese architecture. Most delta towns were flattened by US forces intent on destroying their industries, but the villages are worth exploring – in particular the **craft villages**, which remain more traditional than most you'll find in Vietnam, concentrating on one craft, such as embroidery, wire or noodle-making, to the exclusion of all else. These villages are difficult to get to on your own, but **Bat Trang** pottery village is an interesting example within easy striking distance of Hanoi. Finally, if you're passing by, then **Co Loa** ancient citadel just north of the Red River is worth a pit stop for its historical significance, though there's little to recall its former grandeur.

The Perfume Pagoda

Sixty kilometres southwest of Hanoi the Red River Delta ends abruptly where steep-sided limestone hills rise from the paddy fields. The most easterly of these forested spurs shelters north Vietnam's most famous pilgrimage site, the **Perfume Pagoda**, *Chua Huong*, hidden in the folds of the Mountain of the Perfumed Traces, and said to be named after spring blossoms that perfume the air. The easiest and most popular way to visit the pagoda is on a **day-tour** out of Hanoi (see p.349), or with a hired **car** and driver for the day. Alternatively, it's a two- to three-hour **motorbike** ride: follow Highway 6 through Ha Dong as far as the fourteen-kilometre marker where the highway crosses the rail tracks, then turn left on the D426 heading due south to find Duc Khe village and the Suoi Yen (Yen River) boat station. There's a hefty sightseeing **fee** of $7 to visit the pagoda, though this does include the return boat trip; tickets are sold beside the village post office (*buu dien*). You'll find a few **food stalls** next to the boat station and also where the sampans drop you at the start of the walk to *Chua Thien Chu* (see below).

The Perfume Pagoda, one of many peppering these hills, occupies a spectacular **grotto** over 50m high which is well worth the hot and not particularly interesting walk up the mountain. The start of the journey is a more appealing sampan-ride 4km up a silent, flooded valley among karst hills where fishermen and farmers work their inundated fields. From where the sampan drops you, a stone-flagged path shaded by gnarled frangipani trees brings you to the seventeenth-century *Chua Thien Chu* ("Pagoda Leading to Heaven"), in front of which stands a magnificent, triple-roofed bell pavilion. Quan Am, Goddess of Mercy, takes pride of place on the pagoda's main altar; the original bronze effigy was stolen by Tay Son rebels in the 1770s and some say they melted it down for cannonballs. To the right of the pagoda as you face it a roughly paved **path** leads steeply uphill to the Perfume Pagoda, also dedicated to Quan Am. It's a good idea to bring bottled water for the three-kilometre walk (1–2hr), or put yourself at the mercy of the kids who tag along, lugging cool-boxes of overpriced but very welcome cold cans. The effort is fully rewarded when the gaping cavern is revealed on the side of a deep depression filled with vines and trees reaching for light beneath the inscription "supreme cave under the southern sky". A short flight of steps descends into cool air where gilded Buddhas emerge from dark recesses wreathed in clouds of incense. Despite the constant stream of visitors and band of souvenir sellers, it's a dramatic scene. During the festival months of March and April (from the sixth day of the second lunar month to the end of the third month) thousands of people purify themselves at *Chua Thien Chu* before filing slowly up the mountain, greeting other pilgrims with *Nam mo A Di Da Phat* ("praise to Amitabha Buddha").

Thay Pagoda (the Master's Pagoda)

Thay Pagoda (*Chua Thay*) or the **Master's Pagoda** – also known as *Thien Phuc Tu*, ("Pagoda of the Heavenly Blessing") – was founded in the reign of King Ly Nhan Tong (1072–1127) and is an unusually large complex fronting onto a picturesque lake in the lee of a limestone knobble. Thay Pagoda lies 30km from Hanoi in Sai Son village, between Ha Dong and Son Tay. As this isn't a popular tour destination, you'll probably need to hire a **car** or **xe om** for the excursion, or rent a **motorbike**. The easiest route is via Highway 6, taking a right turn in front of Ha Dong post office (*buu dien*) onto the D72/D70 to Quoc Oai, where you pick up the TL218 heading north. Where the dyke-top road rides high above a medieval collection of village roofs, 24km from Son Tay, the pagoda is signed to the right. The entry **fee** ($1.50) includes one the pagoda's unusually knowledgeable English-speaking guides; note that this is a popular weekend jaunt out of Hanoi, at its busiest on Sundays.

The Master was the ascetic monk and healer **Tu Dao Hanh** (sometimes also known as Minh Khong) who "burned his finger to bring about rain and cured diseases with holy water", in addition to countless other miracles. He was head-monk of the pagoda and an accomplished water puppeteer – hence the lake's dainty theatre-pavilion – and, according to legend, was reincarnated first as a Buddha and then as King Ly Than Tong in answer to King Ly Nhan Tong's prayers for an heir. To complicate matters further, Ly Than Tong's life was then saved by the monk Tu Dao Hanh. Anyway, the Thay Pagoda is dedicated to the cult of Tu Dao Hanh in his three incarnations as monk (the Master), Buddha, and king.

The pagoda is going through the latest of many restorations but its dark, subdued interior retains a powerful atmosphere. Nearly a hundred **statues** fill the prayer halls: the oldest dates back to the pagoda's foundation, but the most eye-catching are two fifteenth-century giant **guardians** made of clay and papier mâché, which weigh 1000 kilos apiece and are said to be the biggest in Vietnam. Behind the prayer floor the first altar holds Buddha images and a thirteenth-century effigy of the Master in yellow garb, while the final sanctuary is reserved for Tu Dao Hanh in all his guises. The monk's remains and a statue with articulated legs repose in a small antechamber which is only unlocked on one day each year (the fifth day of the third lunar month), when the village's oldest male bathes Tu Dao Hanh in fragrant water and helps him to his feet. This event is for the monks' eyes only, but the **water-puppet festival** held on the lake each Tet, from the fifth to seventh days of the first lunar month, is open to all.

In front of the pagoda are two attractive, covered bridges with arched roofs built in 1602: one leads to an islet where spirits of the earth, water and fire are worshipped in a diminutive Taoist temple; the second takes you to a well-worn flight of steps up the limestone hill. When Tu Dao Hanh was near death he followed the same route up to Thanh Hoa cave, now a sacred place hidden behind a screen of aerial banyan roots which lies between a mini-pagoda and a temple dedicated to the monk's parents. Though the sanctuaries themselves are well tended, there's rubbish strewn everywhere and nothing special to see beyond expansive views of a typical delta landscape over the pagoda roofs.

Tay Phuong Pagoda

A few kilometres west of the Thay Pagoda, the much smaller "Pagoda of the West", **Tay Phuong Pagoda**, perches atop a fifty-metre-high limestone hillock supposedly shaped like a buffalo. Tay Phuong can easily be included with the Thay Pagoda (see above) only 6km away to the east, though this journey takes thirty minutes on sometimes rough roads. From the Thay Pagoda, backtrack to Quoc Oai to pick up the DT21B which takes you northwest; after 5km turn left at a crossroads to Thach Xa village and the pagoda.

Among the first pagodas built in Vietnam, Tay Phuong's overriding attraction is its invaluable collection of over sixty jackfruit-wood **statues**, some of which are on view at Hanoi's Fine Arts Museum (see p.329). The highlights are eighteen arhats, disturbingly life-like representations of Buddhist ascetics as imagined by eighteenth-century sculptors, grouped behind the main altar. As Tay Phuong is also an important Confucian sanctuary, disciples of the sage are included on the altar, each carrying a gift to their master, some precious object, a book or a symbol of longevity, alongside the expected Buddha effigies. Tay Phuong's most notable **architectural features** are its heavy double roofs, whose graceful curves are decorated with phoenixes and dragons, its unplastered brick walls and an inviting approach via 237 moss-covered, red-brick steps. At the bottom of the stairway hawkers peddle the local speciality sweetmeat, *banh che lam*, made of sticky-rice pounded together with green bean and sugar.

The craft villages

For centuries villages around Vietnam's major towns have specialized in single-commodity production, firstly to supply the local market and sometimes going on to win national fame for the skill of their artisans. A few communities continue to prosper, of which the best-known near Hanoi are **Dong Ky** woodcarving village (Ha Bac Province) and Bat Trang pottery village. These are well-run, commercial operations where family-units turn out fine, handcrafted products, and are used to foreigners coming to watch them at work, even setting-up salesrooms. Most other villages are far less touristy, and the more isolated tend to treat all visitors with suspicion. Nevertheless, it's worth persevering to gain a rare glimpse into a gruelling way of life that continues to follow the ancient rhythms, using craft-techniques handed down the generations virtually unchanged. Ad hoc "entry-fees" can be a problem, and are better dealt with by a guide, which you'll probably need just to find the place anyway.

BAT TRANG, across the Red River in Hanoi's Gia Lam District, is a manageable ten-kilometre **cycle ride** over the Chuong Duong Bridge, then first right along the levy. While most people come **by road**, the more interesting approach is from the river; *Educulture Tours* (see "Tour agencies" on p.347) puts on **river trips** which include Bat Trang, but only as part of a whole-day tour, making it an expensive venture. Note that some people have been charged an **"entry fee"** of $2–5 when visiting the village independently.

Bat Trang has been producing **bricks** and **earthenware** since the fifteenth century, and the oldest part of the village beside the river has a medieval aura, with its narrow, high-walled alleys spattered with handmade coal-pats (to fire the kilns) drying in the sun. Through tiny doorways, you catch glimpses of courtyards stacked with moulds and hand-painted pots, while all around rise the brick chimneys of the village's 800 kilns. Around 2000 families live in Bat Trang, producing traditional, bright cobalt-blue **ceramics** from small workshops as well as mass-produced plant-pots and highly glazed banisters for Hanoi's building boom. The village has expanded eastwards, away from the river, and this is where you'll find showrooms displaying a motley collection of dusty pots: dig around and you might come across some attractive pieces, though you'll find prices are no cheaper than in Hanoi.

Co Loa Citadel

The earliest independent Vietnamese states grew up in the Red River floodplain, atop low hills or crouched behind sturdy embankments. First to emerge from the mists of legend was Van Lang, presided over by the Hung kings from a knob of high ground, marked today by a few dynastic temples north of Viet Tri (Vinh Phu Province). Then the action moved closer to Hanoi when King An Duong ruled Au Lac (258–207 BC) from an immense citadel at **CO LOA** (Old Snail City), 16km due north of the present capital. These days the once massive earthworks are barely visible and it's really only worth stopping-off here in passing, to take a look at a couple of quiet temples and a thousand-year-old banyan tree that's about on its last leaves.

King An Duong built his citadel inside three concentric ramparts, spiralling like a snail-shell, separated by moats large enough for ships to navigate; the outer wall was 8km long, 6- to 8m wide and at least 4m high, topped-off with bamboo fencing. After the Chinese invaded in the late second century BC, Co Loa was abandoned until 939 AD, when Ngo Quyen established the next period of independent rule from the same heavily symbolic site. Archeologists have found rich pickings at Co Loa including 20,000 iron arrowheads, displayed in Hanoi's History Museum (see p.323), which lend credence to at least one of the Au Lac legends. The story goes that the sacred Golden Turtle gave King An Duong a magic crossbow made from a claw that fired thousands of arrows at a time. A deceitful

Chinese prince married An Duong's daughter, Princess My Chau, persuaded her to show him the crossbow and then stole the claw before mounting an invasion. King An Duong and his daughter were forced to flee, whereupon My Chau understood her act of betrayal and nobly told her father to kill her. When the king beheaded his daughter and threw her body in a well, she turned into lustrous, pink pearls.

The site

Co Loa's temple complex is signposted to the east of busy Highway 3, down a tree-lined road running beside what looks just like any other delta embankment though it's said to be a remnant of the fortifications. First thing you come to after a couple of kilometres is an archer's statue; go 100m further on to find the temples and the banyan tree, the latter held up by a mass of props in a high-walled enclosure. The principal temple, **Den Vua An Duong Vuong**, is a beautiful building furnished with huge, ironwood pillars and ornate gilded carving, where the king and his officers are venerated. Behind the old tree is a smaller temple, **Den My Chau**, where the princess is honoured in the surprising form of a dumpy, armchair-shaped stone clothed in embroidered finery and covered in jewels but lacking a head.

travel details

Buses

*It's almost impossible to give the **frequency** with which buses run. Though scheduled, long-distance public buses won't depart if empty. Moreover, private services, often minibuses or pick-ups, ply more popular routes, and depart only when they have enough passengers to make the journey worthwhile. Highway 1 sees a near-constant stream of buses passing through to various destinations, and it's possible to flag something down at virtually any time of the day. It's advisable to start your journey early – most long-distance departures leave between 5 and 9am, and very few run after midday. **Journey times** can also vary; figures below show the normal length of time you can expect the journey to take.*

Hanoi to: Bai Chay (4hr); Cao Bang (10hr); Haiphong (2hr 30min); Hoa Binh (2hr); Hué (19hr); Lang Son (5hr); Mai Chau (7hr); Nam Dinh (2hr 30min); Ninh Binh (3hr); Son La (12hr); Thai Nguyen (3hr); Thanh Hoa (4–5hr).

Trains

Hanoi to: Da Nang (3 daily; 16hr 40min–22hr); Dong Dang (2 daily; 8–9hr); Dong Ha (2 daily; 14hr–16hr 30min); Dong Hoi (2 daily; 12–14hr); Haiphong (5–6 daily; 2hr–2hr 30min); Ho Chi Minh City (3 daily; 36–44hr); Hué (3 daily; 13hr 30min–18hr); Lao Cai (2 daily; 10–11hr); Nam Dinh (5 daily; 1hr 45min–3hr 10min); Nha Trang (3 daily; 27hr–33hr 30min); Ninh Binh (4 daily; 2hr 20min–4hr); Thanh Hoa (5 daily; 3hr 35min–6hr); Vinh (3 daily; 6hr 30min–8hr 45min).

Flights

Hanoi to: Da Nang (3 daily; 1hr 10min); Dien Bien Phu (2 weekly; 1hr); Ho Chi Minh City (6 daily; 2hr); Hué (2 daily; 1hr 30min); Nha Trang (1 weekly; 2hr 30min); Vinh (3 weekly; 50min).

CHAPTER SEVEN

HA LONG BAY AND THE NORTHERN SEABOARD

The mystical scenery of **Ha Long Bay** is what draws people to the northeast coast of Vietnam. Thousands of limestone islands jut out of the emerald sea, sculpted into such bizarre shapes as to invite comparisons with anything from chickens and dragons to champagne corks or General de Gaulle's nose. Navigating the silent, secretive channels, past bobbing clusters of fishing boats, and stopping to scramble through caves or swim beneath overhanging cliffs is one of the highlights of a trip to Vietnam. The tourist hordes are easily swallowed up in the bay's generous proportions – though **Bai Chay**, the usual jumping-off point, copes less well and a rapidly growing canyon of minihotels detracts from what used to be a pleasantly old-fashioned seaside resort, complete with boulevards, parks and sea-view rooms. Neighbouring **Hong Gai** is a complete contrast: an industrious town with meagre tourist facilities, dedicated to fishing, coal and a profitable cross-border trade, though there's still nearly 150km to go, via the grim mining town of Cam Pha, to reach the booming markets of **Mong Cai** and the Chinese border.

Heading back down the coast, **Haiphong** is north Vietnam's second largest city and its only major port. Broach its industrial outskirts and the city reveals a surprisingly agreeable centre with a cluster of nineteenth-century architecture that merits a stopover. A nearby attraction is the beach resort of **Do Son**, though most travellers are merely passing through Haiphong on the way to **Cat Ba Island**, lying just off the coast. From Cat Ba the southeastern waters of Ha Long Bay are within easy reach and it's worth considering as an alternative base to Bai Chay for touring the bay. The island itself offers some fine scenery as well as being home to **Cat Ba National Park**, a forest and maritime reserve requiring the usual mix of luck and dedication to see anything larger than a mosquito. Hotels are springing up as islanders cotton on to tourism, but for the moment fishing is paramount and a coracle ride around the bustling harbour of Cat Ba Town presents a fascinating glimpse of waterborne communities afloat.

Haiphong and around

Traffic heading out of Hanoi to the northeast coast funnels over the rust-coloured waters of the Red River on Highway 1, before turning east across the northern delta's most prolific rice fields. Container trucks pound the highway, squeaking

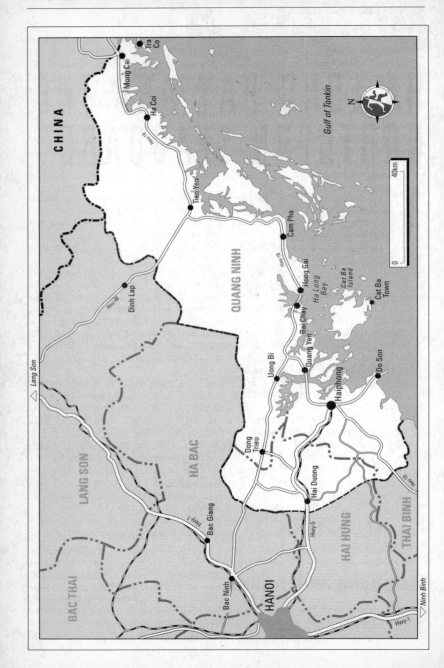

past bicycles and buffalo carts, on the way to **HAIPHONG** where a vast, smoke-belching cement factory dominates the outskirts. But Haiphong isn't to be written off so easily and it comes as a pleasant surprise to find in the centre of this still moderately small, orderly city an older district with low-key sites and subtle charms, shaded by ranks of flame trees. Broad avenues of well-tended colonial villas add to the impression of quiet prosperity and the city has a cosmopolitan flavour, evident in a profusion of import-export companies and suited business-men in hotel lobbies talking deals and joint ventures.

Onward from Haiphong by road is **Do Son**, Hanoi's nearest beach resort and a popular summer destination for wealthy cadres and the nouveaux riches. However, a more interesting destination from Haiphong is Cat Ba Island (see p.364), worth it for the ferry-ride alone, while another recommended ferry journey heads northeast to Hong Gai through the dramatic scenery of Ha Long Bay (see p.368).

Some history

Haiphong lies 100km from Hanoi on the Cua Cam River, one of the main channels of the Red River Estuary. Originally a small **fishing village** and military outpost, its development into a **major port** in the seventeenth century stems more from its proximity to the capital city than from favourable local conditions. In fact it was an astonishingly poor choice for a harbour, 20km from the open sea with shallow, shifting channels, no fresh water and little solid land. The first quay was only built in 1817 and it was not until 1874, when Haiphong was ceded to the French, that a town began to develop. With remarkable determination, the first settlers drained the mosquito-ridden marshes, sinking foundations sometimes as deep as 30m into huge earth platforms that passed for building plots. Doubts about the harbour lingered but then in 1883 the 9000-strong **French Expeditionary Force**, sent to secure Tonkin, established a supply base in Haiphong and its future as the north's principal port was secured.

By 1910 Haiphong, Hanoi and the markets of southern China were connected by rail, and industries began to develop along the Cua Cam River, fed by coal from Cam Pha, but it was not until November 1946 that Haiphong re-appeared in the history books. Rising tensions between French troops and soldiers of the newly declared Democratic Republic of Vietnam erupted in a dispute about customs' control when shots were exchanged over a Chinese junk suspected of smuggling. The French replied with a **naval bombardment** of Haiphong's Vietnamese quarter, killing hundreds of civilians (estimates range from 1000 to 6000), and only regained control of the streets after several days of rioting. But the two nations were now set for war – a war that ended, appropriately, with the citizens of Haiphong watching the last colonial troops embark in 1955 after the collapse of French Indochina.

Merely a decade later the city was again under siege, this time by American planes targeting one of the few industrial centres in North Vietnam and a major supply route for Soviet "aid". In May 1972 President Nixon ordered the **mining of Haiphong harbour** in a futile bid to intimidate the North, but less than a year later America was clearing up the mines under the terms of the Paris ceasefire agreement. By late 1973 the harbour was deemed safe once more, in time for the exodus of desperate **boat people** at the end of the decade as hundreds of refugees escaped in overladen fishing boats.

Arrival, information and city transport

Haiphong **train station** is located on the southeast side of town and within easy walking distance of the centre. For once the station provides left-luggage facilities, making it feasible to do a quick tour of Haiphong while passing through; lockers big enough to take rucksacks are in a "reception room" off the main ticket hall, where you can also buy ferry tickets for Cat Ba Island. The **ferry station**, serving both Hong Gai and Cat Ba, is on the Cua Cam River about 500m north of the city centre along Ben Binh.

Buses from the south and west usually pitch up at Niem Nghia bus station, out in the southwest suburbs on Tran Nguyen Han, about 3km and twelve minutes by cyclo from the centre. Some Hanoi services may drop you closer in at Tam Bac bus station, near the west end of Tam Bac Lake and Sat market. Buses from Bai Chay and the northeast come in to Binh bus station on the north bank of the Cua Cam River, 300m from the cross-river ferry, but if you're coming from this direction the Hong Gai–Haiphong **ferry** is a more scenic alternative.

Leaving Haiphong **by bus**, Hanoi-bound minibuses hang around the ferry station and Tam Bac bus station, where you'll also find public buses to Hanoi; all other buses to the south and west depart from Niem Nghia bus station.

Haiphong's **Cat Bi airport** (flights to Ho Chi Minh City and Da Nang only) is 7km southeast of the city in a restricted military area. *Vietnam Airlines* runs a free minibus to its office on Tran Phu; note that the same service on departure costs $1. Otherwise, a taxi (☎031/841999) to or from the airport should be around $5.

For **information**, head straight for the main office of *Vietnamtourism in Haiphong* at 15 Le Dai Hanh (Mon–Sat 7am–noon & 1.30–5pm; ☎031/842989), though its branch at 57 Dien Bien Phu also offers guides and car rental (☎031/842432). City **maps** are on sale at book stalls on Dien Bien Phu, near the junction with Minh Khai.

Cyclos are easily available and a good way of getting around the central district, although it's quite possible to tackle most of it on foot. As yet there's no official bike rental though you might be able to arrange one through your hotel. For longer distances **car rental** is the only answer: count on $35 per day if renting through *Vietnamtourism*; and slightly less for unmetered taxis, which can usually be found waiting on Nguyen Duc Canh, just south of Tam Bac Lake.

Accommodation

Haiphong has a fair number of hotels in the middle and lower price brackets, though few places can be said to offer great value. Budget accommodation is in short supply and tends to fill up early; single rooms are also at a premium. Most hotels cluster around Dien Bien Phu, the city's main artery, with others near the train and ferry stations.

Bach Dang, 42 Dien Bien Phu (☎031/842444). A big old hotel with a range of rooms, including the cheapest accommodation on the main strip – a few dingy boxes, some of which have bathrooms. If you can afford it, the more cheerful, newly renovated rooms offer better value. ②

Ben Binh, 6 Ben Binh (☎031/842260, fax 842524). An imposing building set in gardens opposite the ferry station. Spacious, high-ceilinged rooms upstairs are more appealing, but it's all rather disappointingly soulless and you get better value at the *Military Zone Guesthouse* (see opposite). ③

ACCOMMODATION PRICE CODES

All accommodation listed in this guide has been categorized according to the following scale:

① under US$10 (under 110,000 dong) ② US$10–15 (110–165,000 dong)

③ US$15–30 (165–330,000 dong) ④ US$30–75 (330–825,000 dong)

⑤ US$75–150 (825–1,650,000 dong) ⑥ over US$150 (over 1,650,000 dong)

Rates are for the cheapest available double or twin room; breakfast is not usually included. During holiday periods, rates are liable to rise, and proprietors may be less amenable to bargaining. Although the law requires prices to be quoted in dong, most hotels also give their rates in US$; payment can be made in either currency. *For a more detailed discussion of accommodation, see pp.31–34.*

Bong Sen, 15–16 Nguyen Duc Canh (☎031/846019, fax 855184). Despite the off-putting entrance through the kitchen, this place is clean, friendly and not overpriced. Smallish rooms come with TV, telephone, hot water and air-con. ②

Cat Bi, 30 Tran Phu (☎031/846306, fax 845181). A pleasant, rambling hotel with reasonable prices which should be worth checking out after its refurbishment. Handy for the train station. ③

Hoa Binh, 104 Luong Khanh Thien (☎031/846909, fax 846907). The clean cell-like rooms in the old block behind are still the cheapest in town, with minimal furnishings and decrepit bathrooms. A smart-looking new extension offers more expensive accommodation (IDD, TV and air-con) though it's already falling apart. ①

Hoang Yen, 7 Tran Hung Dao (☎031/842383, fax 842205). A spruce colonial edifice in an attractive location with a restaurant downstairs. The rooms themselves aren't oozing with character but they're not bad value, offering all the standard facilities and views over town. ③

Hong Bang, 64 Dien Bien Phu (☎031/842229, fax 841044). An aged but friendly, well-run hotel that's popular among businesspeople. Gloomy communal areas but the rooms are large and, except for the cheapest, surprisingly plush, with satellite TV, IDD and fridge. ②–③

Hotel du Commerce, 62 Dien Bien Phu (☎031/842706, fax 842560). An old colonial-style hotel with a certain period charm and helpful staff. Its big, airy rooms have been comfortably refurbished though the paintwork's shoddy. ④

Huu Nghi, 60 Dien Bien Phu (☎031/823244, fax 823245). Haiphong's most glitzy hotel housed in an unsympathetic 11-storey block, the tallest building in town. Top rate gets you a suite with gargantuan bathroom and tasteful high-quality furnishings. Cheaper rooms are just the same, but smaller. ④

La Villa Blanche (also known as the *Navy Guesthouse* or *Nha Khach Hai Quan*), 5 Tran Hung Dao (☎031/841113, fax 842278). A dazzling white building opposite the park, plus two smart new villas behind. Upmarket accommodation providing all the trappings, including video – though the already small, cheaper rooms are over-stuffed with ornate dark-wood furnishings. ④

Military Zone Guesthouse (also known as *Nha Khach Quanh Khu*), 2 Hoang Van Thu (☎031/842492, fax 841017). A large new hotel opposite the GPO. Rooms are well priced, clean and bright, all with satellite TV and air-con. ③

Phuong Dong (*Orient*), 19 Luong Khanh Thien (☎031/855391). A small new hotel right in the station courtyard, that stands out for its relatively good-value accommodation. Everything's sparkling and all rooms include TV and telephone. ②

Thang Nam, 55 Dien Bien Phu (☎031/842820 fax 842674). A popular middle-of-the-road hotel offering spartan rooms with wooden floorboards. But it's all well swept and not badly priced for the central strip. ②–③

Thuy Duong, 4 Cat Cut (☎031/848557). Newly opened mini-hotel, on the edge of things but worth the effort for its good-value roooms with air-con, TV and private bathroom. ①

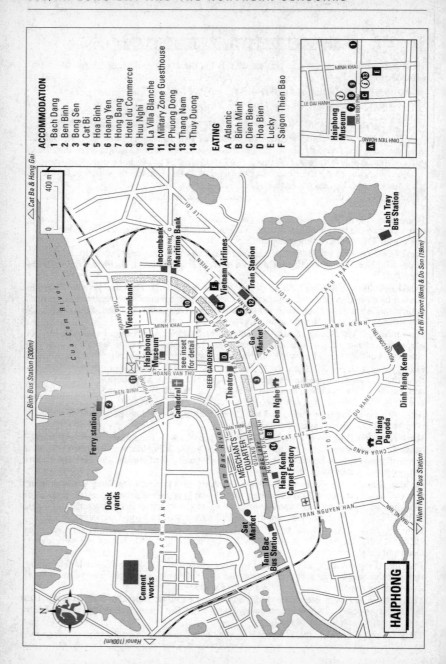

ACCOMMODATION
1 Bach Dang
2 Ben Binh
3 Bong Sen
4 Cat Bi
5 Hoa Binh
6 Hoang Yen
7 Hong Bang
8 Hotel du Commerce
9 Huu Nghi
10 La Villa Blanche
11 Military Zone Guesthouse
12 Phuong Dong
13 Thang Nam
14 Thuy Duong

EATING
A Atlantic
B Binh Minh
C Dien Bien
D Hoa Bien
E Lucky
F Saigon Thien Bao

HAIPHONG

The city centre

Despite its recent history, old Haiphong is surprisingly well preserved. The crescent-shaped nineteenth-century core, which holds most of interest, lies between the curve of the Tam Bac River and the loop of the train tracks. To the north of the main artery, Dien Bien Phu, you'll find an area of broad, sleepy avenues and Haiphong's most attractive **colonial architecture**. On Dien Bien Phu itself are a number of hotels, an uninspiring selection of shops and the classic wine-red facade of the **Haiphong Museum** (Tues, Wed & Sun 8–10am & 2–4pm). Even during its advertised opening hours the museum is often closed due to lack of demand, but you're not missing anything. Instead, head south towards the square tower of Haiphong **cathedral**, built in the late nineteenth century and looking very trim after years of neglect, and continue down bustling Hoang Van Thu to the salmon-pink **theatre**. Constructed of materials shipped from France in the early 1900s, the theatre faces on to a wide, open square – a site remembered locally for the deaths of forty revolutionaries during the street-battles of November 1946 "after a valiant fight against French invaders".

In earlier times the Bonnal Canal ran past this square, linking the Tam Bac and Cua Cam rivers. For most of its length it's now gardens, cutting a green swathe through the city, but the canal's western section survives as Tam Bac Lake. North of the lake you'll find Haiphong's **merchants' quarter**, these days a dilapidated area of street markets, chandlers and ironmongers between Tran Trinh Street and *Cho Sat*. **Sat Market**'s nineteenth-century halls have been replaced by a circular, six-storey block that's been shunned by stallholders who find the rents too high, preferring the bustle and freedom of the streets.

Opposite Cho Sat on the south side of Tam Bac Lake, no. 124 Nguyen Duc Canh is the home of the **Hang Kenh Carpet Factory**, also called *Tapis Hang Kenh* in reference to French entrepreneurs who started producing woollen carpets here in 1929 (Mon–Sat 7–11.30am & 1–5pm, Sun 7–11.30am). The carpets are still handmade on old wooden looms; you can also see the whole production process, starting with heaped rainbow-skeins of wool and ending under the trimmers' glittering scissors. The finished carptets, most of which are exported, vary from delicate Oriental designs in muted tones, to lurid sunsets in Ha Long Bay and Western motifs.

Last stop in the central district is **Den Nghe**, about ten minutes' walk east of the factory along Me Linh. This unusually cramped temple is noted for its sculptures: the finest carvings are on the massive stone table in the first courtyard, but make sure you also look above the perfumed haze of incense for some colourful friezes. General Le Chan, a heroine of the Trung Sisters' Rebellion (see pp.409–410), is worshipped at the main altar; on the eighth day of each second lunar month the general receives a birthday treat – platefuls of her favourite food, crab with rice-noodles.

Across the train tracks

There are a couple of sights of passing interest across the train tracks from Haiphong centre, both about 2km to the south. The more rewarding is **Du Hang Pagoda** located on Chua Hang Street, an appealing lane of old artisans' dwellings. The pagoda, in its present form dating from the late seventeenth century, is accessed through an imposing triple-roofed bell tower. Interestingly, the architecture here reveals a distinct Khmer influence in the form of vase-shaped pinnacles ornamenting the roof and pillars of the inner courtyard – according to Buddhist legend these contain propitious *cam lo*, or sweet dew. A library to the left of the courtyard holds a valuable collection of Buddhist prayer books, and beyond is a small, walled garden of burial stupas.

It's worth going on to **Dinh Hang Kenh**, 1km east on Nguyen Cong Tru, if you haven't yet seen a *dinh*, or communal house. This one is a low, graceful building with a sweeping expanse of tiled roof, facing an ornamental lake; an impressive sight marred by ramshackle gardens and encroaching factories. Thirty-two monumental ironwood columns hold up the roof and populate the long, dark hall which is also noted for its carvings of 308 dragons sculpted in thirty writhing nests – now clothed in the dust of ages.

Eating

Haiphong is well endowed with good **places to eat**. The town's poshest venue by a long chalk is the flashy *Saigon Thien Bao* at 6 Tran Binh Trong (☎031/859152), serving Vietnamese and Western dishes in a spacious dining room – all high-tech chrome and low lighting – to piano accompaniment; prices aren't as outrageous as you'd expect, with main dishes starting at around $4. For something more modest, the *Atlantic* at 30 Dinh Tien Hoang is recommended for its inexpensive home-cooking, including a few eye-watering chilli dishes, rather than its decor. Its handful of tables attract the convivial remnants of Haiphong's Russian community, who stayed on after Comecon collapsed in 1991. Alternatively, try the slightly more expensive *Lucky* at 22 Minh Khai, while both the *Hong Bang* and *Dien Bien* hotels serve generous portions at reasonable prices, and "Western breakfasts", in their echoing dining halls.

A more Vietnamese crowd frequents the ever-popular dining rooms of the *Bong Sen Hotel* on Nguyen Duc Canh and the nearby *Dac San Binh Minh* at no. 60, but for real local atmosphere head for a strip of **beer gardens** and eateries to the west of the theatre on Tran Hung Dao: most are unnamed but nos. 22, 25 (*Hoa Bien*) and 27 get the majority vote. Alternatively, cruise the **food stalls** just east of the train station on Luong Khanh Thien, or near the *Bong Sen Hotel* and in the lanes around Haiphong's largest **market**, *Cho Ga*, where you can snack on sizzling spring rolls. In the evenings, join the throng trawling Nguyen Duc Canh, to pause at an ice-cream parlour or beneath the flickering lights of sugar-cane and coconut-milk vendors.

Listings

Airlines *Vietnam Airlines*, 30 Tran Phu, next to the *Cat Bi Hotel* (daily 8–11.30am, 1.30–5pm).

Banks and exchange All the following banks change currency and travellers' cheques: *Incombank*, 36 Dien Bien Phu; *Indovina Bank*, 30 Tran Phu; *Maritime Bank*, 25 Dien Bien Phu; *Vietcombank*, 11 Hoang Dieu.

Hospital *Ben Vien Viet–Tiep* (Vietnam–Czech Friendship General Hospital), 1 Nha Thuong.

Post office The GPO is at the junction of Nguyen Tri Phuong and Hoang Van Thu, with a sub-post office at 36 Quang Trung.

Taxi For metered taxis call *Haiphong Taxi* on ☎031/841999.

Do Son

Twenty kilometres southeast of Haiphong, the knobbly Do Son Peninsula sticks out into the Gulf of Tonkin like the snout of a seahorse. A string of low limestone hills shelters the three sandy bays of this **beach resort**, where Hanoians and Haiphong day-trippers come to escape the city heat and find cool sea-breezes stirring the casuarina trees. In peak season (June through Aug) rooms are hard to come by and prices double. During the rest of the year, it can be a relaxing place to hole-up for a day or so, but dedicated beach-bums can spare themselves the hour's journey from Haiphong – the sand is none too clean and there's a heavy dose of Red River in the surrounding seas.

DO SON village, before you reach the main resort, hosts an annual **buffalo fighting** contest on the ninth and tenth days of the eighth lunar month. It's not a fight to the death – the loser is the first to run away – but later all the buffaloes are sacrificed and shared among competing villages as *loc*, a gift from the spirits. Do Son village itself holds no interest, other than being where the Haiphong **buses** terminate: services run hourly (6am–5pm) from Haiphong's Lach Tray bus station. On arrival at Do Son bus station, hop on a xe om for the last 2km to the resort hotels; cyclos also do the journey, but cost more, take about thirty minutes and you'll have to walk up the hills. Alternatively, if you take one of the **jeeps** that waits around the Lach Tray bus station (around $5 per person to Do Son village), you might persuade them to take you all the way to the hotels.

Accommodation and eating

Do Son resort is divided into three *khu* or Sections spread over 4km, starting with the congested and unattractive Section 1 in the north. Sections 2 and 3 are more appealing, with a handful of hotels and summer villas set among pine trees; **Section 2** has the better beach plus a choice of hotels and restaurants, all within easy walking distance of each other around the gentle curve of an east-facing bay. You'll most probably be dropped near one of the three hotels owned by *Do Son Garden Resort and Hotels* (☎031/861272, fax 861176): the *Hai Au* and *Hoa Phuong* (both ③) are both modern blocks with comfortable rooms, though the latter offers slightly better prices and sea-view balconies; rooms in the *Garden Resort* (④), six four-bedroom villas set among flame trees and bamboo, are well appointed but not worth the extra. Budget travellers should make straight for the *Van Thong* (☎031/861331, fax 861186; ②), slightly inland at the north end of the promenade, which offers well-priced rooms set round a courtyard – even the most basic have air-con and hot water. All these hotels have reasonable **restaurants** but for more atmospheric eating try the excellent open-air restaurant in front of the *Garden Resort*, or any of the strip along the promenade.

Five hundred metres beyond Section 2, over on the other side of the peninsula, is the west-facing bay of **Section 3**. Its tiny littered beach, best appreciated from the café terrace above, is ringed by a cluster of private houses some of which offer **rooms** (①), with magnificent balconies but minimum furnishings and dodgy bathrooms. Continue for another kilometre to where the former *Hôtel de la Point* perches appropriately at the far end of the promontory. After a gleaming facelift, this 1930s building now operates as a not-very-successful, foreigners-only casino. If the hotel ever re-opens, under its new name of *Van Hoa*, its stunning position will be unbeatable.

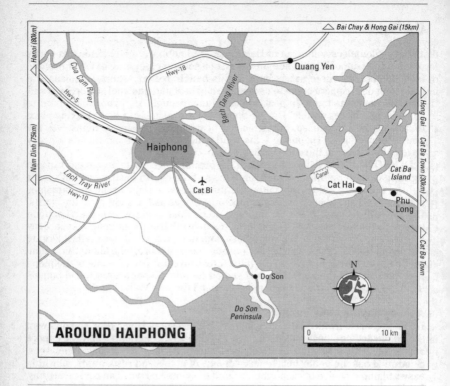

△ Bai Chay & Hong Gai (15km)

Hanoi (80km) ▷

Cua Cam River

Hwy-18

Bach Dang River

Quang Yen

Hwy-5

Nam Dinh (75km) ▷

Haiphong

Hong Gai ▷

Cat Ba Town (30km) ▷

Lach Tray River

Hwy-10

✈ Cat Bi

Canal

Cat Hai

Cat Ba Island

Phu Long

Cat Ba Town ▷

N

Do Son

Do Son Peninsula

AROUND HAIPHONG

0   10 km

Cat Ba Island

Dragon-back mountain ranges mass on the horizon 20km out of Haiphong as the ferry approaches **Cat Ba Island**. The island, the largest member of an archipelago sitting on the west of Ha Long Bay, boasts only one settlement of any size, Cat Ba Town – in reality little more than a fishing village. The rest is unspoilt and largely inaccessible, with just one paved road across a landscape of enclosed valleys and shaggily forested limestone peaks, occasionally descending to lush coastal plains. In 1986 almost half the island and adjacent waters were declared a **national park** in an effort to protect its diverse ecosystems, which range from offshore coral reefs and coastal mangrove swamps to vast tracts of tropical evergreen forest. One of the easiest and most rewarding ways to access the park is by boat from Cat Ba Town, passing through the labyrinth of **Lan Ha Bay**, a miniature version of neighbouring Ha Long Bay but which as yet receives few visitors. Other boat trips venture up into Ha Long Bay itself (see p.368), where most sights are within the scope of a day's outing, or to one of the bay's more dramatic caves, **Ho Ba Ham**. A number of islands in the area sport white coral-sand fringes where the water is noticeably cleaner than elsewhere in the bay, and even Cat Ba Town has a couple of acceptable **beaches** within walking distance.

Archeological evidence shows that humans inhabited Cat Ba's many limestone caves at least 6000 years ago. Centuries later these same caves provided the perfect war-time hideaway – the military presence on Cat Ba has always been strong, for obvious strategic reasons. When trouble with China flared up in 1979, hundreds of ethnic Chinese islanders felt compelled to flee and the exodus continued into the next decade as "boat people" sailed off in search of a better life, depleting the island's population to less than 15,000.

Getting there and around

Two public **ferries** leave **Haiphong** each day for Cat Ba (6am & 1pm; 4–5hr); they're antique vessels crammed to the limits and beyond – weather permitting, it's more comfortable travelling on the roof, and you'll get the best views. Check the ferry goes all the way to Cat Ba Town rather than just to the adjacent island of Cat Hai, which is a particularly unfriendly place with plenty of scams but no accommodation. If you do get dumped there, take the small ferry over to Phu Long village on Cat Ba Island and then get a bus (1hr) or motorbike for the last 30km to Cat Ba Town. From Haiphong the ferry chugs down the Cua Cam River against a procession of wallowing coal barges. Picking its way through a maze of sandbanks and shifting channels, the vessel crosses the **Bach Dang Estuary**, one of the most famous battle sites in Vietnamese history (see box below), before turning south across open sea to the west coast of Cat Ba Island. It's this second half of the voyage that offers the most spectacular scenery as you sail in the shadow of increasingly dramatic cliffs towards Cat Ba Town, tucked into a fold on the island's southern tip.

Ferries between Hong Gai and Haiphong call in at Cat Hai, making it possible in theory to reach Cat Ba **from Hong Gai** (see p.372), or vice versa, but the connections are dicky. If you want to attempt this route, get the early morning sailing and, if nothing turns up in Cat Hai cross over to Phu Long and head for Cat Ba Town overland. At the other extreme, a painless way to visit Cat Ba is to go with one of the travellers' cafés in Hanoi: you can combine the island with a **tour** of Ha Long Bay for just under $40 (see p.349 for more on these options).

Boat tours

Most hotels in Cat Ba Town arrange **boat tours**, with little to chose between them on price, but for the best local knowledge and some interesting variations

---

THE BATTLES OF BACH DANG RIVER

The **Vietnamese Navy** fought its two most glorious and decisive battles in the Bach Dang Estuary, east of Haiphong. The first, in 938 AD, marked the end of a thousand years of Chinese occupation when General **Ngo Quyen** led his rebels to victory, defeating a vastly superior force by means of a brilliant ruse. Waiting until high tide, General Ngo lured the **Chinese fleet** upriver over hundreds of iron-tipped stakes embedded in the estuary mud, then counter-attacked as the tide turned and drove the enemy boats back downstream to founder on the now-exposed stakes.

History repeated itself some three centuries later during the struggle to repel **Kublai Khan**'s Mongol armies. This time it was the great **Tran Hung Dao** who led the Vietnamese in a series of battles culminating in the Bach Dang River in 1288. The ingenious strategy worked just as well second time round when over four hundred vessels were lost or captured, finally seeing off the ambitious Khan.

start with the *Cat Ba Hotel* (ask for Chung). One of the most picturesque trips from Cat Ba is to sail north into Lan Ha Bay, and then either walk into the national park (see facing page) or take a half-day cruise around the maze of limestone islands, stopping at one of the pristine coral-sand beaches for a spot of swimming. The **going rate** for **boat hire** is between $3 and $7 per hour, depending on the season and your negotiating skills; for a half-day **tour** of Lan Ha Bay, you'll be paying roughly $30. Lunch on board rates an extra $2 per person.

Alternatively, it's quite feasible to explore **Ha Long Bay** (see p.368) from here, either as a round-trip or en route to Bai Chay; count on $50 for a full day, plus a little more if you want to be dropped off in Bai Chay.

Cat Ba Town

Caught between green hills and a horseshoe bay alive with coracles scurrying among multicoloured fishing boats, **CAT BA TOWN** faces west – great for sunsets over outlying islands. The town has two sections, separated by a small headland: the tourist facilities are grouped around the new ferry pier; 800m to the west lies the original, workaday fishing village with its market. Directly behind the pier is a small hill topped by the town's war memorial, erected during Ho Chi Minh's visit to the island in 1953; follow a path up the back to find a quiet, breezy spot from which to contemplate the harbour. If you prefer a close-up view of life afloat, hire one of the **coracles**, essentially water-taxis, that hover round the harbour steps; with hard bargaining an hour should cost $1–2.

A set of steep steps just east of the *Cat Ba Hotel* leads to two small, sandy **beaches** hiding on the far side of the peninsula which forms the harbour's easterly arm. The first you come to is the more popular beach, but chances are you'll still have it to yourself outside the Vietnamese peak holiday season of June to early September, and boasts a drinks stall plus some tatty beach huts. Another steep climb, from beside the stall, dissuades most people from continuing to the second beach; you're not missing much, though – it's bigger and wilder but has more litter and no shade.

Practicalities

Cat Ba Town has two ferry piers: for most of the year **ferries** use the new, harbour pier but between May and August, and whenever strong westerly winds blow, they sail round to an old pier on the island's east side, where a bus waits to bring you to the hotels (10min). The town's public **bus** stand is in the village centre near the market place, from where two buses a day ply the island's only road to Phu Long village (1hr; $2). However, for serious exploration, your best bet is a **motorbike**: xe oms congregate round the market place ($2 to the national park; $4 to Phu Long) and rental outlets are ubiquitous. Hotels and restaurants will **change money**, but cash only and at poor rates, so it's best to come prepared. Walk uphill from the market place to find the **post office** on the left.

ACCOMMODATION

Thanks to a low-key building boom, **accommodation** on Cat Ba represents good value: though these are basic budget hotels, they're generally clean, comfortable and most have hot water. Officially all hotels must charge $10 per room (up to 3 beds) in winter and $15 in the peak summer period, but off-season you'll find the majority are willing to bargain. Most are a stone's throw from the new pier and within earshot of the 6am-ferry claxon, but quietest is the well-established *Cat Ba* (☎031/888243). In fact this is three hotels strung out along the seafront to the right of the pier: the *Chua Dong* has the most picturesque site at the far end, but the *Gieng Ngoc*, middle of the three, offers the best rooms. Other recommended hotels, all right by the pier, are the squeaky-clean *Hoang Huong* (☎031/888274), the *Family Hotel Quang Duc* (☎031/888231), friendly and with good local knowledge, and the nicely laid-back *Van Anh* (☎031/888201); these last two both have great roof-terraces. Finally, those who want more atmosphere and are immune to karaoke should try the only hotel in the old town, the *Quang Huan*, also called the *Mini-hotel* (☎031/888225), close to the harbour front and a touch cheaper, owing to shared bathroom facilities. Note that, as yet, the island doesn't have mains electricity and hotels rely on generators, running them for a few hours each evening; a torch comes in handy, especially for those early-morning ferries.

EATING

Despite a limited choice of **restaurants** the quality is excellent and not expensive. Tables set up outside the *Gieng Ngoc Hotel* are a popular spot on fine evenings, facing a harbour full of dancing lights. The food is equally impressive – the day's catch of squid fried with fresh vegetables, or juicy peppered prawns – and few people venture any further, but *Restaurant Huu Dung*, up the road beside the *Van Anh Hotel*, extends a warm welcome and an illustrated menu of soups and seafood, while *Hoang Thu Restaurant*, beside the *Mini-hotel*, is also worth a try.

Across the island to Cat Ba National Park

One of Cat Ba's main draws is its rugged unspoilt scenery. A recommended day's outing is to follow the island's virtually empty road at least as far as the National Park Headquarters, if not the full 30km to Phu Long village on the west coast. The road climbs sharply out of Cat Ba Town, giving views over distant islands and glimpses of secluded coves, and then follows a series of high valleys. After 8km look out on the right for the distinctive **Quan Y Cave**, a gaping mouth embellished with concrete, not far from the road. During the American War the cave became an army hospital big enough to treat 150 patients at a time; for the moment you can't go inside.

Another 8km further on brings you to the gates of **Cat Ba National Park** ($1, plus parking fee). The park's most famous inhabitant is a unique sub-species of the endangered golden-headed langur (*vooc* in Vietnamese), a monkey found only in five isolated communities in the limestone forests of Vietnam and southern China. So far over 700 plant species have been catalogued in the park, including more than one hundred of medicinal value. Although there's no compulsion, it's worth taking a guide into the park ($5 for up to one day), despite occasional incidences of guides demanding more money in mid-trek – or being plain uninterested. Not that it's incredibly wild and woolly, but people have got seriously lost attempting to follow the unmarked paths. With or without a guide, you'll need good boots, lots of water, potent mosquito-repellent, and a compass.

The most popular route is an eight-kilometre walk, two to three hours of hard going, through an area of *kim giao* forest (commonly known as the "chopstick tree" because its wood, said to be sensitive to poisons, was used for the emperors' chopsticks) as far as Ech Lake – most of the frogs (*ech*) for which it's named are presumed to have been eaten. From there an interesting option, offered as a tour by the *Cat Ba Hotel*, is to continue east for another couple of hours to Viet Hai village and the coast, returning to Cat Ba by boat through Lan Ha Bay; meals and accommodation in the village can also be arranged. With luck, on the way back you may even see a langur – they keep mainly to inaccessible cliffs around the shore.

Back at the park gates, the cross-island road continues westwards and drops down onto a pancake-flat coastal plain, home to mangrove swamps and a collection of fish-farms. The last few kilometres are unexciting and it's easy to miss the village of **Phu Long** completely, a few stalls beside a bridge, and to carry straight on to where the road ends at the Phu Long–Cat Hai jetty.

Ha Long Bay

From Guilin in China to Thailand's Phang Nga Bay, the limestone outcrops which typify the scenery of **Ha Long Bay** are not uncommon, but nowhere else do they feature on such an impressive scale: an estimated 1600 islands pepper 1500 square kilometres of Ha Long Bay itself, and two thousand more punctuate the coast towards China. Local legend tells of a celestial dragon and her children, sent by the Jade Emperor to stop an invasion, who spat out great quantities of pearls to form islands and razor-sharp mountain chains in the path of the enemy fleet. After the victory the dragons, enchanted by their creation, decided to stay on, giving rise to the name *Ha Long* ("dragon descending"), and to the inevitable sightings of sea-monsters.

In 1469 King Le Thanh Tong paid a visit to Ha Long Bay and was so inspired by the scenery that he wrote a poem, likening the islands to pieces on a chess board; ever since, visitors have struggled to capture the mystery of this fantasy world. Nineteenth-century Europeans compared the islands to Tuscan cathedrals, while a local brochure opts for meditative "grey-haired fairies" and the bay is frequently referred to as the eighth natural wonder of the world. With so much hyperbole, some find Ha Long disappointing, especially since this stretch of coast is also one of Vietnam's more industrialized regions with a major shipping lane cutting right across the bay to Hong Gai port. The winter weather is also a factor to bear in mind; February and March are the worst months but from November on there can be odd days of cold, drizzly weather when the splendour and romance of the bay is harder to appreciate.

The epicentre of tourism in Ha Long Bay is **Bai Chay**, a beach resort on the north shore, which offers a good choice of accommodation and restaurants plus hordes of boatmen, all conveniently at hand. For those in search of more local colour, or who are put off by Bai Chay's overwhelming devotion to tourism, there are a couple of attractive alternatives. The first is simply to hop across a narrow channel east of Bai Chay to **Hong Gai**, a town which provides only basic tourist facilities but which has a bustling, workaday atmosphere. The other option is to tackle the bay from the south and base yourself on Cat Ba Island (see p.364), with the advantages of a scenic ferry-ride from Haiphong and accommodation located on the edge of an attractive fishing village – but lacking the range of facilities available in Bai Chay.

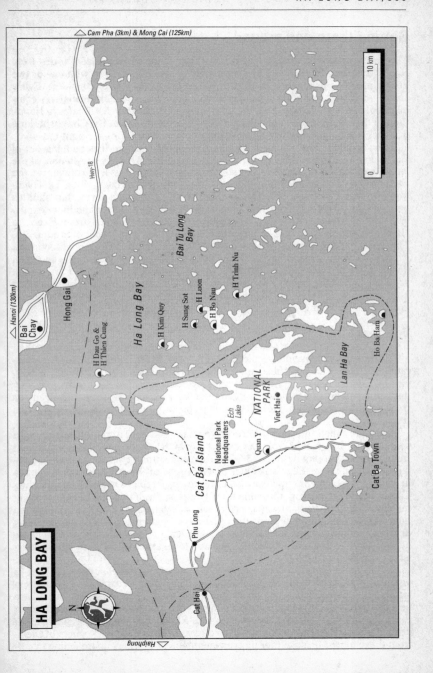

Getting there and around

The vast majority of visitors to Ha Long Bay come on **organized tours** from Hanoi, travelling by road and staying a night or two in Bai Chay, with one or two boat trips in the package (see "Boat trips" below, for factors to consider). Every Hanoi tour agent offers Ha Long Bay excursions (see p.349 for details). In terms of straight cost, it's hard to beat the tours offered by the travellers' cafés in Hanoi, though there have been complaints of chaotic organization in Bai Chay, with long waits for boats and insufficient accommodation on board for overnight tours.

If you'd rather do it yourself, there are frequent **bus** services running out of Hanoi and Haiphong to Bai Chay; these pull in at the Western bus station, at the far end of Ha Long Avenue. Coming from the north, buses terminate at the Eastern bus station; from here, Hong Gai centre is 1km back along Le Thanh Tong, or you can cross over to Bai Chay on the passenger ferry that shuttles between the two bus stations (see map on pp.374–375). A slower and more expensive, but far more interesting approach is to take the **train** from Hanoi to Haiphong and then the public **ferry** to Hong Gai (for a total cost of around $9). The ferry passes through some impressive scenery on the bay's northwest fringes – a dawn voyage on the 6am sailing is particularly stunning – and then docks in Hong Gai's eastern harbour. (See "Travel details" on p.377 for outline schedules of all these services.) Ha Long Bay can also be covered by chartered boat from Cat Ba Town (see p.366), allowing easy access to its less-visited southern fringes, including some of the most unusual formations in the bay.

Boat trips

It's not difficult to **charter** a boat locally, though it works out more expensive than a tour unless you can find people to share costs. Most hotels and some restaurants can help with boat hire, as can the tourist offices (see "Listings", p.375). However, you'll usually get the best rates by going direct to the boatmen: if they don't find you first, head down to the tourist wharves on **Bai Chay** waterfront, or try around the harbour in **Hong Gai**; see p.365 for information on arranging trips **from Cat Ba**.

Rates are much the same wherever you base yourself. In the off-season, with some skilled bargaining, you can expect to pay $4–5 per hour for a small boat (maximum 10 people), rising to $6–7 in the peak summer season and on holiday weekends. An interesting variation is to **overnight on board** (take warm clothes in winter), which means you can also cover the bay's southern reaches, including Cat Ba Island, in one trip; the same hourly rates apply. If you don't fancy sleeping on board, one full day's voyage is preferable to two half-days, as it takes about an hour to get in among the islands. In a **full day**'s boat tour (6–8hr) from Bai Chay or Hong Gai, you'll be able to explore a good deal of the western side, visit some of the caves described below and perhaps take a swing through the eastern islands on the way home.

Engine sizes vary, so if speed is of the essence, make sure your boat is equipped with a powerful engine. **Meals** on board cost an extra $2–4 per person for lunch or dinner, depending on the amount of fresh seafood you opt for, and are usually excellent. Note that you should agree the itinerary in advance and pay at the end of the trip; you may also want to take a look at the boat beforehand, especially if you're going to overnight. There have been occasional reports of thefts from these tourist boats, either by crew-members or hawkers approaching in coracles; as a precaution, have someone stay on the boat all the time or, if your hotel has one, leave valuables in their safe.

The caves and islands

Ha Long Bay is split in two by a wide channel running north–south: the larger, western portion contains the most dramatic scenery and best caves, while to the east lies an attractive area of smaller islands, known as Bai Tu Long or "children of the dragon", though with fewer specific sights. The bay's most famous cave is also the closest to Bai Chay: **Hang Dau Go** ("Grotto of the Wooden Stakes") is where General Tran Hung Dao amassed hundreds of stakes deep inside the cave's third and largest chamber prior to the Bach Dang River battle of 1288 (see box on p.365). Like many of the older caves, Dau Go is marred by rubbish and graffiti but is worth a stop because the same island boasts one of the most beautiful caves. A steep climb up 50m to the entrance of **Hang Thien Cung** ("Grotto of the Heavenly Palace") is rewarded by a rectangular chamber 250m long and 20m high with a text-book display of sparkling stalactites and stalagmites – supposedly petrified characters of the Taoist Heavenly Court.

Continuing south, past hidden bays, needle-sharp ridges and cliffs of ribbed limestone, you sail into an area particularly rich in caves. First choice should be one of the recent finds: **Hang Kim Quy** ("Golden Turtle Grotto"), **Ho Dong Tien** ("Grotto of the Fairy Lake") and the enchanting **Dong Me Cung** ("Grotto of the Labyrinth"). The yawning mouth of **Hang Bo Nau**, ringed with a flotilla of sampans hawking coral and soft drinks, is of fleeting interest as you move on to **Hang Sung Sot**, with good views from the steps and a scramble up to a high second chamber. Next comes the most remarkable in this group, **Hang Luon**, a hollow island accessed via a half-submerged tunnel-cave 30m long: you can take one of the waiting coracles – $1 per person for the return trip, though a group might be able to bargain; or, if it's warm enough, take the plunge and swim through. You emerge into a crater-like lagoon encircled by towering cliffs which echo to the cries of exotic birds in a fair imitation of a lost world. Other caves close by, such as **Hang Trong** ("Drum Grotto") and **Hang Trinh Nu** ("Virgin's Grotto"), are of no particular merit and awash with litter; from here it's about ninety minutes' sail back to Bai Chay.

Of the far-flung sights, **Hang Hanh** is one of the more adventurous day-trips from Bai Chay: the tide must be exactly right (at half-tide) to allow a coracle access to the two-kilometre-long tunnel-cave. Note that the hire of a coracle costs an additional $10 and that powerful torches or caving lamps are also useful here. Finally, Dau Bo Island, on the southeastern edge of Ha Long Bay, encloses **Ho Ba Ham** ("Three Tunnel Lake"), a shallow lagoon wrapped round with limestone walls and connected to the sea by three low-ceilinged tunnels that are only navigable by sampan at low tide. This cave is sometimes included in two-day excursions out of Bai Chay but is easiest to arrange from Cat Ba (see p.365).

Since 1994 fishermen have discovered several **new caves**, prompted by a local initiative granting them the right to charge entry (generally less than $1) for a specified time (usually 3–6 months) on condition that they install lights, stairways and so forth. For up-to-date information and recommendations, the best people to ask are the boatmen themselves – several of whom speak good English – or at the local tourist offices (see "Listings", p.375). A few caverns are still unlit, so take a torch. And if you intend to explore beyond the cave mouths, which usually means scrambling over muddy rocks and through narrow passages, wear shoes with a good grip.

Bai Chay and Hong Gai

In 1994 Hong Gai, Bai Chay and the surrounding districts were amalgamated to create a new provincial capital called **Ha Long City**, the name now used on official documents. For the moment, however, locals still stick to the old names – as do ferry services, minibuses and so on – since this is a useful way to distinguish between the two towns of Bai Chay and Hong Gai, lying on either side of the narrow Cua Luc channel, each with its own distinct character.

Neon signs and flashing fairylights blaze out at night along the **BAI CHAY** waterfront, advertising north Vietnam's most developed resort, though still modest and not too seedy, and with a picturesque backdrop of wooded hills. Apart from strolling the seafront boulevard and a quick look at its very indifferent beach, Bai Chay has nothing to distract you from the main business of touring the bay. **HONG GAI**, on the other hand, has a compelling, raw vitality plus an attractive harbour to the east, crowded with scurrying coracles. Ignoring the western districts, grey with coal dust from the depots surrounding Hong Gai docks, it's worth spending an hour or so wandering the harbourside paths where a picturesque village lies beached-up under the limestone knuckle of Nui Bai Tho. This mountain is named after a collection of poems (*bai tho*) penned in praise of the beauty of Ha Long Bay; these are carved into the rock, kicking off with King Le Thanh Tong's in 1468. Following the cliff-side path clockwise from Long Tien Street, you pass several of the weathered inscriptions as you walk through the fishing village, though no one seems quite sure which are the royal verses.

Accommodation

Despite a rapid increase in the provision of hotels, there are still temporary **room shortages**, particularly during the Vietnamese summer season (June through early Sept) and on holiday weekends. However, during the quieter winter months, when most foreign tourists visit Ha Long Bay, this is less of a problem and room **prices** in the mini-hotels drop (winter rates are given below; mini-hotels may add up to 50 percent during peak periods).

The biggest choice of accommodation is to be found in **Bai Chay**, particularly on Vuon Dao, where it's possible to get real bargains in the off-season, thanks to a building boom that's driven prices down, quality up and aesthetics out. Much of the accommodation in **Hong Gai**, on the other hand, is overpriced and basic, sometimes to the point of squalour. However, there are a number of acceptable budget places which are worth a look before resorting to Bai Chay.

BAI CHAY

Bach Dang, Ha Long Ave (☎033/846330, fax 846026). One of the few hotels at the east end of Bai Chay, now rather aged but clean and friendly. Big rooms, all with sea-view balconies, TV and IDD. ③

Ha Long 1, 2 and 3, Ha Long Ave (☎033/846321, fax 846318). A trio of well-established hotels set among trees. *Ha Long 1* (⑤) offers Bai Chay's most appealing accommodation, in a converted French villa built in 1937. The place has loads of atmosphere but, with only 16 rooms, reservation is a must. Both *Ha Long 2* (④) and *Ha Long 3* (④) are newer blocks popular with tour groups; rooms are furnished to a reasonable standard, with great views from the higher rooms in no. 3, but overpriced.

Heritage, Ha Long Ave (☎033/846888, fax 846999). The Heritage group have revamped an old hotel to create Bai Chay's first truly deluxe accommodation. International ambience doesn't come cheap, though. ⑤

Hoa Binh (*Peace*), Vuon Dao (☎033/846009). One of the better mini-hotels on Vuon Dao, this a clean and welcoming place, with boats for hire. Prices are standard, but the rooms are a cut above the rest. ②

Huong Tram, Ha Long Ave (☎033/846365). A friendly mini-hotel, newly refurbished and with good views. Signposted up a steep track, about 5 minutes' walk east of the post office, this place also offers reasonably priced boat hire plus reliable information about the bay. ②

Minh Tuan, Ho Xuan Huong (☎033/846200). The only cheap beds near the bus station, hidden down a side-street among attractive old houses. Ten small but clean rooms, each with bathroom and hot water, though some lack windows. ①

Ngoc Mai, Vuon Dao (☎033/846123). A reasonably priced, well-run and homely mini-hotel close to the bottom end of Vuon Dao, but far enough from the karaoke cafés. ②

Thanh An, Vuon Dao (☎033/846959). This well-priced hotel claims to be the highest in Bai Chay. Vast, spotless rooms make the walk uphill worth the effort, as do excellent views from the front balconies. Just don't think about typhoons. ②

Yen Ngoc, Ha Long Ave (☎033/846945). A mini-hotel up on the headland, next to the *Huong Tram*. Clean good-value rooms, plus boat tours at competitive prices. ①

HONG GAI

Hai Van, 76 Le Thanh Tong (☎033/826279). A small, friendly guesthouse that offers the best-value accommodation among a strip in central Hong Gai. Rooms are nothing to write home about, but they're clean and come with TV and air-con. ②

Hien Cat, 252 Ben Tau (☎033/827417). Conveniently located right by the ferry pier, this small, spruce guesthouse boasts harbour views from the spacious top-floor room. Smallish rooms lower down aren't bad either, with mini-balcony and use of the most scenic bathroom in town. Meals are available on request and the owner can help with boat hire. ②

Huong Duong, 82 Le Thanh Tong (☎033/827269). If the *Hai Van* is full, try this small guesthouse nearby. The furnishings are aged but well cared for, the bathrooms are clean, and it also offers TV and air-con. ②

Queen, 70 Le Thanh Tong (☎033/826383). Supposedly Hong Gai's poshest accommodation, offering telephone, TV, fridge and air-con. The rooms are small and dark, but at least well kept, and some benefit from sea views. ③

Eating and drinking

Fresh **seafood** is the natural speciality of Hà Long Bay, with excellent lobster, crab and the gamut of fish on offer. Considering the number of tourists visiting Bai Chay, its choice of restaurants is surprisingly meagre, but on the whole the quality of food is high and prices aren't unreasonable. Over in Hong Gai, there are plenty of cheap and cheerful places to choose from.

BAI CHAY

Despite the onslaught of passing traffic and postcard sellers, the most popular places to eat in Bai Chay are a strip of **restaurants** on Ha Long Avenue between the post office and the *Heritage Hotel*. There's nothing much to choose between them, but the *Van Song Restaurant*, at the western end, is recommended for good-value meals and a genial host (who's also an expert on Ha Long's far-flung islands). Alternatively, the *Binh Minh* and *Phuong Vi*, two restaurants nearer the post office, are safe bets and serve decent portions, while cheaper, local eating houses are round the corner on Vuon Dao – the *Anh Tuyet* is clean and friendly. Back on the main road, *Café Indochine* is the place to go for **yoghurts**, fresh milk and a range of **snacks**; it's also recommended for local information and boat hire. At the east end of Bai Chay, the choice is more limited: cheap *com* and *pho* **stalls** cluster round the bus station; otherwise there are two surprisingly reasonable restaurants serving wholesome food, the *Trung Duc* and *Bien Xanh*, a few metres further east.

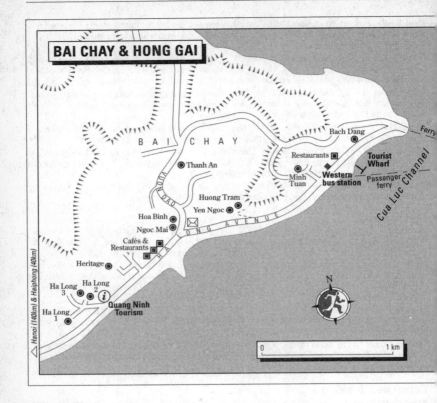

HONG GAI

The best eating in Hong Gai is at the market **food stalls**, where ingredients come fresh from fishing boats in the harbour next door. Otherwise, try one of the many street kitchens on Long Tien or nearby Le Quy Don. *Pho* fans will appreciate an unnamed place behind the Qunimex building; walking east from the *Huong Duong* guesthouse, it's the first stall on the right, after a café. Prices are slightly above the norm, but then so is the quality.

Listings

Banks and exchange The larger hotels in Bai Chay and both post offices change cash, but the only place to handle travellers' cheques is Hong Gai's *Vietcombank*, at the east end of Le Thanh Tong.

Buses Hanoi and Haiphong services depart from the Western bus station, those for Mong Cai from the Eastern. Private minibus services to Hanoi ($4–5) usually wait in the car park opposite the Western terminus, or depart in the early hours from the bottom of Vuon Dao – check with your hotel.

Coal sculptures Examples of this Hong Gai handicraft are sold in a couple of shops opposite the Qunimex Department Store on Le Thanh Tong.

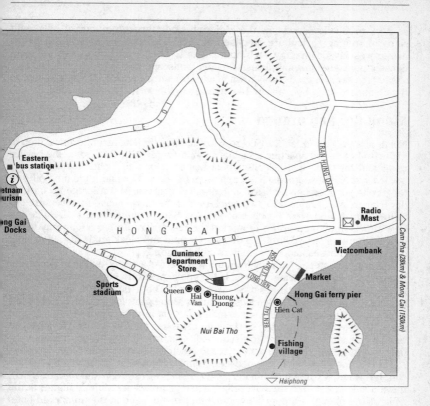

Ferries Boats to Haiphong sail 4 times a day (6am, 8.30am, 11am, 4pm) from the Hong Gai pier; if you're aiming for Cat Ba, take the first morning ferry and hope you connect with one of the Haiphong–Cat Ba Town sailings in Cat Hai (see p.365 for more).

Tourist information *Quang Ninh Tourism* (☎033/846274), beside the entrance to the *Ha Long Hotel*, is the most helpful office; if you're in Hong Gai, *Vietnamtourism* at 2 Le Thanh Tong (☎033/827250), next to the Eastern bus station, is more convenient.

To the Chinese border

There's little to tempt you up Highway 18 to Mong Cai, unless you're looking for a back road to Lang Son or an adventurous route into China (see p.349 for general information on crossing into China). The first stretch with views over Ha Long Bay is promising enough, though the road is choked with trucks from the huge open-cast coal mines of **Cam Pha**, where the whole landscape is shrouded in grey dust. You wouldn't want to linger, but the scenes of masked dock-hands ferrying sacks onto blackened barges or grading the coal with hand-held sieves possess a certain post-apocalyptic power. About 20km beyond Cam Pha the scenery gradually revives, as the highway winds through a spur of hills, with signs of shifting agriculture practised by local Thai people, while down below mangroves invade marshy, saltwater lagoons. Then suddenly you're out onto densely populated coastal plains, a fertile landscape painted every conceivable shade of green, where the only town of any size since Cam Pha, **Tien Yen**, marks the turning to Lang Son, a slow 100km away to the west on a rough road.

Mong Cai and around

North of Tien Yen, it's all flat rice-growing country until an incongruous clump of high-rise hotels and apartment blocks announces **MONG CAI**. Since the border re-opened for trade in 1992, Mong Cai has been booming and its markets are stuffed with Chinese goods, from apples and beer to TVs and huge pink piles of toilet rolls. An open border has also generated local tourist traffic, mostly curious day-trippers from China who do a quick tour of the markets and then venture out to the dismal windswept beaches of **Tra Co**, 8km to the southeast. Despite the best efforts of the authorities to market the resort, Tra Co has a long way to go; its attractions so far are limited to hard grey sand and bleak mud-flats at low tide, a straggle of houses and a coal-miners' holiday home.

Highway 18 enters Mong Cai from the west across a bridge and then peters out in a large, open area. Straight ahead is the public **minibus station** while the **post office** and **bank** (exchanges US$ – cash only) both lie on the south of this unnamed "square". A roof-top clock identifies Mong Cai's focal point, the **covered market**, overflowing into the surrounding streets in a frenzy of commerce that continues late into the evening by the light of hissing paraffin lamps. The **Chinese border** is just 1km away to the north; walk from the bridge through the goods-only bus stand and then follow the river to reach the **border gate** (7am–5pm).

There's not much to choose between Mong Cai's **hotels**, all of which offer air-con, hot water, TV and telephone. Best value is the *Huu Nghi* (no phone; ②–③), down a side-street near the post office, whereas prices are slightly higher at the *Dong A* (no phone; ③), opposite the minibus station, and at the unmarked hotel on the road to the border (no phone; ③). Last resort are several expensive and squalid guesthouses around the central "square", all around the ② mark.

Eating is a happier proposition: streets near the covered market turn into open-air **restaurants** in the evening, each lantern-lit stall thronged with customers. Alternatively, next to the *Dong A* is a friendly restaurant with a display of fresh ingredients to choose from, and cold beers.

travel details

Buses

*It's almost impossible to give the **frequency** with which buses run. Though scheduled, long-distance public buses won't depart if empty. Moreover, private services, often minibuses or pick-ups, ply more popular routes, and depart only when they have enough passengers to make the journey worthwhile. It's advisable to start your journey early – most long-distance departures leave between 5 and 9am, and few run after midday. **Journey times** can also vary; figures below show the normal length of time you can expect the journey to take.*

Bai Chay to: Hanoi (4hr); Haiphong (3hr).
Haiphong to: Bai Chay (3hr); Hanoi (2hr 30min); Nam Dinh (4hr 30min); Ninh Binh (5hr 30min).
Hong Gai to: Mong Cai (5hr).
Mong Cai to: Hanoi (9hr); Hong Gai (5hr).

Trains

Haiphong to: Hanoi (5–6 daily; 2hr–2hr 30min).

Ferries

Cat Ba to: Haiphong (2 daily; 3hr 30min).
Haiphong to: Cat Ba (2 daily; 3hr 30min); Hong Gai (4 daily; 3hr 30min).
Hong Gai to: Haiphong (4 daily; 3hr 30min).

Flights

Haiphong to: Da Nang (3 weekly; 1hr); Ho Chi Minh (1–2 daily; 2hr).

CHAPTER EIGHT

THE FAR NORTH

V ietnam fans out above Hanoi, like the head of a giant pin, to attain its maximum width of 600km, the majority of it a mountainous buffer zone wrapped around the Red River Delta. Two arteries carry road and rail links north from the capital towards China and the border crossings of Lao Cai and Dong Dang. The rest of the region is mostly wild and inaccessible, yet contains some of Vietnam's most awe-inspiring scenery, sparsely populated by a fascinating mosaic of **ethnic minorities**. Most impressive on both counts is the northwest region where Vietnam's highest mountain range and its tallest peak, Fan Si Pan, rise abruptly from the Red River Valley. Within the shadow of Fan Si Pan lies **Sa Pa**, an easily accessible former French hill station, now famous for its weekend market patronized by minority peoples from miles around, and for its superb scenery with opportunities for trekking out to isolated hamlets. The attractions of Sa Pa and the historic battlefield of **Dien Bien Phu**, site of the Viet Minh's decisive victory over French forces in 1954, draw most tourists to the northwest region. However, the little-travelled provinces of east of the Red River Valley also deserve attention, especially the scenery and minority peoples of Cao Bang Province and along the Chinese border. This region is also home to **Ba Be National Park**, where Vietnam's largest natural lake hides among forested limestone crags and impenetrable jungle. Not surprisingly, infrastructure throughout the northern mountains is weak and facilities tend to be thin on the ground.

Some recent history

Remote uplands, dense vegetation and rugged terrain suited to guerrilla activities, plus a safe haven across the border, made this region the perfect place from which to orchestrate Vietnam's independence movement. For a while in 1941, **Ho Chi Minh** hid in Pac Bo Cave on the Chinese frontier, later moving south to Tuyen Quang Province, from where the Viet Minh launched their August Revolution in 1945. These northern provinces were the first to be **liberated** from French rule, but over in the northwest some minority groups, notably from among the Thai, Hmong and Muong, supported the French authorities and it took the Viet Minh until 1952 to gain control of the area. But then, two years later, they staged their great victory over the French at Dien Bien Phu, close to the Lao border. In recognition of these areas' strategic importance and the need to secure their allegiance, soon after Independence Ho Chi Minh created two Autonomous Regions, granting the minorities a degree of **self-government**. In 1975, however, the two regions were broken-up and relegated to the status of ordinary provinces. At the same time the government tried to **assimilate** the minorities into Vietnamese life, though with less success here than elsewhere in Vietnam.

During the late 1970s **Sino-Vietnamese** relations became increasingly sour for various reasons, not least Vietnam's invasion of Cambodia. Things came to a head on February 17, 1979 when the Chinese decided to "teach Vietnam a lesson" – in

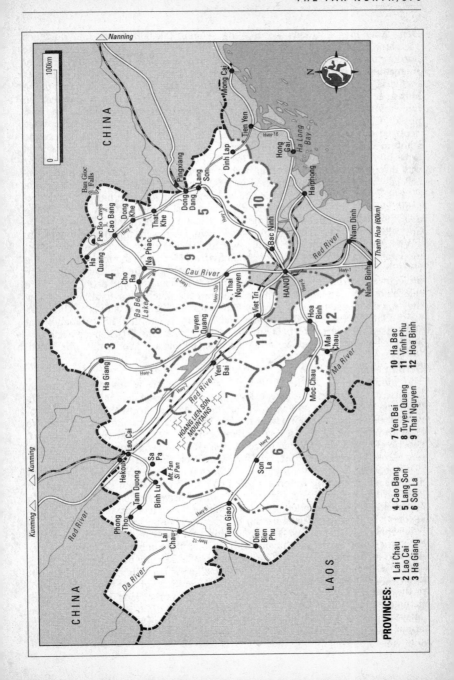

PROVINCES:

1 Lai Chau
2 Lao Cai
3 Ha Giang

4 Cao Bang
5 Lang Son
6 Son La

7 Yen Bai
8 Tuyen Quang
9 Thai Nguyen

10 Ha Bac
11 Vinh Phu
12 Hoa Binh

Deng Xiao Ping's famous words – by sending 200,000 troops into northern Vietnam. The Chinese Army savaged the border region, destroying most of the border towns as well as bridges, roads and crops, but the battle-hardened Vietnamese Army proved they had few lessons to learn, and seventeen days later the invasion force was on its way home, some 20,000 short. Though much of the infrastructural and political damage from the war has been repaired, unmarked minefields along 1000km of frontier pose a more intractable problem. The first phase of mine-clearance was completed in 1995 when 2000 hectares were declared safe and 9000 displaced families returned to their land; making safe the whole area could take several more years. The **border war** put a damper on local cross-border trade but it didn't take long before the smugglers were picking their way through anti-tank mines and barbed wire. In 1989 business resumed semi-officially and was fully normalized in 1992: rice, wheat, metals and ready-made clothes are exported to southern China, in exchange for beer, bicycles, and electronic goods – and an increasingly important local tourist industry is developing alongside. Meanwhile, **smuggling** of electrical equipment into Vietnam continues, with rice and even cars (highly taxed commodities in China) creeping north.

Vietnam is desperately short of power and these relatively sparsely populated mountain areas offer potential for cheap **hydro-electricity**, though so far only the Hoa Binh dam has been built, flooding vast stretches of the Da River Valley. The project was a disaster for the more than 50,000 Thai and Hmong people who were relocated without adequate compensation or even much consideration as to how they were supposed to earn a living. Now a second Da River dam is on the cards for the late 1990s, feasibility studies and funding permitting. It's estimated that 500 square kilometres will be inundated, displacing at least 70,000 people and wiping Lai Chau town off the map – they say it will be managed better this time round.

Getting around

The mountains of northern Vietnam remain relatively unexplored, largely because of the limited road network and the difficulties of getting around by public transport. For the moment, exploration focuses on **two main** navigable **routes**: one round the northwest linking Sa Pa, Lai Chau and Son La, and the other through the northeast via Cao Bang and Lang Son. These routes, which are described in this chapter, can be combined (without returning to Hanoi) by cutting across between Yen Phu and Thai Nguyen on Highway 13a.

It's possible to travel through the northern provinces using local buses but, if finances allow, **renting a vehicle** gives you more freedom to stop at villages or jaunt off along side-tracks. Either a four-wheel drive jeep or Landcruiser, or a motorbike, is recommended; the cost of hiring a jeep and driver (for 3 to 4 passengers) in Hanoi averages around $60 per day, while a motorbike should be between $6 and $12 per day. When **planning** your **route**, note that you'll only find accommodation in the main towns, with the odd place in between; base your itinerary on an average speed of 30km per hour. Whether you travel by public transport or with your own vehicle, you need to allow at least six days' actual **travelling time** to cover the northwestern region; by cutting out side-trips to Dien Bien Phu and Mai Chau you can reduce this to a minimum of four days on the road. Touring the northeast requires four days if you stop off at Ba Be Lake, or three otherwise. Bear in mind, however, that travelling these roads is unpredictable, especially during the rains (see below), and it's advisable to allow some **flexibility** in your programme.

If you've got only limited time, Sa Pa, Mai Chau and Ba Be National Park make rewarding two- or three-day **excursions out of Hanoi**, either by public transport or hired vehicle. The other alternative is to join an organized tour with one of Hanoi's travellers' cafés (see p.347 and 349 for details).

When to go

The **best time** to visit the northern mountains is from September through November or from March to May, when the weather is fairly settled with dry sunny days and clear cold nights. **Winters** can be pretty chilly, especially in the northeast where night frosts are not uncommon from December to February, but the compensation is daybreak mists and breathtaking, sunrise views high above valleys filled with early-morning lakes of cloud. The **rainy season** lasts from May to September, peaking in July and August, when heavy rains wash out bridges, turn unsealed roads into quagmires and throw in the occasional landslide for good measure. Peak season for foreign tourists is from September through November, while the rainy summer months of July and August are when Hanoians head up to the mountains to escape the stifling heat of the delta.

THE ETHNIC MINORITIES

Somewhere around five million minority people (nearly two-thirds of Vietnam's total) live in the northern uplands, mostly in isolated villages. The largest ethnic groups are Thai and Muong in the northwest, Tay and Nung in the northeast, and Hmong and Dao dispersed throughout the region. Historically, all the peoples of northern Vietnam migrated from southern China at various times throughout history: those who arrived first, notably the Tay and Thai, settled in the fertile valleys where they now lead a relatively prosperous existence, whereas late arrivals, such as groups of Hmong and Dao, were left to eke out a living on the inhospitable higher slopes (for more on these diverse groups, see *Contexts*, p.438). Despite government efforts to integrate them into the Vietnamese community, minorities in these remote areas continue to follow a way of life little changed over the centuries. For an insight into the minorities' traditional cultures and highly varied styles of dress, visit the informative **Museum of the Nationalities of Vietnam** in Thai Nguyen (see p.398) before setting off into the mountains.

Visiting minority villages

For many people, one of the highlights of travelling in the far north of Vietnam is the experience of visiting minority villages. This is easiest with your own **transport**. If you're reliant on public services, you'll need to allow more time but, basing yourself in the main towns, it's still possible to get out to traditional villages – notably around Sa Pa, Son La, Mai Chau and Cao Bang, and even to **stay overnight**. Alternatively, a popular, hassle-free option is to join one of the **organized trips** offered by Hanoi tour agencies (see p.349). The usual destinations are Sa Pa, coinciding with the weekly market, or Mai Chau, and the standard package includes guided visits to at least two different minorities plus, in the case of Mai Chau, a night in a stilthouse. The four-day Sa Pa tour costs roughly $50 per person, while two days in Mai Chau is priced at around $25.

If at all possible, it's preferable to visit the minority villages as part of a **small group**, ideally four people or less, as this causes least disruption and allows for

VILLAGE ETIQUETTE

Behaviour that we take for granted may cause offence to some ethnic minority people; remember you're a guest. Apart from being sensitive to the situation and keeping an open mind, the following simple rules should be observed when visiting the ethnic minority areas.

• **Dress modestly**, in long trousers or skirt and T-shirt or shirt.

• Be sensitive to people's wishes when taking **photographs**, particularly of older people; avoid taking close-up shots.

• Only go **inside a house** when invited and remove your shoes before entering.

• Small **gifts**, such as writing materials. are always welcome, although there is a view that this can foster begging. A compromise is to **buy** locally produced **craftwork**, such as embroidery or textiles; note, though, that **jewellery** is usually part of the bride-price and that purchase of antique pieces contributes to the decline of traditional practices.

• Growing and using **opium** is illegal in Vietnam and is punished with a fine or prison sentence; do not encourage its production by buying or smoking opium.

greater communication. There's a whole debate about the **ethics** of cultural tourism and its negative impact on traditional ways of life. Most villagers are genuinely welcoming and hospitable to foreigners, appreciating contact with Westerners and the material benefits which they bring; tourism may also help to protect the minorities against enforced Vietnamization, at least in the short-term, by encouraging greater respect for cultural diversity. Nonetheless, it's important to take a responsible attitude, and to follow the guidelines on etiquette outlined above.

Trekking practicalities

It's only in the last few years that foreigners have been permitted to stay in minority villages, which has opened up the possibility of trekking, and created a small industry focused on Sa Pa. As yet the only **organized treks** are those run by Hanoi's travellers' cafés, which normally visit two or three minorities in a three-day trek, costing around $60 per person for transport, guide and accommodation. When choosing a tour, note that "trekking" sometimes simply means staying in a Sa Pa guesthouse and walking out to minority villages during the day, so check the details carefully. Make sure you know how much walking is required, and over what kind of terrain – and ask about the catering arrangements.

At present, other trekking opportunities are limited. In Hanoi you can arrange an individual programme through a **tour agent**, though it's often difficult to find a guide with a good level of English who is also familiar with the villages and the minorities' cultural traditions. **Tourist offices** in the provincial capitals may be able to help with ad hoc arrangements, if you're prepared to take a chance on the availability of English-speaking guides. Sometimes hotels are a better bet, particularly in Sa Pa where most **guesthouses** offer guides and should be able to suggest an interesting programme. Finally, it is possible to find your own accommodation in the villages by just turning up, but if you go with a local guide you're less likely to cause offence and will probably have a more interesting time.

It's important to wear the right **clothing** when walking in these mountains: strong boots with ankle support are the best footwear, though you can get away with training shoes in the dry season. Choose thin, loose clothing – long trousers offer some protection from thorns and leeches – wear a hat and sunblock; take plenty of water; and carry a basic medical kit. If you plan on spending the night in a village you'll need warm clothing as temperatures can drop to around freezing, and you may want to take a sleeping bag and mosquito net – though these are sometimes provided on organized tours.

THE NORTHWEST

Vietnam's most mountainous provinces lie immediately west of the Red River Valley, dominated by the country's highest range, Hoang Lien Son. Right on the border where the Red River enters Vietnam sits **Lao Cai** town, a major crossing point into China and gateway to the former hill-station of **Sa Pa**, now firmly on the tourist map for its colourful weekly market. From Sa Pa a road loops west across the immense flank of **Fan Si Pan**, the country's tallest peak, to join the Song Da (Black River) Valley running south, through the old French garrison towns of Lai Chau and Son La, via a series of dramatic passes to the industrial town of Hoa Binh on the edge of the northern delta. The only sight as such is the historic battlefield of **Dien Bien Phu**, close to the Lao border, but it's the scenery that makes the diversion worthwhile. Throughout the region, sweeping views and mountain grandeur contrast with ribbons of intensively cultivated valleys, and here more than anywhere else in Vietnam the **ethnic minorities** have retained their traditional dress, architecture and languages. After Sa Pa, the most popular tourist destination in these mountains is **Mai Chau**, an attractive area inhabited by the Thai minority, and within easy reach of Hanoi.

Lao Cai

Follow the Red River Valley northwest from Hanoi and after 300km pushing ever deeper into the mountains, you eventually reach the border town of **LAO CAI**, the railhead for Sa Pa and a popular route into China for travellers heading to Kunming.

Arrival and transport

Most people arriving from Hanoi will pitch up at Lao Cai **train station**, located next to a smart new **post office** on the east bank of the Red River, nearly 3km due south of the Chinese border. Follow the road north from the station towards the border and after 2km you reach Coc Leu Bridge, spanning the river to link up with the bulk of Lao Cai town over on the opposite bank. Immediately across the bridge, turn left for the **bus station** and market, or carry straight on along the town's main axis, Hoang Lien. Getting about is most easily done by motorbike; hordes of xe om shuttle between the train station and frontier or will take you across to the bus station.

For those travelling **on to Sa Pa**, a tourist bus ($2) meets the Hanoi train. Local buses only run this route in the early morning, so the best alternative is to take a jeep ($4–5 per person) or a xe om ($5) all the way; find them at either the train or bus station. **Leaving** Lao Cai **by train**, note that tickets for soft seats and hard sleepers on the night train (which has no soft-sleeper carriages) must be bought in Sa Pa (see p.385); soft-seat tickets on the day train can, however, be bought in Lao Cai.

ONWARD TRAVEL TO CHINA

The border crossing into China is via the Hekou Bridge **border gate** (7.30am–5pm), on the east bank of the Red River. When planning cross-border travel, note that China is **an hour ahead** of Vietnam, and that you need the correct **exit-point** stipulated on your Vietnamese visa (see *Basics*, p.12, for more on this) – and, of course, a visa for China.

At present it's only possible to cross the border **on foot**, but there are plans to re-establish a through train service from Hanoi to Kunming in southwest China. Lines at emigration are longest in the early morning, when local traders get their day pass over to Hekou. Next to the emigration office you'll find an **exchange** desk (7.30am–3pm), which deals in dong, dollars and yuan – but not travellers' cheques. Across on the Chinese side, turn right and Hekou train station is only five minutes' walk away, but floods washed out the Kunming line in 1995 and repairs are not expected to be completed for some time. Until then **bus** is the only option: at least two regular services leave Hekou each day on the twelve-hour journey (520km), but check locally for the latest situation.

Travellers **entering Vietnam** at Lao Cai have occasionally reported problems, usually involving a "fee" of a couple of dollars for paperwork, processing or the like.

Accommodation

Nearly all Lao Cai's **hotels** are found on the road running up to the border, Nguyen Hue. There's not a great choice but standards are improving and the only difficulty is at weekends when rooms fill up with holidaymakers from both sides of the border. If you do need to stay, first stop should be the *Hong Ha Guesthouse* (☎020/830007; ①), only 50m from the border gate on Nguyen Hue, nothing fancy but clean and friendly. If that's full, try *Nha Khach 39* (☎020/830085, fax 823469; ②), a few doors down on the opposite side of the road (look for a sign saying *Lao Cai Imexco*), a big place with moderate prices and a range of rooms. When it's finished, the smartest hotel in Lao Cai will be the *Duyen Hai Hotel*, a new five-storey block going up on the west bank of the Red River.

The town

Lao Cai exudes none of the trading frenzy of other border towns and even its **market**, the only point of interest apart from the border itself, is a small, local affair peddling medicinal leaves, roots and bark from the surrounding forests in greater quantities than Chinese imports. Vietnamese traders head over the border to Hekou market, a mass of ramshackle huts clearly visible across the river; coming the other way, but in smaller numbers, are bevies of Chinese tourists having a day out in Vietnam. There's little reason to linger in Lao Cai – most people make a beeline for Sa Pa or China – but if you need to overnight there are a couple of reasonably comfortable hotels (see above).

Even before the 1979 border war, Lao Cai had seen its fair share of power struggles. The town's most disreputable occupants were the "Black Flags", remnants of the Tai Ping rebel army who fled China to capture Lao Cai in 1868, after a siege lasting almost a year. They were notorious bandits, terrorizing the local population, but when French incursions along the Red River threatened the status quo, Black Flag mercenaries joined forces with the Vietnamese. Though they killed the first two French commanding officers, Garnier and Rivière, the

Black Flags only succeeded in hampering the colonization of northern Vietnam. Lao Cai eventually fell to the French in 1886, though robber bands lived on in the mountains until the end of the nineteenth century.

Eating

The road outside the train station is lined with **food stalls**, as good a place as any to eat in Lao Cai. The market is another obvious hunting-ground, but the only **restaurants** as such are on Nguyen Hue: *Nha Hang Hong Yen* at no. 30 serves basic rice meals in slightly more comfortable surroundings than the competition.

Sa Pa and around

A metalled road climbs slowly westwards away from Lao Cai along the steep, terraced hillsides of the Hoang Lien Son mountain range. Forty kilometres and ninety minutes later, journey's end is **SA PA**, a small market town perched dramatically on the western edge of a high plateau, facing the hazy blue peak of **Fan Si Pan**. The refreshing climate and vaguely Alpine landscape struck a nostalgic chord with European visitors, who travelled up from Lao Cai by sedan chair in the early twentieth century, and by 1930 a flourishing hill-station had developed, complete with tennis court, church and over two hundred villas. Nowadays only a handful of the old buildings remain, the rest lost to time and the 1979 Chinese invasion, but what the modern town lacks in character is more than compensated for by its magnificent scenery and walks out to surrounding **minority villages**. The region is home to a mosaic of ethnic groups, principally Hmong, Dao and Giay (see *Contexts*, p.438, for more on minority peoples).

Sa Pa's invigorating air is a real tonic after the dusty plains, but cold nights make warm clothes essential throughout the year: the sun sets early behind Fan Si Pan, and temperatures fall rapidly after dark. During the coldest months (Dec–Feb), night temperatures often drop below freezing and most winters bring some snow. You'll find the best **weather** from September through November and March to May, though even during these months cold, damp cloud can descend, blotting out the views for several days.

Arrival, information and transport

Many people visit Sa Pa on an organized **tour** from Hanoi (see p.349), and this is a useful option if your priority is trekking to and staying in minority villages. Otherwise Sa Pa is well set-up for individual travel: the most popular routing is **train** to Lao Cai, and then the connecting **tourist bus** ($2) up to Sa Pa; while the night train saves on both time and accommodation, a daylight journey is recommended for great views along the Red River Valley. The tourist bus drops you at Sa Pa's main **post office** on the eastern edge of town, from where it's only a minute's walk into town.

Heading back to Lao Cai, **buses leave** from either *Hotel La Rose* or the post office at 6.30am and 2pm daily. Buy tickets (a day in advance to be sure of a seat) from *La Rose* or the sub-post office, opposite the *Sunrise Hotel*. The sub-post office also sells **train tickets**; note that tickets for hard sleepers and soft seats on the night train can *only* be bought in Sa Pa. **Local buses** go from a dusty junction 2km east of town: between 8 and 9 in the morning there are a couple to Lao Cai, and another two pass by on the route westwards to Tam Duong and Lai Chau at around the same time.

Most guesthouses provide **information** on valley walks and visiting minority villages; guides are available for around $20 per day. First stop should be the *Auberge*, which sells fairly detailed maps of the area and copies of the *Sa Pa* guidebook (published by *The Gioi*; $2), containing suggested walks and information on the local minorities. The bank and most guesthouses **change money** (US dollars only) and the *Auberge* can handle travellers' cheques, but rates are better in Hanoi.

Motorbike taxis can be arranged through your guesthouse, or find them by the top of the market steps; self-drive is available but you need to be an experienced biker to tackle the stony, mountain tracks. It's also possible to hire **jeeps** ($40 per day) via guesthouses, depending on availability, but if you want to tackle the whole northwestern circuit, you'll find cheaper long-term prices in Hanoi.

Accommodation

Since Sa Pa was opened to tourists in 1993, guesthouses have sprung up everywhere, many housed in imitation European villas. In the **summer** months – peak season for local tourists – rooms can be in **short supply**, pushing up prices by as much as fifty percent. **Weekends** during September and November are busy with foreigners but there's usually enough beds to go round. Come mid-week and you'll have your pick of hotels, with the chance of getting a dollar or two knocked off the room rate. All accommodation in Sa Pa tends to be basic, so there's little to choose between most of the places listed below beyond price and location.

Foreigners can now stay in **minority villages**; guesthouses in Sa Pa can help with arrangements.

Auberge Dang Trung, or simply the *Auberge* (☎020/871243). A justifiably popular guesthouse where it's often difficult to get rooms. The three upstairs rooms with roof-top terrace are worth the extra few dollars for some of the most expansive views in town. ①–②

Commercial Guesthouse (☎020/871222). Large and grotty, but offering the cheapest beds in Sa Pa, this place's best feature is a view over the market square from the roof. ①

Darling Hotel, or *May May* (☎020/871349). A new guesthouse just to the north of Sa Pa, perched on the valley edge facing Fan Si Pan, and with a bizarre thatched café on the roof. ①

Forestry Guesthouse (☎020/871230). For those wanting a bit of space this is on the fringes of town among pine trees. Pleasant balconies, great views and newly refurbished bathrooms put prices above the average. ②

Ham Rong Guesthouse (☎020/871305, fax 871303). Owned by Lao Cai Lottery Company and the most upmarket place in Sa Pa, with both TV and telephone. ②

ACCOMMODATION PRICE CODES

All accommodation listed in this guide has been categorized according to the following scale:

① under US$10 (under 110,000 dong)   ② US$10–15 (110–165,000 dong)
③ US$15–30 (165–330,000 dong)   ④ US$30–75 (330–825,000 dong)
⑤ US$75–150 (825–1,650,000 dong)   ⑥ over US$150 (over 1,650,000 dong)

Rates are for the cheapest available double or twin room; breakfast is not usually included. During holiday periods, rates are liable to rise, and proprietors may be less amenable to bargaining. Although the law requires prices to be quoted in dong, most hotels also give their rates in US$; payment can be made in either currency.
For a more detailed discussion of accommodation, see pp.31–34.

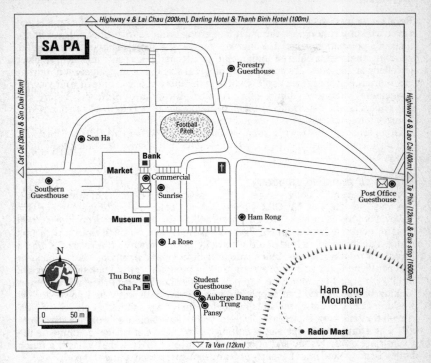

Pansy Guesthouse, or *Nha Nghi Phuong Dung* (☎020/871301). The last building on the track south to Ta Van village. Only four rooms but well kept and friendly. ①

Post Office Guesthouse (☎020/871244, fax 871282). Handy for the tourist bus but a bit out of the centre. Ten big clean rooms above the post office at a variety of prices. ①

Son Ha Guesthouse (☎020/871273). A friendly welcome and useful local information, plus good views and a roof-terrace – but you'll need to bargain the price down a touch. ②

Southern Guesthouse (☎020/871286). West of the market on the road to Cat Cat village, and recommended for its position, roof-top eating area and views to Fan Si Pan rather than the rooms. ①

Student Guesthouse (☎020/871308). Tucked in a corner beside the *Auberge* is this pleasant guesthouse with a flowery terrace, but only three rooms. ①

Sunrise Hotel, or *Binh Minh* (☎020/871331). On the main street, opposite the sub-post office, this hotel has fairly ordinary rooms but it's cheap and cheerful. ①

Thanh Binh Hotel (☎020/871250). To the north of Sa Pa, 300m beyond the *Forestry Guest House*, is this big, welcoming establishment with uninterrupted views south down the valley and a quiet location. ②

The town

Sa Pa itself is ethnically Vietnamese, but its shops and market serve the minority villages for miles around. Activity focuses on the **weekend market**, which runs from noon on Saturday to noon on Sunday, when villagers trek in to pick up a few necessities, meet potential marriage-partners and scrutinize the foreigners. The women in particular come dressed in their finery, the most eye-catching being

Red Dao women wearing scarlet head-dresses festooned with woollen tassels and silver trinkets. Hmong are the most numerous group, at over fifty percent of the district's population – and Hmong women are the most commercially minded, peddling their embroidered indigo-blue waistcoats, bags, hats and heavy, silver jewellery at all hours. It's certainly a colourful scene, but in peak season tourists can outnumber minorities and it's worth scheduling at least some of your visit for a weekday, when everything's more relaxed. Always ask permission before taking photographs, especially of older people; note that Dao in particular resent being photographed and you should respect their wishes.

Unfortunately the town's small **museum**, "Showroom of Sa Pa Minorities Culture", seems permanently closed these days, but it's worth a quick look if you can get in.

Trips to surrounding villages

There are several Hmong villages within easy walking distance of town, of which the most popular is **CAT CAT** village, directly below Sa Pa in the Muong Hoa Valley, roughly 3km away. To get there, follow the track west from the market square, continue past a ruined French villa and then turn left onto a path that drops steeply beside a line of old electricity pylons down to the river. Cat Cat, a huddle of wooden houses, hides among fruit trees and bamboo, where chickens and pot-bellied pigs scavenge among trailing pumpkin vines. Look out for tubs of indigo dye, used to colour the hemp cloth typical of Hmong dress, and for interlocking bamboo pipes that supply the village with both water and power for dehusking rice. Cat Cat waterfall is just below the village, site of an old hydro-electric station and now a pleasant place to rest before tackling the homeward journey. For a longer walk, instead of cutting down to Cat Cat village, continue on the main track up the valley and after 4km you'll reach **SIN CHAI** village, a much larger Hmong settlement (nearly 100 houses) spread out along the path.

You have to venture further afield to reach villages of minorities other than Hmong. One of the most enjoyable treks is to follow the main track from the *Auberge* south down the Muong Hoa Valley for 12km to a wooden suspension bridge and **TA VAN** village, on the opposite side of the river. Ta Van actually consists of two villages: immediately across the bridge is a Giay community, while further uphill to the left is a Dao village. From here, it's possible to walk back towards Sa Pa on the west side of the river, as far as another Hmong village, **LAO CHAI**, before rejoining the main track. If you don't want to walk all the way back up to Sa Pa, you can pick up a motorbike taxi at one of the huts you'll find every 2 to 3km along the track; expect to pay $2–3 one-way (40min). Alternatively, you can take a xe om from Sa Pa for the round-trip, which should work out at roughly $5, including waiting time.

The last recommended excursion is to **TA PHIN** village, which takes you northeast of Sa Pa, along the main Lao Cai road for 6km and then left on a dirt track for the same distance again, past the blackened shell of an old French seminary. Finally a scenic footpath across the paddy leads to a community of Red Dao scattered among a group of low hills; on the way look out for a beautifully engineered rice-husker beside a small stream. The easiest way to find Ta Phin is to take a xe om from Sa Pa ($2–3 each way) and get dropped-off at the start of the footpath; as the leg between Sa Pa and the start of this path isn't so attractive, you might also want to keep it for the return journey.

Hoang Lien Son Nature Reserve and Mount Fan Si Pan

The **Hoang Lien Son Nature Reserve** was set up in 1986 to safeguard remnants of natural forest habitat over an area of 30 square kilometres south and west of Sa Pa. Over the years, trees below an altitude of 1500m have largely been cleared for agriculture, building and firewood, but reforestation programmes are under way, adding commercial timbers in an effort to reduce illegal logging. Of the reserve's 56 mammal species, nearly one third are listed as rare or endangered, among them the clouded leopard, tiger and black gibbon. It's easier to spot some of the 150 bird species, a few of which are unique to the mountains of northwest Vietnam.

Vietnam's highest mountain, **Fan Si Pan** (3143m) lies within the reserve boundary, less than 5km as the crow flies from Sa Pa but an arduous five-day round-trip on foot. The usual route starts by descending 300m to cross the Muong Hoa River, and then climbs almost 2000m on overgrown paths through pine forest and bamboo thickets, before emerging on the southern ridge. The reward is a panorama encompassing the mountain ranges of northwest Vietnam, south to Son La Province and north to the peaks of Yunnan in China. Although it's a hard climb, the most difficult aspect of Fan Si Pan is its climate: even in the most favourable months of November and December it's difficult to predict a stretch of settled clear weather and many people are forced back by cloud, rain and cold. A **guide** is essential to trace indistinct paths, hack through bamboo, and locate water-sources; Hmong guides are said to know the mountain best. Sa Pa guesthouses – notably the *Auberge* and the *Orchid*, both at the southern end of town – can arrange guides and porters as required ($20–30 and $15 per day, respectively), though you'll need to bring your own tents and sleeping bags. Recently, the local authorities have started cashing in on the mountain's popularity, charging $10 per head for a "licence" to climb Fan Si Pan.

Eating

The number of **restaurants** has increased in the last few years, though with the refurbishment of Sa Pa market some old favourites have disappeared. A strip of eating houses at the south end of the main street offers a good choice; *Cha Pa Restaurant* is recommended for both quantity and quality, while *Thu Bong* next door is also popular. The convivial terrace-restaurant of the *Auberge* is the place to while away a sunny afternoon, and they also serve a good range of snacks and main dishes, including an excellent vegetarian set menu each evening. Around the market, a cluster of **food stalls** serve simple rice and noodle dishes.

On to Lai Chau

West of Sa Pa the road climbs over the Hoang Lien Son range and then starts a slow descent along the wall of an immense valley into the least densely populated region of Vietnam's far north. Three hours' drive (80km) later you come to **TAM DUONG**, with a surprisingly good **guesthouse** (no phone; ②) that some people use as an alternative stopover to Lai Chau, particularly as **PHONG THO** village, 30km further west, hosts a Monday **market** rivalling Sa Pa's in size and variety. From here on the route veers south, following the gently attractive Nam Na Valley peopled with Thai villages of impressively solid stilthouses while higher slopes are farmed by groups of Black Hmong and Dao. For much of this stretch, road and river track a wooded gorge before emerging at the confluence with the Da River near the town of Lai Chau, some 200km (8hr) from Sa Pa.

After crossing the Da River the road skirts east of **LAI CHAU**, past a T-junction where the town's one street branches right to the market and **minibus station**, while the regular **bus station** is located further along on the main highway. It's a small sleepy town set among paddy fields on a broad valley floor, with no real centre, just tentacles of buildings stranded above the floodplain. For most travellers this is a one-night stop between Sa Pa and Dien Bien Phu; after a quick walk round the small market, where you can snack on freshly cooked rice cakes, and a wander through the **Black Thai village** on the hillside west of town, there's little else to do – other than enjoy not being on the road. A few years ago Lai Chau lost its status as provincial capital to Dien Bien Phu, since when it's been in slow decline, and may even disappear altogether if plans for a second Da River dam go ahead.

For the moment, though, Lai Chau still has one **hotel**: cross the bridge beside the minibus station and turn left upriver, through the Black Thai village, for about 2km. Up a steep drive on the right is the *Nha Khach Uy Ban*, or *People's Committee Guesthouse* (no phone; ①), where clean, unfussy bungalow-style rooms, some with bathroom and hot water, are set around jaded courtyard-gardens. As a last resort, there's a clutch of *nha tro* or dormitories (no phone; ①) around the minibus station, some of which aren't too bad. The best place to eat in Lai Chau is a **restaurant** conveniently located at the bottom of the hotel driveway.

Dien Bien Phu

South of Lai Chau the road splits: Highway 6 takes off southeast to Tuan Giao and the quickest route to Son La; Highway 12 ploughs on south for more than 100km (4–5hr) to the heart-shaped valley of **DIEN BIEN PHU**, scene of General Giap's triumph in a battle that signalled the end of French Indochina (see box on pp.392–393). The isolated valley is roughly 19km by 8km, oriented north–south and edged by low mountains. Even today Dien Bien Phu has a rather desolate feel, and only a trickle of Vietnamese and foreign tourists are drawn to its historic battlefield. The valley's population is predominantly Thai (53 percent), while only one third are Viet in origin and they are concentrated in the urban area.

Though there are twice-weekly flights from Hanoi, it's a much more interesting journey by road, but this demands a five-day round-trip or an overnight stop on the circuit through Vietnam's northwest. Laos is less than 20km by road to the southeast, but the border here remains firmly closed for the moment.

The town and the battle sites

Highway 12 enters the valley from the north, skirts the airfield 5km out of town and then turns east across the Nam Rom River, to join Dien Bien Phu's main street at a T-junction. Immediately to the left of this junction is the bus station while right takes you past the post office, the biggest building in town, to the museum and Viet Minh cemetery about 800m to the south.

The town's **museum** (Wed, Fri & Sun 8–11am & 2–4pm; $2, includes admission to Hill A1 and de Castries' bunker – see facing page) is set back slightly from the road on the right-hand side as you head south out of town. The forecourt-cum-vegetable garden hosts a display of weaponry including American-made guns of

World War II vintage captured from French troops. Alongside them languish Viet Minh guns, also American-made but newer: these were booty from the Korean War which came via China into Vietnam, to be dragged up the battlefield's encircling hills. Inside the museum's echoing hall, familiar photos of the war-torn valley become more interesting in context, as does the scale-model where a guide describes the unfolding catastrophe – the message is perfectly clear, even in Vietnamese. Also on display is one of the sturdy bicycles capable of carrying 200-kilo loads along the Viet Minh supply trail, along with plenty more examples of ingenious home made weapons and equipment.

Directly opposite the museum is the **Viet Minh Cemetery**, where some of the fallen heroes are buried under grey marble headstones marked only with a red and gold star. In 1993 an imposing imperial gateway was added in time for the fortieth anniversary of the battle; originally there was a wall of names but in the heat and humidity the glued-on letters have fallen off, leaving sad, ghostly outlines on the white marble.

A small hill overlooking the cemetery, known as **Hill A1** to the Vietnamese and as Eliane 2 to French defenders, was the scene of particularly bitter fighting before it was eventually overrun towards the end of the battle. You can inspect a reconstructed bunker on the summit and various memorials, including the grave of a Viet Minh hero who gave his life while disabling the French tank standing next to him, and you also get a panorama over the now peaceful, agricultural valley. Hill A1 is fenced-off and the museum keeps the key; in theory they run weekly guided tours (Thurs 8–10am) but may be persuaded to let you in at other times.

There's even less to see at the last battle site, a reconstruction of **de Castries' bunker**, but it's a pleasant, twenty-minute walk across the river on a track busy with farm carts. To get there, head back into town from Hill A1 for about 300m before turning left opposite the *People's Committee Guesthouse*, down a dirt road signposted to Laos. Cross a bridge, and turn left when you can see the bunker's low, corrugated roof 100m away, surrounded by barbed-wire. Again the museum has the key and gives tours (times as for Hill A1), but all you can do is walk through the empty command post. Around about are captured tanks, anti-aircraft guns and other weaponry rusting away in the fields.

Practicalities

You'll find Dien Bien Phu's **bus station** located on the main street, within walking distance of the town's two main **hotels**. Closest is *Mini-hotel Dien Bien Phu* (no phone; ②–③), an incongruously ornate, three-storey building just north of the bus station. The rooms are cramped but clean, all with TV and fridge, though cheaper ones have shared bathrooms. Walk south from the bus station for about 500m to reach the *People's Committee Guesthouse* (the sign outside says *Nha Khach Guesthouse*; ②), a renovated, three-storey place with bigger rooms, all with bathrooms. If you're on a tight budget, your only choice is the extremely basic *nha tro* (①) at the bus station.

This region's speciality **food** is the Thai minority's black rice (*com gao cam*), which you can sample at Dien Bien Phu's sole Western-style restaurant, located in the *People's Committee Guesthouse*; the *Mini-hotel* restaurant generally caters for groups only. Locals patronize eating houses and food stalls around the bus station and along the main road – your best bet is to look for the biggest crowd – but they all close around 7pm.

THE BATTLE OF DIEN BIEN PHU

In November 1953 General Navarre, Commander-in-Chief in Indochina, ordered the French Expeditionary Force's parachute battalions to establish a base in Dien Bien Phu. Taunted by Viet Minh incursions into Laos, with which France had a mutual defence treaty, Navarre asserted this would block enemy lines through the mountains, force the Viet Minh into open battle and end the war in Indochina within eighteen months – which it did, but not quite as Navarre intended. His deputy in Dien Bien Phu was **Colonel de Castries**, an aristocratic cavalry officer and dashing hero of World War II, supposedly irresistible to women although Graham Greene, visiting the base in January 1954, described him as having the "nervy histrionic features of an old-time actor".

Using bulldozers dropped in beneath seven parachutes apiece, the French cleared two airstrips and then set up nine heavily fortified positions on low hills in the valley floor, reputedly named after de Castries' mistresses – Gabrielle, Eliane, Béatrice, and so on. In fact less than a quarter of the garrison in Dien Bien Phu were mainland French: the rest were either from France's African colonies or the Foreign Legion (a mix of European nationalities), plus local Vietnamese troops including three battalions drawn from the Thai minority. There were also 19 women in the thick of things (a stranded French nurse, plus 18 Vietnamese and Algerian women from the Expeditionary Force's mobile brothel).

Meanwhile, **General Giap**, Commander of the People's Army, quietly moved his own forces into the steep hills around the valley, mobilizing an estimated 300,000 porters, road gangs, and auxiliary soldiers in support of up to 50,000 battle troops. Not only did they carry in all food and equipment, often on foot or bicycle over vast distances, but they then hauled even the heaviest guns up the slopes, hacking paths through the dense steamy forest as they went. Ho Chi Minh described the scene to

Son La and around

East of Dien Bien Phu the road crosses two high, wild passes before reaching a softer landscape of paddy and banana plantations among tree-clad limestone hills, near the small but industrious town of **SON LA**. This provincial capital already has a less parochial air, though it's still a gruelling 300km from Hanoi. Son La's welcoming, low-key charm is enhanced by its valley-edge setting, and it merits more than the usual overnight stop. If time allows, there's enough of interest to occupy a day or two, taking in the old French prison, an underground river system and with forays to nearby Thai and Muong minority villages.

Arrival and information

Son La **bus station** lies about a kilometre southwest of town near the *Son La Hotel*, though coming in from Dien Bien Phu some drivers may let you off by the *Song Da Hotel* at the top of town which saves a walk. The best place to go for **information** is the helpful *Du Lich Cong Doan* ("Trade Union Tourism") in the *Trade Union Guesthouse* (see opposite), where you can also hire transport and English-speaking guides, or arrange to see Thai dancing and sample rice wine. *Vietindebank* at 30 To Hieu will **exchange** dollars; if you then want somewhere to spend it, have a look at local minority handicrafts, including handmade cloth and lively embroideries, on sale in the covered **market**.

journalist William Burchett by turning his helmet upside down: "Down here is the valley of Dien Bien Phu. There are the French. They can't get out. It may take a long time, but they can't get out". In early 1954 Giap was ready to edge his troops even closer, using a network of tunnels dug under cover of darkness. By this time the international stakes had been raised: the war in Indochina would be discussed at the Geneva Conference in May, so now both sides needed a major victory to take to the negotiating table.

French commanders continued to believe their position was impregnable until the first shells rained down on March 10. Within five days Béatrice and Gabrielle had fallen, both airstrips were out of action and the siege had begun in earnest; the French artillery commander, declaring himself "completely dishonoured", lay down and took the pin out of a grenade. All French supplies and reinforcements now had to be parachuted in, frequently dropping behind enemy lines, and when de Castries was promoted to general even his stars were delivered by parachute; at the end of the battle, 83,000 parachutes were strewn across the valley floor. The **final assault** began on May 1, by which time the rains had arrived, hindering air-support, filling the trenches and spreading disease. Waves of Viet Minh fought for every inch of ground, until their flag flew above de Castries' command bunker on the afternoon of May 7. The following morning, the day talks started in Geneva, the last position **surrendered** and the valley at last fell silent after 59 days. A ceasefire was signed in Geneva on July 21, and ten months later the last French troops left Indochina.

The Vietnamese paid a high price for their victory, with an estimated 20,000 dead and many thousands more wounded. On the French side, out of a total force of 16,500, some 10,000 were captured and marched hundreds of kilometres to camps in Vietnam's northeastern mountains; less than half survived the rigours of the journey, diseases and horrendous prison conditions.

Accommodation

The most convenient **accommodation** for those pre-dawn bus departures is the *Son La Hotel* (☎022/852702; ②), which has good-sized rooms and affordable prices, marred by a sour welcome. The alternatives are all in the main part of town where several new hotels are going up, but at the moment the best option is the *Trade Union Guesthouse* (☎022/852244; ②) with a range of accommodation, including a handful of smarter rooms with TV and air-con in two new annexes. Son La's most ritzy establishment, however, is the small *Hoa Ban Hotel* (☎022/852395, fax 852712; ④) at the far end of To Hieu; it's often fully booked despite its high prices. At the other extreme is the *Song Da Hotel* (☎022/852062; ①), a dilapidated place on a hill above town.

The town

The major part of Son La lies off the highway, straggling for little more than a kilo-metre along the west bank of the Nam La River. There's just one main street, To Hieu, where you'll find all the important municipal buildings, including bank and post office. At the far end, in front of the *Hoa Ban Hotel*, a parallel road heads back south on the opposite side of the river, past the new covered **market**, to rejoin Highway 6. Between these two roads the town centre is a green swathe of paddy and vegetable plots.

Son La's principal tourist sight is the **French prison**, *Bao Tang Son La* (Mon–Sat 7–11am & 1–5pm), which occupies a wooded promontory above To Hieu Street. A

sign draped with some chunky prison chains indicates the turning off the highway; walk uphill to find the prison gates and an arched entrance, still announcing "Pénitencier", leading into the main compound. This region was a hotbed of anti-French resistance, and a list of political prisoners interred here reads like a roll-call of famous revolutionaries – among them Le Duan and Truong Chinh, veteran Party members who both went on to become general secretary. Local hero To Hieu was also imprisoned for seditionary crimes but he died from malaria while in captivity, in 1944. Most of the buildings lie in ruins, destroyed by a French bombing raid in 1952, but a few have been reconstructed, including the two-storey kitchen-block (*bep*), beneath which are seven punishment cells. Political prisoners were often incarcerated in brutal conditions: the two larger cells (then windowless) held up to five people shackled by the ankles. Behind the kitchens, don't miss the well-presented collection of prison memorabilia.

Around Son La

Tham Coong Water Cave is promoted as another tourist attraction where, for a small sum, a boatman propels you on a bamboo raft about 40m along a dammed underground river; take a torch if you want to see anything. Though the cave is nothing spectacular, the walk there, among karst hills and paddy fields alive with butterflies, is attractive. Follow the metalled road north from the *Hoa Ban Hotel* for nearly 2km and turn left just before a concrete bridge onto a footpath tracing the river upstream to an ancient stone bridge – according to local legend, built by a Black Thai queen a thousand years ago. Take the first path left on the far side of the bridge, beside a line of pylons, to reach a barbed-wire enclosure where the river emerges from the hillside. There's also a second, dry cave directly overhead – a short scramble up beside the wire – in which you can walk the first 50m of a system said to be 7km long. Just beyond the turning for Tham Coong cave is one of Son La's nearest, though still rarely visited, **minority villages**. Instead of turning left at the concrete bridge continue on the metalled road towards a cliff-face punched with a round cavern, reputed to contain gold, about 70m up. Turn left before the cliff and you pitch up in a Black Thai community of about fifty stilthouses constructed of bamboo, and fenced round with hedges of poinsettia and hibiscus.

If you've got more time, a popular jaunt takes you out to **BAN MONG**, another Thai village six bumpy but scenic kilometres along a luxuriant valley south of Son La. The houses of this village are solid, wooden structures surrounded by gardens of fruit trees rather than vegetables. A scummy pond at the village edge is in fact a hot spring which provides water for bath-house and laundry at a constant 30°C. To get to Ban Mong, take the turning off Highway 6 opposite the prison; the valley becomes completely cut off during the rains and at any time you'll need four-wheel drive, or take a xe om from Son La for the return trip.

Certain minority villages stage events for tour groups, such as traditional Thai dancing or supping the local home brew, a sweet wine made of glutinous rice; it's drunk from a communal earthenware container using bamboo straws, and hence named *ruou can* or stem alcohol.

Eating and drinking

Back in town, both the *Trade Union Guesthouse* and *Hoa Ban Hotel* (see "Accommodation", p.393) have good **restaurants**, the former offering better value though it closes at around 8pm; if you didn't find black rice in Dien Bien Phu, then try it here. There are several local eateries on To Hieu, including the excellent *Son La Beer Factory*, where you can down a refreshing *bia hoi*, with perhaps a snack of *nem chua* dipped in spicy sauce, before eating at the restaurant next door. For caffeine addicts, there's a combined **café** and dentist on To Hieu, opposite the Petrolimex station.

Mai Chau and around

Highway 6 climbs east from Son La onto a high plateau where the cool climate favours tea and coffee cultivation, mulberry to feed the voracious worms of Vietnam's silk industry, and herds of dairy cattle to quench Hanoi's new-found thirst for milk, yoghurt and ice cream. Just over 100km out of Son La, the sprawling market town of **Moc Chau** provides a convenient break at one of the popular roadside restaurants on its eastern outskirts. If you need to overnight here, there's one guesthouse, *Nha Nghi Cong Doan* (no phone; ②), though most people press on – through bleak valleys where the Hmong live in distinctive houses built on the ground under long, low roofs – to reach **MAI CHAU**. The **minority villages** of the Mai Chau Valley, inhabited mainly by Thai people, are close enough to Hanoi (150km) to make this a popular destination. The valley, however, is still largely unspoilt, a peaceful scene of pancake-flat rice fields trimmed with jagged mountains.

Arrival and transport

Most people visit Mai Chau on an organized **tour** out of Hanoi (see p.349), which usually includes overnighting in a minority village, or as part of a longer trip into the northwest mountains by jeep or motorbike.

Mai Chau is not the easiest place to get to by **public transport** but it is possible. From Son La take any bus heading east to Hoa Binh or Hanoi and ask the driver to let you off at the Mai Chau junction, around 65km after Moc Chau; at the junction pick up one of the waiting xe om for the final 6km up the valley. From Hanoi, in theory there's a daily bus (10am) from Ha Dong bus station to Mai Chau, though you may have to change in Hoa Binh (see over); alternatively, take any bus going west on Highway 6 and get off at the Mai Chau junction to pick up a motorbike for the last stretch. A $5 sightseeing charge is levied in an arbitrary fashion at the bottom of the road – those travelling in cars seem more able to avoid it.

A very overcrowded bus **leaving Mai Chau** passes the *Mai Chau Guesthouse* (see over) each day around noon on its way down to Hoa Binh, from where you can pick up a Hanoi bus. Alternatively, take a xe om to the junction with Highway 6 and flag down a bus going in your direction.

Mai Chau village

Mai Chau is the valley's main settlement, though it's still just a village, a friendly, quiet place which suddenly bursts into life for its Sunday **market** when minority people trek in to haggle over buffalo meat, starfruit, sacks of tea or groundnuts. Unlike in Sa Pa, the minorities here have largely forsaken their traditional dress, but there's plenty of colour on the road outside the market where bright hanks of yarn, freshly dyed in primary colours, hang up to dry.

On the south side of Mai Chau is its **hotel**, the new *Mai Chau Guesthouse* (☎018/851812; ②), with nine basic but comfortable rooms. The *Guesthouse* runs a pretty good **restaurant** and there's also an excellent local place in the village with a warm welcome, cold beer and a tasty spread – their marinated meat skewers are highly recommended. To get there, walk back from the *Guesthouse* towards Highway 6, past the playing field and market to a bridge, a total of about 800m; immediately over the bridge look out for a *com pho* sign to your right. For breakfast or a midday snack, head straight for the market where you'll find hawkers selling piping-hot banana fritters and a small café in the far corner.

The Mai Chau Valley

Prosperous Thai communities cultivate the fertile **Mai Chau Valley**, though their wealth is derived from gold-panning supplemented by tourist dollars, rather than farming. The most accessible village is a White Thai settlement of seventy houses (400 people) where you can buy hand-woven textiles, watch performances of traditional dancing and sleep overnight. While too organized for some, this is one of the easiest places to stay in a genuine stilthouse; an edifying experience, particularly at dawn if your sleeping quarters happen to be above the hen-house. The village receives a fair number of tourists, so you can wander around quite freely, but there are also plenty of other, more isolated villages around the valley.

To reach the White Thai village, continue south on the road for 500m beyond the *Mai Chau Guesthouse* and take the first right turn. No one speaks English, but houses displaying cloth outside are most likely to offer accommodation. Expect to pay about $3 per person for the night, plus $1 for a meal depending largely on how much you eat. Alternatively, you can eat at the *Guesthouse*, though you'll have to arrange this when you first arrive.

Hoa Binh

There's one, final pass to go over before Highway 6 leaves the northwest mountains. It's a slow crawl along precipitous hillsides up to a col at 1200m, and then an ear-popping descent to **HOA BINH**, on the edge of the Red River plain. The town's proximity to Hanoi, 76km on a fast road, plus its hotels and easy access to a variety of minority villages mean that Hoa Binh soaks up much of the tourist traffic. Unless you need the bus connections, it's preferable to stop over in Mai Chau or push on all the way to Hanoi.

During the French War Hoa Binh was the scene of a disastrous French raid into Viet Minh-held territory, which reads like a dress-rehearsal for the epic rout of Dien Bien Phu. In November 1951, French paratroop battalions seized Hoa Binh in a daring attempt to hamper enemy supply routes. They met with little resistance and dug in, only to find themselves marooned as Giap's forces cut both road and river access. In February the following year the French fought their way out towards Hanoi in a battle that came to be known as the "hell of Hoa Binh".

The town

The main highway thunders straight through the centre of modern Hoa Binh but a hint of quieter days lingers in its shaded main boulevard, Phuong Lam. Less than 2km above the city to the northwest, the 620-metre-wide **Hoa Binh dam** chokes the Da River to create a lake over 200km long, stretching all the way to Son La. The reservoir is earmarked for tourist development, but its main purpose is to feed Vietnam's largest hydro-electric plant which came on stream in 1994 and has gone some way to solving Vietnam's chronic power shortage. *Hoa Binh Tourism* (at the *Hoa Binh Hotel*) offers guided tours of the complex, but otherwise you get a worm's-eye view of the dam from the pontoon bridge which links Hoa Binh's main street with industrial suburbs across the Da River. Muong, Thai, Hmong and Dao **minorities** all live in the vicinity, but you'll need to arrange a guide and transport if you want to visit them. Again, *Hoa Binh Tourism* can help but at the moment they're geared primarily to tour groups. Their most popular outing is a day's boat trip on the Da River, visiting Muong and Dao villages ($20 per boat), and they can also arrange a night's accommodation in a showpiece Muong village ($10 per person plus food).

Practicalities

Hoa Binh's main **bus station** lies on its eastern edge, where you'll find the usual gaggle of xe om waiting to take you the kilometre back into town. Buses for Hanoi leave every half-hour, but note that some terminate at Ha Dong, where you have to pick up a Hanoi city bus. Keep an eye on your bags as thefts have been reported on this route.

The best **hotel** in town is the *Hoa Binh* (☎018/852051; ③) built on a hillside 2km west of the centre along Highway 6; five stilthouses stand in a garden compound, containing pleasantly furnished, wood-panelled bedrooms. A sixth stilthouse makes a fine restaurant, where you can watch folk dancing and music displays or take a sip of Thai rice wine from the communal pot. In the same complex, you'll find *Hoa Binh Tourism* and a shop selling minority crafts, including a tempting selection of traditional clothes and embroidered textiles. Budget travellers should make straight for *Nha Hang Restaurant* (☎018/852730; ①), actually a three-storey mini-hotel east of the centre – look for a sign on the right saying "Restaurant of the Food Company"; the rooms are spartan but clean.

Hoa Binh fares better on **restaurants**: both the *Hoa Binh Hotel* and *Nha Hang Restaurant* serve excellent food – the latter has fewer frills and is less expensive. There's also a group of local restaurants, cafés and ice-cream parlours at the west end of Phuong Lam Street, about 50m before the T-junction.

THE NORTHEAST

The provinces of northeast Vietnam, from Lang Son looping westwards to Ha Giang and Tuyen Quang, lack the grandeur of their counterparts west of the Red River Valley. In general the peaks here are lower, the views smaller scale and of an altogether softer quality, and getting about is a little easier. Highlights of the northeast are its **agricultural landscapes**, from traditional scenes of green-engulfed villages to the limestone country of Cao Bang, typified by pockets of cultivation squeezed among rugged outcrops whose lower slopes are wrinkled with terraces. However, population densities are still low, leaving huge forest reserves such as **Ba Be National Park** and high areas of wild, open land inhabited by **ethnic minorities** practising swidden farming. While many have adopted a Vietnamese way of life, in remoter parts the minorities remain culturally distinct – particularly evident when local markets, their dates traditionally set by the lunar calendar, are in full swing. The varied local climate supports a wide range of crops, from anise, peach and pear to tea, rubber and the usual gamut of subtropical and tropical species. In addition the hills are rich in largely unexploited reserves of gold, copper, zinc, iron ore and other minerals.

North through Thai Nguyen

Highway 3 forges due north out of Hanoi across the rice lands of the Red River Delta, gradually leaving behind industrial satellite towns and brickworks for the welcome foothills of the northern massif. Only 16km from Hanoi the highway passes right by **Co Loa**, site of the ancient capital of Vietnam (see "Around Hanoi", p.353), but otherwise there's nothing to stop for until you reach **THAI NGUYEN**, 80km from Hanoi on the edge of the delta. This sprawling steel town makes a surprising home for one of Vietnam's more rewarding museums, the **Museum of the Nationalities of Vietnam**, *Bao Tang Van Hoa Cac Dan Thoc Viet Nam* (Tues, Wed & Sun 8–11am & 2–4pm; $2). Usually staff will show foreign tourists around outside the official opening times, but it's best to make a prior arrangement (☎028/855781). The museum is arranged in five rooms according to language group, Viet–Muong, Tay–Thai, Mon–Khmer and so on, with examples of traditional costume and objects from daily life, as well as plenty of photographs and helpful captions in English. Most impressive is the Mon–Khmer room, refurbished with Swedish assistance, which includes video presentations of festivals and excellent architectural models. The museum, an imposing, puce-coloured building built in 1960, stands on a roundabout in the centre of town – north of the post office radio mast – at 359 Duong Tu Minh. Coming north on Highway 3, turn right (northeast) on Hoang Van Thu, then follow directions for Lang Son to find the museum.

Continuing north from Thai Nguyen on Highway 3, after only a few kilometres Highway 13a turns off left, cutting across country to Tuyen Quang, from where it's possible to join the road to Lao Cai (see p.390). Soon after, the main northbound highway starts to climb gently, following the attractive Cau River through a region inhabited by Nung minorities. **NA PHAC**, a small market town with a well-placed clutch of cafés 200km from Hanoi, marks the turning for Ba Be National Park. If you happen to pass through Na Phac on market day (held at five-day intervals, starting on the first day of the lunar month), you'll be treated to an arresting display of minority dress.

Ba Be National Park

Vietnam's largest natural lake, Ho Ba Be, forms the core of **Ba Be National Park**, which encompasses 50,000 hectares of limestone and tropical semi-evergreen forest. The lake is 7km long, up to 30m deep and between 0.5 and 1km wide. A few islands decorate the surface and the whole lot is enclosed by steep, densely wooded slopes, breaking out here and there into white limestone cliffs. Apart from its natural beauty, the park's main attraction is **boat trips** to visit caves, waterfalls and minority villages, with the added bonus of seeing at least a few of the 220 animal, 417 plant and 49 fish species recorded here. Bears, tigers and one of Vietnam's rarest and most endangered primates, the Tonkin snub-nosed monkey (*Rhinopithecus avunculus*), live in a few isolated communities on the fringes of the park, but nearer the lake there's a good chance of spotting the more common macaque monkeys and garrulous, colourful flocks of parrots. Few people are around to disturb the wildlife and outside the months of July and August, when Hanoians take their holidays, you'll usually find only a handful of tourists. What puts many people off Ba Be is difficulty of access by public transport, lack of facilities and expense. With your own transport it becomes easier to justify, especially when combined with one of the minority markets, but even then a two-night stay is probably sufficient.

Getting there and around

The simplest way of getting to Ba Be National Park is to arrange your own transport. Hanoi tour agencies (see p.347) can help with vehicle hire or line up a full programme, either as a three-day excursion or as part of the Cao Bang–Lang Son circuit. Total travelling time from Hanoi to Ba Be is around seven hours: from the Na Phac turning on Highway 3 a road threads west across country to Ba Be (28 km) via **CHO RA**, another small town that comes to life on market days (every five days). If you've got a four-wheel drive vehicle or motorbike, you can take an interesting alternative route on a rough back-road through stunning rural landscapes: just north of Phu Thong on Highway 3 (near the 174km marker), turn left and 30km (90min) later you'll come out beside Cho Ra's *Ba Be Hotel* (see "Accommodation and eating", below). **Public transport** to Ba Be is a more tricky proposition but your best option is probably the Cao Bang bus from Hanoi, disembarking at Na Phac, followed by a xe om to Cho Ra, or to Ba Be.

On arrival, first stop for every visitor is the park headquarters just inside the boundary gates, where you pay a sightseeing fee ($5) and can get **information**, English-speaking **guides** ($10 per day) and boat hire. A popular boat trip takes you south to **PAC NGOI**, a Tay village of 80 houses (300 people) strung along the valley-edge above flourishing plots of rice, maize and vegetables. From here you can walk into the forest or to villages higher up the valley, and it's also possible to stay overnight (see below). Alternatively, take a boat north up the lake to **Hang Puong**, where the Nang River has tunnelled a 300-metre-long, bat-filled cave through a mountain, and to various waterfalls. Boat hire is charged at $3 per hour (maximum 10 people per boat). In a full day (6–8hr) you'll be able to visit the village, cave and a waterfall but with little time to spare at each stop. On a tight schedule it's probably best to stick to the village plus a waterfall with a forest-walk; count on two hours for a round-trip to the village and three to the top of the lake and back – these boats don't hurry. The boat landing, also the local ferry pier, is a manageable 2500m from the park headquarters; motorbikes waiting by the lake will give you a lift back uphill for a small charge.

Accommodation and eating

Cho Ra now boasts its own mini-hotel, the friendly *Ba Be Hotel* (☎026/876115; ②), on the east side of town near a cluster of small eating houses; as it's only another 13km (30min) to Ba Be, this makes a feasible base for the park.

Actually **within the park** is a choice of accommodation managed by the park administration (☎026/876127). The *Guesthouse*, part of the headquarters complex, offers simply furnished rooms sharing a well-scrubbed bathroom (hot water in the evenings only), plus a newer block in stilthouse style (②). It also has a few very basic rooms in a rundown block with no shower facilities next to the boat station (①). There's a **restaurant** next door to the *Guesthouse* serving well-priced set meals, usually including fish fresh from the lake, while the small café beside the boat station might rustle up a noodle soup.

Lastly, the most interesting option is to take a twenty-minute boat ride down to **Pac Ngoi** village at the south end of the lake and stay in a real Tay stilthouse (②); the park authorities insist you take a guide to help with the preliminaries. Accommodation consists of a sleeping mat, blankets, pillow and mosquito net, and meals can be provided for $1–2 per person but, unless you've booked in advance, it's a good idea to bring the first night's food. You'll also want a torch: Pac Ngoi has no mains electricity, relying on a generator in the evenings and paraffin lamps at other times.

Cao Bang and around

North from Na Phac, Highway 3 climbs up to a high pass (800m), called **Col des Vents** by the French, which marks the watershed between the Red River Valley to the south and China's Pearl River in the north. Over the col lies a region of metamorphic rocks typified by big, rounded hills and denuded summits, known as the **Ngan Son Mountains**. This is the domain of several ethnic minorities, among them the Nung, Dao and San Chay (whose women carry a broad, curved knife tucked in the back of their belts). There are few villages in sight on these wild uplands, just the occasional split-bamboo hut selling wild honey (*mat ong*) beside the road. In fact, apart from **Ngan Son**, lost in a vast, treeless valley, there's no settlement of any size between Na Phac and journey's end, 80km later in **CAO BANG**.

Cao Bang is a likeable place: it's small, off the beaten track and, though the town has little intrinsic beauty, its riverside setting backed by sugar-loaf mountains helps to blur the edges. The Chinese border is now only 30km away, as the crow flies, but fortunately Cao Bang is too much of a backwater to be troubled by the frontier atmosphere of Lang Son (see p.403). Few travellers venture as far north as Cao Bang, but those who do get up here usually make the pilgrimage out to **Pac Bo Cave**, where Ho Chi Minh lived on his return to Vietnam in 1941, and the classic limestone scenery of the region is worth exploring. The province is home to several ethnic minorities, notably the Dao, Nung and Tay who still maintain their traditional way of life in the more remote uplands.

Arrival and information

Cao Bang's **bus station** is on the main street, 400m east along the river from the market hall, while private minibuses hang around the crossroads on the far side of the river. The **post office**, on the main highway near the centre of town, is immediately recognizable from its radio-mast, while the **bank** (exchange facilities for cash only) lies opposite it across a park.

Accommodation

One disadvantage of backwaters is their lack of **accommodation**, and Cao Bang is no exception. Of the two hotels in town, first choice should be the *Cao Bang Mini-hotel* (☎026/852237; ①), which has only three rooms – two of which have partition walls and shared bathrooms – but it's clean, friendly and sensibly priced. To find it coming in on Highway 3, look out on the left for a small notice pronouncing, "Mini-hotel for Foreigners; it'll really you please", just after the road takes a sharp right turn along the river. A little further along the same road but on the opposite side, next to the bus station, is the government-run *Phong Lan Hotel* (☎026/852260; ①), predictably grey and overpriced, though its top-rate rooms are at least clean and boast en suite bathrooms.

The town

Cao Bang is built on the southwestern bank of the **Bang Giang River**, nearly 300km due north of Hanoi. Highway 3 drops steeply down from the hills and enters town from the west on a tree-lined avenue of self-important edifices, including People's Committee, theatre, bank and post office, before turning right along the river. Until the highway is sealed, walking this busy main road is akin to taking a dust bath, from which a small grid of backstreets and the **market** hall (next to where a modern bridge spans the river) provide welcome relief. Held daily, the enormous market forms the town's focal point: if possible, try to visit around sunrise when minority women trek into town and bamboo rafts laden with produce dock beside the bridge. Once you've exhausted the market, the only thing to do is head for the hills north of town.

Pac Bo Cave

Such a lot is made of **Pac Bo Cave** that it comes as a surprise to learn that Ho Chi Minh only lived in it for seven weeks, during February and March 1941. If you're not a fan of Ho memorabilia then neither the cave nor the small museum justifies the fifty-kilometre excursion (2hr each way), though the first part of the journey, passing minority villages moored in rice-paddy seas against craggy blue horizons, is a memorable ride.

To get to Pac Bo from Cao Bang, head northwest across the Bang Giang River on the Ha Quang road until you see a signpost directing you off to the right. From this junction it's another 4km to the **ticket** gate ($2.50, including a guide and admission to the museum; small additional charge for parking), along a valley dotted with memorials to heroes and heroines who died protecting Ho's hideaway. Getting to the cave by public transport is not easy as few buses ply the route between Cao Bang and Ha Quang. If you do take a bus, ask to be dropped off at the turning for Pac Bo, two hours from Cao Bang, where you can pick up a xe om for the last leg ($1). An easier but more costly alternative is to hire a motorbike or jeep – $10 and $30 per day, respectively – at the *Mini-hotel* in Cao Bang (see "Accommodation", above).

Pac Bo is situated right on the border with China. When **Ho Chi Minh** walked over from Guangxi Province in January 1941 he took his first steps on Vietnamese soil for thirty years. At first he lived in a Nung village but soon left for the nearby cave where he set about co-ordinating the independence movement, translating the history of the Soviet Communist Party into Vietnamese and, in his spare time, renaming local landmarks: a spring beside the cave became Lenin Stream, while the mountain above he rechristened Karl Marx Mountain. However, the French soon discovered his hideaway and Ho had to move again, this time to a jungle hut not far away where the Viet Minh was founded in May 1941. Later that same year he left for China, to drum up support for his nascent army, and when he next returned to Pac Bo it was after Independence, as a tourist, in 1961.

The **cave** today is a strange mixture of shrine and picnic spot, set in a peaceful wood full of birds and butterflies but marred with rubbish. The guides – none of whom speak English – will walk you up beside Lenin Stream to the cave mouth, pointing out where Uncle Ho fished, cooked, worked, wrote poetry, even where he sat in 1961. Inside the cave, which it's said Chinese troops vandalized during the border war, you can gaze on a replica wooden bed and a stalagmite bearing an uncanny resemblance to Karl Marx. Unfortunately, exhibits in the small **museum** have no English labels: there's much of interest for the keen student of Vietnamese history, but even an amateur will be able to identify Ho's *Hermes Baby* typewriter, bamboo suitcase and *Mauser* pistol.

Over the Ma Phuc Pass

If revolutionary relics aren't your thing, take the road north towards Tra Linh and Quang Uyen and lose yourself among sugar-loaf scenery beyond the **Ma Phuc Pass**. The road from Cao Bang, in unusually fine condition, shoots straight up the valleyside and after a disappointing start you're suddenly looking down on a tortured landscape of scarred limestone peaks and streamless valleys typical of karst scenery. The region is inhabited by Nung people who cultivate the valley-floors and terraced lower slopes, living in distinctive wooden houses that are built partly on ground level and partly raised on stilts. Even if you don't have time to explore further, views from the top of the pass – a mere 20km (30min) out of Cao Bang – more than repay the effort. Just before the top, the road splits: pick either direction for some great scenery but the right fork takes you to the only specific sight in the area, the **Ban Gioc Falls**, whose location exactly on the frontier with China made them a bone of contention during the border war. At over 90km and three hours' driving each way, Ban Gioc is a full day's outing; note that the falls are less than spectacular in the dry season.

Eating

For some reason, Cao Bang has an abundance of dentists and dog restaurants, but fortunately there are other alternatives when it comes to eating. Small **restaurants** are found in the backstreets near the market, up the road beside the *Phong Lan Hotel* and on Highway 4 near the bridge. First stop on cold mornings should be a **breakfast soup** ladled from the huge steaming cauldrons in the market.

Southeast to Lang Son

At Cao Bang you join **Highway 4**, an ambitious road that was originally part of a French military network linking the isolated garrisons right across northern Vietnam's empty mountain country. Much of the highway is no longer navigable, but east of Cao Bang there are some surprisingly good stretches, and the 140-kilometre journey to Lang Son takes a leisurely six hours, leaving plenty of time to enjoy the scenery. Beyond **Dong Khe**, a nondescript town roughly 40km (90min) out of Cao Bang, the virtually traffic-free road climbs through a gorge of claustrophobic limestone cliffs before cresting the dramatic **Dong Khe Pass**. In 1950 this pass was the scene of a daring ambush in which the Viet Minh gained their first major victory over the French Expeditionary Force. In the ensuing panic, forts all along the border were abandoned, an estimated 6000 French troops were killed or captured, and the Viet Minh netted 950 machine guns, 8000 rifles and a few hundred trucks.

From **THAT KHE**, the only other town of any size on the journey, the route follows the pretty Ky Cung Valley, inhabited by Nung and Tay; their bamboo rafts and huge wooden waterwheels, which form part of sophisticated irrigation works, grace the river. Though That Khe lies exactly halfway between Cao Bang and Lang Son, this last stretch is far quicker, taking a mere two hours to cover the final 70km to Lang Son, entering town from the north on Highway 1.

Lang Son

Redeeming features are few and far between in the small, scruffy provincial capital of **LANG SON**, but for most people this is merely an overnight stop on the journey through the northeast or en route to China, only 18km away to the north. A stroll through Lang Son's oversized Ky Lua market, stuffed with down-jackets and bicycles, confirms the proximity of China, as does Chinese script outside hotels and shops where they accept yuan as readily as dollars. Even before cross-border trade was legalized, Lang Son had been doing very nicely from smuggling, but now its economy is booming on the strength of enthusiastic capitalism and a resilient black-market. This combination rarely brings out the best in a place, and Lang Son has its share of prostitutes and hustlers. Really, the only reason to stop is for the trappings of civilization – hotels, banks, and a post office. For the intrepid, Lang Son is the start of a little-travelled backroad cutting across 100km of empty country to Tien Yen on the east coast, offering a route to (or from) Ha Long Bay – but one passable only by four-wheel-drive vehicles or motorbikes.

ACROSS THE BORDER TO CHINA

The majority of people taking this route into China travel **by train**, using one of the two services per week direct from Hanoi to Beijing via Nanning (see p.349 for details). Though it may be difficult to get a reservation, it's possible to join this train at Dong Dang (or get off here if heading south); tickets can be bought in Hanoi, or in Dong Dang itself.

Alternatively, you can still use the **road crossing** known as the Friendship Gate (*Huu Nghi Quan*), which lies 18km north of Lang Son and 4km from Dong Dang at the end of Highway 1. If you're travelling by **local bus**, your best bet is to overnight in Lang Son (see over) and then take a motorbike all the way to the border gate ($2–3). Otherwise, **minibuses** shuttle between Lang Son's Le Loi Street and Dong Dang town, but you'll then have to hop on a motorbike for the last leg. **Local trains** from Hanoi terminate at Dong Dang station, 800m south of the main town, from where you can take a xe om up to the border ($1); station shopkeepers will usually **change money**, but at poor rates.

The **border gate** is open between 7am and 6pm and there's a walk of less than 1km between the two check points. On the Chinese side, take a bus or taxi (about 20 yuan) the 20km to Pingxiang, from where frequent buses run to Nanning (4hr), or catch a slightly slower train; note that China is **one hour ahead** of Vietnam.

Whether you cross the border by train or road, you must have a Chinese **visa** (see p.349), and the correct **exit** (or entry) **point** on your Vietnam visa – Dong Dang checkpoint for the train crossing, Huu Nghi for the road – which can't be arranged on the spot (see *Basics*, p.12, for more on the formalities).

Arrival and information

Nearly all Lang Son's facilities are found on the north bank of the river. The **post office** lies near the Ky Lua bridge, a couple of hundred metres east of the highway down Le Loi Street. Next door is the provincial **bus station**, though most long-distance buses will drop you on the main road. If you're travelling on to China (see box on previous page), there's no reason to stop in Lang Son, unless you need accommodation (see below). Most hotels **exchange** dollars and yuan, or cross over to the south side of the Ky Cung River to find a couple of banks on the corner of Tran Hung Dao (Highway 1) and Quang Trung streets.

Accommodation

Market forces have spawned new **hotels** and Lang Son is fairly well provisioned with inexpensive accommodation, although at weekends rooms still fill up with holidaymakers, mostly male, trekking over from China. Budget travellers should head straight for the clean, friendly and well-priced *Hoa Phuong Guesthouse* (☎025/871233; ①) on the highway between the bridge and Ky Lua market. A few hundred metres further north, opposite the market entrance, are two well-kept older hotels with large comfortable rooms and little to choose between them: the *Tam Thanh* (☎025/870979; ②) and *Hoa Binh* (☎025/870807; ②–③). If you're looking for something off the main road, try the *Thanh Tung* (☎025/871195; ②), just west of the highway beside the Ky Lua bridge, which offers four floors of tiny but spruce and well-equipped rooms, or the new *Gia Phong Hotel* (☎025/873396; ②) on Le Loi.

The town

Lang Son started life as a Chinese citadel and has been disputed ever since by Vietnamese, Chinese, French and Japanese armies. The Ky Cung River splits the town in two, leaving the main bulk on the north side of the Ky Lua bridge and provincial offices to the south. Highway 1, the town's main north–south artery, is called Tran Dang Ninh, and along here you'll find all that Lang Son has to offer. Bustling **Ky Lua market** is in the thick of things, just east of the highway, and is well worth investigating, especially in the early morning when Tay, Nung and Dao women come to trade. Chinese imports dominate – flowery eiderdowns, fabrics and plastic toys – alongside an amazing array of local produce, from freshwater fish to nuts, vegetables, fruit, and golden bowls of silk-worm larvae, according to the season. From the market, walk 1km downhill to the river and take a quick look at the small temple, **Den Ky Cung**, tucked under the bridge on the north bank. Founded over 500 years ago, this temple is dedicated to Quan Tuan Tranh, an army officer of the border guard who is reputed to have slain hundreds of Chinese in battle before he himself fell. There's nothing much to see inside apart from a photo of Uncle Ho visiting Lang Son in 1960.

Eating

Options in Lang Son are limited, to say the least. The old *Bac Son Hotel* on Le Loi has a passable **restaurant**, but street kitchens round the corner on Tran Dang Ninh are more interesting – no. 28 is recommended, opposite the junction with Tam Thanh. In the evenings a handful of rice and noodle **food stalls** set up on Le Loi near the highway.

South to Hanoi

Leaving Lang Son to head south, road and rail shadow each other for the roughly 150-kilometre journey to Hanoi, taking four hours via Highway 1 and an unbelievably leisurely eight to ten hours by train. The route climbs out of the gentle Ky Cung Valley into an area of low limestone hills which provide a singularly undramatic setting for one of Vietnam's historic victories over the Chinese. On this occasion it was the Ming Chinese who were defeated in 1427, losing thirty thousand men (a third of their force) to the rebel hero Le Loi during an ambush in the **Chi Lang Pass**. The battle is commemorated with a prominent war memorial and two nondescript walls beside the road in a bleak valley roughly 60km out of Lang Son.

A few kilometres further on, the hills begin to fade out on the edge of the Red River Valley as you enter **HA BAC**, a densely populated province famed for its folksy woodblock prints (those from Dong Ho village are especially prized) and **festivals**. The most endearing festival is held in Lim village, 20km outside Hanoi near **BAC NINH** town, on the thirteenth to fifteenth days of each first lunar month, in anticipation of spring. Young men and women compete in *quan ho* or alternate singing, unaccompanied and usually improvised love duets, ranging from the coy to the suggestive, which were traditionally flung back and forth as a prelude to courtship. But the festival at **Den Ba Chua Kho**, 1km west of Bac Ninh, is more in keeping with the times: hopefuls flock out of Hanoi on the fourteenth and fifteenth days of the second lunar month to pray for wealth at this temple dedicated to an exemplary businesswoman of the Ly dynasty. The goddess grants "loans" of paper money or gold leaf which must be repaid, with interest, by the end of the year, either in real money or in reproduction dollar bills.

travel details

Buses

*It's almost impossible to give the **frequency** with which buses run. Though scheduled, long-distance public buses won't depart if empty. Moreover, private services, often minibuses or pick-ups, ply more popular routes, and depart only when they have enough passengers to make the journey worthwhile. It's advisable to start your journey early – most long-distance departures leave between 5 and 9am, and few run after midday. **Journey times** can also vary; figures below show the normal length of time you can expect the journey to take.*

Cao Bang to: Hanoi (10hr); Lang Son (6hr).
Dien Bien Phu to: Lai Chau (5hr); Son La (8hr).
Hoa Binh to: Hanoi (2hr); Mai Chau (4hr); Son La (10hr).
Lai Chau to: Dien Bien Phu (5hr); Sa Pa (8hr).
Lao Cai to: Sa Pa (1hr 30min–2hr).
Lang Son to: Cao Bang (6hr); Hanoi (5hr).
Mai Chau to: Hoa Binh (4hr).
Sa Pa to: Lai Chau (8hr); Lao Cai (1hr 30min–2hr).
Son La to: Dien Bien Phu (8hr); Hanoi (12hr); Hoa Binh (10hr), via the Mai Chau junction (8hr).

Trains

Dong Dang to: Hanoi (2 daily; 8–10hr).
Lao Cai to: Hanoi (2 daily; 10–11hr).

Flights

Dien Bien Phu to: Hanoi (2 weekly; 1hr)

PART THREE

THE

CONTEXTS

Entrance tecket: 12.000d

THE HISTORICAL FRAMEWORK

Vietnam as a unified state within its present geographical boundaries has only existed since the early nineteenth century. The national history, however, stretches back thousands of years to a legendary kingdom in the Red River Delta. From there the Viet people pushed relentlessly down the peninsula of Indochina on the "March to the South", *Nam Tien*. The other compelling force, and a constant theme throughout its history, is Vietnam's ultimately successful resistance to all foreign aggressors.

THE BEGINNINGS

The earliest evidence of human activity in Vietnam can be traced back to a Paleolithic culture that existed some 500,000 years ago. Over the following centuries these hunter-gatherers slowly developed agricultural techniques, but the most important step came about 4000 years ago when farmers began to cultivate irrigated rice in the Red River Delta. The communal effort required to build and maintain the system of dykes and canals spawned a stable, highly organized society, held to be the original Vietnamese nation. This embryonic kingdom, **Van Lang**, emerged sometime around 2000 BC and was ruled over by the semi-mythological Hung Kings from their capital near today's Viet

Tri, northwest of Hanoi. Archeological finds indicate that by the first millennium BC these people, the Lac Viet, had evolved into a sophisticated Bronze Age culture whose influence spread as far as Indonesia. Undoubtedly their greatest creations were the ritualistic **bronze drums**, discovered in the 1920s near Dong Son, and revered by the Vietnamese as the first hard evidence of an indigenous, independent culture.

In the mid-third century BC a Chinese warlord conquered Van Lang to create a new kingdom, **Au Lac**, with its capital at Co Loa, near present-day Hanoi. For the first time the lowland Lac Viet and the hill peoples were united. After only fifty years, around 207 BC, Au Lac was itself invaded by a Chinese potentate and became part of **Nam Viet** (Southern Viet), an independent kingdom occupying much of southern China. For a while the Lac Viet were able to maintain their local traditions and an indigenous aristocracy. Then, in 111 BC the Han emperors annexed the whole Red River Delta and so began a thousand years of Chinese domination.

CHINESE RULE

A millennium under Chinese rule had a profound effect on all aspects of Vietnamese life, notably the social and political spheres. With the introduction of **Confucianism** came the growth of a rigid, feudalistic hierarchy dominated by a mandarin class. This innately conservative elite ensured the long-term stability of an administrative system which continued to dominate Vietnamese society until well into the nineteenth century. The Chinese also introduced technological advances, such as writing, silk production and large-scale hydraulic works, while Mahayana Buddhism first entered Vietnam from China during the second century AD.

At the same time, however, the Viet people were forging their national identity in the continuous struggle to break free from their powerful northern neighbour. The local aristocracy, though they prospered under the Chinese, increasingly resented their vassal status and the heavy taxes demanded in tribute. Much is made of the various insurrections that marked the period, but on at least three occasions the Vietnamese ousted their masters. The first and most celebrated of these short-lived independent kingdoms was established by the **Trung sisters** (Hai Ba Trung) in 40 AD. Following the murder of Trung Trac's husband by the Chinese, the two sisters rallied the local lords and peasant farmers in the first popular insurrection against foreign domination. The Chinese fled, leaving Trung Trac ruler of the territory from Hué to southern China until the Han emperor dispatched 20,000 troops and a fleet of 2000 junks to quell the rebellion three years later. The sisters threw themselves in a river to escape capture, and the Chinese quickly set about removing the local lords. Though subsequent uprisings also failed, the Trungs had demonstrated the fallibility of the Chinese and earned their place in Vietnam's pantheon of heroes.

Over the following centuries Vietnam was drawn closer into the political and cultural realm of China. The seventh and eighth centuries were particularly bleak as the powerful Tang dynasty tightened its grip on the province it called **Annam**, or the "Pacified South". As soon as the dynasty collapsed in the early tenth century a series of major rebellions broke out, culminating in the battle of the **Bach Dang River** in 938 AD. In this famous victory Ngo Quyen, leader of the Vietnamese forces, lured the Chinese Navy into the estuary and, as the tide turned, chased them onto stakes embedded in the river mouth (see p.365). Ngo Quyen declared himself ruler of **Nam Viet** and set up court at the historic citadel of Co Loa, heralding what was to be nearly ten centuries of Vietnamese independence.

FUNAN AND CHAMPA

Meanwhile, in the south of Vietnam it was the Indian civilization rather than the Chinese which dominated, though as a cultural influence rather than a ruling power. From the first century AD Indian traders sailing east towards China established Hindu enclaves along the southern coast of Indochina. The largest and most important of these city-states was **Funan**, based on a port-city called Oc Eo, near present-day Rach Gia in the Mekong Delta (see p.150). By the early third century, Funan had developed into a powerful trading nation with links extending as far as Persia and even Rome. But technological developments in the fifth century enabled larger ships to sail round Indochina without calling at any port, and Funan gradually declined.

At around the same time another Indianized kingdom was developing along the narrow coastal plains of central Vietnam. Little is known about the origins of **Champa**, but Chinese records indicate the creation of a "barbarian" state in the area towards the end of the second century. Champa's subsequent history is a complicated tale of shifting allegiances between its Chinese, Khmer and, later, Vietnamese neighbours (see box on p.204). For most of its existence, however, Champa was a Hindu kingdom, based on wet-rice farming and maritime trade, ruled over by divine kings who worshipped first Shiva and later embraced Buddhism. Until the late tenth century, Champa extended from the Hoanh Son Mountains, north of Dong Hoi, down to the Mekong Delta. Their power-base was largely the territory around today's Da Nang, and their spiritual heartland the temple complex of My Son. Cham kings sponsored a vast array of sacred buildings and the red-brick ruins of their towers and temples can be seen all along the coast of south-central Vietnam. While they never attained the magnificence of Angkor, their greatest legacy is a striking architectural style characterized by a wealth of exuberant sculpture.

In general the Chinese tolerated the relatively weak kingdom on their borders, though they exacted tribute and plundered Champa on several occasions. After the mid-tenth century, however, Vietnamese independence changed the situation dramatically as the Viets, in search of new land, turned their attention southwards. By the end of the eleventh century Champa had lost its territory north of Hué and four centuries later the whole kingdom became a vassal state under Viet hegemony. For a while Cham princes continued as nominal rulers until the state was finally absorbed into Vietnam in the nineteenth century.

INDEPENDENT VIETNAM

Back in the Red River Delta, the period immediately following independence from Chinese rule in 939 AD was marked by factional infighting. Ngo Quyen died after only five years on the throne and Nam Viet dissolved in anarchy while twelve warlords disputed the succession. In 968 one of the rivals, Dinh Bo Linh, finally united the country and secured its future by paying tribute to the Chinese Emperor, a system which continued until the nineteenth century. Dinh Bo Linh, however, took the additional precaution of moving his capital south to the well-defended valley of Hoa Lu, where it remained during the two short-lived Dinh and Early Le dynasties.

THE VIETNAMESE DYNASTIES

Ngo	939–965 AD
Dinh	968–980
Early Le	980–1009
Ly	1009–1225
Tran	1225–1400
Ho	1400–1407
(Ming Chinese	1407–1428)
Later Le	1428–1789
Nguyen and Trinh lords	1592–1788
Tay Son	1788–1802
Nguyen	1802–1945

These early monarchs laid the framework for a centralized state. They reformed the administration and the army, and instigated a programme of road building. But it was the following **Ly dynasty**, founded by the great **Ly Thai To** in 1009, that consolidated the independence of **Dai Viet** (Great Viet) and guaranteed the nation's stability for the next four hundred years. Ly Thai To and his successors were ardent Buddhists; the ideological basis for their administrative and political reforms, however, was solidly Confucian and borrowed heavily from the Chinese. One of the first actions of the new dynasty was to move the capital back into the northern rice-lands, founding the city of Thang Long, the precursor of modern Hanoi. The construction of more sophisticated irrigation systems in the Red River Delta led to a significant improvement in the national economy. At the same time, reform of both land-tenure and the provincial administration created an emerging class of hereditary landowners and provided a stable tax base for the state coffers. In 1076 a Ly king founded Vietnam's first national university in Hanoi's great temple to Confucius, Van Mieu, in order to supply the state with its senior mandarins through competitive examination.

Ly Thai To's successor, Ly Thai Tong (1028–54), carried out a major reorganization of the national army, turning it into a professional fighting force, able to secure the northern borders and also to start expanding southwards. So confident was this new power that in 1076 the army of Dai Viet, under the revered General Ly Thuong Kiet, launched a pre-emptive strike against the Sung Chinese and then held off their counterattack. But this was a mere skirmish compared with what the next dynasty, the Tran, had in store, as Kublai Khan swept his armies down through southern China in the late thirteenth century.

The **Tran dynasty**, which ousted the declining Ly clan in 1225, largely retained the existing administrative system and continued to increase the power of the centralized state. But the Tran's crowning achievements were their spectacular military victories against three successive **Mongol invasions** in the space of thirty years. On the first two occasions, in 1257 and 1284, Mongol forces briefly occupied the capital before having to withdraw, while the last battle, in 1288, is remembered for a re-run of Ngo Quyen's ploy in the Bach Dang River. This time it was the brilliant General Tran Hung Dao, a prince in the royal family, who led Viet forces against the far superior armies of Kublai Khan. While the Mongol Navy foundered in the Bach Dang River, its army was also being trounced and the remnants driven back into China; soon after, the Khan died, and with him the Mongol threat.

By the end of the fourteenth century constant warfare – mostly against the Chams – and high taxes had bled the country dry. Famines plagued the northern delta while powerful feudal lords amassed ever larger land-holdings, creating a rebellious population of landless slaves, serfs and peasant farmers. In the confusion that marked the end of the Tran dynasty, an ambitious court minister, Ho Qui Ly, usurped the throne in 1400. Though the **Ho dynasty** lasted only seven years, its two progressive monarchs launched a number of important reforms. They tackled the problem of land shortages by restricting the size of holdings and then rented out the excess to landless peasants; the tax system was revised and paper money replaced coinage; ports were opened to foreign trade; the judiciary was overhauled and public health care introduced. Even the education system came under review and was broadened to include mathematics, agriculture and other practical subjects along with the classic Confucian texts.

Just as the Ho were getting into their stride, so the new Ming dynasty in China were beginning to look south again across the border. Under the pretext of restoring the Tran, Ming armies invaded in 1407 and imposed direct rule a few years later. This time, however, the **Chinese occupation** faced a much tougher problem as the Viet people were now a relatively cohesive force, united by their growing sense of national identity. The Chinese tried to dismantle the Viet culture by outlawing local customs and destroying Vietnamese literature, works of art and historical texts. Economic conditions were equally harsh and rebellions erupted throughout the country. Slowly, Vietnamese resistance gravitated towards the mountains of Thanh Hoa, south of Hanoi, where a local landlord and mandarin, **Le Loi**, was preparing for a war of national liberation. For ten years Le Loi's well-disciplined guerrilla force harassed the enemy until he was finally able to defeat the Chinese Army in open battle in 1427.

Le Loi, as King Le Thai To, founded the third of the great ruling families, the **Later Le dynasty**, and set in train the reconstruction of Dai Viet, though he died after only five years on the throne. It was the fourth Le monarch, **Le Thanh Tong** (1460–97), who is regarded as the greatest of the Le kings. Under Le Thanh Tong agricultural reforms increased grain production and vast new tracts of land were opened up as the Champa kingdom was pushed south. This new-found prosperity, coupled with a relatively peaceful era, allowed Le Thanh Tong to conduct a national census and a geographical survey of the entire kingdom. He also instigated a new civil and criminal code which formed the basis for Vietnamese law right into the nineteenth century. In other ways, however, Le Thanh Tong was a deeply conservative monarch who promoted Confucian doctrine above all else.

THE NGUYEN AND TRINH LORDS

Initially the Le dynasty reaped the economic rewards of its expanding empire, but eventually their new provinces spawned wealthy semi-autonomous rulers strong enough to challenge the throne. As the Le declined in the sixteenth century, two such powerful clans, the **Nguyen and Trinh**, at first supported the dynasty against rival contenders. Towards the end of the century, however, they became the effective rulers of Vietnam, splitting the country in two. The Trinh lords held sway in Hanoi and the north, while the Nguyens set up court at Hué; the Le remained monarchs in name only. Sporadic civil war between the two clans lasted until 1674 when they signed a hundred-year truce and formally partitioned the country at the Gianh River, near Dong Hoi.

At around the same time the Nguyen lords completed their conquest of the Mekong Delta,

seizing territory from the fading Khmer empire, and by the mid-eighteenth century Viet people occupied the whole peninsula down to Ca Mau. Nevertheless, severe famines, exacerbated by land shortages in the north and corrupt officials everywhere, plagued Vietnam throughout the eighteenth century. Insurrections rumbled away until the general discontent focused on an uprising at Tay Son in 1771. For a while the rebels held sway, but there was now a new factor in the balance of power.

THE ARRIVAL OF THE WEST

The first Western visitors to the Vietnamese peninsula were probably **traders** from ancient Rome who sailed into the ports of Champa in the second century AD. After the fifth century, however, the main trade routes between East and West bypassed Indochina. Marco Polo sailed up the coast in the thirteenth century on his way to China, but more significant was the arrival of a Portuguese merchant, Antonia Da Faria, at the port of Fai Fo (Hoi An) in 1535. Fai Fo was then one of southeast Asia's greatest ports, crammed with vessels from China and Japan. The Portuguese established their own trading post at Fai Fo, in the land they called Cochinchina, soon to be followed by other European maritime powers. At this time Vietnam was breaking up into regional factions and the Europeans were quick to exploit growing tensions between the Nguyen and Trinh lords, providing weapons in exchange for trading concessions. However, when the civil war ended in 1674 the merchants lost their advantage. Gradually the English, Dutch and French closed down their trading posts until only the Portuguese remained in Fai Fo.

With the traders came the **missionaries**. Portuguese Dominicans had been the first to arrive in the early sixteenth century, but it wasn't until 1615, when Jesuits set up a small mission in Fai Fo, that the Catholic Church gained an established presence in Vietnam. The mission's initial success in the southern, Nguyen territory encouraged the Jesuits to look north. The man they chose for the job was a 28-year-old Frenchman, **Alexandre de Rhodes**, a gifted linguist who, only six months after arriving in Fai Fo, in 1627, was preaching in Vietnamese. His talents soon won over the Trinh lords in Hanoi, where de Rhodes gave six sermons a day and converted nearly 7000 Vietnamese in just two years. During this time de Rhodes was also working on a simple romanized script for the Vietnamese language, which otherwise used a formidable system based on Chinese characters. De Rhodes merely wanted to make evangelizing easier, but his phonetic system eventually came to be adopted as Vietnam's national language, *quoc ngu*.

The missionaries found a ready audience, especially among peasant farmers and others near the bottom of the established Confucian hierarchy. It didn't take long before the ruling elite felt threatened by Christianity's subversive ideas – undermining loyalty to the emperor and denouncing polygamy worried them in particular. Missionary work was banned after the 1630s and many priests were expelled, or even executed. But enforcement was erratic and missionaries came and went according to the political climate. By the end of the seventeenth century the Catholic Church, and particularly the French Society of Foreign Missions, claimed several hundred thousand converts. Then, towards the end of the eighteenth century, the Catholic missions also provided an opening for French merchants wishing to challenge Britain's presence in the Far East. When a large-scale rebellion broke out in Vietnam in the early 1770s these entrepreneurs saw their chance to establish a firmer footing on the Indochinese peninsula.

THE TAY SON REBELLION

As the eighteenth century progressed, insurrections flared up throughout the countryside. Most were easily stamped out, but in 1771 three brothers raised their standard in Tay Son village, west of Qui Nhon, and ended up ruling the whole country. Their **Tay Son rebellion** gained broad support among dispossessed peasants, ethnic minorities, small merchants and townspeople attracted by the brothers' message of equal rights, justice and liberty. As rebellion spread through the south, the Tay Son army rallied even more converts when they seized land from the wealthy and redistributed it to the poor. By the middle of 1786 the rebels had overthrown both the Trinh and Nguyen lords, again leaving the Le dynasty intact. When the Le monarch called on the Chinese in 1788 to help remove the Tay Son usurpers, the Chinese happily obliged by occupying Hanoi. At this the middle brother (Nguyen Hue) declared himself

Emperor Quang Trung and quick-marched his army 600km from Hué to defeat the Chinese in a glorious battle at Dong Da, on the outskirts of Hanoi. With Hué as his capital, Quang Trung set about implementing his promised reforms, but when he died prematurely in 1792, aged 39, his ten-year-old son was unable to hold on to power.

One of the few Nguyen lords to have survived the Tay Son rebellion in the south was Prince Nguyen Anh. The prince made several unsuccessful attempts to regain the throne in the mid-1780s. After one such failure he fled to Phu Quoc Island where he met a French bishop, Pigneau de Béhaine. With an eye on future religious and commercial concessions, the bishop offered to make approaches to the French on behalf of the Nguyens. A treaty was eventually signed in 1787, promising military aid in exchange for territorial and trading concessions, though France failed to deliver the assistance due to a financial crisis preceding the French Revolution. The bishop went ahead anyway, raising a motley force of 4000 armed mercenaries and a handful of ships. The expedition was launched in 1789 and Nguyen Anh entered Hanoi in 1802 to claim the throne as **Emperor Gia Long**. Bishop de Béhaine didn't live to see the victory, nor to enforce the treaty: he died in 1799 and received a stately funeral.

THE NGUYEN DYNASTY

For the first time **Vietnam**, as the country was now called, fell under a single authority from the northern border all the way down to the point of Ca Mau. In the hope of promoting unity, Gia Long established his capital in the centre, at Hué, where he built a magnificent citadel in imitation of the Chinese emperor's Forbidden City. The choice of architecture was appropriate: Gia Long and the **Nguyen dynasty** he founded were resolutely Confucian. The new emperor immediately abolished the Tay Son reforms, reimposing the old feudal order under a strongly centralized state in which the monarch became increasingly isolated from his subjects. Land confiscated from the rebels was redistributed to loyal mandarins, the bureaucracy was reinstated and the majority of peasants found themselves worse off than before; numerous rebellions were ruthlessly suppressed. Gradually the country was closed to the outside world and to modernizing influences which might have helped it withstand the onslaught of French military intervention in the mid-nineteenth century. On the other hand, Gia Long and his successors did much to improve the infrastructure of Vietnam, developing a road network, extending the irrigation systems and rationalizing the provincial administration. Under the Nguyens the arts, particularly literature and court music, also flourished.

By refusing to grant any trading concessions, Gia Long disappointed the French adventurers who had helped him to the throne. He did, however, permit a certain amount of religious freedom, though his successors were far more suspicious of the missionaries' intentions. After 1825 several edicts were issued forbidding missionary work, accompanied by sporadic, occasionally brutal, persecutions of Christians, both Vietnamese converts and foreign priests. Ultimately, this provided the French with the excuse they needed to annex the country.

FRENCH CONQUEST

French governments grew increasingly imperialistic as the nineteenth century wore on. In the Far East, as Britain threatened to dominate trade with China, France began to see Vietnam as a potential route into the resource-rich provinces of Yunnan and southern China. Not that France had any formal policy to colonize Indochina; rather it came about in a piecemeal fashion, driven as often as not by private adventurers or the unilateral actions of French officials. In 1847 two French naval vessels began the process when they bombarded Da Nang on the pretext of rescuing a French priest. Reports of Catholic persecutions were deliberately exaggerated until Napoleon III was finally persuaded to launch an armada of fourteen ships and 2500 men in 1858. After capturing Da Nang in September, the force moved south to take Saigon, against considerable opposition, and the whole Mekong Delta over the next three years. Faced with serious unrest in the north, Emperor Tu Duc signed a treaty in 1862 granting France the three eastern provinces of the delta plus trading rights in selected ports, and allowing missionaries the freedom to proselytize. Five years later French forces annexed the remaining southern provinces to create the colony of **Cochinchina**.

France became embroiled in domestic troubles and the French government was divided on whether to continue the enterprise. But the administrators of Cochinchina, backed by the commercial lobby, had their eyes on the north. The first attempt to take Hanoi and open up the Red River into China failed when its leader, the charismatic explorer Francis Garnier, was killed in 1873. In 1882 a larger force was dispatched under the command of Henri Rivière; within a few months, France was in control of Hanoi and the lower reaches of the Red River Delta. Spurred on by this success, the French parliament financed the first contingents of the **French Expeditionary Force** just as the Nguyens were floundering in a succession crisis following the death of Tu Duc. In August 1883, when the French fleet sailed into the mouth of the Perfume River, near Hué, the new emperor was compelled to meet their demands. **Annam** (central Vietnam) and **Tonkin** (the north) became protectorates of France, to be combined with Cochinchina, Cambodia and, later, Laos to form the **Union of Indochina** after 1887. Though the emperor in Hué retained a semblance of power, for the next seventy years Vietnam was once again under foreign occupation.

FRENCH RULE

Despite much talk of the "civilizing mission" of imperial rule, the French were more interested in the economic potential of their new possession. One of the key architects of colonial policy was Paul Doumer, governor-general from 1897 to 1902. Doumer launched a massive programme of **infrastructural development**, constructing railways, bridges, roads and draining vast areas of the swampy Mekong Delta. These public works were funded by raising punitive taxes, including state monopolies on opium, alcohol and salt, which between them accounted for seventy percent of government revenues. As far as the colonialists were concerned this was a promising start and private capital began to flow into the colony in ever larger amounts, reaching a peak in the 1920s.

Much of this economic development, however, was built on shaky foundations, and during the Great Depression of the 1930s markets collapsed and commodity prices tumbled. The shift to large-scale rice production for export had not only eroded Vietnam's traditional social systems and undermined the local economy, but also meant that per capita food consumption actually decreased under French rule. Peasants were forced off the land to work as indentured labour in the new rubber, tea and coffee estates or in the mines, often under brutal conditions. Heavy taxes exacerbated **rural poverty** and any commercial or industrial eneterprises were kept firmly in French hands, or were controlled by the small minority of Vietnamese and Chinese who actually benefited under the new regime.

On the positive side, mass vaccination and health programmes did bring the frequent epidemics of cholera, smallpox and the plague under control. Education was a thornier issue: overall, education levels deteriorated during French rule, particularly among unskilled labourers, but important reforms saw the introduction of *quoc ngu*, the romanized script of Alexandre de Rhodes. In addition, a small elite from the emerging urban middle class received a broader, French-based education and a few went to universities in Europe. Not that it got them very far: Vietnamese were barred from all but the most menial jobs in the colonial administration. It was this frustrated and alienated group, imbued with the ideas of Western liberals and Chinese reformers, who began to challenge French rule.

THE ANTI-COLONIAL STRUGGLE

For a population brought up on legends of heroic victories over superior forces, the ease with which France had occupied Vietnam was a deep psychological blow. The earliest resistance movements naturally focused on the restoration of the monarchy, such as the "Save the King" (*Can Vuong*) movement of the 1890s. But any emperor showing signs of patriotism was swiftly removed by the French administration. Gradually the nationalists saw that a more radical approach was called for. One of the most influential leaders of the early twentieth century was **Phan Boi Chau**, who eventually called for the violent overthrow of the colonial regime. Like many young Asian revolutionaries he was deeply affected by the Japanese defeat of a Russian fleet in 1905, the first Asian victory over a European power. For several years Phan Boi Chau lived in Japan where he organized the Eastward Movement, providing dissident intellectuals with a political and military education. Later, he moved to south China, where Sun Yat Sen's 1911 revolution was another source of inspiration to many Vietnamese nationalists.

Up until the mid-1920s Vietnam's various anti-colonial movements tended to be fragmented, disorganized and were easily controlled by the *Sûreté*, the formidable French secret police. On the whole the nationalists' aims were political rather than social or economic, and most failed to appeal to the majority of Vietnamese. But in the late 1920s more radical organizations appeared, drawing on the ideas of Phan Boi Chau. The most important of these was the **Vietnam Nationalist Party** (*Viet Nam Quoc Dan Dang*, or VNQDD), established in Hanoi in 1927 and modelled on the Chinese Nationalist Party, the Kuomintang. The new party was pledged to the violent overthrow of the French regime and the establishment of a democratic republic. In February 1930 the VNQDD launched an attack against military outposts in Yen Bai and the north of Vietnam. But the uprising was badly co-ordinated and ended in disaster when it failed to attract widespread support: most of the VNQDD leaders were captured and executed, after which the organization gradually faded from the scene.

Meanwhile, over the border in southern China, a more significant event had occurred a few years earlier, with the foundation of the **Revolutionary Youth League** in 1925. Not only was this Vietnam's first Marxist–Leninist organization, but its founding father was **Ho Chi Minh**. Born in 1890, the son of a patriotic minor official, Ho was already in trouble with the French authorities in his teens. He left Vietnam in 1911, then turned up in Paris after World War I under one of his many pseudonyms, Nguyen Ai Quoc ("Nguyen the Patriot"). In France, Ho became increasingly active among other exiled dissidents exploring ways to bring an end to colonial rule. At this time one of the few political groups actively supporting anti-colonial movements were the communists; in 1920 Ho became a founding member of the French Communist Party and by 1923 he was in Moscow, training as a communist agent. His task was to unite the nascent Vietnamese anti-colonial movements under one organization, the Revolutionary Youth League. Among his many talents, Ho Chi Minh was an intelligent strategist and a great motivator; though he was now committed to Marxist–Leninist ideology, he understood the need to appeal to all nationalists, downplaying the controversial goal of social revolution (see pp.294–295 for more on the chequered life of Ho Chi Minh).

Although many other subsequently famous revolutionaries worked with Ho, it was largely his fierce dedication, single-mindedness and tremendous charisma that held the nationalist movement together and finally propelled the country to independence. The first real test of Ho's leadership came in 1929 when, in his absence, the League split into three separate communist parties. In Hong Kong a year later, Ho persuaded the rival groups to unite into one **Indochinese Communist Party** whose main goal was an independent Vietnam governed by workers, peasants and soldiers. In preparation for the revolution, cadres were sent into rural areas and among urban workers to set up party cells. The timing couldn't have been better: unemployment and poverty were on the increase as the Great Depression took hold, while France became less willing to commit resources to its colonies. But perhaps most importantly, Vietnamese workers were themselves becoming politically active, largely under the influence of some of the 100,000 Vietnamese soldiers and auxiliaries returning from World War I with ideas about the power of organized labour.

Throughout the 1930s Vietnam was plagued with strikes and labour unrest, of which the most important was the **Nghe Tinh uprising** in the summer of 1930. The precise role of the Communist Party in the revolt, during which French planes bombed a crowd of 20,000 demonstrators marching on Vinh, has never been made clear. But within days villagers had seized control of much of the surrounding countryside and, in some cases, set up revolutionary councils to evict wealthy landlords and redistribute land to the peasants. Some of these "soviets" held out against the authorities for six months while the movement spread to other districts. The uprising had demonstrated the power of socialist organization but it proved disastrous in the short term. Thousands of peasants were killed or imprisoned, the leaders were executed and the Communist Party structure was badly mauled. Most of the ringleaders ended up in the notorious penal colony of Poulo Condore (Con Dao Island), which came to be known as the "University of the Revolution". It's estimated that the French held some 10,000 Vietnamese communists and other activists in prison by the late 1930s.

WORLD WAR II

The German occupation of France in 1940 suddenly changed the whole political landscape. Not only did it demonstrate to the Vietnamese the vulnerability of their colonial masters, but it also overturned the established order in Vietnam and ultimately provided Ho Chi Minh with the opportunity he had been waiting for. The immediate repercussion was the **Japanese occupation** of Indochina after Vichy France signed a treaty allowing Japan to station troops in the colony, while leaving the French administration in place. By mid-1941 the region's coal mines, rice fields and military installations were all under Japanese control. Some Vietnamese nationalist groups welcomed this turn of events as the Japanese made encouraging noises about autonomy and "Asia for the Asians". Others, mostly communist groups, declared their opposition to all foreign intervention and continued to operate from secret bases in the mountainous region that flanks the border between China and Vietnam.

By this time Ho Chi Minh had reappeared in southern China, from where he walked over the border into Vietnam, carrying his rattan trunk and trusty Hermes typewriter. The date was February 1941; Ho had been in exile for thirty years. In **Pac Bo cave**, near Cao Bang, Ho met up with other resistance leaders, including Vo Nguyen Giap, to start the next phase in the fight for national liberation. The key element was a nationalist coalition, the League for the Independence of Vietnam (*Viet Nam Doc Lap Dong Minh*), better known as the **Viet Minh**, founded in May 1941. The organization was again specifically designed to win broad popular support for independence, followed by moderate social and democratic reforms. The second critical decision reached in Pac Bo was to mobilize mass support with a nationwide propaganda campaign.

Over the next few years Viet Minh recruits received military training in southern China and the first regular armed units were set up, which formed the nucleus of the **Vietnamese Liberation Army** in 1945. Gradually the Viet Minh established liberated zones in the northern mountains to provide bases for future guerrilla operations. Then, as Japanese defeat looked ever more likely, Ho Chi Minh set off once again into China to seek military and financial support from the Chinese and from the Allied forces operating out of Kunming. Ho also made contact with the American Office of Strategic Services (forerunner of the CIA), which promised him limited arms, much to the anger of the Free French who were already planning their return to Indochina. In return for **American aid** the Viet Minh provided information about Japanese forces and rescued Allied pilots shot down over Vietnam. Later, in 1945, an American team arrived in Ho's Cao Bang base where they found him suffering from malaria, dysentery and dengue fever; it's said they saved his life.

Meanwhile, suspecting a belated French counterattack, Japanese forces seized full control of the country in March 1945. They declared a nominally independent state under the leadership of Bao Dai, the last Nguyen emperor, and imprisoned most of the French Army. The Viet Minh quickly moved onto the offensive, helped to some extent by a massive famine that ravaged northern Vietnam that summer. Then, in early August, US forces dropped the first atom bomb on Hiroshima, precipitating the **Japanese surrender** on August 14.

THE AUGUST REVOLUTION

The Japanese surrender left a power vacuum which Ho Chi Minh was quick to exploit. On August 15 Ho called for a national uprising, which later came to be known as the **August Revolution**. Within four days Hanoi was seething with pro-Viet Minh demonstrations and in two weeks most of Vietnam came under their control. Emperor Bao Dai handed over his imperial sword to Ho's provisional government at the end of August and on September 2, 1945 Ho Chi Minh proclaimed the establishment of the **Democratic Republic of Vietnam**, cheered by a massive crowd in Hanoi's Ba Dinh Square. For the first time in eighty years Vietnam was an independent country. Famously, Ho's Declaration of Independence quoted from the American Declaration: "All men are created equal. They are endowed with their Creator with certain inalienable rights, among these are life, liberty and the pursuit of happiness". But this, and subsequent appeals for America's help against the looming threat of recolonization, fell on deaf ears as America became increasingly concerned at communist expansion.

The **Potsdam Agreement**, which marked the end of World War II, failed to recognize the new Republic of Vietnam. Instead, Japanese troops south of the Sixteenth Parallel were to surrender to British authority, while those in the north would defer to the Chinese Kuomintang. However, by the time these forces arrived, the Viet Minh were already in control, having relieved the Japanese of most of their weapons. In the **south** rival nationalist groups were battling it out in Saigon and French troops had also joined in the fray. The situation was so chaotic that the British commander proclaimed martial law and, amazingly, even deployed Japanese soldiers to help restore calm. Against orders, he also re-armed the 6000 liberated French troops and Saigon was soon back in French hands. A few days later General Leclerc arrived with the first units of the French Expeditionary Force, charged with re-imposing colonial rule in Indochina.

Meanwhile, things were going more smoothly in the north, though 200,000 Chinese soldiers on Vietnamese soil worried the new government. The soldiers acted increasingly like an army of occupation against which the Viet Minh could muster a mere 5000 ill-equipped troops. Forced to choose between the two in order to survive, Ho Chi Minh finally rated French rule the lesser of the two evils and commenced negotiations with the French commissioner. Ho is reputed to have commented, "I prefer to smell French shit for five years, rather than Chinese shit for the rest of my life". In March 1946 Ho's government signed a treaty allowing a limited French force to replace Kuomintang soldiers in the north. In return France recognized the Democratic Republic as a "free state" within the proposed French Union; the terms were left deliberately vague. The treaty also provided for a referendum to determine whether Cochinchina would join the new state or remain separate.

While further negotiations dragged on during the summer of 1946 both sides were busily re-arming as it became apparent that the French were not going to abide by the treaty. By late April the Expeditionary Force had already exceeded agreed levels, and there was no sign of the promised referendum; in September 1946 the talks effectively broke down. Skirmishes between Vietnamese and French troops in the northern delta increased as tensions rose, until they boiled over in a dispute over customs control in Haiphong. To quell the rioting, the French navy bombed the town on November 23, killing thousands of civilians. This was followed by the announcement that French troops would assume responsibility for law and order in the north. By way of reply, Viet Minh units attacked French installations in Hanoi on December 19, and then, while resistance forces held the capital for a few days, Ho Chi Minh and the regular army slipped away into the northern mountains.

THE FRENCH WAR

For the first years of the **war against the French** (also known as the First Indochina War, or Franco-Viet Minh War) the Viet Minh kept largely to their mountain bases in northern and central Vietnam. While the Viet Minh were building up and training an army, the Expeditionary Force was consolidating its control over the Red River Delta and establishing a string of highly vulnerable outposts around guerrilla-held areas. In October 1947 the French attempted an all-out attack, an ambitious assault against the enemy headquarters. It soon became obvious that this was not a conventional war, but rather a "war without fronts" where Viet Minh troops could simply melt away into the jungle whenever threatened. In addition, the French found they had no secure areas; the enemy taunted them with hit-and-run attacks deep within the delta, protected by a local population who either actively supported or at least tolerated the Viet Minh.

The terrain certainly didn't favour the French, encumbered as they were with tanks and massed battalions, but perhaps most important was the political aspect of the war – as the Americans were to learn twenty years later. As outsiders fighting a war of recolonization, the French were already disadvantaged; they compounded the problem by failing to provide a viable political alternative to the Viet Minh. Non-communist nationalists, particularly in the south, were increasingly disenchanted with the communists, who were not above using terrorist tactics and even murdering their opponents. Attempting to capitalize on this, the French persuaded Bao Dai to return as head of the Associated State of Vietnam in March 1949. Unfortunately, most Vietnamese regarded Bao Dai as a mere puppet of the French and his gov-

ernment won little support. On the other hand the Viet Minh continued to attract new recruits to the **people's war**.

By 1948 a stalemate had been reached, but the communist victory in China in 1949 proved to be a turning point in the war. Almost immediately both China and Russia recognized the Democratic Republic of Vietnam and military aid started to flow across the border. Bao Dai's shaky government came to be seen as the last bastion of the free world and America was drawn into the war, funding the French military to the tune of at least US$3 billion by 1954. As the war entered a new phase, the Viet Minh recorded their first major victory, forcing the French to abandon their outposts along the Chinese border and gaining unhindered access to sanctuary in China. Early in 1951, equipped with Chinese weapons and confident of success, the Viet Minh launched an assault on Hanoi itself. In the first pitched battle of the war the Viet Minh suffered a massive defeat. They lost over 6000 troops in a battle that saw napalm deployed for the first time in Vietnam. But Giap had learnt his lesson, and for the next two years the French sought in vain to repeat their success.

The French were already tiring of the war and in 1953 made contact with Ho Chi Minh to find some way of resolving the conflict. The Americans were growing increasingly impatient with French progress, and at one stage threatened to deploy tactical nuclear weapons against the Viet Minh, while the Russians and Chinese were also applying pressure to end the war. The two sides agreed to discussions at the Geneva Conference, due to take place in May the next year to discuss the Korean peace. Meanwhile in Vietnam, a crucial battle was unfolding in an isolated valley on the Laotian border, near the town of **Dien Bien Phu**. Early in 1954 French battalions established a massive camp here, deliberately trying to tempt the Viet Minh into the open. Instead the Viet Minh surrounded the valley, cut off reinforcements and slowly closed in (see p.392 for the full story). After 59 days of bitter fighting the French were forced to surrender on May 7, 1954, the eve of the Geneva Conference. The eight years of war proved costly to both sides: total losses on the French side stood at 93,000, while an estimated 200,000 Viet Minh soldiers had been killed.

THE GENEVA CONFERENCE

On May 8, a day after the French capitulation at Dien Bien Phu, the nine delegations attending the **Geneva Conference** trained their focus upon Indochina. Armed with the knowledge that they now controlled around 65 percent of the country, and with such a decisive win under their belt, the Viet Minh delegation, led by Pham Van Dong, arrived in buoyant mood. The lasting peace they sought wasn't forthcoming. Hampered by distrust, the conference succeeded only in reaching a stopgap solution, a necessarily ambiguous compromise which, however, allowed the French to withdraw with some honour and recognized Vietnamese sovereignty at least in part. Keen to have a weak and fractured nation on their southern border, the Chinese delegation, headed by Chou En-Lai, spurred the Viet Minh into agreeing to a division of the country; reliant upon Chinese arms, the Viet Minh were forced to comply.

Under the terms of July 1954's **Geneva Accords** Vietnam was divided at the Seventeenth Parallel, along the Ben Hai River, pending nationwide free elections to be held by July 1956; a demilitarized buffer zone was established on either side of this military front. France and the Viet Minh, who were still fighting in the central highlands even as delegates machinated, agreed to an immediate ceasefire, and consented to a withdrawal of all troops to their respective territories – communists to the north, non-communists plus supporters of the French to the south. China, USSR, Britain, France and the Viet Minh agreed on the accords, but crucially neither the United States nor Bao Dai's government endorsed them, fearing that they heralded a reunited, communist-ruled Vietnam.

Long term, the Geneva Accords served to polarize deep divisions within the country and to widen the conflict into an ideological battle between the superpowers, fought out on Vietnamese soil. The immediate consequence, however, was a massive exodus from the north during the stipulated 300-day period of "**free movement**". Almost a million (mostly Catholic) refugees headed south, their flight aided by the US Navy, and to some extent engineered by the CIA, whose distribution of scaremongering, anti-communist leaflets was designed to create a base of support for the puppet government it was concocting in Saigon (see below). Approaching 100,000 **anti-French guerrillas** and sympathizers moved in the opposite direction to regroup, though as a precautionary measure, between 5000 and 10,000 Viet Minh cadres remained in the south, awaiting orders from Hanoi. These dormant operatives, known to the CIA as "**stay-behinds**" and to the communists as "winter cadres", were joined by spies who infiltrated the Catholic move south.

In line with the terms of the ceasefire, Ho Chi Minh's troops marched into Hanoi on October 9, 1954, even as the last French forces were still trooping out.

DIEM TAKES THE HELM

The Geneva Accords were still being thrashed out as Emperor Bao Dai named himself President and **Ngo Dinh Diem** ("Zee-em") Prime Minister of South Vietnam, on July 7. A Catholic, and vehemently anti-communist, Diem knew that Ho Chi Minh would win the lion's share of votes in the proposed elections, and therefore steadfastly refused to countenance them. His mandate "strengthened" by an October 1955 **referendum** (the prime minister's garnering of 98.2 percent of votes cast was more indicative of the blatancy of his vote-rigging than of any popular support), Diem promptly ousted Bao Dai from the chain of command, declared himself President of the Republic of Vietnam, and knuckled down to consolidating his position.

Diem inherited a political climate that was far from stable, and for a while his heavy-handed approach to government bore fruit. In the countryside, the militias maintained by the **Hoa Hao** and **Cao Dai** religious sects wielded great influence; while a Mafia-like crime syndicate called the **Binh Xuyen** ruled Saigon. By 1956, Diem had emasculated both the Hoa Hao and the Cao Dai, and a few months later the Binh Xuyen were efficiently subdued, though only after pitched battles on the streets of Saigon. Diem was able to turn his attention later the same year to Viet Minh dissidents still in the South, but in this case the iron-fist approach was hopelessly misguided. Although the subsequent **witch-hunt** decimated Viet Minh numbers, the brutal and indiscriminate nature of the operation – all dissenters were targeted (Viet Minh, communist or otherwise), as were those who simply resisted the extortion rackets of Diem's corrupt officials – caused widespread discontent that the president's bare-faced **nepotism** and insensitive land reforms did nothing to quell. As the supposed "free world democracy" of the South mutated into a police state, over 50,000 citizens died in Diem's pogrom.

BACK IN HANOI...

In Hanoi, meanwhile, Ho Chi Minh's government was finding it had problems of its own as, aided by droves of Chinese advisers, it set about constructing a socialist society. Years of warring with France had profoundly damaged the country's infrastructure, and now it found itself deprived of the South's plentiful rice stocks. Worse still, the **land reforms** of the mid-1950s, vaunted as a Robin Hood-style redistribution of land, saw many thousands (some historians set the number as high as 100,000) of innocents "tried" as landlords by ad hoc **People's Agricultural Reform Tribunals**, tortured, and then executed or set to work in labour camps. "Reactionaries" were also denounced and punished, often for such imperialist "crimes" as possessing works of the great French poets and novelists. The **Rectification of Errors Campaign** of 1956 at least released many victims of the reforms from imprisonment, but as Ho Chi Minh himself said, "one cannot wake the dead".

With Hanoi so preoccupied with getting its own house in order and, at least until 1956, with being seen to be sticking to Geneva's terms, Viet Minh guerrillas south of the Seventeenth Parallel were for several years left to fend for themselves. For the most part, they sat tight in the face of Diem's reprisals, although guerrilla strikes became increasingly common towards the end of the 1950s, often taking the form of assassinations of government officials. Only in 1959 did the erosion of their ranks, witnessed first-hand by Le Duan, prompt Hanoi to shift up a gear and endorse a more overtly military stance. Conscription was introduced in April 1960, cadres and hardware began to creep down the **Ho Chi Minh Trail** (see p.286), and at the end of the year Hanoi orchestrated the creation of the **National Liberation Front** (NLF), which drew together all opposition forces in the South. Diem dubbed its guerrilla fighters **Viet Cong**, or VC (Vietnamese Communists) – a name which stuck, though in reality the NLF rep-

resented a united front of Catholic, Buddhist, communist and non-communist nationalists. Numbers were further boosted by erstwhile members of the Binh Xuyen, and the Hoa Hao and Cao Daist militias. Despite its eclectic make-up, the NLF worked in tandem with Hanoi, from where it received its directives.

AMERICA ENTERS THE FRAY

American dollars had since 1950 been supporting the French war effort in Indochina. In 1954, President Eisenhower wrote of donating an "intelligent program of aid" as a means to "maintaining a strong, viable state", and in early 1955 the White House began to bankroll Diem's government and the training of his army, the **ARVN** (Army of the Republic of Vietnam). Behind these policies lay the fear of the chain reaction that could follow in southeast Asia, were South Vietnam to be overrun by communism – the so-called **Domino Effect** – and, more cynically, what this would mean for US access to raw materials, trade routes and markets. No change in policy accompanied President John F Kennedy's short-lived tenure of the White House. Kennedy, who had once described Diem's government as a "finger in the dyke" that held communism at bay, increased the build-up of military advisers and the financial shoring of the Southern regime and, though he balked at the prospect of large-scale American intervention, by the summer of 1962 there were 12,000 American advisers in South Vietnam.

Yet, despite all these injections of money, Diem's incompetent and unpopular government was losing ground to the VC in the battle for the **hearts and minds** of the population. Particularly damaging to the government was its **Strategic Hamlets Programme**. Formulated in 1962 and based on British methods used during the Malayan Emergency, the programme forcibly relocated entire villages into fortified stockades, with the aim of keeping the VC at bay. Ill-conceived, insensitive and open to exploitation by corrupt officials, the programme in fact had the opposite effect: as Nguyen Van Hieu, a high-ranking member of the Southern resistance, told Western journalist Wilfred Burchett, "Terror and brutal repression are driving everyone into the arms of the resistance". The majority of strategic hamlets were empty within two years, as villagers drifted back to their **ancestral lands**.

Militarily, things were little better. If America needed proof that Diem's government was struggling to subdue the guerrillas, it came in January 1963, at the **Battle of Ap Bac** (see p.124), where incompetent ARVN troops suffered heavy losses against a greatly outnumbered Viet Cong force. Four months later, Buddhists celebrating Buddha's birthday were fired upon by ARVN soldiers in Hué, sparking off riots and demonstrations against religious repression, and provoking **Thich Quang Duc**'s infamous self-immolation in Saigon (see p.83). Diem had become a liability. Fearing that the communists would gain further by his unpopularity, America tacitly sanctioned the November 1 **coup** that ousted him; Diem and his brother escaped to Cholon, only to be shot the following day (see p.87).

THE ESCALATION OF THE WAR

Three weeks later, Kennedy was dead. Whatever private misgivings his successor Lyndon B Johnson had about **continuing involvement** in what he called "that bitch of a war", still he was determined not to be responsible for America's losing a war to the communists. "Nothing", he said, "would be worse than that". By the end of 1963, America was involved to the tune of US$500 million a year.

The generals who superseded Diem proved no more efficacious, their **factional struggles** through 1964 and into 1965 igniting street demonstrations and riots that crippled Saigon. The capital staggered from coup to coup, but corruption, nepotism and dependence upon American support remained constant. In the countryside, meanwhile, the Viet Cong were forging a solid base of popular support. Observing Southern instability, Hanoi in early 1964 proceeded to send battalions of **NVA** (North Vietnamese Army) infantrymen down the Ho Chi Minh Trail, with 10,000 Northern troops hitting the trail in the first year. For America, unwilling to see the communists granted a say in the running of the South, yet unable to envisage Saigon's generals fending them off, the only option seemed to be to **"Americanize"** the conflict.

In August 1964, a chance came to do just that, when the American destroyer the USS *Maddox* allegedly suffered an unprovoked attack from North Vietnamese craft; two days afterwards, the *Maddox* and another ship, the *C Turner Joy*, reported a second attack. Years later

it emerged that the *Maddox* had been taking part in a covert mission to monitor coastal installations, and that the second incident almost certainly never happened. Nevertheless, reprisals followed in the form of 64 **bombing** sorties against Northern coastal bases. And back in Washington, senators voted through the **Tonkin Gulf Resolution**, empowering Johnson to deploy regular American troops in Vietnam, "to prevent further aggression". To Johnson, seeking re-election at the time, this stand against communism was grist to the publicity mill.

OPERATION ROLLING THUNDER

An NVA attack upon the highland town of Plei Ku in February 1965 curtailed several months of US procrastination about how best to prosecute the war in Vietnam, and elicited **Operation Flaming Dart**, a concerted bombing raid on NVA camps above the Seventeenth Parallel. Increasingly, the military argument swayed the decision-makers: General Curtis Le May, Commander of the US Air Force, graphically compared previous policy in Vietnam to "swatting flies", when "going after the manure pile" would be more effective. **Operation Rolling Thunder**, a sustained carpet-bombing campaign, kicked in a month later; by the time of its suspension three and a half years later its 350,000 sorties had seen twice the tonnage of bombs dropped (around 800 daily) as had fallen on all World War II's theatres of war. Despite such impressive statistics, Rolling Thunder failed either to break the North's sources and lines of supply, or to coerce Hanoi into a suspension of activities in the South. Bombing served only to strengthen the resilience of the North, whose population was mobilized to rebuild bridges, roads and railways as quickly as they were damaged. Moreover, NVA troops continued to infiltrate the South in increasing numbers, so that by 1967 over 100,000 a year were making the trek south.

As far back as 1954, the American politician William F Knowland had warned that "using United States ground forces in the Indochina jungle would be like trying to cover an elephant with a handkerchief — you just can't do it." His words fell on deaf ears. The first regular **American troops** from the 3rd US Marine Division landed at Da Nang in March 1965, and their original brief to defend its air base there was soon widened to embrace offensive action in the field. By the end of 1965, 200,000 GIs were in Vietnam – a figure that was to double within a year and approach half a million by the winter of 1967; in addition, there were large numbers of **Free World Military Forces**, comprising substantial contingents of Australians (Australian military advisers had been in South Vietnam since 1962) and South Koreans, plus smaller units of New Zealanders, Thais and Filipinos.

The American mission was largely confined to keeping the NVA at bay in the central highlands – as in the battle for the **Ia Drang Valley** during the autumn of 1965 – and neutralizing the guerrilla threat in the South, particularly the Mekong Delta and the region north of Saigon, the Viet Cong power-bases. The war these troops fought was a dirty, dispiriting and frustrating one: for the most part, it was a guerrilla conflict against an invisible enemy able to disappear into the nearest village, leaving them unable to trust even civilians. Missions to flush active Viet Cong soldiers out of villages, which were initiated towards the end of 1965, became known as **Search and Destroy** operations; the most infamous of these resulted in the **My Lai massacre** (see p.220–221). Other jargon was coined, too, and added to the lexicon of conflict: in the highlands, **fire bases** were established, from where Howitzers could rain fire upon NVA troop movements; elsewhere, **free fire zones** – areas cleared of villagers to enable bombing of their supposed guerrilla occupants – were declared; and **scorched earth**, the policy of denuding and razing vast swathes of land in order to rob the Viet Cong of cover, was introduced. And all the while, generals in the field were quick to establish that most symbolic arbiter in this insane war, the **body count**, according to which missions succeeded or failed.

HEARTS AND MINDS

Predictably, it was the **civilians** who suffered most as the conflict in Vietnam rolled on. In the **North**, outrage at the merciless bombing campaign meted out by a remote foreign aggressor engendered a sense of anti-colonial purpose – especially when Hanoi's propaganda machine got into gear. But in the **South**, there was only disorientation. To some, the enormity of the US presence seemed to preclude the possibility of a protracted conflict, and was therefore welcome; to others, it felt so much like an invasion, especially when GIs began to uproot them and

destroy their land, that they supported or joined the NLF. The Viet Cong themselves were no angels, though, often imposing a reign of terror, augmented by summary executions of alleged traitors. What's more, successive Saigon governments were corrupt and unpopular, but the alternative was the Northern communists so gruesomely depicted by American propaganda.

To survive, villagers quickly learned to react, and to say the right thing to the right person. The American policy of **Pacification**, by which was meant the provision of such commodities as education and health care, was introduced to win civilian confidence. But once the Americans had returned to their bases at night, the Viet Cong would commandeer the villages they vacated. Trying to appease the two sets of soldiers they encountered in the space of a day was like treading a tightrope for villagers, creating a climate of hatred and distrust that turned neighbours into informants; and, since children were conscripted by whichever side reached them first, brothers and sisters often found themselves fighting on opposing sides.

THE TET OFFENSIVE

On January 21, 1968, around 40,000 NVA troops laid siege to a remote American military base at **Khe Sanh**, near the Laotian border northwest of Hué. Wary that the confrontation might become an American Dien Bien Phu – an analogy that in reality held no water, given the USA's superior air power – America responded, to borrow the military jargon of the day, "with extreme prejudice", notching up a communist body count of over 10,000 in a carpet-bombing campaign graphically labelled "Niagara". However, such losses were seen as a necessary evil by the communists, for whom Khe Sanh was primarily a decoy to steer US troops and attention away from the **Tet Offensive** that exploded a week later. In the early hours of January 31, a combined force of 70,000 communists (most of them VC) violated a New Year truce to launch offensives on over a hundred urban centres across the South. The campaign failed to achieve its objectives of sparking a revolt against the Saigon regime and imposing VC representation in the Southern government as a first step towards reunification. Only in Hué did VC forces manage to hold out for more than a few days; moreover, communist losses were so devastating as to leave the VC permanently lamed.

But success *did* register across the Pacific, where the offensive caused a sea change in popular perceptions of the war. Thus far, Washington's propaganda machine had largely convinced the public that the war in Vietnam was under control; events in 1968 flew in the face of this charade. Around 2000 American GIs had died during the Tet Offensive; but symbolically more damaging was the audacious assault mounted, on the first day of the offensive, by a crack VC commando team on the compound of the **US Embassy in Saigon**. The communists had pierced the underbelly of the American presence in Vietnam: by the time the compound had been secured over six hours later, five Americans had died – and with them the popular conviction that the war was being won.

This shift in attitude was soon reflected in President Johnson's **vetoing** of requests for a massive troop expansion. On March 31, he announced a virtual cessation of bombing; a month later, the first bout of diplomatic sparring that was to grind on for five years was held in Paris; and before the year was out, a full end to bombing had been declared.

Further proof – if any were needed – of the futility of the American involvement in Vietnam came in the form of the battle for **A Shau Valley**, west of Da Nang in the central highlands, early the next year. One of the exit points for NVA troops labouring down the Ho Chi Minh Trail, the valley had been under communist control for three years. After two abortive attempts to retake the valley, by May 1969 the Americans had finally made some headway, bottling the NVA troops into its western end, where many of them dug in on Hill 937 (Ap Bia hill). The combined efforts of the American and ARVN troops to take the hill led to the loss of an estimated 700 lives, and earned it the graphically descriptive name of **Hamburger Hill** – because it turned fighting men into hamburger meat. Once defeat became inevitable, NVA forces simply retreated into Laos, and the valley was abandoned by the South.

NIXON'S PRESIDENCY

Richard Nixon's ill-starred term of office commenced in January 1969, on the back of a campaign in which he promised to "end the war and win the peace". His quest for a solution that would facilitate an American pull-out without tarnishing its image led Nixon to pursue the strategy of **"Vietnamization"**, a gradual US withdrawal coupled with a stiffening of ARVN forces and hardware. Though the number of US troops in Vietnam reached an all-time peak of 540,000 early on in 1969, 60,000 of these were home for Christmas, and by the end of 1970 only 280,000 remained. Over the same time period, ARVN numbers almost doubled, from 640,000 to well over a million. As part of America's buttressing of the South, Nixon persisted with Johnson's controversial **Phoenix Programme**, which undermined the communist infrastructure in the Mekong Delta by infiltrating Viet Cong cells. Thousands of VC cadres were tortured, imprisoned or killed in the process. Furthermore, the quota system to which agents worked meant that many of the estimated 50,000 people assassinated were in fact innocent.

Nixon didn't limit his attacks to South Vietnam. The NVA had for several years been stockpiling both men and supplies in **Cambodia**, and in March 1969 US covert bombing of these targets commenced. Codenamed **Operation Menu**, it lasted for fourteen months, yet elicited no outcry from Hanoi since they had no right to be in neutral Cambodia in the first place. The following spring, an American-backed coup having replaced Prince Sihanouk of Cambodia with Lon Nol and thus eased access for US troops, a **task force** of 20,000 soldiers advanced on communist installations there. The American public was outraged: dismayed that Nixon, far from closing down the war, was in fact widening the conflict, they rallied at massed anti-war demonstrations. At one such demo at **Kent State University**, Ohio, national guardsmen fired shots into the crowd, killing four marchers – an action that spurred 100,000 demonstrators to gather in Washington. As for the forays into Cambodia, they were failures both in terms of their missions, and in the sense that the ineptitude of the ARVN proved beyond doubt that Vietnamization wasn't working – something underlined by an abortive strike on an NVA base in Laos, codenamed **Lam Son 719**.

Meanwhile, the stop-start **peace talks** in Paris dragged along, now with Nixon's National Security Adviser Henry Kissinger at the American helm, and Le Duc Tho representing the North (Ho Chi Minh had died on September 2, 1969). Two stumbling blocks hindered any advancement: the North's insistence on a coalition government in the South with no place for the current president, Thieu, and the US insistence that all NVA troops should move north after a ceasefire. Tit-for-tat military offensives launched early in 1972 saw both sides attempting to strengthen their hand at the bargaining table: Hanoi launched its **Easter Offensive** on the upper provinces of the South; while Nixon countered with a resumption of **bombing of the North** – at first targeting routes of strategical importance, but swiftly homing in on Haiphong and Hanoi. Towards the year's end, negotiations recommenced, this time with Hanoi in a mood to compromise – not least because Nixon let rumours spread of his **Madman Theory**, which involved the use of nuclear weaponry. Tragically, the draft agreement produced in October (Nixon was keen to see a resolution before the US elections in November) was delayed by President Thieu in Saigon, and by the time it was finalized in January 1973, Nixon had flexed his military muscles one last time, sanctioning the eleven-day **Christmas Bombing** (see p.334) of Hanoi and Haiphong, in which 20,000 tonnes of ordnance was dropped, and 1600 civilians perished.

Under the terms of the **Paris Accords**, signed on January 27 by the United States, the North, the South and the Viet Cong, a ceasefire was established, all remaining American troops were repatriated by April, and Hanoi and Saigon released their PoWs. The Paris talks failed to yield a long-term political settlement, instead providing for the creation of a **Council of National Conciliation**, comprising Saigon's government and the communists, to sort matters out at some future date. The agreements allowed the NVA and ARVN troops to retain whatever positions they held. For this fudged deal, Kissinger and Le Duc Tho were awarded the Nobel Prize for peace, though only Kissinger accepted.

THE FALL OF THE SOUTH

The Paris Accords accomplished little beyond smoothing the US withdrawal from Vietnam and, with the NVA allowed to remain in the South, it was only a matter of time before **renewed aggression** erupted. Thieu's ARVN, now numbering a million troops and in robust shape thanks to its new US-financed equipment, soon set about retaking territory lost to the North during the Easter Offensive. The com-

munists, on the other hand, were still reeling from losses accrued during that campaign. As for the Viet Cong, Tet had resulted in what Henry Kamm calls "enormous bloodletting" within their ranks – 40,000 deaths is a popular estimate – and the Phoenix Programme resulted in many more; increasingly, the NVA took over the struggle.

By 1974, however, things were beginning to sour for the South. An economy already weakened by heavy **inflation** was further drained by the **unemployment** caused by America's withdrawal; corruption in the military was rife, and unpaid wages led to a burgeoning ARVN desertion rate. By the end of the year, the South was ripe for the taking.

Received wisdom in Hanoi was that a slow build-up of arms in the South, in preparation for a conventional push in 1976, would be the wisest course of action. Then, over the Christmas period of 1974, an **NVA drive** led by General Tran overran the area north of Saigon now called Song Be Province. Duly encouraged, Hanoi went into action, and towns in the South fell like ninepins under the irresistible momentum of the **Ho Chi Minh Campaign**. Within two months, communist troops had occupied Buon Me Thuot, taking a mere 24 hours to finish a job they'd anticipated would require a week. Hué and Da Nang duly followed, and by April 21, Xuan Loc, the last real line of defence before Saigon, had also fallen. ARVN defiance disintegrated in the face of the North's unerring progress: a famous image from these last days shows a highway scattered with the discarded boots of fleeing Southern soldiers. President Thieu fled by helicopter to Taiwan, and leadership of Saigon's government was assumed by **General Duong Van Minh** ("Big Minh"). Minh held the post for just two days before NVA tanks crashed through the gates of the Presidential Palace and Saigon fell to the North on April 30. Only hours before, the last Americans and other Westerners in the city had been **airlifted out** in the frantic helicopter operation known as "Frequent Wind" (see p.79).

The **toll** of the American War, in human terms, was staggering. Of the 3.3 million Americans who served in Vietnam between 1965 and 1973, over 57,600 died, and more than 150,000 received wounds which required hospitalization. Today, it is estimated that 500,000 veterans suffer from Post Traumatic Stress

Disorder and that veteran suicides have now exceeded the total number of US fatalities during the conflict. The ARVN lost 250,000 troops. Hanoi declared that over 2 million Vietnamese civilians, and 1 million communist troops, died during the war. Many more on both sides are still listed as "missing in action" (MIA).

POST-REUNIFICATION VIETNAM

For the first time since the French colonization in the 1850s, Vietnam was once again a **unified nation**. So severely had Tet and the Phoenix Programme weakened the NLF that it was effectively a force of wholly Northern soldiers that brought about the fall of Saigon. At first they trod softly, softly in order to impress the international community, but Southerners eyed the future with profound apprehension. Their fears were well founded. Hanoi was in no mood to grant Saigon autonomy: the Council of National Reconciliation, provided for by the Paris Accords, was never established, and the NLF's **Provisional Revolutionary Government** worked beneath the shadow of the Military Management Committee, and therefore Hanoi, until the **Socialist Republic of Vietnam** was officially born, in July 1976. The impression of a conquering army was exacerbated when northern cadres – the *can bo* – swarmed south to take up all official posts. More than one commentator on the war suggested that, in some way, this seizing of the reins of power harked back to earlier centuries and represented the revenge of the Trinh over the Nguyen (see p.413).

Monumental **problems** faced the nascent republic. For many years, the two halves of Vietnam had lived according to wildly variant political and economic systems. The North had no industry, its agriculture was based on co-operative farms, and much of its land had been bombed on a massive scale. In stark contrast, American involvement in the South had underwritten what John Pilger describes as "an 'economy' based upon the services of maids, pimps, whores, beggars and black-marketeers", buttressed by American cash that dried up when the last helicopter left the embassy in Saigon.

The slow, cautious merger of economies that the NLF had in mind found no favour in Hanoi, whose top ranks were intent on ushering in a rigid socialist state. At the **Fourth Communist Party Congress** held in December 1976, southern Vietnam was economically restructured in line with the north: privately owned land was confiscated; collectivization of agriculture, based on unwieldy Eastern bloc models, was introduced; and citizens were relocated and gathered into communal farms. The state took control of industry and trade, output dwindled, and some farmers slaughtered cattle rather than rear them only for donation to the cause. Productivity wasn't helped any by the **devastation** wreaked on the nation's forestry and farmland by the lingering effects of chemical warfare waged by the Americans (see "Environmental issues", p.453).

The changes that swept the country weren't limited to economics. Bitterness on Hanoi's part towards its former enemies was inevitable; yet instead of making moves towards national conciliation, and despite the fact that many families had connections in both camps, recriminations drove futher wedges between the peoples of north and south. The dissident novelist Duong Thu Huong succinctly states: "Our people are strong in times of war...But to live in a civil society, with a full awareness of individual value, our people are still very young and naive. Notions like democracy, the rights of man, are seen as something very distant, luxuries." Anyone with remote connections with America was interned in a **re-education camp** (in reality, a labour camp), along with Buddhist monks, priests, intellectuals, and anyone else the government wanted rid of. Hundreds of thousands of southerners were sent, without trial, to these camps, and some remained for over a decade. Discrimination against those on the "wrong side" in the war continues today, in areas as diverse as health care, education and job opportunities – even cemeteries containing southerners' remains have been razed.

Talks aimed at normalizing relations between Vietnam and the United States began in March 1977, but the meetings came to nothing. Instead, 1970's **Trading with the Enemy Act**, which made it a crime for Americans to do business in or with Vietnam, was upheld. In addition, and largely due to American pressure, Vietnam was, until 1993, unable to look to the IMF, World Bank or Asian Development Bank for **development loans**. Soviet aid was all that was available to the country; in 1978, Vietnam joined **COMECON**, the Eastern European economic community.

THE "BOAT PEOPLE"

In 1979 the attention of the world was caught by images of bedraggled fishing boats packed with Vietnamese **refugees** seeking sanctuary in Hong Kong and other southeast Asian harbours. An untold number – some say a third – fell victim to typhoons, starvation and disease or pirates, who often sank the boats after seizing the refugees' meagre possessions and raping the women. Others somehow fetched up on the coast of Australia or were picked up by passing freighters. The prime destination, however, was Hong Kong, where 68,000 asylum-seekers arrived in 1979 alone. The exodus was at its peak in 1979, but it had been going on, largely unnoticed, since reunification four years earlier, and continued up to the early 1990s. Over this period an estimated 840,000 boat people left Vietnam, of whom more than 750,000 were resettled overseas.

The first refugees were mostly **southerners**, people who felt themselves too closely associated with the old regime or their American allies and feared communist reprisals. Some were former nationalists and a few were even ex-Viet Cong, disillusioned with the new government's extremism. Then, in early 1978, nationalization of private commerce was instituted in the south, hitting hard at the **Chinese** community, which controlled much southern business and the all-important rice trade. Anti-Chinese sentiment took hold and thousands made their escape in fishing boats, initially from the south but, as relations between China and Vietnam deteriorated in 1979, the panic spread northwards. Large numbers fled across the border on foot, while others paid huge sums – including bribes to local officials – for a passage on the risky voyage to Hong Kong. Though the majority were ethnic Chinese, in the late 1970s more **Vietnamese** began to leave, driven by a series of bad harvests, severe hardship and the prospect of prolonged military service in Cambodia.

By 1979 the situation had become so critical that the international community was forced to act, offering asylum to the more than 200,000 refugees crowding temporary camps around southeast Asia. Under the auspices of the UN, the **Orderly Departure Programme** (ODP) has also enabled legal emigration of political refugees (mainly former American employees, Amerasian children and those seeking to be re-united with their families) to the West, resettling 500,000 in over forty Western countries.

It seemed that the crisis was over, until 1987, when suddenly the South China Sea was once again full of Vietnamese people in overcrowded boats. This **second wave** were mostly northerners and – often inflamed by tales of wealth from relatives already overseas and seemed to be fleeing desperate poverty rather than fear of persecution. Hong Kong again bore the brunt of new arrivals: in 1989, 34,000 boat people entered the camps, bringing the total to 56,000, few of whom had any real chance of resettlement. But governments were less sympathetic this time round and, in an attempt to halt the flow, from early 1989 boat people were denied automatic refugee status. Instead, a screening process was introduced to identify "genuine" refugees, the rest, designated "economic migrants", were encouraged to return under the **Voluntary Repatriation Scheme**, which offered concrete assistance with resettlement. Despite numerous complaints about the screening procedures, more than 70,000 boat people have returned since 1990, keen to leave the prison-like camps and reassured by the changes occurring in Vietnam. Meanwhile, in Hong Kong, which is under pressure to clear the camps before China takes over in 1997, the first **forced repatriations** took place in 1989, causing a storm of protest around the world and threats of mass suicide from the camps' occupants.

Returnees in Vietnam are monitored by staff of the UN High Commission for Refugees (UNHCR), who say there is no evidence of persecution or discrimination. However, others claim that the **monitoring** is inadequate and ineffective, and cite examples of returnees being imprisoned. Despite the controversy, in early 1996 all parties finally agreed that the only "viable solution" was to send the 40,000 failed asylum-seekers still in southeast Asian camps back home as quickly as possible. Under the agreement, most UNHCR funding stops at the end of 1996, after which all camps should be closed within two years. However, this is just the latest of several deadlines, and those people remaining – including a hard core of criminals whom nobody wants – are becoming increasingly desperate. In theory **deportations** are to take place "without threat or use of force", but clashes with local security forces are turning more violent, especially in Hong Kong.

The other unknown is how quickly Vietnam will be able to absorb another 40,000 people, even with the promised international aid.

The quagmire Vietnam found itself in after reunification prompted many of its citizens to flee the country and blunder across the oceans in unseaworthy vessels, hoping to wash up on the shores of a friendly nation (see box opposite).

A RETURN TO WAR

Three weeks before the fall of Saigon in 1975, **Pol Pot**'s genocidal regime had seized power in Cambodia; within a year his troops were making **cross-border forays** into regions of Vietnam that had once fallen under Khmer sway, around the Mekong Delta and north of Ho Chi Minh City (as Saigon had been renamed). One such venture led to the massacre at **Ba Chuc** (see p.147), in which almost 2000 people died. Reprisals were slow in coming, due to the tacit support Pol Pot enjoyed from the Chinese. Towards the end of the war against America, Hanoi had shifted its allegiances away from Beijing and closer to Moscow; conflict in Cambodia was bound to ruffle feathers in Beijing and so heighten the Sino-Vietnamese tensions that already existed.

However, by 1978, Vietnam could stand back no longer, and on Christmas Day of that year, 120,000 **Vietnamese troops invaded Cambodia** and ousted Pol Pot. Whatever the motives for the invasion, and even though it brought an end to Pol Pot's reign of terror, Vietnam was further ostracized by the international community. In February 1979, Beijing's response came in the form of a punitive **Chinese invasion** of Vietnam's northeastern provinces; Chinese losses were heavy, and after sixteen days they retreated. Meanwhile, Pol Pot had withdrawn across the Thai border, from where his army was able to continue attacking the Vietnamese army of occupation. The Vietnamese remained in Cambodia until September 1989, by which time an estimated 50,000 troops had died, the majority of them southern conscripts.

DOI MOI... AND THE FUTURE

A severe famine in 1985 and the 775 percent inflation that crippled the country in 1986 were just two of the many symptoms of the **economic malaise** threatening to tear Vietnam apart during the late 1970s and early 1980s. An experimental hybrid of planned and market

economies tried out in 1979 came to nothing, and by the early 1980s the only thing keeping Vietnam afloat was Soviet aid.

The Party's conservative old guard resisted change for as long as it could, but the death of General Secretary Le Duan in 1986 finally cleared the way for more reformist politicians to attempt to reverse the country's fortunes. At the Sixth Party Congress in December, the reformist **Nguyen Van Linh** took over as general secretary, and sweeping economic reforms, known as **doi moi** or "renovation", followed. Collectivization and central planning were abandoned, a market economy was embraced, agriculture and retail were privatized, and attempts were made to attract foreign capital by liberalizing foreign investment regulations. Political reforms came a poor second, although the congress did instigate purges on corrupt officialdom and gave the press freer rein to criticize. With the **collapse of communism** across Europe in 1989 though, the press was again silenced, and in a keynote speech Nguyen Van Linh rejected the concept of a multi-party state; all economic reforms, however, remained in place. **Soviet aid**, which by the end of the 1980s amounted to US$2 billion a year, continued to provide an important lifeline until it ran dry in 1991. Realizing that Vietnam would henceforth need to stand alone, that year's **Seventh Party Congress** strengthened its commitment to economic reform and set in motion efforts to end Vietnam's isolation.

International rehabilitation, which had already begun with the withdrawal of troops from Cambodia in 1989, gathered momentum in the 1990s, as efforts to aid the US search teams looking for remains of the 2000-plus American soldiers still unaccounted for (MIAs) were stepped up. In 1993, a year after the reformist **Vo Van Kiet** became prime minister, the Americans duly lifted their veto on aid, and Western cash began to flow. By year's end, inflation was down to five percent. The rapprochement with the US continued into 1994, as the US trade embargo was lifted by President Clinton, and in February 1995 the two countries opened liaison offices in each other's capitals. Vietnam was admitted into **ASEAN** (the Association of Southeast Asian Nations) in July 1995, and the same month saw full **diplomatic relations restored** with the **US**.

As Vietnam moves **towards the millennium**, its future looks far rosier than anyone could have hoped for a decade ago, with oil, manufacturing and tourism just three of the many causes for optimism. Yet huge problems still block the way forward. The economic upturn has so far benefited city-dwellers (and in particular residents of Ho Chi Minh) far more than those living in rural areas, and this is encouraging a steady drift to the cities, combined with dissatisfaction in the countryside. Moreover, families of wartime supporters of the South continue to suffer repression in the form of limited job and education opportunities; corruption is rife, and political pluralism elusive. The modest manifestations of dissent that occasionally reach street level are quickly snuffed out, but many are watching with interest to see if the government can reconcile the inherent contradictions between the economic and political structures, and satisfy the growing aspirations of the Vietnamese people.

RELIGION AND BELIEFS

The moral and religious life of most Vietnamese people is governed by a complex mixture of Confucian, Buddhist and Taoist philosophical teachings interwoven with ancestor worship and ancient, animistic practices. Incompatibilities are reconciled on a practical level into a single, functioning belief system whereby a family may maintain an ancestral altar in their home, consult the village guardian spirit, propitiate the God of the Hearth and take offerings to the Buddhist pagoda.

The primary influence on Vietnam's religious life has been Chinese. But in southern Vietnam, which historically fell within the Indian sphere, small communities of Khmers and Chams still adhere to Hinduism, Islam and Theravada Buddhism brought direct from India. From the fifteenth century on, **Christianity** has also been a feature, represented largely by Roman Catholicism but with a small Protestant following in the south. Vietnam also claims a couple of home-grown religious **sects**, both products of political and social turmoil in the early twentieth century: Cao Dai and Hoa Hao.

The **political dimension** has never been far removed from religious affairs in Vietnam, as the world was made vividly aware by Buddhist opposition to the oppressive regime of President Diem in the 1960s. After 1975, the Marxist–Leninist government of reunified Vietnam declared the state atheist while theoretically allowing people the right to practise their religion under the constitution. In reality, churches and pagodas were closed down, religious leaders sent for re-education, and followers discriminated against if not actively persecuted. Since 1986 the situation has eased, accompanied by the release of most prisoners held on religious grounds, while Party leaders have publicly demonstrated the new freedoms by visiting pagodas and churches. Though the government continues to exercise control through such practices as monitoring appointments and publications, many Vietnamese are once again openly practising their faith. Indeed, as Vietnam faces the onslaught of new ideas and the "social evils" spawned by the breakdown of its moral codes, people are looking to religion both for personal guidance and as a stabilizing force in society.

ANCESTOR WORSHIP

One of the oldest cults practised in Vietnam is that of ancestor worship, based on the fundamental principles of filial piety and of obligation to the past, present and future generations. No matter what their religion, virtually every Vietnamese household, even hard-line communist, will maintain an **ancestral altar** in the belief that the dead continue to live in another realm. Ancestors can intercede on behalf of their descendants and bring the family good fortune, but in return the living must pay respect, perform prescribed ceremonies and provide for their ancestors' well-being. At funerals and subsequent anniversaries, quantities of paper money and other **votive offerings** (these days including television sets and cars) are burnt, and choice morsels of food are regularly placed on the altar. Traditionally this is financed by the income from a designated plot of land and it is the responsibility of the oldest, usually male, member of the family to organize the rituals, tend the altar and keep the ancestors abreast of all important family events; failure in any of these duties carries the risk of inciting peeved ancestors to make mischief.

The ancestral altar occupies a central position in the home. On it are placed several wooden tablets, one for each ancestor going back five generations. One hundred days after the funeral, the deceased's spirit returns to live in their tablet. People without children to honour them by burning incense at the altar are condemned to wander the world in search of a home. Some childless people make provision by paying a temple or pagoda to observe the rituals, while the spirits of others may eventually take up residence in one of the small shrine houses (*cuong*) you see in fields and at roadsides. Important times for remembering the dead are **Tet**, the lunar new year, and **Thanh Minh** ("Festival of Pure Light"), which falls on the 5th day of the third lunar month.

SPIRIT WORSHIP

Residual animism plus a whole host of spirits borrowed from other religions have given Vietnam a complicated mystical world. The universe is divided into **three realms**, the sky, earth and man, under the overall guardianship of Ong Troi, Lord of Heaven, assisted by spirits of the earth, mountains and water. Within the hierarchy are four **sacred animals** who appear everywhere in Vietnamese architecture: the dragon, representing the king, power and intelligence; the phoenix, embodying the queen, beauty and peace; the turtle, symbol of longevity and protector of the kingdom; and the mythical kylin, usually translated as unicorn, which represents wisdom.

In addition each village or urban quarter will venerate a **guardian spirit** in either a temple (*den*) or communal house (*dinh*). The deity may be legendary, for example the benevolent horse-spirit Bach Ma of Thang Long (modern Hanoi; see p.322), and will often come from the Taoist pantheon. Or the guardian may be a historical figure such as a local or national hero, or a man of great virtue. In either case people will propitiate these tutelary spirits – represented on the altar by a gilded throne – with offerings, and will consult them in times of need. The *dinh* also serves as meeting-house and school for the community.

BUDDHISM

The Buddha was born **Siddhartha Gautama** to a wealthy family some time during the sixth century BC in present-day Nepal. At an early age he renounced his life of luxury to seek the ultimate deliverance from worldly suffering and strive to reach **nirvana**, an indefinable, blissful state. After several years Siddhartha attained enlightenment while sitting under a bodhi tree, and then devoted the rest of his life to teaching the **Middle Way** that leads to nirvana. The Buddha preached that existence is a cycle of perpetual reincarnation in which actions in one life determine one's position in the next, but that it is possible to break free by following certain precepts, central to which are non-violence and compassion. The Buddha's doctrine was based on the **Four Noble Truths**: existence is suffering; suffering is caused by desire; suffering ends with the extinction of desire; the way to end suffering is to follow the eightfold path of right understanding, thought, speech, action, livelihood, effort, mindfulness and concentration.

THE HISTORY OF BUDDHISM IN VIETNAM

It's estimated that up to **two-thirds** of the Vietnamese **population** consider themselves Buddhist. The vast majority are followers of the Mahayana school which was introduced to northern Vietnam via China in the second century AD. Within this, most Vietnamese Buddhists claim allegiance to the Pure Land sect (*Tinh Do*), which venerates A Di Da or Amitabha Buddha above all others, while the meditational Zen sect (*Thien*) has a moderate following, predominantly in northern Vietnam.

In fact Buddhism first arrived in southern Vietnam nearly one hundred years earlier as **Theravada** or the "Lesser Vehicle", following Indian trade routes through Burma and Thailand. Theravada is an ascetical form of the faith based on the individual pursuit of perfection and enlightenment, which failed to find favour beyond the Khmer communities of the Mekong, where it still claims about 400,000 followers. One of the salient features of **Mahayana** Buddhism, in contrast, is the belief that intermediaries, **bodhisattvas**, have chosen to forgo nirvana to work for the salvation of all humanity, and it was this that enabled Mahayana to adapt to a Vietnamese context by incorporating local gods and spirits into its array of bodhisattvas. The most well-known bodhisattva is Avalokitesvara, usually worshipped in Vietnam as **Quan Am**, the Goddess of Mercy. Mahayana Buddhism spread through northern Vietnam until it became the **official state religion** after the country regained its independence from China in the tenth century. The Ly kings (1009–1225) in particular were devout Buddhists who sponsored hundreds of pagodas, prompting a flowering of the arts, and established a hierarchy of scholar-monks as advisers to the court. Great landowning monasteries came into being and Buddhist doctrine was incorporated into the civil service examinations along with Confucian and Taoist texts as part of the "triple world-view", *Tam Giao*. At the same time it became apparent that Buddhism was unable to provide the unifying ideology required by a highly centralized state constantly fighting for its survival. Consequently, by the mid-fourteenth century Buddhism had lost its political and economic influence, and when the Le dynasty came to power in 1428 Confucianism finally eclipsed it as the dominant national philosophy.

But by then Buddhism was too deeply rooted, particularly in the folk-religion of the countryside, to lose its influence completely. Buddhism enjoyed brief periods of **royal patronage**, notably during the seventeenth and eighteenth centuries when new pagodas were built and old ones repaired. To many people it still offered a spiritual element lacking in Confucian doctrine and during the colonial era Vietnamese intellectuals turned to Buddhism in search of a national identity. Since then the Buddhist community has been a **focus of dissent**, not least in the 1960s when images of self-immolating

Buddhist monks focused world attention on the excesses of South Vietnam's Catholic President Diem. At the time, protesting Buddhists were accused of being pro-communist, but their standpoint was essentially neutral. In the event they experienced even greater repression **after reunification** when pagodas were closed, and monks and nuns were sent to re-education camps. Buddhist leaders have persisted in their denunciations of the regime, campaigning for human rights and causing the government acute embarrassment as it seeks international approval. In general, though, the Party has made good its promises of **greater religious freedom** under *doi moi*. In the last few years the Buddhist community, currently estimated at 20,000 practising monks and nuns, has been able to resume its social and educational pro-

---

THE BUDDHIST PAGODA

The Vietnamese word *Chua*, translated as "pagoda", is an exclusively Buddhist term whereas a temple (*den*) may be Taoist, Confucian or house a guardian spirit. **Pagoda architecture** reached a pinnacle during the Ly and Tran dynasties, but thanks to Chinese invasions and local, anti-Buddhist movements, few examples remain. A majority of those still in existence are eighteenth- or nineteenth-century constructions, though many retain features of earlier designs. Generally pagoda **layout** is either an inverse T or three parallel lines of single-storeyed pavilions. The first hall is reserved for public worship, while those beyond, on slightly raised platforms, contain the prayer table and principal altar. Other typical elements are a **bell-tower**, either integral to the building or standing apart, and a **walled courtyard** containing ponds, stone stelae and, particularly in Mahayana pagodas, the white figure of Quan Am symbolizing charity and compassion.

The most interesting feature inside the pagoda is often the **statuary**. Rows of Buddhas sit or stand on the main altar, where the Buddhist trinity occupies the highest level: A Di Da or Amitabha, the Historical Buddha; Thich Ca Mau Ni or Sakyamuni, born Siddhartha Gautama, the Present Buddha; and Di Lac, or Maitreya, the Future Buddha. Lower ranks comprise the same Buddhas in a variety of forms accompanied by bodhisattvas: look out for pot-bellied Maitreya as the laughing carefree Buddha who grants wishes; the omnipotent Avalokitesvara of a "thousand" arms and eyes; and the Nine Dragon Buddha (Tuong Cuu

Long). This latter is a small statue, found more often in northern Vietnam, of Sakyamuni encircled by dragons, standing with one hand pointing to the sky and the other to the earth. According to legend, nine dragons descended from the sky to bathe the newborn Buddha, after which he took seven steps forward and proclaimed "on earth and in the sky, I alone am the highest".

Two unmistakable figures residing in all pagodas are the giant **guardians of Buddhist law**: white-faced "Mister Charitable" (Ong Thien), holding a pearl, and red-faced "Mister Wicked" (Ong Ac). Ong Thien sees everything, both the good and the bad, while Ong Ac dispenses justice. From an artistic point of view, some of the most fascinating statues are the lifelike representations of arhats, ascetic Buddhist saints; the best examples are found in northern pagodas, where each figure is portrayed in a disturbingly realistic style. Finally, Mahayana pagodas will undoubtedly welcome in a few **Taoist spirits**, the favourites being Thien Hau, the Protectress of Sailors, and Thanh Mau, the Mother Goddess. Somewhere in the pagoda halls will be an altar dedicated to deceased monks or nuns, while larger pagodas usually maintain a garden for their burial stupas. Traditionally Buddhists would bury their dead, but increasingly they practise cremation.

The **best times to visit** a pagoda are the 1st and 15th days of the lunar month (new moon and full moon) when they are at their busiest. Note that it's customary to remove your shoes when entering the main sanctuary.

grammes. Life is slowly returning to the pagodas, many of which are being renovated after twenty or more years of neglect.

CONFUCIANISM

The teachings of Confucius provide a guiding set of moral and ethical principles, an **ideology** for the state's rulers and subjects onto which ritualistic practices have been grafted.

Confucius is the Latinized name of K'ung-Fu-Tzu (Khong Tu in Vietnamese) who was born into a minor aristocratic family in China in 551 BC. At this time China was in turmoil while the Zhou dynasty dissolved into rival feudal states battling for supremacy. Confucius worked for many years as a court official, where he observed the nature of power and the function of government at close quarters. At the age of fifty, he packed it all in and for the next twenty years wandered the country spreading his ideas on social and political reform in an effort to persuade states and individuals to live peacefully together for their mutual benefit. His central tenet was the importance of **correct behaviour** and **loyal service**, reinforced by ceremonial rites whereby the ruler maintains authority through good example rather than force. Important qualities to strive for are selflessness, respectfulness, sincerity and non-violence; the ideal person should be neither heroic nor extrovert, but instead follow a "golden mean". Confucius remained silent on spiritual matters, though he placed great emphasis on observing ancient rituals such as making offerings to heaven and to ancestors.

Confucian **teachings** were handed down in the Analects, but he is also credited with editing the Six Classics, among them the Book of Changes (*I Ching*) and the Book of Ritual (*Li Chi*). Later these became the basic texts for civil service examinations, ensuring that all state officials had a deeply ingrained respect for tradition and social order. Though Confucianism ultimately led to national inflexibility and the undermining of personal initiative, its positive legacy has been an emphasis on the value of education and a belief that individual merit is of greater consequence than high birth.

After the death of Confucius in 478 BC the doctrine was developed further by his **disciples**, the most famous of whom was Mencius (Meng-tzu). By the first century AD, Confucianism, which slowly absorbed elements of Taoism, had evolved into a cult and also become the state ideology whereby kings ruled under the Mandate of Heaven. Social stability was maintained through a fixed hierarchy of interdependent relationships encapsulated in the notion of filial piety. Thus children must obey their parents without question, wives their husbands, students their teacher, and subjects their ruler. For their part the recipient, particularly the king, must earn this obedience; if the rules are broken, the harmony of society and nature is disturbed and authority loses its legitimacy. Therefore, by implication, revolution was justified when the king lost his divine right to rule.

THE HISTORY OF CONFUCIANISM IN VIETNAM

Confucian thinking has pervaded Vietnamese society ever since Chinese administrators introduced the concepts during the second century BC. Reinforced by a thousand years of Chinese rule, Confucianism (*Nho Giao*) came to play an essential role in Vietnam's political, social and educational systems. The philosophy was largely one of an intellectual elite, but Confucian teaching eventually filtered down to the village level where it had a profound influence on the Vietnamese family organization.

The ceremonial **cult of Confucius** was formalized in 1070 when King Ly Thanh Tong founded the Temple of Literature in Hanoi. But it was not until the foundation of the later Le dynasty in 1428 that Confucian doctrine gained supremacy over Buddhism in the Vietnamese court. The Le kings viewed Confucian ideology, with its emphasis on social order, duty and respect, as an effective means of consolidating their new regime. In 1442 they overhauled the education system and based it on a curriculum of Confucian texts. They also began recruiting top-level mandarins through doctoral examinations which eventually gave rise to a scholar-gentry class at the expense of the old landed aristocracy. Confucian influence reached its peak during the reign of King Le Thanh Tong (1460–97), which heralded a golden age of bureaucratic reform when public service on behalf of both community and state reached a noble ideal. At the same time, however, a strongly centralized administration, presided over by a divine ruler and a mandarin elite, eventually bred corruption, despotism and an increasingly rigid society. The arrival of Western ideas and French rule in the late nineteenth century finally undermined the political dominance of Confucianism, though it managed to survive as the court ideology until well into the twentieth century. The cult of Confucius continues in a few temples (*Van Mieu*) dedicated to the sage, and he also appears on other altars as an honoured ancestor, an exemplary figure remembered for services to the nation.

Many **Confucian ideals** have been completely assimilated into Vietnamese society. After Independence, the Communist Party struggled against inherent conservatism and the supremacy of the family as a political unit; indeed, leaders can still be heard railing against the entrenched "feudal" nature of rural Vietnam. But the Party was also able to tap into those elements of the Confucian tradition that suited their new classless, socialist society: conformity, duty and the denial of personal interest for the common good. Today, however, Confucian ideals are seriously threatened by the invasion of materialism and individual ambition.

TAOISM

Taoism is based on the **Tao-te-ching**, the "Book of the Way", traditionally attributed to **Lao Tzu** (meaning "Old Master"), who is thought to have lived in China in the sixth century BC. The Tao, the Way, emphasizes effortless action, intuition and spontaneity; the Tao is invisible and impartial; it cannot be taught, nor can it be expressed in words. It is the one reality from which everything is born, universal and eternal. However, by virtuous, compassionate and non-violent behaviour, it is possible to achieve ultimate stillness, through a mystical and personal quest. Taoism thus preached non-intervention, passivity and the futility of academic scholarship; it was viewed by Confucians as suspiciously subversive.

Central to the Tao is the **duality** inherent in nature; the whole universe is in temporary balance, a tension of complimentary opposites defined as **yin** and **yang**, the male and female principles. Yang is male, the sun, active and orthodox; yin is female, the earth, flexible, passive and instinctive. Harmony is the balance between the two, and experiencing that harmony is the Tao. Accordingly all natural things can be categorized by their property of yin or yang, and human activity should strive not to

disrupt that balance. In its pure form Taoism has no gods, only emanations of the Tao, but in the first century AD it corrupted into an organized religion venerating a deified Lao Tzu. The new cult had popular appeal since it offered the goal of immortality through yogic meditation and good deeds. Eventually the practice of Taoism developed highly complex **rituals**, incorporating magic, mysticism, superstition and the use of geomancy (see box above) to ensure harmony between man and nature; while astrology may be used to determine auspicious dates for weddings, funerals, starting a journey or even launching a new business. Ancient spirit worship, the cult of ancestors and the veneration of legendary or historic figures all fused happily with the Taoist idea of a universal essence.

The vast, eclectic pantheon of Taoist **gods and immortals** is presided over by Ngoc Hoang, the Jade Emperor. He is assisted by three ministers: Nam Tao, the southern star who records all births; Bac Dau, the north star who registers deaths; and Ong Tao, God of the Hearth who reports all happenings in the family household to Ngoc Hoang at the end of the year. Then there is a collection of immortals, genies and guardian deities, including legendary and historic figures. In Vietnam among the most well-known are Tran Vo, God of the North, Bach

Ho, the White Tiger of the West, and Tran Hung Dao, who protects the newborn and cures the sick. Confucius is also honoured as a Taoist saint. A distinctive aspect of Taoism is its use of **mediums** to communicate with the gods; the divine message is often in the form of a poem, transmitted by a writing brush onto sand or a bed of rice.

Chinese immigrants **brought** Taoism (*Dao Giao*) **to Vietnam** during the long period of Chinese rule (111 BC–939 AD). Between the eleventh and fourteenth centuries the philosophy enjoyed equal status with Buddhism and Confucianism as one of Vietnam's three "religions", but Taoism gradually declined until it eventually became a strand of folk-religion. A few Taoist temples (*Quan*) exist in Vietnam but on the whole its deities have been absorbed into other cults. The Jade Emperor, for example, frequently finds himself part of the Buddhist pantheon in Vietnamese pagodas.

CHRISTIANITY

Vietnam's **Catholic community** is the second largest in southeast Asia after the Philippines. Exact figures are hard to come by but estimates vary between five and eight million (7–10 percent of the population), of which perhaps two-thirds live in the south. In the early twentieth century **Protestantism** was introduced by American missionaries working in southern Vietnam, particularly among the ethnic minorities of the central highlands. Nowadays there are reckoned to be as many as 400,000 adherents to the Protestant faith, know as *Tin Lanh*, or the Good News.

The first Christian **missionaries** to reach Vietnam were Portuguese and Spanish Dominicans who landed briefly on the north coast in the sixteenth century. They were followed in 1615 by French and Portuguese Jesuits, dispatched by the Pope to establish the first permanent missions. Among the early arrivals was the Frenchman Alexandre de Rhodes, a Jesuit who impressed the northern Trinh lords and won, by his reckoning, nearly 7000 converts. The inevitable **backlash** against Christianity, which opposed ancestor worship and espoused subversive ideas such as equality, was not long in coming. In 1630 the Trinh lords expelled all Christians, including de Rhodes, who returned to France where he

helped create the Society of Foreign Missions (*Société des Missions Etrangères*). This society soon became the most active proselytizing body in Indochina; by the end of the eighteenth century it claimed thousands of converts, particularly in the coastal provinces.

Official attitudes towards the Catholic religion waxed and waned over the centuries, though the Vietnamese kings were generally suspicious of the Church's increasingly political role. The most violent **persecution** of Christians occurred during the reign of Minh Mang (1820–41), an ardent Confucian, and reached a peak after 1832. Churches were destroyed, the faces of converts were branded with the words *ta dao*, meaning "false religion", and many of those refusing to renounce their faith were killed; 117 martyrs, both European and Asian, were later canonized. Such repression, much exaggerated at the time, provided the French with a pretext for greater involvement in Indochina, culminating in full colonial rule at the end of the nineteenth century.

Not surprisingly, Catholicism **prospered** under the French regime. Missions re-opened and hundreds of churches, schools and hospitals were built. Vietnamese Catholics formed an educated elite among a population that counted some two million faithful by the 1950s. When partition came in 1954 many Catholics chose to move south, partly because of their opposition to communism and partly because the new leader of South Vietnam, President Ngo Dinh Diem, was a Catholic. Of the estimated 900,000 Vietnamese who left the North in 1954, it's said that around two-thirds were Catholic; many of these became refugees a second time in the 1970s.

Diem actively discriminated in favour of the Catholic community, which he viewed as a bulwark against communism. As a result he alienated large sections of the population, most importantly Buddhists whose protests eventually contributed to his downfall. Meanwhile in North Vietnam the authorities trod fairly carefully with those Catholics who had chosen to stay, allowing them freedom to practise their religion, but the Church was severely restricted and there were some reports of persecution.

After reunification, churches were permitted to function but still came under strict **surveillance** with all appointments controlled by the government, and members of the Church hierarchy frequently received heavy jail sentences for opposition to the regime. Since 1986 the Party has been working to reduce the tension by re-opening seminaries, allowing the Church to resume its social work and releasing some clergy from prison. Catholics throughout Vietnam now regularly attend Mass and when the Cardinal of Hanoi died in 1990 thousands attended the funeral in the largest postwar demonstration of Catholic faith. The government, however, still insists on vetting all appointments: the position of Cardinal remains vacant, but in 1994, after several years of acrimony, the government and Vatican finally agreed on a mutually acceptable Archbishop of Hanoi.

CAO DAI

Social upheaval coupled with an injection of Western thinking in the early twentieth century gave birth to Vietnam's two indigenous religious sects, **Cao Dai** and Hoa Hao. Of the two, Cao Dai claims more adherents, with an estimated following of two million in south Vietnam, plus a few thousand among overseas Vietnamese in America, Canada and Britain. The sect's headquarters, the **Holy See**, resides in a flamboyant cathedral at Tay Ninh (see p.110), where they also maintain a school, agricultural co-operative and hospital. Vietnam's most northerly Cao Dai congregation worships in Hué.

The religion of Cao Dai (meaning "high place") was revealed by the "Supreme Being" to a middle-aged civil servant working in Phu Quoc called **Ngo Van Chieu** during several trances over a period of years from 1919 to 1925. What Chieu preached to his followers was essentially a distillation of Vietnam's religious heritage: elements of Confucian, Taoist and Buddhist thought, intermixed with ancestor worship, Christianity and Islam. According to Cao Dai beliefs, all religions are different manifestations of one **meta-religion**, Cao Dai; in the past, this took on whatever form most suited the prevailing human need, but during this century can finally be presented in its unity. Thus the **Supreme Being**, who revealed himself in 1925, has had two earlier manifestations, always in human guise: the first in the sixth century BC, appearing as various figures from Buddhism, Taoism and

Christianity among many other saints and sages; secondly as Sakyamuni, Confucius, Jesus Christ, Mohammed and Lao Tzu. In the third manifestation the Supreme Being has revealed himself through his divine light, symbolized as an all-seeing Eye on a pale-blue, star-spangled globe.

Cao Dai **doctrine** preaches respect for all its constituent religions and holds that individual desires should be subordinate to the common interest. Adherents seek to escape from the cycle of reincarnation by following the five prohibitions: no violence, theft or lying – nor indulgence in alcohol or sexual activity; priests are expected to be completely vegetarian though others need only eschew meat on certain days of the lunar month. The Cao Dai **hierarchy** is modelled on that of the Catholic Church, and divides into nine ranks, of which the Pope is the highest. Officials are grouped into three branches, identifiable by the colour of their ceremonial robes: the Confucian branch dresses in red, Buddhist in saffron and Taoist in blue. Otherwise practitioners wear white as a symbol of purity, and because it contains every colour.

The **rituals** of Cao Dai are a complex mixture of Buddhist and Taoist rites, including meditation and seances. Prayers take place four times a day in the temples (6am, noon, 6pm and midnight) though ordinary members are only required to attend on four days per month and otherwise can pray at home. Note that shoes should always be removed when entering a Cao Dai temple or mansion. At the start of the thirty-minute-long ceremony, worshippers file into the temple in three columns, women on the left, men in the middle and on the right; they then kneel and bow three times – to the Supreme Being, to the earth and to mankind. Cao Dai's most important **ceremony**, a sort of feast day for the Supreme Being, takes place on the 9th day of the first lunar month; other special observances are the day of Taoism (15th day of the second month), Buddha's birthday (15th of the fourth lunar month), the day of Confucius (28th of the eighth lunar month) and Christmas Day.

The religion of Cao Dai is further enlivened with a panoply of **saints**, encompassing the great and the good of many countries and cultures: Victor Hugo, Joan of Arc, William Shakespeare, Napoleon Bonaparte, Lenin,

Winston Churchill, Louis Pasteur and Sun Yat Sen, alongside home-grown heroes such as Tran Hung Dao and Le Loi. These characters fulfil a variety of roles from prophet to bodhisattva and even spirit medium, through which followers communicate with the Supreme Being. Contact can occur by means of a ouija board, messages left in sealed envelopes or through human mediums – who enter a trance and write using a *planchette* (a pencil secured to a wooden board on castors, on which the medium rests his hand, sometimes known as a *corbeille à bec*). Apparently Cao Daists once appointed an official to take down the further works of Victor Hugo by dictation from his spirit.

The ideology, which had widespread appeal, attracted **converts** in their hundreds of thousands in the Mekong Delta, but only gained official recognition from the French colonial authorities in 1926. Over the next decade the Holy See developed into a **semi-autonomous state** wielding considerable political power and backed by a paramilitary wing which mustered around 50,000 men in the mid-1950s. Although originally nationalist, Cao Daists clashed with communist troops in a local power struggle, and the sect ended up opposing both the North Vietnamese and President Diem's pro-Catholic regime. Diem moved quickly to dismantle the army when he came to power and exiled its leaders; then after 1975 the communists purged the religious body, closing down Cao Dai temples and schools, and sending priests for re-education. However, Cao Dai survived as a religion and has gained some **new adherents** since 1990 when its temples and mansions, approximately 400 in all, were allowed to re-open.

HOA HAO

The second of Vietnam's local sects, **Hoa Hao**, meaning "peace and kindness", emerged in the late 1930s near Chau Doc in the Mekong Delta (see p.143). The movement was founded by a young mystic, **Huynh Phu So**, who disliked mechanical ritual and preached a very pure, simple form of Buddhism that required no clergy or other intermediaries, and could be practised at home by means of meditation, fasting and prayer. Gambling, alcohol and opium were prohibited, while filial piety was once more invoked to promote social order.

As a young man Huynh Phu So was cured of a mysterious illness by the monks of Tra Son Pagoda near his home town of Chau Doc. He continued to live at the pagoda, studying under the monk Xom, but returned to his home village after Xan died. During a storm in 1939, So entered a trance from which he emerged to develop his own Buddhist way. The sect quickly gained followers and, like Cao Dai, was soon caught up in **nationalist politics**. To the French, So was a mad but dangerous subversive; they committed him to a psychiatric hospital (where he promptly converted his doctor to Hoa Hao), and then placed him under house arrest. During World War II Hoa Hao followers were armed by the Japanese and later continued to fight against the French while also opposing the communists. At the end of the war Hoa Hao members formed an anti-Marxist political party, prompting the Viet Minh to assassinate So in 1947.

However, the movement continued to grow, its **private army** equalling the Cao Dai's in size, until Diem came to power and effectively crushed the sect's political and military arm. The sect then splintered, with some members turning to the National Liberation Front, while most sided with the Americans. As a result, when the communists took over in 1975 many Hoa Hao leaders were arrested and its priesthood was disbanded. Nevertheless some claim that there are now up to 1.5 million Hoa Hao practising in the Mekong Delta. Members are kept under close supervision since some are allegedly still engaged in anti-government activities.

HINDUISM AND ISLAM

Indian merchants carried **Hinduism** to Vietnam in the early years of the millennium, travelling along the coast of Siam (now Thailand) and down the Mekong to reach the Indianized kingdom of Champa. Cham subjects worshipped the Hindu god Shiva, represented by a *lingam*, but when Arab traders became paramount during the sixteenth century most Chams converted to **Islam**, though retained certain elements of their Hindu tradition.

Islam currently claims more followers: several thousand Cham and Khmer Moslems live along Vietnam's central coast between Nha Trang and Phan Thiet. There is also a sizeable group in Ho Chi Minh City and a tiny Moslem community in Hanoi. None of these profess a particularly devout form of the religion: prayers are reduced to once on Fridays, Ramadan lasts only three days, no one goes on the Hajj, and there are no restrictions on alcohol – although most do not eat pork; few Vietnamese can read or speak Arabic and little of the Koran has been translated. Both Hindus and Moslems make offerings to Hindu *linga* as well as to animist spirits. Ho Chi Minh City has a few Hindu temples which are currently undergoing something of a revival.

VIETNAMESE DEITIES

BUDDHIST DEITIES

A Di Da or **Amitabha** The Historical Buddha, the most revered member of the Buddhist pantheon in Vietnamese pagodas.

Avalokitesvara A bodhisattva often represented with many arms and eyes, being omnipotent and all-powerful, or as Quan Am (see below).

Di Lac or **Maitreya** The Future Buddha, usually depicted as chubby, with a bare chest and a huge grin, sitting on a lotus throne.

Ong Ac or **Trung Ac** One of the two guardians of the Buddhist religion, popularly known as Mister Wicked, who judges all people. He has a fierce red face and a reputation for severity – of which badly behaved children are frequently reminded.

Ong Thien or **Khuyen Thien** The second guardian of Buddhism is Mister Charitable, a white-faced kindly soul who encourages good behaviour.

Quan Am The Goddess of Mercy, adopted from the Chinese goddess, Kuan Yin. Quan Am is a popular incarnation of Avalokitesvara. She is usually represented as a graceful white statue, with her hand raised in blessing.

Thich Ca Mau Ni or **Sakyamuni**. The Present Buddha, born Siddhartha Gautama, who founded Buddhism.

OTHER CHARACTERS

Ngoc Hoang The Jade Emperor, ruler of the Taoist pantheon who presides over heaven.

Ong Tau God of the Hearth, who keeps watch over every family and reports on the household to the Jade Emperor every New Year.

Quan Cong A Chinese general of the Han dynasty revered for his loyalty, honesty and exemplary behaviour. Usually flanked by his two assistants.

Thanh Mau The Mother Goddess.

Thien Hau Protectress of Sailors.

Tran Vo Properly known as Tran Vo Bac De, Taoist Emperor of the North, who governs storms and general harmful events.

VIETNAM'S ETHNIC MOSAIC

The population of Vietnam currently numbers some 73 million people, of whom nearly 90 percent are ethnic Vietnamese (known as Viet or Kinh), while approximately one million are Chinese in origin (Hoa) – see box on p.445. The remaining six to seven million people comprise an estimated 54 ethnic groups divided into dozens of subgroups, some with a mere hundred or so members, giving Vietnam the richest and most complex ethnic make-up in the whole of southeast Asia.

The vast majority of Vietnam's minorities live in the hilly regions of the **north**, down the Truong Son mountain range, and in the **central highlands** – all areas which saw heavy fighting in recent wars. Several groups straddle today's international boundaries, spreading across the Indochinese peninsula and up into southern China.

Little is known about the origins of many of these people, some of whom already inhabited the area before the ancestors of the **Viet** arrived from southern China around four to five thousand years ago. At some point the Viet emerged as a distinct group from among the various indigenous peoples living around the Red River Delta and then gradually absorbed smaller communities until they became the dominant culture. Other groups continued to interact with the Viet people, but either chose to maintain their independence in the highlands or were forced up into the hills, off the ever-more-crowded coastal plains. Vietnamese legend accounts for this fundamental split between **lowlanders** and **highlanders** as follows: the Dragon King of the south married Au Co, a beautiful northern princess, and at first they lived in the mountains where she gave birth to a hundred strong, handsome boys. After a while, however, the Dragon King missed his watery, lowland home and decamped with half his sons, leaving fifty behind in the mountains – the ancestors of the ethnic minorities.

Vietnam's ethnic groups are normally differentiated according to three main **linguistic families** – Austronesian, Austro-Asian and Sino-Tibetan – which are further subdivided into smaller groups, such as the Viet–Muong and Tay–Thai language groups. Austronesians, related to Indonesians and Pacific Islanders, were probably the earliest inhabitants of the area but are now restricted to the central highlands. Peoples of the two other linguistic families originated in southern China and at different times migrated southwards to settle throughout the Vietnamese uplands.

Despite their different origins, languages, dialects and hugely varied traditional dress, there are a number of similarities among the highland groups that distinguish them from Viet people. Most immediately obvious is the **stilt-house**, which protects against snakes, vermin and larger beasts as well as floods, while also providing safe stabling for domestic animals. The communal imbibing of **rice wine** is popular with most highland groups, as are certain **rituals** such as protecting a child from evil spirits by not naming it until after a certain age. Most highlanders traditionally practise **swidden farming**, clearing patches of forest land, farming the burnt-over fields for a few years and then leaving it fallow for a specified period while it recovers its fertility. Where the soils are particularly poor, a semi-nomadic lifestyle is adopted, shifting the village location at intervals as necessary.

If you're interested in learning more about Vietnam's ethnic diversity, pick up a copy of the slightly dated *Ethnic Minorities in Vietnam*, which is on sale in Hanoi and Ho Chi Minh City.

SOME RECENT HISTORY

Traditionally, Viet kings demanded tribute from the often fiercely independent ethnic minorities but otherwise left them to govern their own affairs. This relationship changed with the arrival of Catholic missionaries, who won many converts to Christianity among the peoples of the central highlands – called **montagnards** by the French. Under colonial rule the minorities gained a certain degree of local autonomy in the late nineteenth century, but at the same time the French expropriated their land, exacted forced labour and imposed heavy taxes. As elsewhere in Vietnam, such behaviour sparked off rebellions, notably among the Hmong in the early twentieth century.

THE NORTHERN MOUNTAINS

The French were quick to capitalize on ancient antipathies between the highland and lowland peoples. In the northwest mountains, for example, they set up a semi-autonomous Thai federation, complete with armed militias and border guards. When war broke out in 1946, groups of Thai, Hmong and Muong in the northwest sided with the French and against the Vietnamese, even to the extent of providing battalions to fight alongside French troops. But the situation was not clear cut: some Thai actively supported the Viet Minh, while Ho Chi Minh found a safe base for his guerrilla armies among the Tay and Nung people of the northeast. Recognizing the need to secure the minorities' allegiance, after North Vietnam won independence in 1954 Ho Chi Minh created two **autonomous regions**, allowing limited self-government within a "unified multi-national state".

THE CENTRAL HIGHLANDS

The minorities of the **central highlands** had also been split between supporting the French and Viet Minh after 1946. In the interests of preserving their independence, the ethnic peoples were often simply anti-Vietnamese, of whatever political persuasion. After partition in 1954, anti-Vietnamese sentiment was exacerbated when President Diem started moving Viet settlers into the region, totally ignoring local land rights. Diem wanted to tie the minorities more closely into the South Vietnamese state; the immediate result, however, was that the Bahnar, Jarai and Ede joined forces in an organized opposition movement and called a general strike in 1958. Over the next few years this well-armed coalition developed into the United Front for the Liberation of Oppressed Races, popularly known by its French acronym, **FULRO**. They demanded greater autonomy for the minorities, including elected representation at the National Assembly, more local self-government, school instruction in their own language and access to higher education. While FULRO met with some initial success, the movement was weakened after a number split off to join the Viet Cong. An estimated 10,000 or more remained, fighting first of all against the South

Vietnamese and the Americans, and then against the North Vietnamese Army until 1975. After this FULRO rebels and other anti-communist minority groups, mainly Ede, operated out of bases in Cambodia. The few who survived Pol Pot's killing fields later fled to Thailand and were eventually resettled in America.

During the **American War**, those minorities living around the Seventeenth Parallel soon found themselves on the front line. The worst fighting occurred during the late 1960s and early 1970s, when North Vietnamese troops were based in these remote uplands and American forces sought to rout them. Massive bombing raids were augmented by the use of defoliants and herbicides which, as well as denuding protective forest cover, destroyed crops and animals; this chemical warfare also killed an unknown number of people and caused severe long-term illnesses. In addition, villages were often subject to night raids by Viet Cong and North Vietnamese soldiers keen to "encourage" local support and replenish their food supplies. It's estimated that over 200,000 minority people, both civilian and military, were killed as a result of the American War, out of a total population of around one million. By 1975, 85 percent of villages in the highlands had been either destroyed or abandoned, while nothing was left standing in the region closest to the Demilitarized Zone. At the end of the war thousands of minority people were living in temporary camps, along with Viet refugees, unable to practise their traditional way of life.

POST-REUNIFICATION

After reunification things didn't really get much better. Promises of greater autonomy, made by both sides, came to nothing; even the little self-government the minorities had been granted was removed. Those groups who had opposed the North Vietnamese were kept under close observation and their leaders sent for re-education. The new government pursued a policy of **forced assimilation** of the minorities into the Vietnamese culture and glossed over their previous anti-Viet activities: all education was conducted in the Vietnamese language, traditional customs were discouraged or outlawed, and minority people were moved from their dispersed villages into permanent settlements. At the same time the government created **New**

Economic Zones in the central highlands and along the Chinese border, often commandeering the best land to resettle thousands of people from the overcrowded lowlands. According to official records, 250,000 settlers were moved into the New Economic Zones each year during the 1980s. The policy resulted in food shortages among minorities unable to support themselves on the marginal lands, and the widespread degradation of overfarmed upland soils.

Doi moi brought a shift in policy in the early 1990s, marked by the establishment of a central office responsible for the ethnic minorities. Minority languages are now officially recognized and can be taught in schools; scholarships enable minority people to attend institutes of higher education, and there is now greater representation of minorities at all levels of government. Cash crops such as timber and fruit are being introduced as an alternative to illegal hunting, logging and opium cultivation. Other income-generating schemes are also being promoted and health-care programmes upgraded. All this has been accompanied by moves to preserve Vietnam's **cultural diversity**, driven in part by the realization that ethnic differences have greater appeal to tourists. However, in many areas the minorities' traditional lifestyles are fast being eroded.

MINORITIES IN THE NORTHERN HIGHLANDS

The mountains of northern Vietnam are home to a large number of ethnic groups, all of them originating from southern China. The dominant minorities are the Tay and Thai, both feudal societies who once held sway over their weaker neighbours. These powerful well-established groups farm the fertile, valley-bottom land; while Hmong and Dao people, who only arrived in Vietnam at the end of the eighteenth century, occupy the least hospitable land at the highest altitudes. These isolated groups have been better able to lead an independent life and to preserve their traditional customs, though most exist at near-subsistence levels. Local **markets**, usually held at weekly intervals, fulfil an important role in social and economic life in the highlands; the best known is at Sa Pa, though there are others throughout the area (see *The Far North* chapter, starting on p.378, for details). Most groups

maintain a tradition of **alternate singing**, which is performed at ceremonies and festivals.

TAY

The **Tay** are Vietnam's largest minority group living in the highlands, with an estimated population of 1.2 million, concentrated in the northeast, from the Red River Valley east to the coastal plain, where they settled over 2000 years ago. Through centuries of close contact with lowlanders, Tay society has been strongly influenced by Viet culture, sharing many common rituals and Confucian practices. Many Tay have now adopted Viet architecture and dress, but it's still possible to find villages of thatched stilthouses, characterized by a railed balcony around the building. Nowadays it's largely the women who still wear the Tay's traditional long, belted dress of indigo-dyed cloth, with a similarly plain, knotted headscarf peaked at the front and set off with lots of silver jewellery. Tay farmers are famous for their animal husbandry, and they also specialize in fish-farming and growing high-value crops, such as anise, tobacco, soya and cinnamon. The Tay have developed advanced irrigation systems for wet-rice cultivation, including the huge water wheels found beside rivers in the northeast. They have had a written language since the sixteenth century, fostering a strong literary tradition; alternate singing is also popular, as are theatrical performances, kite-flying and a whole variety of other games. Some Tay groups in the more remote regions occasionally erect a funeral house, decorated with fluttering slips of white paper, over a new grave.

THAI

The **Thai** minority numbers just over 1 million, and is the dominant group in the northwest mountains from the Red River south to Nghe An, though most live in Lai Chau and Son La provinces. They are distantly related to the Thai of Thailand and to groups in southern China, their ancestral homeland. However, Thai people have been living in Vietnam for at least 2000 years and show similarities with both Viet and Tay cultures. Traditional Thai society was strongly hierarchical, ruled over by feudal lords who controlled vast land-holdings worked by the villagers. Their written language, which is based on Sanskrit, has furnished a literary legacy dating back five centuries, including epic poems, histories and a wealth of folklore. The Thai are also famous for their unique dance repertoire and finely woven brocades decorated with flowers, birds and dragons, which are on sale in local markets. From their early teens women learn how to weave and embroider, eventually preparing a set of blankets for their dowry. Thai houses are often still constructed on stilts, with wood or bamboo frames, though the architecture varies between regions.

There are two main subgroups: **Black Thai** (around Dien Bien Phu, Tuan Giao and Son La) and **White Thai** (Mai Chau, Lai Chau), whose names are often attributed to the traditional colour of the women's shirts, though this is open to dispute. In fact, the women of both groups tend to wear similar clothes, consisting of long sarong-like skirts, either black or very dark indigo blue, perhaps with a brightly coloured sash or brocade panels. Their shirts are fastened with beautiful silver clasps, fashioned in the shape of butterflies or other insects, and on formal occasions they don intricately woven headscarves.

MUONG

The lower hills from the Red River Valley south through Yen Bai, and Son La down to Thanh Hoa are the domain of the **Muong** ethnic minority, with the majority now living in Hoa Binh Province. Muong people, totalling just under 1 million, are believed to share common ancestors with the Viet. It's thought that the two groups split around 2000 years ago, after which the Muong developed relatively independently in the highlands. Society is traditionally dominated by aristocratic families, who distribute communal land to the villagers in return for labour and tax contributions; the symbols of their authority are drums and bronze gongs. Muong stilthouses are similar to those built by the Thai, and the main staple is rice, though fishing, hunting and gathering are all still fairly important. Muong people have a varied cultural tradition, including alternate singing and epic tales, and they are famed for their embroidery, typically creating bold geometric designs in black and white. Older Muong women continue to wear the traditional long black skirt and close-fitting shirt; a broad, heavily embroidered belt is the main accessory, and many women also wear a simple white headscarf.

NUNG

Nung people are closely related to the Tay, sharing the same language and often living in the same villages. Their population is estimated at 700,000, mostly in Cao Bang and Lang Son provinces, where they have a long tradition of cultivating wet rice, using water wheels for irrigation. Nung farmers terrace the lower slopes to provide extra land, and are noted for the wide variety of crops they grow, including maize, groundnuts and a whole host of vegetables. In fact, the Nung are reckoned to be the best horticulturalists in Vietnam, while their blacksmiths are almost as renowned. Unusually, the traditional Nung house has clay walls and a tiled roof, and is built either flat on the ground or with only one section raised on stilts.

Most Nung are Buddhist, worshipping Quan Am, though they also honour the spirits and their ancestors. They are particularly adept at alternate singing, relishing the improvised double entendre. Not surprisingly, Nung traditional dress is similar to the Tay, though hemmed with coloured bands. Women often sport a neck scarf with brightly coloured fringes and a shoulder bag, embroidered with the sun, stars and flowers, or woven in black and white interspersed with delicately coloured threads.

HMONG

Since the end of the eighteenth century groups of Miao people have been fleeing southern China, heading for Laos, Burma, Thailand and Vietnam. Miao meant "barbarian", whereas their new name, **Hmong**, means "free people". In Vietnam the Hmong population now stands at around 600,000, living in the high areas of all the northern provinces down to Nghe An. The poor farming land, geographical isolation and their traditional seclusion from other people has left the Hmong one of the most impoverished groups in Vietnam; standards of health and education are low, while infant mortality is exceptionally high. Hmong farmers grow maize, rice and vegetables on burnt-over land, irrigated fields and terraced hillsides. Traditionally they also grow poppies, though this is now being discouraged by the government. Hmong people raise cattle, buffalo and horses, and have recently started growing fruit trees, such as peach, plum and apple. They are also skilled hunters and gather forest products, including honey, medicinal herbs, roots and bark, either for their own consumption or to trade at weekly markets. Hmong houses are built flat on the ground, rather than raised on stilts.

Until recently there was no written Hmong language, but a strong oral tradition of folk songs, riddles and proverbs flourishes. Perhaps the Hmong are best known, however, for their handicrafts, particularly weaving hemp and cotton cloth which is then coloured with indigo dyes. To achieve the right intensity of blue, the cloth may be dyed up to thirty times, and then beaten until the surface takes on a lustrous, almost metallic sheen. Many Hmong people still wear traditional indigo apparel: men wear baggy, tubular trousers with a loose shirt, a long waistcoat of burnished cloth and silver or bronze necklaces; female attire is generally a knee-length skirt, an apron, leggings and a waistcoat, plus a collection of chunky silver earrings, bracelets and necklaces. Hmong women often adorn their shirt sleeves with embroidered bands, while the skirts of some groups may also be highly decorated. The main subgroups are **White**, **Red**, **Green**, **Black** and **Flower Hmong**. Though the origin of the names is unknown, there are marked differences in dialect and social customs as well as dress and hairstyle, especially among the women.

DAO

The **Dao** (pronounced "Zao") ethnic minority is incredibly diverse in all aspects of life: social and religious practices, architecture, agriculture and dress. Small, localized groups settled in the northern border region after leaving China some 200 years ago. Dao people now number some 500,000 in Vietnam, with related groups in Laos, Thailand and China.

Long ago the Dao adopted the Chinese writing system and have a substantial literary tradition. One popular legend records the origin of the 12 Dao clans: Ban Ho, a powerful dog of five colours, killed an enemy general and was granted the hand of a princess in marriage, who gave birth to twelve children. Ban Ho is worshipped by the Dao and the five colours of Dao embroidery represent their ancestor. The Dao boast a particularly striking traditional dress, characterized by a rectangular patch of embroidery sewn onto the back of their jackets, and both men and women sport silver or copper jewellery and tasselled shoulder bags. Dao women wear elaborate headgear, usually a triangular-shaped tur-

ban, either embroidered or decorated with silver coins, beads and coloured tassels; it's also common for Dao women to shave their eyebrows and sometimes the whole head, coating the skull with wax. Dao people live at all altitudes, their house style and agricultural techniques varying accordingly. While groups living at lower levels are relatively prosperous, growing rice and raising livestock, those in the high, rocky mountains live in considerable poverty.

GIAY

The **Giay** (pronounced "Zay") are a relatively small minority group, with a population of just under 40,000, living at high altitudes in Lao Cai and Lai Chau provinces. Traditional Giay society is feudal, with a strict demarcation between the local aristocracy and the peasant classes. All villagers work the communal lands, living in closely knit villages of stilthouses. A few Giay women still wear the traditional style of dress, distinguished by the highly coloured, circular panel sewn around the collar and a shirt-fastening on the right shoulder; the shirt itself is often of bright green, pink or blue. On formal occasions, women often also wear a chequered headscarf or turban.

MINORITIES IN THE CENTRAL HIGHLANDS

Nearly all minority groups living in the central highlands are indigenous peoples: most are matrilineal societies with a strong emphasis on community life and with some particularly complex burial rites. Catholic **missionaries** enjoyed considerable success in the central highlands, establishing a mission at Kon Tum in the mid-nineteenth century, and then early in the twentieth century Protestantism was also introduced to the region. Most converts came from among the Ede and Bahnar, though other groups have also incorporated Christian practices into their traditional belief systems. Likewise, **Vietnamese influence** has been stronger here than in northern Vietnam, while the **American War** caused severe disruption. Nevertheless, their cultures have been sufficiently strong to resist complete assimilation.

JARAI (OR GIA-RAI)

The largest minority group on the central highlands is the **Jarai**, with a population of roughly 250,000. It's thought that Jarai people left the coastal plains around 2000 years ago, settling on the fertile plateau around Plei Ku. Some ethnologists hold that Cham people are in fact a branch of the Jarai, and they certainly share common linguistic traits and a matrilineal social order. Young Jarai women initiate the marriage proposal and afterwards the couple live in the wife's family home, with children taking their mother's name. Houses are traditionally built on stilts, facing north. The focus of village life is the communal house or *rong*, where the council of elders and their elected chief meet. Animist beliefs are still strong and the Jarai world is peopled with spirits, the most famous of which are the kings of Water, Fire and Wind, represented by shamans who are involved in rain-making ceremonies and other rituals. Funeral rites are particularly complex and expensive: after the burial, a funeral house is built over the grave and evocative sculptures of people, birds and objects from everyday life are placed inside. The Jarai also have an extensive musical repertoire, the principal instruments being gongs and the unique *k'longput*, made of bamboo tubes into which the players force air by clapping their hands.

During the American War the majority of Jarai villagers moved out of their war-torn homeland; many have been resettled in Plei Ku, and others are only now slowly returning.

EDE (OR RHADÉ)

Further south, towards Buon Me Thuot, around 200,000 people of the **Ede** minority live in stilthouses grouped together in a village or *buon*. These longhouses, which can be up to 100m in length, are boat-shaped with hardwood frames, bamboo floors and walls, and topped with a high thatched roof. As many as a hundred family members may live in a single house, under the authority of the oldest or most respected woman, who owns all family property, including the house and domestic animals; wealth is indicated by the number of ceremonial gongs. Other much-prized heirlooms are the large earthenware jars used for making the rice wine drunk at festivals. Like the Jarai, Ede people worship the kings of Fire and Water among a whole host of animist spirits, and also erect a funeral house on their graves. Both the original longhouse and its grave-site replica are often decorated with fine carvings.

The Ede homeland lies in a region of red soils on the rolling western plateaux. In the nine-teenth and twentieth centuries French settlers introduced coffee and rubber estates to the area, often seizing land from the local people they called Rhadé. Traditional swidden farming has gradually been disappearing, a process accelerated by the American War and the forced relocation of Ede into permanent settlements.

BAHNAR (OR BA-NA)

Bahnar people trace their ancestry back many centuries to communities co-existing on the coastal plains with the Cham and Jarai. Now the Bahnar minority, numbering some 140,000, mostly live in the highlands east of Plei Ku and Kon Tum.

The most distinctive aspect of a Bahnar village is its *rong* or communal house, the roof of which may be up to 30m high and slightly curved. The *rong* is the centre of village cultural and ceremonial life, and also the home of adolescent boys, who are taught Bahnar history, the skills of hunting and other manly matters. The village houses grouped around the *rong* are typically stilthouses with a thatched or tiled roof, and are often decorated with geometric motifs. For centuries Bahnar people have traded with the Cham and later the Viet people of the lowlands, and as a result have little tradition of handicrafts. However they are well-known for their animal husbandry and horticulture, growing maize, sweet potato or millet, together with indigo, hemp or tobacco as cash crops. Bahnar groups also erect funeral houses and decorate them with elaborate carvings, though they are not as imposing as those of the Jarai. Some time after the burial, wooden statues, gongs, wine jars and other items of family property will be placed in the funeral house.

SEDANG (OR XO-DANG)

According to their oral histories, **Sedang** people once lived further north but are now concentrated in the area between Kon Tum and Quang Ngai, comprising a community of nearly 100,000. The Sedang were traditionally a war-like people whose villages were surrounded with defensive hedges, barbed with spears and stakes, and with only one entrance. Intervillage wars were frequent and the Sedang also carried out raids on the peaceable Bahnar, mainly to seize prisoners rather than territory. In the past, Sedang religious ritual involved human sacrifices to propitiate the spirits – a practice that was later modified into a profitable business, selling slaves to traders from Laos and Thailand. In the 1880s, an eccentric French military adventurer called Marie-David de Mayréna, established a kingdom in Sedang territory by making treaties with the local chiefs (see p.183). A few decades later, the French authorities conscripted Sedang labour to build Highway 14 from Kon Tum to Da Nang; conditions were so harsh that many died, provoking a rebellion in the 1930s. Soon after, the Viet Minh won many recruits among the Sedang in their war against the French. In the American War some Sedang groups fought for the Viet Cong while others were formed into militia units by the American Special Services. But when fighting intensified after 1965, Sedang villagers were forced to flee and many now live in almost destitute conditions, having lost their ancestral lands.

Traditionally, membership of a Sedang village was indicated by the use of a common watersource. Each extended family occupies a longhouse, built on stilts and usually facing east; central to village life is the communal house where young men and boys sleep, and where all the major ceremonies take place. Because villages historically had relatively little contact with each other, there are marked variations between the social customs of the subgroups and so far seventeen Sedang dialects have been identified. Agricultural techniques are more consistent, mainly swidden farming supplemented by horticulture and hunting. Some Sedang farmers employ a "water harp", a combined bird-scarer, musical instrument and appeaser of the spirits. The harp consists of bamboo tubes linked together and placed in a flowing stream to produce an irregular, haunting sound.

KOHO (OR CO-HO) AND LAT

The Di Linh plateau at the very southern end of the central highlands is the home of the **Koho** minority. The community of some 90,000 is subdivided into six highly varied subgroups, including the **Lat** people of Da Lat.

The typical Koho house is built on stilts with a thatched roof and bamboo walls and flooring. Inside the house, above the entrance door, is the co nao, an intricately carved board used in ancestor worship. Despite the fact that many Koho were converted to Christianity in the early

twentieth century, spirit-worship is widely practised and each family adopts a guardian spirit from the natural world. Catholic missionaries developed a phonetic script for the Koho language but the oral tradition remains strong. Unlike many minorities in this region, dance is an important element of the Koho's religious rites; a variety of musical instruments, such as gongs, bamboo flutes and buffalo horns, are also involved. Subgroups of the Koho minority are famed for their pottery and ironwork, whereas Lat farmers have a reputation for constructing sophisticated irrigation systems.

MNONG

The **Mnong** ethnic minority is probably best known for its skill in hunting elephants and domesticating them for use in war, for transport and for their ivory. Mnong people are also the creators of the lithophone, a kind of stone xylophone thought to be among the world's most ancient musical instruments; an example is on show at the Lam Dong Province Museum in Da Lat (see p.166). The Mnong have lived in the southern central highlands for centuries, and now around 67,000 people are concentrated in the region between Buon Me Thuot and Da Lat. Mnong houses are usually built flat on the ground and, though the society is generally matrilineal, village affairs are organized by a male chief. Mnong craftsmen are skilled at basketry and printing textiles, while they also make the copper, tin and silver jewellery worn by both sexes. In traditional burial rituals a buffalo-shaped coffin is placed under a funeral house which is peopled with wooden statues and painted with black, red or white designs.

BRU AND TA-OI

Two related minority groups had the extreme misfortune to live on the Seventeenth Parallel, near the border with Laos: the **Bru** (or Bru Van-Kieu), these days numbering around 40,000, and the **Ta-oi**, with a population of only 26,000. Bru people were caught up in the battle of Khe Sanh (see p.287) – both as refugees and as part of an American militia force – while the Ta-oi, amongst others, helped keep open the Ho Chi Minh Trail for the North Vietnamese Army. During the worst years of fighting, refugees fled south to Ede country or crossed over into Laos, and many never returned. Those that did move back found Viet people settled on their best land – the Khe

Sanh plateau was declared a New Economic Zone – and were forced into marginal areas.

Of the two groups, Bru people have always had greater contact with the outside world since the ancient Lao Bao trade route passes through their territory to Laos. Bru houses can usually be distinguished by their rounded shape, likened to a tortoise shell, and are occasionally decorated with carved birds or buffalo horns at each end. Both groups are patrilineal, practise swidden farming and worship a huge range of spirits, though ancestor worship is also central to their belief systems.

MINORITIES IN THE SOUTHERN LOWLANDS

As the Viet people pushed down the coastal plain and into the Mekong Delta they displaced two main ethnic groups, the Cham and Khmer. Up until the tenth century powerful **Cham** kings had ruled over most of southern Vietnam (see p.410); nowadays, there are less than 100,000

Cham people, mostly living on the coast between Phan Rang and Phan Thiet, or on the Cambodian border around Chau Doc, with a small number in Ho Chi Minh City. The coastal communities are largely still Hindu worshippers of Shiva and follow the matrilineal practices of their Cham ancestors; they earn a living from farming, silk weaving and crafting jewellery of gold or silver. Groups along the Cambodian border are Islamic and, in general, patrilineal. They engage in river-fishing, weaving and cross-border trade, with little agricultural activity. On the whole, Cham people have adopted the Vietnamese way of life and dress, though their traditional arts, principally dance and music, have experienced a revival in recent years.

Ethnic Khmers are the indigenous people of the Mekong Delta, including Cambodia. Nowadays only about 900,000 remain in the eastern delta under Vietnamese rule, and some of these only arrived in the late 1970s as refugees from Pol Pot's brutal regime in

HOA AND VIET KIEU

Ethnic Chinese people, known in Vietnamese as **Hoa**, form one of Vietnam's largest minority groups, estimated at around 1 million. Throughout the country's history Chinese people, mostly from China's southern provinces, have been emigrating to Vietnam, as administrators and merchants or as refugees from persecution. In the mid-seventeenth century the collapse of the Ming dynasty sent a human deluge southwards, and there were other large-scale migrations in the nineteenth century and then the 1940s. Until the early nineteenth century all Hoa, even those of mixed blood, were considered by the Viets to be Chinese. After that date, however, they were admitted to public office and gradually became integrated into Vietnamese society, so that now most have Vietnamese nationality. Nevertheless, the Hoa remain slightly apart, living in close communities according to their ancestral province in China and preserving elements of their own culture, notably their language. The Hoa have tended to settle in urban areas, typically becoming successful merchants, artisans and businesspeople, and playing an important role in the economy. Ninety percent of Hoa now live in southern Vietnam, predominantly in Cholon, with small groups scattered through the Mekong Delta and the central highlands.

Viet people have tended to distrust the Hoa, mainly because of their dominant commercial position and their close links with China. After 1975 the Hoa were badly hit when socialist policies were enforced, in what amounted to an anti-Chinese persecution. Tensions rose even further when China invaded Vietnam in 1979 and thousands of Hoa left the country, to escape reprisals, with Hoa people forming a large majority of the "boat people" (see box on p.426). It's estimated that up to one-third of the Hoa population eventually left Vietnam. Many settled in America, Australia and France, where they joined earlier refugees to become what the Vietnamese call **Viet kieu**, or overseas Vietnamese, of whom there are perhaps as many as 2 million worldwide. In the last few years Viet kieu have been allowed back to visit relatives and can now send money to family members still in Vietnam, providing an important source of extra income for individuals and becoming increasingly valuable in the wider economy, especially in southern Vietnam. Not surprisingly, however, the attitudes of those who stuck it out in Vietnam towards Viet kieu are ambivalent, and the government itself is unsure about how to handle relations with the Viet kieu; in general their money and expertise are welcomed but not necessarily their politics, nor their Western ways.

Cambodia. Khmer farmers are noted for their skill at irrigation and wet-rice cultivation; it's said that they farm nearly 150 varieties of rice, each suited to specific local conditions. Traditionally, Khmers live in villages of stilt-houses erected on raised mounds above the flood waters, but these days are more likely to build flat on the earth, along canals and road-ways. The pagoda, however, is still a distinctive feature of Khmer villages, its brightly patterned roofs decorated with images of the sacred ancestral dragon, the neak. Although ancient beliefs persist, since the late thirteenth century the Khmers have been devout followers of Theravada Buddhism, as practised in Cambodia, Laos and Thailand. Local craftspeople produce fine silk and basketry, and Khmers have retained their tradition of satirical stories, proverbs and folk songs – and still wear their distinctive red-and-white scarves.

MUSIC AND THEATRE

The binding element to all Vietnam's traditional performing arts is music, and particularly singing (*hat*), which is a natural extension to an already musical language. The origins of Vietnamese music can be traced back as far as the bronze drums and flutes of Dong Son (see p.324), and further again to the lithophone (stone xylophone) called the *dan da*, the world's oldest-known instrument. The Chinese influence is evident in operatic theatre and stringed instruments, while India bestowed rhythms, modal improvisations and several types of drum. Much later, especially during the nineteenth century, elements of European theatre and music were co-opted, while during this century most Vietnamese musicians received a classical, Western training based on the works of Eastern bloc composers such as Prokofiev and Tchaikovsky.

From this multicultural melting-pot Vietnamese artists have generated a variety of musical and theatrical forms over the centuries, though, surprisingly dance is less developed than in neighbouring Thailand, Cambodia and Laos. One of the most famous home-grown performance arts is water puppetry, Vietnam's unique contribution to the world of marionettes, where puppeteers work their magic on a stage of water. The folk tradition is particularly rich, with its improvised courtship songs and the strident, sacred music of trance dances, to which the more than fifty ethnic minorities add their own repertoire of songs and instruments.

Traditionally the professions of artists or performers were hereditary; sadly, the wars and political upheavals of this century have contributed to the loss of much of this largely oral tradition. Many musicians and actors are now into their eighties, while the younger generation is more interested in higher-paid professions and Vietnamese pop. As revolutionary (red) music has waned since 1986, so pre-1975 music from the South, previously outlawed as "decadent and reactionary", is back with a vengeance, mixed with a sprinkling of artists from other Asian countries and the West.

THE TRADITIONAL STRAND

Vietnam's traditional theatre, with its strong Chinese influence, is more akin to opera than pure spoken drama. A musical accompaniment and well-known repertoire of songs form an integral part of the performance, where the plots and characters are equally familiar to the audience. Nowadays, however, the two oldest forms, **Cheo** and **Tuong**, are struggling to survive, while even the more contemporary **Cai Luong** is losing out to television and the video recorder. Other traditional arts have seen something of a revival, though, most notably **water puppetry** and folk-song performances. The stimulus for this came largely from tourism, but renewed interest in the trance music of **Chau Van** and the complexities of **Tai Tu** chamber music has been very much home-grown.

THEATRE

Vietnam's oldest surviving stage art, **Hat Cheo**, or "Popular Opera", has its roots in the Red River Delta where it's believed to have existed since at least the eleventh century. Performances consist of popular legends and everyday events, often with a biting satirical edge, accompanied by a selection of tunes drawn as appropriate from a common fund. Though the movements have become highly stylized over the centuries, Cheo's free form allows the actors considerable room for interpretation; the audience demonstrates its approval, or otherwise, by beating a drum. Cheo has the reputation of being anti-establishment, especially its buffoon character who comments freely on the action, the audience and current events. So incensed were the kings of the fifteenth-century Le dynasty that Cheo was banned from the court, while artists and their descendants were excluded from public office. Nowadays, the few Cheo ensembles that still exist in northern Vietnam rely on scenes from unrelated libretti.

Hat Tuong (known in southern Vietnam as *Hat Boi*), probably introduced from China around the thirteenth century, evolved from classical Chinese opera, and was originally for royal entertainment before being adopted by travelling troupes. Its story lines are mostly historic events and epic tales dealing with such Confucian principles as filial piety and relations between the monarch and his subjects. Tuong, like Cheo, is governed by rigorous rules in which the characters are rendered instantly recognizable by their make-up and costume. Setting and atmosphere are conjured not by props and scenery but through nuances of gesture and musical conventions with which the audience are completely familiar – and which they won't hesitate to criticize if badly executed.

While performances of Cheo and Tuong are rare events these days, if you see a large building with peanut and candy sellers outside, the chances are that there's a performance of **Hat Cai Luong**, or "Renovated Theatre", going on inside. Cai Luong originated in southern Vietnam in the early twentieth century, showing a French theatrical influence in its spoken parts, with short scenes and relatively elaborate sets. The action is a tangle of historical drama (such as *The Tale of the Kieu*) and racy contemporary themes from the street (murder, drug deals, incest, theft, revenge, denouement). Its music is a similar hodgepodge: eighteenth-century chamber music played on amplified traditional instruments for the set pieces; electric guitar, keyboards and drums during the scene changes. Cai Luong's use of contemporary vernacular has made it highly adaptable and enabled it to keep pace with Vietnam's social changes.

WATER PUPPETRY

The origin of **water puppetry**, *roi nuoc*, is obscure beyond that it developed in the murky rice paddies of the Red River Delta, and usually took place in spring when there was less farm work to be done. The earliest record is a stele in Nam Ha Province dated 1121 AD, suggesting that by this date water puppetry was already a regular feature at the royal court. Obscured behind a split-bamboo screen, puppeteers standing waist-deep in water manipulate the wooden puppets, some weighing over 10kg, attached to the end of long poles hidden beneath the surface. Dragons, ducks, lions, unicorns, phoenixes and frogs spout smoke, throw balls and generally cavort – miraculously avoiding tangling the poles. Brief scenes of rural life, such as water-buffalo fights, fishing or rice-planting, take place alongside the legendary exploits of Le Loi and the promenade of fairy-like immortals. Even fireworks emerge to dance upon the water, which itself takes on different characters, from soft-focus and placid to seething and furious during naval battles.

The art of water puppetry was traditionally a jealously guarded secret handed down from father to son; women were not permitted to learn the techniques in case they revealed them to their husbands' families. This contributed to its decline until the art seemed in danger of dying out altogether. Happily a French organization, *Maison des Cultures des Monde*, intervened and, since 1984, with newly carved puppets, a revamped programme and more elaborate staging, Vietnam's water puppet troupes have played various international capitals to great acclaim – and can be seen nightly in Hanoi (see p.343) and Ho Chi Minh City (see p.100). Where before gongs and drums alone were used for scene-setting and building atmosphere, today's national troupes often maintain a larger ensemble, similar to Hat Cheo, including zithers and flutes. The songs are also borrowed from the Cheo repertoire, particularly declamatory styles and popular folk tunes, and the show often includes a short recital of traditional music before the puppets emerge to create their own unique illusion.

MUSIC AND SONG

One of Vietnam's oldest song traditions is that of **Quan Ho**, or alternate singing, a form which thrives in the Red River Delta, particularly Ha Bac Province, and has parallels among the north's ethnic minorities. These unaccompanied songs are usually heard in spring, performed by young men and women bandying improvised lyrics back and forth. Quan Ho traditionally played a part in the courtship ritual and performers are applauded for their skill in complimenting or teasing their partner, earning delighted approval as the exchange becomes increasingly bawdy.

Hat Chau Van is an ancient, sacred ritual music that's instrumental in goddess worship during trance possession ceremonies. Statues of a pantheon of goddesses are placed in shrines to the Mother Goddess, Thanh Mau, found in both Buddhist pagodas and village temples. Throughout the performance of hypnotically rhythmic music (the performers may be one or many, male or female) a medium enters a trance state and is possessed by a chosen deity. Because of the anti-religious stance of the Vietnamese government until 1986, the style was practised in secret, though some pieces were adapted for inclusion in state-sponsored Cheo theatre. Chau Van is currently being revived by older practitioners in its original religious setting, promoted by a class of nouveau riche keen for the goddesses to intercede and protect their business interests.

Although the song tradition known as **Ca Tru**, or **Hat A Dao**, dates back centuries, it became all the rage in the fifteenth century when the Vietnamese regained their independence from China. According to legend, a beautiful young songstress, A Dao, charmed the enemy with her songs of the verdant countryside and the way of life in the villages. Fascinated by her voice, the soldiers were encouraged to drink until they became incapacitated and could be pushed into the river and drowned. The lyrics of Ca Tru are often taken from famous poems and are traditionally sung by a woman. The singer also plays a bamboo percussion instrument, and is accompanied by a 3-chord guitar (*dan day*) and drum. She has to master a whole range of singing styles, each differentiated by its particular rhythm, such as *Hat noi* (similar to speech) and *Gui thu* (a more formal style, akin to a written letter). Ca Tru is closely related to the song tradition of Hué, **Ca Hué**, which is now performed for tourists on sampans on the Perfume River (see p.277).

The traditional music accompanying Cai Luong theatre originated in eighteenth-century Hué. Played as pure chamber music, without the voice, it is known as **Nhac Tai Tu**, or "skilled chamber music of amateurs". This is one of the most delightful and tricksy of all Vietnamese genres: the players have a great degree of improvisational latitude over a fundamental melodic skeleton. They must think and respond quickly, as in a game, and the resulting independently funky rhythms can be wild. Although modern conservatory training fails to prepare students for this most satisfying of all styles, there is now a resurgence of interest by young players in learning the demands of Tai Tu.

TRADITIONAL INSTRUMENTS

A visiting US general once stepped off a plane with the intention of smoothing relations by attempting a little Vietnamese, a tonal language. Instead of "I am honoured to be here", listeners heard "the sunburnt duck lies sleeping". The voice and its inherent melodic information are behind all Vietnamese music, and most instruments are, to some extent, made to do what voices do: delicate pitch bends, ornaments and subtle slides. According to classical Confucian theory, instruments fall into eight **categories of sound**: silk, stone, skin, clay, metal, air, wood and bamboo. Although few people play by the rules these days, classical theory also relates five occasions when it is forbidden to perform: at sunset, during a storm, when the preparations have not been made seriously, with improper costumes, and when the audience is not paying attention.

Many instruments whose strings are now made of steel, gut or nylon originally had **silk** strings; silk is now out of fashion, more for acoustic than ecological reasons. The most famous of these, and unique to Vietnam, is the monochord **dan bau** (or *dan doc huyen*), an ingenious invention perfectly suited to its job of mimicking vocal inflections. It is made from one string (originally silk obtained by yanking apart the live worm), stretched over a long amplified sounding box, fixed at one end. The other end is attached to a buffalo-horn "whammy bar" stalk which can be flexed to stretch or relax the string's tension. Meanwhile the string is plucked with a plectrum at its harmonic nodes to produce overtones that swoop and glide and quiver over a range of three octaves. The most common string instruments include the *dan nguyet* moon-shaped lute, the *dan tranh* 16-string zither, *dan nhi* (2-string fiddle with the bow running between the strings), *dan day* (an open shoe-box head with a long fingerboard used in Ca Tru and also unique to Vietnam), and the *dan luc huyen cam*, a regular guitar with a fingerboard scalloped to allow for wider pitch bends.

The *dan da* **stone** lithophone is the world's oldest instrument, consisting of six or more rocks struck with heavy wooden mallets. Several sets have been found originating from the one slate quarry in the central highlands where the stones sing like nowhere else. The oldest *dan da* is now in Paris, but an identical set exists in Ho Chi Minh City, where it still produces pure ringing tones; there's also one on display in Da Lat (see p.166).

Various kinds of **drums** (*trong*) are used, played with acrobatic use of the sticks in the air and on the sides. Some originated from China, while others were introduced from India via the Cham people, such as the double-headed "rice drum" (*trong com*), which was developed from the Indian *mridangam*; the name derives from thin patches of cooked rice paste stuck on each membrane.

Representing **clay**, four thimble-size teacups are held in the fingers and often played as percussion instruments for Hué chamber music. Representing **metal**, the *sinh tien*, **coin clappers**, are another invention unique to Vietnam, combining in one unit a rasping scraper, wooden clapper and a sistrum rattle made from old coins. Bronze **gongs** are occasionally found in minority music, but Vietnam is the only country in southeast Asia where tuned gamelan-type gong-chimes are not used.

Air, wood and bamboo furnish a whole range of wind instruments, such as the many side- and end-blown flutes used for folk songs and to accompany poetry recitals; or the *ken*, a double-reed oboe common across Asia and played, appropriately, in funeral processions and other outdoor ceremonies. Five thin bones often dangle from the *ken* player's mouthpiece to suggest the delicate fingers of a young woman, while disguising the hideous grin necessary to play the instrument. The *song lang* is a slit drum, played by the foot, used to count the measures in *Tai Tu* skilled chamber music, while the *k'longput*, consisting of racks of bamboo pipes, is the only percussion instrument you don't actually touch but clap in front of. Another instrument from the same folk tradition is the *t'rung*, made of ladders of tuned bamboo.

NEW FOLK

Turn on the TV during the Tet Lunar New Year festivities and you can't miss the public face of Vietnamese traditional music: ethnic-costumed dancers, musicians and singers smilingly portraying the happy life of the worker. Swell arrangements of well-known tunes from all over the country, including some token minorities' music, are spiced up with fancy hats and bamboo pianos. This choreographed entertainment known as **Modernized Folk Music** (*Nhac Dan Toc Cai Bien*) has only been "traditional" since 1956, when the Hanoi Conservatory of Music was founded and the teaching of folk music was deliberately "improved".

For the first time, music was learned from written Western notation (leading to the neglect of improvisational skills while opening the way for huge orchestras), and conductors were used. Tunings of the traditional eight modes were tempered to accommodate Western-style harmonies, while bizarre new instruments were invented to play bass and to fill out chords in the enlarged bands. Schools, with the mandate of preserving traditional music through "inheritance development", took over from the families and professional apprenticeships which had formerly been passed on via the oral tradition.

Not surprisingly a new creature was born out of all this. Trained Conservatory graduates have spread throughout the country, been promoted through competitions and state-sponsored ensembles on TV, radio, and even in the lobbies of classier hotels. The new corpus of music and song arrangements has become an emblem of national pride and scientific improvement. Folk songs, melodies from the ethnic minorities, Mozart and Chinese tunes are all ripe fodder for the arranger's pen. Much to the chagrin of the few remaining traditional musicians outside this system, this is now the predominant folk-based music generally heard in public. A friend visiting the central highlands asked the local tribal musicians how they felt about their music being "improved". At first they replied what an honour it was for their music to be considered by city people, but after the official interview they privately confessed their horror.

Music for new folk is entertaining and accessible, albeit risking tawdriness; at its best, though, it can be an astonishing display of a lively new artform. One family of six brothers (and one sister-in-law), led by Duc Loi, forms a percussion group in Ho Chi Minh City under the name **Phu Dong**, whose members spent time in the highlands learning the instruments of several minorities. Since 1981 they have played together and developed an infectious musical personality. Circular breathing and lightning-speed virtuosity are just some of the dazzling features of a performance, and their instrumentarium is like a zoo of mutant bamboo. Most striking, though, is their use of the lithophone (*dan da*), a replica of the original, 6000-year-old marimba made of rocks. The effect of awakening this ancient voice, whatever changes in performance practice there may have been over the last six millennia, is shattering.

There is no lack of extraordinary recordings of Vietnamese folk music made over the last sixty years; on the contrary, there are over 4000 of them. They are, however, all but totally inaccessible in the guarded bowels of a converted pagoda in Hanoi. The tapes, their rusty dandruff particles floating off with each playing, have lain uncatalogued for the last few decades, although a New York Foundation (The Asian Cultural Council) is now helping. Recently recognized as a national treasure because of the lost traditions they contain, they are being studied on condition that no copies be made; the fears are that someone might make a lot of money out of publishing them abroad, and that their technical quality is embarrassing when compared to modern CDs. The inspired solution is to begin making new field recordings of what's left (which of course does nothing to rescue the lost traditions from their rapidly deteriorating archive).

"YELLOW MUSIC": VIETNAMESE POP

They pedal from gig to gig, or sit side-saddle on a Honda Dream if they are famous: the pop singers of Ho Chi Minh City. Emerging from the traffic, they park their wheels, sit behind a tree near the stage and wait for their turn at the mike, carefully preening their rumpled *ao dai* or suit. If you want to hear the current play-list during the course of one evening, all you have to do is visit one of the many café-bar-hotels where there is a live band. One by one the singers take turns to come on stage, sing a song (two, if they are well known – one slow, one fast) before hopping down the road to repeat the routine.

While there is no shortage of pop-star wannabes in Vietnam (witness the karaoke boom), the star-making industry is less than effi-

cient and the public usually recognizes the songwriter before the performer. Paris-trained Pham Trong Cau, jungle-trained Diep Minh Tuyen and Thanh Tung (a business mogul who doubles as the best-known writer of film scores) are all famous songwriters, but **Trinh Cong Son** is the undisputed number one. Joan Baez was not far off when she dubbed him "the Vietnamese Bob Dylan": the tunes are catchy and the lyrics right on. His first songs were written while in hiding from the military draft, and in 1969, when his album *Lullaby* sold over two million copies in Japan, Son's works were banned by the South Vietnamese government, who considered the lyrics too demoralizing. Even the new government sent him to work as a peasant in the fields, but since 1979 he has lived in Ho Chi Minh City, drinking and painting, writing apolitical love songs and celebrating Vietnam's natural wonders, with over 600 songs to his credit.

In recent years the Pop Rock genre (Misery-Pop to some) has returned with sweet determination, in which a search for Vietnam's answer to Charles Aznavour would be hotly contested. Bryan Adams and John Denver have already played Vietnam, but the real mania would be reserved for a visit by Kenny G or Richard Clayderman. Heavy metal and other music that raises the blood pressure have yet to be widely accepted, but the influence from the Asian pop field – wryly referred to as "Yellow Music" – is strong, with cassettes from the Hong Kong, Thai and Taiwanese markets bootlegged on the street you wait.

The standard band consists of a singer (who may admit of a few modest gyrations), bass guitar and one or two electronic keyboards, hailed throughout the country as the greatest labour-saving device, despite their cheesy sound. Indeed, in rural areas where there is no electricity, these portable keyboards run happily on batteries, and all the rhythm buttons that are so rarely used elsewhere – rumba, tango, bossa nova and surf-rock – are here employed liberally. The ubiquitous slap-echo on the singer's microphone is intentional; without it, they say, it sounds "unprofessional". Each evening, when the traffic noise dies down, you can hear the mournful laments of neighbouring karaoke bars mingling together, the ghostly echoes of lonely pop singers reverberating from another dimension.

DISCOGRAPHY

Many recordings are not yet available outside Vietnam; the best places to shop are Ben Thanh market in Ho Chi Minh City and Hang Bai Street in Hanoi.

TRADITIONAL

Various *The Music of Vietnam* (Celestial Harmonies, US). Although it doesn't really explore contemporary popular styles, this 3-CD set includes some unique music from the Imperial Court in Hué, and is the most varied and approachable introduction to the richness and diversity of Vietnamese music, all presented with freshness and a sense of discovery.

Various *Stilling Time* (Innova, US). A sampler of field recordings from all over Vietnam, including songs from ethnic minorities and the only Phu Dong on CD. An introduction to the many surprises in store for the musical traveller, recorded and compiled by Philip Blackburn.

Kim Sinh *The Art of Kim Sinh* (World Music Library, Japan). Blind guitarist plays it blue. Cai Luong theatre songs at their best; you can smell the dust in the air. This recording has influenced a whole generation of young guitarists in California.

Tran Van Khe *Vietnam: Poésies et Chants* and *Le Dan Tranh* (Ocora, France). Master-musician Tran Van Khe, dreamy zithering and floating poetry make these discs central to any Vietnamese collection.

Various *Music from Vietnam* (Caprice, Sweden). Examples of fine performances of several main genres: Quan Ho, Cai Luong, Hat Cheo, Hat Chau Van, Nhac Dan Toc Cai Bien. Improvisers conjure up wafting images of a surreal Vietnam.

Various *Vietnam: Ca Tru* and *Quan Ho, Tradition of the South* (Anthology of Traditional Music, France). Two CDs produced by veteran musician and scholar Tran Van Khe. Not the best recorded sound but invaluable documents of important genres: Ca Tru, Quan Ho and Nhac Tai Tu.

Dr Phong Nguyen Ensemble *Eternal Voices: Traditional Vietnamese Music in the United States* (New Alliance Records, US). Double set of folk songs and chamber music expertly played. Includes the most informative booklet around.

Various *String Instruments of Vietnam* (World Music Library, Japan). Ravishing sounds of lushly stroked strings with plenty of atmosphere to boot.

POP

In a world of cheaply self-produced albums by karaoke addicts, look for anything by these artists to ensure quality: Khanh Ha (Vietnam's answer to Barbra Streisand); Y Lan (a raunchy, occasionally scandalous, performer); Tuan Ngoc (a star of yesteryear). Any song by Tring Cong Son, Van Cao or Pham Duy is also a plus.

Thu Hien *Ai Ra Xu Hué* (Hué, Vietnam). Mellowest Hué pop music starring the perfumed voice of Thu Hien.

Don Ho *Ru Em* (Thuy Nga, US). Heart-throb lullabies from one of California's hottest singers.

Nguyen Thanh Van *Beo Giat May Troi* (Diem Xua, US). Passion and pathos by one of the up-and-coming stars of the Vietnamese pop world.

With contributions by Philip Blackburn
(abridged from *The Rough Guide to World Music*).

ENVIRONMENTAL ISSUES

Vietnam is endowed with a wide variety of fauna and flora, including an unusually high number of bird species and a rich diversity of primates. Current estimates suggest 12,000 plant species, 280 mammals, 770 birds, 130 reptiles, 80 amphibians and perhaps 2500 species of fish, though remote areas are still being explored. Over the last few years, in the forest reserves bordering Laos, the identification of two mammals previously unknown to scientists has caused a sensation in the scientific community.

Such diversity is largely attributable to Vietnam's range of habitats, from the sub-alpine mountains of the north to the Mekong Delta's mangrove swamps, in a country that is 75 percent mountainous, has 3200km of coastline and extends over 16 degrees of latitude. However, the list of endangered species is also long — over 80 mammals and 90 types of bird — as their domains are threatened by population pressure, widespread logging and pollution, particularly of the coastal zone. One of the biggest environmental challenges facing Vietnam is to preserve its rapidly diminishing forest areas by establishing methods of sustainable use. Happily, the government does at least seem to recognize the value of Vietnam's biodiversity and the need to act quickly on such issues.

ECOLOGICAL WARFARE

The word **"ecocide"** was coined during the American War, in reference to the quantity of herbicides dropped from the air to deprive the Viet Cong of their safe areas, deep under the triple-canopy forest, and their food crops. The most notorious defoliant used was **Agent Orange**, along with agents Blue and White, all named after the colour of the respective storage containers. Their active ingredient was **dioxin**, a slowly dissolving poison that has a half-life of 8 to 10 years in the environment — but remains much longer in human tissue. Between 1962 and 1970 it's estimated that over 70 million litres of these defoliants were sprayed from American planes crisscrossing the forests and mangrove swamps of South Vietnam. Figures

vary, but somewhere between 20 and 40 percent of the South's land area was sprayed at least once and in some cases more frequently, destroying up to a quarter of the forest cover.

The environmental impact was perhaps greatest on the **mangrove forests**, which are particularly susceptible to defoliants. Mangroves were a valuable resource for the guerrillas, not only for their cover and firewood but also because the young shoots — which remove the salt from sea water — could be chewed to provide a vital supply of fresh water. Spraying destroyed about one-half of all Vietnam's mangrove swamps and the forests; since these don't regenerate naturally, they're having to be replanted by hand, a slow operation with a low success rate. In other areas vast tracts of forest also died, along with the wildlife population, and **crop destruction** left the local people malnourished or starving. Initially, bamboo thickets and "American grass" were the only plants able to tolerate the sun-baked, chemical-soaked soils and only recently have efforts at reforestation been successful. Still now, fires sweep through the dead forests and brittle grasses each dry season, after which monsoon rains wash away the exposed topsoil.

The herbicides also had a severe impact on **soldiers**, both Vietnamese and American, and **villagers** who were caught in the spraying or absorbed dioxins from the food chain and from drinking water. Children and old people were the worst affected: some died immediately from the poisons, while others suffered respiratory diseases, skin rashes and other ailments. Soon, however, it became apparent that the dioxins were also causing abnormally high levels of miscarriage, birth defects, neurological disease and cancers. For years doctors in Saigon's Tu Do Hospital, supported by international experts, have been trying to convince the American government of the link between the use of defoliants and these medical conditions, in the hope of claiming **compensation** for the victims. American war veterans who were exposed to dioxins have also been seeking reparations. In 1984 a group of ex-servicemen won an out-of-court settlement from the manufacturers; though the government refused to accept culpability, they were later forced to reimburse the chemical company following legal proceedings.

Apart from using herbicides, American and South Vietnamese troops cut down swathes of forest land with specially adapted bulldozers, called **Rome Ploughs**. These vehicles were capable of slicing through a three-metre-thick tree trunk, and were used to clear roadsides and riverbanks against ambushes, or to remove vestiges of undergrowth and trees left after the spraying. Finally, there were the **bombs** themselves – an estimated 13 million tonnes of explosives were dropped during the course of the war, leaving a staggering 25 million bomb craters, the vast majority in the South. In addition to their general destructive power, explosions compact the soil to the point where nothing will grow, and napalm bombs sparked off forest fires. The worst single incident occurred in 1968 when U Minh forest, at the southern tip of Vietnam, burned for 7 weeks; 85 percent of its trees were destroyed.

Since the war Vietnamese scientists, led by Professor Vo Quy of Hanoi University, have instigated **reforestation programmes**, slowly coaxing life back into even the worst-affected regions. This has involved pioneering work in regenerating tropical forest, planting native species under a protective umbrella of eucalyptus and acacia. In 1987 a record 500 million trees were replanted over 160,000 hectares, though not all survived and large areas of Vietnam remain denuded of forest cover or support only stunted growth. A symbolically significant success of local environmentalists has been the **return of the Sarus crane** to the Plain of Reeds (see p.124), on the Cambodian border. The crane, a stately bird with an elaborate courtship dance, abandoned its nesting grounds when the Americans drained the wetlands, dropped herbicides and then napalm in their attempts to rout Viet Cong soldiers from the marshes. After the war thousands of landless farmers were settled in the area and continued digging canals for rice cultivation and transport. However, the acid soils proved difficult to farm and the provincial governor, Muoi Nhe, succeeded in re-establishing a portion of the wetlands to support commercial crops of melaleucas (tea trees), as well as restoring the natural habitat. The first Sarus cranes reappeared in 1986, after which Tam Nong Bird Sanctuary (see p.124) was set up to protect the crane and other returning species. Now well over 1000 Sarus cranes overwinter in the wetlands.

POST-WAR DEFORESTATION

It's estimated that more than 2 million hectares of Vietnam's forest reserves were destroyed during the American War as a result of defoliation, napalm fires and bombing. However, over the last twenty years as much again has been lost to commercial **logging**, agricultural **clearance**, firewood collection – and **population pressure**. Originally perhaps 75 percent of Vietnam's land area would have been covered by forest: by 1945 this had dwindled to 44 percent and it now stands at less than 25 percent, of which only a small percentage is natural primary forest. Despite some of the world's most ambitious reforestation programmes, the reserves are still shrinking. Each year somewhere between 100,000 and 200,000 hectares of woodland are felled or burnt, while replanting efforts can cover at most 100,000 hectares annually.

The **worst-affected areas** are Vietnam's northern mountains, the central province of Nghe An, and around Plei Ku in the central highlands. In these areas soil erosion is a major problem, and countrywide floods are getting worse as a result of deforestation along the watersheds. Many rare hardwoods are fast disappearing and the fragile ecosystems are no longer able to support a wildlife population forced into ever-smaller pockets of undisturbed jungle. Much of the blame for this rapid reduction in the forest cover is often laid on the **ethnic minorities** who traditionally clear land for farming and rely on the forests for building timber and firewood. Increased population pressure, exacerbated by lowland Vietnamese settling in the mountains, has meant extending the cultivated area and reducing the fallow period, when natural regeneration would normally have taken place. In response, the government has been trying to encourage forms of sedentary agriculture around permanent village sites. But perhaps a greater threat to the forests is the highly lucrative **timber trade**, both legal and illegal. By **replanting**, it's hoped to create sustainable forests for commercial logging and to protect the remaining areas of primary forests, but **enforcement** is hampered by lack of resources. Recently the authorities have been experimenting with new ideas of conservation, devolving the management and protection of

CONSERVATION AND THE NATIONAL PARKS

Vietnam recognized the need for conservation relatively early, establishing its first national park in 1962 and adopting a **National Conservation Strategy** in 1985. The more accessible or interesting of Vietnam's **national parks** are listed below, with page references to the *Guide* where there's more information about visiting them. Unless you're prepared to spend a lot of time in the parks, it's unlikely that you'll see many animals. Birds, insects and butterflies, however, are more readily visible and often the dense tropical vegetation or mountain scenery are in themselves worth the journey.

Ba Be (see p.398). A national park of 50,000 hectares, containing Vietnam's largest natural lake – and a few extremely rare Tonkin snub-nosed monkeys. The park has limited tourist facilities, but boat trips, jungle walks and overnight stays in a minority village are generally possible.

Bach Ma (see p.279). A small park (25,000ha), Bach Ma sits on the climatological divide between the tropical forests of the south and the northern sub-tropical zone, and contains Vietnam's most lush tropical rainforests. It is also home to a wide variety of bird species, including several rare pheasants, and over 500 recorded flora species. Bach Ma is currently being developed for tourism.

Cat Ba (see p.367). Cat Ba National Park covers only 15,000 hectares, but 4000 of these are important marine reserves, including areas of coral reef. The limestone island supports a broad range of habitats, a wealth of medicinal plants, and some golden-headed langurs. The park is accessible to tourists either on foot or by boat from Cat Ba Town.

Cat Tien, Dong Nai Province. This 35,000-hectare park, together with neighbouring Cat Loc Nature Reserve, is most famous for its small population of Javan rhino, the only ones known in mainland Asia. Otherwise the park's wetlands are a haven for water birds, including the white-winged duck

and the woolly necked stork, as well as forest birds. Although it's relatively close to Ho Chi Minh City, Cat Tien is fairly inaccessible and tourist facilities are limited; *Gateway Tours*, based in Ho Chi Minh City (75 Le Thanh Ton; ☎08/844 1167), specializes in treks to the park.

Cuc Phuong (see p.301). Vietnam's first national park, Cuc Phuong was established in 1962 in an area of limestone hills relatively close to Hanoi. The reserve covers 22,000 hectares and contains a number of unique, ancient trees and also functions as a national research and training centre. This is one of the most accessible parks, where it's possible to hike and stay overnight.

Yok Don (see p.177). Lying on the border with Cambodia, Yok Don constitutes a 60,000-hectare reserve carved out of Vietnam's most extensive forests. The area is also one of the most biologically diverse in the whole of Indochina, supporting rare Indochinese tigers and Asian elephants. Visitors can overnight in minority villages or camp; elephant-back rides and boat trips are also on offer.

Note To support environmental programmes already taking place in Vietnam, contact the following organizations:

Birdlife International, Wellbrook Court, Girton Rd, Cambridge CB3 0NA, UK (☎01223/277318); Vietnam office: 17M13 Lang Trung, Dong Da District, Hanoi.

Frontier, 77 Leonard St, London EC2I 4QS, UK (☎0171/613 1911) e-mail: enquiries@Frontier. mailbox.co.uk (see also p.5 for more on field trips organized by *Frontier*).

International Crane Foundation, Baraboo, Wisconsin, USA (☎608/356 9462).

WWF International, Avenue du Mont-Blanc, 1196 Gland, Switzerland.

WWF UK, Panda House, Weyside Park, Godalming, Surrey GU7 1XR, UK.

---

the forest reserves to local communities, with some success. In 1991 the Vietnamese government announced its intention to establish protection areas covering 6 million hectares of forest, provide for 11 million hectares of productive woodland, and restore forest reserves over forty percent of Vietnam's land area by the year 2010.

WILDLIFE

Forest clearance, warfare, pollution and economic necessity have all contributed to the loss of natural habitat and reduced Vietnam's broad species base. In 1994, when Vietnam signed the **Convention on International Trade in Endangered Species** (CITES), which bans the traffic in animals or plants facing extinction, the species list identified 365 animal species in need of urgent protection. Among these, the Javan rhino, the world's rarest large mammal, is reduced to a mere ten or fifteen animals, while one of the world's most endangered primate species, the Tonkin snub-nosed monkey, survives in small isolated communities in the northern forests. Other severely endangered species include the François langur, Indochina tiger and Asian elephant.

Hunting continues to be a vital source of local income, as a walk round Vietnamese markets soon reveals. Wild animals and birds are sought after for their meat or to satisfy the demand for **medicinal products** and live specimens, an often illegal (but extremely lucrative) business. Since the border with China was re-opened in the early 1990s, smuggling of rare species has increased, among them the Asiatic black bear, whose gall bladder is prized as a cure for fevers and liver problems; relentless hunting has decimated the population to small numbers in the north. Similarly, Vietnam's population of wild Asian elephants is now reduced to some 300 individuals, down from 2000 in the 1970s. Not only has their habitat along the Cambodian border declined, but after 1975 poachers began hunting elephants for their tusks. Conservationists hope to maintain two or three viable populations in Dak Lak Province, where domesticated elephants are still used for transport and forestry work.

Nevertheless, quite large areas of the Vietnamese interior remain amazingly untouched, especially the Truong Son Mountains north of the Hai Van pass, the southern central highlands and lowland forests of the Mekong Delta. These isolated areas are rich in **biodiversity** and have yielded spectacular discoveries in recent years, with much still to be explored. In 1992, Dr John MacKinnon and a team of Vietnamese biologists working in the Vu Quang Nature Reserve, an area of steamy, impenetrable jungle on the Lao border, identified a species of ox new to science, now known as the saola. Two years later the Giant Muntjac, a previously unknown species of deer, and a new carp were found in the same region.

An all-out effort is being made to protect this "biological gold mine" and other similar areas both within Vietnam or over the border in Laos. After the saola was discovered, the reserve was put strictly off limits and the total **protected area** enlarged to almost 160,000 hectares, with buffer zones and corridors linking the reserve to conservation areas in Laos. The task is fraught with difficulties, such as achieving cross-border co-operation and establishing effective policing of the reserve – especially against poaching and illegal logging – with inadequate personnel and financial resources. At the same time, the authorities have been working to find alternative sources of income and food for people living in or near the reserve, and carrying out educational work on the importance of conservation and its relevance to their daily lives.

With additional material supplied by the WWF Vietnam office, Hanoi.

BOOKS

Of the vast canon of books written on the subject of Vietnam, the overwhelming majority concern themselves, inevitably, with the American War. Indigenous attempts to come to terms with the conflicts that have caused Vietnam such pain are only now beginning to filter through the country's overcautious censorship; the few novels that have reached the West in recent years are reviewed below. French-speakers will have a wider choice of titles.

For a decent copy of a book on Vietnam, your best bet is to scour bookshops before you set off from home – only Hanoi and Ho Chi Minh City have ranges of literature of any breadth, and then only in photocopied offprint form. The only exceptions to this are books distributed by Hanoi's *Foreign Languages Publishing House*, which you'll have difficulty finding outside Vietnam.

TRAVELLERS' ACCOUNTS

Maria Coffey *Three Moons in Vietnam*. Delightfully jolly jaunt around Vietnam by boat, bus and bicycle. Coffey conspires to meet more locals in one day than most travellers do in a month, making this a valuable snapshot of modern Vietnam.

Graham Greene *Ways of Escape*. Greene's global travels in the 1950s took him to Vietnam for four consecutive winters; the coverage of Vietnam in this slim autobiographical volume is intriguing, but tantalizingly short, its memories of dice-playing with French agents over Vermouths and opium-smoking in Cholon evidently templates for scenes in *The Quiet American*.

Norman Lewis *A Dragon Apparent*. When in 1950 Lewis made the journey that would inspire his seminal Indochina travelogue, the Vietnam he saw was still a land of longhouses and imperial hunts, though poised for renewed conflict; the erudite prose of this doyen of travel writers reveals a Vietnam now long-gone.

W Somerset Maugham *The Gentleman in the Parlour*. The fruit of Maugham's grand tour from Rangoon to Haiphong to recharge his creative batteries, *The Gentleman in the Parlour* finds him less than enamoured by Vietnam, his last stop. Nevertheless, his accounts of the Hué court teetering on the brink of extinction, and of a run-in with an old acquaintance in a Haiphong café, are vintage Maugham.

Gontran de Poncins *From a Chinese City*. Believing that "the ancient customs of a national culture endure longer in remote colonies than in the motherland", de Poncins opted for a sojourn in Cholon as a means to a better understanding of the foibles of the Chinese; the resulting document of life in 1955 Cholon is a lively period piece, backed up by fluid illustrations.

Paul Theroux *The Great Railway Bazaar*. His elaborate circumnavigation of Europe and Asia by train took Theroux, in 1973, to a South Vietnam still bewildered by the recent American withdrawal. In bleak sound-bite accounts of rides from Saigon to Bien Hoa and Hué to Da Nang, he describes the war's awful legacy of poverty, suffering and infrastructural breakdown, but marvels at the country's unbowed, and unexpected, beauty.

Gabrielle M Vassal *On and Off Duty in Annam*. An enchanting wander through turn-of-the-century southern Vietnam, penned by the intrepid wife of a French army doctor. A stint in Saigon is followed by a boat trip to Nha Trang (where she was carried ashore "on the backs of natives through the breakers") and a gutsy foray into the central highlands; amazing prints of the Vietnamese and *montagnards* she encountered further enhance the account.

John White *A Voyage to Cochin China*. Memoirs of a pioneering voyager, who stepped ashore at Saigon several decades before the French took control.

Justin Wintle *Romancing Vietnam*. Wintle's genial but lightweight yomp upcountry was one of the first of its kind, post-*doi moi*, and remains a pleasing aperitif to travels in Vietnam.

VIETNAMESE ABROAD

Donald Anderson (ed.) *Aftermath: An Anthology of Post-Vietnam Fiction*. As the war's tendrils crept across the Pacific to America, they touched not only the people who fought, but also those who stayed at home. In their depictions of Americans, Amerasians and Asians regathering the strands of their lives, these short stories run the gamut of emotions provoked by war.

Le Ly Hayslip *Child of War, Woman of Peace*. In this follow-up to *When Heaven and Earth Changed Places* (see p.460), Hayslip's narrative shifts to America, where the cultural disorientation of a new arrival is examined.

Robert Olen Butler *A Good Scent from a Strange Mountain*. Pulitzer prize-winning collection of short stories that ponder the struggles of Vietnamese in America to maintain the cultural ley lines linking them with their mother country, and the gulf between them and their Americanized offspring. War veteran Olen Butler's assured prose ensures the voices of his Vietnamese characters find perfect pitch.

VIETNAMESE LITERATURE

Bao Ninh *The Sorrow of War*. This is a groundbreaking novel, largely due to its portrayal of communist soldiers suffering the same traumas, fear and lost innocence as their American counterparts.

Alastair Dingwall (ed.) *South-East Asia Traveller's Literary Companion*. Among the bite-sized essays inside this gem of a book is an enlightening 30-page segment on Vietnam, into which are crammed biopics, a recommended reading list, historical, linguistic and literary backgrounds. Excerpts range from classical literature to the writings of foreign journalists in the 1960s.

Duong Thu Huong *Novel Without a Name*. A tale of young Vietnamese men seeking glory but finding only loneliness, disillusionment and death, as war abridges youth and curtails loves; a depiction of dwindling idealism, and a radical questioning of the political motives behind the war.

Ho Chi Minh *Prison Diary*. Hanoi's *Foreign Languages Publishing House* also publishes a sawdust-dry, four-volume *Collected Works*, but the touching poems Ho penned while behind bars in 1942, in which he looks to birds' songs and moonlight to ease the loneliness of prison life, are more compelling.

Nguyen Du *The Tale of Kieu*. Vietnamese literature reached its zenith with this tale of the ill-starred love between Kieu and Kim.

Nguyen Huy Thiep *The General Retires and Other Stories*. Perhaps Vietnam's pre-eminent writer, Nguyen Huy Thiep in these short stories articulates the lives of ordinary Vietnamese – instead of following the prevailing trend of re-imagining the lives of past heroes.

Vietnamese Literature. Weighty anthology of classic Vietnamese literature available from street-sellers in Hanoi and Ho Chi Minh City.

NOVELS SET IN VIETNAM

Marguerite Duras *The Lover*. A young French girl encounters a wealthy Chinese from Cholon on a Mekong Delta ferry; the ensuing affair initiates her into adulthood, with all its joys and responsibilities. The novel's depiction of a dysfunctional, hard-up French family in Vietnam provides an interesting slant on expat life, showing it wasn't all Vermouths and tennis.

Graham Greene *The Quiet American*. Greene's prescient and cautionary tale of the dangers of innocence in uncertain times, which second-guessed America's boorish manhandling of Vietnam's political situation by several years, is still the best single account of wartime Vietnam. Its regular name-drops of familiar locales – Tay Ninh, the *Continental*, Dong Khoi – make it doubly enjoyable.

Anthony Grey *Saigon*. Vietnamese history given the blockbuster touch: a rip-roaring narrative, whose Vietnamese, French and American protagonists conspire to be present at all defining moments in recent Vietnamese history, from French plantation riots to the fall of Saigon.

Tim O'Brien *Going After Cacciato*. A highly acclaimed, lyrical tale of an American soldier who simply walks out of the war and sets off for Paris, pursued by his company on a fantastical mission that takes them across Asia. The savage reality of war stands out vividly against a dream-world of peace and freedom.

PREHISTORY AND HISTORY

William J Duiker *The Communist Road to Power in Vietnam*. One of America's leading analysts of the political context in Vietnam takes a long close look at why communist Vietnam won its wars – as opposed to why France and America lost.

Bernard Fall *Hell in a Very Small Place*. The classic account of the siege of Dien Bien Phu, capturing the claustrophobia and the fear, written by a French-born American journalist.

Bernard Fall *Street Without Joy*. Another masterpiece by Fall, charting the French debacle in Indochina, which became required reading for American generals and GIs – though it didn't prevent them committing exactly the same mistakes just a few years later.

David Halberstam *Ho*. Diminutive, sympathetic and highly readable biography of Vietnam's foremost icon, though no attempt is made to apportion blame for the disastrous land reforms of the 1950s.

Charles Higham *The Archaeology of Mainland Southeast Asia*. Covering the period from 10,000 BC through to the close of the Angkor Empire, this is an immensely scholarly work that touches on all periods of Vietnam's prehistory and early history, from the hunter-gatherers of the Red River Delta to the Empire of Champa.

Stanley Karnow *Vietnam: A History*. Weighty, august tome that elucidates the entire span of Vietnamese history.

Michael Maclear *Vietnam: The Ten Thousand Day War*. A detailed yet accessible account of the French and American wars, from Ho's alliance with Archimedes Patti, to the fall of Saigon.

David G Marr *Vietnamese Anti-Colonialism, 1885–1925*. Well worth rooting out for its contextualization of Vietnam's struggles against France and America.

Nguyen Khac Vien *Vietnam: A Long History*. Published by Hanoi's *Foreign Languages Publishing House*, and therefore heavily weighted in favour of the communists, but easier to get hold of in Vietnam than most histories.

Keith Weller Taylor *The Birth of Vietnam*. As a GI, Taylor was struck by the "intelligence and resolve" of his enemy. This meticulous account of the dawn of Vietnamese history, trawling the past from the nation's first recorded history up to the tenth century, is the result of his attempt to uncover their roots.

THE AMERICAN WAR

Mark Baker *Nam*. Unflinching firsthand accounts of the GI's descent from boot camp, into the morass of death, paranoia, exhaustion and tedium. Gut-wrenchingly frank at times, the book depicts war as a rite of passage, and moral deterioration as a prerequisite to survival.

Michael Bilton and Kevin Sim *Four Hours in My Lai*. Brutally candid and immaculately researched reconstruction of the events surrounding the My Lai massacre of 1968; as harrowing a portrayal of the depths plumbed in war as you'll ever read.

Philip Caputo *A Rumour of War*. One of the classics of the American War, Caputo's straightforward narrative is a powerful account of the numbing daily routine of the ordinary US soldier's life, the strange exhilaration of combat, and the brutalization that accompanies war.

Michael Clodfelter *Mad Minutes and Vietnam Months*. Combat reminiscences from a man who found war's false promise of "courage, sacrifice, glory and adventure" displaced by monotony and, occasionally, atrocity.

Shirley Dicks *From Vietnam to Hell*. For the subjects of Shirley Dick's 23 case studies, the war has never ended; her interviews with sufferers of Post Traumatic Stress Disorder paint a heartbreaking picture of men and women torn apart by their own memories.

W D Ehrhart *Going Back: An Ex-Marine Returns to Vietnam*. A veteran of the battle for Hué, Ehrhart returned to Vietnam in 1985. *Going Back*, a record of that trip, mixes diary, memory and Ehrhart's own poetry to very readable effect.

James Fenton *All the Wrong Places*. In Vietnam at the moment of Saigon's liberation, Fenton somehow managed to hitch a lift on the tank that rammed through the palace gates; his easy prose and poet's eye for detail make his account an engrossing one.

Le Ly Hayslip *When Heaven and Earth Changed Places*. For giving a human face to the slopes, dinks and gooks of American writing on Vietnam, this heart-rending tale of villagers trying to survive in a climate of hatred and distrust is perhaps more valuable than any history book.

Michael Herr *Dispatches*. Infuriatingly narcissistic at times, Herr's spaced-out narrative still conveys the mud, blood and guts of the American war effort in Vietnam.

Peter King (ed.) *Australia's Vietnam*. American troops weren't the only foreigners dragged into the mire of the Vietnam conflict: the Australian role is chronicled in this compendium of essays.

Tom Mangold and John Penycate *The Tunnels of Cu Chi*. The most thorough, and the most captivating, account yet written of the guerrilla resistance mounted in the tunnels around Cu Chi.

Robert Mason *Chickenhawk*. Few people can be better qualified than Mason to deliver an account of the American War: a helicopter pilot with over 1000 missions under his belt, his blood-and-guts, bird's-eye account of the war is harrowing but compelling.

Tim O'Brien *The Things They Carried*. Through a mix of autobiography and fiction O'Brien lays to rest the ghosts of the past in a brutally honest reappraisal of the war, his own actions and the events he witnessed (see also O'Brien's novel *Going After Cacciato*, reviewed on p.458).

Frank Palmos *Ridding the Devils*. In 1968, Australian correspondent Palmos was the lone survivor of a Viet Cong ambush of a jeep carrying five journalists in Cholon. Twenty years later he returned to Vietnam to seek out the man who had tried to kill him – and allay his nightmares; his story highlights both the mental toll his investigations took, and the plight of Australian veterans.

Barry Petersen *Tiger Men*. In the run-up to the American War, Australian Barry Petersen was working in the central highlands, forming members of the Ede (Rhadé) minority into a crack fighting force, part of a covert CIA programme to deny the Viet Cong control of the villages.

John Pilger *Heroes*. Pilger's systematic dismantling of the myth that America's role was in any way a justifiable "crusade" makes his Vietnam reportage required reading.

William Prochnau *Once Upon a Lonely War*. Now that all the journos ever to set foot in Vietnam have published memoirs, Prochnau presents a new twist – the intriguing story of the people who wrote the stories of Vietnam.

Jonathan Schell *The Real War*. Acute and assured reportage, relaying the devastating ferocity of the American war effort in Vietnam – first the onslaught on the village of Ben Suc (in the Iron Triangle), then the laying waste of Quang Ngai Province.

Neil Sheehan *A Bright Shining Lie*. This monumental and fluently rendered account of the war, hung around the life of the soldier John Paul Vann, won the Pulitzer Prize for Sheehan; one of the true classics of Vietnam-inspired literature.

Justin Wintle *The Vietnam War*. Written in reaction to the shelves of long-winded texts available on the subject, Wintle's succinct overview manages to condense this mad war into less than 200 pages.

Tobias Wolff *In Pharaoh's Army*. A former adviser based in My Tho, Wolff's honest, gentle autobiographical tale takes a wry look at life away from the "front line".

POST-WAR VIETNAM

Bui Tin *Following Ho Chi Minh*. An erstwhile colonel in the North Vietnamese Army, Bui Tin effectively defected to the West in 1990, since when he has been an outspoken critic of Vietnam's state apparatus. These, his memoirs, don't flinch from addressing the underside – corruption, prejudice, naivety and insensitivity – of the Party.

Adam Fforde and Stefan de Vylder *From Plan to Market*. Highbrow, laudably researched book plotting the route Vietnam has taken from Stalinist central planning to market economy: Fforde and de Vylder hold the fabric of *doi moi* up to the light for examination.

Tim Page *Derailed in Uncle Ho's Victory Garden*. The war photographer with a legendary ability to defy death, returns to Vietnam; buried among the flashbacks and meandering discourse, Page's eye for detail and his delight in the bizarre gives a flavour of modern Vietnam.

Neil Sheehan *Two Cities: Hanoi and Saigon*. Sheehan returned to Vietnam in 1989 to witness firsthand the legacy of the war. Down south, the memories really begin to flow as encounters and travels trigger wartime flashbacks, interspersed with commentary on re-education camps and other deprivations of the dark, pre-*doi moi* years.

Michael C Williams *Vietnam at the Crossroads*. Though several years out of date already, this meticulously detailed and knowing study of the changes wrought by *doi moi*, written by a veteran of the BBC's *World Service*, is still a most valuable account of a country in flux.

CULTURE AND SOCIETY

Dang Nghiem Van, Chu Thai Son and Luu Hung *Ethnic Minorities in Vietnam*. Comprehensive, if a little dry and dated, round-up of Vietnam's minorities; available at street-sellers in Hanoi and Ho Chi Minh City.

Lou Dematteis *A Portrait of Viet Nam*. A stunning photographic record of daily life in Vietnam.

Claire Ellis *Culture Shock! Vietnam*. A cultural bible detailing how to avoid such faux pas as sticking your chopsticks into your food, pointing the sole of your foot at somebody and arranging a business meeting for an inauspicious day of the month...Invaluable if you're doing business in Vietnam, interesting even if you aren't.

Gabriel Gobron *History and Philosophy of Cao Daism*. Standard text on Cao Daist history and beliefs, readily available from street-sellers in Ho Chi Minh City.

Gerald Cannon Hickey *Shattered World*. The latest of several detailed but readable accounts of ethnic minorities living in Vietnam's central highlands, by one of the region's leading ethnologists. A fascinating analysis of the minorities' tragic struggle to survive both war and peace.

Pierre Huard and Maurice Durand *Vietnam: Civilization and Culture*. Sections on topics as diverse as teeth-blackening, ear-cleaning, literature, fishing and astrology make this a cornucopia of trivial info and hard fact. Chunks are now out of date, but in areas such as social relations, festivities and rice cultivation, there's still much of value.

Henry Kamm *Dragon Ascending*. Rather than relying upon the endless self-aggrandizing anecdotes favoured by many reporters, Pulitzer prize-winning correspondent Kamm prefers to let the Vietnamese − art dealers, ex-colonels, academics, doctors, authors − speak for themselves. This they do eloquently, resulting in a convincing portrait of contemporary Vietnam.

Norma J Livo and Dia Cha *Folk Stories of the Hmong*. The Hmong's fading oral tradition is captured in this unique collection, gleaned from US immigrants, while its scene-setting introduction offers a valuable overview of Hmong culture, accompanied by illustrations of traditional costume and embroidered "storycloths".

Christina Noble *Bridge Across My Sorrows*. Life-affirming autobiography by a Dublin woman spurred by a dream to channel her considerable strengths into helping Ho Chi Minh City's *bui doi*, or street children.

Philip Rawson *The Art of Southeast Asia*. In this attractive glossy volume, crammed with colour plates, Vietnam is represented by chapters on Indochina and Champa.

VIETNAM ON FILM

Gilbert Adair *Hollywood's Vietnam: From the Green Berets to Full Metal Jacket*. Adair's excitable prose guides you past the fire-fights, f-words and R&R hijinks, to a real appreciation of how Hollywood reflected shifting American attitudes to the war.

Jeremy Devine *Vietnam at 24 Frames a Second*. Among the 400-plus films covered in this, the most wide-ranging analysis of Vietnam movies, are more recent releases such as *Scent of Green Papaya* and *Heaven and Earth*.

Linda Dittmar and Gene Michaud (ed) *From Hanoi to Hollywood*. Collected essays on the way the Vietnam War encroached on Hollywood.

NATURAL HISTORY AND ECOLOGY

Elizabeth Kemf *Month of Pure Light*. One of very few accounts looking at the long-term environmental impact of the American War and the subsequent "re-greening" of Vietnam. Written as a travelogue rather than a scientific survey, with an optimistic message of rebirth underscored by a personal story of renewal.

Ben King, Martin Woodcock and Edward Dickinson *Field Guide to Birds of South East Asia*. Seminal study of the region's ornithological diversity.

SIPRI *Ecological Consequences of the Second Indochina War*. A scholarly study of the emasculation of Vietnam's terrain by American ordnance and chemicals.

VIETNAM IN THE MOVIES

The embroilment of France and the US in Vietnam and its conflicts has spawned hundreds of movies, ranging from fond soft-focused colonial reminiscences, to blood-and-guts depictions of the horrors of war. As a means of brushing up on your Indochinese history, their value is questionable: for the most part, they're hardly objective. Yet, through the reflections they cast of the climates in which they were created, these films amplify the West's efforts to come to terms with what went on there, and for this reason they demand attention.

EARLY DEPICTIONS

Hollywood was setting movies in Indochina long before the first American troops splashed ashore at Da Nang. As early as 1932, Jean Harlow played a sassy Saigon prostitute to smouldering Clark Gable's rubber-plantation manager, in the steamy pot-boiler, **Red Dust**. At this early stage, however, Vietnam was no more than an exotic backdrop.

Even by the mid-1950s, as the modest beginnings of American involvement elicited from Hollywood its first real moves to acquaint itself with Vietnam, the country was often treated less as a nation with its own discernible identity and unique set of political issues, and more as a generic Asian theatre of war, in which the righteous **battle against communism** could

be played out. In its portrayal of noble and libertarian French forces, aided by American military specialists, confronting the evil of communism, **China Gate** (1957) is an early example of this trend. Dedicated to the French colons who "advanced this backward society to its place as the rice bowl of Asia", its laboured plot, concerning an attempt to destroy a Viet Minh arms cache, is of much less interest than its heavy-handed politics.

Vietnam provided Hollywood with a golden opportunity to project its militaristic fantasies, and a chance to tap into the prejudices brought to the surface by more than a decade of anti-Japanese World War II movies – prejudices that painted American involvement as a reprise of past battles with the inscrutable **Asian hordes**. Rather more depth of thought went into the making of **The Quiet American** (1958), in which Michael Redgrave played the British journalist and cynic, Fowler, while Audie Murphy (America's most-decorated soldier in World War II) played Pyle, the eponymous "hero" of Graham Greene's novel. To Greene's chagrin, Pyle was depicted not as a representative of the American government, but of a private aid organization – something which the author felt blunted his anti-American message; nevertheless, the movie retained its source's sense of the futility of attempting to make sense of Vietnam's political quagmire.

GUNG HO!

The military mandarins who led America into war failed to get the message, though: with American troops duly deployed in a far-flung corner of the globe by 1965, it was only a matter of time before **John Wayne** produced a patriotic movie to match. This came in the form of the monumentally bad **The Green Berets** (1968), in which a paunchy Wayne starred as "Big" Bill Kirby, a lovable colonel leading an adoring team of American soldiers into the central highlands. That Wayne, while on a promotional trip out to Vietnam, handed out cigarette cases inscribed with his signature and the message "Fuck communism", speaks volumes about the film's subtlety. Kicking off with a stirring marching song ("Fighting soldiers from the sky, Fearless men who jump and die..."), the movie depicts **American soldiers** in spotless uniforms and perma-grins fighting against no less a threat than total "Communist domination of the world", yet still abiding, as the critic Gilbert Adair has it, "by Queensberry rules". In stark contrast to the squeaky-clean GIs are the barbaric **Viet Cong**, depicted as child-abusing rapists who whoop and holler like madmen as they overrun a US camp, all to the strains of suitably eerie Oriental music.

SWEEPING VIETNAM UNDER THE CARPET

The war in Vietnam was a much dirtier affair than *The Green Berets* made it seem, its politics far less cut and dry. As the struggle turned into tragedy and popular support for it soured, movie moguls sensed that the war had become **taboo**. "Vietnam is awkward," said the journalist, Michael Herr, "…and if people don't even want to hear about it, you know they're not going to pay money to sit there in the dark and have it brought up." It was to be a full decade before another major combat movie was released. Instead, film-makers trained their gaze upon returning Vietnam veterans' doomed attempts to ease back into society. The resulting pictures were low in compassion: America's national pride had been collectively compromised by the failure to bring home a victory, and sympathy and forgiveness were at a premium.

A raft of **exploitation movies** was churned out, boasting names such as *Born Losers* (1967), *Angels from Hell* (1968) and *The Ravager* (1970), in which the mental scars of Vietnam provided topical window-dressing to improbable tales of martial arts, motorbikes and mayhem. At best, vets were treated as dysfunctional vigilantes acting beyond the pale of society – most famously in **Taxi Driver** (1976), which has Robert De Niro's disturbed insomniac returnee, Travis Bickle, embarking on a one-man moral crusade to purge the streets of a hellish New York. At worst, they were wacko misfits posing a threat to smalltown America. With veterans being portrayed as anything but heroes, it was left to the stars of the **campus riot movies**, and films lionizing **draft-dodgers**, to provide role models.

COMING TO TERMS WITH THE WAR

Only in **1978** did Hollywood finally pluck up courage enough to confront the war head-on, and so aid the nation's healing process – **movies-as-therapy**. In the years since John

Wayne's *Green Berets* had battened down the hatches against communism, America had first lost sight of justification for the war, and then effectively lost the war itself. Movies no longer sought to make sense of past events, but to highlight their futility; for the generation of young Americans unfortunate enough to live through Vietnam, mere survival was seen as triumph enough. As audiences were exposed to their first dramatized glimpses of the war's unpalatable realities, they were confronted by disaffected troops seeking comfort in prostitution and drug abuse, along with far more shocking examples of soldiers' fraying moral fibre.

Such themes were woven through the first of the four movies of note released in 1978, **The Boys in Company C**, which follows a band of young draftees through their basic training stateside, and then into action. In one particularly telling scene, American lives are lost transporting what turns out to be whiskey and cigarettes to the front. A similar futility underpins **Go Tell the Spartans**, in which Burt Lancaster's drug- and alcohol-hazed troops take, and then abandon, a camp – an idea re-used nine years later in *Hamburger Hill*.

Coming Home (1978), which cast Jane Fonda as a military career-man's wife who falls in love with a wheelchair-bound veteran (Jon Voight), was significant for its sensitive consideration of the emotional and physical tolls exacted by the war, and initiated the trend for more measured and intelligent vet movies. Similarly concerned with the ramifications of the war, both home and away, was **The Deer Hunter**, in which the conscription of three friends fractures their Russian orthodox community in Pennsylvania. The friends' "one-shot" code of honour, espoused on a last pre-Vietnam hunting trip, contrasts wildly with the moral vacuum of the war, whose random brutality is embodied in the movie's central scenes of Russian roulette. The picture's ending, with its melancholy rendition of *God Bless America* by the central characters, is only semi-ironic, and alludes to the country's regenerative process. For all its power, *The Deer Hunter* is marred by overt **racist stereotyping** of the Vietnamese who, according to John Pilger, are dismissed as "sub-human Oriental barbarians and idiots". The Vietnamese we see are grotesque caricatures interested only in getting their kicks from gambling and death, and there's a strong sense that American youths ought never to have been exposed to such primordial evil as existed across the Pacific.

Francis Ford Coppola's hugely indulgent but visually magnificent **Apocalypse Now** (1979) rounded off the vanguard of post-war Vietnam combat movies. Described by one critic as "Film as opera... it turns Vietnam into a vast trip, into a War of the Imagination", the picture's Dantean snapshots of the war rob Vietnam of all identity other than as a "heart of darkness". Fuelled by his desire to convey the "horror, the madness, the sensuousness, and the moral dilemma of the Vietnam war", Coppola totally mythologizes the conflict, rendering it not so much futile as insane. The usual elements of needless death, casual atrocity, moral decline and spaced-out soldiers leaning heavily on substance abuse are all here, played out against a raunchy soundtrack. However, with its stylized representation of *montagnards* as **generic savages** deifying Westerners, and its depiction of the Viet Cong as butchers who happily lop the arms off children who have had "American" inoculations, *Apocalypse Now* is little more enlightened than *The Deer Hunter*. Coppola subsequently compared the creation of the film itself to a war: "We were in the jungle, there were too many of us. We had access to too much money and too much equipment and little by little, we went insane" – a process graphically depicted in **Hearts of Darkness: AFilmmaker's Apocalypse** (1991).

RETURNING HOME

The precedent set by *Coming Home* of sympathetic consideration for **returning veterans'** mind-sets spurred many movies along similar lines in subsequent years. These focused on the disillusionment and disorientation felt by soldiers coming back, not to heroes' welcomes, but to indifference and even disdain.

One of the first of these movies was **First Blood** (1982), which introduced audiences to Sly Stallone's muscle-bound super-vet, John Rambo. As we witness Rambo's torment in small-town America, the picture is more shoot 'em up than cerebral. Yet its climax, in which Rambo's former colonel becomes a surrogate father-figure to him, underscores the tender ages of the troops who fought the war. Other movies of the genre – among them Alan Parker's **Birdy** (1984) and Oliver Stone's **Born on the**

4th of July (1989) – reiterated the message of stolen youth and innocence by screening idyllic, elegiac scenes of childhood. Stone has his hero (played by Tom Cruise) swallowing the anticommunist line, and returning to an indifference symbolized by the squalor of the army hospital in which he recuperates and by the breakdown of his relationship with his mother. In *Birdy*, doctors at a loss as to how to treat a catatonic patient turn to a fellow vet for help – this sense of America's inability to relate to returnees subsequently resurfaces in **JackKnife** (1989).

REWRITING HISTORY

Not content with squaring up to the war in Vietnam, Hollywood during the 1980s attempted, bizarrely, to rewrite its script, in a series of **revisionist movies**. Richard Gere had made the armed forces hip again in 1982's weepie **An Officer and a Gentleman**; and a year later the first of an intriguing sub-genre of films hit cinemas, in which Americans returned to Vietnam, invariably to rescue MIAs, and "won". Given a righteous cause (and what could be more righteous than rescuing fellow soldiers), and freed from the chains of moral degradation that had shackled him in previous movies, the US soldier could now show his true mettle. In stark contrast to the comic-book superhuman Americans of these pictures, are the brainless **Vietnamese**, who appear only as cannon fodder.

Uncommon Valor (1983), a rather silly piece about an MIA rescue starring Gene Hackman, kicked things off, closely followed by **Missing in Action** (1983), in which Chuck Norris, the poor man's Stallone, karate-kicks his way towards the same resolution with sufficient panache to justify a speedy follow-up. The mother of them all, though, was **Rambo: First Blood, Part II** (1985), in which the hero of *First Blood* gets to settle some old scores. "Do we get to win this time?" asks Rambo, at the top of the movie. As he riots through the Vietnamese countryside in order to extricate a band of American PoWs, he answers his own question by slaying Vietnamese foes at an approximate rate of one every two minutes.

"IT DON'T MEAN NOTHING"

The backlash to the patent nonsense of the revisionist films came in the form of a series of shockingly realistic movies which attempted, in the words of the director Oliver Stone, to "peel the onion" and reveal the **real Vietnam**, routine atrocities, indiscipline and all. There are no heroes in these GI's-view movies, only fragile, confused-looking young men in fatigues, emphasizing that this was a war that affected a whole generation – not just its most photogenic individuals.

In **Platoon** (1986), Oliver Stone, himself a foot-soldier in Vietnam, created the most realistic cinematographic interpretation of the American involvement yet. Filmed on location in the Philippines, this movie reminded audiences that killing gooks wasn't as straightforward as Rambo made it seem. As well as portraying the depths to which humankind can sink, Stone shows the circumstances under which it was feasible for young American boys to become murderers of civilians. Its oppressive sensory overload powerfully conjures the paranoiac near-hysteria spawned by fear, confusion, loss of motivation and inability to discriminate between friend and foe. Inherent in its shadowy, half-seen portrayal of the enemy is a grudging respect for their expertise in jungle warfare.

If *Platoon* portrays a dirty war, in **Hamburger Hill** (1987), which dramatizes the taking of Ap Bia hill during May 1969's battle for the A Shau Valley, it has degenerated into a positive mudbath. As troops slither and slide on the flanks of the hill in the highland mists, they become indistinguishable, and the image of an entire generation stumbling toward the maws of death is strengthened by the fact that the cast includes no big-name actors – the men who fall on the hill are neighbours, sons or brothers, not film stars. American losses are taken in order to secure a useless hill, a potent symbol of the futility of America's involvement in the war; as one soldier says, time after time, in a weary mantra, "it don't mean nothing, not a thing". Stanley Kubrick's **Full Metal Jacket** (1987) picks up *Hamburger Hill*'s theme of the war's theft of American youth in its opening scene, as the camp barber strips conscripts of their hair and, by implication, their individuality. A brutal drill-sergeant completes the alienation process by replacing the soldiers' names with nicknames of his choosing, and then sets about expunging their humanity – on the grounds that it will only hamper them when they experience firsthand the insanity of the war. However, as US troops plod wearily through a smouldering Hué in the

movie's final scene, the usual macho marching tunes are replaced with a plaintive echo of youth: "Who's the leader of the club that's made for you and me, M-I-C, K-E-Y, M-O-U-S-E".

MOVIES OF THE 1990S

French cinema only began to tackle the subject of Vietnam in the 1990s. If in **Dien Bien Phu** (1992) it confronted its own ghosts, on the whole its output has been limited to visually captivating colonial whimsies, to which the Vietnamese setting merely adds an exotic tang. For example, **The Lover** (1992) works not because it does justice to Marguerite Duras's poignant rites-of-passage novella, but because its extended interludes of heaving flesh are cloaked with a veneer of Oriental mystique created by location filming in Ho Chi Minh City and Sa Dec. **Indochine** (1993) starts off in similarly rose-tinted fashion amid the seductively rarefied atmosphere of a French colonial rubber plantation, and from there it veers off to take full advantage of the romantic possibilities of Ha Long Bay.

Even **The Scent of Green Papaya** (1993), filmed entirely in Paris by **Vietnamese director** Tran Anh Hung, is a fondly nostalgic period piece in which the East's languorous elegance and beauty are shown, minus its squalor, and nothing of import is said about the war experience. Tran Anh Hung's latest offering, **Cyclo** (1996), is an altogether different matter, a grimy tale of murder and prostitution tacked onto an Oriental setting.

In **Hollywood**'s output, Vietnamese people have mostly been noticeable by their absence, or through the filter of blatant stereotyping. **Heaven and Earth** (1993), the final part of Oliver Stone's Vietnam trilogy, went some way towards rectifying this imbalance. Its depiction of a Vietnamese girl's odyssey (based on the life of Le Lay Hayslip; see pp.458 and 460), from idyllic early childhood to the traumas of life as a wife in San Diego symbolizes the trials and tribulations of the country as a whole, and acts as a timely reminder that not only Americans suffered during the struggle.

SOME TO LOOK OUT FOR...

Apocalypse Now (1979). Vietnam becomes one long trip in this all-powerful picture in which Martin Sheen is dispatched upriver towards the Cambodian border to assassinate

Kurtz (played by Marlon Brando), an American colonel who, destabilized by the horrors of the war, has set himself up as leader of a tribe of *montagnards*.

Birdy (1984). When post-traumatic stress leads Birdy (Matthew Modine) to believe he's one of the birds of which he was so fond as a child, his buddy Al (Nicolas Cage) is called in to try to snap him out of his spell and coax him back into the real world.

Born on the 4th of July (1989). Having skipped off to war head-full of anti-communist ideals, Ron Kovic (Tom Cruise) returns home having lost the use of his legs, and taken the life of a fellow American in a friendly-fire incident. Oliver Stone's rendering of his tortuous passage through guilt, confession, redemption and finally regeneration is harrowing and affecting.

Coming Home (1978). A career soldier's departure for Vietnam leaves his wife with time on her hands to help out at a local hospital. There she meets a paraplegic veteran played by Jon Voight, and commences a love affair that wildly alters life for all three of them.

Cyclo (1996). An impoverished cyclo driver working Ho Chi Minh City's mean streets takes to a life of crime to supplement his income. Made by the same director as *The Scent of Green Papaya*, though a world away from it in style and content.

Dear America: Letters Home from America (1987). Enormously moving documentary in which readings from soldiers' correspondence home are intercut with contemporary footage of the war.

The Deer Hunter (1978). Three friends from the same steeltown in Pennsylvania are captured by Viet Cong and forced to play Russian roulette. One is terribly wounded in the ensuing escape and returns home in a wheelchair; another (played by Christopher Walken) continues to dice with death in Saigon; and the third, played by Robert De Niro, returns to rescue him.

Dien Bien Phu (1992). Tens of thousands of Vietnamese extras see to it that this epic reconstruction of France's darkest Indochinese hour impresses. Director Pierre Schoendoerffer, himself a veteran of Dien Bien Phu, intercuts the battle scenes with depictions of the last days of colonial Hanoi.

First Blood (1982). Ignoring a small-town sheriff's order to leave ironically named Hope lands Vietnam vet John Rambo in prison; there, illtreatment induces a Vietnam flashback, a jailbreak and a gripping manhunt in which Rambo's jungle-warfare training pays dividends.

Full Metal Jacket (1987). A film of two halves, and gripping from start to finish. The first half showcases the brutality of an American army boot camp and its tragic effect on an overweight conscript; the second focuses on an incountry unit's attempts to neutralize a sniper.

Good Morning Vietnam (1987). Robin Williams shines as a military DJ who ruffles feathers by trying to enliven broadcasts and so heighten morale; the movie is little more than a vehicle for his hilarious monologues – pleasing, but ultimately lightweight.

Hamburger Hill (1987). Powerful, unremittingly depressing dramatization of the taking of Ap Bia hill in the A Shau Valley (see p.423).

Heaven and Earth (1993) By following a young Vietnamese girl on her personal odyssey from childhood in a village near Da Nang, through prostitution, to married life in America, this film concerns itself with the war's renting of the physical, social and spiritual fabric of Vietnamese family life.

Indochine (1993). Catherine Deneuve as a plantation owner whose lover (a naval officer) falls for her adopted Vietnamese daughter. With the lover's posting in Tonkin and the daughter's flight after him, the movie shifts to Ha Long Bay. Visually sumptuous.

JackKnife (1989). Robert De Niro again, this time turning in a typically fine performance as Vietnam veteran Megs, whose blossoming relationship with the sister of wartime buddy Dave sprouts tensions that say much about the loneliness of veterans.

The Lover (1992). Steamy interpretation of Marguerite Duras's novella, in which a young French girl living in the Mekong Delta enters into a passionate affair with a wealthy Chinese from Cholon. The story of her sexual awakening and its repercussions, is told through the melancholy narrative of the girl herself, now grown up.

Platoon (1986). Life on patrol as described in the letters home of wide-eyed new boy, Chris (Charlie Sheen), whose platoon is torn in two by its divided allegiance to sergeants Barnes (Tom Berenger) and Elias (Willem Dafoe), symbolizing the dark and light, the animal and human, sides of American involvement in Vietnam.

The Quiet American (1958). During the final days of of colonial Saigon, a young American's naive vision of ending the war by arming a "third force" has disastrous results. Graham Greene disapproved of this version of his famed Vietnam novel, but it's lent a wonderful glaze of authenticity by the location shooting in Saigon.

Rambo: First Blood, Part II (1985). *First Blood*'s John Rambo again, this time single-handedly hauling a band of MIAs out of their jungle captivity and to safety – and blowing away a staggering number of Vietnamese in the process.

The Scent of Green Papaya (1993). A country girl called Mui is sent to work as servant to a Saigon family, and soon develops an unspoken love for the son of the house; years later, she keeps house for him. A dignified and nostalgic glance back at a Saigon before the Americans.

Taxi Driver (1976). Hollywood's most famous veteran (barring John Rambo), insomniac cabbie and angst-ridden social misfit Travis Bickle (Robert De Niro) turns moral crusader, with a mission to "wash all the scum off the streets".

LANGUAGE

Linguists are uncertain as to the exact roots of Vietnamese, though the language betrays Thai, Khmer and Chinese influences. A tonal language, it's extremely tricky for Westerners to master, though the phrases below should help you get by. English has, in fact, superseded Russian as *the* language to learn since the sweeping changes of *doi moi*, so increasingly you'll find that Vietnamese isn't called for. Then again, nothing will endear you to locals as much as showing conversational willing.

Vietnamese was set down using Chinese characters until the fourteenth century, when an indigenous **script** called *chu nom* was created; this, in turn, was subsequently dropped in favour of *quoc ngu*, a Romanized script developed by a French missionary in the seventeenth century, and it's this form that's universally used today – though you'll still occasionally spot lavish *chu nom* characters daubed on the walls of more venerable pagodas and temples.

Three main **dialects** – northern, central and southern – are used in Vietnam today, and although for the most part, they are pretty similar, pronunciation can be so wildly variant that some locals have trouble understanding each other. Bear in mind, too, that Vietnam's minority peoples have their own languages, and may look blankly at you as you gamely try out your Vietnamese on them.

If you want more scope than the expressions below allow, invest in a **phrasebook**. *Vietnamese: A Rough Guide Phrasebook* is the last word in user-friendly phrasebooks, combining useful phrases and expressions with a dictionary section and menu reader, all with phonetic transliterations. Otherwise, you should have no trouble picking up a copy of the Hanoi Foreign Languages Publishing House's *Speak Vietnamese* in either Hanoi or Ho Chi Minh City. The same applies to the *Tu Dien Anh-Viet* or *English-Vietnamese Dictionary*, though if you can find it, go for the excellent **dictionary** compiled by Nguyen Dinh Hoa. If you're determined to master the basics of spoken Vietnamese, *Audio Forum* (Microworld House, 2–6 Foscote Mews, London W9 2HH; ☎0171/266 2202) produces a decent **teaching pack**, *Language '30*, comprising two cassettes and a booklet.

PRONUNCIATION

The Vietnamese language is a **tonal** one, that is, one in which a word's meaning is determined by the pitch at which you deliver it. Six tones are used – the mid-level tone (syllables with no marker), the low falling tone (syllables marked `), the low rising tone (syllables marked '), the high broken tone (syllables marked ~), the high rising tone (syllables marked ´) and the low broken tone (syllables marked ,) – though you'll probably remain in the dark until you ask a Vietnamese person to give you spoken examples of each of them. Depending upon its tone, the word *ba*, for instance, can mean either three, grandmother, poisoned food, waste, aunt or any – leaving ample scope for misunderstandings and diplomatic incidents.

With tones accomplished, or at least comprehended, there are the many vowel and consonant sounds to take on board. These we've listed below, along with phonetic renderings of how they should be pronounced.

Vowels

a	'a' as in f**a**ther
ă	'u' as in h**u**t (slight 'u' as in unstressed English 'a')
â	'uh' sound as above only longer
e	'e' as in b**e**d
ê	'ay' as in p**a**y
i	'i' as in -**i**ng
o	'o ' as in h**o**t
ô	'aw' as in **aw**e
o'	'ur' as in f**u**r
u	'oo' as in b**oo**

u'	'ơ' closest to French 'u'
y	'i' as in -i**ng**

Vowel combinations

ai	'ai' as in Th**ai**
ao	'ao' as in M**ao**
au	'a-oo'
âu	'oh' as in **oh**!
ay	'ay' as in h**ay**
ây	'ay-i' (as in 'ay' above but longer)
eo	'eh-ao'
êu	'ay-oo'
iu	'ew' as in f**ew**
iêu	'i-yoh'
oa	'wa'
oe	'weh'
ôi	'oy'
ơi	'uh-i'
ua	'waw'
uê	'weh'
uô	'waw'
uy	'wee'

u'a	'oo-a'
u'u	'er-oo'
u'ơi	'oo-uh-i'

Consonants

c	'g'
ch	'j' as in **j**ar
d	'y' as in **y**oung
g	'g' as in **g**oat
gh	'g' as in **g**oat
gi	'y' as in **y**oung
k	'g' as in **g**oat
kh	'k' as in **k**eep
ng/ngh	'ng' as in si**ng**
nh	'n-y' as in ca**ny**on
ph	'f'
q	'g' as in **g**oat
t	'd' as in **d**ay
th	't'
tr	'j' as in **j**ar
x	's'

WORDS AND PHRASES

GREETINGS AND BASIC PHRASES

How you greet and then speak to somebody in Vietnam depends very much on their sex, and on their age and social standing, relative to your own. As a general rule of thumb, if you address a man as *ông*, and a woman as *bà*, you can be sure you aren't being impolite. If you find yourself in conversation, either formally or informally, with someone of your approximate age, you can use *anh* (for a man) and *chi* (for a woman).

Hello	*chào ông/bà*	Where do you come from?	*ông/bà ơ dâu dến?*
How are you?	*ông/bà có khỏe không?*		
Fine, thanks	*tôi khỏe cám ơn*	I come from	*tôi ơ (nước Anh/nước*
Pleased to meet you	*hân hạnh gặp ông/bà*	(England/America/	*Mỹ/nước Úc)*
Goodbye	*chào, tạm biệt*	Australia)	
Good night	*chúc ngủ ngon*	What do you do?	*ông/bà làm gì?*
Excuse me (to say sorry)	*xin lỗi*	Do you speak English?	*ông/bà biết nói tiếng*
Excuse me (to get past)	*xin ông/bà thứ lỗi*		*Anh không?*
Please	*làm ơn*	I don't understand	*tôi không hiểu*
Thank you	*cám ơn ông/bà*	Could you repeat that?	*xin ông/bà lập lại?*
Thank you very much	*cám ơn nhiều*	Yes	*vâng* (north);
Don't mention it	*không có chi*		*dạ* (south)
What's your name?	*ông/bà tên gì?*	No	*không*
My name is...	*tên tôi là...*		

EMERGENCIES

Can you help me?	*ông/bà có thể giúp tôi không?*	Please call a doctor	*làm ơn gọi bác sĩ*
		hospital	*bệnh viện*
There's been an accident	*có một vụ tai nạn*		

GETTING AROUND

Where is the...?	...ở đâu?	bus	xe buýt
How many kilometres is it to...?	bao nhiêu cây số thì đến...?	bus station	bến xe buýt
		train station	bến xe lửa
How do I get to..?	tôi phải đi...bằng cách nào?	taxi	tắc xi
		car	xe hơi
We'd like to go to...	chúng tôi muốn đi...	filling station	trạm xăng
To the airport, please	làm ơn đưa tôi đi sân bay	bicycle	xe đạp
		baggage	hành lý
Can you take me to the...?	ông/bà có thể đưa tôi đi....?	bank	nhà băng
		post office	sở bưu điện
Where do we catch the bus to...?	ở đâu đón xe đi....?	passport	hộ chiếu
		hotel	khách sạn
When does the bus for Hoi An leave?	khi nào xe Hội An chạy?	restaurant	nhà hàng
		Please stop here	xin dừng lại đây
Can I book a seat?	tôi có thể đặt ghế trước không?	over there	bên kia
		here	đây
How long does it take?	phải tốn bao lâu?	left/right	bên trái/bên phải
ticket	vé	north	phía bắc
aeroplane	máy bay	south	phía nam
airport	sân bay	east	phía đông
boat	tàu bè	west	phía tây

ACCOMMODATION AND SHOPPING

Do you have any rooms?	ông/bà có phòng không?	room with a private bathroom	một phòng tắm riêng
How much is it per night?	mỗi đêm bao nhiêu?	cheap/expensive	rẻ/đắt
How much is it?	bao nhiêu tiền?	single room	phòng một người
How much does it cost?	cái này giá bao nhiêu?	double room	phòng hai người
Can I have a look?	xem có đực không?	single bed	giường một người
Do you have...?	ông/bà có không...?	double bed	giường đôi
I want a...	tôi muốn một...	air-conditioner	máy lạnh
I'd like...	cho tôi xin một...	fan (electric)	quạt máy
How much is this?	cái này bao nhiêu?	mosquito net	cái màn
That's too expensive	đắt quá	toilet paper	giấy vệ sinh
Do you have anything cheaper?	ông/bà còn gì rẻ hơn không?	telephone	điện thoại
		laundry	quần áo dơ
Could I have the bill please?	làm ơn tính tiền?	blanket	chăn (north) mền (south)
room with a balcony	một phòng có bao lơn	open/closed	mở cửa/đóng cửa

TIME

What's the time?	mấy giờ rồi?	tomorrow	mai
noon	buổi trưa	yesterday	hôm qua
midnight	nửa đêm	now	bây giờ
minute	phút	next week	tuần tới
hour	giờ	last week	tuần vừa qua
day	ngày	morning	buổi sáng
week	tuần	afternoon	buổi chiều
month	tháng	evening	buổi tối
year	năm	night	ban đêm
today	hôm nay		

NUMBERS

Note that for numbers ending in 5, from 15 onwards, *lăm* is used in northern Vietnam and *nhăm* in the south, rather than the written form of *năm*. Also, bear in mind that an alternative for numbers that are multiples of ten is *chục* – so, for example ten would be *một chục*, twenty would be *hai chục*, etc.

zero	*không*	eleven	*mười một*	twenty-one	*hai mười một*
one	*một*	twelve	*mười hai*	twenty-two	*hai mười hai*
two	*hai*	thirteen	*mười ba*	thirty	*ba mười*
three	*ba*	fourteen	*mười bốn*	forty	*bốn mười*
four	*bốn*	fifteen	*mười làm*	fifty	*năm mười*
five	*năm*		*/nhăm*	one hundred	*một trăm*
six	*sáu*	sixteen	*mười sáu*	two hundred	*hai trăm*
seven	*bảy*	seventeen	*mười bảy*	one thousand	*một ngàn*
eight	*tám*	eighteen	*mười tám*	ten thousand	*mười ngàn*
nine	*chín*	nineteen	*mười chín*		
ten	*mười*	twenty	*hai mười*		

A GLOSSARY OF WORDS AND ACRONYMS

Agent Orange Defoliant herbicide used to deprive guerrillas of forest cover.

Annam ("Pacified South") A term coined by the Chinese to refer to their protectorate in northern Vietnam before 939 AD; the French later applied the name to the middle reaches of their protectorate, from the southern central highlands to the edge of the Red River Delta.

ao dai Traditional Vietnamese dress for women, comprising baggy pants and a long, slit tunic.

arhats Ascetic Buddhist saints, whose statues are found in northern pagodas.

ARVN (Army of the Republic of Vietnam) The army of South Vietnam.

ben xe Bus station.

Bo doi Northern soldiers

boat people Ethnic Chinese who fled Vietnam by boat in the late Seventies to escape persecution at the hands of the communists.

bodhisattva An intermediary who has chosen to forgo Buddhist nirvana to work for the salvation of all humanity.

body count Term coined by the Americans to measure the success of a military operation, determined by the number of dead bodies after a battle.

bonze Buddhist monk.

buu dien Post office.

Cao Daism Indigenous religion, essentially a hybrid of Buddhism, Taoism and Confucianism, but hinged around an attempt at unification of all earthly codes of belief (see p.111).

Champa Indianized Hindu empire that held sway in much of the southern half of Vietnam until the late seventeenth century (see p.204).

cho Market.

chua Pagoda (Buddhist place of worship).

Cochinchina A Portuguese term adopted by the French colonial government for their southern administrative region.

chu nom Classic Vietnamese script, based upon Chinese.

colon French colonial expatriate.

cyclo Three-wheeled bicycle with a carriage on the front.

cyclo mai A motorized version of a cyclo.

dao Island.

DRV (Democratic Republic of Vietnam) The North Vietnamese state established by Ho Chi Minh following the August Revolution in 1945.

den Temple (Taoist or other non-Buddhist place of worship).

dinh Communal meeting hall.

DMZ ("dee-em-zee") The Demilitarized Zone along the 17th Parallel, marking the border between North and South Vietnam.

doi moi Vietnam's economic restructuring.

duong Avenue.

FULRO (United Front for the Liberation of Oppressed Races) An opposition movement formed by the ethnic minorities of the central highlands, demanding greater autonomy.

Funan Indianized empire, a forerunner of the great Khmer empires.

GI (General Infantryman) Soldier in the US Army.

gopuram Bank of sculpted deities over the entrance to a Hindu temple.

"grunt" American infantryman.

gui xe Bicycle compound.

hang Cave.

ho Lake.

Ho Chi Minh Trail Trail used first by the Viet Minh and later by the North Vietnamese Army to transport supplies to the South, via Laos and Cambodia.

Hoa Ethnic Chinese people living in Vietnam.

Honda loi Motorized version of a *xe dap loi* (see below).

Honda om Literally "Honda embrace" – a motorbike taxi.

"Huey" Nickname given to American helicopter, the HU-1.

Indochina The region of Asia comprising Vietnam, Laos and Cambodia.

kalan Sanctuary in a Cham tower.

khach san Hotel.

Khmer Ethnic Cambodian.

kylin Mythical, dew-drinking animal (often translated as unicorn); a harbinger of peace.

Lien Xo Translating as "Soviet Union", this is used as a term of abuse – and may still be hurled at foreigners in more remote regions.

lingam A phallic statue representing Shiva, often seen in Cham towers.

mandapa Meditation hall in Cham temple complex.

MIAs (Missing in Action) Soldiers who fought – on both sides – in the American War, but have still not been accounted for.

montagnards French term for Vietnam's ethnic minority peoples.

mua roi nuoc Water puppet show.

mui Cape.

mukha lingam Lingam fashioned into the likeness of a deity.

napalm Jellied fuel dropped by US forces during the American War, and capable of administering terrible burns.

ngo Alley.

nha hang Restaurant.

nha khach Hotel or guesthouse.

nha nghi Guesthouse.

nha tro Basic dormitory accommodation, usually found near stations.

NLF (National Liberation Front) Popular movement formed in South Vietnam in 1960 by opponents to the American-backed Southern regime.

nui Mountain.

A DIRECTORY OF STREET NAMES

In travelling around Vietnam, it doesn't take long before you can recite the street names, a litany of the principal characters in Vietnamese history. Just a few from this cast list of famous revolutionaries, Party leaders, legendary kings and peasant heroes are given below. Other favoured names commemorate the glorious victories of Bach Dang and Dien Bien Phu, and the momentous date when Saigon was "liberated" in 1975: 30 Thang 4 (30 April).

Hai Ba Trung The two Trung sisters led a popular uprising against the Chinese occupying army in 40 AD and established a short-lived kingdom (see p.409).

Hoang Hoa Tham (or De Tham) Famous pirate with a Robin Hood reputation and anti-French tendencies, assassinated in 1913.

Hung Vuong The semi-mythological Hung kings ruled an embryonic kingdom, Van Lang, around 2000 BC.

Le Duan General Secretary of the Communist Party, 1960–1986.

Le Hong Phong Leading communist and patriot who died from torture in Poulo Condore prison (Con Son Island) in 1942.

Le Loi One of the most revered Vietnamese heroes, Le Loi defeated the Ming Chinese in 1427, and then ruled as King Le Thai To.

Ngo Quyen First ruler of an independent Vietnam following his defeat of the Chinese armies in 939 AD (see p.410).

Nguyen Hue Middle member of the three Nguyen brothers who led the Tay Son rebellion in the 1770s (see p.413), and then ruled briefly as Emperor Quang Trung.

Nguyen Thai Hoc Founding member of the Vietnam Nationalist Party (VNQDD), executed in 1927 following the disastrous Yen Bay uprising (see p.415).

Nguyen Thi Minh Khai Prominent anti-colonialist revolutionary of the 1930s, the wife of Le Hong Phong (see above) and sister-in-law of General Giap.

Nguyen Trai Brilliant strategist who helped mastermind Le Loi's victories over the Chinese. His ideas on the popular struggle ("it is better to conquer hearts than citadels") were used to good effect by Northern leaders in the French and American wars.

Pham Ngu Lao General in the army of Tran Hung Dao (see below).

Phan Boi Chau Influential leader of the anti-colonial movement in the early twentieth century (see p.415).

Tran Hung Dao Thirteenth-century general who beat the Mongols twice in the space of four years, and reached the ripe old age of 87.

Tran Phu Founding member and first general Secretary of the Indochinese Communist Party (see p.416), he died in prison in 1931 at the age of 27.

nuoc mam Fish sauce.

NVA (North Vietnamese Army) The army of the Democratic Republic of Vietnam.

Oc Eo Ancient seaport of the Funan Empire, east of modern-day Rach Gia in the Mekong Delta.

ODP (Orderly Departure Programme) A United Nations-backed scheme enabling legal emigration of Vietnamese refugees.

paddy Unharvested rice.

PoW Prisoner of war.

R&R ("Rest and Recreaton") Term coined during the American War to describe a soldier's temporary leave of duty.

quan District.

roi nuoc *see* mua roi nuoc.

rong Communal house of ethnic minorities in the central highlands.

RVN (Republic of Vietnam) The official name for South Vietnam from 1954 to 1976.

sampan Flat-bottomed cargo boat.

song River.

SRVN (Socialist Republic of Vietnam) The post-liberation amalgamation of the DRV and RVN, and the official name of modern Vietnam.

tai chi Chinese martial art, commonly performed as early morning exercise.

Tet Vietnam's lunar new year.

thung chai Coracles.

Tonkin The third administrative region of French colonial Vietnam, from Ninh Binh northwards.

tunnel rats American soldiers trained for warfare in tunnels such as those at Cu Chi.

VC (Viet Cong) Literally "Vietnamese communists"; used to describe the guerrilla forces of the NLF.

Viet kieu Overseas Vietnamese.

Viet Minh Shortened version of *Viet Nam Doc Lap Dong Minh*, the League for the Independence of Vietnam, established by Ho Chi Minh in 1941.

VNQDD Acronym for *Viet Nam Quoc Dan Dang*, the Vietnam Nationalist Party, founded in 1927.

xe dap loi Yet another variation on the cyclo theme, where passengers are pulled along in a "wagon" tagged behind a bicycle.

xe lam Motorized three-wheeler buggy carrying numerous passengers.

xe om Northern equivalent of the Honda om, a motorbike taxi.

direct orders from

Amsterdam	1-85828-218-7	UK£8.99	US$14.95	CAN$19.99
Andalucia	1-85828-219-5	9.99	16.95	22.99
Australia	1-85828-220-9	13.99	21.95	29.99
Bali	1-85828-134-2	8.99	14.95	19.99
Barcelona	1-85828-221-7	8.99	14.95	19.99
Berlin	1-85828-129-6	8.99	14.95	19.99
Belgium & Luxembourg	1-85828-222-5	10.99	17.95	23.99
Brazil	1-85828-102-4	9.99	15.95	19.99
Britain	1-85828-208-X	12.99	19.95	25.99
Brittany & Normandy	1-85828-224-1	9.99	16.95	22.99
Bulgaria	1-85828-183-0	9.99	16.95	22.99
California	1-85828-181-4	10.99	16.95	22.99
Canada	1-85828-130-X	10.99	14.95	19.99
China	1-85828-225-X	15.99	24.95	32.99
Corfu	1-85828-226-8	8.99	14.95	19.99
Corsica	1-85828-227-6	9.99	16.95	22.99
Costa Rica	1-85828-136-9	9.99	15.95	21.99
Crete	1-85828-132-6	8.99	14.95	18.99
Cyprus	1-85828-182-2	9.99	16.95	22.99
Czech & Slovak Republics	1-85828-121-0	9.99	16.95	22.99
Egypt	1-85828-188-1	10.99	17.95	23.99
Europe	1-85828-159-8	14.99	19.95	25.99
England	1-85828-160-1	10.99	17.95	23.99
First Time Europe	1-85828-270-5	7.99	9.95	12.99
Florida	1-85828-184-4	10.99	16.95	22.99
France	1-85828-228-4	12.99	19.95	25.99
Germany	1-85828-128-8	11.99	17.95	23.99
Goa	1-85828-275-6	8.99	14.95	19.99
Greece	1-85828-131-8	9.99	16.95	20.99
Greek Islands	1-85828-163-6	8.99	14.95	19.99
Guatemala	1-85828-189-X	10.99	16.95	22.99
Hawaii: Big Island	1-85828-158-X	8.99	12.95	16.99
Hawaii	1-85828-206-3	10.99	16.95	22.99
Holland	1-85828-229-2	10.99	17.95	23.99
Hong Kong	1-85828-187-3	8.99	14.95	19.99
Hungary	1-85828-123-7	8.99	14.95	19.99
India	1-85828-200-4	14.99	23.95	31.99
Ireland	1-85828-179-2	10.99	17.95	23.99
Italy	1-85828-167-9	12.99	19.95	25.99
Jamaica	1-85828-230-6	9.99	16.95	22.99
Kenya	1-85828-192-X	11.99	18.95	24.99
London	1-85828-231-4	9.99	15.95	21.99
Mallorca & Menorca	1-85828-165-2	8.99	14.95	19.99
Malaysia, Singapore & Brunei	1-85828-232-2	11.99	18.95	24.99
Mexico	1-85828-044-3	10.99	16.95	22.99
Morocco	1-85828-040-0	9.99	16.95	21.99
Moscow	1-85828-118-0	8.99	14.95	19.99
Nepal	1-85828-190-3	10.99	17.95	23.99
New York	1-85828-171-7	9.99	15.95	21.99
Norway	1-85828-234-9	10.99	17.95	23.99
Pacific Northwest	1-85828-092-3	9.99	14.95	19.99

around the world

Paris	1-85828-235-7	8.99	14.95	19.99
Poland	1-85828-168-7	10.99	17.95	23.99
Portugal	1-85828-180-6	9.99	16.95	22.99
Prague	1-85828-122-9	8.99	14.95	19.99
Provence	1-85828-127-X	9.99	16.95	22.99
Pyrenees	1-85828-093-1	8.99	15.95	19.99
Rhodes & the Dodecanese	1-85828-120-2	8.99	14.95	19.99
Romania	1-85828-097-4	9.99	15.95	21.99
San Francisco	1-85828-185-7	8.99	14.95	19.99
Scandinavia	1-85828-236-5	12.99	20.95	27.99
Scotland	1-85828-166-0	9.99	16.95	22.99
Sicily	1-85828-178-4	9.99	16.95	22.99
Singapore	1-85828-135-0	8.99	14.95	19.99
Soutwest USA	1-85828-239-X	10.99	16.95	22.99
Spain	1-85828-240-3	11.99	18.95	24.99
St Petersburg	1-85828-133-4	8.99	14.95	19.99
Sweden	1-85828-241-1	10.99	17.95	23.99
Thailand	1-85828-140-7	10.99	17.95	24.99
Tunisia	1-85828-139-3	10.99	17.95	24.99
Turkey	1-85828-242-X	12.99	19.95	25.99
Tuscany & Umbria	1-85828-243-8	10.99	17.95	23.99
USA	1-85828-161-X	14.99	19.95	25.99
Venice	1-85828-170-9	8.99	14.95	19.99
Vietnam	1-85828-191-1	9.99	15.95	21.99
Wales	1-85828-245-4	10.99	17.95	23.99
Washington DC	1-85828-246-2	8.99	14.95	19.99
West Africa	1-85828-101-6	15.99	24.95	34.99
More Women Travel	1-85828-098-2	10.99	16.95	22.99
Zimbabwe & Botswana	1-85828-186-5	11.99	18.95	24.99

Phrasebooks

Czech	1-85828-148-2	3.50	5.00	7.00
French	1-85828-144-X	3.50	5.00	7.00
German	1-85828-146-6	3.50	5.00	7.00
Greek	1-85828-145-8	3.50	5.00	7.00
Italian	1-85828-143-1	3.50	5.00	7.00
Mexican	1-85828-176-8	3.50	5.00	7.00
Portuguese	1-85828-175-X	3.50	5.00	7.00
Polish	1-85828-174-1	3.50	5.00	7.00
Spanish	1-85828-147-4	3.50	5.00	7.00
Thai	1-85828-177-6	3.50	5.00	7.00
Turkish	1-85828-173-3	3.50	5.00	7.00
Vietnamese	1-85828-172-5	3.50	5.00	7.00

Reference

Classical Music	1-85828-113-X	12.99	19.95	25.99
European Football	1-85828-256-X	14.99	23.95	31.99
Internet	1-85828-198-9	5.00	8.00	10.00
Jazz	1-85828-137-7	16.99	24.95	34.99
Opera	1-85828-138-5	16.99	24.95	34.99
Reggae	1-85828-247-0	12.99	19.95	25.99
Rock	1-85828-201-2	17.99	26.95	35.00
World Music	1-85828-017-6	16.99	22.95	29.99

In the USA, or for international orders, charge your order by Master Card or Visa (US$15.00 minimum order): call 1-800-253-6476; or send orders, with complete name, address and zip code, and list price, plus $2.00 shipping and handling per order to: Consumer Sales, Penguin USA, PO Box 999 – Dept #17109, Bergenfield, NJ 07621. No COD. Prepay foreign orders by international money order, a cheque drawn on a US bank, or US currency. No postage stamps are accepted. All orders are subject to stock availability at the time they are processed. Refunds will be made for books not available at that time. Please allow a minimum of four weeks for delivery.

NORTH SOUTH TRAVEL

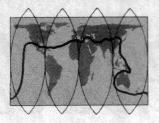

DISCOUNT FARES

PROFITS TO CHARITIES

- North South Travel is a friendly, competitive travel agency, offering discount fares world-wide.
- North South Travel's profits contribute to community projects in the developing world.
- We have special experience of booking destinations in Africa, Asia and Latin America.
- Clients who book through North South Travel include exchange groups, students and independent travellers, as well as charities, church organisations and small businesses.

To discuss your booking requirements: contact Brenda Skinner between 9am and 5pm, Monday to Friday, on (01245) 492 882: Fax (01245) 356 612, any time. Or write to: North South Travel Limited, Moulsham Mill Centre, Parkway, Chelmsford, Essex CM2 7PX, UK

Help us to help others – Your travel can make a difference

Our Holidays Their Homes

Exploring New Destinations?
Ever wondered what that means to the locals?
Ever seen things you're uncomfortable with?
Ever thought of joining Tourism Concern?

Tourism Concern is the only independent British organisation seeking ways to make tourism just, participatory and sustainable · world-wide.

For a membership fee of only £15 (£8 unwaged) UK, £25 overseas, you will support us in our work, receive our quarterly magazine, and learn about what is happening in tourism around the world.

We'll help find answers to the questions.

Tourism Concern, Southlands College, Wimbledon Parkside, London SW19 5NN UK Tel: 0181-944 0464 Fax: 0181-944 6583.